Yates Phalanx:

The History of the
Thirty-Ninth Regiment,
Illinois Volunteer Veteran Infantry,

in the War of the Rebellion,

1861–1865

Charles M. Clark, M.D.
(Late Surgeon)

Edited by
Frederick Charles Decker

HERITAGE BOOKS
2015

HERITAGE BOOKS
AN IMPRINT OF HERITAGE BOOKS, INC.

Books, CDs, and more—Worldwide

For our listing of thousands of titles see our website
at
www.HeritageBooks.com

Published 2015 by
HERITAGE BOOKS, INC.
Publishing Division
5810 Ruatan Street
Berwyn Heights, Md. 20740

Copyright © 1994 Frederick Charles Decker

All rights reserved. No part of this book may be reproduced or transmitted in any form or by any means, electronic or mechanical, including photocopying, recording or by any information storage and retrieval system without written permission from the author, except for the inclusion of brief quotations in a review.

International Standard Book Numbers
Paperbound: 978-0-7884-0152-7
Clothbound: 978-0-7884-6229-0

Courtesy of Mr. & Mrs. Fred A. Decker

Private Hugh Rippy Snee
1838-1927
Company E, 39th Illinois Volunteer Veteran Infantry

DEDICATION

TO THE CHILDREN, THE SONS AND DAUGHTERS OF THE VETERAN SOLDIERS OF THE THIRTY-NINTH REGIMENT ILLINOIS VETERAN VOLUNTEERS, WHO SO NOBLY RESPONDED TO THE CALL OF THEIR IMPERILED COUNTRY IN THE TIME OF HER NEED; AND WHO SUFFERED UNTOLD PRIVATIONS, DANGERS, AND THE SHEDDING OF THEIR BLOOD, THAT "GOD'S BEST COUNTRY" MIGHT BE PRESERVED AND HANDED DOWN IN ITS INTEGRITY TO THE DEAR ONES, FOR THEIR INHERITANCE.

This book is dedicated
to my Civil War relatives:

Private Hugh Rippy Snee
Company E, 39th Regiment
Illinois Volunteer Infantry
who survived the war
and the horrors of Andersonville,

and

Private Moses F. Shreffler
Company E, 39th Regiment
Illinois Volunteer Infantry
who survived the war but died
shortly thereafter
as a result of his wounds,

and

Private Nathan W. Snee
Company I, 76th Regiment
Illinois Volunteer Infantry
and the
4th Division, 17th Artillery Corps
who survived the war,

and

Private Noah A. Decker
Company G, 5th Regiment
Wisconsin Volunteer Infantry
who survived the war.

TABLE OF CONTENTS

CHAPTER	TITLE	PAGE
1.	"Into United States Service"	1
2.	"Off for St. Louis.	5
3.	Making Encampment	13
4.	"The hour has not yet come"	21
5.	"The Rebel Force"	29
6.	"Fight under any circumstances"	43
7.	"The scene of the battlefield is awful"	55
8.	"Death was busy reaping a rich harvest"	67
9.	"At half past two the Ball opened"	77
10.	"But at what a cost!"	91
11.	"Veterans".	111
12.	Return to the army.	117
13.	"In the Army of the James.	121
14.	"Rally on the rifle-pits!".	127
15.	"We will drive those rebels to hell!"	143
16.	"Charge those works!"	157
17.	"Where are the rest?"	169
18.	Reorganization.	185
19.	"There was some terrible hot work going on"	193
20.	"End of this wicked rebellion".	201
21.	"On to Richmond!".	209
22.	"School is out!".	217
	The Wilmington Monument.	221
	Testimonial to Dr. Clark.	223

APPENDIX I.	Hugh R. Snee Letter to his grandchildren	225
APPENDIX II.	Trial Testimony of Hugh R. Snee	233
APPENDIX III.	Federal Forces - May 16, 1864	237
APPENDIX IV.	Confederate Forces - May 16, 1864	243
APPENDIX V.	Company Histories & Summary of Casualties	249
APPENDIX VI.	Regimental Band	267
APPENDIX VII.	Roster	271
INDEX		413
ERRATUM		

LIST OF ILLUSTRATIONS AND PHOTOGRAPHS

NA - National Archives

#	TITLE	PAGE
1.	Private Hugh Rippy Snee	iii
2.	Flag No. 1 - The Agricultural Flag (unrestored) (Camp Lincoln)	xxii
3.	Flag No. 1 - The Agricultural Flag (restored)	xxiii
4.	Flag No. 2 - Governor Yates Flag (unrestored) (Camp Lincoln)	xxiv
5.	Flag No. 2 - Governor Yates Flag (restored)	xxv
6.	Flag No. 3 - Blue Silk Regimental Flag (unrestored) (Camp Lincoln)	xxvi
7.	Flag No. 3 - Blue Silk Regimental Flag (restored)	xxvii
8.	Off to the Front	4
9.	The Sutlers	6
10.	Supper at Pittsburgh	9
11.	The Camp Kitchen	14
12.	Thomas O. Osborn (NA)	17
13.	Muhlenburg's Guns on Warm Spring Ridge	30
14.	The Retreat from Alpine Station	40
15.	Bivouacking at Cedar Creek	54
16.	Fresh Pork for Supper	59
17.	On the March	63
18.	Review by President Lincoln at Falmouth	64
19.	Gunboats on James River	68
20.	On Picket	71
21.	Band boys foraging	74
22.	Counting the scars	76
23.	Scene of operations in South Carolina	82
24.	Fort Sumter after bombardment	83
25.	300-pounder battery on Morris Island	93
26.	Beacon House	94
27.	Fort Wagner - point of first assault	95
28.	Fort Wagner - sea front	96
29.	Bomb-proof	99
30.	Fort Sumter in ruins	100
31.	Requa Battery manned by Thirty-Ninth Illinois (Curran)	101
32.	Section of Requa Battery	102
33.	Swamp Angel	106
34.	Long Bridge - examining a pass	119

TITLE	PAGE
35. Line of defense - Bermuda Hundred	122
36. Map of Richmond and Petersburg area	128
37. Pierre G. T. Beauregard (NA)	130
38. Benjamin F. Butler (NA)	131
39. Quincy A. Gillmore (NA)	132
40. The Hospital Steamer	137
41. The Field Hospital	149
42. Dutch Gap Canal	151
43. Pontoon Bridge guarded by the Thirty-Ninth Illinois (NA)	163
44. Scene of assault, August 16, 1864	165
45. The assault	174
46. Collecting the wounded	176
47. Winter quarters at Chaffin's Farm	182
48. Officers quarters at Chaffin's Farm	182
49. The assault of Fort Gregg, April 2, 1865	195
50. McLean's house	206
51. Regimental Band (Curran)	270

PREFACE

As a boy, my parents often told me about my maternal great-great-grandfather, Hugh Rippy Snee, and his experiences during the American Civil War. I was told he served in the Thirty-Ninth Illinois Volunteers. I was also informed he was wounded during a battle in Virginia and of his capture and imprisonment in the Confederate Military Prison at Andersonville, Georgia and of his ultimate escape from that place of horror. However, information regarding where the battle was, or when the battle occurred, was lacking.

Occasionally I attempted to research Grandfather Snee's story, but without success. It was not until many years later that I could piece together the puzzle that these statements had created for me: I was given his hand written account of his capture and subsequent escape from Andersonville Prison. With this document, I began a personal quest to learn about his participation in the Civil War. This led to a fascination with the history of Hugh Snee's regiment, "Yates Phalanx." The Thirty-Ninth Illinois Volunteer Infantry. The "battle in Virginia" became the attack on Fort Darling at Drewry's Bluff. The date of the battle was May 16, 1864, and 128 years later this date commemorates the date of my first grandchild's birth. This effort is in memory of Hugh Rippy Snee and for his great-great-great-great-grandson, Alexander Taylor Burden.

My mother subsequently gave me Grandfather Snee's copy of The History of the Thirty-Ninth Regiment Illinois Volunteer Veteran Infantry, by Charles M. Clark, M.D. As I read, I began to realize that the firing on Fort Sumter had caused more than shell holes and shrapnel. It set into motion a gigantic plan for organizing the vast armies needed to preserve the Union. From the United States Congress and the legislatures of the Northern States came the call to arms. The handbills designed to inspire the creation of companies and regiments manned by able-bodied patriots are now yellow and faded, but in September 1861, when a Lieutenant of the Thirty-Ninth Illinois came to Rockville to recruit, the bold black print was timely, vivid, and enticing. Enticing and patriotic enough that Mr. Hugh Rippy Snee became Private Hugh Rippy Snee, Company E, Thirty-Ninth Illinois Volunteer Infantry. If he died in battle, so much for that, you only live once, and besides, it would be a clean wound of fatal but heroic significance. The cause was just. Private Snee and the other 50-plus men of Company E would join in battle and preserve the Union. Certainly a cause worth giving one's life. Yet, if he survived! He would surely have something to tell his grandchildren. The only losers would be the Confederate States. In the Spring of 1861 the sound of drum and bugle was louder than musket and cannon. Spirits were high and the Union would truly be saved!

The genesis of the Thirty-Ninth Illinois began shortly after the attack on Fort Sumter. Key individuals gathered to discuss the forming of companies. One such group of men, including Thomas Osborn & Charles Clark, met in Osborn's law office in Chicago before the smoke had cleared from that battered old fort in Charleston Harbor. These individuals decided to organize an infantry regiment to support the Union cause. Money was raised and men were sent into the cities, towns and villages to recruit able-bodied volunteers. Within six weeks over 1,300 men responded to the call to arms. However, they were not yet to be a regiment. When they sent the register of names to the Adjutant-General of Illinois, the organizers were notified that the State had already filled its quota and the recruits could not be accepted as a regimental organization at that time. Disappointed, most of the volunteers went to other states to apply for service. This left the Chicago group enough men to form one company.

On May 3, 1861, President Lincoln authorized a second call for troops; this time 500,000 additional men were needed. When this occurred, Governor Yates of Illinois forwarded the muster-roll of this uncommitted company of roughly fifty men to the Adjutant-General of Illinois. The Thirty-Ninth Illinois Infantry Regiment, under the temporary command of Lieutenant-Colonel Osborn, was organizing in Chicago and the company was offered a place.

In the latter part of July, shortly after the first battle of Bull Run, Governor Yates received notice that the Thirty-Ninth was to be accepted, and additional recruiting began immediately. On August 10, 1861, this company was mustered into the service of the United States as Company A, Thirty-Ninth Illinois Volunteer Infantry. The remainder of the companies, B through I and K, followed in short order. The Regiment had decided to bear the name of the Governor of the State and became known as "Yates Phalanx."

The original complement of 806 men was formed and sworn into the service of the United States on October 11, 1861. After the swearing in, they boarded a train and were on their way to the Camp of Instruction at Benton Barracks, St. Louis, Missouri.

After several days of instruction, the men began to realize that life in the army was different from prior experience. Yet, some rural boys thought they had never had it so good. Young men straight off the farm believed the uniform was the best suit of clothes they ever had. Others said they had never seen so much food, although, it was not very good.

For many, however, the confusion of thousands of men, in close quarters, strange surroundings, and the drastic change in their diets created havoc. They learned that badly cooked salt pork, rancid pickled beef, beans and hardtack were the staff of life for the soldier. This change in their dietary habits would develop into chronic diarrhea that would continue through their army service. Moreover, some tainted water contained the germs that created amoebic dysentery. For Hugh Snee and many of his compatriots, this disease would affect their entire lives.

On October 26, 1861 the Regiment was ordered to Hagerstown, Maryland for further instruction, drilling, and a continuing acclimation to military life. On November 7, the Regiment continued to Williamsport, Maryland where they finally received their weapons, the legendary Springfield rifle.

With their training over, the Regiment broke camp and departed for Hancock, Maryland, arriving the next day on December 16. They crossed the Potomac River to Alpine Station, in what is now West Virginia, where they were ordered to guard the Baltimore and Ohio Railroad depot. This lonely and seemingly insignificant spot in the road was where their war was to begin.

In early January, Generals William W. "Old Blizzard" Loring and Thomas Jonathan "Stonewall" Jackson led a Rebel force of approximately 15,000 men with forty pieces of artillery down the Shenandoah Valley. Their orders were to cross the Potomac at Alpine Station and raid through the borders of Maryland and Pennsylvania.

The Thirty-Ninth Illinois "saw the elephant" in a furious action with Jackson's troops near Alpine Station at Warm Spring Ridge on January 3, 1862. They repulsed a brigade of the enemy holding them in check for several hours and made good their retreat under cover of darkness.

Preface

For the next few months, the Thirty-Ninth slugged it out with the Rebels up and down the Shenandoah Valley. They participated in the victory over Stonewall's army at Winchester on March 23, 1862. In early May orders were received to march to Fredericksburg and report to General McDowell who had 40,000 troops under his command and was actively preparing for a move on Richmond.

About May 25, the Thirty-Ninth was ordered to return to the Shenandoah to support General Banks. Before they were half way there they were notified of Bank's defeat. They were then ordered to Alexandria, Virginia, which they reached on July 12, 1862 to be given a recuperative rest from a march of over 360 miles. However, this respite turned out to be short lived for McClellan's army was soon engaged with Lee's in what has been recorded as the "Seven Days Battle." Therefore, according to Dr. Clark, " . . . like the Wandering Jew, the Regiment moved on" toward their destiny at Fort Wagner, Drewry's Bluff, Ware Bottom Church, Darbytown Cross-Roads, Deep Bottom Run, Fort Gregg and Appomattox Court-house.

On June 26 they were ordered to Harrison's Landing on the James River and arrived in time to take a small part in the battle of Malvern Hill that took place on July 1, 1862. Then for the next few weeks all companies of the Thirty-Ninth were detailed to outpost duty at the front.

New orders were issued on August 13. The Thirty-Ninth were to be the rear guard of the Union army that a month before had been mobilized to take Richmond. Now, the Union force was retreating to Yorktown, its trailing wagons protected by the Thirty-Ninth Illinois. The Regiment marched for five days. The pulverized clay of the road was suffocating. They had little water and nothing to eat except dry hardtack. When they reached Yorktown, they gratefully camped on the same ground made historic by the battles of their Revolutionary forefathers.

After a few days rest the Regiment proceeded to Suffolk where it participated in three different engagements on the Blackwater River, and in a reconnaissance to the Dismal Swamp.

On April 1, 1863, the Regiment was called upon to take part in General Hunter's expedition to Confederate held Folly Island. They took the fortification with little opposition and settled in.

Over the next three months the constant picket and fatigue duty had worn out the men of the Thirty-Ninth. Finally, on July 7, they were ordered to Cole's Island for a rest. However, on the following day orders were received to attack the enemy fortifications on Morris Island, South Carolina. The principal target was Fort Wagner. The assaults began on July 11, and continued until July 18, when a charge led by Colonel Robert Gould Shaw and the Fifty-Fourth Massachusetts (Colored) Infantry was thrown back with terrible losses. History has recorded the courage, heroism and "Glory" displayed at Fort Wagner that evening. The Thirty-Ninth Illinois had taken part in these assaults and listed fifty-three members of its units as killed or wounded.

Supporting these assaults was a group of soldiers assigned to special duty. These men were responsible for the handling of a device known as "The Billinghurst-Requa battery." Among those detailed was Private Snee. The Requa Battery description will be found in the text of the book.

During the next thirty days, the Thirty-Ninth was given the assignment of building and repairing the sand forts and batteries on Morris Island. They were continuously under fire from the Rebel forts Sumter, Wagner, Gregg and the batteries on Sullivan's Island. During this period, on August 16,

1863, while standing guard duty in front of Beacon House, a building near the end of the island, Hugh Snee's best friend and future brother-in-law, Moses Sheffler, was seriously wounded in the head by a Rebel musket ball. The wound caused multiple skull fractures and depressed a large piece of bone that partially paralyzed him. Sheffler was transported to the military hospital near Petersburg for surgery.

The Regiment formed the advance of their Brigade and occupied the trenches on the night it was discovered Fort Wagner was being evacuated. When this was known, the Thirty-Ninth entered the fort, captured the enemy's rearguard, cut several fuses designed to blow up the structure on the approach of the Union troops, and planted the Regimental colors on the parapet some two hours before the time appointed for the general charge.

After helping in strengthening and remodeling the defenses on Morris Island, (including the building and naming of the "Swamp Angel"), the Thirty-Ninth returned to Folly Island, and soon embarked for Hilton Head, South Carolina where the regiment remained for several weeks. During this period the Thirty-Ninth became the first organization in the Department to accept Veteran honors. It left Hilton Head on Veteran furlough for Chicago, on January 1, 1864 with only 350 men left, the minimum required to be a veteran regiment.

After the regiment had been recruited to full strength, it left Chicago in early March 1864 for Washington, DC, and from there sailed to Georgetown, where it was assigned to the First Brigade, First Division, Tenth Army Corps, Army of the James. It then embarked on May 5, 1864 with General Butler's expedition to the James River, Richmond, and Petersburg. Upon reaching Bermuda Hundred Virginia, the Regiment took the advance on the march into the interior. After several miles the Armies of the James 40,000 troops were halted and fortifications were built. Remaining a day or two, the entire column moved forward to Drewry's Bluff, Virginia.

The battle for Drewry's Bluff was a small, apparently meaningless engagement when compared with a large scale conflict such as Antietam where in one day 6,000 men died, and another 17,000 were wounded. [More than twice as many Americans lost their lives in that one day than fell in combat in the War of 1812, the Mexican War, and the Spanish-American War combined. The casualties at Antietam numbered four times the total suffered by American soldiers on the Normandy beaches during the D-day invasion, June 6, 1944. There were also Gettysburg, Vicksburg, and Cold Harbor, Virginia where Union forces lost 7,000 men in twenty minutes.] Yet, no battle of the Civil War was truly insignificant. Every man, every musket, every horse or cannon the South lost was irreplaceable. The Southern agrarian-based society could not hope to compete with the more populous, industrialized North. Moreover, this undertaking at Drewry's Bluff was important for additional reasons: it was the first large scale battle for the Thirty-Ninth Illinois, and extremely important in the life of my great-great-grandfather, Hugh Rippy Snee.

The violent battle lasted over thirteen hours. In many respects it was a remarkable engagement, considering the early morning hour in which it began, the dense fog, the drizzling, sometimes heavy rain that obscured the combatants, and the large number of defenders unexpected by the Union command. There were many hand-to-hand encounters, bayonet charges, and acts of heroism than cannot be fully recounted here. There was also the first extensive, defensive use of heavy telegraph wire which was strung from timber to fence post to tree-stump [all a foot off the ground] much like today's barbed wire entanglements.

Early in the evening of May 15, 1864, the Army of the James began moving into position. General Butler ordered General Gillmore to align the regiments of the Tenth Army Corps (approximately 12,000 men) from left of the Richmond and Petersburg railroad tracks to the edge of the Richmond-Petersburg Turnpike, a distance of approximately 2,000 yards. Gillmore formed the 550 men of the Thirty-Ninth Illinois on the extreme left of his line and the other twenty-three regiments of infantry were spread across the remaining distance to the turnpike. Across the turnpike was Smith's Eighteenth Army Corps and its thirty regiments of infantry, cavalry and various batteries of artillery. (See Appendix IV)

Opposite the Thirty-Ninth were battle hardened veterans, the Third North Carolina Cavalry and General Montgomery Corse's Brigade of the Fifteenth, Seventeenth, Eighteenth, Twenty-Ninth and Thirtieth Virginia Infantries.

The occasional rain on the night of May 15, 1864 had turned the earth to thick, clinging mud. The night fog surrounding Drewry's Bluff, Virginia thickened in the early morning hours. The Union soldiers lay in a shallow trench behind the small ridge they had quickly pushed up with their hands. They had been awakened at 3:30 in the morning when the Rebels began their shelling. They now waited for an enemy they could not see. Private Hugh Snee of Company E and the balance of the Thirty-Ninth Illinois Volunteer Veteran Infantry were prepared for the inevitable. They knew that in front of them a sizable Confederate force was preparing to charge. This was the first large scale battle for the Thirty-Ninth and they were ordered to defend their position until ordered otherwise.

General Butler had planned to attack the Confederate positions on the morning of the 16th, but Beauregard had anticipated him. Under cover of darkness and the thick obscuring mist, Beauregard's troops made a violent assault on Butler's right flank. The heavy fog had provided a curtain through which the graybacks came yelling and shooting. Beauregard's attack had been successful, the opaque mist contributing largely to his efforts. However, the heavy loss of men left him in no position to follow the Federals in their retreat. By ten o'clock in the morning the fighting for the day was over on the right flank.

Meanwhile, as the fog began to thin, the Thirty-Ninth Illinois observed two columns of the Fifteenth Virginia with their red battle flags spread to the morning breeze, slowly making their way from their rifle-pits near the railroad and attempting to advance to the Thirty-Ninth's position on the ridge. Another enemy column, the Eighteenth Virginia, was also approaching the left of the Thirty-Ninth along the fence.

The center of the Union line was undergoing a series of five charges by the Rebel troops and was finally forced to fall back toward Bermuda Hundred. The orders, however, never reached the officers of the Thirty-Ninth. Left to hold the position alone when the other regiments had been ordered to the right, the 550 soldiers from Illinois had been overlooked in the confusion of the general retreat.

The Fifteenth Virginia, who were advancing along the railroad tracks and protected by high banks, came abreast of the Union troops and opened fire "which made the position of the Thirty-Ninth regiment untenable." Overpowered, those who remained alive took to the woods through heavy fire. Finding shelter in the timber, and being under the impression that the balance of the line was still secure, the Thirty-Ninth was ordered to "Charge on the trenches!" and a simultaneous charge was made by all companies of the Regiment. The Rebels were forced back and out of the Union lines. Meanwhile, the enemy had closed on the Thirty-Ninth from the front and left. The Rebel column on the tracks moved into the woods to the Thirty-Ninth's rear to prevent their retreat. An order was shouted, "Rally on the Rifle-Pits!", and again, under appalling fire, the Thirty-Ninth had to cross the open field between their trenches and the woods. Every man for himself, firing as he could, ran for the apparent safety of the timber, but many traveled only a short distance before they were cut down by enemy bullets and left on the field where they fell. [It was discovered later that the order to "Rally on the Rifle Pits!" had been shouted by a rebel officer commanding his own troops.]

One of those to fall was Private Hugh Snee. Early in the battle he had received a head wound cause by a Rebel saber, and now he was wounded in the cheek by a musket ball. Later, after Snee regained consciousness and was considered a "walking wounded" by the Union doctors, he was sent back with some of his companions to pick up the more seriously injured from his Company. As they carried the wounded back to the railroad cars they were suddenly charged by the Third North Carolina Cavalry from the woods on their right. When the cavalry cut them off, this group of Union men ran up the tracks towards Petersburg, however, they were quickly surrounded and forced to surrender. Private Snee and forty-five men of the Thirty-Ninth were taken prisoner that day. Their destination was to be Andersonville Prison in Georgia. Butler's badly crippled force returned to their camp at Bermuda Hundred.

During the battle of Drewry's Bluff, the Army of the James lost 4,500 men, including 1,478 who were listed as missing. The Thirty-Ninth suffered 127 casualties killed, wounded, captured or missing. (Hugh Snee was listed as missing).

On May 20 the Thirty-Ninth and the balance of the Brigade attacked Beauregard's troops at Ware Bottom Church, Virginia. The loss sustained by the Regiment amounted to seventy killed and wounded with the overall loss to the Brigade of 300. On June 2 the Regiment sustained a similar loss in men in an engagement on the same ground. During the middle of June the command fought General Longstreet's Corps and the Regiment lost thirty-five men. In those two weeks the Thirty-Ninth Illinois had lost over 50% of its troops and presented a sorry image on June 22 when President Lincoln, accompanied by General Butler, rode along their entrenchments. From June 16 until October 13 the Regiment fought again at Ware Bottom Church, and then Deep Run, Chaffin's Farm, and Darbytown Cross-Roads, losing another 177 soldiers that were either killed or wounded. At the end of the day on October 13, 1864, only three officers were left in the Regiment. By this date, the regiment had suffered 489 killed, wounded, captured or missing of the 550 that formed in line of battle at Drewry's Bluff just five months earlier.

During the winter, additional recruits arrived and by Spring a new regiment had been formed. In that period the Regiment took part in the military movements which finally wrestled the strongholds of Petersburg and Richmond from the Rebels.

On April 2, 1865, the Regiment led the charge on Fort Gregg, the key to the fortifications around Petersburg and Richmond. This fort was surrounded by five other forts, redoubts and a ditch six feet deep and 12 feet wide. It was the Thirty-Ninth's assignment to make this charge and take the fort. Only by digging with swords and bayonets could footholds be secured on the slippery slope to the parapet. Here a desperate hand-to-hand struggle ensued and lasted until the fort was captured. The Thirty-Ninth was the first regiment to gain the waterway and plant its flag.

After the capture of Fort Gregg, the Regiment took the advance of the Army of the James in the pursuit of Lee. After a series of forced marches (by a wide detour) the Regiment succeeded in heading off the Army of Northern Virginia, and had the proud satisfaction of seeing the final surrender at Appomattox Court House.

The Regiment was then ordered to take control of the captured enemy equipment and weapons and see to it's return to the North. The next few months were spent on provost duty in Richmond; during this time they had to quell several riots between the cavalry and newly freed slaves over food.

On December 6, 1865, while at Norfolk, Virginia, the Regiment was mustered out and its remarkable career ended.

Shortly after the end of the war, the Thirty-Ninth sent a report to the Adjutant-General of the State of Illinois which gave the Regiment the dubious honor of ranking third in killed or wounded in the list of 156 Regiments of Infantry which took to the field from Illinois during the Civil War. The Regiment had traveled a total of 6,463 miles: 5,038 miles by rail and water and 1,425 miles by marching over hills, through valleys, across rivers and streams, and at some times over extremely difficult terrain.

By the end of the war two of their officers, Orrin Mann and Thomas Osborn had been promoted to General.

In September, 1861, the youngest enlistee was Private Charles W. Beam, 15, and the oldest was Private Alexander Gaurley, who was 67.

Corporal John Kipp, famous for his naming of the "Swamp Angel," did not survive the war. On October 13, 1864, when the Regiment was repulsed and fell back after storming the fortifications at Darbytown Cross-roads, Kipp brought back the Regimental flag. One of Kipp's arms was shattered, but with the other he carried the flag and his musket. When an officer offered to help Kipp, ". . .he told the officer if he was so anxious to assist that he might carry his gun, but the flag never." Kipp died of his wounds November 5, 1864 and is buried in the U. S. National Cemetery at Hampton, Virginia, near Fort Monroe.

Private Henry M. Day of Company A was awarded a Medal of Honor for his efforts in planting the colors of the Regiment at Fort Gregg on April 2, 1865.

Private Abner P. Allen of Company K was a member of the color-guard and carried the State Flag at the formal surrender of General Lee. He accompanied General John Gibbon to Washington, DC, with seventy-six stands of Rebel colors where the young trooper was presented a Medal of Honor by Secretary of War Stanton for meritorious conduct in front of Petersburg.

George Hayworth of Company E was one of the last men captured and then paroled by the Army of Northern Virginia. Both experiences occurred on the final day of the Civil War for the men of the Thirty-Ninth Illinois, April 9, 1865.

YATES PHALANX

Private Hugh Snee returned from sick leave after his ordeal at Andersonville and was one of the men mustered out with the Regiment. His tale of imprisonment and escape is one of great deprivation, pain and terrible suffering. Yet, filled too, with strength, determination and courage. [See Appendix I]

Hugh Snee, his friend Moses Sheffler, and the balance of the Thirty-Ninth Illinois were ordinary men. They were farmers, shopkeepers, bankers, clerks, doctors and lawyers who simply believed in perpetuating the Union. Many were not affected by, or knew little about, slavery, the South, or states rights, but when their country called, they answered.

Most of their deeds of glory are well documented in the history books. Yet, not every soldier fought in a battle, not all died of heroic wounds. Many fought the terrible ravages of disease and did not die a romanticized gallant hero's death. However, they were all heroes for having suffered the systematic savagery of the American Civil War.

Grateful acknowledgment is made to my good friend Phil Reilley who helped me begin. Also to my daughter and son-in-law Kathleen and Jeffry Burden who were so kind to help research the National Archives. Special thanks to Pat, my wife and partner, for without her tireless efforts I would never have been able to complete this endeavor.

Frederick C. Decker
Ventura, California

THE REGIMENTAL FLAGS

There were three Regimental flags and they were individually presented when the Regiment massed for its final muster at Springfield, Illinois in December 1865. The flags were all literally in ribbons, and bore incontrovertible evidence of the fiery ordeal through which they had passed.

Number One was a "prize flag," awarded to the Regiment by the State Agricultural Society as an award for superior drill and discipline, and was called "The Agricultural Flag." The bronze eagle, ball and socket attached to the flag staff were presented by Major-General John Gibbons, who commanded the Twenty-Fourth Army Corps, for gallant conduct in the assault on Fort Gregg, near Petersburg, Virginia, April 2, 1865.

Number Two had been presented to the Regiment by Governor Yates, and contained a life-size picture of His Excellency.

Number Three, a blue silk battle flag, in its tattered, riddled and ragged condition, bores unmistakable traces of original beauty, and was a gift of a young lady named Miss Helen Arion, and had been tenderly and sacredly regarded for her sake.

The photographs of these flags were kindly provided by Mr. Charles W. Munie, C.W.4, IL ARNG (Ret), Historian and Curator of the Illinois Department of Military Affairs Museum, Camp Lincoln, Springfield, Illinois.

Special acknowledgement is given to Mr. Tom Roe, Ventura College Art Department Chair. Special recognition is given to his student, Mr. Evan Donn, who computer scanned and painstakingly restored the flags in the photographs to show what they may have looked like when they were originally issued. I have included both versions—one to show the condition as they existed at the end of the war and the restored version.

In the restored version, no attempt was made to remove the battle award which was sewn on the flag's red stripes.

YATES PHALANX

FLAG NUMBER ONE

PRIZE FLAG AWARDED BY THE STATE AGRICULTURE SOCIETY

As it looked in December 1865

FLAG NUMBER ONE

PRIZE FLAG AWARDED BY THE STATE AGRICULTURE SOCIETY

As it may have looked in April 1861

YATES PHALANX

FLAG NUMBER TWO

REGIMENTAL BATTLE FLAG PRESENTED BY GOVERNOR YATES

As it looked in December 1865

FLAG NUMBER TWO

REGIMENTAL BATTLE FLAG PRESENTED BY GOVERNOR YATES

As it may have looked in January 1863

YATES PHALANX

FLAG NUMBER THREE

SILK BATTLE FLAG PRESENTED BY MISS ARION

As it looked in December 1865

The Regimental Flags

FLAG NUMBER THREE

SILK BATTLE FLAG PRESENTED BY MISS ARION

As it may have looked in October 1861

INTRODUCTORY

Comrades:

It was with feeling of great diffidence and misgiving that I approached the task of writing the history of **THE THIRTY-NINTH REGIMENT OF ILLINOIS VETERAN VOLUNTEERS** during its four years and two months of active service in the field; and now that the task (not its history) is completed, I feel more than ever my disqualification for undertaking it. I was a medical officer, and therefore not always acquainted with the real object of your movements, and seldom present as a participant when they were carried into execution. (I have reference to your movements on the battlefield, not the marches or the many other matters incidental to the life of the soldier.) In my feeble and imperfect way, however, I managed to keep track of you, and with the kind assistance of Major Homer A. Plimpton have given a fair recital of your deeds, both offensive and defensive, when confronted by the enemy. This history will be read by many of the men who personally helped to make it, and doubtless they will see errors and discrepancies, and will note the absence of many details and incidents connected with the movements and operations of the regiment. This must necessarily have been the case under the most favorable circumstances; but it must be borne in mind that the writer has had but little cooperation in the compilation of the facts presented, although the most earnest solicitation has been frequently made to all concerned, in order to make this history as complete and satisfactory as possible.

The "Roster" of officers and men was transcribed from the books of the Regimental Adjutant at Norfolk, Virginia in 1865, by Lieutenant John L. Ripple, and they were found to be very incomplete, and full of errors. This has been rectified in so far as possible, and has required a great deal of research and much time. It is yet imperfect in many respects.[1]

I have tried to be generous and just to all; and I do not think that I have given to any one man or to any one company more than his share of the glory they participated in. Where all did their duty so well, it is impossible to individualize.

This history was commenced in 1871, and completed in 1872; but for reasons not necessary to mention it was laid aside and practically abandoned. At the solicitation of many of the members of the regiment it was again taken in hand in 1887, and in most part has been rewritten, and much interesting matter added.

The discouragements encountered in the efforts to get the history published have been immense. That you now possess it is wholly due to the unwearied efforts of the writer, and the generous subscriptions of a few members of our Veteran Association.

Acknowledgment is due for the generous gift of money by Comrade N. B. Kendall, generous subscriptions from Comrades Mann, Sweetser, Baker, Savage, McGregor, and others.

---

[1] The Adjutant-General of the State of Illinois published a much more detailed report in 1901. This report, the Regimental History, and the National Archives Pension Files were used by the Editor for the Roster.

This book, Comrades, will recall and refresh many half-buried recollections of the days when you were soldiering. It will revive memories of much suffering, hardship, and perhaps may cause some old wound to ache and grumble. It will remind you of old comrades who fell at your side, and who now lie far away from their homes in hurried graves you made for them. Your children, I hope, will appreciate this record of your achievements at a time when the very foundations of this Government were being undermined and threatened with destruction, and Human Liberty was poised in the balance; and may it teach them a greater love for their country.

To all, or any, who may care to read it, I hope that it may teach them the great Brotherhood of Man.

I am deeply conscious of its imperfections, but it is the best I could do under the circumstances. Treat it with all the indulgence you can, and with the charity and consideration that is meted out to one who has faithfully tried to do his duty.

Charles M. Clark, M.D.
Chicago, Illinois
July 1, 1889

"This history of the Thirty-Ninth has been written, not for you alone for your satisfaction, but for the gratification of your children and your children's children, who will hand it down to still remoter generations with the pride and boast of an ancestry who fought and died and were crippled in order to sustain and perpetuate the Union of the States of North America."

Charles M. Clark, M.D.
Chicago, Illinois
1889

REVEILLE

The day-star shines upon the hill,
The valleys in the shadows sleep;
In wood and thicket, dark and still,
My comrades lie in slumber deep.
Far in the east a phantom gray
Steals slowly up the night's black pall,
And, herald of the coming day,

I can't get 'em up,
I can't get 'em up,
I can't get 'em up in the morning;
I cant' get 'em up,
I cant' get 'em up,
I can't get 'em up at all!

A thought of motion at the sound —
As though the forest caught its breath,
And belted sleepers on the ground
More restless, like life in death,
And slumbering echoes, here and there,
Awaken as the challenge floats,
And louder on the morning air
Ring out the cheery bugle notes —

I can't get 'em up,
I can't get 'em up,
I can't get 'em up in the morning;
I cant' get 'em up,
I cant' get 'em up,
I can't get 'em up at all!

And as the shrilling strains prolong,
Flames into rose and gold the day,
And springing up, with shout and song,
Each soldier welcome march or fray,
Through wooded vale, o'er wind-swept hill,
Where camp-fires gleam and shadows fall,
Louder and clearer, cheerily still,
Rings out the merry bugle call —

I can't get 'em up,
I can't get 'em up,
I can't get 'em up in the morning;
I cant' get 'em up,
I cant' get 'em up,
I can't get 'em up at all!

Robert J. Burdett.

Reveille

CHAPTER ONE

"Into United States Service"

THE THIRTY-NINTH REGIMENT had its birth during that period of great excitement and the intense feeling of indignation that followed upon the opening act of the rebellious States, the firing upon Fort Sumter, Charleston Harbor, South Carolina, Friday, April 12, 1861.

A party of gentlemen, some of whom were afterwards prominently identified with this regiment, had assembled in the law offices of Moore & Osborn in the old Tremont building on Dearborn Street, Chicago, to give expression to the feelings engendered by this outrage and insult to the flag of our common country, when we thought a company of infantry be raised at once and tendered to the Governor of the State.

Action was immediately taken, and the names of Thomas O. Osborn, Frank B. Marshall, Dr. Samuel C. Blake, Joseph A. Cutler, George Coatsworth, Dr. Charles M. Clark and a few others enrolled as members. Soon the idea occurred it might be as easy to organize and raise a regiment as a company, and measures were taken to that end. Money was obtained and men selected to go to various portions of the State to enlist men and secure companies that had already been formed and were awaiting acceptance in some organized regiment.

Meanwhile, Orrin L. Mann, William H. Ranstead, William Dircks and others became associated with us, and active recruiting commenced in the city and suburbs. In less than six week's time we had some 1,300 men ready and impatient for muster into the United States service. Unfortunately for us the State had filled its quota under the first call for troops, and it was found that we could not be accepted as a regimental organization at that time, but were requested to await the next call, which, it was expected, would soon be made; but the men were impatient to get to the front and into active service, and learning that the State of Missouri was behind in raising its proportion of men, the Regiment was tendered to the Governor of that State, but with a like result.

Somewhat discouraged, and there being no certainty as to when it would be accepted, the Regiment became, in part disorganized, some companies withdrawing for acceptance into other regiments that had not their full complement of men but had been accepted, and many men joining other companies that were about ready to take the field.

The Regiment had decided upon bearing the name of Governor of the State, Richard Yates, and became known as the **"Yates Phalanx."** Governor Yates manifested an earnest desire to have this Regiment brought into U. S. Service and sent Orrin Mann, then recruiting a company, to Washington with strong complimentary letters to the President and the Secretary of War, urging the acceptance of this body of men, but it was not until the President had been authorized by Congress to make a call for 500,000 additional troops that hope revived and measures were taken to recruit our losses.

In the latter part of July 1861, after the disaster to our army at the first battle of Bull Run, Virginia, notice was received from Washington that the Regiment had been accepted and to prepare at once for muster into the services of the United States. More active measures were immediately put forward to increase our membership, and soon there were some 300 men quartered in the old Republican Wigwam on Market Street. Company A, Captain Munn, was the first full company to report, and they were quickly followed by Company C, Company D, and Company G. In succeeding chapters more explicit mention of the company organizations will be given.

In the latter part of July, Austin Light, who had seen considerable service in the United States Army, came to us well recommended as an organizer and as being well-posted in military affairs, army requirements and regulations, and to him was given the duty of perfecting the organizations of the Regiment, and it was conceded that he should have been made the colonel, although no election for field officers had as yet taken place.

On or about August 10, the necessary tents and camp equipment having been furnished, encampment was made on Indiana avenue near 26th street, and named "Camp Mather" in honor of the Adjutant General of the State, and were soon inducted into some semblance of military life and duty.

Daily drill was inaugurated, by company in the mornings and battalion in the afternoons. Awkward squads could be seen maneuvering at most all times. The Regimental Band, organized by Phillip M. Lace at Pontiac, Illinois, had joined us, and their music served to enliven the somewhat dull monotony of the camp, and especially did it serve as an attraction for visitors at the time of dress parade.

The camp was pleasantly situated, with plenty of open prairie ground about us; and in our near vicinity, to the south and east of us, was what was called the Douglas Brigade, then in state of formation.

On pleasant days there was no lack of visitors of both sexes, but especially were we overrun with peddlers and traders of every conceivable sort; agents from various arms manufactories soliciting orders for revolvers and ammunition; dealers in horses, who wished to supply the field and staff; drummers from tailoring establishments, etc.

In the early part of September, the State Commissioners of Agriculture, while in session at Chicago, voted a flag to be presented to the best drilled company of soldiers in camp at Chicago, and the regimental officers decided to enter competition for it; and Adjutant Frank B. Marshall, formerly a member of the Ellsworth Zouaves, was selected to organize and command a company made up of men of his choosing from any soldiers in the regiment. This he at once went on to do, and within ten days' time, by patient and persistent work with his men he brought them to that perfection in the manual of arms and in field evolutions, which on the day appointed for the contest and the adjudication they won an easy victory and were awarded the flag.

In the closing days of September, the precise date is forgotten, there was an order issued for the election of field officers. It had been very well understood for a long time who was the choice for the positions of colonel and lieutenant-colonel, and, in fact, these officers had already received their commissions; but it was evident that there were in the field for the position, Orrin L. Mann and William H. Ranstead, both of whom had been active in organizing and recruiting for the Regiment.

There were two factions; pretty evenly divided in support of the two men; that in favor of William Ranstead was the most noisy and belligerent and consisted of what was termed the "bummer" element of the Regiment; the party in favor of Orrin Mann was more peaceful and orderly, but fully as determined. On the day of the election, the officers gathered in one of the larger tents and prepared for the ballot, selecting Doctor Clark as judge of elections. Slips of paper bearing the name of each candidate were prepared and the voting proceeded, each slip being dropped into a hat on the table before the judge. When the votes were counted, it was found to be a tie, but the judge of elections had not yet voted, and who should be the Major wholly depended on his decision; and amid a most profound quiet and anxious, questioning glances, he declared for Captain Mann. As soon as the result became known among the men it was evident that trouble was brewing. Ranstead, who was present on the grounds, was soon surrounded by his admirers and supporters and was lifted upon their shoulders, and as they paraded him around, it was declared that he should be major or they would leave the Regiment. Some disgraceful scenes and a few acts of violence followed in the course of the day, but by nightfall matters became quieted down. Captain Mann was not present, being absent sick, and it perhaps was best so, for there were many threats of violence made against him, principally due to whiskey. Ranstead declared that he should contest the matter to the extent of his ability, and did exert all the influence that he could bring to bear upon the Governor; but it proved to no avail. Captain Mann received the commission of Major.

On October 8 the order that we had anxiously and patiently looked for came to hand. We were to immediately prepare to muster into the United States Service for three years, and to hold ourselves in readiness to move at a moment's notice.

Absentees were notified and gathered in, and everything made in readiness for the change awaiting us. A grateful surprise, however, was in store, before leaving Chicago, which was the presentation of a beautiful silk flag, by Miss Helen Arion, daughter of C. P. Arion, who had taken a lively interest in our affairs from the first. The presentation was made at the close of dress parade, on the evening of October 10, by Fernando Jones, of Chicago, and the flag was received by Lieutenant-Colonel Osborn, who in a few well-chosen words thanked the fair donor in behalf of the Regiment, and finally ended by naming her the "Daughter of the Regiment."

October 11, 1861, at seven o'clock in the morning, the officers and men were formed for inspection and for "muster in" by Captain Webb, U. S. A.

There were 806 officers and men were in line, all being present except Company H, which was in process of recruiting. Some little time was occupied by the inspection, and at the last, when the order was given to raise the right hand and be sworn, the sight was solemn and inspiring as this body of stalwart and eager men took the oath to defend and ever uphold the government of the United States of America.

The orders received directed us to report to General S. R. Curtis, commanding the Camp of Instruction at Benton Barracks, St. Louis, Missouri, transportation being furnished via the Chicago, Alton, and St. Louis Railroad. At eleven a.m., we bade a last adieu to Camp Mather, and commenced the march to the depot, stepping out to the spirited strains from the band of "The Girl I Left Behind Me." We were at last "off to the wars," and thus commenced the first of a series of long and often disastrous marches unattended by such pleasurable emotions as at this time filled our hearts.

The Regiment proceeded by way of Cottage Grove avenue to 22nd Street, turning into Michigan avenue, thence to Madison street, and to the cars. The men put their best foot forward, making a most creditable and soldierly appearance, although without muskets, gratefully and proudly receiving the admiring plaudits of the thousands who gathered to witness the departure of the Thirty-Ninth.

"Off to the Front."

We were escorted from the camp to the depot by the Chicago Zouaves in command of Captain E. L. Brand, and highly appreciated the compliment.

After the men had been assigned and comfortable disposed of on board the cars, the officers, through the courtesy of Mr. C. Pratt, one of the officials of the railway, were invited to partake of lunch at the Briggs House, where they as one proceeded, and with good appetites soon showed their appreciation of this kindness. After the meal, Mr. George C. Bates, an old soldier and a prominent lawyer of Chicago, arose, and in behalf of the citizens spoke to us about courage, glory and honor.

At the conclusion of the remarks of, Lieutenant-Colonel Thomas O. Osborn arose, and with a heart full of emotion and in words of burning eloquence, responded in behalf of the Phalanx and its officers. He told of the obstacles in its infancy, the embarrassments in its equipment, and of its successful and perfect organization, and pledged the Regiment and its officers to either maintain and defend the cause of the Union or to leave every man of it on the field of battle and of duty.

A short and stirring speech was then made by Captain Hooker, when the order was given to "Fall-in!" and the officers proceeded to their posts. An excellent light meal was also provided by the railroad company for the Regiment and Captain Brand's escort, at the depot, which was discussed with eminent satisfaction and elicited universal sentiments of gratitude for the generosity which had anticipated their wants.

CHAPTER TWO

"Off for St. Louis"

After leaving the Briggs House our steps were directed to the railroad cars, where, after bidding adieu to the many friends who had accompanied us, the order was given to move, and we were soon separated from all the blandishments of Chicago, and bade a long goodbye to home scenes and comforts.

The occasion was one that enlisted the energy of thought, and as the train moved forward and onward a mournful silence seemed to take possession of us all, relieved only by the swift rolling wheels and jar and clatter of motion; but the reaction soon took place, and the jovial element of some of our comrades asserted a preeminence that we could not control, and in mirthful song and strange story we soon forgot the past.

We reached the city of Alton the following afternoon, where a most desirable change awaited us in the shape of a steamboat ride down the river.

The transfer was soon made, and "all aboard!" soon proclaimed, when we heard the cry of "man overboard!" All rushed to see what was the matter, but thanks to the crew of the steamer the man was already landed, and proved to be one of the men who had imbibed too freely of the milk of "human weakness," and he came aboard again dripping and sputtering about a bath in the Mississippi.

The city of St. Louis was reached about seven p.m. and the command disembarked and formed for the march to Benton Barracks, our destination. It was some time, however, before a guide was found, and then we learned that a march of several miles was before us.

The Regiment started out, marching by platoons up through the narrow and deserted streets with no one to cheer and no one to make afraid. Occasionally some belated traveler or vagrant would turn to watch our progress. It was not until the band had come together and commenced a lively air that the streets were enlivened by the lights from door and window, but they were generally quickly closed again, for it was nothing but a "Yankee parade" in the opinion of the majority.

We reached the barracks in the early morning, but received no accommodations at all until eight o'clock, when quarters were assigned to the field and staff officers and to each company.

Benton Barracks, at this time, was a Camp of Instruction and were occupied by several regiments of infantry and one regiment of cavalry under the command of Brigadier-General S. R. Curtis, U.S.A. The barracks were named at the request of Major-General Fremont in honor of his father-in-law. They were pleasantly located, some three miles west of the city, and were very extensive, including the old Fairgrounds and some 300 acres beside it. The barracks proper was constructed on the border of an oblong square enclosing 100 acres used for parade and drill purposes, and the appearance presented here, at times, was calculated to awaken enthusiasm in the most obtuse.

For the first few days, there seemed to be a general revulsion of mind occasioned by the strange scene and the consciousness of having suffered a great change in social and culinary arrangements. We had but just begun to realize that pork, beef, beans and hardtack were the "staff of life" for the soldier, and the continuous use of this provender, badly cooked, was calculated to engender a bad temper. The Post Sutler was the only alternative, and the extortionate prices for little delicacies in the way of fruit and cakes made one wonder, besides making him sick. All were soon familiar with the new routing of life; and in going through camp, scenes of contented comfort and enjoyment were apparent.

The Sutlers.

The soldier is ever the creature of circumstances, and we had made up our minds to take "things as they came," and let care go drifting; and the leisure time was enjoyed through out camp in games at cards, dancing, and practical jokes.

Private George Riddle, of Company I, enlisted on September 17, 1861. He later recalled;

> "My first night in camp, and breakfast the next morning, somewhat disappointed me. I was taken to a tent and told that I could sleep there. They didn't even ask me if I preferred to sleep alone or with someone, but just told me that I could sleep there. So I rolled myself up in a wisp of straw and managed to pass the night quite comfortably. In the morning

I heard a rattling of drums all around me and the boys all tumbled out 'hollering' 'Roll call! Roll call!' So I rolled out too. They told me to 'get in line there!' And I got into line same as the rest. They then called 'breakfast!' And I saw all the boys run, and I followed, and got around a table made out of some rough boards put on sticks driven in the ground for legs. I found a piece of fat meat on a tin plate, and a tin cup with some black stuff in it, and a little 'hunk' of bread. The 'boys' 'pitched in!' But I thought I'd wait until breakfast was ready. I didn't see no sugar, no cream or butter—no potatoes; in fact, nothing but a little fat meat, and bread, and the little tin of what they called coffee. I still kept waiting, thinking they would soon bring on some thing like what us boys had been use to. By this time the 'boys' had 'downed' the meat and bread. They shouted out for me to 'grab hold' and make myself at home. And then I did."

Arms for the Regiment were received October 16, 1861, but as they were of an inferior type the men protested against them. General Curtis said that they were for drill purposes and for the protection of the camp, and that as soon as possible they should receive better ones; which explanation was satisfactory.

Private Riddle continued, "My first night on guard (it happened that during our stay in Chicago I did not have to go on guard duty) came at Benton Barracks. I got along fine in the daytime, but Oh, Lord! The trouble I had that night! They gave me an old carbine that Santa Anna had in the Mexican War! And put me on a 'beat' close to a little lot that had corn in it, and gave me the 'countersign' which I never will forget; but I forgot it that night. They told me that I must keep a good 'look out!' For they were looking for Price's[2] whole army to come on us.

"My relief was put on at 12 o'clock that night, and I had to look out for Price and the 'grand rounds' both, and it kept me so busy that I forgot part of the 'counter-sign,' which was *Santomingo*. I could think of *Sango*, but for my life I couldn't think of *mingo*, so I walked to the other sentinel and asked him what it was. He said, "By golly! I've forgot it too!" but he said it was *mingo* something. 'All right!' I said, 'I've got it now—*Sangomingo*!'

"It wasn't long then before the 'grand rounds' came. I could hear the other sentinels halt them, and my heart began to flutter. I let Price and his army go to thunder and I stuck to the 'countersign' and the 'grand rounds.' When they came up within speaking distance I cried out, 'Halt!' And they halted, and for the life of me I couldn't think of what else to say, and they still halted! I thought I must say something, so I says 'Come on with your grand rounds!' And they came up, and I saw it was Lieutenant-Colonel Osborn and Dr. Clark; and the Colonel says, 'Soldier! Don't you know the duties of a sentinel?' 'Yes, sir,' says I. 'Well, I don't think you do,' says he; 'and I'll report you to your company commander.' This kind of flustrated me, for I thought I had halted them all right—just as good as a soldier of 1812.

---

[2] Brigadier-General Sterling Price - Confederate States Army

"Soon after I heard a noise in the cornfield nearby, and I, Price and his men are coming! I listened closely, and felt sure I could hear them, and cocked the old carbine to be ready; but they never came. But I'll tell you, if they had come, I would have cleaned them out right then and there and gone to camp faster than a bank cashier going to Canada."

After being in barracks for some days, sickness among the men became manifest, and it was not unusual matter to have 150 report at "sick call" in the morning. Many of this number were pure malingerers, of course, and reported merely for the purpose of being excused from duty, which was becoming too onerous and 'played out,' in their parlance, and wishing to escape drill, they reported to the surgeons for an excuse.

It had been intimated, and we had reason to believe that we were to be sent to General Sigell's division, but while waiting for transportation, Colonel Ward H. Lamon, Marshal of the District of Columbia, arrived on October 26 with an order from General Fremont for us to proceed to Williamsport, Maryland, to join Ward H. Lamon's Brigade, which was then organizing, and was to be assigned to General Bank's Division of the Army of the Potomac.

The order directed us to leave camp on October 29 and proceed to Leesburg on the Potomac via Alton, Terre Haute, and Indianapolis. Our wish would have been, by the way of Chicago; but it was considered that too much risk would be run in the matter of losing men.

For some reason the departure of the Regiment from St. Louis was deferred until October 31, 1861, and the destination changed to Hagerstown, Maryland.

The journey from St. Louis to Hagerstown occupied thirty-six hours. The incidents of the trip were diverse and exciting. Everywhere along the line we met with hearty welcome, amounting to ovations in some instances. At the isolated farmhouses, the inmates came to the portal waving us onward and giving us God-speed to our destination and our mission.

At Indianapolis a light meal was bountifully spread and partaken of with thankful hearts, seasoned as it was with cheering words at the hand of youth and beauty (feminine gender). The Regimental band under the enthusiastic Lace gave them some patriotic airs, and we sped onward, traversing a beautiful and picturesque country down the valley of the Beaver and Ohio Rivers until we reached Allegheny City at four p.m., November 1, 1861.

We crossed the river, and were soon in Pittsburgh, where a delegation from the "Soldier's Aid Committee" escorted the Regiment to rooms over the city market and where we were plentifully fed with the staples of life, to say nothing of the luxuries.

The boys put away the "hash," as they termed it, with decided relish under the waiting hands and smiles of the patriotic women of Pittsburgh.

At this point we were transferred to the Pennsylvania Railroad, under the gaze of curious thousands who had gathered to look at an Illinois regiment.

As we moved off, the grand hurrahs of the men and the encouraging smiles of the women were sufficient to satisfy even the most apathetic among us. The cars provided for us were very comfortable, and numbered some twenty-six aside from the baggage train, and three locomotives were attached to draw us onwards.

In passing through the train we found the men to be unanimous in the opinion of having been well treated in Pittsburgh, and it was amusing to a great degree to listen to their talk. Some were convinced that old Pennsylvania was the most hospitable State in the Union. "Didn't they treat us well!" says one who had a box of cigars, a package of tobacco and a drinking cup had been presented to him. Others would only admit it was second to Indianapolis. "For didn't they do it brown for us in Indianapolis!" There was gratitude on every side, and we were thankful that the generous people had been so thoughtful for us.

SUPPER AT PITTSBURGH.

At midnight we commenced the ascent of the mountain and many were the wishes that the darkness of night might be changed to day until the passage was made, that we might enjoy the scenery.

Some hours were occupied in making the transit, and occasionally we caught glimpses of awful chasms and frightful precipices; sometimes were whirling along unbroken ridges, then thundering through dismal tunnels cut through massive rock; then as we commenced the descent, our speed was sometimes alarming; but the only satisfaction obtained was the clangor of the chained wheels as they slid along the rails, awaking shudders for our safety.

November 2, at three p.m., we reached Harrisburg, after following along the historic Juniata and the broad and beautiful Susquehanna Rivers.

We remained sufficiently long to transfer our train to the Cumberland Valley Railroad, and were soon rolling on again, and reached Mechanicsburg, a lively and very pleasant city, and one that will remain "green" in the memory of more than one connected with the "Phalanx," for as we entered the town a large number of young ladies met us at the depot, from the Seminary near by, each bearing the colors we go to maintain.

Some of the officers and men were so fascinated that they jumped from the train and hastened to pay their respects, thus taking lead of the Field and Staff, who were so importuned that at last they consented to show themselves—all being modest and retiring men.

A merry time was had in the few moments that we were permitted to stop. The whole population of the town had seemingly turned out to greet us, and those who remained behind were seen at the doors and windows with fluttering handkerchiefs and waving hats.

At half-past six p.m. we reached Carlisle, our Colonel's old home, and who called our attention to the barracks where he had spent many years as a soldier.

On reaching the station we proceeded to the hotel for supper, much to the annoyance of the engineers, who blandly told us that they would not stop longer than five minutes; but we soon ended the controversy by asserting that we would remain until our supper was finished, well knowing that their duty would not be compromised, as there were not trains to meet and no trouble to encounter except their willfulness; and we enforced our point by giving orders to have the brakes put "hard down" in case they attempted to start, and many of the boys who had been up the "trick" before, were only too glad to obey; and the train was soon under "martial law."

On leaving the supper-table we found the noncommissioned staff and men enjoying themselves heartily in making the acquaintance of the many ladies who had gathered along the train and who were presenting edibles and smiles in one motion gratuitously; and there are many of the old "Phalanx" who will cherish thoughts of that occasion for all time.

Carlisle lies about fifty miles from the border of Virginia, and in the track of rebel invasion, and the inhabitants of the town were in constant fear of such a disaster as was realized in the partial destruction of their place in 1863, during the passage of Lee's army through to Gettysburg. The railroad runs through the main street of the town, and notwithstanding the lateness of the hour, the streets were full of people to welcome troops who were going to the front to place themselves between them and danger. The ladies seemed to preponderate, and the boys when they left the train to stretch their legs, were quite taken by surprise to find so much beauty and such a loving welcome as was extended. One would have thought that they had all come to meed some long-absent brother or son, so demonstrative was their greeting. The boys, after recovering from their surprise, rather enjoyed the affair, and much regretted that it could not be continued indefinitely or taken along.

It was eight o'clock before we were started again, and it will be remembered that every town we passed through was illuminated with bonfires and lights placed at the windows and portals of the houses—in fact a perfect ovation had been tendered the command from its first starting out to the end of the journey.

We reached Hagerstown at midnight, but did not leave the cars until morning, on account of the rain which had commenced to fall some hours previously.

At six o'clock we removed from the cars, during a temporary lull in the storm, to the market house, which was kindly placed at our disposal and where the morning ration was disposed of. The city was very quiet; but few of the citizens (principally Negroes) gathered around to look at us. At midnight, November 7, the baggage train and ambulances reported from Williamsport. The train was speedily loaded and we started out, in a drenching rain, for our destination. The march occupied two hours time, but it was not a gloomy one notwithstanding the heavy rain and driving wind. There was no complaining, for every man behaved himself as a soldier, and the vivacity of spirit and elasticity of step was wonderful in consideration of all the circumstances. Officers and men were soon wet to the skin, and it was only occasionally that some of the more effeminate reported back to the ambulance for shelter.

Williamsport, the "Omega" of our tramp, was reached at three p.m., and we proceeded to take quarters in several vacant warehouses on the banks of the canal, as it was deemed impossible to pitch the tents on account of the high wind and incessant rain.

But one incident had occurred to mar the pleasure of our progress from St. Louis, Missouri to Williamsport, Maryland. Before leaving Pittsburgh, Private Daniel Neal, of Company K, while the car in which he was riding was at rest upon a bridge (the train having stopped for repairs), missed his footing upon the platform and was precipitated down through the trestle-work a distance of forty feet. Fortunately the bed of the stream beneath was shallow, and he escaped drowning; but when picked up it was found that he had suffered a severe concussion of the spinal column, with fracture of two of the processes of the dorsal vertebrae. The lower limbs were paralyzed. He was taken aboard the cars again and made as comfortable as circumstances would permit, and on reaching Pittsburgh he was placed under competent care at Dr. Waller's Surgical Infirmary. He rejoined the Regiment at Arlington Heights, Virginia in 1864 and was discharged by reason of physical deformity.

CHAPTER THREE

Making Encampment

After a good night's rest in our provisional quarters we removed to a camping-ground about one mile from the town, it being located on the summit of a broad ridge near the river, from which and the enemy's pickets it was closed from view by a belt of heavy timber.

The Regimental Hospital was established in the town, having appropriated a large brick structure, formerly a hotel, for the purpose. It was capable of containing about 100 patients, and was soon completely full by reason of an epidemic of measles which broke out about this time among the men of the command, aside from other and frequently recurring diseases incident to camp life. The medical officers of the Regiment treated some 300 cases of measles in this hospital without the loss of a single life; but afterwards, the sequelae frequently occasioned death.

While here, First-Lieutenant Joseph W. Richardson, of Company A, was taken sick with typhoid fever. He received the best of care at the Globe Inn, where he was quartered, but after a painful illness he succumbed to the disease, November 7, 1861. The ladies of the house contributed a very pretty wreath of flowers, and the Regimental colors, furled with crepe, were hung at the window of the room where he lay. He was buried with military honors on the banks of the Potomac River, between the two hostile armies—the friends and foes of the Union.

The Regiment had no weapons at this time, and upon request to Colonel Leonard, commanding the Thirteenth Massachusetts and the Post, to send a firing party, he responded with his whole regiment, which turned out with the Thirty-Ninth to do the last sad offices for the dead lieutenant. This, perhaps, is the only instance during the war where two regiments, at the front, attended the burial of a soldier, no matter of what rank. Chaplain McReading read the impressive burial service of the Masonic Order, to which the deceased belonged, and soon after the hills echoed the salute which Massachusetts fired over the grave of a patriot son of Illinois.

The medical officers remained in town for the reason that the hospital was located there, but each morning either the surgeon or the assistant rode out to camp at seven a.m. to hold "sick call." There seemed to be an organized fellowship among members of the several companies to give the "doctor" a warm reception at each visit, and no sooner did we reach the outline of camp than a perfect howl was sent up in which could be distinguished expressions such as "Here comes old Salts! Castor O-i-l! Quinine!" etc., etc., and which were echoed and re-echoed from one end of camp to the other, making a most unpleasant strain upon the sensitive eardrums of the doctors.

The medical officers, however, had the opportunity for revenge among the large numbers always presented for excuse from duty (mainly malingerers), by repeating the doses of salts and oil and quinine, and personally attending the administration.

The practice of cathartics among the men was rendered almost absolute by reason of the continual gormandizing of indigestible rubbish from the sutlers, and it was a matter of surprise that no more sickness was brought about from the inordinate stuffing that was continually practiced; and, be it known, a six months supply was consumed in the short space of six weeks.

THE CAMP KITCHEN. (FROM PHOTOGRAPH.)

Opposite the Potomac House in the town, was a quaint structure that possessed more than common interest, and around which many reminiscences of the past clustered that are still dear to every American heart. It was in this building that General George Washington, while looking for a site for the National Capitol, made his headquarters and remained for the space of two weeks. Williamsport was a locality he had in view at one time, but some circumstance changed it to the present region.

We were close upon the rebels here, and could see their pickets daily pacing along the high ridges of the opposite shore of the Potomac River, and sometimes we had a view of large numbers of cavalry who were scouting and continually driving the Union-loving men and women from their homes, besides plundering and destroying their property.

Williamsport was full of refugees that had been forced to leave their homes on account of their loyal sentiments. It was also full of spies, who, under the most strict surveillance, managed to communicate with the enemy on the opposite shore. There were rebels in the town, too, but they were securely lodged in the guardhouse.

The Regiment, at this time, still had no muskets, but were daily expecting them, and as a consequence we felt ourselves to be in a very lame condition, with no means of offense or defense except what nature could provide.

The Thirteenth Massachusetts Volunteers, then quartered in town, were armed with the Enfield rifle, and besides, there were several companies of cavalry well-mounted and armed, and a section of battery of rifled cannon.

It was promised that two more regiments, one from West Virginia and one from Pennsylvania, would soon join us, and then it was proposed to cross the river, proceed to Martinsburg, thirteen miles distant, where there was some 5,000 of the enemy with heavy ordnance, and we, of course, were going to dislodge them and establish a new base of operations; but

> "The well-laid plans of mice and men
> Gang aft aglee;"

and so in this instance we suffered disappointment. Had we crossed the river, the example of General Patterson, who was our predecessor, would not have been followed, for we had no sympathy with the rebellion.

November 10, 1861, there was some indication of an attack, judging from the preparation they were making on the opposite bluffs, but it eventuated in nothing but a scare.

A little episode in our history grew out of the matter, however, which was very personal in its application. At about nine p.m. the "long roll" sounded through camp, and it being our first experience with it, and unusual excitement and commotion was soon established. Every man fully believed that the "Secesh" were coming full tilt, from the fact that various rumors during the day had prepared them to give credence to almost everything. While the alarm was being sounded, the men were seen slinging their knapsacks and grasping anything that would serve as a weapon before taking their place in the line that forming, and, strange to say, a perfect alignment was made in the space of three minute's time. The band came out with their instruments in one hand and a carpetbag in the other, each member looking somewhat bewildered. The females in camp, and there were several, the wives of enlisted men, who had come out as laundresses, was in a maze of bewilderment and fluttered about with bundles of clothing in their arms and slung over their backs, fully intent on preserving their effects from what would soon be (in their belief) a plundered camp.

After the line was formed, the Regiment was put in motion and maneuvered about for some little time, when it was dismissed by the Colonel with some explanations.

The men were unanimous in considering it a good joke, but confessed to a bitter disappointment that their fears had not been realized.

While we were at Williamsport we made the acquaintance of David Strother, but more familiarly known as "Porte Crayon" from his pen and pencil sketches. He at the time was engaged in scouting, and frequently made his appearance at the Potomac House where he would spend a social evening. We took much pleasure in entertaining him, well knowing him as a literary acquaintance and a staunch Union man in his sentiments and actions. He was afterwards on the staff of Major-General Banks, and before the close of the war had the commission of Colonel. In the later part of November

1861, Colonel Austin Light left the Regiment by order of the War Department. The reasons for his dismissal are well known to many who were present with the Regiment at the time, and therefore it would serve no-good purpose to repeat them here.

What was reported as to Colonel Light's conduct while a Corporal in the U. S. Army, may or may not have been true. Even if it were, it is the opinion of the writer (who was acquainted with all the circumstances) that there was no justification for his removal.

The order caused a painful surprise. The men had become much attached to him, for he was an efficient officer and a kind-hearted man. The men marched in a body to headquarters to bid him goodbye. The Colonel thus addressed them:

> "Fellow Soldiers, Officers and Gentlemen of the Thirty-Ninth: It has pleased the War Department through the influence of some political intrigue, I know not how else, to deprive your Colonel of his command. As I leave you, I must say that I have found you soldiers such as command my respect and such as I should be proud to lead against the rebels now in arms. I must now bid you farewell."

As he passed through the ranks, on his departure, every head was bared and much sorrow expressed in many ways.

As soon as it was known that our "Light" had gone out we went to work to get a new Colonel.

The company officers were at first bitterly opposed to supplying the vacancy by promotion, and held a meeting on the night of December 4, in the parlors of the Potomac Hotel for the purpose of choosing a man to fill the vacancy. The first choice was William J. Wyatt, of Illinois, and the second Thomas Morgan, of the same State; but notwithstanding this action on their part, the Governor promoted Lieutenant-Colonel T. O. Osborn to Colonel, Major Orrin L. Mann to Lieutenant-Colonel and Captain S. W. Munn of Company A, to Major, and matters were soon adjusted to the satisfaction of all parties.

December 5, Colonel Leonard of the Thirteenth Massachusetts Regiment, commanding the post, received orders from Washington to send forward, without delay, all the troops he could to reinforce General Kelly, at Romney, West Virginia, who was said to be creeping down to engage the rebels and reopen the Baltimore and Ohio Railroad.

We had not as yet received our arms, although assured that they were at Hagerstown, and consequently could not go to the assistance of General Kelly.

The health of the command at this time was excellent, the measles having run their course, 353 cases having been treated in the short space of two months, aside from other diseases.

The mortality list was small indeed, the only deaths in the command being Lieutenant Joseph Richardson, from typhoid fever; Private William Parrish, of Company G, from organic disease of the heart; and Private Henry Hoisington, Company B, from tuberculosis.

Thanksgiving Day came, bringing with it a suspension of all but necessary duties, and likewise a considerable number of turkeys and chickens whose age, lineage and previous history were not especially inquired into, having been provided by the genius who watches after the wants of the soldier. Several officers were invited to dinner in town with the officers of the Thirteenth

Massachusetts; others dined at the house of Captain Kennedy, of the First Maryland Infantry. In the evening a grand ball was held at the Globe Inn, and largely attended, but did not prove particularly interesting, on account of the scarcity of women for partners. But a "stag" dance being better than no dance at all, the fun was continued until the small hours of a very foggy morning in more senses than one.

Colonel Thomas O. Osborn

Courtesy of the National Archives

Reminiscences of Surgeon S. C. Blake

"When the Regiment arrived at Williamsport, Maryland, two female spies came into camp and asked to see the commander of the post. These two women were sisters. One of them was a single woman and the other was a widow. From their appearance, they had been exposed to severe weather, and had been on a hard tramp. They had also evidently been camping in the woods, as their clothes were soiled and badly torn, and they looked as if they had no opportunity to wash their faces and hands for a number of days. These women claimed to be Union spies, and told our commander that they had important information to impart in reference to the strength, condition, and position of the enemy on the other side of the river in Virginia. It turned out that the women were what they represented themselves to be. We found out that they were sisters, born and reared in Martinsburg, West Virginia, but had been faithful to the Union and loyal to their country, and were ready to sacrifice even their lives for its preservation. The oldest sister, some few weeks after they came to us, while making a visit to the enemy's camp, were arrested and tried as a spy, but were so ably defended by a Confederate officer, a companion and friend, from childhood, of the brave and loyal women, and who was also a very able lawyer, that she escaped punishment.

"These were remarkable women—intelligent, brave, and loyal to the cause of the Union. They had been loyal to the Nation from the commencement of its trouble, and did not fail to make known their patriotism to their neighbors. As soon as the war commenced these patriotic women placed the National Flag over their front door, and would not allow it to be taken down, although it was often undertaken; but the brave women defended it, saying they would defend it with their lives; and although a military guard was placed at their house and kept there until our army entered Martinsburg, the guard allowed it to remain rather than have a fight with women. So all persons who entered their house had to pass under the United States flag.

"For some weeks before our army entered Martinsburg we had missed the return of our fair spies, and had come to the conclusion that they had been arrested and perhaps executed, but we found them safe and ready with a warm welcome for us. They had been so perfectly guarded since the trial of one of them for being a spy that they could not come to us.

"It so happened that the lady who was tried for being a spy had an opportunity to show her gratitude to her Confederate friend who so ably and gallantly defended her. When our Regiment entered Martinsburg, this friend, who was a Major in the Confederate army, was captured with a friend who was a surgeon in that army. When Major Munn and Surgeon S. C. Blake arrived at Martinsburg, these ladies besought them to use their influence with the commanding officer of the place to secure a parole for these officers, who were then occupying a cell in the county jail. In consideration of the services rendered by the gallant Major in behalf of our loyal friend, which no one else would undertake for her, Munn and Blake gladly used their offices to secure their parole, and succeeded, to the delight of all, especially the lady whose life had been saved by the Major's earnest efforts.

"These brave and patriotic women should certainly have a prominent place in the history of our country."

The following incident will show how little true conception our volunteer army had of the discipline and rigid enforcement of army regulations necessary for efficient and effective service in actual warfare. Soon after we arrived at Williamsport, Maryland, an extensive epidemic of measles broke out in our Regiment. About 500 of the Regiment had the disease, most of them, however, in a mild form; and as it was mild and pleasant weather, only about ninety were obliged to be taken care of in the hospital.

Of course there was no regular hospital in a small village like Williamsport, consequently Surgeon Blake was obliged to extemporize a hospital. The ninety patients in this hospital were very sick and caused the attending surgeons a great deal of anxiety. Among others, Company A had quite a number of very sick members. Captain Munn, of this Company, afterwards Major of the Regiment, was very solicitous about his men, and anxious that they should have the best of care. He, like many other officers, had recruited his company from among his neighbors and acquaintances, and was prompted by his warm heart and patriotic zeal to promise the wives, sisters, and sweethearts of the recruit that he would see that they were well-taken care of, and especially when they were sick or wounded; and now it seemed to these officers the time had come for the fulfillment of this promise.

Surgeons Blake and the writer fully appreciated the responsibility so suddenly thrown upon them, and were obliged to make very stringent rules for the government of the hospital, and in order to prevent interference with their duties, Surgeon Blake issued an order that no one should visit the hospital unless having a pass either from the Surgeon or Assistant Surgeon. As soon as these officers learned this fact they were very angry, and boldly announced that no damned surgeons were going to interfere with their looking after their men, and that they would soon convince these surgeons that they would visit the hospital when they pleased.

Consequently a number of officers, headed by Captain Munn, in a very determined and boisterous manner started for the hospital. Upon arriving at the door of the hospital they were halted by a guard, who of course had not seen much real service, and as his superior officers demanded to pass, the guard was trying to persuade them to desist and first get a pass; but Captain Munn told the guard that he would give him to understand, and also Surgeon Blake, that no damned surgeon could keep them from visiting their men when they please. DeNormandie, who was then Hospital Steward, hearing the noise at the door of the hospital went to discover what the trouble was, and Captain Munn informed him, the Doctor taking up his new Springfield rifle and stepping back a few feet, placed the gun to his shoulder, saying, "Captain Munn, you are my friend and the Captain of my company, and you ought to know better than to attempt to force a guard; and I can assure you that unless you have a pass from one of the surgeons you cannot enter his hospital, and if you attempt it I will put a bullet through your body or the body of anybody else who attempts it."

Captain Munn afterwards said that the "old Doc," as he called him, showed by his eye that he meant business. These officers, now more enraged than ever, started for the headquarters of the Commander of the Regiment, Colonel T. O. Osborn. As it happened, Colonel Osborn, with the Colonel of the Thirteenth Massachusetts Regiment, and other officers, was visiting Surgeon Blake at his quarters, and while pleasantly conversing about affairs of the command, in rushed Captain Munn with his fellow officers, and in great excitement began to abuse the surgeons and especially Surgeon Blake, telling the Colonel what an outrage had been committed towards himself and comrades. To the great chagrin of both Captain Munn and his comrades, the Colonel coolly informed them that he had no control over the medical department and look at the Army Regulations, and see what sort of a position they had placed themselves in.

On the next morning after this episode, as Surgeon Blake was sitting on the front porch of his quarters, he saw coming down the street a little squad of officers, but they looked very meek and were apparently in very earnest conversation about some serious affair. When they saw the Surgeon, Captain Mann called him to one side, and in a most anxious manner asked him what he was going to do about the affair of last night. The Surgeon, with an apparently offended air, very coolly said to the Captain that he had not yet determined what he would do about it. Whereupon the Captain in an excited manner replied that he had heard that the Surgeon intended to have them all court-martialed; and then in a most imploring way, said, "Blake, do you know that if you call a court-martial we shall all be shot? The regulations say that to attempt to force a guard while in active service shall be punished by death! For God's sake, let's settle the matter". We made damned fools of ourselves, and will assure you that we will never be guilty of such foolishness again.

Surgeon Blake, after keeping them on the anxious seat for a few days, never had occasion to mention the matter again.

This incident did more to establish discipline in the Regiment than anything that ever happened to it.

It is gratifying to be able to state that every man who was sick at that time recovered, and that this severe attack of sickness thoroughly established the surgeons in the confidence of the entire Regiment, which was never lost during the war.

CHAPTER FOUR

"The hour had not yet come"

The days passed uneventfully by, the hours filled out with the monotonous routine of camp duties, with the exception of the stir occasioned on arrival of arms for the Regiment in the early part of December. They were the Springfield rifle, a most excellent and serviceable weapon, and the men were jubilant over the possession, having considered that they were only half soldiers with no means of offense or defense.

December 15, 1861, the Regiment broke camp and departed for Hancock, Maryland, some 16 miles distant, the camp and garrison equipment being transported by canal-boat. It arrived at Hancock on the following day, after bivouacking at Clear Spring over night, and at once crossed the Potomac River to Alpine Station, West Virginia, having orders to guard the Baltimore and Ohio Railroad.

The various companies of the command were distributed as follows: Companies A, B, C, and F at Alpine Station and vicinity; Company E at Sir John's Run, six miles distant up the road in the direction of Cumberland; Company G, at Great Cacapon Bridge; and Companies D, K and I at Bath (also known as Berkeley Springs), six miles in the interior, back from the river. The Regimental Headquarters were established at Alpine, taking possession of the vacant house belonging to Johnson Orrick, then a member of the Confederate Congress, and who had removed his family to Richmond. The hospital was also established at this place. The Orrick mansion was spacious and roomy; but nothing had been left behind to facilitate the comforts of keeping house, being an exception to the quarters found by the company officers at Bath and other places. There was, however, good stabling for horses, with plenty of hay and grain.

The cold December days and long dreary nights here were full of surmises and expectancy, with now and then a stirring rumor of the approach of the enemy. Aside from this, there was nothing to excite or amuse. By way of variety, an occasional dance would be indulged in, and many will remember that it was while quartered in the Orrick house that Colonel Osborn learned his first steps in the contra-dance from Phil Lace, the band leader; and so captivating did it prove for the gallant Colonel that it was reported that he was often seen, in the dead of night, careering around with his shadow reflected on the wall by the light of a candle. But this, doubtless, was somewhat imaginative.

Alpine Station consisted of a few straggling houses. The only family of any prominence left there was the Swan family, made up of father, mother, and two daughters—all pronounced rebel sympathizers. The old gentlemen was such a dyed-in-the wool rebel that he was accommodated with quarters in the calaboose over at Hancock in charge of Captain Fox, who commanded a detachment less bitter in her hatred of the Yankees, and there was little reason to doubt that she possessed among her other accomplishments, that of a spy, and she was placed under constant surveillance. The Western men found considerable more favor in her eyes, however, than those from Massachusetts, and at time she was disposed to be most gracious. The Assistant Surgeon of the Regiment had especially ingratiated himself, and she had so worked upon his sympathies that he received permission from Captain Fox to take her father home to spend Christmas day; and in this way the doctor and a few others got a solid dinner. But the doctor did not enjoy it overmuch, having to keep the old gentlemen in mind all the time, being responsible for his safe return at a specified hour.

Some earthworks were thrown up near the Orrick house, for the protection of headquarters it was supposed, that was christened Fort Osborn; but there was never occasion for their use.

The men of the various companies stationed at Alpine and other places were kept constantly busy, often being sent out in scouting parties and frequently returning with prisoners and horses, or whatever else was considered contraband of war. The men rather seemed to enjoy it, too; for in this way the commissariat was often replenished with something more palatable than pork and hardtack. It will be remembered that when a scouting party under command of Lieutenant-Colonel Mann was out on the road leading to Martinsburg they overhauled the house of a noted secessionist, bringing to light from the cellar some five barrels of old applejack, which, by order of the Colonel, was condemned to make a puddle in the road, notwithstanding it was fifteen years old and the party very thirsty. All they succeeded in getting, however, was a good long smell.

Information received almost daily from various sources gave indication that the enemy was preparing to attack in force. Encounters frequently took place with the rebel cavalry and we were kept in a state of constant expectancy and vigilance. Night alarms were frequent—generally resulting, however, in nothing more than a momentary panic and a disturbance of rest among those off duty. "The hour had not yet come," but we felt it to be approaching. The detached companies at Bath were exceedingly well provided for. Company D, Captain Linton, was quartered near the bathhouses. Whether they improved their opportunities to keep clean is somewhat uncertain. Company I, Captain Phillips, was stationed upon Warm Spring ridge, over looking the town, and the captain and his lieutenants occupied a large three-story stone house, the former occupants of which had left behind much costly and elegant furniture, such as mahogany bedsteads, large mirrors, marble-top tables, etc.; and when we had occasion to visit his quarters the Captain did the honors in regal style. Company K, Captain Woodruff, was also stationed on the ridge, and fared sumptuously, while Lieutenant Muhlenburg, in command of a section of battery of the Fourth U. S. Artillery, occupied the courthouse. He used to remark that court was in session every day and at all hours, and that there was a standing invitation to call up and see his friend Judge Applejack at any time.

All will remember Muhlenburg and the good service he rendered with his two pieces at Bath and Hancock, January 3 and 4, 1862. He was small in quantity but immense in quality a jovial, breezy fellow, and a smart, intelligent and brave officer. Death claimed him sometime in 1863.

Bath, or Berkeley Springs, had been the great "watering place" and summer resort for Southern people, and the inhabitants had received their principal support from the many pleasure seekers. It is situated at the foot of Warm Spring ridge, and lovely scenery surrounds the place. The house at the Springs was occupied by the Strother family, and in it was a large collection of paintings executed by "Porte Crayon" and mostly sketched by him while on a tour through Italy. The Strothers were a loyal family, as was also that of Judge Pendleton, living near by. They always extended a hearty welcome and fully sympathized with our presence among them.

On January 2 an expedition was sent out from Bath to reconnoiter and ascertain the whereabouts of the enemy. After proceeding out on the Martinsburg Road some six miles it returned without encountering anything in the shape of armed rebels.

During the morning of the ensuing day a Negro came into camp and reported to Major Munn that the whole of Jackson's army was moving on Bath and that the advance could not be more than five miles distant.

Acting upon this information, Captain Linton, of Company D, with sixty men, was ordered out on another scout. Major Mann, with several cavalrymen, accompanied it. After proceeding some four or five miles in the direction of Martinsburg, the advance of what proved to be Jackson's forces was met and a lively skirmish ensued, which resulted in one man being wounded and nine taken prisoner. The enemy was held in check for some time by the excellent management of Captain Linton, who divided his command into some five or six sections, each under command of a sergeant, and made a show of a much larger force than was present, and by their excellent knowledge of the skirmish drill, for which this company was noted, it made good its retreat from the large and constantly increasing numbers of the enemy. Major Mann, who was wounded, had a narrow escape from capture; the good running qualities of his young stallion saved him. The company made good its return to Bath, reaching there after dark, and was not followed by the rebels.

The news reached camp in a very exaggerated form, and by the time it reached Alpine Station it had become alarming. The writer had gone, late in the afternoon, to visit some patients in the hospital across the river at Hancock, and was returning when he met Surgeon Blake and Colonel Bowles, the latter of whom gave an invitation to go over to his house and listen to some music that Lieutenant Brucker and his daughter were executing in great style.

We accepted, remaining at the house until nine p.m., when we started to cross the river to Alpine. On reaching the ferry we heard a great call for the ferryman from the opposite shore. The first voice recognized was that of Chaplain McReading, who was vociferating most lustily, "O-o-o ferryman! Ferryman! For God's sake come over quick! The Thirty-Ninth has been cut all to pieces!" Then followed a stronger and more excited voice that we recognized as belonging to Lieutenant Belcher, of Company K. He was shouting like a "Stentor"—notwithstanding the presence of the chaplain: "Ferryman! O-o-o ferryman! God damn your soul, why don't you hurry up with that boat! Do you want to have us all gobbled up?" The ferryman was in his shanty, but had retired for the night and was totally oblivious to all the noise; but we speedily roused him, thinking that some great disaster had overtaken the troops at Bath, and were soon in the skiff and across to the opposite shore, where we met two of the most frantic and impatient men ever encountered. All that could be learned was that all the troops at Bath were all cut to pieces, Major Munn a prisoner, and that they were going for the Eighty-Fourth Pennsylvania regiment, that had that afternoon reached Hancock from Williamsport.

Doctor Blake returned with them and followed them to the headquarters of Colonel Murray, commanding the Eighty-Fourth. The Colonel was found, and as he afterwards stated, "The two men acted as if they were crazy; I could get no definite idea of what had occurred, or where it had occurred, or by whose orders they were sent to me." As soon as Blake appeared on the scene he gave the Colonel the topography of Bath, and matters explained and made more satisfactory. Colonel Murray said that his regiment was in a poor condition for a fight, as they had just received their guns (the Belgian musket), and they were full of tallow, and his men were now busy thawing them out, but he was ready to obey orders.

The writer, when he reached the Virginia shore, proceeded to headquarters but found no persons except the members of the regimental band and a few other noncombatants, all of whom were much excited, and getting their traps together for a retreat on the first appearance of danger.

A snowstorm had set in during the early part of the evening which did not add much comfort to the situation. The Swan family was greatly excited, and no doubt was much pleased with the prospect of getting rid of the Yankees. They, however, called for protection—not from any fear of the rebels, but they were afraid that our boys, in case they were driven across the river, might commit some overt act in the spirit of revenge. They were not gratified, however, the only satisfaction given was to place a guard at the house to prevent any member of the family leaving the premises.

On the morning of January 4 we received some intelligent information of what had transpired the previous day, and which has already been given to the reader. Early in the day we caught the sound of artillery firing and knew that the enemy was advancing on Bath. No medical officer being at that post, Assistant Surgeon Clark was ordered to proceed there at once, which he did, reaching there safely, but found only one wounded man—Private Lankinaw of Company D, and he had been shot through the calf of the leg on the previous evening. There was a cessation of hostilities toward noon and Doctor Clark returned to Alpine for instruments and dressings. The official report of Colonel Osborn regarding this affair is here inserted.

"Headquarters Thirty-Ninth Illinois Regiment
Hancock, Maryland, Jan 8, 1862

"TO GENERAL LANDER, Commanding Division.
Sir: I have the honor to submit a report of our late skirmish with the rebel forces under General Jackson.

"While we were guarding the Baltimore and Ohio Railroad from Hancock or Alpine Station, Virginia, to Great Cacapon, on the 19th of December 1861, in obedience to orders from General Kelly, then commanding division, the Thirty-Ninth Regiment of Illinois Volunteers under my command crossed the Potomac at Hancock to the Virginia side and were stationed as follows: Companies A, B, C and F, at Alpine Station, Company E at Sir John's Run, Company G with Captain Dike's Company (Second Maryland Volunteers) at Great Cacapon; while Companies D, K, I and Lieutenant E. D. Muhlenburg with one section of Captain Best's Battery stationed at Bath, Virginia, being the advanced position, and the key to our whole line.

"The position of the artillery was such as to command the Martinsburg and Winchester roads. Scouts were sent out daily at different points along our whole line, but no intimation of the approaching rebels was received until the third day of January at four p.m. when information reached us that a large force of the enemy was advancing on our lines. For the purpose of ascertaining their whereabouts Captain Russell (who reported to me the day before, by order of General Kelly) was detailed with thirty of his cavalry to scout in the direction of Martinsburg from Alpine Station. Major O. L. Mann and Captain Linton with thirty of his men and five of Captain Russell's cavalry proceeded from Bath on the Winchester road, and Captain Slaughter with a small portion of his command took position upon Great Cacapon mountain, commanding a view of the valley between Great Cacapon and Warm Spring mountains, a distance of three miles, where he discovered a rebel force which he estimated at 3,000. Captain Russell reported a force of from 600 to 800 infantry and two cavalry companies which were bivouacked on the Martinsburg road seven miles from Alpine Station.

"Major O. L. Mann and his party had proceeded about four miles on the Winchester road, when they discovered some fifteen of the rebel cavalry whom they pursued until they were fired upon by about 150 rebel infantry who in ambush had awaited until our men had passed, doubtless, designing to cut off their retreat; but they were disappointed. Our brave boys returned their fire, driving them from their position, killing five of the rebels, including one lieutenant, wounding several and making good their retreat with the loss of three slightly wounded and eight taken prisoner.

"In anticipation of a general attack by a much superior force at an early hour on the succeeding morning, our men were kept in readiness for immediate action. I telegraphed General Kelly for support, who promptly replied that the Thirteenth Indiana Volunteers would come to our assistance by eight o'clock the next morning, and also instructed me to call on Colonel Murray of the Eighty-Fourth Pennsylvania Volunteers, who was lying at Hancock on the opposite side of the Potomac. At ten o'clock Colonel Murray, who had just received his arms, which were in rather a greasy condition for immediate action, crossed the Potomac 550 strong and proceeded to Bath to strengthen that position.

"A four o'clock on the morning of the 4th of January, our forces at Bath took position on Warm Spring Ridge, over looking Bath, and near our artillery.

"At Hancock Station Company A took position on the hill commanding the road to Winchester; Companies B and C commanding the road to Martinsburg and Sleepy Creek; and Company F, Mount Alpine, with Company G (Captain Slaughter), at Great Cacapon, with a detachment of twenty-two men under Lieutenant Rudd, at Great Cacapon mountain.

"At about nine o'clock the rebel cavalry made a demonstration by driving our pickets on the Martinsburg Road leading to Alpine, when Captain Russell with twenty-five of his cavalry, and Lieutenant Sellards of Company B with sixty infantry, was ordered to proceed in that direction to check their advance. At the same time the rebels appeared in the woods on the left of our forces at Bath, and a lively skirmishing fire was kept up on both sides; but our position was such that we lost no men, but a number of rebels fell under the fire of the artillery and our long-range Springfield rifles, Lieutenant Muhlenburg doing good service in holding the enemy at bay much longer that we could otherwise have done.

"At about three p.m. the rebels appeared in full force, variously estimated at from ten to fifteen thousand, with twenty-two pieces of cannon. Colonel Murray, fearing being surrounded by such an overwhelming force, and believing that he would not be able to hold his position at Bath, ordered a retreat by way of Sir John's Run, which was accomplished in good order, Companies I, K, and D of the Thirty-Ninth covering the retreat.

"The Thirteenth Indiana Volunteers were met near Sir John's, but too late to afford any assistance. At this point the artillery, together with the companies above mentioned, forded the river (there being no other means of crossing), Captain Hooker with forty men remaining to defend the point from the Maryland side, the Eighty-Fourth Pennsylvania Volunteers proceeding down the railroad to Hancock.

"In the meantime a column of the enemy, consisting of three regiments of infantry and two pieces of artillery, advanced upon our position at Great Cacapon. Lieutenant Rudd, of Company G, being posted upon the mountain, selected a position near a bend in the narrow road which he knew the column must pass. He and his men knelt and awaited its approach, and not until the foremost files were within fifty yards was their presence suspected. At this critical moment they coolly delivered their fire, and several of the enemy were seen to fall, while the head of their column was thrown into confusion. Taking advantage of this, they retreated to another shelter on the road, thus holding them at bay until the darkness of night covered them before the rebels dare descend the mountain.

"At about six o'clock the enemy succeeded in planting their cannon and opened fire upon the Union troops stationed at Hancock, and which were placed behind a natural barricade of brick walls aligned on the principal street. The ball opened at last, and the command was kept in a most horrid situation for the following twelve hours by the booming of Jackson's cannon and the reply of our two pieces of ordnance of the Fourth U. S. Artillery commanded by Lieutenant Muhlenburg, U.S.A. We held our own and were receiving reinforcements.

"The next morning there was a signal for a 'flag of truce,' from the command of Jackson and Loring. Lieutenant-Colonel O. L. Mann with proper escort and a boat went over to Alpine Station, and brought back with him Colonel Ashby, of the cavalry, blindfolded. He was taken to headquarters under an escort, and made known his wishes and demands, which, of course, were not acceded to.

"The day was spent in desultory firing, and as evening approached a huge bonfire was lighted, consuming all our stores except what could be carried away, and the few buildings, with the exception of Swan's and Orrick's, were soon in ruins. The next morning there was no enemy in sight.

Very Respectfully,
Your Obed't servant,
T. O. Osborn,
Colonel Thirty-Ninth Illinois, Commanding"

General Jno D. Imboden, in his article on "Stonewall Jackson in the Shenandoah," in the June Century Magazine, 1885, says:

"Jackson's only movement of any note in the winter of 1861 was an expedition at the end of December to Bath and Romney, to destroy the Baltimore and Ohio Railroad and a dam or two near Hancock, on the Chesapeake and Ohio canal. The weather set in to be very inclement about New Year's, with snow, rain, sleet, high winds and intense cold. Many in Jackson's command were opposed to the expedition, and as it resulted in nothing of much military importance, but was attended with great suffering on the part of his troops, nothing by the confidence he had won by his previous service saved him from personal ruin.

"In that terrible winters' march and exposure, he endured all that any private was exposed to. One morning, near Bath, some of his men having crawled out from under their snow-laded blankets, half frozen, were cursing him as the cause of their suffering. He lay close by under a tree, also snowed under, and heard all this; but without noticing it, presently crawled out too, and shaking the snow off, made some jocular remark to the nearest men, who had no idea he had ridden up in the night and lain down amongst them. The incident ran through the little army in a few hours, and reconciled his followers to all the hardships of the expedition, and fully reestablished his popularity."

CHAPTER FIVE

"The Rebel Force"

The force under Generals Thomas Jonathan "Stonewall" Jackson and William Wing "Old Blizzard" Loring was estimated to be between 12,000 to 15,000 men with forty pieces of artillery, and the object of the movement was supposed to be, in the first place, to capture the Thirty-Ninth Illinois, then cross the Potomac at Alpine, make a raid through the border of Maryland and Pennsylvania, and by moving rapidly through Cumberland, get in the rear of our forces under General Kelly at Romney, West Virginia, and by severing their communications, and cutting off their retreat, compel the surrender of the entire Federal force operating in Maryland and Northern Virginia.

Bath was the key to the position held by the Thirty-Ninth, and was naturally a very strong position and easily defended. On the north of the town was a range of high hills, or they might be classed as mountains, that extended for many miles from this point up and down the Potomac River. At this point for some miles in either direction was the only gap through which a military force could reach the river. These lofty heights commanded all the roads leading from the interior into Bath, and the Gap itself was favorable for a vigorous defense.

We will now go back a little so that we may arrive at a better understanding of this affair at Bath.

On the morning of the January 3, 1862, Captain Samuel S. Linton of Company D was ordered to make a reconnaissance by Lieutenant-Colonel Mann, commanding at Bath, and after he had proceeded about five miles in the direction of Martinsburg he encountered the advance of General Jackson's army.

A brisk skirmish ensued, in which the enemy was checked with considerable loss, and Captain Linton fell back on Bath with a loss of only nine men. The morning of January 4 Jackson advanced his whole force. The three companies of the Thirty-Ninth which had been reenforced on the previous day by the Eighty-Fourth Pennsylvania Volunteers, took up a position on the heights of Warm Spring ridge, the artillery of Muhlenburg planted in a commanding position. A brisk action took place lasting for the period of an hour, and notwithstanding the overwhelming number of the enemy under the command of one of the best of the Confederate generals, the position taken by our force was so strong and "sucker" grit so far above the average that every attempt made by the enemy to carry the heights was repulsed with heavy loss. During the entire day the rebels were held in check, and it was not until the shades of evening were gathering, and learning that the rebels were flanking the position some distance above, that our weary men fell back in good order to Sir John's Run and crossed the river into Maryland. The enemy's force then divided, one portion following on to Sir John's Run and Great Cacapon, the other taking the direction to Alpine Station. At Sir John's Run there was but little fighting, if any, as our men had already retreated, but at Great Cacapon where Captain Slaughter with Company G was stationed, a number of sharp skirmishes took place. Night was already setting in when Lieutenant Rudd of Company G, in order to allow the balance of the command to retreat, called for twenty volunteers, and proceeded at their head to take position in a narrow defile through which the enemy must pass, and here he awaited the advance of General John "Prince John" Magruder's Brigade, which had already commenced the descent of the mountain, planting two pieces of artillery, and commenced firing.

Muhlenburg's Guns in Action on Warm Spring Ridge.

Lieutenant Rudd awaited patiently until the advance was within 100 yards of his line, when he gave the order to fire, which had the effect of turning the rebel advance into a complete rout, when the Lieutenant and his men retreated in good order, safely rejoining their comrades who had fallen back to the Cumberland road on the Maryland shore.

In corroboration of what has been said in relation to this affair there is presented here the statement of William C. Dutcherage, of Dove Park, Arkansas, who was a member of the Third Arkansas Volunteer Infantry that participated in this raid. He wrote up the history of his regiment some years ago and it was published by installments in the *Washington World* before it became merged into the *National Tribune*. He says:

"After some brisk skirmishing with the Yanks at Bath, in which a number were captured and we had compelled them to retreat, Stonewall Jackson divided up his command—he going in person with two brigades to clean out the Yanks at Sir John's Run and the Yankee force opposite Hancock on the Virginia side, while the brigade that I belonged to was ordered to Big Capon to burn the railroad bridge. We left Bath about six o'clock in the evening, reaching the Big Capon mountain about seven o'clock. There General Magruder ordered the regiments to form in line of battle, the Third Arkansas taking the advance. We had two pieces of light artillery. We muffled the wheels, so the Yanks would not hear us coming down the mountain, and had a good deal of fun among ourselves thinking how nicely we were going to outwit the Yankees. We slipped down the old Bath Pike leading to Big Capon, and could see dim lights once in a while at the bridge. We slipped along carefully until within about 150 yards [of the bridge, it is presumed] and opened fire with both pieces of artillery, and several volleys of musketry. The Yanks returned the fire so quickly and sharply that we retreated out of range of their guns, leaving our artillery on the field. The next morning we advanced to the Big Capon, but not a Yank in sight. Some of the natives at Big Capon hooted at us for being such cowards as to let about 100 Yankees get away with such a big crowd as you'uns.

"We had five men wounded and one killed; his name was John Kelly, a New Yorker. We buried him where he was killed, destroyed the bridge and then returned to Bath."

The following is from the pen of Lieutenant Amos Savage, who participated in the skirmish at Great Cacapon, and will give some needed information. He says:

"About twenty-five men of Company E, from Sir John's Run, under Lieutenant Whipple, joined us just before the fight. These men, with about as many more of Company G, were stationed at the railroad trestle-work bridge. About twenty-five men under my command were stationed at the ford, 600 or 800 yards above the bridge, the balance of Company G being stationed along the Cacapon between the two points before mentioned, under Captain Slaughter.

"The rebel force attacking us was the Third Arkansas and Thirty-Seventh Virginia, with two pieces of artillery, and was commanded by Colonel Rust, of the Third Arkansas.

"The attacks at the bridge and ford were nearly simultaneous and were made, as near as I could judge, by a regiment at each place. Both were repulsed, and the affair appears to have been regarded as quite serious by them, as it was not until the next morning when reinforced by General Loring that they ventured to renew the attack on the bridge, which, being no longer held by our men, was occupied by them with no other annoyance than that occasioned by the fire of a squad of men who had waded the Potomac and opened a scattering fire on them from the north bank of the river."

Private George Riddle of Company I later wrote for the Regimental History:

"The first time I was drawn up in line of battle and ordered to 'load at will,' I would much rather have taken the time to come home to load, for I was somewhat scared. My heart got between my teeth and I couldn't bite my cartridge, so I finally got it torn off; and the trouble was then to hit the gun-barrel with the cartridge, for the muzzle of the gun wasn't half large enough. If it had been as large of an iron kettle, I don't think I could have got my cartridge in it; but I finally got her loaded, but had a hard time returning the rammer. You may think I was scared! But I got 'er there all the same, Eli!"

At Alpine Station on January 4 all was excitement. We knew that our boys were engaged with the enemy at Bath, but as to what extent and how progressing nothing was known. Colonel Osborn spent most of his time at the telegraph office, sending dispatches to Generals Frederick Lander and Kelly for reinforcements and receiving orders.

Dr. Clark returned from Bath about noon for instruments and supplies and reported that at the time he left all was quiet and our forces were holding its own, and it was supposed that the enemy was trying to flank the position. He started again for Bath at two o'clock and had proceeded some five miles, reaching a position overlooking the town, when he saw that it was useless to proceed farther as the rebel cavalry was swarming over the hills to the west of the town, and taking position on the road leading to Alpine. Nothing could be seen of our troops and he presumed that they had retreated in the direction of Sir John's Run. He immediately turned and made his way back to Alpine, nor hesitated long on the order of the going, reaching Alpine soon after four o'clock. He reported to the Colonel what he had seen, and acting on this information Osborn ordered Major Munn with two companies, A and F, to take position in ambush commanding the defile through which the enemy must pass in order to reach Alpine. In the meantime there was great activity and more confusion at the various quarters. There were urgent calls upon the quartermaster for transportation. He had but two wagons, and one of these was over on the Maryland side of the river, and the other was already loaded with quartermaster and commissary stores' but room was finally made for officers' baggage and it was started over the river. The hospital stores had to be abandoned, all that was saved being a few books and instruments. Orders to hurry up intermingled with considerable profanity at the seeming stupidity and slowness of servants and orderlies, with shouts now and then that the rebels were coming, all this was certainly calculated to turn ones head, be it ever so well balanced, and especially when was added the certainty of there being an enemy in our immediate front, and a wide river in which ice was already forming in our rear. The evening was decidedly chilly and the duskiness of night fast closing about us as the rebel cavalry approached and prepared for a charge. And soon they came down the road with a yell and a clatter, but had not proceeded more than a hundred yards, when the command under Major Munn with a well-directed volley of musketry gave them such a surprise and proved so effective that the rebels concluded not to advance any farther, only a few riderless horses carrying out the original intention, which were captured. The enemy had been so effectively checked that time was allowed for the four companies of the Thirty-Ninth Illinois and the Eighty-Fourth Pennsylvania Volunteers, who had retreated to this point from Bath via Sir

John's Run, to cross the river to Hancock. Three-fourths of the command were compelled to wade, the water reaching to the shoulders of the tallest, while the shorter ones were almost submerged. One man belonging to the Eighty-Fourth Pennsylvania Regiment was reported drowned in making the passage.

Private William O. L. Jewell, Company E later wrote:

"On January 4, 1862, half of our company was sent from Sir John's Run to guard a railroad bridge across the Big Bethel. I was some five or six miles up the Potomac River from Sir John's Run. The detail was in command of Lieutenant Lewis T. Whipple, a gallant and excellent officer and man. Some of us took position behind a pile of railroad ties we had arranged near the bridge. Jackson was coming upon us, our pickets had been driven in and we were awaiting events. The Thirteenth Indiana Volunteer Regiment had come down from Cumberland and had built fires to cook supper, some quarter of a mile above us. Lieutenant Whipple had started for the Indiana camp, and the rebels had muffled the wheels of a cannon and brought it to the end of the bridge about fifty yards from us, unheard and unnoticed, and discharged a shot at the Indiana encampment. This was about nine p.m., and very dark. The shot passed over the head of Lieutenant Whipple, and just as the report of the gun reached him he caught his toe in a snag, and fell. Thinking himself shot, and not fully realizing his position, and withal desirous of telling the boys how to dispose of his body, he called, 'Bury me where I lay, boys!' Only a moment elapsed, when, finding himself more scared than hurt, he quietly arose and proceeded on his journey, saying nothing more about the disposition of his body.

"We at the pile of ties fired a number of rounds at the place we had seen the flashes of the gun, but the firing soon ceased on their part, and we were ordered to retreat across the Potomac, and wading that swift stream in the darkness, was no laughing matter. We emerged, and went rattling through the weeds on the Maryland shore, encased in sheets of ice, until several hours march we reached an inn where we stirred up big fires and thawed out."

The passage of the river at a temperature considerably below the freezing point was a most trying ordeal, and resulted afterwards in much sickness. As the men emerged from the water, the frosty air gave their clothing a most uncomfortable stiffness.

There was no time for a change of clothing, for the command was immediately marched up into the town and placed in alignment along the main street, running parallel with the river, to afford shelter from the shot and shell of the enemy, who had by this time planted several cannons on the edge of the bluff opposite Hancock and commenced throwing shot and shell. No fires were allowed, and the condition of some of the men was most pitiable. Muhlenburg had already got his two guns in position and returned the fire for the space of an hour or more with so much effort that the rebel guns were silenced for the night. Fortunately but few of the enemy's shells had exploded and but little damage occasioned. The citizens of Hancock were badly frightened, and those who could, were busily engaged in removal. Thus passed the night. Shelter and opportunity was given the men as far as possible to change or dry their clothing and prepare coffee. Reinforcements were constantly arriving through the night, and early the following day, General Williams with a brigade arrived; also General Lander, who assumed command. We were astir early on the morning of January 4 and patiently awaited developments. The enemy could be plainly seen over at Alpine and on the bluffs, but all was peaceful.

At ten a.m. a white flag was raised and seen advancing to the border of the river on the opposite side, which indicated that the enemy wished to communicate, and Lieutenant Colonel O. L. Mann, who had been appointed provost-marshal that morning, with a small detachment in command of Sergeant Myers was ordered to cross the river to receive it. He soon returned bring Colonel Turner Ashby, of some cavalry fame at that time, and proceeded direct to General Lander's headquarters, Ashby being blindfolded. On the way over he inquired of the boys, "What regiment do you belong to?" he was answered "The Thirty-Ninth Illinois!" "My God!" He said, "Where in hell is not the Thirty-Ninth Illinois! They seem to be ubiquitous." He doubtless was thinking of the many different places he had encountered the Thirty-Ninth on the previous day.

General Lander received Colonel Ashby in a room in which was the telegraph office, and thinking that Ashby might understand telegraphy removed to another room where he read the communication from General Jackson. In this message Jackson demanded the surrender of the Union forces, saying that he had 15,000 men and it was his intention to cross the river, and that if he were opposed that he should bombard the town. It also stated that two hours' time would be given noncombatants to leave the place, at the termination of which he would open fire. General Lander read it carefully through and his reply was at once emphatic, forcible and characteristic. Turning to Ashby, he said: "Colonel Ashby, give my compliments to General Jackson and tell him to bombard and be damned! If he opens his batteries on this town he will injure more of his friends than he will of the enemy, for this is a damned Secesh place, anyhow." Lieutenant-Colonel Mann, thinking the interview terminated, commenced to replace the bandage over Ashby's eyes prior to leading him forth, when General Lander, having reflected somewhat on his answer, said: "Hold on! Take a seat, Colonel Ashby. General Jackson has addressed me in a polite and soldierly manner and it demands a like reply. I take back all that I have said and will write that I have to communicate." This was done, and as Lander placed the missive in his hand, he said: "General Jackson and yourself, Colonel Ashby, are gentlemen and brave men, without a question, but you have started out in a God Damn bad cause!" and shaking hands with him, Ashby departed. He was returned safely to his lines, and afterwards, without making much preparation, we patiently awaited events. The citizens were busily engaged, meanwhile, in hustling out of town, bringing into service all sorts of vehicles and conveyances. Our forces were so placed as to be concealed from view, and we had a very respectable one, sufficient at all events to prevent the enemy crossing the river at this place. At the expiration of the two hours the garrison flag of the Thirty-Ninth was run up to the top of the old liberty pole standing in town and we anxiously waited for the opening of the promised bombardment. At last two shots were fired over, one of which, a small six-pounder solid shot, was picked up and is now in the possession of Captain Hiram Phillips, of Bloomington, Ill. These shots did no damage, and only served as an invitation for our batteries to respond, which they did in a brisk manner and kept it up for the space of an hour. The enemy did not return the fire, but we could see their troops in motion and it was evident that the enemy was busy in sacking Alpine, as fires were lighted in many places and soon all the houses save the Swan and Orrick property was in conflagration, lighting up the surrounding country for miles.

The following day a reconnaissance was made over the river by some of the Thirty-Ninth, who found matters and things at the station pretty badly demoralized. The Swan family had removed, bag and baggage, and no one was found to give us any information. The Swan house, as well as the Orrick, was found to have received the many compliments in shape of shot and shell that we had sent over, and both were badly damaged. The railway had been torn up and the rails twisted and bent with fire, and all the railway property destroyed. Where our medical dispensary had stood there was nothing but a mound of ashes. All was ruin and desolation.

Proceeding up along the road to Bath we found a number of newly-made graves, and several of them were occupied by soldiers who had perished from cold, for the weather had been exceedingly severe and the men in Jackson's command from Georgia, Alabama and Arkansas had suffered extremely.

Many notes addressed to the Thirty-Ninth were found. Some were couched in terms of bitterness and hostility, some complimentary and conciliatory, but all exhibiting evident respect for the pluck and fighting qualities of Western men.

Here is a sample copy of one that was addressed;

"TO THE BOYS OVER THE WAY."

"We are about to leave you, and our comfortable quarters to your tender mercies. If you should happen to pick up anything lying around here, I expect that you will want to keep it as a slight token of your regard, or send it home. How much better it would be for the 'liberty boys' if they would go home themselves and leave us poor rebels to enjoy freedom in their own way.

Company G, First Reg't Georgia Vol's."

"P.S. We are poor rebels and cannot offer a more valuable keepsake, but hope you will prize it from the spirit in which it was given.

Col. J. W. Ramsey, First Georgia Vol's."

"P.S. Go home, boys! Go home! We owe you no ill will further than result from your efforts to conquer the Freeman of the South. We will go home gladly when we have effectually defended our borders.

Company G."

Jackson's army that had started out on this raid from Winchester animated, no doubt, with high hopes of easily gobbling up an Illinois regiment, and cheered by the prospect of foraging among the quiet hills and valleys of "My Maryland" and the neighboring border of prosperous Pennsylvania, had been most grievously disappointed. He had gained absolutely nothing; but had lost seriously by battle and exposures, and certainly he had not won any renown, but instead had experienced the bitter mortification of having been held at bay with his entire army of 15,000 men for nearly a day at Bath, and for hours at different points by mere detachments from an Illinois regiment, who by delaying his progress have ample time for the Federal forces to concentrate their strength and turn him back empty-handed from the very threshold of Maryland and victory. This affair might have had a more sorrowful and tragic ending had Jackson fully understood the number of our troops and their disposition.

On January 3 his cavalry had captured several of our men, one of whom was taken before Jackson who questioned him closely about the number of the Union forces in his front. This man proved to be an able diplomat and was equal to the occasion. In reply to the question as to the number of troops, he stated (and it must have been believed) that we had on the Virginia side of the river between 6,000 and 7,000 men, and that before leaving camp that morning it was reported that General Bank's army had reached Williamsport on its way to reinforce Lander. It was possible, and could have been accomplished with comparative ease, for Jackson with his large force to have captured us all by making a vigorous push on January 3, but the cautious feeling of his way proved our salvation.

We recrossed the river, after having accomplished our mission, and went into quarters at the Old Tannery, most of our tents and garrison equipment having been lost for the want of transportation.

A hospital had been established by Surgeon Blake up in Pennsylvania, near the border, having found a suitable building that had served the purpose of a church or school house. The Doctor had located there at the time of the threatened bombardment of Hancock by Jackson, and it was not thought best to make any change as our stay at Hancock was very uncertain.

The Thirty-Ninth was pursuing a sort of independent existence, it not having been brigaded as yet. The brigade that was to have been organized by Ward H. Lamon and to which it was to have been assigned was never more heard of after reaching Williamsport.

We remained at Hancock until the evening of January 11, 1862, when orders were received to march to Cumberland, Maryland. The reason for this move was said to be that Jackson was after the military supplies stored at Romney, Virginia, and General Kelly had ordered the Thirty-Ninth, the Eighty-Fourth Pennsylvania, and the 110th Pennsylvania Volunteers to make a forced march to the assistance of the force already there and that were to be concentrated at New Creek, Virginia.

In concluding this chapter I give room to General O. L. Mann's version of the skirmish and retreat from Bath, as follows:

"In the afternoon of January 3, 1862, Major Mann, who was stationed at Bath in command of three companies of the Thirty-Ninth, received a call from a very excited Negro who urged him 'In de name of de Lawd' to get out of the town at once. The African had traveled about ten miles on the road from Winchester and was overflowing with startling news. He said that General Jackson with his entire army was moving on Bath, and could not be more than five miles away. A scouting party had been out about seven miles on that road in the morning and had returned without having seen the enemy. Major Mann took Captain Linton and sixty men, and after marching about four miles out met the advance of Jackson's army. Captain Linton deployed his men to the right of the road and Major Mann and Lieutenant Belcher of Company K, who were mounted, and two cavalry couriers kept the road. In a short time the men were briskly engaged by rebel cavalry and infantry. Seeing that they were largely outnumbered, Captain Linton retreated after a brisk skirmish and the loss of nine men taken prisoner.

"Major Mann was cut off from his road of retreat and was nearly made a prisoner by Ashby's cavalry, but the good running and jumping qualities of his young stallion helped him to gain shelter in the thick timber and finally to reach camp, bringing with him Lankinaw of Company D, who had been shot in the leg. (He was the first man in the Regiment to be wounded by the enemy.)

"Captain Woodruff of Company K, who had heard the firing from his position at Bath, had so disposed of his troops as to make the best defense possible. The rebels, however, did not follow up the retreat that night.

"It is now known that one of the men who had been captured (his name is forgotten) proved himself a most accomplished liar, for when taken before General Jackson, the interview is believed to have resulted much to our advantage. He assured the rebel chieftain that General Kelly had not over 5,000 men at Bath, but that he understood before leaving camp that General Banks was crossing his entire army at Sir John's Run and at Hancock, and was expected at Bath that evening. The man knew that he was dealing out large lumps of 'taffy' to the General, but that it was also a military 'necessity.' Jackson must have given some credence to these 'whoppers,' for he ordered a halt, and sending for his subordinates ordered them to camp in line of battle and be ready for action at any moment. Before midnight of the 3rd, two Pennsylvania regiments (the Eighty-Fourth and the 110th) arrived. Colonel Murray, commanding the Eighty-Fourth, by virtue of rank assumed the command, and on being advised of the state of affairs and the location of the enemy, deployed his troops to the north and east of the town, and an anxious night was passed with rain, sleet and snow. The following day was devoted to skirmishing until late in the afternoon, when the enemy, being doubtless convinced that the strength of the Union forces had been magnificently estimated by their prisoner, determined to surround our forces if possible. The position was naturally a strong one, and the two pieces of artillery operated by Lieutenant Muhlenburg did excellent service throughout the day in keeping the rebels in check. General Kelly, at Cumberland, had advised Colonel Murray early in the day that the Thirteenth Indiana Volunteer Infantry would reach us from the place by rail, bringing a fresh supply of ammunition, of which Major Mann's command was getting short. At sundown, no help reaching us, and the rebels developing great strength, Colonel Murray ordered a retreat to Sir John's Run, on the Baltimore and Ohio Railroad, distant about two miles, and where it was feasible to ford the Potomac River to the Maryland side. As they neared the station, the Thirteenth Indiana Volunteers, commanded by Lieutenant-Colonel Robert S. Foster, was met. A short council was held which resulted in an order to 'about face' and fight. After the first part of this order had been executed, Major Mann asked Colonel Foster for ammunition and was surprised to learn that the officer had but two rounds to his men, and had been told that he would get ammunition at Bath. This intelligence resulted in another 'about face,' for the Thirty-Ninth had but two rounds left, and the Pennsylvania regiments being armed with guns of a different caliber their supply was of no use. Colonel Foster at once ordered his men aboard the cars and returned to Cumberland, and the detachments of the Thirty-Ninth and the artillery forded the river. The two Pennsylvania regiments retreated down the railroad to Alpine Station, only to ford the river later on. After fording the Potomac, a part of Captain Woodruff's company (K) volunteered to remain there to protect the bridge and station. This they did most effectually, the enemy not being able to accomplish this vandalism under the fire of Company K's sharpshooters. The other companies proceeded on to Hancock."

The official report of Captain William B. Slaughter, who was in command of the companies at that point is here inserted. His report, dated January 6, 1862, says:

"The afternoon of Friday, the 3rd, I spent with a small part of my company, and Lieutenant Rudd, in a careful reconnaissance from the top of Big Cacapon mountain, taking observations from prominent points, for a distance of two and a half miles. From these points, we could plainly see indications of the presence, in the valley between us and Warm Spring mountain, of a large force of the enemy. We estimated it at not less than 3,000, and in the distance could be seen extensive camps. I accordingly extended my pickets on the mountain during the night, and ordered my men to sleep on their arms.

"On Saturday, I threw out a party of twenty-one men, under Lieutenant Rudd, to the top of the mountain, with instructions to observe the enemy, (which we knew to be approaching Bath in great force), and embarrass the approach of any force that might be sent against us. About eleven o'clock, information was brought that a column of three regiments was approaching by the Bath road. It was thought probable that another force would be brought against us, by the Long Hollow from Bloomery Gap. This supposition was enhanced by the fact, which I had learned, that the movements against Bath were simultaneously made, by large forces by way of Sleepy Creek and the valley east of the Big Cacapon. I therefore directed Captain Dircks, with his company, to occupy the approaches by the Long Hollow and points across to the bluffs of the Great Cacapon creek, and took measures to defend the bridge and ford with my company, and the detachment from Company E, under Lieutenant Whipple.

"Breastworks of timber and railroad ties had been constructed during the day, on each side of the bridge, and strong defenses planted along the bluffs of the creek. Lieutenant Whipple, with thirty men, were posted at the bridge, and the balance of my force, except the detachment under Lieutenant Rudd, disposed on the bluffs, under command of Lieutenant Savage. Valuable service was rendered during the day by the detachment under Lieutenant Rudd. Having the whole valley west of the Big Cacapon mountain before him, he was able to see every movement and disposition of the enemy, and to perceive their strength.

"The column advancing against us consisted of three regiments of infantry and one piece of artillery. To check so large a force was a desperate undertaking for twenty-two men, but, as the event showed, not impossible one. Selecting a position near a bend in the narrow road, which they knew the column must pass, our boys knelt on one knee, and awaited its approach. Not until the foremost files were within fifty yards, was the presence of our party suspected, and then, at the critical moment when the discovery had caused hesitation, the men coolly delivered their fire. Several of the enemy were seen to fall, and the head of the column was thrown into confusion. Our party retired to another shelter. The enemy was thus held at bay for three hours, and it was not until the darkness of the night covered them, that they ventured to descent the mountain. Lieutenant Rudd expresses the highest admiration for the coolness and determination of the men. The whole execution of his part was such as to reflect the highest honor upon him.

"Colonel Foster, with the Thirteenth Indiana, arrived on the ground at Big Cacapon about six p.m., but he declined to take the command, and our plans were not changed. Had the enemy descended the west side of the mountain before dark nothing could have saved the Thirteenth, as its retreat would have been effectually cut off. I am fully convinced that its salvation is due to the courage and skill of the detachment that occupied the mountain road.

"About seven p.m., we became aware of the fact that the enemy was fixing a gun in position to attack us. Deeming it probable that we should be obliged to retire before their superior force, I ordered all the company baggage and stores to be placed in the cars, so as to facilitate our retreat when it should become necessary. Our loading was not completed, when the enemy opened on us with his cannon. The engineer immediately started the train, and moved around the curve about two miles, where it could lie in safety. The Thirteenth Indiana, being in the cars, was carried along. Our men, stationed at the bridge, under command of Lieutenant Whipple, could distinctly see the position of the enemy's gun. They answered its fire with their muskets. After the second shot the gun was deserted, and gave us no further trouble.

"A large force of their infantry at the same time made its appearance at the creek, and replied with muskets. Our men, being well protected, were able to maintain their position with impunity. The skirmishing continued for about three-fourths of an hour after the train had left. A company of cavalry, and a regiment of infantry, made a show of purpose to cross the ford opposite the bluff occupied by Lieutenant Savage, but they were handsomely repulsed. I was confident the position could be maintained at Big Cacapon, provided the Indiana regiment could return and take part in the defense. I accordingly dispatched a message to Colonel Foster, with the request that he would bring down his force and assume command. Before the messenger reached him, however, I received word that the enemy had crossed the creek a mile and a half above, and were likely to cut off our retreat. I therefore ordered a retreat, which was effected in good order. Since the above was written, we have reliable information that the enemy lost seventeen men in the Big Cacapon affair, including Dr. Wilson, a distinguished and influential citizen of Morgan county, and surgeon in the rebel army."

Captain E. C. Myers of Company K reminiscences:

"On the night of January 4 all of the troops had crossed the river by eight o'clock excepting the Pennsylvania regiment, which followed the railway to Alpine Station, and the last company to cross was Company K, of the Thirty-Ninth.

The Retreat from Alpine Station the Night of Jan. 4, 1862. (From a Sketch made at the time by Dr. Clark.)

"Captain Woodruff and myself, I was then a Sergeant, lingered a little with the hope of securing a boat, as one or two had been in use ferrying over the sick and disabled. The idea of fording the river was not at all inviting that cold night. While waiting and watching for a boat I discovered quite a number of muskets lying around, perhaps a dozen or more, that had been purposely thrown away by some of the men before they took to the water. They were all loaded. I gathered them together and said to the Captain, who was becoming impatient and somewhat fearful of the enemy's approach, that we had the means for making a fair defense, even if we were attacked; and as the night was quite dark the enemy could not estimate our force, and by the rapid discharge of our dozen muskets they could be held in check, anyhow, until we crossed the river.

"Soon I saw a boat near the opposite shore with a man in it, and I called to him to come over; but he paid no attention whatever. I then aimed a gun at him and told him to bring that boat over or I would shoot. This proved a bad move on my part, for the man, doubtless thinking us to be rebels, left his boat and sprang up and over the canal bank for shelter. There was then no hope from that direction, and we had about concluded to ford the river when I saw a man in a boat coming across from another direction. He evidently had not seen us, and passed by, landing some yards below where we stood.

"It was now so dusky that we could not distinguish who or what the man was, whether a soldier or civilian, and did not much care, being more exercised about getting safely over the river with a dry skin than aught else. The man in the boat, after landing, drew it up on the shore and immediately started through the woods at a lively pace, as though he had some important business, and I have since thought that he was a spy.

"We immediately went to the boat and took possession, and after putting the muskets on board, started across the river. Landing safely, we found a portion of our men still there, and after disposing of the muskets we started for Hancock. On reaching the hotel after midnight, I sought a place to rest myself, and going upstairs entered a room which was occupied by Lieutenant-Colonel Mann, who was stretched out on the bed, boots and all, and with permission I laid down beside him, hoping for a little rest. The room we occupied had early in the evening been pierced by a six-pounder solid shot fired by the enemy, and in its passage had cut off the footboard. It was then occupied by the chaplain of the Eighty-Fourth Pennsylvania regiment, who naturally got out, and it was owning to this circumstance that the Lieutenant-Colonel had secured the bed. The night passed quietly enough except for the noise made by the men down below, who were busy in drying their clothing and making a resting-place on tables, chairs, and floor."

CHAPTER SIX

"Fight under any circumstances"

We moved out of Hancock at six p.m. ahead of the two Pennsylvania regiments. The night was cold, with some considerable snow on the ground. The distance to Cumberland was forty miles, our route lying over the mountains. The experience of the past two weeks had been amply sufficient to warrant us in drawing the conclusion that the funny and agreeable part of our soldier life had gone glimmering down the vista of time, and we saw little before us but hardship and peril. The boys stepped out gaily and briskly, singing, shouting and making merry for the first few miles, but the grade in the ascent of the first mountain soon subdued them into paying strict attention to the business in hand.

We had left behind all our sick and tender-footed with Surgeon Blake, who had been assigned to the charge of the hospital by Dr. Antisel, the Chief Medical Officer of William's Brigade that remained at Hancock.

Every few miles a halt was ordered for rest, but many men, instead of resting, took advantage of the occasion to forage for something to eat, and opportunities were not wanting, as the country was well settled by thrifty farmers whose larders must have suffered severely, judging from the amount of provender of all varieties and descriptions that found its way back and was distributed along the line. We reached Cumberland at four p.m. January 12, eight hours in advance of the Pennsylvania regiments which left Hancock at the same hour with ourselves.

Here the men were distributed in churches and other places, until other arrangements could be made; some of the officers, however, took rooms at the St. Nicholas Hotel. Russell's Cavalry Company and Muhlenburg with his artillery had preceded us, and we found these officers already established and ready to show their friends about the city. After remaining at this point for the period of five days, during which time new clothing was issued to the men, and many of our losses made good, we, on January 17, were put on board a train of box and platform cars and started for New Creek, West Virginia, after having been placed in the Second Brigade of General William Starke Rosencrans Division, commanded by Colonel Dunning, of an Ohio regiment, acting Brigadier-General.

New Creek, West Virginia was a small station of the Baltimore and Ohio Railroad, some seventeen miles from Cumberland. It was situated in a mountainous region and made up of about a dozen buildings, including a depot. When we reached there the whole place was a sea of mud, and we were given the privilege of either remaining and making our quarters on board the train of cars or making encampment in the open field. Owing to the condition of the ground it was decided to remain on the cars, and the boys went to work transforming them into "sleepers" and dining cars "a la" Pullman, as fast as their limited resources would allow. The officers were privileged to lodge and find meals wherever they could. Only one tent was erected, and that served for the Adjutant's office. We found a regiment of cavalry here which had been guarding the long trestle railroad bridge at this point, and as frequent attempts to burn this structure had been made it was ordered that, instead of proceeding to Romney, the Regiment should remain here.

Soon after arriving at New Creek we were joined by the Sixty-Second Ohio Volunteers, Colonel Pond, and the Sixty-Seventh Ohio Volunteers, commanded by Colonel A. C. Voris, and from whom we were never afterwards separated until they were mustered out of the service. The officers and men of both commands were fully up to the standard and our ideal of what should constitute good soldiers and "bon camaraderie." The record they made in after years and left as an inheritance to coming generations has more than justified these few words of feeble praise.

Rain fell continuously during the first week of our sojourn here, giving encouragement to those feelings of "nostalgia" and general discomfort that, up to this time, we had been comparatively free from. Sickness came as a floodtide upon us, and after confinement in those horrid box cars it became necessary to take a building and establish a provisional hospital, which was soon completely filled with cases of pneumonia, malaria and typhoid fevers. Dr. Clark, the Assistant Surgeon, was the only medical officer with the Regiment, the Surgeon and the Hospital Steward, Anthony DeNormandie, having remained at Hancock.

The experiences of both officers and men at New Creek, will be remembered as among the saddest and most sorrowful of any that were encountered in their history as soldiers. On or about January 25 a portion of the Regiment participated in a reconnaissance in the direction of Romney and came in contact with a small body of rebel cavalry. A short but brisk skirmish ensued which resulted in no particular advantage to either side. It was undertaken more for the purpose of diverting the minds of the men and giving them needed exercise, and at the same time to let the Johnnies know that the Thirty-Ninth was "still on deck," than aught else. When practicable as well as necessary the old camelback locomotive that was attached to the train and always ready for duty in case of need, would take some of us into Cumberland for supplies or carry sick to general hospital.

On February 7 a most welcome order came to proceed to Patterson's Creek, thus retracing our steps back through Cumberland in the direction of Martinsburg. We were again to be assigned to the command of General F. W. Lander. Colonel Osborn had been offered, however, his choice of three different positions; either to remain where we then were and construct barracks, or go to Cumberland in command of that post or report to General Lander at Patterson's Creek, and take the lead on to Winchester and reconstruct the railway and bridges of the Baltimore and Ohio Railroad as we went along. Upon consultation with his officers it was decided to accept the latter proposition as offering the best means to get into more active service. Before we could leave, it became necessary to stop and repair the bridge at New Creek, which the day previous had become warped and twisted by reason of a flood in that stream. This occupied the most part of two days, and when at last we did pass over it was very crooked and far from safe.

The Regiment reached Patterson's Creek, thirty-four miles distant, safely, February 11, 1862, still occupying the old and dilapidated freight and cattle cars. On reaching this place, the Regiment was placed in the First Brigade of Lander's Division. A large brick structure near the station was occupied as headquarters and another building taken for the hospital.

On Washington's birthday, February 22, after dress parade, the Regiment was formed in "hollow square" that they might more easily hear the reading of some resolutions that had been drawn up expressive of our feelings in relation to the great victory at Fort Donelson and the bravery of our "Western boys."

RESOLUTIONS.

WHEREAS: Intelligence has been received announcing in detail the victories gained in the valley of the Mississippi, in which our fellow soldiers of Illinois took such a conspicuous part, showing a courage unsurpassed by that of the heroes of modern or ancient times, and a love for the Union stronger than the love of life; therefore,

RESOLVED: That we, the officers and men of the Thirty-Ninth Regiment of Illinois Volunteers, having assembled to celebrate the birthday of the Father of our country, do seize upon this the most appropriate occasion to express to them our sincere and heartfelt thanks for the noble and heroic conduct which they have everywhere exhibited on the field of battle; and that we most heartily congratulate them upon their glorious achievements.

RESOLVED: That we, as soldiers of the Government of the United States of America, will never lose sight of the heroic and patriotic examples placed before us by our fellow soldiers of the West; but by our conduct whenever and wherever we meet the enemy we will endeavor to emulate them, and thus sweep rebellion before us, until peace is restored to this fair land, and the Stars and Stripes again wave over every city, village and hamlet of the thirty-four states of America.

RESOLVED: That while we rejoice over the late victories of our troops we shed tears of sympathy for the fathers, mothers, wives, sisters, brothers, daughters and sons of those who have so nobly fallen in the defense of our country; and that our prayer shall ever be, God protect and comfort them in their affliction, and give them the happy assurance that our civil wars will soon cease forever, and that no more of their friends shall fall in unnatural and fraternal strife.

RESOLVED: That the inauguration of that traitor Jefferson Davis as president of the so-called Southern Confederacy upon this, the birthday of the immortal Washington, is an insult of the deepest dye to the memory of the "Father of Our Country" and to every lover of free institutions, and that we pledge ourselves to avenge the insult whenever and wherever we meet him or his emissaries.

The resolutions were adopted amid vociferous cheering and were followed by some speech-making, after which the men were dismissed and we returned to our quarters.

Malaria was abundant, and it became necessary to give the men daily rations of quinine and whiskey. In all our after experience we never encountered so much sickness as existed among the men of the Regiment at this time. We were detained here until March 1, by reason of repairs necessary to be made to the railroad and especially the construction of a bridge over the creek, before we could advance with the train. The order to move was received after midnight, and was accompanied by the following characteristic letter from General Lander:

"Headquarters, 1 a.m., March 1, 1862

"Colonel Osborn: I have entrusted you with a highly important service—that of opening the railroad to Martinsburg. If threatened by the enemy, call on Colonel Pond, or on General Williams at Hancock; the latter may be on the road to Williamsport. You will provide for my tents, camp equipage, horses and forage for them at Cherry Run turnout; but it will be time enough to look out for this when they arrive.

"If the rebels come on you in force, fight under any circumstances, and if you are taken prisoner I will release you tomorrow morning. I start on a forced march across the country to cut them off from Winchester. I commend to your favorable notice Mr. Quincy, who goes down in charge of the repairs of the road. Afford him and the telegraph company all the aid they may require.

F. W. Lander, Brigadier-General"

General Lander's headquarters were then located at Paw-Paw, West Virginia, and this letter is perhaps one of the last he ever penned, for on March 3, while at Alpine Station, intelligence reached us of his sudden death. We were painfully surprised and affected, as we lost in him a valued friend and good counselor. It was presumed that his death was caused by an apoplectic seizure. He had retired on the night preceding in usual health and was found dead by his servant in the morning. The remains were sent to Washington, DC, under proper escort.

General Mann (then a Lieutenant-Colonel) later related a story for Dr. Clark for the Regimental History:

"The troops had all been sent forward from Patterson's Creek, West Virginia, to Paw-Paw Tunnel, except the Thirty-Ninth, which General Lander said he ordered left there to guard the bridge and to send forward material for reconstructing the railroad. The General and his full staff were about ready to leave when I was sent for, in the absence of Colonel Osborn, who had gone to Cumberland.

"General Lander met me in the hall of his headquarters and directed my attention to a very stringent and vigorous order he had published, prohibiting marauding on the part of our troops, and ordered me to see that it was obeyed. I had seen some Generals before that, and have seen a great many since, but I think I never saw one who appeared at that time. His splendid tall form was the commanding figure in a field of which his large, well-equipped staff was the impressive background. I listened to the General's instructions, and realized that weighty responsibilities were crowding heavily upon my shoulders. I was fresh, and had never before stood face to face with a live General. when he concluded what he had to say, I promptly saluted and boldly said, 'General, I will try and see your order's obeyed.'

"'Try! God damn your soul to hell! Try! What in hell do you mean, Sir, by such talk? Is that any language for a soldier to use, damn you!' and each oath was emphasized by a terrible stamp of his foot.

"I looked for a way to escape from his severe presence a large rat-hole in the floor afforded momentary hope; but at last my wits came to my rescue, and straightening myself up to more than full height, as I now remember, I gave the most graceful salute possible, and in tones that I meant should be heard, I said, 'General Lander, your orders shall be obeyed to the letter!'

"The General immediately extended his long, sinewy hand, and clasping mine warmly, said, in subdued tones, 'That is right, Colonel; that is soldierly! I bid you good bye, and hope we shall soon meet again.'

"But we never did. General Lander was a corpse ten days later, but his impressive lesson was of great service to me. I never thereafter allowed myself to think of trying to execute a military order."

General Mann also wrote, "At this same post (Patterson's Creek) Captain S. W. Munn was ordered to Paw-Paw to fill detail on a 'general court-martial' to try Colonel Ansel, of the First Virginia Cavalry. General Lander had started his troops from Paw-Paw across the country to attack Jackson at Winchester, and was anxious to get there before General Banks should from Harper's Ferry. Ten miles out, he met the enemy at Bloomery Gap, and ordered Colonel Ansel to 'Charge' them. It was charged that the enemy showed some 'pluck,' and Colonel Ansel fell back with his regiment in great confusion.

"General Lander was rushing to the front, and meeting Colonel Ansel, ordered him in arrest, and taking command of the Regiment led it in person to a nice victory, capturing some seventy-five rebels and dispersing the rest. Lander wired the facts to Secretary Stanton, and asked for instructions. Secretary Stanton had just assumed the duties of the War Office, and was not as familiar with military law as he became in later years. He telegraphed Lander to order the Colonel tried by court-martial, and if found guilty of cowardice in presence of the enemy, have him shot at once. The entire army and the country at large were shocked at the order, for at that time no persons could be legally executed for military offenses, except on the approval of the sentence by the President of the United States.

"The court-martial was ordered, however, when Captain Munn arrived he found that Colonel Ansel had no counsel to defend him. Munn's high ideas of law and justice led him to suggest that counsel be furnished the accused before he was forced to trial, and arrangements were consummated whereby Munn was relieved from the court and assigned to the defense of the accused. Colonel Ansel was found guilty as charged, but Munn succeeded in getting him off with loss of pay and rank, and dismissal from the service. The Captain's good reputation made at home as a criminal lawyer now became noised abroad in army circles in the field, and he was frequently called upon to defend delinquents."

We left Patterson's Creek on March 1 on board the same old train of cars, our duty being to protect the workingmen while making repairs to the road. The first stop for any length of time was made at Sir John's Run in the early morning of March 2. Taking advantage of this halt, Lieutenant-Colonel Mann and Dr. Clark got permission to go over to Bath, and getting their horses from the car started.

On arriving at Bath a great many changes were noticeable in the appearance of things since January 4, the date of the advent of the rebels. Old Colonel Strother had died, his death being hastened by the outrages committed by Jackson's troops in consequence of the outspoken sympathies of his family for the Union cause. His home had been pillaged from cellar to garret and much valuable property destroyed.

Judge Pendleton and family were still there and gave them hearty welcome, together with the sad tale of the wholesale destruction of the effects of the Union sympathizers in the town. Bath was neutral ground at this time, and they did not care to tarry long, especially after learning that the rebel cavalry frequently made a dash into the town; but regarding the importunities of their friends consented to remain during the night and were furnished with a room in a remote part of the big house by a Mr. Randolph, a son-in-law of Strother. In the early morning they returned safely via Alpine Station, where the Regiment had proceeded.

On leaving Alpine the train passed on to a point called Back Creek where a bridge needed repair, and here it was obliged to remain for some time.

While patiently awaiting a forward movement it was apparent that the larder of the field and staff was about depleted, and something must be done in the matter of compensation, otherwise known as foraging. We made up a party of four persons, exclusive of the guide who was to conduct us to the plantation of a noted secessionist six miles distant. We started at sundown, well mounted and armed "*cap-a-pie*," for it was rather a dangerous experiment, knowing the enemy's scouts to be in the vicinity but it suited our adventurous and somewhat reckless dispositions, and especially our brave Adjutant Walker, who led the party. Reaching the place after an hour's ride we rode into the yard, dismounted, and the Adjutant and Doctor Clark approached the door, leaving our companions on guard outside. The door was opened by the lady of the house, who bade us enter, which we did and stated our business as being in search of articles of contraband of war, and an officer of the rebel army that was supposed to be in the house. We were told to search and satisfy ourselves.

On opening the door of an adjoining room we were somewhat startled to find seated at the supper table three stalwart men, and on the wall were slung several guns. We were a trifle disconcerted at this discovery, but speedily regaining our equilibrium we held a moment's consultation, the result of which was for Clark to step to the door and order, in their hearing, an imaginary sergeant to take a file of men and examine the premises surrounding, the Adjutant at the same time placing the occupants of the house in arrest and forbidding them leaving their seats. We had absolutely surprised this group of men, and by a little strategy kept them in subjection; otherwise, some little unpleasantness might have occurred. After a little time Clark left the house to participate in the search for provender, leaving Walker on guard. He found that the balance of the party outside had secured several chickens and had disturbed a family of ducks, and to-a-man, were busy in chasing them about the yard, hurling stones and other missiles until a half dozen or more were captured. The noise and clatter of the chase from men and ducks could be heard plainly, and did not exactly tally with the profession we had made, and Walker's position in the house was not envied; however, it was carrying out our plan of operations. After visiting all the outhouses our plunder, when we were ready to start, amounted to six chickens, six ducks, a tub of link sausage, a pot of honey and a sack of hickory nuts, which were all bagged and sent forward to camp. Now, how to get away was the question. It was finally agreed that two of us should go in and announce loudly to Walker the result of our search and state that we considered it necessary under the circumstances to place a guard about the house for the night, or until we could receive instructions from headquarters. This arrangement, Walker said, met with his views, and he would himself go and consult superiors. On leaving the house we loudly admonished the sentinels (imaginary) to allow no one to leave it, and them mounting our horses sped back to camp, or rather the railway train, which we reached in safety.

Before leaving the house, however, a noise under the bed attracted our attention, and on lifting the valence we beheld a young lady who prayed us to spare her life. On assuring her that we had no intention of committing any outrage, she came out, stating that "she would rather be killed than scared to death!" She was much frightened, but soon regained something like composure.

We remained at this place for several days, guarding the road, making expeditions to various points and watching the heavy-laden trains of soldiers passing on to Martinsburg.

While at this point Lieutenant Rudd came in from a scouting expedition bringing two prisoners, two horses, and a large number of turkeys, chickens, etc. One of the prisoners was a member of the Virginia Legislature, and the other, a member of Colonel Ashby's cavalry who was home on furlough. The experiences of the party were pleasing to hear. His first captive was found in a bin of oats, the man having covered himself completely, and his appearance when called upon to report was most ludicrous.

After the repair of the bridge at Back Creek we advanced several miles to Cherry Run where another bridge spanning the deep and narrow stream needed reconstructing, and the Regiment left the cars and made a temporary encampment.

General Shields had been appointed to the command of our Division, taking the place made vacant by the death of General Lander, and he had been expected to report for several days. None were more eager for his arrival than the Thirty-Ninth, for we knew him to have been a former resident of our State, and many of us were familiar with his record and reputation made during the war with Mexico.

Lieutenant Simon S. Brucker, of Company C, had been left with a detail of men near the railway station and he had established his headquarters in a large residence near the depot. About nine p.m. the quiet of camp was broken by the report that rapidly spread to the effect that General Shields had just arrived at the headquarters of Lieutenant Brucker. The night was so mild and bright that Colonel Osborn could not resist the temptation to immediately pay his respects to the old hero.

Lace and the Band were summoned and directed to accompany an informal march of a majority of the Regiment to the place where the General was said to be stopping. Colonel Osborn had instructed Lace to play soon after he and his staff should enter the house, and in due time General Shields should enter the house, and in due time General Shields should also be called upon for a speech. Osborn was met at the entrance to the mansion by Lieutenant Brucker, who, in response to inquires from his colonel, replied, "Yes, General Shields is in the parlor. Walk in!" The party removed their hats, and put on their most soldierly appearance and walked into the room—it was vacant. On the parlor table rested a volume which proved to be a history of the Mexican War, and which Lieutenant Brucker, in answer to many questioning glances, proceeded to open, revealing a fine portrait of General Shields and which he introduced to Colonel Osborn and staff.

The pith of the joke was at once visible to all, and while the Colonel was deliberating just how best to compensate his subordinate for the "chestnut" he had proffered him the band burst out in the most approved style, "Hail to the Chief!"

It was known that calls for Shields would soon follow, and Osborn ordered the Adjutant to notify the command of the disappointment. To this Major Munn entered his demurrer, saying the sell was too good not to be shared by the rank and file. He insisted that as Lieutenant-Colonel Mann could imitate the Irish brogue and blarney to perfection, that he should take his place, at the call for Shields, in the shade of the veranda, and, surrounded by the officers, should make a speech. Colonel Osborn, after muttering a mild reprimand to Brucker, finally acquiesced. The music soon ceased, when "Shields!" "Shields!" "General Shields!" was shouted by several hundred voices.

Without the formality of an introduction the Lieutenant Colonel with approved Celtic accent, retaining his position well in the background, said:

"Me brave boys of the Thirty-Ninth Illinois Infantry—"

Here the balmy air was rent with three cheers and a tiger for General Shields, who by proxy continued to say:—

"Me lips will not express the deep gratification I feel in meeting you tonight. [*Cheers*] I was once a resident of your great State, and was associated in many public movements with our great Commander-in-chief, Abraham Lincoln. [*Cheers*] It was my good fortune to lead troops from that great State against the enemy in Mexico, and more gallant men never marched to the music of the Union that were they."

This seemed to electrify Captain Phillips of Company I, who had served under Shields in Mexico, and he shouted out, "That's so! General Shields, and there are several of them chaps here tonight."

"I am profoundly glad to meet you, veterans and heroes of the Mexican struggle," continued the General, "and only hope that you and your new comrades in arms will prove just as brave and serviceable when, under my humble lead, you face the frowning forts at Richmond, as you did at Monterey. The eyes of the civilized world are on men from Illinois today; and believing your acts will ever honor your State, I bid ye all, Good-night!"

Lace, the leader of the band, was the first to discover the little deception, and he was anything but amiable until he learned that the joke had reached and been shared by all alike. The men enjoyed it.

On March 9, 1862, we received orders to prepare to leave the cars that had been our home for so long a time, and to march forward to Martinsburg, ten miles distant. We had reconstructed the road up to this point, and were now to join the balance of the division which had already passed by us and met General Shields (for a fact, this time), who was to take command of our division at Martinsburg. On March 10 a regiment of loyal Virginia soldiers arrived to take our place, and we moved forward, reaching Martinsburg at four p.m., and were directed to proceed to the courthouse, where, with the greater part of the whole division, we were massed in solid column to receive some remarks from General Shields on the occasion of his assuming the command. His speech is not sufficiently well remembered to give it place in this history.

It will perhaps be remembered that when our forces first entered Martinsburg, the rebellious inhabitants had barricaded the doors of the courthouse, and cut the halyards from the flagstaff with the avowed purpose that no Union flag should float over it. The Thirty-Ninth was determined that the Stars and Stripes should fly there notwithstanding that the people of the town had announced that sudden death awaited those who dare attempt it. A member of Company B, of the Thirty-Ninth, Private Lee Harvey, volunteered to do the business, and was soon seen getting up the side of the building by the aid of the lightning-rod, bearing with him a flag. He reached the roof and with the same energy he climbed the flagstaff and to the top of it nailed the Stars and Stripes where so lately had flaunted the Stars and Bars of the so-called Southern Confederacy. This brave act made him the hero of the hour.

After General Shields' address the command moved out a short distance from town on the Winchester Pike, and bivouacked for the night. The following morning at nine we resumed our march toward Winchester, and when within two miles of that city went into camp, at four in the afternoon. The following morning, March 12, 1862, after guard mount and the duties of the day were disposed of, attention was given to a general cleaning up, which was sadly needed after so long a confinement in filthy cars.

Several officers, after "slicking up," as it was termed, and which mainly consisted in having their boots blacked or greased and attaching a clean paper collar to the shirt, received permission to ride into the city of Winchester to satisfy a curiosity to see the late stronghold of Secession, and the base of operations of Jackson's army.

General Nathaniel Banks' command was encamped near by and the Thirteenth Massachusetts Volunteers was on provost-marshal duty in the town.

After a few days of rest in camp, the Thirty-Ninth was ordered to take part in an expedition up the valley; and leaving knapsacks and all camp equipment we filed out on the morning of March 18, 1862, to join the balance of our Brigade, which was already in line, and at half-past nine commenced to move, preceded by a company of pioneers bearing axes and followed by twenty pieces of artillery.

During a short halt made in the city, Major S. W. Munn, who was riding a horse that had been captured at Bath on January 3, was approached by a young and comely lady and a loyal rebel, who after the preface of some pleasant smiles and words, remarked that he was riding her horse and proceeded forthwith to state the circumstances that led to its being captured, and ended by saying that she presumed the Major would have the courtesy to return the horse to its owner. The Major as we all know, was an exceedingly gallant and gracious man and especially so when a handsome woman was concerned. After recovering somewhat from his surprise he said in reply, "Well, Madam, I do not know about this. The horse, if yours, was found in very bad company, and is a legitimate capture from an officer in open rebellion against the Government of the United States. It is a contraband and confiscation of war and is now the property of the government. I am riding it on the present occasion, being sadly in need of a horse; perhaps the accidents of war may restore it to you. Otherwise it will be turned in to the quartermaster and sold. I am very sorry that I cannot have the pleasure of turning it over to you, but it is not within my leaving." The woman much chagrined at her failure and doubtless with a less favorable opinion of the "Yanks" than she had before.

The circumstances attending the capture of this horse were as follows: During a reconnaissance on January 3 near Bath, under the immediate command of Captain S. S. Linton, also accompanied by Lieutenant-Colonel Mann and several cavalrymen, Sergeant Hopkins, of Company D, with a squad of men surprised an officer who seemed to be out prospecting in a neighboring field, and who, as was afterwards learned, was the Adjutant-General of Loring's Brigade. The Sergeant commanded him to halt, dismount, and surrender! The officer quickly dismounted, and taking down some of the top rails of the intervening fence, gave the horse a stoke that sent him over and into our lines, while the officer, taking advantage of the momentary diversion and approach of some of the rebel cavalry, sneaked away under cover of the fence and escaped. The horse was captured and turned over to Major Munn, who had been without a horse since his promotion. It was afterwards jointly used by him and Lieutenant-Colonel Mann, whose horse had been severely injured on this expedition while leaping a ditch in efforts to escape capture. At Suffolk, Virginia, the horse was turned in to the quartermaster, and an order was procured for its sale, when it was bought by money contributed by the officers of the Regiment and forwarded to Governor Yates as a present—Major Munn taking it to Springfield in December 1862, when he left the service.

As we passed through the streets of Winchester many dark and gloomy faces peered at us from doors and windows, and some among the gentler sex were even tearful, thinking perhaps of our mission and their many dear friends in the Confederate service whom we might encounter.

The streets through which we passed were lined with soldiers from General Banks' command who greeted us as we passed with cheering words. At times a familiar voice would admonish us to "take care of yourself, old boy!" and "don't get shot in the back!"

The spectacle presented by this moving column, fully 10,000 strong, was grand and imposing—the glorious old Stars and Stripes waving to the breeze—the various bands discoursing lively Union music, and the well-clothed and orderly soldiers trampling onward in measured steps.

> "'Twere worth ten years of peaceful life,—
> One glance of their array."

We passed at a quickstep through the city and were soon joined by General Shields and staff, who took position at the head of the column, which was preceded by the Fifth Ohio Infantry and a portion of the First Michigan Cavalry, who acted as skirmishers.

Along our line of travel we constantly saw traces of the enemy, who, as we approached, had hastily decamped, leaving their campfires still burning and their forage scattered. We found enough of hay and oats to give our horses a good feed. At a distance of eight miles we reached the small village of Newtown, the only remarkable feature of which was the absence of the male population. The women were, as it seemed, the sole occupants, and exhibited themselves freely at the windows and porches of the houses, and it pleased them to wear a most forbidding countenance. The only delighted and happy expressions were seen in the shining faces of the many Negroes who had gathered together in little groups at various points.

Several miles further brought us to Middletown, before reaching which, however, we noticed a dense column of smoke from what we soon learned was the bridge spanning Cedar Creek, and which had been set on fire by the retreating rebels. Soon after we heard the booming of cannon, and an order came to open ranks and let the artillery pass, which came at flying speed; then closing up, we rushed forward at double-quick to the scene of the action, but found no enemy to fight. One of the Michigan Cavalry was badly wounded by Colonel Ashby, in the thigh, and the bone was so badly shattered that amputation was necessary.

We were obliged to bivouac at this point for the night, the Thirty-Ninth being ordered to flank the artillery. No fire was allowed, and as the night was cold, dark and rainy, it was supremely disagreeable; but it being a "military necessity" we stood it out patiently.

The following morning we were up and stirring by the time "reveille" sounded, and after sharpening our teeth on hardtack passed on to Strasburg, a temporary bridge having been provided to cross the creek. Our approach, however, was careful and well considered, for now and then a shell would come over in our vicinity, which plainly gave us to understand that the enemy was not far off. We halted a mile from town; the sharpshooters and cavalry were sent ahead together with a portion of the artillery, and for the space of an hour a brisk skirmish was kept up with Ashby's cavalry. We finally entered Strasburg, and proceeded two miles beyond, taking the field instead of the road, as we were afraid of masked batteries, and with reason, too, for they were soon discovered, and in such position that had we kept the road they would have done great damage. The enemy constantly directed their fire upon us, but without effect, as but very few of their shells exploded. We had expected to meet a large force and consequently were drawn up in line of battle, and anxiously awaited the commencement. Quickly twelve pieces of artillery were put in position, and opened fire, but soon ceased, for we could discover in the distance an attempt to stampede and Ashby's cavalry preparing for a charge upon the Fifth Ohio in order to give opportunity for a successful retreat.

We waited impatiently for operations to commence, but there was no commencement, and we advanced until darkness when the order came to bivouac; and to add to the discomfort a drizzly rain set in and continued through the night. In the morning nothing could be seen of the enemy and at nine a.m. we were ordered back to our former camp, which was reached at eight p.m., after a very fatiguing march of twenty-one miles through the rain, which still continued to fall.

BIVOUACKING AT CEDAR CREEK—IN THE RAIN.

CHAPTER SEVEN

"The scene of the battlefield is awful"

At Newton, on our return, we met with Doctor J. W. Owens, who invited the Surgeon of the Thirteenth Indiana and Dr. Clark to his house, where a good dinner was furnished, with the "et cetera." Before dining he took much pride in showing us some of his correspondence with Daniel Webster and several European celebrities. We found him to be a man of culture and refinement. He was a widower; the splendid residence occupied by him being chiefly in care of his much-attached slaves. He showed up a miniature picture of his late wife, who was a descendant of the Washington family, and which he carried in a fold of his pocketbook, for the reason, as he stated, that he did not know when he might be taken prisoner, and he wished to have it with him. He was a most bitter secessionist and owned some twenty slaves which, he said, he would soon free.

On our return we met with our old friend, David Strother (Porte Crayon). He is attached to the cavalry service and was stationed at Manassas, but had been detached and put upon General Bank's staff and was proceeding to Strasburg by invitation of General Shields, who wished to avail himself of his topographical knowledge. In speaking of the late affair at Bath, he stated that the rebels had done him great damage, having destroyed a valuable cabinet of minerals—defaced all his paintings and stolen all his sketches, a loss irreparable, and one that money could not replace.

We reached our camp near Winchester at eight p.m., and were glad to get under the shelter of our tents.

Lieutenant S. S. Brucker was later to write:

"As your are probably not aware that I had the honor to open the battle of Winchester, I will give you a brief account of the matter.

"On the Friday evening, March 21, 1862, before the battle, I was detailed to report, with fifty men of Company C, at the headquarters of General Shields. Upon arrival, I was ordered to await a detail of fifty men from the Thirteenth Indiana Volunteers, who would report to me, and I was then to proceed out a distance of about two miles on the Front Royal road to relieve picket outposts belonging to General Bank's army, which was preparing to move on Centreville.

"In having rained almost continuously the preceding three days, the roads were in bad condition and almost impassable, and being a very dark night our progress was necessarily slow. After marching nearly four hours, I concluded that it was about time we found the pickets that we were to relieve, so I halted my command near the border of some timber, where we found a large plantation-house and outbuildings.

"As was usual in such cases, in less than fifteen minutes the "boys" had ascertained that there were several fine horses and saddles in the stable. I borrowed three of them without taking the trouble of asking permission, and mounting a sergeant and two men, sent them forward to find out if the pickets were still in advance of us. In an hour's time they returned, having failed to discover them. After a short rest I ordered my men to fall back toward Winchester, and having taken about the proper distance I deployed them in regular picket-line between the Front Royal and Strasburg Pikes, leaving a small reserve and both ends of the line.

"We had barely got our line fully established as day began to break, and I concluded to take some rest; but before I could accomplish this, my attention was called by the Corporal of the Guard, who said that he could see Banks' pickets coming in; and looking I could perceive some fifteen cavalrymen, dressed in the Federal uniform, coming toward us from the Front Royal Road. They continued to approach until within fifty yards, when they raised their carbines and opened fire, but their aim being hurried no one was hurt. After the volley they immediately whirled about and rode off at a gallop. Everyone seemed to be surprised, having little doubt but that they were our own men, and the pickets that we had been in search of, and that perhaps they were playing a joke upon us. Nevertheless, I instructed my men to return the fire in case of a repetition.

"One half hour later they returned with an increased force, and quite a lively skirmish took place for an hour's time. I soon found a more advantageous position behind a stone fence, such as are found in that locality, and where I had a better chance to pepper into them without exposing my men, and shortened the distance between the two roads.

"The enemy must have realized the fact that our position was such that they could not dislodge us with their tactics, and to our great surprise an artillery fire was opened, throwing shells. This was continued quite lively for a while in order to distract our attention from the cavalry, who in the meantime attempted to flank our position, but without success, as we kept them at bay and held the position. Meanwhile we were looking toward Winchester for reinforcements, and wondered why none came, for we reasoned that the firing must have been heard, and I had sent a messenger to General Shields' headquarters some time before; and yet no sign of answer, and we were beginning to despair. But at last, about eleven a.m., we heard the welcome sounds of the bugle and fast-galloping troopers coming down the Strasburg Pike to our assistance. They found us still masters of the situation.

"We had been attacked and had successfully repulsed the enemy's pickets and skirmishers at least a dozen times, and it was surprising that we had escaped with so small a loss, which was, one killed and three wounded of the Thirteenth Indiana Volunteers, and two wounded and five prisoners taken from the Thirty-Ninth Illinois Volunteers. The Confederate loss, as I was afterwards credibly informed, was three killed and fifteen wounded.

"When I reported at General Shields' headquarters the following evening, I found him confined to his bed suffering from a shattered arm, caused by a fragment of shell from the enemy's guns, received early in the evening of the 22nd. I gave him a detailed account of the occurrences of my two days and one night's outpost duty, and inquired why no support was sent me after the firing was heard. He replied that he had heard the firing of musketry and artillery, and on inquiring the cause had been informed that our artillery and infantry were drilling and practicing. He was very angry when he learned that General Banks' pickets had left their posts without waiting to be relieved. He highly complimented us and our noble Regiment, and expressed the great interest he took in the old brigade, remarking that if the balance of the army consisted of such material the war would soon end."

This reconnaissance in force was not attended with the results that were anticipated, except that we gained a knowledge of the enemy's strength and location and cleared the way for the advance of General Banks' army, which was moving on Centreville.

The night of March 22, the "long roll" was sounded, and the various regiments of our Division turned out and were soon in line and on the march toward Winchester. The scene of the affray was located about one mile beyond the city, and was occasioned by a body of Ashby's cavalry who had dismounted and were advancing as infantry, under the impression that the Union forces had left, as they had undoubtedly witnessed the departure of General Banks' army. They came howling and yelling like so many demons, but were gallantly met by the First Maryland Cavalry, who delivered a fire that killed nineteen of the rebels who fell like stones to rise no more. The Thirty-Ninth Illinois and the Fifth Ohio Infantry took position on the Romney Pike, fortunately their services were not demanded, for the enemy soon retreated.

During the little skirmish one of our artillerymen was killed, and also the horse he was riding. General Shields was also wounded by a fragment of shell which broke his left arm. He was soon conveyed to the rear in an ambulance.

During the day Captain Gray of Company C had been stationed some three miles in advance with his company, on outpost duty, and when we met with him, after this skirmish, he told us that he had been engaged more or less during the whole day with the advance of Ashby's cavalry and had lost two men.

The whole Division was kept on duty during the entire night, and the retreating rebels were followed up by some five companies of cavalry.

The succeeding day (March 23, 1862) ushered in the battle of Winchester, with Ashby's cavalry and the whole force of Jackson to combat. The engagement commenced at ten a.m., and did not terminate until darkness had set in. The Thirty-Ninth occupied the extreme left and was not called into action, but did good service in supporting a battery during the engagement.

The scene of the action was in the vicinity of Kernstown, some four miles in advance of Winchester on the Strasburg Pike. Our Division was posted as follows: the Brigade of General Nathanial Kimball on the extreme right, General Tyler in the center, and General Jeremiah Sullivan on the left. General Kimball had command, owing to the disability of General Shields. The battle opened with a fierce artillery duel which continued until about three in the afternoon, when the infantry became engaged, and resulted in a complete victory for our troops after fighting almost hand-to-hand over a distance of two miles.

The carnage was frightful, our Division having 150 men killed and 300 wounded, while the enemy's loss amounted to some 900 in killed and wounded, 236 taken prisoner, and the abandonment of two field-pieces and four caissons, together with 1,000 small arms and several stands of colors. (The battle and the victory at Winchester were considered so important, occurring as it did so soon after the Bull Run disaster, that President Lincoln and his cabinet paid a visit to the battleground. The victory at Winchester was bravely won, but not without the sacrifice of many good and valiant men. The troops were complimented by General McClellan, and General Shields personally complimented them upon opening the campaign on the Potomac, and advised us to inscribe Winchester upon our banners.)

General Jackson, it was said, had made the boast in the morning that he would enter Winchester in time for evening service at the churches; and so confident were the women that he would be successful that they were preparing a banquet for him, but it proved as true in this case as in many others that "There's many a slip between cup and lip;" and instead of entering Winchester he was fast retreating on Strasburg with a crippled army. It was at this battle that General Jackson received the "Soubriquet" of "Stonewall Jackson" from the fact of his having taken up with a position behind a stone wall which resulted most disastrously to our men while making a charge. [Editors' note: In reality, Stonewall Jackson earned his "soubriquet" during the first battle of Bull Run].

Our men had nothing to eat since early morning and it was not until nine p.m. that the commissary reported with rations.

The men lay on their weapons all night, and a bitter cold night it was. The following morning General Banks returned, but too late to be of any service except in the matter of directing the pursuit, and it devolved upon the Thirty-Ninth to lead the advance, which was continued to Strasburg. Our march during the day was continually interrupted and made disagreeable by the continued assaults of the rearguard of the enemy, who with two pieces of artillery, were throwing shells amongst us but their fire was returned with interest, and as we advanced we could perceive that our fire had been effectual from the number of dead and wounded that had been left to our mercy.

We bivouacked for the night at Cedar Creek. The pursuit was continued the following morning (Tuesday, March 25), and as we pushed forward the rebel cavalry and artillery seemed to have disappeared; but more or less skirmishing was kept up with the enemy's rearguard until we went into camp near Woodstock. This town was a county-seat and was built up along one street, and as we entered at one end the rebels left at the other. The enemy had planted a battery of artillery upon a hill at the further side, and our artillery took position on a rise of ground opposite, the town lying between, and a brief but lively cannonading took place. A shell from one of our guns struck a large brass ball upon the cupola of the court-house, splitting it in halves. General Ashby's horse was also killed under him.

We soon moved on and went into camp at the town of Edinburg, and here, as we were sadly short of rations, permission was given to forage; and as the woods were full of hogs there was soon no lack of provender in the flesh line.

We remained at this place until April 1, when we were called upon at one in the morning to advance. We passed through the town, our advance guard driving the pickets of the enemy. The rebels, however, made but little resistance. About sunrise we reached Mount Jackson, a town of some 600 inhabitants, and here the enemy set fire to the cars and the bridge before retiring; but our cavalry hastened forward and after a light skirmish in which one man was killed and three taken prisoners the bridge was saved. Jackson endeavored to make a stand on the heights across the river, but Shields succeeded in flanking his position and he moved on toward Staunton.

FRESH PORK FOR SUPPER.

Here it was that the Thirty-Ninth made its first, if not its most brilliant charge. On Rude's Hill, nearly a mile distant, there was discovered what was supposed to be a masked battery. No men were visible, only the mouth of a large gun, at least a 32-pounder, could be seen. This battery must be taken, and the Thirty-Ninth was assigned that duty. At the word of command the boys started out on the "double-quick," but cautiously, making a detour so as to conceal the movement and take the battery in flank. When sufficiently near, the order came to charge, and with a cheer and hurrah they made a grand rush upon the formidable battery, which was found to consist of an old piece of smokestack or pipe that had been abandoned by the roadside and was well supported by any number of trees standing in martial order behind it. We then moved on to Strasburg and went into camp.

As stated in <u>Fifteen Years Ago: or the Patriotism of Will County</u> by George H. Woodruff, Joliet, 1876, 156-158, about the battle of Winchester:

"Being posted at the extreme left, the Thirty-Ninth did not come into the thickest of the fight, and suffered very little. Its part in the battle is thus told by a member of the Regiment, (name unknown), writing to the Wilmington Herald at the time. Under date of March 29, near Strasburg, he writes:

"Everything remained quiet after that, until Sunday noon, when the long roll sounded again. We marched out on the Strasburg road, and within two miles of Winchester, turned off to the left, and marching through the fields and woods until we came in sight of the enemy. We halted and were ordered to lie flat. Meanwhile the enemy's cannon on the front and right was speaking loud and fierce. Some of our artillery were planted on a hill to the right, and replied with good effect. The position of the enemy was in the woods to the right and left of a little village called Kernstown. All around there were patches of timber in which the enemy concealed themselves as much as possible. Their main force seemed to be in the edge of a wood on a hill, northwest of the town. Most of our force was on a ridge northeast of the town. The rebels opened fire on our Regiment from a battery in front, but few shells reached us. They then moved to the left and nearer, and the shells burst thick and fast around us. Two cannon came to our rescue, and soon silenced the rebel guns. We now moved to the left, and took position close to the enemy, so as to command their position, and they immediately drew back.

"About five o'clock we hear a heavy roll of musketry, and another, and another in quick succession, then one continued roar and crash, and the smoke rises thick above the trees where the battle is raging. The roar and smoke continued without abatement, but it moves farther and farther off, and we conclude our forces are driving the enemy. As night comes on we see the flash of the guns, as the messengers of death fly fast from line to line, and as the darkness increases, the noise dies away, until it ceases altogether. We lie down on the field with our guns beside us, not knowing when we may be called upon to renew the conflict. All night long the men are moving about with torches in search of the wounded and dead. Many poor fellows on both sides have gone to their long rest. Many more are crippled for life. The Union loss is said to be from fifty to 100 killed, and 300 or 400 wounded. The enemy's loss is not known, but said to be 300 killed.

"The scene of the battlefield is awful. Dead men lying in heaps here and there, limbs off, and dead horses lying in every direction. In a little hollow behind a battery four rebels were playing cards. They had just dealt, and each held his hand, when a shell burst in their midst, and killed all of them. In other places the wounded are groaning and crying for help. Such is a battlefield! Although the shells fell thick around us, and Company D was skirmishing all the afternoon, none of our Regiment was injured. Next morning before light we moved on, the artillery occasionally throwing shells. All day we followed the retreating rebels, till we came to Cedar Creek, when our artillery threw shells across at the rebels who were cooking their supper. They gathered up in haste and fled; one shell killed one man and wounded three. Next morning as we passed over the ground of the rebel bivouac, we found it strewn with half-filled barrels of flour, cakes half baked, and tents half burned, and things scattered very generally. We passed on without much skirmishing, to our present position, three miles from Strasburg."

This was the limit of our pursuit as directed by General Banks. It was rumored at this time that the enemy had been largely reinforced by Generals Smith and Longstreet, but his proved incorrect at this time. Our force on this occasion consisted of four brigades of infantry, one regiment of cavalry (The Third U. S.) and forty pieces of artillery. On the evening of April 4 the Sutler reached our camp, bring several casks of ale, and it is hardly necessary to add that it was soon transferred from the barrels to the thirsty throats of its admirers. The same evening some of the officers, accompanied by the band, proceeded to pay their respects to Colonel Nathan Kimball, commanding, who was found wrapped in the drapery of his blankets and who declined to listen to any music, as it was not military at such a time, and furthermore, would prevent us hearing an alarm if one was sounded. The General being too much engaged with his fears, we left him and proceeded to the headquarters of General Williams, who courteously invited us in and gave us a hearty welcome.

April 7, the Regiment was called upon for duty at the outpost, to support a battery of artillery, and a sorry time we had, bivouacking out in the cold drizzly rain; but in the space of twenty-four hours we were relieved by the Seventh Indiana and proceeded back to our old quarters where there was more solid comfort.

April 12, General Shields had so far recovered as to be able to review his command. On being congratulated upon his recovery, he stated that he was again ready to give the rebels another chance at him, supported as he would be by his gallant troops.

While we were encamped at Strasburg Surgeon Blake and Major Munn rejoined the Regiment. The Major had been absent sick since March 22, and Surgeon Blake since the battle, having been detailed to the hospital. Considerable speculation was indulged in as regarded in our next move, but nothing could be learned from any source. It was evident, however, what we should not remain long idle.

At one a.m., April 17, orders came to at once prepare to march, and we were soon in readiness for any destination. We left camp before daylight and during the morning crossed the south branch of the Shenandoah River, our skirmishers having now and then a little brush with the rebel cavalry; but they retreated rapidly after burning bridges, railroad cars and other property that might give aid and comfort to the enemy. Our cavalry in the advance had several brisk skirmishes, resulting in the capture of a few prisoners. During the day we forded the Shenandoah River, the water being waist deep and having a very strong current. A large number of the men removed their clothing for this purpose, remembering their experiences at Hancock, Maryland with wet garments.

We reached New Market after a tedious journey over the worst road that we had as yet traveled, and bivouacked. The following morning, April 19, the Regiment was ordered to cross the Massanuton Mountain to guard the bridges upon the river which were spanning the south fork of the Potomac. One half of the Regiment was stationed at Columbia Bridge, while the other part guarded the White House Bridge, some six miles distant. The duty at the White House Bridge was shared by two companies of the First Vermont Cavalry, who were daily busy in making raids. On April 23 we organized a raid to proceed to the village of Luray, some six miles distant, but did not accomplish anything except giving the inhabitants a thorough scare and driving from town a small force of the enemy. We remained in the town some few hours, and while there the larders of its citizens suffered somewhat severely by helping ourselves to something for eating and drinking, which was by no means abundant.

The six companies that were stationed at Columbia Bridge, under the command of Major Munn, had quite a lively skirmish with two companies of rebel cavalry at the time they took possession, getting some seventeen prisoners. The Major posted his men in such manner as to hold the place. This bridge as well as the White House was a covered one, and of great length, and it was impossible to determine the character of any persons in the bridge by those approaching, and this circumstances soon gave them another prisoner. It seems that a rebel officer had been off down the river to see his best girl, and in his absence the bridge had fallen into our hands. He was totally ignorant of the fact, and was returning on his horse in a very leisurely and unconcerned manner. He came along singing and chirping and was doubtless in a very happy frame of mind, just back from seeing his charmer. Our boys noticed his coming and one of them drew up his gun to fire, but was stopped in time by the Major, who said, "Let him alone and we will give him a surprise;" and they withdrew back in the deeper shadow of the bridge. The man continued to approach, wholly unsuspicious of danger. He was allowed to come quite close before the word was given to "Halt!" "Halt!" He sang out, thinking the matter a joke. "What in the hell are you halting me for? I'm no damned Yankee!" "Well, we are. Halt!" And the boys stepped forward presenting their muskets. The surprise and astonishment of this man can better be imagined than described. He was almost paralyzed, but yielded gracefully to circumstances and the fortunes of war.

April 22, Major Collins, commanding several companies of the First Vermont Cavalry stationed near us at White House Bridge, invited several officers of the Thirty-Ninth to accompany him on an expedition made for the purpose of arresting a Colonel Boswell, of the Confederate army, who was known to be at his home several miles distant in the country. At the head of two companies we started off on the gallop. An hour's ride brought us to the house, and attended by a file of troopers we proceeded up to the door, and were met by a lady very much excited and frightened. "Is this the residence of Colonel Boswell, Madam?" the Major asked. "It is, sir." "Is the Colonel at home?" "No, Sir." "Can you inform us as to his whereabouts?" "I think he has gone to join the army; but, are you Northern or Southern soldiers?" "We are soldiers in support of the majesty of the United States Government, Northern men, Madam, and, if you please, genuine Yankees; and you will please be quite certain that your husband is not here, for we intend to search the house and premises." "I tell you the truth, Sir, if I die the next minute; but I do hope you will not kill him in case you should ever meet with him, and I do pray that you will not turn myself and daughters out of our home on such a day as this is." "No fear, Madam. We came solely to seek your husband, whom we were informed was here on a visit. You or your home shall not suffer in the least, and we do not war against women and children."

We then proceeded to make a thorough search of the house and outbuildings, but failed to find the Colonel. He must have been apprised of our coming and fled.

After overhauling all his papers and correspondence and appropriating what seemed of importance we returned to our camp very much chagrined at the failure.

The probabilities were that we would remain at the vicinity of the White House Bridge for several weeks and consequently had ordered forwarded all our camp and garrison equipment. Our life was full of novelty and excitement, and the hours and days passed smoothly away. While here, we were visited by a large and motley group of slaves belonging to the adjacent farmers, and to witness their delight and the well-pleased expressions that beamed from every polished face—their large eyes rolling in a frenzy of amazement and their thick lips shrinking back from the gleaming ivory in merry grins at what they witnessed of company drill and camp scenes, were funny to behold. The Regimental Band played some lively airs for their especial benefit, awaking in them all the harmony of their natures, which expressed itself in every bone and muscle, and occasionally it found vent in words: "Lor, bless dis y'er time! Chile, jis listen to dat ar! it am mighty fine." They remained until after "dress parade," which "capped the climax."

May 4, the detachment located at White House Bridge was ordered to Columbia Bridge to support the Thirteenth Indiana and First Virginia regiments, which were guarding the bridge. On the 5th rumors of the advance of Jackson were circulated, and finally confirmed by the appearance of large numbers of rebel cavalry on the opposite side. The troops were ordered to sleep on their muskets and be in readiness at a moment's warning to either fight or retreat.

May 6 brought nothing new except that Companies D and G of the Thirty-Ninth were sent out as skirmishers and we were reinforced with five regiments of infantry, one regiment of cavalry, and two batteries of artillery.

At one o'clock the following morning the whole command was ordered forward for a reconnaissance of the enemy's position, which resulted in a severe skirmish with the vanguard of the enemy, wherein the Thirteenth Indiana, which led the advance, lost about fifty men in killed and wounded and taken prisoners. We found their force to be greatly superior to our own and were compelled to make a hasty retreat. The report had reached us that Yorktown had been evacuated, and the force opposite to us was indeed a part if not the whole of that army. During the night the summit and sides of the Blue Ridge for miles were glittering with the campfires and signal-lights of the rebel host. In order to mislead the enemy hundreds of unnecessary fires were lighted up on our hillsides.

ON THE MARCH.

The signal corps were kept busy all night telegraphing across the mountain to General Banks, who had been forced to retire from Harrisonburg by reason of the advance of the large army under Johnson and Jackson.

May 10, orders came to prepare for a march to Fredericksburg and report to General McDowell. The following morning at an early hour we had commenced a weary march, and for four continuous days the rain was unceasing. After crossing the Blue Ridge we met a party of some 600 rebel cavalry, and a brisk skirmish ensued which delayed our progress for a few hours. This march had extended across the peninsula and through the wilderness of Virginia, and had been undertaken with the expectation of forming, with the army of General McDowell, the right wing of McClellan's army.

General McDowell had a force of 40,000 men under his command, and at the time of our arrival they were in active preparation for a move "On to Richmond," and we were ordered to at once trim ourselves for the movement. All of our tents were ordered turned over; the baggage train to be diminished to four wagons; our heavy winter clothing to be packed and sent to Washington; all disabled men to be discharged from the service, and those requiring hospital treatment to be sent to Alexandria, Virginia. There was to be a general purging out of Shield's Division, and his rough Western men must subscribe more fully and obey more strictly "army regulations," so they might harmonize more fully with the popinjay soldiers from Massachusetts and the Eastern States, whom we often noticed looking scornfully and disdainfully at us, until there were several broken heads among them to teach them better manners.

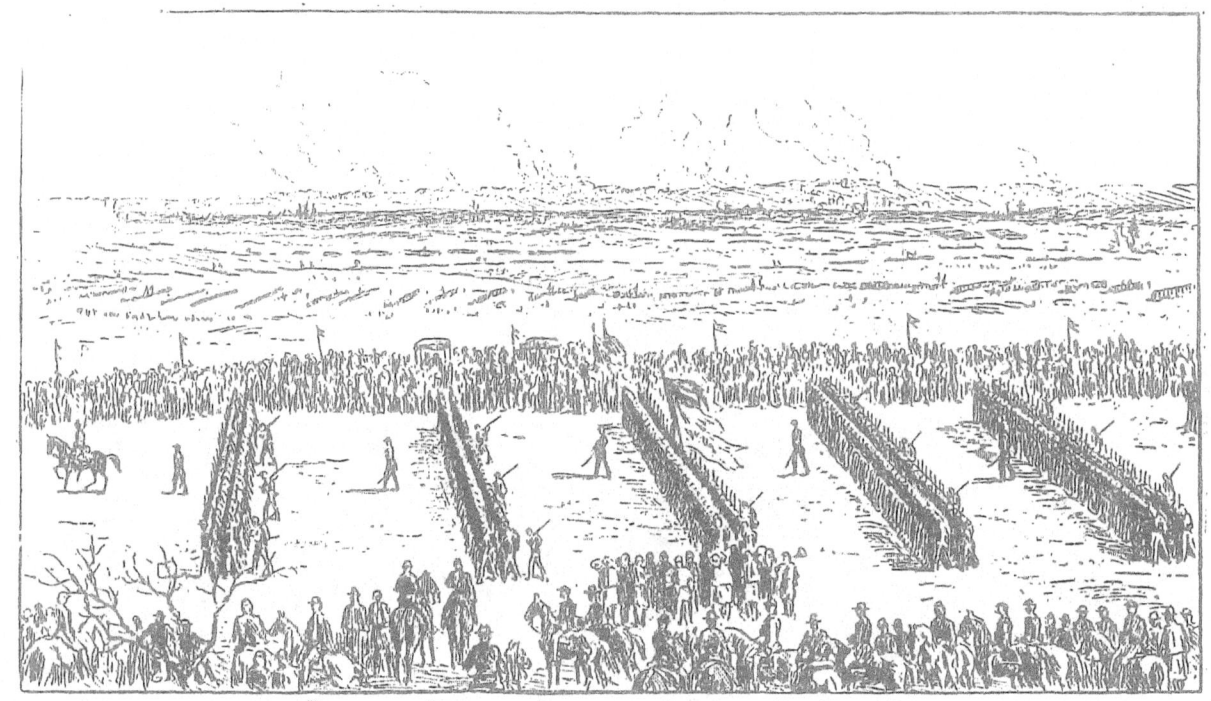
REVIEW BY PRESIDENT LINCOLN AT FALMOUTH, VA., MAY 1862.

President Lincoln, Secretary Edwin Stanton, Lord Lyons of the British Embassy, and other distinguished persons, were present here, and the next day there was to be a grand review of the army, and there was a great deal to do in order to prepare for a close inspection and the parade. On the afternoon of May 24, the troops, numbering some 50,000, were paraded for review. As President Lincoln rode down our lines at a gallop in company with General McDowell and his brilliant staff, his eye caught sight of our flag, which had our name and number emblazoned upon it, and partly turned and stopped and called out, "What Regiment is that?" "Thirty-Ninth Illinois!" was answered. "Well! You boys are a good ways from home, ain't you?" and passed on down the line. After the review and we had returned to our camp the President came and made a tour through the Regimental quarters, shaking hands with many and asking numerous questions. He seemed delighted to find a regiment from his own state in the Army of the Potomac.

The lines of army discipline were drawn pretty taut at this juncture, and the duties of officers and men were onerous in the extreme. Dr. Clark was the only medical officer with the Regiment, as Dr. Blake had remained at New Market in charge of our sick, and had afterwards been assigned to duty in Banks' army in charge of a hospital near Mount Jackson, Virginia. Major Munn was also absent on detached service as provost-marshal at Warrenton Junction. The Regimental Quartermaster, Joseph A. Cutler, was also behind somewhere, and Lieutenant J. F. Linton, of Company D, was acting in his place, and was much more efficient and gave much better satisfaction. Disabled men were being examined and discharged and the sick sent to the hospital, and the heavy clothing and overcoats of the men were got in readiness to be sent to Washington.

About May 23, it began to be rumored that General Banks was being driven back and surrounded by the rebels under Generals Bushrod Johnson, Stonewall Jackson and Richard Ewell, who were making every effort to tear the Baltimore and Ohio Railroad again, and Shields' Division received orders to march back to his relief; and on the morning of May 25, at six o'clock, we started on a return forced march. Prior to leaving, however, four captains and two lieutenants from different companies of the Regiment went to Dr. Clark for examination and a certificate of disability on which to base an application to enable them to present the resignation of their commissions—right in the face of the enemy, as it were. Dr. Clark, upon examination of these six officers, found that he could not accede to their wishes, and they, after some slight unpleasantness with the Doctor, were obliged to return, but soon afterwards tendered their resignations and left the service.

On the return march some trouble occurred between General Irvin McDowell and Shields, with the result that General Shields left his command. At Warrenton Junction we heard of General Bank's defeat and utter route from the valley, and there being no further necessity for our joining him, our brigade, which then consisted of the Thirty-Ninth Illinois, Sixty-Seventh Ohio and Thirteenth Indiana Volunteers, was ordered to Alexandria.

There were many sick and footsore, and they were given transportation on the railroad. Proceeding on from this point, the march became more and more tedious and monotonous. We were yet on the road formerly traversed, noticeable by many signs, chief of which, was the complete demolition of the rail-fencing marking our former bivouacs, which had been used for fuel or shelter, and in many instances for a bed, in order to keep out of the mud. The rail fences of Virginia were a great boon to the soldiers of both armies.

The Thirty-Ninth, with the balance of the Division, reached Alexandria about June 12, where a rest was given us to from so long a march; but it was not to be a protracted or even a sufficient one, for McClellan's army was engaged with Lee's in what has been recorded in history as the "Seven Days'" fight, in front of Richmond, and like the Wandering Jew we must move on.

June 26 we were ordered on board transports and were soon enroute for Harrison's Landing on the James River, arriving there in time to take some small part in the battle of Malvern Hill, July 1, 1862; but fortunately our positions and duty were such that we lost no men from the Regiment.

It should have been mentioned in its proper connection that when we reached Luray, Virginia, on our return march from Fredericksburg, a portion of our brigade was sent to Port Republic to hold or, if need be, to destroy the bridge across the South Branch of the Shenandoah River, where it met a large force of the enemy and a disastrous battle took place. The Thirty-Ninth was ordered there but did not reach the place in time to take part, but assisted in taking care of the wounded, numbering 100 or more.

The march to and from Fredericksburg had occupied some three weeks' time, and we had covered 360 miles of distance. It was a distressingly long march and one that tried the patience and endurance of the men beyond anything in our former experience as soldiers, and crippled many.

CHAPTER EIGHT

"Death was busy reaping a rich harvest"

We were assigned after reaching Harrison's Landing to the Corps commanded by General Erasmus Darwin Keyes, but were yet in General John James Peck's Division, and General Orris Sanford Ferry commanded our Brigade, and the eminent surgeon Dr. Frank H. Hamilton was the Medical Director. The weather for the most part of the time that we remained at this place was almost unendurable, the temperature often reaching 102° in the shade. The dry soil was so destitute of all moisture that it was fissured in all directions. Many of the camps were so destitute of all shade; the water scarce and totally unfit for use; in numerable flies by day destroyed all comfort for man and beast, and myriads of mosquitoes disturbed sleep at night. Sickness in many forms was widespread, and Death was busy reaping a rich harvest in the Army of the Potomac. It will be remembered that we had considerable sickness in the Regiment but lost no men by death at this time. A contract assistant surgeon, Dr. J. H. Strobridge, a Canadian, had been assigned to duty with the Regiment and rendered very efficient service. The Sanitary and Christian Commissions came very opportunely to our aid at this juncture, furnishing abundance's of ice and delicacies for the sick, and in no small degree contributing to their comfort and return to health. The Thirty-Ninth for the most part was put on outpost duty at the front, remaining out for a week at a time, and this duty was much more desirable than remaining in camp, near the river.

July 26, Captain W. B. Slaughter, Company G, resigned his commission, and Lieutenant Amos Savage was promoted to the position. Captains Gray, Company C, Wilmarth, Company B, and Hooker, of Company E, had previously resigned; also Lieutenants Holderman, Company B, and Nicholson, of Company K. Adjutant Frank B. Marshall, who had been absent from the Regiment for a considerable time on recruiting service, had also resigned, Sergeant-Major Joseph D. Walker being promoted to fill the vacancy. Surgeon S. C. Blake had resigned June 3, Assisting Surgeon C. M. Clark being promoted.

Company H, commanded by Captain Williams, joined the Regiment here, together with recruits for other companies, on or about the July 12, 1862.

August 9 there was general commotion in General McClellan's Army, and a move in some direction seemed imminent. The gunboats went up the river and assailed Fort Darling, and much of the infantry, artillery and cavalry was in motion, but as yet we had received no orders. The "*Celestial Picket*" up in a balloon, anchored near McClellan's headquarters, reported the enemy advancing and estimated to be some 60,000 strong. About midnight there was a terrific cannonading. The whole camp was roused by the rapid bursting of shells in the very midst of our encampment, which produced, as can be imagined, a very lively commotion and scattering, in a closely packed camp of about 50,000 men. It was soon discovered that the shells came from a battery across the James River. In 20 minutes time, however, a few of our guns had completely silenced it.

Gunboats on James River.

Aside from the large amount of actual sickness in McClellan's army, there was noticeable, and especially among commissioned officers, a large amount of nostalgia, or home sickness. Large numbers sent in their resignations, but as a rule they were disapproved. Many feigned sickness, and one instance is known where a valiant officer hired two men to carry him to the hospital boat on a stretcher, and he succeeded in getting North to a hospital. The camp was a harvest for the sutlers. These vampires charged double prices for everything they sold, and nothing was sold for a less price than 10 cents, if it was a stick of candy.

On August 2 General Joseph Hooker's Brigade moved toward Malvern and attacked the enemy near Glendale, and on the 15th the army was in bustle and confusion, and commenced to move somewhere.

August 16 we received orders to march, having no idea to our destination, but soon found out that we were the tail-end and rearguard of that magnificent army that a month or two before had been mobilized for the purpose of taking Richmond; and now it was ingloriously retreating to Yorktown, its rear protected by a Western brigade. After five days of weary marching under the fierce rays of a vertical sun, and through clouds of pulverized clay that rolled so thickly around and about us as to obscure the men in our rear, and was almost suffocating; water very scarce, and nothing to eat but dry "hardtack" and a few straggling ears of corn that had escaped capture by the preceding multitude; having to sleep shelterless, and awaking in the morning to find our blankets and clothing saturated with the moisture of the heavy falling dew, we reached the vicinity of Yorktown and encamped on ground made historic by the early struggles of our Revolutionary fathers for that freedom and that country that we are now striving to perpetuate. Before leaving Harrison's Landing, there came into our possession in some manner a specimen of camp poetry, a paraphrase on Poe's "Raven," and penned evidently by some one who was no admirer of McClellan. It is reproduced here, not because we endorse its sentiments, but as a fair specimen of a campaign lyric.

"THE CRAVEN."

"On that mighty day of battle, 'mid the booming and the rattle,
Shouts of victory and of anguish, wherewith Malvern's Hill did roar,
Did a General, now quite fameless, who in these lines shall be nameless,
Show himself as rather gameless, gameless on the James' shore?
Safely smoking on a gunboat, while the tempest raged on shore—
　　　Only this, and nothing more.

The congressional committee, sat within the Nation's city,
And each Congressman so witty, did the General implore:
"Tell us if thou, at that battle, 'mid the booming and the rattle,
Was on gunboat or in saddle, while the tempest rag'd ashore?"
Answer'd he: "I don't remember; might have been." What more?
　　　Only this, and nothing more.

"By the truth which is eternal, by the lies that are diurnal,
By our Abraham paternal, General, we thee implore,
Tell the truth and shame the devil, parent of old Jeff and evil—
Give us no more of such drive—Tell us, were thou on the shore?"
"Don't remember; might have been,"—Thus spake he o'er and o'er,
　　　Only this, and nothing more.

"On that day, Sir, had you seen a gunboat of the name Galena,
In an anchorage to screen a man from danger on the shore?
Was a man about your inches, smoking with those two French Princes,
With a caution with evinces care for such a 'garde de corps'
Were you that man on the gunboat?" "Don't remember; might have been."
"The bore!"
　　　Only this, and nothing more."

We remained at Yorktown, pleasantly encamped near the waters of Chesapeake Bay, until August 30 when orders came to march; and the prevailing opinion seemed to be that we were destined again to the valley of Virginia to cooperate with General John Pope's army, as it was reported that the enemy was endeavoring to cross the Potomac into Maryland.

We were, however, to proceed in another direction. We marched to Fort Monroe and there took transport across to the Nansemond River, up which we proceeded to Suffolk, Virginia, reaching there September 3, 1862, and made encampment just out side the town.

Suffolk is pleasantly situated on the Nansemond River, which is navigable to this place. Before the war it had a population of 1,600, the majority of whom were slaves. The great Dismal Swamp stretched out from its eastern and southern boundaries, connected with the town by canal. Suffolk was burned during the Revolutionary War, but was again rebuilt, and its appearance was quite pleasing and decidedly antique or ancient. The few families left in town were or had been wealthy, and those who found "entree" met excellent society. The female portion were very shy and retiring, however, and on the approach of a Union soldier plainly showed how distasteful and unwelcome he was.

The Regimental Hospital was located in the town for the better accommodation of the sick, having selected a large two-story structure which proved admirably adapted for the purpose. On or about September 9 two assistant surgeons reported from Illinois, having been assigned to the Thirty-Ninth. There were Doctor James Crozier, First Assistant, and William Woodward, Second Assistant. Doctor Strobridge still remained with us, and for the first time in the history of the Regiment we had more than the necessary supply of what the men facetiously termed "pill shooters." Lieutenant-Colonel Mann returned from a "leave of absence" that he had received at Harrison's Landing, about this time, bringing with him his bride, and inducted her into the mysteries of "camping out."

The first Sabbath spent at Suffolk was ushered in with a peal of church bells which we, for a long, long time, had been strangers to. Sunday, in our "calendar," was the day when all marches were commenced, and battles fought, and we had grown to consider it as the most exacting day of the week. In all our previous history, and on an active campaign, there was nothing to herald its approach, and absolutely nothing to distinguish it from the other days, except perhaps the feeble workings of a conscience, and, at remarkably long intervals, the announcement that the chaplain had arrived and would hold services.

In the early part of September a reconnaissance in force was made around the Dismal Swamp, but for some reason it was recalled before having accomplished the mission it had started upon. The Thirty-Ninth was kept busy in cutting timber, throwing up entrenchments and forts, and occasionally participating in expeditions out to the Blackwater River, eighteen miles distant, where there was quite a force of the enemy.

On one of these reconnaissances the Thirty-Ninth had a lively brush with the enemy, capturing two pieces of artillery and forty prisoners, with the loss of one man.

Lieutenant S. S. Brucker later wrote for the Regimental History:

"While proceeding on a scouting expedition to the Dismal Swamp, the Thirty-Ninth was accompanied by two cavalry companies and one battery of artillery. After marching all the day and until about dark, we made camp on what was termed an island in the swamp. Major Munn was 'Officer of the day and pickets.' Before going to the front with my detail, the Major gave me strict orders to be vigilant, as we were near where a large body of the enemy was reported to be, and as our command was small, he said 'We cannot afford to give the rebels a chance to surprise or capture us. You are therefore commanded to fire on any body of men that advances from the road in the swamp coming toward you, and without giving the usual warning of halt!'

"I proceeded to the post assigned to me, established my picket line, and left my reserves about 100 yards in the rear. In order to understand the nature of the surroundings it is necessary to state that the road was built of logs, a 'cross-way' in the midst of a swamp for miles ahead and to the right of us, and no one could approach towards us except on the 'cross-way.' About midnight, while visiting my outpost, my attention was called to a slight noise as if made by a body of horse in the distance. It became more and more distinct, and the clang of metal (such as the clatter of sabers makes) left no doubt in my mind that a large body of cavalry was advancing upon us. We quietly fell back upon our reserves, who had also heard the approach and were on the alert. I first cautioned my men to silence, and to have their guns ready and bayonets fixed, but not to fire under any circumstances until I have the word of command.

"I had my orders implicit and strict, yet I hesitated to fire. I cannot tell even to this day what possessed me, but something seemed to whisper 'Do not fire until after you have challenged them.' The time was passing quickly and they came nearer and nearer. We could

ON PICKET.

neither see them, or they us, as the night was very dark, but we were conscious that a few seconds of time would bring them up to our position. I then called out loudly and distinctly,
'Halt!' The command must have surprised and startled them wonderfully, judging from the almost instantaneous check given the horses and rattle of the sabers. I was quickly answered 'Friends!' to which I replied, 'Advance, Friend, and give the countersign!'

'Who are you?' was asked.

'We are friends,'

'Friends of whom?'

'Friends of the Union!' I replied,

'So are we!' he said.

"I then asked 'What rank do you hold? Where are you from, and where going?'

'Captain! From Chowan River, and enroute to Suffolk!' he replied.

"Knowing, of course, that we held Suffolk, I felt satisfied they were not rebels, yet I called upon the Captain to dismount and advance twenty paces, and I would meet him which we did. Satisfying myself that he was all right, I yet ordered my men to hold the cavalry while I escorted the Captain to headquarters, where he proved to be a Captain Wyland of a New York cavalry regiment on a scout from Beaufort, North Carolina, to report to headquarters of the Commanding General at Suffolk, Virginia. When Major Munn stated to the Captain the instructions he had given me, that officer turned a few shades paler and was ready to embrace me for joy at his narrow escape. It was disobedience to orders, but proved a great mercy."

Many of the veterans will remember "Aunt Sally," a tall, angular Negress, a familiar character about the camp and hospital, full of her oddities and pranks, coming daily with milk, eggs, chickens and oysters to sell. She was a most singular person, possessing a great deal of assurance as well as impudence and a wonderful amount of "lip." She stuttered and stammered badly, and was exceedingly sensitive in regard to this defect—so much so, that the least appearance of mocking at it would render her furious, and then she could hardly articulate intelligibly at all. Every morning she would come ambling and shuffling along the street with a milk pitcher perched on the top of her woolly head, and with pails or baskets swinging from her arms, and singing "We'll be gay and happy still!" "In a voice that would do credit to a Stentor;" and if the music at guard mount was sounding, she would stop to execute a "pas de seul" to the infinite amusement of the bystanders. "M-m-mawing, boss! Want s-s-s-s-ome f-f-fine ostahs or c-c-chickens foh yo' s-s-sick, dis m-m-mawing?" Poor old Aunt Sally! We wonder if you survived "de wah?"

The New York papers were received daily via Norfolk, and the war news was scanned with the utmost interest. At this date (September 13, 1862,) the news is most discouraging from all points. In the whole of the past year's campaign nothing has been satisfactorily accomplished. The rebels have driven our armies back and back until the Union forces occupy but a very small portion of their territory, and what is still more humiliating and shameful, they have invaded our border and bid fair to make good their threat of dictating their own terms of settlement. The policy of our leaders seems to be to wait while the rebels win, and the frequent mistakes of our generals are taken advantage of and turned to good account. While we are planning, they are boldly executing. Their army, inferior as it is in numbers, poorly fed and badly clothed, has a vigor and determination that makes us tremble, and troubles us every where.

The people of the North never properly appreciated the magnitude of the rebellion; they have always undervalued the resources of the South, and have consoled themselves with the idea that there was no possibility of failure. Our armies can never be victorious until the whole North, laying aside all party prejudices and the *"irrepressible nigger question,"* unites as one man, and the unity of purpose proceeds to the work of speedily vindicating the "old flag" and reestablishing the only government worth living for.

The Regiment lost two men at Suffolk—one killed by being struck by a falling tree while at work with his comrades in felling timber for use in constructing redoubts; the other dying from typhoid fever. The work devolving upon the soldiers at this post was immense, and very seldom was there a day that could be devoted to rest or amusement for when not engaged in work on the entrenchments and forts, there was sure to be an alarm from the advance guard of the enemy's approach, and the men held in constant readiness for defense.

About December 1, Major S. W. Munn resigned from the service by reason of poor health, Captain S. S. Linton being promoted to the position. At the same time Colonel Osborn was granted a "leave of absence" and proceeded home to Chicago. New Year's Day came in bright and beautiful, and the officers of the Division celebrated it by taking a gallop through town in force, led by Colonel R. S. Foster, of the Thirteenth Indiana Volunteers. Later in the day there was prepared a grand dinner, and in the evening a dance, with a sufficient number of ladies to make it interesting.

The mean strength of the Regiment at this time was—officers, thirty-seven; enlisted men, 730.

January 3, 1863, it became noised around that orders had been received to prepare for a march and change of base, and such proved to be the case; and on January 5, after the usual turning over of camp and garrison equipment and the cutting down of the means of transportation, our Division moved out for the Chowan River, seventy-five miles distant. The weather was fine and the spirits of the men fresh and elastic. During the first day's march the advance of our column encountered a small body of rebel cavalry that occasioned a slight delay. On the second day the novelty of the change had considerably worn off, and there was a little more straggling and weariness. During a halt in the afternoon, just over the state line in North Carolina, a Negro was discovered crouching in a fence corner and apparently badly frightened. The soldiers in the vicinity, in the spirit of mischief, ordered him to "come out of that!" which he immediately did, badly demoralized by fear. "Strip off that coat!" "Now take off your vest!" "Skin off that shirt!" all of which commands were readily obeyed; and had not the order to "fall in" sounded just then, there is no telling what else he would have been ordered to do. He soon mastered all his fear and seemed to relish the fun at his expense, and finally consented to come along as servant to one of the company officers. Large numbers of carts, mules and horses were gathered in by the men on this march, and before reaching our destination nearly every company possessed a mule and cart, which was utilized to carry knapsacks and blankets. It was no uncommon sight to see soldiers mounted on mules and horses, and they, to accommodate their less fortunate comrades, would consent to take their shelter tents, canteens, knapsacks, etc., until there was place for no more, and the appearance presented was most ludicrous.

They called themselves "Mounted Infantry." This sport did not continue for any great length of time, for when the matter reached the notice of the commander, each horse, mule and cart was turned over to the owner, who in most instances had followed on after them.

Tobacco raising and manufacturing seemed to be the leading industry of this section of country, and we came across large quantities of it in all shapes. On one plantation a large barn near the road we were following was found well stocked, and by order of the General commanding, many hogsheads, casks and boxes of it were rolled down to the roadside, the heads of the casks broken in, and the boys were permitted to help themselves, which they did without much ceremony, although they were not allowed to stop; but it was grab and march on. Some were content with a twist or two of the natural leaf for smoking and a plug or so for chewing, but there were others so avaricious that they grabbed and scrambled for all they could carry, and were then sorry that they could not take it all. Many were afterwards seen with at least fifteen or twenty pounds of plug tobacco in their arms or slung to their backs, while their haversacks and pockets were bulging with hunks of the natural leaf. The day was decidedly warm, and as mile after mile passed you could notice that those very greedy chaps, who were scrambling and almost fighting for the lion's share, were eager to lighten their load by giving it away to whoever wanted it, and many were glad to throw it all away before the bivouac was reached. It was most excellent tobacco, and it seemed a sin and a shame to have it so wantonly wasted.

The country through which we were passing furnished excellent advantage for foraging, and men were specially detailed for the purpose from each company; besides, there were those who went off on their individual responsibility. The members of the band had become experts, and some will remember that on one occasion during this march they captured a young pig, and in order to bring it along secure from notice they placed it inside the big drum and thus brought in to the night camp.

BAND BOYS FORAGING.

Orders were usually very strict regarding individual and indiscriminate foraging, nevertheless men would take the chances.

George Riddle of Company I tells a little of his experience while on this march. He says:

"One day when we had halted for dinner, a comrade and myself left the ranks and started out to look for a little change of diet for supper. We soon found a little sandy shoat, [a young, weaned pig], and my comrade had just 'stuck' it, when, looking up the road, we saw General 'Sandy' Foster, of the Thirteenth Indiana Volunteers, coming. My comrade ran away, but I held on to the pig, and had it be the throat as the General came up and said 'What are you doing with that pig?' I told him that fellow running yonder had cut its throat and I was trying to stop the blood from staining its bristles. He looked at me a moment quite sharply, and then asked, 'What regiment do you belong to?' 'Thirty-Ninth Illinois,' I answered. 'Well,' said he, 'the blood will be damned apt to stop by the time a 'Sucker' gets through with it; but don't you let anybody see you with that pig, or you may get into trouble; and,' he continued, 'you'll know where to find my quarters tonight, won't you?'"

The afternoon of January 8 we reached the Chowan River, where preparations were made to embark on transports for New Bern, North Carolina, which was reached the following morning. We were now in the Department commanded by General A. J. Foster. Colonel Osborn was placed in temporary command of the Brigade here. We were sent some three miles out of the city to make encampment, and selected a timber grove after removing the dense undergrowth.

The men were supplied with a small "A" or button tent, often called the "dog tent" at this time, no other tents being furnished except for hospital use. Many of the officers found accommodations for meals and for sleeping in the neighboring houses. One plantation house was quite near our camp and was occupied by a family of the poorer class, who stated that they had been left in charge by the owner, who had removed with his family when New Bern was first occupied by Union soldiers. The house was beautifully furnished throughout, and here it was that a few of us got accommodations that were quite home like. A grand piano had been left behind, and with the musical talent that we had with us, quite entertaining and swell concerts were given.

While at New Bern the Regiment received an elegant flag from Governor Richard Yates of Illinois, bearing his portrait, and on the day of its reception, at the hour of "dress parade," it was placed in the hands of the "color-guard" with appropriate ceremonies. Short speeches were made by several of the officers, the sum and substance being, "Never submit to its dishonor or permit its capture by the enemy!" The history of the Thirty-Ninth Illinois shows how well it was guarded and cared for by the many brave men who have constituted the "color-guard" during the long and bloody years they were called upon to sustain it.

Fully two-thirds of the guard who first received the flag were killed while supporting it at the battles of Drewry's Bluff, Hatcher's Run, and Darbytown Cross-Roads, and it with the other colors of the Regiment was honorably and proudly borne back to the "muster-out" at the capitol of the State in December 1865, their folds scarred and rent with rifle balls, but covered all over with glory. The archives of the State contain no better symbols of the bravery and devotion of her sons than the banners of the "Yates Phalanx."

COUNTING THE SCARS IN THE COLORS.

On January 18, 1863, we were notified that we were to be sent into South Carolina, and everything was made in readiness for the trip; wives of the officers were sent home, horses, wagons, and ambulances turned in to the Post Quartermaster, and the sick and disabled of the command sent to general hospital. On the 20th we took the cars for Morehead City, a distance of twenty miles, where we were to embark for Hilton Head, South Carolina. The harbor was full of shipping of all kinds and descriptions, and we were granted permission to select our vessels. A small side-wheel steamer was at first pointed out to us as one of our vessels, but on inspection by the Colonel and Surgeon it was found to be unseaworthy, and beside, would not accommodate one-half the Regiment.

We next visited a craft lying near the opposite shore, a two-masted propeller. We reached her in due course by a small boat, but soon condemned it, for on descending into the hold we found her timbers rotten, and the clap-boarding of her upper deck (could not be dignified by any other name) in a most shameful condition. We finally took up with two small propellers that were seaworthy, and a small schooner to carry our baggage and horses. These vessels were soon brought to the wharf and Companies A to E, together with a portion of the field and staff and the band, embarked on the *General Meigs*. The other companies of the Regiment went on board the *City of Bath* and the schooner *Skirmisher*, and towards evening we started out as a part of the Foster Expedition for South Carolina, the State that first inaugurated the Rebellion.

CHAPTER NINE

"At half past two the Ball opened"

We passed Fort McAllister at sundown and were soon on the billows of the broad Atlantic. The storm that had been brewing since early morning now broke in all its fury, and we got more than a taste of old Ocean in one of its tragic moods. The storm increased in violence, and the vessel labored heavily in its passage through the heavy seas. Fully two-thirds of the officers and men were settling up accounts with "Neptune," with a large balance in his favor, and felt most thoroughly depleted and disconsolate. The few officers who kept their "sea legs" and a clear head, engaged in games of whist and euchre in the Captain's saloon, and in this way passed the night; and a most protracted and gloomy night it was, the rolling and pitching of the vessel often capsizing us from our chairs, and it did seem at times as if the vessel itself would roll over. At last the welcome morning dawned, and as the sun arose, the wind and waves abated, yet the long and heavy swells of water kept large numbers on the sick list. At inspection in the morning the hold of the vessel was found to be in a most foul and filthy condition. The men were ordered on deck and the ship's crew with hoses and brooms were put to work cleaning. During the afternoon the sea became as smooth as a mirror and the many seasick soldiers came from their beds into the fresh and bracing sea air for enjoyment. Some got out their fishing tackle, other baited for sharks, of which we saw numbers, and all found pleasure in watching the antics of the porpoises and the gulls.

While we are at sea it may be well to take an "account of stock," as it were, and find out what the condition of the Thirty-Ninth then was. We had been in the United States service one year, three months and ten days up to January 22, 1863. We left Chicago with 806 officers and enlisted men, October 11, 1861. In the meantime we had received 147 recruits, including Company H, which joined us at Harrison's Landing, Virginia, making a total of 953. From this number nineteen officers have resigned their commissions; two officers have been dismissed the service; one officer had died; thirty-two men have been left behind on marches; thirty-nine men have deserted; thirty-one men have been sent to the general hospital; eighteen men have died, leaving 767 officers and men for active service in the new field to which we are hastening.

We reached Hilton Head early in the morning of January 22, and lay in the harbor for several hours, awaiting, as we afterwards learned, the settlement of some difficulty between Generals Foster and David Hunter, the latter of whom was in command of the Department of South Carolina.

Without going into the details of their controversy concerning rank and position, which in itself is not pertinent to this history, but which was of prime interest to the two generals, we take up the thread of our personal history again.

During the afternoon we were sent down to a landing place on St. Helena Island, where the men disembarked. The schooner carrying our baggage and livestock could not reach the improvised pier during flood-tide, and our horses were pushed overboard and made to swim ashore, which they did in gallant style, and were fully as glad as ourselves in reaching terra firma once more.

We bivouacked for the night; but the following day had quarters assigned to us about one mile from the river, and as all our equipment for camp and garrison had followed us, we soon had all our tents pitched and camp furniture in place.

General O. S. Ferry remained as our Division General, and Dr. Sol Van Etten the Division Surgeon. General Hunter commanded the Department; Surgeon Crane, U. S. A., was Medical Director, and Dr. J. J. Craven the Medical Purveyor, and attached to Hunter's command was General Charles Halpine, otherwise knows as *Miles O'Reilly*, who was not only a wit but a poet of no mean order.

While we were stationed on St. Helena Island some soldiers from General James Nagle's command made a foray on Parris Island and killed a bull, the only one on the island, and its owner came to the headquarters of General Hunter sadly lamenting his loss. The occasion inspired General Halpine to issue the following:

"BALLAD OF PARRIS ISLAND."

Dear General Hunter, my heart is full,
Lamenting for my butchered bull: —
The only bull our Island had,
And all my widowed cows are sad.

With briny tears and drooping tails,
With loud boo-hoo's and bovine wails,
My cows lament with wifely zeal
Their perished hopes of future veal.

Sad is the wail of human wife
To see her partner snatched from life:
But he—the husband of a score—
For him the grief is more and more!

No future hope of golden cream!
Even milk in tea becomes a dream: —
Whey, bonny-clabber, curds and cheese
Are now, ah, me! mere idle words!

> The cruel soldiers, fierce and full
> Of reckless wrath, have shot my bull;
> The stateliest bull—let scoffers laugh—
> That e'er was "father" called by calf!
> A bull as noble, firm and fair
> As that which aided Jove to bear
> Europa from the flowery glade
> Where she amidst her maidens played.
>
> Dear General Hunter, accept my vows,
> And oh! take pity on my cows,—
> With whom, bereft of wifely ties,
> All tender hearts must sympathize.
>
> Quick to Van Vliet your order send
> (By Smith's congenial spirit penned)
> And order him in language full,
> At one to send me down a bull: —
>
> If possible, a youthful beast,
> With warm affections yet unplaced,
> Who to my widowed cows may prove
> A husband of enduring love.

 Great attention was paid to the matters of drill and discipline while located on this island, the whole Regiment being exercised twice daily in field evolutions and the manual of arms. Two hours of the morning were spent in company drill, and the same length of time in the afternoon was devoted to battalion exercise. Great proficiency was attained in this manner, and the officers and men of the regiments enjoyed the proud satisfaction of being reported at Department Headquarters by an experienced U. S. General Inspector as the best drilled and disciplined Regiment in the Department of the South.
 The leisure hours that were at our disposal, and when permission could be obtained, were spent in making excursions to Hilton Head or the surrounding islands. Hilton Head Island, the headquarters of General Hunter, was at this time quite a city in a business aspect if in no other. The general hospital was located here, together with the quartermaster's and commissary's depot, and the medical purveyor's store; and beside, there were scores of traders in all sorts of merchandise who had built large structures for containing and bartering goods. Several photographic galleries were in full operation and abundantly patronized. One in particular was conducted by a German by name of Hass, and some of us will remember the name distinctly for the reason that we reached his gallery just at a period when he was about sailing for New York on the steam ship *Arago*, to replenish his chemicals and other stocks. He was a burly and phlegmatic Teuton, and was slipping away without saying

"goodbye" to his wife, who called out to him in sorrowful tones, "Ain't you going to kiss me, Hass, before you go?" The old chap, when thus reminded, removed the pipe from his lips and said, "It ish no time to sthop fooling now. I musht get aporad as quick as never I can. Vait 'till I gets back, my dear!!" and off he went in an excited flurry, under the midday sun and through the sand, to get "apoard mit the steamer."

Sometimes a trip was made up Broad River to Beaufort where the Sanitary and Christian Commissions had headquarters. This place was also the location of the "Freedman's Bureau," and there were two or three hospitals, one of which was under the matronship of Mrs. General F. W. Lander—more generally known as Julia Davenport, the actress.

In passing, this estimable lady is worthy of a more extended tribute for her disinterested devotion and care of the sick and wounded soldiers under her charge at not only this place, but at all other points where her sympathy or hand could reach them. It was our privilege to have the personal acquaintance of this lady, for she frequently visited the various troops in the department, and our Regiment, at one time under the command of her brave husband, entertained the greatest respect for one so lately bereaved and who still in her widow's weeds remained within the circle of the army, giving time, money and patience and the attributes of a sympathetic nature to the care of disabled men. Whatever laurels Mrs. Lander may achieve before the footlights as a tragedienne will never be brighter, fresher, or greener than those won in hospital service on a more tragic state—the bloody fields of the great strife for National existence.

At other times we would gratify our passion for fishing and hunting by proceeding up the island to a large plantation house which had been turned over to the Freedman's Bureau and the plantation worked by giving a certain percentage on the sale of products to the Negro, or else paying him or her so much a day for labor. There was a school established there, but we were never fully satisfied that the Negroes appreciated their advantages. The Negroes on this and adjoining islands were the most obtuse and thickheaded that we came in contact with. They came regularly to camp each morning with something for sale—sweet potatoes, oysters, clams, shrimps, etc., and such gibberish, such unintelligible mutterings were never heard before. We might as well have attempted the translation of the "Congo" dialect as try to understand the "lingo" of these "mokes" of both sexes. It must be confessed that we had some respect for the Negro as we had seen him in Virginia and at home, but here, there was nothing but approximation to the monkey tribe, and call the thick-lipped, monkey-faced Negro with his gibberish, a fellow "well met" on all occasions was more than could be expected.

At the plantation house before mentioned, we would secure a boat and a guide and sail down the inlet to the sea. On the way and while passing through the rice swamps we often found wild ducks and reed birds for our sport, and with the use of a trolling hook and line would manage to catch good fish, to say nothing of the crabs fastened to the line at each haul.

In the latter part of the month of March 1863, we were called upon to make preparations for a move, and on April 1 we embarked on steamers to take part in General Hunter's expedition to Folly Island. For several weeks previous to starting the men had been drilled in the management of surf boats. On the morning of April 3 we arrived opposite Stono Inlet, but the storm, which had been furious during the night had not abated, and we were compelled, together with the balance of the fleet, to lie-to for several hours; and besides, several of the transports had lost their surf-boats during the gale. We were in close proximity to the blockading squadron off Charleston Harbor, and the scene presented at this time was novel and exciting. Matters began to look like business again, and we were all glad to have the dull and monotonous routine of camp-life dissolved. About noon of this day we steamed up to Edisto Island and soon came to anchor in the quiet waters of Edisto River, where we found seven monitors and five gunboats, aside from other craft. During the day the steamer *Ben DeFort* came in and anchored near us, bring General Hunter and Admiral Samuel Francis DuPont. Early the succeeding morning we got under way again and had a comparatively smooth passage to Stono Inlet, at the mouth of which we found a tug *Harriet Weed* in waiting to pilot us up the river to Cole's Island, where we commenced disembarking by means of the surf-boats and rafts. The men made rather bungling work at first in handling their oars, but soon came down to work. The Thirty-Ninth was the first to reach the island, where we found the 100th New York Volunteers already in camp. The Sixty-Second Ohio, Sixty-Seventh Ohio and Eighty-Fifth Pennsylvania Infantry soon followed us.

We made our encampment near the shore and close to Folly Island, which was in possession of the rebels. The entire camp equipment was landed before sunset, and the tents soon pitched, and supper, the first decent meal of the day, partaken of. Near the camp were several old forts and entrenchments, and during the evening some of us took up position on the parapets of a fort where we could plainly see the campfires of the rebels—their signal lights and rockets, which were flashing out intelligence of our approach.

April 5, the Brigade commenced the work of throwing up rifle-pits, and otherwise fortifying the position, for an attack at any moment was possible. From the head of the island, a mile or so distant from camp, the rebel pickets could plainly be seen, together with squads of men here and there, busy in perfecting their line of earthworks, and mounting cannon. At seven p.m. of this day an order came to put out all lights, as General Ferry was under the impression that we would be shelled by the rebels. At ten p.m. orders came to strike tents and move to the landing, and at midnight we got on board the tug *Harriet Weed* and were ferried over in detail of companies to Folly Island. On landing, the Regiment stacked arms and lay down for a little rest. At sunrise the following morning we commenced moving up the sea-beach, preceded by a large body of skirmishers, and two pieces of 12-pounder artillery under the charge of marines and drawn by hand. Several halts were made in our progress, which were necessitated by the slow movements of our skirmishers, they being spread out across the island in order to make a clean sweep. The slow movement was mostly attributable to the dense undergrowth, trailing vines, hedges, etc., that had to be cut away by the pioneers before progress could be made. At noon the Regiment halted in a palmetto grove for dinner, and a siesta was taken until three p.m.; then we started on again and continued until four p.m., when an order came to bivouac. There was an implicit order against building fires, and a cold lunch of ham and hardtack sufficed for supper.

At ten a.m. we were awakened with a muffled order to "fall in" and march, and were soon enroute again, with nothing to disturb the quiet except the song of the mocking bird and the thud-thud of the many footsteps along the level beach—the clatter of canteens against the knapsack or the gun; but all this was drowned, except to the participants in the march, by the dull and monotonous cadence of the ocean, whose waves often washed over our footsteps. We reached the head of the island at daybreak without meeting the enemy. Our fears had been greatly excited at times from the fact that the skirmishing party would exercise us by firing of their guns, and at one time we thought that we had been attacked in the rear, all occasioned by the careless handling of firearms. At the head of the island we reconnoitered Morris Island by peeping through the thick foliage that skirted Light House Inlet.

Folly Island is some seven miles in length and was densely timbered with palmetto, pine and magnolia trees, together with a dense growth of underbrush throughout the greater portion. There was no habitation except at the foot of the island, consisting of a two-story frame house and one or two outbuildings, all of which were later used for our accommodations—the house for the General's headquarters and the out-buildings for hospital purposes.

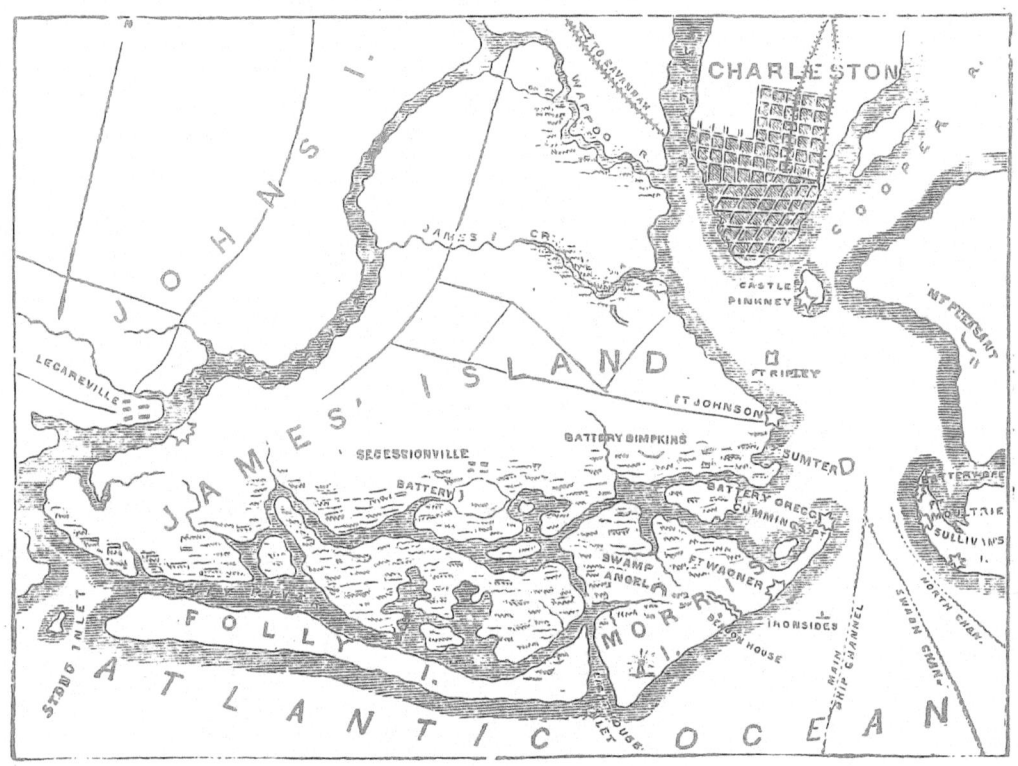

Scene of Operations in South Carolina.

In our position at the head of the island we had a full view of Forts Sumter, Moultrie, Johnson, and the various sand batteries on Morris and Sullivan's Islands, and in the foreground were numerous "graybacks" perched on the sand hills intently engaged in looking in our direction. At times they would approach the water's edge on the opposite shore and fire their muskets toward us. We had an unobstructed view of the blockading squadron seaward, and the monitor fleet that was entering the ship channel to engage the various harbor batteries. At two p.m. the monitor fleet, led by the *New*

Ironsides, were seen in motion, with the *Weehawken* as skirmisher to dispose of obstructions. After the *Ironsides* came the *Passaic, Montauk, Patapsco, Catskill, Nantucket, Nahant,* and *Keokuk*. The fleet paid no attention to the batteries on Morris Island, but pressed forward to the northwest face of Fort Sumter.

At half past two o'clock the ball opened, the first shot being fired from Fort Sumter. Soon the batteries on Sullivan's Island and Morris Island opened most fiercely, followed by broadsides from Sumter, and the din and roar was deafening, which together with the flash and smoke from each gun made up a scene that was deeply interesting to distant spectators; but when we consider the animosity that pointed each gun from the fort that inaugurated the rebellion we pause to contemplate the fiendishness of it.

FORT SUMTER AFTER BOMBARDMENT.

Through some mistake of orders the *Weehawken* missed her course and the line of battle became confused so that the whole power of our fleet was not manifest for a long time. It was impossible for the monitors to get nearer than 800 feet of the fort because of the numerous floating torpedoes, yet the monitor *Keokuk* succeeded in gaining a nearer position, and in consequence was completely disabled, having received ninety shots in the course of half an hour. By means of her pumps she was brought out from the fray, and finally sank near the entrance of the harbor—her smoke-stack reaching just above the surface of the water. The other monitors were not essentially damaged.

At half-past four p.m. the whole fleet withdrew and, with the exceptions of the *Ironsides*, proceeded to Hilton Head or Port Royal. The number of guns that had been brought to bear upon this little squadron was fully 300, and for rapidity of fire and weight of metal they were never surpassed.

We watched this combat with the greatest interest, even climbing trees for a better view. Fort Sumter seemed to be a sheet of flame from the successive discharge of her numerous guns. About once a minute there would be the discharge of a gun from the turret of a monitor and we would watch the effect of the heavy ball as it struck the fort. All that we could discover was a cloud of dust and a fall of debris—no breach being apparent. We have ever considered this naval duel as one of the most novel and exciting episodes of our life and never shall forget it, in any of its details. The wounded in the engagement were principally on the *Keokuk*, and they were put on board the hospital ship by her own crew.

April 8 opened up gloriously as far as sun, sky and good temperature were concerned, but the want of food from the failure of the commissary to report was intensely felt, and a pall as thick as mud fell like an incubus on our spirits. We had some hardtack left which was washed down with the mere apology for coffee. During the forenoon heavy cannonading was again heard, but mostly confined to remove the rust from their guns. On bring our glasses to bear on Fort Sumter, three flags were seen—one the National flag of the Confederacy, one the State flag bearing the Palmetto, and the third one was made out as a black flag, or looked like one. At two p.m. orders were received to remove our camp back some three miles for a permanent position. We picked out a suitable site and finally pitched the tents agreeably to army regulations, and soon were in quarters for a sleep, with the roar of the ocean for a lullaby.

April 9, General Vogdes came with authority from General Hunter to assume command of the forces on this island, thus superseding Colonel Howell, who had been acting as Brigadier-General. General Vogdes, prior to the war, was a captain in an artillery regiment and a graduate of West Point. At the battle of "Bull Run" he was taken prisoner and lingered in prison at Richmond for some thirteen months. When exchanged he was promoted to the rank of Brigadier-General.

General Israel Vogdes will long be remembered by his command on Folly Island for his remarkable eccentricities of manner and speech. He was a great stickler for discipline and exacted from the soldiers all the honors due his rank and position. Although it was his invariable habit to saunter around camp in a blouse or in his shirt-sleeves, yet he was so puffed out with egotism that he excused no one for not recognizing him as the Commanding General. The soldiers had taken a dislike to him on general principles and neglected no opportunity to annoy and vex him. One night he was caught out while near the head of the island without the "word" or "countersign," and was delayed some two hours on one pretext or another, although it was well-known who he was.

At one time when Private Lankinaw of Company D, a stalwart German who had seen service in the Prussian army, was on guard duty near headquarters, the General happened to pass just at sundown and Lankinaw paid no attention whatever. This was so gross a breach of discipline and respect that Vogdes could not pass it by, and the officer of the day was sent for. Colonel Howell, of the Eighty-Fifth Pennsylvania, a very suave and polite old gentlemen, was on duty, and when he reported, Vogdes said: "Colonel, these damned Western volunteer soldiers do not know their duty, sir. I was passing the sentinel just know, sir, and he did not salute or pay the least attention to his commanding general, and you will at once relieve and punish him, sir."

"Yes, sir; great disrespect to the commanding officer," said Howell. "Will see to it at once, sir, at once!" and he started to interview Lankinaw.

"Soldier, the general commanding reports that you did not 'present arms' when he lately passed you. Don't you know your duty?"

"Vell, Colonel Howells, I shalutes no man, by tam, ven it pees sundown."

"Sundown, was it? If so, you were in the right, sir, and will so report."

Colonel Howell returned to the General, saying: "General Vogdes, the soldier says the sun was down when you passed him, and according to the army regulations, you know, the sentinel is not obliged to pay salute to anybody."

"Yes, yes, I know; but I do not think the sun was down, at least, I do not think that it was quite down. However, let it pass; but see to it that these volunteers are better instructed in their duties."

The Regiment by detail was kept constantly busy in throwing up entrenchments and building forts, and from this severe labor, in connection with the miasma of the marshes, a large number of men constantly reported on the "sick list." Many were sent to the hospital at the foot of the island, and when accommodations failed, or they could be benefited by a change, they were sent aboard the hospital ship *Cosmopolitan* and transferred to Northern hospitals. The *Cosmopolitan* came each month to receive our sick and wounded. It was under the charge of Surgeon Otis, United States Volunteers.

April 11, under cover of the dark night, some 300 of the enemy approached the island in boats in the endeavor to surprise our outposts, but were discovered and driven back, but not until they had wounded one man of the 100th New York Volunteers and captured two others.

General Truman Seymour had succeeded General Vogdes in command of the whole force, and on the evening of this day there was a detail from the Thirty-Ninth to deploy as skirmishers across the island. General Ferry went to Port Royal and the fleet of transports there sailed for the same destination, taking with them the whole force with the expedition of five regiments under command of Vogdes.

April 12, the Thirty-Ninth went to the head of the island to relieve the 100th New York, which was ordered to Cole's Island to relieve the Sixty-Second Ohio, ordered back to Folly Island.

A great deal of sickness was prevalent at this time, and as a prophylactic measure whiskey and quinine was ordered to be given the men each morning.

April 13 was the anniversary of the capture of Fort Sumter by the rebels, and we notice that they are having a jubilee not only at the fort but on Morris Island. We occasionally see officers accompanied by women that must have come from Charleston, and from our point of observation the officers were engaged in pointing out the position of the "Yanks," and doubt less remarking to their lady friends how easy it will be to dislodge them when the proper time arrives (?).

Soon after the occupation of Folly Island a post hospital was established in a vacant two-story building near the head quarters of General Vogdes, and Surgeon Clark was placed in charge.

There was considerable sickness among the soldiers at this time from the incessant fatigue and exposure attending the erection of batteries and the constant picket duty; and besides, men were continually being wounded by the enemy's shells or by accident and carelessness. It is remembered that among the first to be admitted for wounds were two men belonging to the Sixth Ohio Volunteers. They, it seems, had found a shell when they were on duty and had brought it with them to their quarters, and when about to cook their dinners had utilized it as a support for their wood fire.

They had not, in their stupidity, ascertained whether it was loaded or not, but were soon informed, for it exploded with great force, wounding four men, two of them very seriously, one having to suffer amputation of a leg.

April 15 the steamer *Cossack* arrived, bringing a company of the First Maryland Cavalry, in command of Lieutenant Holt. On the 16th Quartermaster Friedly of General Ferry's staff, arrived on the steamer *Secor*, bringing an order for the Thirty-Ninth to report at Hilton Head; but toward evening, on the arrival of the steamer *Nellie Baker*, the order was countermanded, much to our satisfaction, as we wished to remain until after the assault on Morris Island, for which we had long been making preparations.

Work was steadily progressing in fortifying at the head of the island, under the direct superintendence of Captain Crusoe, of the New York Engineer Battalion, and the rebels apparently had no idea of our plans, so well were they guarded and screened from observation by the thick undergrowth and sand dunes. The rebels were also active in throwing up batteries on the opposite shore of the inlet. Each day brought some new excitement to enliven the dullness of the camp. Either the rebels would open up a lively artillery fire, or the gunboat stationed in Stono River (the *Pawnee* and *McDonough*) would proceed, in company with the mortar schooner, up the Stono to Folly River and shell the woods and adjacent islands, accomplishing very little, but invariably provoking the enemy to respond in our direction.

Majors Moore and Mason, Paymasters, U. S. A., put in an appearance about this time, and were gratefully welcomed, and we did what was proper in the matter of entertainment, and received "Uncle Sam's" promises-to-pay in the shape of crisp "greenbacks." The Paymaster was always a welcome visitor, and especially to the sutler, who then received payment for the truck he had credited the soldiers at most exorbitant prices.

The Thirty-Ninth had a sutler at this time who was a most singular character, but possessed of active and energetic qualities for business, often bringing schooner loads of merchandise into the department and disposing of the same, at a great advance from New York prices, to his more impecunious brothers in trade. He had two great passions. One was his intense love for barter, in which the desire for gain often led him to be unscrupulous; it was only the "monish," as he expressed it, that he wanted. The other was his passion for a periodical spree, which generally lasted for a week or ten days, dependent on circumstances and associations. The periodic habit of exalting himself with "schnapps" came near ending his career on several occasions. It will be remembered that when we first reached the department after leaving St. Helena Island, the captain of our transport had permission to proceed up to Beaufort for a supply of coal, as the bunkers of the steamer were about exhausted. On reaching Beaufort we made fast to the schooner having the coal, and which was moored to the wharf, there being a space bridged over by a single plank from the vessel to the shore. As we were to remain overnight, a party of us, in company with the sutler, proceeded up into the hotel, where found a gay and jovial assemblage of officers, mostly "regulars." Something to drink was in order, which was continued in force during the evening. The sutler, in the meantime, had become quite exhilarated, loquacious and combative, and soon was quarreling with a captain on the staff of General O. O. Howard, over the relative merits and bravery of the volunteer and regular soldiers. The sutler was insisting, and would maintain at any cost, that the volunteers who had responded to the call of the President, to uphold and maintain the integrity of the Federal Government, had accomplished more in generalship, in valorous actions, and had done more fighting, marching and effective work so far, that all the "regulars" he had ever seen, met, or heard of.

The captain was just as emphatic and abusive in his denial, until finally the matter culminated in a challenge for a duel, and they were about to adjourn to a room upstairs to fight it out, when another party of officers arrived and put a stop to the disgraceful proceeding. The captain was ordered to his quarters, and the sutler was prevailed upon to return to the steamer. We started out, followed by the sutler, who was still spluttering about having "shatisfacshun out of that reg'lar for his 'spersions against the volunteers."

It was ten o'clock and the night was very dark when we reached the wharf and commenced the ascent of the plank to the schooner, and had nearly accomplished the passage when the sutler made a miscalculation in his footing (although we had use all precaution to help him over safely), and plunged down into the water. We hurriedly called for ropes and a lantern, and it seemed an age before they came, and we begun to fear the man was lost, for no answer had been returned to our frequent calls to know if he was safe. Looking down, after the arrival of the light, he was at last discovered astride a big hawser, but submerged to his shoulders, and the first words of greeting were, "Shay, you fellows! going to let a man drown?" A rope was secured under his arms and he was lifted aboard the schooner, a wetter but a more sober man. His escape was almost a miracle, under the circumstances. Poor fellow! After amassing a small fortune as a sutler, he established a bank at Richmond, Virginia, after its evacuation, and subsequently a banking business in Chicago, where he died some twelve years ago in very reduced circumstances.

Up to May 11 the troops on Folly Island had desisted from sounding "reveille," or giving the "calls," and at this time were only permitted the use of a drum and fife, for "You know the rebels would know where to shoot, you know!" as General Vogdes explained. On this day several officers of the Regiment, on invitation, paid a visit to the *New Ironsides*, one of the blockading fleet, taking passage on the little steamer *Nantucket* in company with a large number of naval officers who were reporting for duty from the North. We were very courteously received and shown over the vessel by Surgeon Duval and others. Our attention was directed to the injuries received by the vessel during the bombardment of Fort Sumter, which were very slight, consisting of a few saucer-like indentations in her armor.

May 13 we received intelligence and a few particulars of the battle fought at Fredericksburg, Virginia, which accounts for the firing of minute guns by the enemy today. Later in the day a Charleston paper was received, by means of a float, from the "Johnnies." It contained the news of the death of Generals Hill and "Stonewall" Jackson, and the information that "the Yankees lost 20,000 men and 8,000 prisoners at the battle." On the margin of the paper was also scribbled, "If you 'Yanks' expect to stay on Folly Island to combat the sandflies and fleas until you drive us into the Union, you will have to stay there until hell freezes over!"

Quite an amicable understanding had and still existed between the soldiers on both sides of the inlet, and a good deal of barter was carried on, exchanging coffee for tobacco and trading newspapers, which was accomplished by constructing little "dugouts" and "floats" and attaching a sail, and when the wind and tide were favorable, sending them adrift freighted with whatever was to be exchanged; and everything was conducted on the "square," but it had to be carried on "sub rosa." When an officer on duty approached, all was changed, and fierce picket firing was indulged in.

The men on advance guard duty at the head of the island and along the border of Folly River had strict instructions how to deal with persons who could not satisfactorily account for themselves, and it was dangerous to be abroad, especially at night, without the countersign; and then it was necessary to be prompt in answering a challenge from the sentinel. It will be remembered that Captain Rodgers, of the Sixty-Second Ohio Volunteers, when Officer of the Day, and when making "grand rounds" at night, was challenged, and failing to answer promptly, was shot while advancing, and died soon afterwards.

In the latter part of May the blockage running steamer *Ruby*, was stranded on the bar at the mouth of Light House Inlet. She had stranded about midway between Morris and Folly Island and had been abandoned by her crew. The rebels had already made several excursions to her, carrying away a good deal of merchandise, and several officers of the Thirty-Ninth had decided to make a voyage of discovery, under cover of night, and see what was to be found. A boat crew was collected under the command of Major Linton, and they started out, moving with a good deal of care so as not to be discovered and thus draw fire from the rebels. The vessel was reached without any mishap, and they were soon in undisputed possession. But what was their chagrin and annoyance when they discovered that all the matches they had brought along had become wet and therefore useless. Nevertheless, they were not going back without making some kind of examination to find out the character of the cargo. They went to work upon their senses of feeling and smelling and were soon rewarded by finding some pineapples and cigars, and last, but not least, some bottles of fine Scotch whiskey. Helping themselves to as much as they could carry, they left and got back all right.

This expedition proved so successful that after a few days it was followed by another, being accompanied by the two assistant-surgeons of the Regiment. The visit was so timed as to take advantage of the ebb tide. They proceeded out to the bar, where the boat was left in charge of one of the party, while the others clambered aboard.

The man who had remained with the boat as sentinel had secured the "painter" by placing his foot upon it, and was so intent on some other matters that he had not noticed the incoming tide, and before he was aware, the water was bubbling at this feet and the boat floated away, painter and all. The party on board the *Ruby* were hastily notified, and prepared for the return trip before the tide should effectually cut off retreat. It was a most ludicrous as well as disagreeable position to be placed in, and no telling when the rebels might appear. They could now wade for some distance along the bar, but before reaching the shore there was a stretch of deep water that would necessitate swimming. All of the party excepting the Second Assistant-Surgeon, Doctor Woodward, reached the shore without much trouble, and Woodward came along gallantly until within thirty feet of the shore when he found his strength ailing him and cried, "Help! Help!! I sink!!!" The large number of men on the beach who had been watching the enterprise now made an effort for his recovery, and some twenty men, joining hands, walked off into the water in his direction, and the foremost link of this human chain succeeded in grasping this old disciple of ancient God of Medicine and Healing, *Aesculapius*, helped him to dry land; but what was the chagrin of man and the laughter of others when they found him to be weighted down with a heavy plate looking-glass slung about his neck, and several pineapples in his coat pockets, together with other small trash that he had accumulated while on board, but not least of all was a calf skin hat-box containing a hat that he had kept possession of, and it is presumed that if he had sunk beneath the waves, that hat-box would have been his companion.

The doctor's troubles did not end here, however, for the next morning the matter came to General Vogdes' ears, and he in his supreme majesty ordered the doctor under arrest, and to report at once to headquarters. Under the shadow of two bayonets the doctor walked down to the foot of the island to confront the General. The result of the examination was that Doctor Woodward should report to the head of the island and remain until further orders, without daring to transgress limits. The head of the island was constantly exposed to the shot and shell that were daily thrown from Morris Island, and the troops, in order to protect themselves, erected bomb-proof shelters over excavations in the sand, and it was in a place of this character that our second assistant surgeon was located for some six weeks.

Occasionally a number of us would ride up to the head of the island after sunset to see our friend and get some idea of the progress of operations, and would invariably call to see the doctor, who was making the best of his banishment, but pleading meantime, most energetically for a reprieve. We could not stop long in endeavors to console him, for shot and shell were flying briskly around us; however, we gave him encouragement, and would do our utmost to get a pardon from the General. His looking-glass was still present and reflecting upon him; also the hat and hat-case; but the pineapples had been gobbled. After the doctor's release, which happened a few days after this visit, he magnanimously fractured the looking-glass, and after rubbing off the film of quicksilver, took several pieces down to the foot of the island and had an ambrotype taken on them of himself—portrayed with a pipe in his mouth and a very distressed look, as commemorating his vigils at the head of Folly Island.

The doctor might have escaped this punishment if he had used a little diplomacy by sharing the fruits of his gathering with the General. Vogdes had heard of these expeditions and what had been captured, and he one day remarked to an officer, "Colonel, I hear that the men at the head of the island are going out to that blockade runner and get lots of fruit, cigars and liquor. It's a little strange that none of it has found the way to these headquarters." He felt slighted, and the accidents of this last expedition gave him the opportunity to visit vengeance on someone, and Woodward proved to be the one. After this he authorized an expedition to go aboard and take what cargo was left, but it proved too late to get any of the delicacies. It, however, brought from the vessel a large quantity of white cotton cloth, which was mostly turned over to the medical department for bandages and dressings.

CHAPTER TEN

"But at what a cost!"

June 1, 1863, Private Fowler of Company K was seriously injured by the falling of a heavy branch from a tree severed by the passage of a shell fired by the enemy. Several accidents of a similar nature occurred while we were on the island. Some days previously a Negro boy, servant to one of the regimental officers, had been killed by the passage of a shell through camp.

When our soldiers were not busy with the spade or on picket duty, they spent a large portion of their leisure, even intruding on bed hours, in playing poker or some other game of chance, and many were the dollars lost and won. Beans were the prevailing currency until the Paymaster arrived, when each individual bean, representing so much value, was cashed. These set-downs or squat-downs to a game of poker, euchre or "seven-up" were frequent among both officers and men, and the invariable accompaniment was a canteen of commissary whiskey or some vile concoction from the Sutler. Gatherings of this character were sometimes attended with unpleasant results. Some Veterans will remember the shooting of a Lieutenant of the 100th New York Volunteers at the quarters of Lieutenant Holt of the First Maryland Cavalry in a wrangle over a game of cards. A witness to the affair thus described it to Doctor Clark, who was called to attend the wounded man: "You see, they were drunk! and got into a skirmish over the game, and all at once Lieutenant Holt, of the cavalry, snatched a pistol from the table and said, 'Damn you!' 'I will shoot you!' And sure enough, the pistol exploded and we thought we had a dead man; but he rallied. The Lieutenant was badly shot through the face. He was taken into the hospital, and after recovery received a leave of absence for sixty days. He never returned to his regiment, resigning his commission. He was badly disfigured for life.

Gambling was prohibited in the command. Yet it was not and could not be wholly suppressed, although a careful watch was always kept and punishment often inflicted. The regimental sutlers also came under surveillance from the fact that they were constantly selling intoxicating liquors under false names, which were brought into the department in cases that were variously marked as "boots and shoes," "preserved fruits," etc., and it was found necessary to appoint a "Board of Administration" to examine their goods and govern their prices. This board convened as occasion justified, but generally once a month. The sutlers protested vigorously against the rulings of this "Board," but it was futile. It was doing a much-needed service to the soldier who with his $13 per month could ill afford to pay such outrageous prices as were demanded for little comforts. Beside, their traffic in sweets and other indigestible goods wonderfully increased the sick list, pandering to the perverted appetites of the soldiers with their displays of edibles, giving, as it were, "stones for bread."

June 14, Generals Gillmore and Seymour made their appearance on the island, and clearly operations were to be commenced in earnest. Since the bombardment of Fort Sumter, when nothing of importance was accomplished, there had been but little done in the matter of effecting the reduction of the forts in Charleston Harbor. Gillmore had succeeded General Hunter in the command of the land forces, and Admiral John Dahlgren had superseded DuPont, who had never been very sanguine after his first attempt and failure. It was fully understood that Gillmore should pursue his own plans, untrammeled by any outside influences, and he and Dahlgren were to cooperate.

Troops were arriving daily in large numbers, and we began to consider than an active campaign was about commencing in which there would be some serious fighting. There were in the Department of the South at this time some 18,000 troops, all well drilled and disciplined, and of the very best material, all being volunteers who had enlisted in 1861 for the purpose of putting down the Rebellion—not hirelings or drafted men. Only about 11,000 of these troops could be concentrated for active service, for it must be remembered that Gillmore had a coast line of 2,500 miles to picket and garrison.

The plan of operations to be pursued was, first, to take the south end of Morris Island; second, to reduce the forts on Morris Island; third, to destroy Fort Sumter, and then, with the help of Dahlgren, to threaten and demand the surrender of Charleston. These plans were all feasible and were eventually most effectually carried out, but required a vast sacrifice of life, as is now known.

Heavy ordnance and ordnance stores were continually arriving, chiefly 100-pounder Parrott guns and 15-inch mortars. The battery at the head of Folly Island, made of sand and marsh sod, was soon completed and ready for its guns, and by July 1 there were forty-eight heavy guns were in position; and so quietly did the work progress that the rebels were totally unconscious that such a thing existed until it was uncovered on July 10, and spoke for itself in a way that produced much discomfiture to the rebels. The enemy undoubtedly knew that we were being reinforced, for they were more active and annoying, not a day passing without their opening up with a shower of shot and shell, which would continue for an hour or two, and at intervals during the night.

The men of the Thirty-Ninth were about worn out by constant picket and fatigue duty, with loss of sleep, and were ordered to Cole's Island for a rest, the Sixty-Second and Sixty-Seventh Ohio Volunteers taking its place at Camp Seymour. July 7, the Field Hospital was organized near the head of the Island, and prepared to receive wounded men, Surgeon William Brown, of the Seventh New Hampshire Volunteers being placed in charge, and Surgeon M. S. Kittinger, of the 100th New York Volunteers, and Surgeon Clark, of the Thirty-Ninth, detailed as operating surgeons. The weather was generally fair, with a temperature ranging from 87° to 96° in the shade, but the nights were cool, and it was always comfortable to sleep underneath a blanket.

July 8, orders were received to be prepared to move at a moment's notice. Tents were struck and all the camp equipment placed in care of the quartermaster. The sick and wounded were ordered sent away to Northern hospitals, and the ambulances and hospital tents were taken to the field hospital. This was all accomplished on the evening of the 9th, and we patiently awaited the signal to attack. Meanwhile General Alfred H. Terry, in command of some 3,000 men, among whom was the Thirty-Ninth Illinois, was sent over on James Island to divert the attention of the enemy.

Brigadier-General George C. Strong had already selected six regiments to make the assault on Morris Island. They were the Forty-Eighth New York, Seventy-Sixth Pennsylvania, Sixth and Seventh Connecticut, Third New Hampshire, and Ninth Maine Volunteers, and they were in place on Folly River where the boats were in waiting to convey them across the inlet. General Vogdes had command of the reserve force, consisting of the Sixty-Second and Sixty-Seventh Ohio, Eighty-Fifth Pennsylvania, 100th New York, and Battery B, First U. S. Artillery. The batteries at the head of the island were commanded by Lieutenant-Colonel Jackson and Major L. L. Langdon, First U. S. Artillery.

THREE HUNDRED-POUNDER PARROT GUN BATTERY ON MORRIS ISLAND, S. C.
Operated by Detail from Thirty-Ninth Illinois, in Command of Lieutenant A. B. HOFFMAN, Co. F.

The hours of the night of the 9th passed very slowly and very quietly away, but at sunrise, the morning of the 10th, thirty-two guns and fifteen mortars opened fire upon the Confederates, and a few minutes later four monitors had taken position and opened with 15-inch and 11-inch guns on the rebel left, and four howitzer-launches pulled into position and opened on the enemy's right; and for three hours the fire of sixty guns was concentrated on the rebel position. About seven o'clock General Strong was signaled to advance, which was done in a gallant and vigorous manner, and in twenty minutes his boats were in the surf on the Morris Island shore, with the loss of only one boat and two men wounded. The regiments formed quickly after leaving the boats, and, with General Strong at their head, pressed forward, driving the rebels out of their first and second line of rifle-pits. On they swept, victorious, over the sand dunes, past the old Beacon House and up to within rifle shot of Fort Wagner, where the rebels had hurriedly retreated and made a stand. Dr. Kittinger and the writer witnessed most of this assault from the "Lookout" near the head of Folly Island, and only retired when the wounded were brought to the hospital, which was near by.

BEACON HOUSE.

Three-fourths of Morris Island was now in our possession, and the whole of it might have been had the troops pushed on, according to a rebel account, which says: "Only a little dash on the part of the Union army would have given them the whole of the island. All they had to do was to press on with even one-half of the troops they had landed. In my opinion it did not justify their excess of prudence; fortunately, however, it saved us."

Our losses in this affair were fourteen killed and thirty-nine wounded. The Confederate loss was 294, of whom 127 were prisoners. We captured twelve guns, several flags, and many tents and small arms. A pontoon bridge was now thrown across the inlet, and the reserves and other troops ordered across. Another hospital was also established at the other end of the island.

The first wounded men to receive attention were two gunners who were injured by the premature explosion of a gun. They were so mangled that they suffered amputation of both arms; and besides, their sight was destroyed. The wounded were attended to as speedily as possible and sent to the hospital boat *Cosmopolitan*, at the foot of Folly Island, for transfer to Hilton Head.

It was decided that Fort Wagner should be carried by assault the next morning, and three regiments were selected, the Ninth Maine, Seventh Connecticut and Seventy-Sixth Pennsylvania Volunteers, and General Strong were to lead them. At daybreak on the 11th he had formed the assaulting column of the regiments mentioned with the Third and Seventh New Hampshire Volunteers as reserves. The Seventh Connecticut led the advance and strictly followed the orders given; "But unfortunately," says General Strong in his report, "when the enemy opened fire along the whole line, and within range of 200 yards, the Seventy-Sixth Pennsylvania halted and lay down upon the ground. Though they remained in this position but a few minutes, and afterwards moved gallantly forward, some of them even to the ditch, that halt lost the battle, for the interval was lost and the Seventh Connecticut, unsupported, was driven from the parapet and the force retired."

Our losses were eight officers and 332 men. The loss to the enemy was one officer and five men killed, and one officer and five men wounded. The Confederate force in Wagner at the time was about 1,200 officers and men.

FORT WAGNER. POINT OF FIRST ASSAULT.

The following Confederate account of this assault was taken from a Charleston paper of July 18, and was written by Colonel Rian, who commanded the rebel picket line that morning:

"At peep of day my attention was called to a dark mass approaching my front. When about twenty-five yards off I ordered the videttes to fire by file, which they did; then the whole battalion rose, formed lines, and gave an almost simultaneous yell. This meant for me 'all right for Battery Wagner,' 'They are coming.' My first line had come to a ready; we could see the beard on the faces of the Federals. Aim! Fire! Then a sheet of flame burst into the advancing line; this doubles up their front, but on comes the body at a double-quick. We fall back, loading as we retire, and form on the left of the second line, coming to a ready, aim-fire! and we poured another volley into their faces. Their front staggers, but on come the survivors at a stately double-quick. We fall back to the third line, the whole battalion coming to a ready; they are now within ten steps of us. Aim! Fire! for the last time. The effect is terrific—it appears as when a wind strikes the stalks of a wheat field. I actually felt sorry for them. It was war, hence fair, but it did seem to me that we were taking unfair advantage of them; they could not stop to fire upon us, for time was all-important to them; their success depending on reaching the battery without delay, and hence they had to receive these dreadful volleys without responding. The enemy dashed on, but barely gave us time to reach the inside of the works before they were repulsed."

After this repulse General Gillmore and Admiral Dahlgren consulted and it was decided that no more assaults should be made until works had been built, and Wagner destroyed by bombardment; and work at once began, building batteries. The Thirty-Ninth had taken no part in these assaults. It returned from James Island on the 11th and made encampment about midway between Fort Wagner and the south end of the island. The Eighty-Fifth Pennsylvania Volunteers had been attached to our brigade at St. Helena Island, and Colonel Joshua B. Howell, its commander, being senior in rank, was acting Brigadier-General.

Morris Island is a narrow ridge of sand formed by accumulations from the beach, having an area of about 400 acres. It is wider at its southern than in its northern part, the extremity on Lighthouse Inlet being about 1,000 yards in width. Its surface is irregular and broken by sand ridges or dunes, affording excellent shelter for troops. It gradually slopes inward, terminating in a series of marshes. The northern extremity was very narrow, terminating in what is called Cummings Point, and distant from Charleston about five and a half miles. The main channel into the harbor was some 1,200 yards distant and parallel to the island. On Cummings Point was located Battery Gregg, and about 2,000 yards this side (south) was Fort Wagner. Heavy details were made every few days from the Regiment to work in the entrenchments and for grand guard duty at the front. Fort Sumter and the batteries on Sullivan's Island kept us and almost continuous fire across Fort Wagner upon our trenches and not a day passed that one or more men were not killed or wounded. Gillmore, however, soon had some 26 heavy guns in position and vigorously returned the enemy's fire, and in great part put a stop to this constant annoyance, enabling our men to more easily, rapidly and safely push forward the work. Lines of rifle-pits were thrown across the island in front of the batteries and were constantly advanced. Fort Wagner was never silent.

Work thus continued, preparing for the great assault that was soon to take place. At last the morning of the July 18, 1863 dawned and gave promise to a hot, sultry day. In the early morning the fleet of ironclads and other vessels, under the command of Admiral Dahlgren, was seen in motion moving up the channel towards Battery Wagner, prepared for the great bombardment. The *New Ironsides* led, followed by the monitors' *Weehawken, Patapsco, Nantucket, Montauk* and *Catskill*, and the wooden vessels' *Seneca, Paul Jones, Ottawa, Chippewa*, and *Wissahickon*, with six mortar boats. They were soon in position and opened fire upon Fort Wagner. Our land batteries opened fire simultaneously, and over some eleven hours an incessant firing was kept up from over 100 guns, and within this time over 9,000 shells were hurled against Wagner. The enemy's firing was also rapid, throwing from their various forts an average of fourteen shots per minute. The shells thrown from our guns were so timed that when they struck or reached Battery Wagner they exploded, raising vast columns of sand and burying many guns, and uncovering to a great extent the bombproofs. The bombardment as witnessed by many of us from the summit of the sand hills above our camp was grand and terrifying, and when the mind contemplated the assault that was to take place, with the inevitable loss of life that must follow, it was filled with sorrowful foreboding and sickening fears that brought pallor to the face and tears to the heart, if not to the eye.

FORT WAGNER. SEA FRONT.

At seven p.m. the assaulting columns commenced forming at a distance of 1,350 yards from the fort. General Strong's brigade had the advance and was composed as previously in the assault of the 11th, with the addition of a regiment of colored troops—the Fifty-Fourth Massachusetts, commanded by Colonel Robert Gould Shaw. Why this regiment of colored men was chosen and placed at the head of the assaulting party is unknown. It may have been for political reasons, or to allow a race so lately emancipated from slavery to share in the glory of this undertaking; or again, it may have been to infuriate the rebels. But no matter what the reason was, placing them in this position and at the last moment, took up valuable time.

Darkness was approaching, made more dusky by a storm that threatened. Putnam's brigade was in support of Strong's and Stephenson's followed. The balance of the troops on the island was also under arms, back midway of the island. The whole of the assaulting force was under the command of General Seymour. General Gillmore was back, on the island.

At half-past seven p.m. the order to charge on the double quick was given by General Strong, and is thus described by an eyewitness and one who participated in it:

"The Fifty-Fourth Massachusetts (Colored), 640 strong, at the command 'charge!' started out on the 'double-quick' in columns of 'wings,' with the right resting on the sea, and passed obliquely to the left towards the land face of the fort. They were met by fully twice their number in the garrison, who opened upon them when within 100 yards of the battery with a terrific volley of grape, shrapnel and musketry which had the effect of turning back the majority of the Regiment. A small number, however, still followed their brave Colonel across the moat or ditch and up the side of the fort, and succeeded in planting their flag upon the ramparts; there Colonel Shaw was shot dead together with many of his brave men; the others were panic-stricken, and fled.

"General Strong with the balance of his brigade remained still standing in columns of companies awaiting orders. It was not until the Negroes had been repulsed that he again gave the order 'Column, forward! Double-quick, march!' and forward the brigade rushed, the 6th Connecticut leading. All was quiet as the grave save the clatter of our tramp; not a gun was fired; the darkness of night was fast closing around us. As we neared the ditch, which contained some three feet of water, the parapet of the fort seemed to swarm with the enemy, who gave a fearful 'yell' and then opened a withering fire with cannon and musketry. The column reeled and swayed, and many fell; it was light as day with the incessant flashes of the guns; the air was filled with the cheers of the living and the moans of the dying as they fell under the deadly missiles of the enemy until they lay in rows and heaps far up the fatal slope of the battery. The solid column of a few moments ago had melted away, with here and there a man standing in the gathering gloom; but they continued to press forward, stumbling over spikes, spearheads and wire entanglements that had been placed with fiendish ingenuity to impede progress. We reached the southeast bastion, the strongest part of the works, drove the rebels from their guns; followed them over the terrace, and over the superior slope, and at last stood upon the parapet—140 men, a mere handful —victorious! But at what a cost! We stood there in the darkness, awaiting orders and reinforcement, but none came. Nearly three hours passed, each man acting for himself, until the enemy, having been reinforced, made an assault which we could not withstand and had to surrender."

The Second Brigade, commanded by Colonel Putnam, had in the meantime made a furious charge to reinforce those in the fort, but it was now dark, and they were driven back; and at last, late in the night, the shattered remnant of these brigades fell back, with Fort Wagner no nearer taken that it had been in the morning. General Strong was mortally wounded. Colonel Putnam was killed just as he reached the fort. Colonel Shaw had been killed at the first assault and was buried the next morning in a pit along with his dead Negroes. Over 800 of our dead were left behind and rudely buried in the sand the next morning by the Confederate soldiers. General Seymour was also wounded. Every field officer at the front, with the exception of Major Plympton of the Third New Hampshire, had been killed or wounded, and the entire Union loss in this assault was fully 2,500 officers and enlisted men, although it was never fully ascertained. General Gillmore's quarterly report ending July 20, 1863, showed that since the commencement of his operations on Morris Island he had lost 33 percent of his troops (13,000) in killed, wounded, missing and sick. The Sixth and Seventh Connecticut and the Forty-Eighth New York had been more than decimated in number.

Was this assault a sacrifice of life to incompetence? There were many bad, almost stupid blunders in the management of this assault, but it is not the intention of the writer to point them out or attempt an explanation, even were he competent. It was considered by the country a most disastrous failure, and history has never done full justice to the courage and heroism there displayed.

The hospital at the south end of the island, consisting chiefly of shelters for the operating tables, presented a most distressing and sickening sight even to the experienced surgeon during the whole night of the 18th and a part of the following day. As fast as the wounded could be cared for they were placed upon the hospital transport to be taken to Hilton Head.

In a few days many of the Eastern troops were ordered away to Hilton Head and some to Florida, but our division remained, under the command of Brigadier-General A. H. Terry.

Work was at once commenced again at the front with the spade (which was becoming known as the "Gillmore rifle"), and sapping and mining and running parallels was vigorously prosecuted by heavy details of men from the various brigades both night and day, and exposed to constant fire from the enemy. Numbers of heavy guns were also arriving, mostly 300-pounder Parrotts, and were hauled up the beach by teams of twenty or more horses to the positions they were to occupy.

In our hours of rest by day we were called upon to fight innumerable nuisances in the shape of sand-flies, fleas, and other pests; and besides, the heat was most intense and debilitating. At night the mosquitoes made it lively for us, and after an uneasy sleep it was no unusual thing to awaken with the eyes, nose, and mouth filled with sand that had drifted in through the various openings of the tent. During the night and when there would be unusual activity at the forts we would ascent the high sand-hills and watch the shells as they came towering up and over and then bursting with a dull, heavy sound and a scintillation that was brilliant in the extreme. Our details at the front were protected by heavy bombproofs which afforded them shelter from the storms and security from the enemy's shot and shell. Occasionally, however, a litter would come back bearing some poor wounded mortal to the hospital.[3]

---

[3]Hugh Snee's best friend and future brother-in-law, Moses Sheffler, was one of those "poor wounded mortals" to be carried back to the hospital. He received a musket ball wound in the skull that partially paralyzed him.

BOMB-PROOF.

August 20, Colonel Howell, of the Eighty-Fifth Pennsylvania, who temporarily commanded our Brigade, was injured severely by the collapse of a bomb-proof under which he was sheltered, causing concussion of the brain and scalp wound. After receiving the necessary attention and he was able to travel he was given leave of absence and departed for his home near Philadelphia, Colonel Osborn of the Thirty-Ninth succeeding him in command of the brigade.

The location of our quarters gave a splendid view of the whole scene of operations. In our front were our heavy batteries, and almost continually in exercise, with Forts Sumter, Wagner, Gregg and the batteries on Sullivan's Island. At our right was the imposing fleet, under command of Admiral Dahlgren, and at night the ships were splendidly lit up with signal lights and rockets. The scene presented was enjoyable, but when we thought all of this combination engaged in active and fratricidal warfare, a shade of sadness would involuntarily creep over us, and we turned to our beds wondering as to the result. During the subsequent operations on the parallels, and while Colonel Osborn was inspecting, as "Officer of the day," the various batteries, he was partially stunned by the premature discharge of a 300-pound gun, and was laid up for several days in consequence.

The second parallel was opened up by the flying sap at 750 yards from the fort on July 23; the third parallel at 450 on August 9; and beyond this point the trenches were pushed forward rapidly, sometimes by the flying sap and sometimes the full sap, as occasion required. The fourth parallel, at 200 yards, was finished and a ridge wrested from the enemy August 26. Beyond this point there was not a front enough for a parallel, and the approach was made by zigzags with sharp angles.

Fort Sumter had been continuously bombarded, and on August 24 General Gillmore reported it a mass of ruins. It was curious to watch the heavy solid shot and shell when they struck the fort, as they invariably did, the range being so perfect; and when they did strike, a heavy cloud of debris was lifted, and as it settled we could plainly see the break it had made in the wall of the fort.

In the latter part of August it was discovered that the enemy had a number of sharpshooters in some strong rifle-pits just in advance of Fort Wagner, and it wad determined to dislodge them. There were 250 picked men from the Twenty-Fourth Massachusetts Volunteers were selected to do this business. They crept quietly to the head of the sap, and upon the order being given dashed from there

Fort Sumter in Ruins.

over the open space, and soon found themselves at the rifle-pits in close contact with the rebels. The enemy opened fire from both Wagner and Gregg, and for a short time the air was full of death.

The Union boys received the fire from the rifle-pits, which did but little execution—the aim had been too high, and before the "gray-backs" could reload, seventy-five of them were taken prisoners. From that time until the fall of Wagner no Confederates ventured outside the fort in our direction.

Supporting these assaults were a number of "Requa Batteries."[4]

In case of an assault at short range, each section or piece of the battery was intended to be as effective and would throw as much lead as a regiment of men in a given time. Sections of this battery were stationed along the advanced lines at the siege of Fort Wagner, and proved to be especial service in protecting the sappers and miners while extending their parallels. The men required to operate it were detailed from various regiments, and at the time it was photographed, as shown, the full battery was manned by details from the Thirty-Ninth Illinois, Third Vermont, and Ninth Maine Regiments, and was commanded by First Lieutenant A. W. Wheeler, Company K, and Second Lieutenant E. Kingsbury, Company E, of the Thirty-Ninth Illinois. Among the detail from the Thirty-Ninth were Sergeant Daniel Smouse, of Company K, Corporal George Burton, and Privates W. W. Ely, Charles C. Hudson, Thomas Kinney and Hugh R. Snee, with some few others whose names are not recalled.

---

[4] More properly known as the Billinghurst-Requa, these batteries consisted of six pieces, each piece or section comprising 25 heavy rifled gunbarrels, mounted on a two-wheeled carriage. The barrels could be elevated or depressed and spread fan-shaped to cover a greater lateral range if necessary. It was loaded at the breech, the cartridges being fixed upon a bar and taken from the caisson in that manner, the bar, in fact, being the breech of the gun, and all the cartridges were exploded simultaneously by pulling a lanyard.

"Regina Battery" manned by a Detachment of the
39th Regiment Alabama during the Siege of Charleston S.C.

Hugh R. Enex - 39th Reg. Ill.
1861 - 1865

Civil War 1861-65

SECTION OF REQUA BATTERY.
Commanded by Lieutenants WHEELER and KINGSBURY, Thirty-Ninth Illinois.
Morris Island, S. C., 1863

The section in charge of Corporal Burton, and Privates Ely and Snee did excellent service in support of the charge made by the Twenty-Fourth Massachusetts that evening during August 1863, to dislodge the rebel sharpshooters in front of Wagner, the rapidity of firing and the well-directed aim of the piece rendering it very unsafe for the rebels within the fort to go to the assistance of their sharpshooters in the rifle-pits outside, and they were easily captured. But as soon as the battery disclosed its whereabouts, Forts Gregg and Moultrie and the mortars at Sumter opened a most vigorous fire upon it for a short time, but without effecting much damage.

One section of the battery was placed on a platform built in the water some distance from the beach, and protected by sand bags. It was often the target for the enemy's guns.

September 1, a large number of light mortars were taken to the front, and the position for the sharpshooters was enlarged; and on the morning of the 5th another heavy bombardment by the land batteries was commenced, and continued for a period of forty-two hours, the whole fire being concentrated upon Battery Wagner. On the evening of the 6th, five companies of the Thirty-Ninth were ordered to the front as "grand guards" at the trenches, and a like number from some of the other regiments, all under the command of Lieutenant-Colonel Mann. At or near midnight a young man, an Irishman, small in stature, and whose clothing was dripping with sea brine, was brought by a corporal of the guard before the commanding officer as a deserter from Fort Wagner, and who stated that the fort was being evacuated by the rebels. Upon being questioned, he said,

> "I deserted because I have no love for the rebels or their cause. I was taken some few months ago from a vessel that had run the blockade from the Bermudas', and placed in Fort Wagner as a soldier, and I want to go home. The majority of the garrison have gone, leaving a squad of men to set fire to the fuse connecting with the powder magazines, with the intent to blow you all up, and I escaped and made my way by swimming around to you in order to give the information."

He was told that the matter would be immediately inquired into, and if the intelligence he brought proved true that he would be rewarded and sent home; if otherwise, he would certainly be shot. "Well, sor, I'll take the chances!" said he.

He was given in charge of the guards, to be taken to General Gillmore, but not before a rough plan of the fort was drawn, with a request for him to point out the location of the magazines, which he did. Just previous to the arrival of this man, General Gillmore had sent up a dispatch from his headquarters on Folly Island, inquiring about the working of the calcium lights that had recently been placed in position. The answer had been returned, and Lieutenant-Colonel Mann, in his hurry and excitement over the good news, sent the following dispatch to General Gillmore direct, forgetting the courtesy due the Division Commander, Brigadier-General Terry, through whom it should have been sent:

"12:05 a.m.

General Gillmore: A deserter just in from Wagner reports that they have evacuated the fort, except a few men left to blow up magazines, says they have gone to Fort Gregg. Shall I turn my guns on it? Prisoner is Irish, and swam in. Have sent him to you.

Lt.-Col. O. L. Mann."

To this the following answer was returned:

"12:15 a.m.

Lieutenant-Colonel Mann: Turn all your batteries on Gregg.

General Gillmore."

"1:10 a.m.

Lieutenant-Colonel Mann: Cease fire on Gregg and open on Wagner actively for about fifteen minutes; then gradually slacken; then cease. When you have ceased, send five resolute men from the head of the sap into the fort to ascertain whether it is evacuated. If it is evacuated send in twenty men to seize any men who may be lurking there to blow up the magazine.

General Q. A. Gillmore."

"1:20 a.m.

Lieutenant-Colonel Mann: If the fort is evacuated send the calcium light up to Wagner and put it on the parapet of the sea-face, so that it will be sheltered from James Island and Fort Johnson. Let the light be thrown on Gregg and the intervening ground.

General A. H. Terry"

"3:30 A.M.

General Gillmore: One of the five men sent in has returned and reports all is quiet. Captain James Wightman and twenty have gone in and the colors of the Thirty-Ninth Illinois are planted on the ramparts.

Lt.-Col. O. L. Mann."

The telegraph line was now ordered to be extended and taken into Fort Wagner. At five a.m. General Terry had his division under arms and in motion proceeding to Fort Wagner and Gregg. One regiment was left to garrison Fort Gregg and the Second Brigade, 1,000 strong, was put into Fort Wagner, while the balance of the troops were sent back to quarters.

At eight a.m. the telegraph line was completed to Fort Wagner by Lieutenant Dana, and the first dispatch to be sent over the completed line was the following:

"General Gillmore: The general officer of the trenches sends his compliments and congratulations to the General commanding from the bombproof in fallen Fort Wagner. His confidence in God and General Gillmore is unshaken."

Among the five men who volunteered to enter the fort after the news of its being evacuated, was

Private Cornelius Cox of Company G, and with the view of giving as much information as possible concerning the occupation of this formidable battery, the brief and modest account of Cox is here inserted.

STATEMENT OF CORNELIUS COX.

"Some time after midnight September 7, a man came in from battery Wagner, having swam out in the water to elude detection, and reported to the commanding officer of the trenches that Wagner was being evacuated. Soon after, Major Linton came around and called for volunteers from each company to enter the fort and ascertain whether the report was true or false. I volunteered for Company G. There were five of us. We separated, and passed around on top of the parapet until opposite each other, and then came through the fort and met in the center. While we were doing this, the rebels fired two shots from their small mortars, which was the last of them. After looking around and finding some of the guns spiked, one of the five was sent back to report the fort evacuated; after which the Regiment marched in and took possession. This was just at daybreak. I did not see any lighted fuse, but was informed afterwards that one of the five before mentioned did find a lighted fuse, supposed to lead to the magazine, and cut it. I do not think any particular officer, man or company is entitled to credit for first occupying the fort after the fact had been established that it had been evacuated. I do not write this because I wish to figure as a hero, for I am aware that it would be unjust to mention names, unless all that did their duty could be mentioned; but I do think five men from the Regiment, regardless of any particular company, are entitled to the credit of first entering Fort Wagner under very perilous circumstances.

"I may add that we each received a complimentary 'furlough' of thirty days endorsed by General Quincy A. Gillmore and Lieutenant-Colonel Orrin L. Mann."

There was great rejoicing over the downfall of this great earthwork—the most formidable of ancient or modern times, which had successfully withstood the combined efforts of both army and navy for nearly three months, and would have still held out had there been a larger force for its defense. The event was soon heralded in song.

"Yes, Wagner is ours! Oh, glory, hurrah!
Won't all those head rebels feel gay!
And the greatest arch-traitor the world ever saw—
Old Jeff—will feel tickled today.
All honor and fame to the gallant and brave,
Who have forced the 'rebs' out of their holes;
Bring out the old banner, and proud let it wave,
With the sun shining bright on its folds.
Then, hurrah, boy! hurrah! shout glory and sing,
For the traitors look sadly forsaken;

Our glorious old Eagle is still on the wing,
For Wagner is taken! boys, taken!"

The possession of the whole of Morris Island placed Sumter and many of the enemy's other forts, and the lower part of the city of Charleston within reach of our guns, and these forts were soon abandoned. The city of Charleston, however, had been reached by shot and shell some weeks previously by a little battery known as the "Swamp Angel." This battery had been constructed about the middle of July. General Gillmore ordered Colonel Surrell of the New York Engineer Regiment and Major P. S. Michie to explore the marsh lying between Morris and James Islands in the direction of Charleston, and report if it was feasible to erect a small battery there whose shots could reach the city. After three days' patient investigation a favorable report was made, and an order was given to one of Colonel Surrell's subordinate officers, Captain Crusoe, to make the necessary requisitions and proceed with the work.

"SWAMP ANGEL."

This officer, after exploring the marsh and finding the mud not less than fifteen feet deep, closed his requisition by asking for 100 men, eighteen feet high, to do work in a marsh into which they were liable to sink eight feet. The officer was arrested instead of being promoted for his witticism, but the work was begun.

Planks were laid from the island westward across the marsh for nearly two miles to the spot on a small creek designated for the battery, and anchored down by sandbags to keep them from floating off in high tide. Over this pathway, in single file, details of soldiers carried bags of sand from which, with the aid of timbers floated up the creek from Folly Island, a small fort with capacity for one gun was in due time constructed, and all done under cover of darkness.

As soon as ready, a 100-pounder Parrot gun was floated there on a scow boat, under the same cover, and placed in position. On August 18 General Gillmore, under flag of truce, notified General Beauregard of the Confederate forces that he was prepared to reach the heart of the city with his guns, and that unless Forts Wagner, Gregg and Sumter were surrendered to the authority of the

United States, he should bombard the city; and further suggested that if his demand was not recognized the women and children should be removed from the city. General Beauregard thought this to be all nonsense on the part of Gillmore and refused.

The next day the "Swamp Angel" was trained on the spire of St. Michael's Church, plainly visible, and at two o'clock the following morning the first shot was fired. Those who witnessed the occurrence could trace the shell by its burning fuse as it went over on its mission. Shot succeeded shot until the third, whose shell exploded in the city of Charleston, and soon flames were seen ascending. It was learned the next day by the "exchanges" received by the courtesy of the pickets, that this shell charged with Greek Fire [similar to Napalm], had fallen through the roof of a large building filled with medical supplies and had started a serious fire that consumed an entire block of buildings before extinguished. The succeeding shots that were fired reached the city, but none proved so disastrous a did the third one. At the thirty-second shot, the reinforcement or rear portion of the gun was blown out, and this accident ended the brief but brilliant career of this famous little battery. The gun was never replaced, for before a new one could have been placed in position, Forts Wagner and Gregg had fallen, which brought us within easy range of the city.

This little battery took its unique name from a remark made by a member of the Thirty-Ninth Regiment of Illinois Volunteers. As a Chicago paper said at the time of the fall of Wagner, " . . . the Thirty-Ninth Illinois Regiment being the only one in that military department from Illinois, it of course was expected to furnish a name for the most famous little fort ever erected, and be the first to plant its colors on the strongest earthworks ever constructed." Late at night the adjutant of the Regiment made a detail of fifty men to help construct the pathway across the marsh. When they returned the next morning, all covered with mud and slush, Corporal John Kipp of Company K, a good deal of a wag, was asked where on earth he had been and what he had been doing to get so bespattered. "I will tell you," replied the jolly corporal. "We have been out in the great marsh, and as nearly as I can guess we have been constructing a pulpit of sand for some swamp angel to preach from." From this little incident the battery took on a name by which it was known as far as intelligence could reach.

The "Swamp Angel" gun at the close of the war, or when the forts on Morris Island were dismantled, was sent North to be broken up, and was taken to the Arsenal at Trenton, New Jersey. It was not to meet so ignoble a fate, however, for while lying at the Arsenal it was recognized by some one as the "Swamp Angel," and measures were at once taken to insure its preservation. It was repaired, nicely mounted and inscribed and placed in the public square of the city of Trenton, a most interesting relic of the "War of the Rebellion."[5]

The Thirty-Ninth garrisoned Wagner and also Battery Gregg in their turn for a long time after their evacuation, and during the time lost several valuable men. On the night of September 23, Captain Joseph Woodruff of Company K was struck with a fragment of shell that had been thrown from Sullivan's Island. The piece entered his abdomen, wounding the intestines, but he continued breathing for several hours. The Captain was one of our bravest officers; quiet and sedate in his manner, but always genial and sociable in his intercourse with both officers and men. After his death

---

[5] April 12, 1961, the "Swamp Angel" was moved to Cadwalader Park in Trenton and rededicated on the 100th anniversary of the start of the Civil War.

the officers of the Regiment were convened and the following resolutions drafted and adopted as expressive of our sense of the irreparable loss that had befallen the Regiment:

RESOLUTIONS

WHEREAS, On the night of September 23, 1863, Captain Joseph Woodruff, of Company K, Thirty-Ninth Regiment Illinois Volunteers, while on duty as officer in command at Fort Gregg, and when about to be relieved from said duty, was wounded by a shell from Fort Moultrie which carried away a large portion of his right side, causing his death in less than two hours after the receipt of the injury; therefore,

Resolved, That while we recognized the hand of God in all things, we can but mourn the loss of our brother officer, and one of our country's noble defenders; and, while we so deeply regret the violent death that snatched from us one whose every act endeared him to all—whose loyalty, patriotism and bravery proclaimed him a true man and soldier, we cannot but feel that our loss is his gain, and that he has left a world of suffering and gone to join that band of noble patriots that have fallen before him in their country's defense.

Resolved, That we tender our heartfelt sympathies to the family and friends in this sad bereavement of a kind husband, father, and generous companion, and trust that they may find consolation in the fact that he fell while at his post and in the discharge of his duty; and that in dying, he evinced, while sensible, that spirit of resignation which bespeaks the faith of a Christian.

Resolved, That as a token of our respect and esteem, the officers of this Regiment wear the usual badge of mourning for the next thirty days, and that a copy of the foregoing preamble and resolutions be sent to the family of the deceased, and that a copy of them be sent for publication to the Chicago Press and the Ottawa papers and the two papers of this Department.

    The captured forts were enlarged and new batteries were erected, which still kept our men busy at work both night and day. The rebels still gave us at intervals a galling fire and was very troublesome, although doing no very great damage. The forts of the enemy were constantly bombarded and the shelling of Charleston was continued. The vessels constituting the naval force at times consented to join in, but as a general thing they more most gloriously inactive.
    It was considered by us landsmen that after the taking of Forts Wagner, Gregg, and the reduction of Fort Sumter, our fleet would push forward to the city of Charleston and demand its surrender or level it to the ground, but we were mistaken; and the plea for their hesitation was, that the channel was full of chains and torpedoes. But what if it was! Could they not sacrifice a ship or two and a few lives in common with us in the endeavor to abbreviate and crush out the headquarters of this audacious rebellion? We were assured time and again that a portion of the channel was free from all

obstructions, and the fact was reported to Dahlgren, but he put no faith in the statement. He made the assertion that he believed there were cables submerged in that direction, to entrap his vessels, and declared that he would not make the attempt under any circumstances.

A serious difficulty, in consequence, sprang us between General Gillmore and Dahlgran, and the troops on the island were gradually withdrawn, whereby General Gillmore divested himself and his gallant troops of the responsibility of the future of the siege.

September 16 the following General Order was received from General Gillmore congratulating his troops and announcing the destruction of Fort Sumter:

"Department of the South, Headquarters in the Field, Morris Island, S. C., September 15, 1863.

GENERAL ORDERS.

It is with no ordinary feeling of gratification and pride that the Brigadier-General commanding is enabled to congratulate this army upon the signal success which as crowned the enterprise in which it has been engaged. Fort Sumter is destroyed. The scene where our country's flag suffered its first dishonor, you have made the theater of one of its proudest triumphs.

"The fort has been in possession of the enemy for more than two years; it has been his pride and boast; has been strengthened by every appliance known to military science and has defied the assaults of the most powerful and gallant fleet the world ever saw. But it has yielded to your courage and patient labor. Its walls are now crumbled to ruins; its formidable batteries are silenced; and though a hostile flag floats over it, the fort is a harmless and helpless wreck.

"Forts Wagner and Gregg, works rendered memorable by their protracted resistance and the sacrifice of life they have cost, have also been wrested from the enemy by your persevering courage and skill, and the graves of your fallen comrades rescued from desecration and contumely.

"You now hold in undisputed possession of the whole of Morris Island, and the city and harbor of Charleston lie at the mercy of your artillery from the very spot where the first shot was fired at your country's flag and the rebellion itself was inaugurated.

"To you, the officers and soldiers of this command, and to the gallant navy which has cooperated with you, are due the thanks of your commander and your country. You were called upon to encounter untold privations and dangers; to undergo unremitting and exhausting labors; to sustain severe and disheartening reverses. How nobly your patriotism and zeal have responded to the call the result of the campaign will show, and your commanding General gratefully bears witness.

Q. A Gillmore, Brig. Gen'l Commanding."

CHAPTER ELEVEN

"Veterans"

The Thirty-Ninth were soon ordered back to Folly Island and went into camp where company drill and battalion exercise occupied the most part of the time. We remained here very pleasantly under the shade of the magnolia and palmetto, with considerable diversion by way of fishing and hunting and paying visits to our friends. While here, Lieutenant-Colonel O. L. Mann was ordered on recruiting service and departed for Chicago on November 10, with several subordinate officers. That they made good use of their time was manifest when some 250 recruits joined our ranks on our return to the front after our veteran furlough in February 1864. We still retained our Regimental Hospital organization and all sick who could not be comfortably cared for were sent to St. Augustine, Florida.

About December 1 we were ordered to report at Hilton Head and went into camp there. The same drills and exercises were continued, with a little more attention to discipline and the police of camp. Otherwise our life was as automatic as could be. While here, an order came to re-vaccinate the whole command, and the detail of surgeons to accomplish the matter was made. We were receiving large numbers of Negro troops, and they had brought with them the smallpox. Every man in each regiment of our brigade was vaccinated, and some curious scenes occurred; but this is no place to give the results of this forced vaccination.

During the time that we remained on the island the Regiment was induced to reenlist for three years or the continuance of the war, with the exception of about 100 who preferred to remain in this department until the term of their service expired and then proceed home for good. Many of those who were willing to reenlist could not be accepted because of physical disability. Each man had to undergo a rigid and thorough examination at the hands of the regimental surgeon. During the few days that the examination was in progress the sick call was but slimly attended, and it was exceedingly wonderful to notice how rugged and healthful men would appear and represent themselves, who had formerly been the best patrons of the dispensary, and all through their eagerness to reenlist and get the opportunity of going home. Each regiment that enlisted as a body was granted a furlough, and the Thirty-Ninth was the first in the Department to accept these veteran honors.

All was in readiness on the morning of January 28, 1864, to move down to the wharf for the purpose of embarking for home, but it was fully afternoon before the march was commenced, and this delay was occasioned from the fact that three brigades of the Division were preparing to escort us, a compliment that gratified every man of the Regiment. Our progress to the wharf was a perfect ovation, all the troops in the department turning out to greet us with a "bon voyage." The Regiment numbered at this time 450 men—the minimum number of a regiment that could retain its organization and received "leave of absence" from the Department for the purpose of proceeding home to recruit.

The Thirty-Ninth was deservedly popular and a favorite in the Department of the South, as evinced on all sides at this time, and the following letters given to Colonel Osborn by Generals Gillmore and Seymour for Governor Yates plainly showed the esteem of our commanders.

"Headquarters, Hilton Head (Pulaski),
January 25, 1864.

To His Excellency, the Governor of Illinois:

Sir: The Thirty-Ninth Regiment Illinois Volunteers, Colonel T. O. Osborn, having reenlisted as a 'Veteran Regiment,' has been furloughed and will soon proceed homeward. I cannot permit it to leave my command without expressing, so far as I am able, my entire satisfaction with its conduct under all circumstance.

"It will display to you, possible, a state of discipline and excellence of instruction that will not be diminished by contrast with the very best of our volunteer regiments, and you may justly be proud of its past and present efficiency, for which Colonel Osborn, a most excellent officer, deserves great praise.

"Your Excellency will, I am sure, afford Colonel Osborn every reasonable facility for filling his command, and you can entrust the interests of your citizen-soldiers to no better hands. And I am

Your Excellency's Obedient Servant,
T. Seymour, Brig. Gen'l Commanding."

On the back of this letter was the following endorsement by General Gillmore:

"I heartily endorse everything Brigadier-General Seymour says of the Thirty-Ninth Regiment Illinois Volunteers, and their commanders, and hope the Governor of Illinois will use his influence to have the regiment returned to my command when recruited, unless Colonel Osborn prefers some other.

Q. A. Gillmore, Maj. Gen'l Commanding."

Two large propellers, the *Mary Boardman* and *City of Bath*, had been assigned to carry us to New York, and the Regiment was divided for the passage. The right wing of the Regiment and the regimental staff took passage on the *City of Bath*, while the other wing took the *Mary Boardman*. We left the harbor at about ten o'clock p.m. The sea was tranquil and the weather most enjoyable during the night, and the morning was ushered in with a glorious "sunburst" and a clear sky, with the ocean as smooth as glass. About nine o'clock in the morning we neared the "Frying Pan Shoals," and those on deck had their attention called to what was considered a school of porpoises disporting, but we were not quite certain in the matter, and went forward to the pilothouse to make inquiry. The man at the wheel did not know exactly what it was, at least he said so, but as we approached nearer and nearer we became convinced that it was shoal water; and our guesses and fears were more than realized in a moment more when the ship struck the bar with a dull heavy thud that brought us to our knees. After striking, the ship careened over at an angle of 45°, and we all rushed to the opposite side in the endeavor to balance her. The sea was calm and smooth when we struck, but there was evidence of an approaching storm in the light puffs of wind that occasionally reached us, and the increasing ripple on the wide undulating billows around.

There was no panic among the men, and the only concern manifested was on the part of the captain, who got a little excited as hour after hour wore away without much progress made in getting off. The Colonel and Dr. Clark descended the hatch ways into the lower hold to see if there was any sign of leak or damage to the ship's bottom, but could not find anything to alarm them.

But here we were, aground on a sandbar—no land in sight, the nearest being twenty miles distant, and no progress made in our constant efforts to back off. Under the orders of the captain we rushed from side to side of the ship and full steam was put upon the reversed propeller. The wind continued to freshen and the waves became quite respectable in size, and we began to feel a little uneasy at the prospect, when all at once, at the expiration of the third hour, the cry came, "She moves! She moves!!" and sure enough we were soon free again and moving in a direction that gave the shoal a wide berth. Such a glad shout of thanksgiving as went up from the hearts of 250 war-worn soldiers never was listened to before or since. We had struck the bar with great force while under the momentum of a full head of steam, and had grounded along for the distance of two ship's lengths, and our good fortune in getting off was mainly due to the rising tide and the coming storm. It was a piece of gross carelessness that we were brought into the difficulty, but the captain explained that he wished to make a quick trip and had taken an unfrequented channel with the hope of getting through, and that the pilot at the wheel had missed it.

The captain of our vessel was an Englishman and had in conversation expressed his sympathy for the South, and when we struck the bar we did not know but what it was a preconcerted plan to wreck us. We held a short consultation and came to the conclusion that, if he did not make the proper endeavor to extricate the vessel or show a pretty liberal interest in our safety, we would, before compelled to leave the vessel, hang him and his officers to the yardarm. The poor man, however, was more frightened at his situation than we were, and we accepted his explanation readily, but not without informing him of our suspicions. He was a jolly and good-natured tar, and after this did everything he could to afford us pleasure and comfort.

Our trip was destined to be an eventful one, for in a short time after the late disaster we discovered the ship on fire around the smokestack on the second deck, but a few pails of water sufficed to extinguish it.

The storm came on fast, and as we rounded Cape Hatteras it seemed to reach its greatest fury and it became impossible to keep a footing. The vessel rolled fearfully, and at times we had some fears of completely rolling over, especially when our course led us into the trough of the sea. To add to the horrors of our situation, word was brought by a seaman that Dr. Clark's horse had broken loose from his stall and was in the hold among the men. The Doctor crept up to the deck, and then crawling dog-fashion on all fours succeeding in reaching the forward hatch and descended to the hold, and, sure enough, there was the poor horse, reeking with perspiration and frightened out of his senses. At each roll of the ship he would go sliding along the deck, each muscle braced to the utmost tension; and bang! he would strike against the side; and this was repeated many times before we were able to throw and secure him on a bed of hay prepared for the purpose.

Still later in the day, another and more grievous calamity befell some of the men of Company I, who were located in the vicinity of some huge watercasks which broke away from their lashings and came like an avalanche upon them. Six men were seriously injured; broken ribs, arms and collar bones, and it was with the utmost difficulty that we got them aft into the cabin where their injuries could be attended to. It being impossible to transport them up and over the deck, we with the consent of the captain knocked down a partition separating the cabin from the hold, and soon had them in berths where they were as comfortable as possible until our arrival in New York, when four of them were taken to the hospital on David's Island.

A dense darkness overtook us before reaching Sandy Hook and no pilot-boats were visible, and after vain efforts to signal one by the use of rockets for fully the space of an hour, our captain determined to try and make the outer harbor, for it seemed madness to anchor and try and ride out the storm until daylight on such a dangerous coast; and the captain succeeded, much to our delight, and we were soon at anchor in quiet waters.

In the early morning we steamed up to the city and made fast to the pier at the foot of Cortland street, where we speedily disembarked and marched to the Park barracks, where we found the other companies of the Thirty-Ninth which had reached the harbor some twelve hours previously. Their vessel had not encountered all the trials that we had been subjected to, yet their progress had been marked with some disagreeable incidents, for their ship had twice caught fire, which had given some alarm, but fortunately it was discovered soon enough to be easily extinguished.

The Regiment remained in Park barracks on Chatham square until the following morning, February 3, 1864, when it took up the line of march for the New York and Erie Railroad depot. The Regiment presented a fine appearance after the rest afforded, and the brushing and cleansing they had received; and their passage to the ferry was witnessed by thousands eager to see an Illinois regiment, and their plaudits were incessant as the veterans passed with even, measured step—proudly erect and conscious of the honor paid them.

The passage over the North river was soon made, and we were speedily aboard an elegant train of cars awaiting us in the depot, and after a few moments delay to await stragglers were rolling out of Jersey City for home. We passed on swiftly and safely, enjoying the rare and beautiful scenery along this line of railway, with nothing to mar the pleasure of the trip except the attendant fatigue that must necessarily accompany so long a journey by rail.

Every man had $400 to $500, and was prepared to have a "good time." After leaving New York City, when roll was called to take cars for Chicago, there were fourteen men missing. They were back in the city. There was one from Company A, one from Company B, four from Company E, two from Company D, three from Company F, one from H, one from I and three from Company K.

Colonel Mann detailed Sergeant Slagle, of Company K, to return and hunt up and bring on these stragglers in a great city. The Sergeant was introduced to Mr. C. H. Vaness, who would assist him in getting the transportation to Chicago. He then found out from each company where these men were last seen, and returned to the city. Inside an hour and a half he succeeded in finding all. The man from Company B got away, and stayed for some time after.

These men were loud ones, and with plenty of money were bent on having a good time, and did;

but many of this number were good soldiers, and lost their lives during the battles of the following summer. All were "painting the city red." One had rooms at the Astor House; another at the Fifth Avenue Hotel. They were a jolly and loud set as they were escorted down to the ferry by a squad of Broadway police. They then boarded the train for Chicago. They then took a car for themselves, had big times, reaching Chicago in good shape in advance of the Regiment.

Sellick's Brigade, Christ, Deacon, Preacher, Grubby, Pretty, Motsey, The Brute, The Longest Corporal, Old Scullion, Happy Jack, Uncle Hubbard, were characters in Company K. All except one or two were good soldiers. *Sellick's Brigade* did not gain much of a record. One time he got into trouble for making a suggestion to Colonel Light, at Indianapolis, when enroute for the East. Cars were limited to two on a seat, and no change to do better. Colonel Light was passing through the cars and placing the men, seeing that there were no reserved seats, when Sellick, in an officious way, said to him, "Colonel, damn it, if you will put the fire out of the stove, you can seat two men on the stove!" The Colonel had Sellick placed under arrest, and a man to guard him, and made room for two without disturbing the stove.

Some little delay was always consequent to our stopping places, for the men would ramble and stray about, glad of a little opportunity to stretch their limbs and seek refreshment both solid and liquid, and when all were "on board" again there were merry times in which "King Gambrinus" took no small share.

As we neared our destination a telegram came for us to "hurry up!" as the ladies of the Soldier's Rest and the citizens of Chicago generally were waiting to give us a reception, and we did hurry—the train fairly flying over the rails; but it was midnight before we reached Chicago, and it was supposed that we would have to go supperless to bed. All haste was made in the disembarkation and the line was soon formed. Marching up to Clark Street, the Regiment pursued its course to the Tribune building where three cheers were given for the loyal press, and then countermarched to Bryan Hall, where a good supper awaited us at the hands of the lovely, loyal and patriotic ladies of Chicago. After a feast of good things seasoned with the loving smiles of our pretty waiters, some speech-making was indulged in by Lieutenant-Colonel Mann and Colonel Osborn, and the festivities closed with a song or two by the regimental glee club. The men then marched to North Market Hall and bivouacked for the night. The following morning, February 7, the Regiment again repaired to Bryan Hall for breakfast, and were more than satisfied with what they received at the hands of the ladies.

It would appear like base ingratitude, and it certainly would be doing great injustice to the lady manager of the Chicago Soldier's Rest, did we not give them more than a passing mention in this volume, and we are sure that the surviving members of the Thirty-Ninth (to say nothing of the shades of our many dead heroes) would never be satisfied unless we meted out to them some measure expressive of their common gratitude. The patriotic devotion of these ladies—their incessant labor both day and night in endeavors to give a cheering and homelike reception to the many weary soldiers who were constantly coming and going. Their care, patience and watchful kindness for the sick and disabled that were sheltered and fed and clothed, enshrined them in the hearts of the soldiers.

There are not a great many of that devoted band left now—they have gone up higher. The writer cherishes a grateful memory of them all—Mrs. Livermore, Mrs. Hoge, Mrs. James B. Bradwell, Mrs.

Dr. Hamill, Mrs. Dickinson, Mrs. Sayres, Mrs. Blane and a score of others whose names are not so easily recalled. There was one, Miss Julia R. Hamill, who after the war became the writers' wife, and who proved a most devoted and loving companion until death claimed her in 1871. Her many virtues and loving character have been a cherished memory these many long and wearisome years.

After our breakfast the boys were given furloughs to go on to their homes and report back to Camp Fry, Chicago, within ten days or else be considered deserters.

Active measures were taken to recruit, and within the period of thirty days we have received about 250 men, making our aggregate strength nearly 780.

The long days and nights at Camp Fry (now Wright's Grove) will long be remembered as making a sum-total of misery that was lily borne; for a large city was near that afforded pleasure and enjoyment, and to be guarded in a circumscribed camp was unendurable. Passes were freely given to visit the city and return within twenty-four hours, but each man was prone to think he was entitled to more freedom, and taking advantage of the Colonel's sympathies and good nature often remained for forty-eight.

Nothing of especial interest occurred during our stay in Chicago excepting, perhaps, the appearance on the boards of McVicker's Theater of our second assistant surgeon, Dr. Woodward, who volunteered his services at the benefit of Mr. Warren, the treasurer, in the third act of "Hamlet."

The morning papers of the following day took some notice of the Doctor's performance, and all spoke of it in a good-natured way except the Times, which in the course of its comment remarked: "If the Doctor of the Thirty-Ninth Illinois murders the men of his regiment in the same manner he did Hamlet last night, he had better leave the service." Woodward felt quite indignant over this "slur" and always Wilbur F. Storey and his dramatic critic when the subject was mentioned.

CHAPTER TWELVE

Return to the Army

Before our return to the army the Regiment assembled at Bryan Hall to listen to words of encouragement, congratulation and counsel from Governor Yates. The night was stormy and the mud and slush in the streets made our march to the hall anything but comfortable. Despite the inclemency of the weather the hall was filled with men and women and hundreds were unable to get in even for a standing position.

Upon the appearance of His Excellency Governor Yates the applause was loud, prolonged and deeply earnest. He commenced his address by alluding to the activity that had been evinced from the time of the rebel eruption until the present hour, by the people of that glorious commonwealth, Illinois. From the moment of the booming of the incendiary gun, directed at the heart of the nation, rolled over the land, the cities, towns, villages, hamlets and prairie's of the great Northwest gave, without stint or limit, men; and he was proud to say that his State was foremost in the response for hands and hearts to uphold the constitution, the country, and the laws.

He spoke of those who, in the Spring of 1861, came ready and willing into the ranks, and leaving behind them homes, comforts, loved ones and dear kindred, to meet a deadly and vindictive foe. He alluded to the flags that the people of Chicago had entrusted to the Thirty-Ninth Regiment, and then pointed to them as they were being unfurled by the men who had borne them in the hour of strife and deadly conflict. "You see them there," he said, "tattered and torn, riddled by shot and shell, and stained by the blood of brave men, but you will find no blot upon their escutcheon." The applause that followed this remark lasted for a long time, the ladies joining heartily in the evidence of patriotic and loyal approval.

After the discourse of the Governor short speeches were made by Colonel Osborn, Lieutenant-Colonel Mann and others, and then we departed for our quarters at Camp Fry.

On February 28 we received orders to return to the army and were instructed to report at Washington. It was again a sorrowful time, to break loose from the home ties that bound us, but the remorseless clutch of war had its grip upon every one of us, and it was forward, march!

We left Camp Fry at seven o'clock on our march to the depot of the Pittsburgh and Fort Wayne Railroad, and on the march were the observed of all observers, more especially after we had reached the south side, were the most of our friends were congregated. The Regiment never looked better or marched with more precision of step and soldierly bearing than on this trip to the depot. The train provided for us was comfortable and we had a pleasant journey to Pittsburgh, where a change of cars was required. The only train that we could get at the time was made up from the debris of the rolling-stock of the road and consisted of old, worn-out cattle and stock cars with rough pine boards for seats arranged around the sides, for the men, and a secondhand coach for the officers. The majority of the officers were justly indignant at such treatment, when their transportation called for first-class, and they came in a body to Dr. Clark, to have a protest made, based on sanitary reasons. He went to the Colonel, who was busy talking with the Superintendent of the Road, and opened his battery of wrath (backed by all the mutineers), saying that a protest had been made by all the commissioned officers against submitting to such indignity for themselves or men, adding that he, in his capacity of surgeon, charged with the sanitary condition of the enlisted men, most strenuously objected to the train, which was fit only for the transportation of cattle and hogs. "Go away," says the Colonel, "and mind your business!" This settled it. There was no further use in trying to get a change of cars, and the Doctor left the Colonel's presence, merely remarking that if he persisted in accepting that train he might ride alone. Before the train started some of the officers relented and jumped aboard, leaving some nine or more behind to await the express train. After loitering around the city until fairly tired, and with the conviction that we had been guilty of a great breach of discipline as well as being very silly, we made steps for the depot at midnight and took the express. We overtook our train on the other side of the mountain, at Altoona, where the Regiment had stopped for breakfast, and rejoined them with very guilty feelings as well as looks. After breakfast we got aboard the proper train, and were soon enroute for Chambersburg.

After a little the Colonel sent his orderly around with invitations for such and such a officer to report, and on reporting, they were invariably placed under arrest to await a future disposition. At last the Colonel sent his orderly with his compliments, and would be glad to see Dr. Clark at his headquarters on board the train. The Doctor mustered his courage and dignity, and amid the smiles of his comrades in the same fix went up the aisle to the front of the car and took a seat beside his superior officer—the Colonel, who said, "Why did you, sir, disobey my orders when told to get aboard the train?" "Well, sir," replied the Doctor, "Why did you pay no attention to the protest, which was made in the interest of your command? I am entrusted with their health and felt in duty bound to remonstrate against their being huddled together like so many dumb brutes, and still maintain my position in the matter."

"Well, sir," said Osborn, "you have disobeyed my orders, and I shall write to the Surgeon-General concerning your conduct."

"All right, sir," replied the Doctor, who said he also would write, detailing particularly all the circumstances. As was expected, before reaching Washington all the disobedient officers had been released from arrest and everything was again pleasant and serene, although it would have served us right to have been more severely punished for this mutinous conduct. The discipline in a majority of the volunteer regiments for infractions of this character were more apparent than real. It was impossible for a superior officer of the same command to enforce the rigid discipline of the regular army and tyrannize over men who, at home, were fully his equals, if not more, in all relations of a social or financial character, and as the war would not last forever there might come a reckoning for past grievances in the shape of insults and punishments given and taken while dressed in a "little brief authority" and protected for the time by military law. This, however, would be no excuse where the good of the service would be compromised, and in all well-disciplined regiments the disobedience of a subaltern of whatever grade, or the refusal to do duty while in the face and front of the enemy, was most rigidly punished.

We have heard men speak most scandalously of their officers, using all the disreputable epithets they could call to mind when being punished for some infraction of duty, and many examples might be given, but as this was seldom the case in the Thirty-Ninth their mention is not relevant to this history.

We reached Baltimore after a safe and speedy passage, on the morning of March 3, and were obliged to remain several hours to await means of transportation to Washington. Our destination was reached in the afternoon and we were provided with temporary quarters in the barracks adjoining the "Soldier's Rest," where we passed the night in comparative comfort.

The following day, March 4, 1864, we had orders to cross the Potomac into Virginia, and were soon on the tramp again, passing down Pennsylvania avenue to the Long Bridge which was crossed, and a march of several miles brought us into camp at Arlington Heights on a side hill at the foot of Fort Barnard, which was garrisoned by two companies of the First Connecticut Heavy Artillery under the command of Major George B. Cook, a very pleasant and gentlemanly officer, who did all that was possible to make our camp agreeable, giving us lumber for flooring, bunks, desks, etc., from the unoccupied barracks above the fort.

The Long Bridge - Examining a pass

The weather during our stay was most disagreeable, raining almost every day, and being located on the hillside great care was necessary in ditching to conduct the water to the little creek below in order to prevent the flooding of the tents at the foot of the hill where the hospital and headquarters were located. The soil was a mixture of clay and sand, and it was seldom that we could step outside without sinking to our ankles in the mud, which adhered most tenaciously to our boots. Soon after reaching this place Colonel Osborn was stricken down with double pneumonia and was a very sick man for some days, and had not Major Cook of the Artillery given up his comfortable bed and quarters for the use of the Colonel, the Colonel would never have helped to place the finishing touch on the rebellion at Appomattox. A large number of men were taken sick at this camp with pneumonia, typhoid and remittent fevers, and six of them died. The Augur General Hospital at Camp Distribution was near by, and the most serious cases were sent there to be treated.

There were in the Regiment quite a number of both officers and men who belonged to the Masonic Fraternity, and the idea was conceived of opening a lodge in one of the many unused buildings at Fort Barnard. After a dispensation had been received from the Illinois Grand Lodge a lodge was opened and soon in working order, several of us being initiated into the mysteries of this ancient body.

After leaving this camp our lodge was broken up, for active operations in the field commenced, and during the succeeding months at the front the majority of the officers of our lodge were either killed or wounded—Captain Chauncey Williams, Company H, our Worthy Master, being killed in action August 16, 1864; and two other officers of the lodge, Captain Leroy A. Baker, Company A, and Lieutenant Norman C. Warner, Company E, were each so seriously wounded at the same time that amputation of their legs became necessary, and they were discharged.

Tents were struck, extra baggage turned over to the acting quartermaster, Lieutenant N. C. Warner, and we were in readiness to leave camp on the morning of April 25. At ten a.m. the march to Alexandria was commenced; there we took transports and proceeded to Gloucester Point on the York river where we were assigned to the First Brigade, First Division of the Tenth Army Corps, temporarily commanded by Brigadier-General Robert S. Foster, or "Sandy" Foster, as we termed him, while the corps was temporarily under the care of General Alfred H. Terry. We remained at this point for several days, reorganizing the regiments, brigades and divisions of the corps, turning over all surplus equipment and baggage, even to our extra clothing, which was boxed up and either stored away or sent home—thus reducing the command to a fighting condition.

CHAPTER THIRTEEN

"IN THE ARMY OF THE JAMES"

Everything at last was ready, and on the Morning of May 4 we embarked on the transports to accompany General Butler's expedition up the James River to City Point. Meanwhile, the Medical Department had been entirely revised. The Ambulance Corps was organized under the command of a lieutenant, an Antenneith Dispensing Wagon attached to each division, details made for the carrying of hospital knapsacks and stretchers or litters, with two wagons to convey the medical supplies for each brigade. Details were also made of medical officers, hospital stewards, and men for the flying hospital, so that when we took the field everything would be arranged and everybody knows their duty in the active campaign before us. Surgeon Clark was temporarily detached as Chief Medical Officer of the Division an ordered to report to General Foster, which he did on the evening of May 3, Dr. Kurtz of the Eighty-Fifth Pennsylvania supplying his place as Brigade Surgeon.

There was some delay in getting the ambulances and other transportation connected with the Division aboard, but at last everything was ready by 10 p.m. May 4. During the afternoon of this day the steamship *Arago* came in bearing General Gillmore and staff, who was to assume command of the troops at this point. After all was aboard, we moved out into the stream and anchored for the night. We spent some hours on the deck of our steamer in company with General Foster and staff, during the evening, enjoying the scene presented by this vast fleet of vessels at anchor in the river. It seemed like a fairy scene—the brilliant lights of varied colors swinging from the masts; bands of music here and there discoursing lively tunes, and the glorious Stars and Stripes above all, floating and flaunting in a delicious breeze.

At daylight, May 5, the whole fleet got under way and went gallantly down the York River to Chesapeake Bay, reaching Fort Monroe at nine a.m. We halted just long enough to get instructions that ordered us to proceed up the James River. The day was lovely, and we enjoyed the scenery along the river, which was beautiful; often recalling to mind, as we journeyed along, the many reminiscences attaching to General McClellan's campaign on the Peninsula, especially Harrison's Landing, where we could point out the location of our camp in 1862, and the view called up many pleasing as well as sorrowful recollections.

We reached City Point about four p.m. where there were the ruins of some recently burned buildings and where the advance of our fleet had a skirmish with a small body of the enemy. Our

Division did not stop, but proceeded on to Bermuda Hundred, so called from the fact that a settlement was made there by 100 persons from the Island of Bermuda many years ago.

We were now in the "Army of the James," consisting of the Tenth and Eighteenth Army Corps, under the command of General Benjamin F. Butler. General Grant, now Lieutenant-General, [first to hold this position since George Washington] had taken the supreme command of all the Union forces, and with the Army of the Potomac was preparing to move against General Lee by way of the Wilderness, and the Army of the James had been organized for the purpose of moving on Petersburg and Richmond while the attention of the Confederate army was being diverted by Grant.

We landed at Bermuda Hundred and bivouacked for the night in an open field. We were now within 15 miles of Richmond, and only seven from Petersburg. At daybreak we took up the line of march in the direction of Drewry's Bluff. Our progress was very slow, owing to frequent halts made necessary to await the action of the skirmishers. We were almost a full day in making a distance of six miles, and finally bivouacked on the night of May 6, and the following morning made encampment. The men were soon put to work throwing up entrenchments, spades having once more turned up as the trump card in the game. The policy of our commander seemed to be to act on the defensive and to prevent reinforcements being sent to Lee by tearing up the Richmond and Petersburg Railroad, which ran some three miles in front of our position.

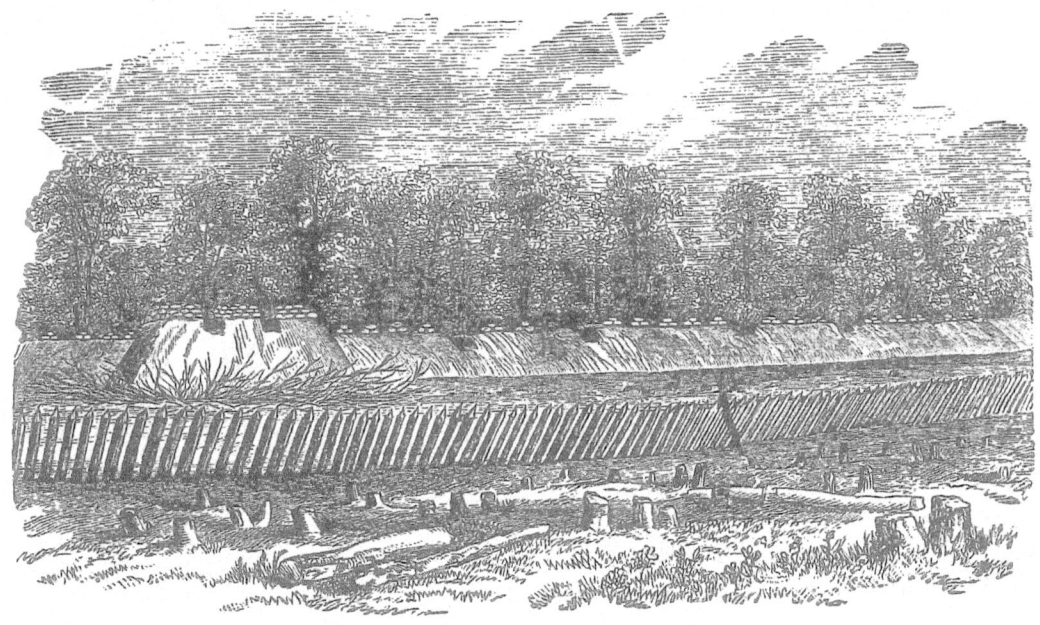

LINE OF DEFENSE—BERMUDA HUNDRED.

The Second Division of the Tenth Corps, in command of General Turner, was ordered out for this purpose on the 7th, and a brisk skirmish with the enemy took place near Chester Heights. Our force succeeded in reaching the railroad and destroyed it for some distance, but gained no other advantage after losing some 250 men. General Beauregard, who commanded the Confederate forces in our front, had succeeded in reinforcing Petersburg the previous night; otherwise, the results would have been different.

General Mann recalled some years later:

"When Butler's expedition up the James river landed at Bermuda Hundred, Virginia, the Thirty-Ninth Illinois was the first regiment to debark, and was immediately deployed on either side of the road leading to Petersburg; skirmishers were sent forward, and the Regiment was gradually advanced to make room for the other troops of the expedition. Evening found us about two and a half miles from the landing.

"About this time I heard great cheering at the rear, which was renewed several times, each time coming nearer; and looking for the cause, I saw General Butler and his entire staff approaching on the main road. When they reached my outer line I halted them. General Butler asked if we had seen any 'rebs' in the front. I told him that several squads of cavalry had appeared about a quarter of a mile distant. After examining a large chart the General said that he desired to go forward to a creek with a small church beside it, thence down the creek about one-fourth mile, and back to our line, forming, as he said, a triangle in the scout. I offered to advance my command to the creek, saying to the General that it would be safer for his party. I was thanked and told to hold my men as they were, but to instruct them to admit his party on their return. I looked for an episode, and it soon came.

"Butler and staff galloped to the front. The country was quite level (called the Ware Bottoms), and excepting scattering pine trees was quite open for some distance around us. Securing a commanding view from a tree stump, I soon saw the General's party halt on the banks of 'Butler's Creek' (as it was subsequently called by the men of the Thirty-Ninth), close to Ware Bottom Church. Field-glasses were brought into use and the 'unpenetrated beyond' was carefully explored. Soon the party turned to the left, intending to run out the base of their triangle, but it was never completed. At this moment there sprang from behind a dense thicket of alder bushes on the opposite side of the creek a squad of rebel horse, who yelled 'Halt!' and fired their carbines. Butler had no armed escort and but two mounted orderlies, both of whose horses fell dead to the ground and their riders were taken prisoners. Butler and his staff came dashing through the tall pines back to our lines with more regard to speed than order of coming. The prisoners were taken to Petersburg that night, and the name and fame of their chief, who had so narrowly escaped death or capture, was revealed. Before the next night the *Petersburg Morning Index* was in our lines where we saw a full account of the affair.

"It appears that a Confederate Major, with over 200 horsemen, was carefully concealed beyond the creek, eagerly waiting for General Butler and his staff to cross over. The papers scored the Major most fearfully, for not capturing the 'beast,'[6] and called on the authorities at Richmond to discipline him for neglect of duty. It is quite safe to conclude that General Butler was seldom found in front of the skirmish line after this experience."

Doctor Clark also reminiscences that, "After landing at Bermuda Hundred the Thirty-Ninth were advanced out on the Petersburg road, and Captain O. F. Rudd, of Company G, had charge of the skirmish line. About two p.m. a man approached on horseback, and of course was halted; and upon being questioned, stated that he was a Doctor, and said that he had a very sick patient near the landing whom he desired to visit. He was quite a venerable-looking fellow, very polite, and seemed honest. He was placed under guard, however, and sent to General Butler, who, on learning his business, also furnished him with a military escort, to visit his patient. House after house was visited, but no invalid was to be found, and matters began to wear a suspicious look. Upon a close examination into the case, and feeling satisfied that the doctor had some other motives in passing our lines than the one given, General Butler ordered him in arrest and sent him to the '*Rip Raps*' off Fort Monroe. This man proved to be Dr. Howlett, whose splendid mansion a short distance up the James river soon give name to the celebrated Howlett House Battery, planted the by the Confederates to enliven Butler's proceedings on the 'Dutch Gap' canal."

On May 12 General Butler sent out a still heavier force under Generals Gillmore and "Baldy" Smith, which forced the rebels back on Fort Darling, where they were entrenched. At two o'clock on the morning of May 14 the Thirty-Ninth were ordered to advance, being called upon to guard an ammunition train to the front. We reached the front at two p.m. and at five o'clock received orders to advance to the extreme left of General Gillmore's line to support a battery of artillery quite near the railroad. While advancing, the rebels opened up a lively firing with grape and canister, and the men were ordered to lie down. Colonel Osborn, however, still remained upon his horse, "Old Mack," and here it was that he received a wound in the right elbow-joint the first and last hit of the war, and which confined him to hospital for some months, and today he carries a stiff arm with the "souvenir" the rebels gave him somewhere embedded in the joint. Colonel Osborn remained on the field until his Regiment occupied the desired position, and then reported at the field hospital, only because forced to do so from pain and loss of blood. Patient search was made for the ball which had lodged in the joint, but it could not be found; and after giving the limb a dressing the Colonel was directed to go back to our camp within the entrenchments. The following morning, without waiting for another examination, he mounted his horse and rode to Bermuda Hundred landing, where he took

---

[6]The South hated General Butler and called him the "Beast of New Orleans" because of Butler's treatment of the citizens of New Orleans during the Federal occupation. Butler wrote an order that inflamed the Confederacy. This notorious Order Number 28 stated: "As the officers and soldiers of the United States have been subject to repeated insults from the women (calling themselves ladies) of New Orleans in return for the most scrupulous noninterference and courtesy on our part, it is ordered that hereafter when any female shall by word, gesture, or movement insult or show contempt for any officer or soldier of the United States she shall be treated as a women of the town plying her avocation."

the hospital boat and was conveyed to Chesapeake Hospital at Fort Monroe. Lieutenant-Colonel Mann, who had been on the sick list for several days, accompanied him for the purpose of giving him assistance and for instruction before going to the front to take command. The Colonel, however, strongly advised him to stay back, for he said "The rebels are going to give us h-e-l-l! The Regiment is fully officered, Major Linton will handle it well; and bear in mind you will soon have a chance to command it in battle."

Notwithstanding this advice, which was emphasized most strongly by the Colonel's painful wound, Lieutenant-Colonel Mann, after seeing Osborn safely to the boat, returned and made his way to the front, reaching there as the Regiment, or what was left of it, was falling back, bravely fighting for each foot of ground almost singlehanded, their support on either flank having retreated almost an hour before.

On his way back the Lieutenant-Colonel saw Sutler Brown, who had become demoralized and shut up shop, and was doubtless on his way to the boat. Brown was reclining at the foot of a tree with his carpet-sack under his head, and was fast asleep.

Colonel Mann, familiar with Brown's habits and concluding that he must have a large sum of money with him, and thinking to give him a good wholesome scare as well as a lesson, removed the gripsack from under his head and placed it behind an adjoining tree. Then remounted his horse he awoke the sutler from his slumbers. Brown's first concern on awaking was his satchel, and finding it gone, he instantly exclaimed in his quick, incisive manner: "Where's my satchel? Where's my satchel? My God! $30,000 in that satchel! and I'm ruined, Sir, RUINED!" and he bustled about like a crazy man. In a few moments the Lieutenant-Colonel, thinking that a sufficient lesson on his folly had been given the now thoroughly frightened man, pointed out the resting place of the wealth, and with one bound the sutler cleared the space that separated him from his god Money, and took up his march to the landing, a wiser man. Begging pardon for this digression, we now resume the thread of our narrative.

The Regiment lay in support of the battery in command of Major S. S. Linton during the night, and on the morning of the 15th, having been provided with spades, dug a trench, throwing up rifle-pits the whole length of their line, for they were exposed to a almost constant fire from the enemy. During the whole of the 15th an intermittent firing was kept up from sharpshooters on both sides, and no sooner would a man expose himself, that he was sure of becoming a target. William H. Jenkins, of Company C, in his enthusiasm, and curious to see what was going on, received the compliments of some watchful "Johnny" in the shape of a bullet in his neck which made a clean passage through his "meat pipe;" and before falling, another ball grazed his shoulder. Jenkins received four different wounds while in the service, the last one of which (October 13, 1864) resulted, after two years of painful suffering, amputation of the thigh, which was done at the "Soldiers Home" in Chicago, after vain endeavors to save the limb.

During the afternoon of the 15th Surgeons Clark and Kittinger had orders to advance with a section of the field hospital nearer the front and prepare for the reception of the wounded from the general assault that had been ordered for the next day. Their tables and shelters were advanced nearly half a mile, having selected a grove near General Butler's headquarters.

At night the surgeons and assistants occupied the Second story of one of the brick outbuildings for a dormitory, and retired early in order to be refreshed for the work of the morrow. All was peaceful until three a.m. when a "Whitworth bolt" from the enemy came crashing through the building just over their heads, scattering bricks and debris in all directions. This was the first gun—the prelude to the opening to the battle of Drewry's Bluff, May 16, 1864, and proved a decided "eye-opener" for the doctors, who scampered out into a dense, foggy atmosphere that completely veiled everything.

CHAPTER FOURTEEN

"Rally on the rifle-pits!"

May 16, 1864

Confederate General Beauregard had anticipated General Butler, and under cover of the fog and darkness made a furious assault on the right of our lines, which unfortunately was a weak point and poorly prepared to receive the shock. The rebel column came on with terrible yells and forced their way through our lines, becoming badly mixed up with our men. Beauregard had evidently discovered the weak point in Butler's right wing the evening before; the extreme right for the distance of a mile to the river being thinly picketed by a single Negro regiment.[7] Beauregard's attack had been successful, the dense fog contributing largely to his efforts. But he was in no condition to follow our forces in their retreat, and by 10:00 a.m. the fighting for the day was over.

It is probably a fact that for a distance of one-half mile beginning at the river there were absolutely no pickets whatever, hence the Confederates were massed on the right flank and in the rear of General Hickman's Brigade, and easily captured a large portion of it.

The surgeons remained in the grove, where bullets began to splatter against the trees thick and fast. They did not know which way to turn, and could see nothing, but could distinctly hear the roar of combat. While debating what course to pursue an "Aid" of General Butler's came hurriedly by, and seeing them, halted and said, "You damn fools! If you don't want to be captured by the enemy, you had better make tracks from here, and lively too! They're closing fast upon us!" The surgeons did not stop to resent this unmannerly address, for the gentlemanly Aid and they retreated to the rear, after securing their instruments and horses, and were soon back to their old place of the preceding day, feeling badly demoralized.

Affairs remained comparatively quiet until eight a.m., when Beauregard advanced on Gillmore's troops occupying the position behind their breastworks at Drewry's Bluff. Massing his column,[8] he made three successive and desperate charges upon our line and each time the enemy was driven

---

[7] 150 mounted men of the Second U. S. Colored Cavalry

[8] Beauregard's column consisted of the General Montgomery Corse's Third North Carolina Cavalry. Moving to the right were the infantry regiments of the Fifteenth, Eighteenth, Thirtieth and Seventeenth Virginia. Continuing across the front to the Chesterfield Courthouse Road were the infantry regiments of the Sixty-First and Fifty-First North Carolina. Across the road were the Twenty-Fourth, Forty-Ninth, Thirty-First, and Eighth North Carolina, the Twenty-Fifth, Forty-Fourth, Sixty-Third, Seventeenth and Twenty-Third Tennessee Infantry Regiments..

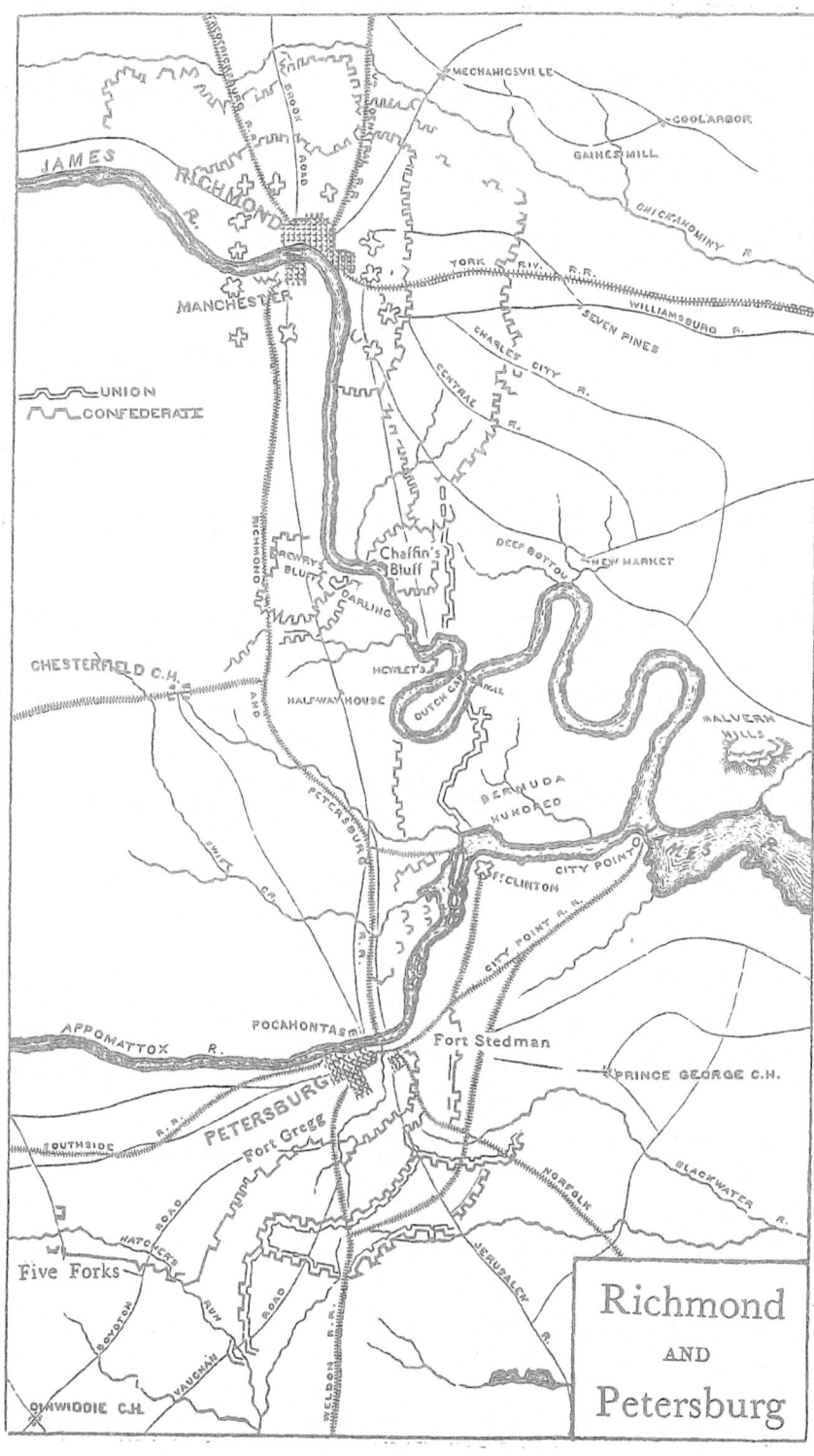

back.[9] The position occupied by the Thirty-Ninth was along an extended line of ridge running through an open field from the Richmond and Petersburg Railroad to a piece of timber on the left. In front was piece of low, open ground. The line of our troops across the railroad was through the timber and extending somewhat in advance of it. The left of the Regiment was entirely unsupported even by a cavalry squad.[10] In order to present a detailed account of the part the Thirty-Ninth took in this battle, the narrative of Captain Homer A. Plimpton is here inserted.

"The Thirty-Ninth was called out early on the morning of the 14th and ordered to guard an ammunition train to the left of the line of advance. At four a.m. it left camp and marched two miles to the Richmond and Petersburg Pike, thence to the railroad a mile farther at Chester Station, where it halted some two hours waiting the arrival of several coal cars that had been discovered up the track. At last it started up the railroad toward our line of battle, which was over two miles in the advance, but it only advanced a short distance when the looked-for cars arrived, and Companies G and I were detached from the Regiment to push the cars to the front for the wounded who had been gathered up and laid by the roadside; the main portion of the Regiment remained near Chester Station to guard the ammunition train. The hotel there was transformed by our surgeons into a hospital for the wounded. As fast as the coal cars would be loaded with the wounded a dozen men or more would push them up to Chester Station and unload, and return to the front for more. Such were the duties of Companies G and I. They had succeeded in removing all of the wounded up to one p.m. when they received orders from General Gillmore to report to him at the front immediately. The balance of the Regiment was brought forward and moved to the left of the line, where in a short time it was assigned to the duty of supporting a portion of the First New Jersey Battery[11]. There was some delay in posting the battery, owing to the incessant and heavy firing of the enemy's skirmishers and sharpshooters, during which time our Regiment had quite a number wounded. The battery having got into position on a rise of ground just to the left of the railroad and in good view and easy range of the rebel fortifications, opened with decided effect.

"Then began a hot contest between the rebel forts and our batteries along the whole line, which continued until darkness set in.

---

[9] Gillmore had strung telegraph wire from timber to fence post to tree stump, all a foot off the ground. They knew that the wire would not stop the Rebels but it would at least slow them down. However, there was none in front of the Thirty-Ninth.

[10] Immediately to the right of the Thirty-Ninth, were the infantry regiments of the Eighty-First and the Ninety-Sixth New York, the Fourth New Hampshire, the Fifty-Fifth Pennsylvania, the 100th New York, the Seventh Connecticut, the 117th New York, Fortieth Massachusetts, and the Sixth Connecticut spread across the lines to the Chesterfield Courthouse Road.

[11] The Fifth Battery of the New Jersey Light Artillery

General Pierre Gustave Toutant Beauregard

Major-General Benjamin F. Butler

Major-General Quincy A. Gillmore

"During the heat of the engagement the Thirty-Ninth moved from the timber in rear of the battery, every man lying flat on the ground for protection as he got his place in line. All of this occurred on the 14th. In passing from the timber and over the open field for a distance of eighty yards the crashing of shells and whiz of balls was terrific, and quite a number of the Regiment were wounded. Colonel Osborn, who was on horseback, was struck in the right elbow by a shrapnel shot, fracturing the bone at the point of the elbow. He continued on duty until dark, when the command of the Regiment was turned over to Major S. S. Linton, the Lieutenant-Colonel, O. L. Mann being in camp sick. The New Jersey battery plied their guns well and bravely, but lost heavily in men and horses. At dark the battery went to the rear and the Thirty-Ninth moved to the right, and the right of the first company (I) rested on the railroad; the Eighty-Fifth Pennsylvania, being the next in line on the right, rested its left on the railroad opposite our right.

"At daylight on the 15th the Regiment retired from the top of the ridge where it had remained during the night and formed a line parallel with its first one, about twenty-five yards to the rear, again lying flat on the ground to avoid the rebel missiles. Companies I and G, being on the right and most exposed, threw up a slight ridge of earthworks in front of them, sufficient to protect the front rank; the other companies did the same, so that by evening a little ridge extended along the front to the extreme left of our line of battle, there being two other regiments on the left of the Thirty-Ninth.

"The day was very quiet until late in the afternoon, when the enemy opened upon us with artillery, doing some mischief. Two men of Company E were killed—Silas Benton and Elisha Karr, and two severely wounded, by one shell.

"The ground between the Thirty-Ninth Illinois and the rebel rifle-pits, about six hundred yards off, was descending, with now and then a shrub to obstruct the vision. On the right was the railroad, along which ran a rail fence, almost obscured by tall grass and shrubs, extending to the rebel rifle-pits; and on the left was a board fence reaching the rebel rifle-pits on the left just at the edge of a small grove of about three acres in area. Beyond the rifle-pits of the enemy the ground was ascending to their line of forts about 400 yards farther back, bringing them on a level with us.

"The night of the 15th was spent by the Regiment in strengthening the works in our front in order that the two ranks might be secure from rebel shell and shot.

"The 16th dawned and the fog was so dense until seven o'clock that it was impossible to discover a man thirty yards off. About four o'clock in the morning the rebels opened on the right, where the Eighteenth Army Corps was stationed, and the firing continued to increase towards the left until seven o'clock, when the regiments on the left of the Thirty-Ninth were ordered to another point, the supposition with us being that a charge was about to be made on a rebel fort just to our right. The Thirty-Ninth then formed in single rank and occupied their own and most of the left trenches, and prepared to do its part should the rebels' make a demonstration in that direction. As the fog arose, we gazed toward the rebel lines to observe their maneuvering, and as a sudden fierce and loud renewal of the strife to our right began we saw slowly wending their way from their pits near the railroad and endeavoring to advance by the flank up the track, two columns of the enemy with flags spread to the breeze, evidently determined on attacking us[12]. Another column was also approaching the left of our Regiment along the fence.[13] All nerved themselves for the contest, believing that much depended upon their holding the position they had been placed in, and knowing that if the enemy attacked them in front they were equal to twice or thrice their own number. But on the columns came, steady and apparently confident; the combat on our right which had raged with great fierceness had become reduced to desultory firing; the men we had out as skirmishers along the fence by the railroad were driven back hurriedly to our breastworks, when we opened on the enemy from the entire line. They returned the fire, and the fighting commenced with energy and determination.

"In the meantime all of the other troops had retired, and an order had been received by our Major for the Thirty-Ninth to retreat; but before he could communicate the order he was severely wounded through the left side, and the Regiment remained in ignorance of the condition all around it, but resolved to hold its own or be driven to some desperate strait. But the column on the railroad was protected from our fire by the high bank on either side, and therefore advanced rapidly and securely; as it got even with our flank resting on the railroad a severe fire was suddenly opened lengthwise with the trench which made the position of the Regiment untenable, and hence the men 'took for the woods' the shortest way under a raking fire of musketry from front and flank. On getting a short distance into the timber, and being under the impression that the balance of the line was perfect, and that by our leaving the position we held the whole line might be flanked, the order was given to 'charge on the trenches,' thus hoping to regain our works. That order was repeated immediately by a dozen voices, and a simultaneous charge, through every one for himself, was made by Companies I, G, and C. The rebels were driven from our line, and by rushing up to the railroad and concentrating our fire on the column passing along it our forces cut it in two, driving half of it back to their works whilst the portion in advance continued on its way within our lines, as we thought.

"The left of our Regiment having by that time learned that a retreat had been ordered, did not come back to the trenches; so the three companies before mentioned were left to triumph in a victory which proved to be of short duration. The column which we had sundered had 'about-faced,' and was coming back slowly and steadily on the railroad track, of which fact we were speedily apprised and also assured that we were surrounded—that our whole line had fallen back. Captain Rudd went to the bank above the railroad at the edge of the timber and ordered the rebels to surrender; they lowered the muzzles of their pieces but advanced slowly, their eyes fixed upon the Captain and the small squad about him as if in doubt what to do. Our men were cautioned not to shoot, a dozen singing out the word at a time. Still the 'rebs' came on, when a shot heedlessly or inadvertently fired by one of the men brought on a volley from the rebel column which set all parley aside. The Captain and his squad

---

[12] The Fifteenth Virginia Infantry Regiment.

[13] The Eighteenth Virginia Infantry Regiment.

turned just in time to escape the rebel bullets. A brisk skirmish then ensued, but the fight was unequal, for the enemy had closed upon us from front and left and the column on the track began to spring into the woods to our rear to prevent our retreat, and we again had to cross the open space between our trench and the timber under a most galling fire. Every man for himself, firing as he could, struck for the timber, but many went but a short distance when they were cut down in their career by the bullets of the enemy and left on the field where they fell. [One of those to fall wounded was Hugh R. Snee]

"The loss in the Regiment was 119 enlisted men and eight officers killed, wounded and missing. Adjutant J. D. Walker and Captain James Wightman, Company C, were mortally wounded. The entire force which so successfully on the 13th retired within our lines of fortifications returned to their camp on the evening of the 16th, badly crippled, and almost decimated in numbers. General Butler assured us, however, that the objects of the move were fully achieved and the whole affair was satisfactory. However that may be, it leaves the bitter cup of sorrow to be drained by many friends and relatives of those who have met a sad fate, meted out to them by the stern realities of battle."

The account of Major (then Captain) Plimpton is, with a few exceptions, correct. The errors have been pointed out to the writer by a letter received from Major S. S. Linton and which in part is here presented.

"Minneapolis, Minn., December 28, 1887.
Dr. C. M. Clark — Dear Comrade:
I find Plimpton's account of the battle of Drewry's Bluff, Virginia, May 16, 1864, to contain a few errors. For example, we never received an order to fall back. The only order we ever received was to 'fill the trenches and hold them,' and that order was received in the early morning.

"Again: — Captain Wightman, of Company C, and Adjutant Walker were both wounded and taken off the field before I was wounded. Also Companies I, G, and C went to the rear on my order to reform in the woods, my idea being to fall back as soon as my command was closed up in two ranks, as we were then in one very thin rank; but they evidently misunderstood my order, as they went back in confusion. I ordered them to halt, in a loud voice, and ran after them in the woods; but not seeing them I ran slowly towards the left of the Regiment and came upon the rear of Company D, which was the center company of the Regiment, intending to order the left wing of the Regiment to fall back, but as I crossed the open space I saw that the right wing had returned to the trenches and were in vigorous combat with the rebels. As I crossed the open space I was struck by a bullet. I saw at once that we must drive the enemy back before we could retreat in order, and I immediately turned to go to the right and assist in driving them back when I got my second and lung wound. I was aware that we were flanked on the right by the rebel line across the road, by seeing the Pennsylvania Regiment in retreat. The Regiment fell back inside of twenty minutes after I was wounded. The men who undertook to carry me back were captured, and it was not over five or ten minutes time before I saw Captain Baker, Company A, with the left wing, and they carried my off the field. Yours, etc., S. S. Linton."

The battle of Drewry's Bluff was in fact the first real battle that the Thirty-Ninth was engaged in, and it lost in killed, wounded and missing 119 officers and enlisted men; and the loss to Butler's army numbered over 3,000. It lasted fully thirteen hours, and was most hotly contested, and in many respects it was a remarkable battle, considering the early morning hour in which it began, the dense fog that obscured the combatants up to seven o'clock, and the surprise and the great superiority in the numbers of the assailants. There were many hand-to-hand encounters and bayonet charges, and many acts of heroism that will never be recounted. The Thirty-Ninth was at one time nearly surrounded by reason of the retreat of the Seventy-Sixth Pennsylvania on the right of the line, but they heroically cut their way out, bringing with them a large number of prisoners. The rebel loss greatly exceeded ours and it was a great disappointment to the rebel leader that he did not crush and destroy Butler's army. The deportment of the Regiment in this battle was such that it received the personal thanks of the General commanding for their display of heroism and endurance. There were many incidents connected with this fight, some painful, but several rather pleasing in character. Adjutant Joseph D. Walker was mortally wounded, and also Captain James Wightman of Company C, at the time that the assault of the second line of rebels had been gallantly repulsed. These officers were so elated with the success of our "boys" that they sprang upon the embankment of earth in front of the pits waving their swords, and calling for cheers, when they were shot down by a volley from rebels on the flank.

Captain N. B. Kendall of Company G (then Corporal) was wounded by a rifle bullet which struck him on the head, causing a severe scalp wound and a great confusion of ideas. McKee of that company says that he passed him just after he was hit, and Kendall was crying out "O! I'm dead! I'm dead!" and the presumption is, that anybody under the same circumstances would have been somewhat "mixed up" as regarded their condition.

After the rebels had succeeded in flanking the position, the right wing fell back, and after getting back some 100 yards, near the timber, an order came to "Rally on the rifle pits!" This order was supposed to have been given by Major Linton, but it proved to be from a rebel officer on the flank. Captain Leroy A. Baker, Company A, was with the Colors at this time, and the boys at this command followed him back with cheers, and on arriving at the pits found the third line of the enemy within short range, and advancing with the confidence of securing an easy victory; but our men, flushed with the pride of two successive victories over the assaulting rebels, and feeling that the honor of the State of Illinois must be maintained by its sole representative in the Army of the James, delivered a steady, well-directed and deadly volley which quickly upset all their calculations, and in a few moments they were in retreat; then turning their attention to the flanking column they succeeded in cutting their way through them, and returned to the entrenchments at Bermuda Hundred.[14]

---

[14] Left to hold the position alone when the other regiments had been ordered to the right, the 550 soldiers from Illinois had been forgotten in the confusion.

At the time the enemy was flanking the line of the Thirty-Ninth, Assistant-Surgeon James Crozier, who had accompanied the Regiment to their position, and Phillip M. Lace, the leader of the band, and who had supervision of the stretcher bearers, thought it about time that they should be retiring from the front, and the following is the version of that attempt as given to the writer by Lace, afterwards;

"You see, Doc, we were laying back some 250 yards from the rifle-pits, watching and waiting for something to 'turn-up.' The 'boys' were all doing their 'level best' and giving the Johnnies particular hell every time they came up. Soon we saw the Regiment on the right of the Thirty-Ninth give way—couldn't stand the pressure, you know; and a body of rebels came swooping around on the flank of 'our boys' and they delivered a lively fire that swept the trenches. Some stray shots came in our direction, and we could see the 'rebs' just more than jumping up around us. Then, Doc, Crozier just went off on a tangent! with coattails flying! and I after him; and when the bullets came singing and whizzing by, we would just drop down and go it on all-fours; then when there would come a little lull and quiet, we would up again, and those long legs of Crozier's would just go flying like a jackass rabbit's. I wish you could have seen us about the time of our liveliest gait! nothing more than shadows, and then half the time invisible by reason of ducking and stumbling. We finally reached a safe position back among our troops, and after so long a chase thought we'd take a little 'nip' of 'Frumenti;' but there was 'nary drop' in the canteen, for a bullet had pierced it and let the whiskey all out."

The Hospital Steamer.

We reached our old camp back of the entrenchments late in the afternoon, where Walker and Wightman had been taken, together with some other wounded men of the Regiment. Wightman was found to be insensible and dying. Adjutant Walker was suffering with a wound in the abdomen, the ball having penetrated the bowels. He was quite anxious about his condition, and wished to be told if he could live. When told that it was impossible, he merely said, "It is well!" which were the last words he spoke to Doctor Clark. He died two hours later. Lieutenant Kingsbury's wound in the arm was of such a nature as to require amputation. Major Linton's wound through the lung was at first considered mortal, but happily he made a good recovery in general hospital. Our wounded were sent as soon as possible to Bermuda Hundred and there placed on transports and taken to Fort Monroe.

Private Ezra A. Cook, Company G later wrote for the Regimental History,

"As we came into line of battle Saturday afternoon, [May 14, 1864] in easy range and in plain sight of the rebel works, a shell burst amongst us, a piece of it striking Colonel Osborn's elbow, and a large piece, the force of which was nearly spent, striking a comrade near me on his side, and though it knocked him over, as it was the smooth or rounded side that struck him, he was simply bruised by it. There we lay till dark, under an incessant fire of both artillery and infantry, and if ever a lot of men got weary lying on the ground, we certainly did. But the darkness hid us, and during the night some one got hold of a shovel, and with the single shovel (I think there was but one) a ditch was dug which, with the dirt from it, made a great protection to all who chose to sit or kneel in the ditch.

"Bullets were constantly whizzing by us, and several were hit. A comrade close by me, had his throat cut by a bullet on Sabbath morning, while eating his breakfast.

"The Richmond and Petersburg Railroad ran through the battlefield, the main body of the army extending from the railroad to the James river on the right, but the Thirty-Ninth extended from the railroad to the left. Early Monday morning, in a dense fog, the rebels made a furious attack on the entire line and the right seemed to yield at once. Skirmishers in front of our line gave the alarm and we were ready for them and opened on them 'fire by file!' Under our incessant fire the line soon wavered and broke. The lifting fog gave us a good view of them. Line after line formed and advanced to the same fate. The sound of battle, however, soon told us that the battle line on our right had been forced back of us, and a galling fire was opened on our flank by a force just across the railroad. We retreated in good order to the edge of the woods, a few yards away, when every man seemed to yell, Halt! We paid our respects to the 'Johnnies' across the railroad, who soon ran, and then the cry was passed, 'Hurrah for our ditch!' I think the man who started that cry was a new recruit close by me, for I first heard it from him, but it was echoed all along the line. He furnished us an excellent example of valor without discipline. Noticing that his bayonet was not fixed I told him to fix bayonet and was not surprised to learn, on asking him, that his gun was empty. He loaded quickly, and was ready to start with us by the time our rallying cry had passed down the line, and away we went, and hustled out the few rebels who had got into our ditch. Brave Captain Rudd was the only commissioned officer I saw with us. Soon after our return to our ditch a rebel force appeared directly in our rear and close at hand.

"Surrender!" yelled the rebel leader. 'Surrender yourself!' answered Captain Rudd. 'Fire!' yelled the rebel, and every man of us fell flat. 'Up and at them!' commanded Captain Rudd, and with a volley, a yell, and the bayonet, that rebel force was cleared out in less time than it takes to recount the fact. It was evidently time for us to join the main body of the army, then far in our rear, as we could tell by the noise of battle; so we leisurely withdrew, following the course of the railroad.

"Sergeant Spencer brought up the rear, and when out of sight of the rebels behind us, he stepped up to the railroad, which was there about breast high, and seeing a squad of 'Johnnies,' let drive, and called to me asking if I did not want a good shot. I ran over, and as he stood loading I threw my gun into the fork of a sapling and took deliberate aim at one of the squad just across the railroad. With the report of my gun, I heard Spencer yell, 'Cook!' and turned to find a large rebel force right on to me, certainly not fifteen feet away. The dense underbrush had concealed their approach. Just as I faced them one of them fired and shattered my right hand, and the stock of my gun just in front of the lock. The ball and two of the three buckshot tore through the inside of my hand, and nipped the end of the little finger. I then turned and ran the gauntlet of a perfect cyclone of bullets, amid yells of 'Halt!' 'Surrender!' 'Shoot him!' 'Kill him!' and other choice greetings. The dense underbrush favored me, and through bullets through my clothing told how narrow was my escape, I speedily overtook Sergeant Spencer and we were soon our of sight of our pursuers.

"On seeing that I was wounded, Sergeant Spencer insisted on taking my gun which I still held on to, and then I saw he had lost his. He said that on hearing a noise behind him he turned, and, seeing the rebels, started to run, when he found his gun caught by a root or branch, and so he left it.

"I had become much attached to that rifled musket, and hoped to take it home with me, as we were told we would be allowed to buy them, but I have not seen it since, as poor Spencer received a wound from which he died, but a short time afterwards.

"Before we overtook the Company I became very weak from loss of blood, and but for the fact that I got a chance to soak my wound in the cold swamp-water, and wrap it in a large handkerchief also wet, I should probably have soon fainted. As it was I could hardly keep my feet with the aid of a comrade.

"Some coal-cars had been captured, and in these many of the wounded were conveyed towards the field hospital. I was helped into one of these, and soon felt better, as the chill from the cold water had checked the bleeding. When we came to another group of wounded men and I saw there was not room for them all, I climbed out and started on foot for the camp at Bermuda Hundred, walking just behind an ambulance. Just a we got in sight of the hospital the cry was raised, 'Rebel cavalry! Rebel cavalry are coming!'

"The fields and roads were full of stragglers, most of them Colonel Dandy's New York Regiment [100th New York Volunteers], and as this rebel cavalry cry was raised I saw Colonel Dandy trying to rally his men. Pointing his revolver at a group of men on the run towards camp he would yell 'Halt!' and they would stop till he turned to another squad, when they ran on again. A moment after, the rebels with a yell and a volley were upon them, and doubtless most of them were captured. A squad of rebels even fired into the ambulance that I had been following, and though they may not have hurt any one in it the did wound one of the horses. I think this ambulance escaped capture, for from my hiding place in the underbrush I saw them dashing along at a furious rate, one horse apparently on three legs, he was so badly wounded.

"As I was not in fighting trim, though I had picked up a sword, which I carried into camp, I kept out of sight till the cavalry dash was over, and then quietly proceeded to camp.

"The coal-car in which I rode a short distance was captured with its occupants, and poor Luscomb, of my own company, whom I left in it, with a wound in the arm, died in the rebel hospital at Petersburg.

"During that night what was left of the Thirty-Ninth arrived in camp, and the next morning I was glad to restore to its owner the sword I had picked up on the battlefield. It belong to Lieutenant Kingsbury, of Company E, whose arm was being amputated when I sent the sword to his tent for him.

"Though my wound was then painful, I had no idea that it was of so serious a character as it proved to be. The following morning the rebels attacked our camp, and with the bullets whistling around me I was sent to the Brigade Field Hospital, thence to Fort Monroe, and from there by boat to the great Government Hospital on David's Island, New York harbor. By this time I began to realize my right hand was a mass of torn flesh; gangrene soon developed, and I became very weak and restless from the intense pain, especially when the flesh was being burned with bromide, as it was daily.

"To my rigid temperance principles I owe my right hand, without doubt. Whiskey was sent in for my use, as it was for all the severely wounded, and I feared I would be forced to take it. On appealing to Surgeon Thompson he said I should have the best wine there was in the hospital instead of whiskey. I stated my objections to all stimulants, and was not a little astonished to find that Dr. Thompson's views exactly coincided with mine. He explained that he was under authority and had orders to furnish stimulant to those who were weak from wounds, but was not under orders to force men to take them; so it was agreed that I should take none, and the decision was rigidly adhered to. I bore the terrible pain of cutting and burning my wound without anything to deaden it. The flesh was cut and burned away clear to the bone, leaving the large cords on the right side of my hand entirely bare, the flesh around and beneath them being removed, and while dressing the wound one morning an artery burst, and Dr. Thompson worked over me the entire day, not less than seven hours consecutively, not leaving even for his dinner. The gangrene had at last been cut and burned away, and my hand began to heal, and was a marvelous sight. Hundreds, many of soldiers who had lost a limb, came to look at it when it was being dressed. It seemed as if you could see the new flesh grow while you were looking at it. I was assured by the hospital attendants that the saving of my hand seemed almost miraculous. They supposed, as soon as they saw it, that it would have to be amputated, and did not believe Dr. Thompson could save it. While I was there limbs less seriously wounded were daily amputated, and an officer with a flesh wound in the arm died of lockjaw. The muscles of my hand contracted so as to draw my hand around at nearly a right angle with my arm, and it was double its normal thickness when it was healed five months after I was wounded, and I had very imperfect control of my fingers. Dr. Thompson recommended that I should, whenever I could, whether sitting or standing, gently strain on my hand and fingers till they were straight, and the plan proved effective, though it took fully five years to accomplish it.

"It was evident that my days of military service were over, and I learned soon after I reached the hospital that my discharge was recommended, but it did not reach me till August 23, just eleven days before my time was out, when I naturally hurried home."

Private Martin Van Buren Peters of Company F also wrote for the Regimental History:

"I was in the terrible battle at Drewry's Bluff, Virginia, where so many of our Regiment were killed and wounded. I was also on the skirmish line at Bermuda Hundred, Virginia, where stumps and trees were in good demand. Some minie balls had whistled were close to me, when a comrade sung out, 'Don't you see that reb shooting at you?' 'No!' said I; 'where?' and just then along came another, and it struck a small sapling close by and went so near through it as to bulge the bark on the opposite side. I saw the smoke of the gun that fired it, then saw his head appear from behind his tree; then his neck and breast; he was looking for me, and I had changed position. Then I let him have the contents of my gun; but whether I hit him or not, he did not trouble me any more.

"Ere long, as I was loading, a shot came from another direction, the bullet striking me at the outside corner of my left eye, tearing the flesh away and chipping the bone. It turned my partly around. I did not know what had struck me at first—thought my comrade and struck me, and asked him what he did it for. 'I didn't strike you!' he said; 'You're wounded, man!' and by this time I began to think so, too, as the blood was streaming down my face in a rivulet. It was a close call. I was soon all right again, however.

"In October, 1864, I was transferred to Company F, Eleventh Regiment of the Invalid Corps, and assisted in guarding the assassins of our noble President."

First Sergeant Emile Guntz, Company K had been a photographer at the outbreak of the war. He was to take many of the soldiers tin-types on Folly and Morris Island. He later related to Dr. Clark for the Regimental History:

"...I was captured at the battle of Drewry's Bluff, May 16, 1864. That was the time my hardships commenced. We were in retreat at the time, and got onto the railroad track, when we saw a lot of cavalry coming towards us and thought they were our men, but we got badly fooled. The first thing we knew we were ordered to throw down our guns, 'You Yankee sons of bitches.' We were driven like a lot of hogs on a run, with revolvers at our heads. We were taken to Macon, Georgia, and there robbed of all we possessed, them telling us they would return everything in a few days, when we would be paroled; but that day had never come. Stayed there a few days and were then taken to Savannah, Georgia, and put in a bull pen—hardly enough room to stand in; no shelter of any kind and nothing to eat for 24 hours; and when we did get anything it was a pint of cornmeal and about two ounces of bacon.

"We stayed there about two weeks, when we received orders to get ready—that we were going to be exchanged; and oh! weren't we happy! A happier lot of men you never saw. But we were to be disappointed. We were put on board a train of cattle and open cars, packed in like so many hogs, and away we went, not to our lines, but to that hell-hole, Andersonville, the most God-forsaken place that men were ever put in—not fit for cattle.

"I don't think there is any use of my giving a detailed account of our hardships and sufferings while there, for I imagine there is not a person in the United States who has not heard of or read about it. I might fill a book twice as large as this one.

"At one time we received the news that Sherman coming to set us free. Then they moved us to Millen, and in going there the train ran off the track and I was thrown out of the car and received a severe bruise that I feel to this day. We were then taken back to Andersonville, when Wirz said it was a pity that it had not killed all of us 'Yankee sons of bitches.' After that we received hardly anything to eat except about half a pint of cornmeal a day, and not fit for hogs to eat.

"I don't see how any of us ever lived to get out of there. Many of our brave soldiers were left there. We used to quarrel to get a chance to carry out one of our dead comrades, so that we could get a little wood to cook our cornmeal.

"At last we received notice that we were going to be exchanged. We were taken to Savannah again, where we found out that instead of being exchanged they were going to take us to Mobile, Alabama, excepting those who could not move any further, and these were to be paroled, and I managed to get among them. We were put on board and taken out to where 'Uncle Sam' was waiting for us, and that was the happiest moment of my life, when I saw the old Stars and Stripes one more.

"I think that is where our Government made a great mistake—letting our soldiers starve in those Rebels Hells. They might just as well have exchanged us, and I don't think it would have helped the Confederacy any. Wirz made his brags that he could do more for the cause by killing our men in prisons than they could in battle.

"I was, in all, in prison nine months, and it seemed to me so many years. I don't see how anybody who went through those rebel prisons can ever forget. I never will, for I lost part of my hearing, and my eye-sight has been very poor since, and is getting worse, all from exposure when there.

"We then received a furlough to go home, and in about three months I joined the Regiment again, when I went through all the hardships with them, until we were mustered out at Springfield, Illinois, in 1865."

CHAPTER FIFTEEN

"We will drive these rebels to hell!"

General Butler's force numbered some 26,000 men when it was again behind the entrenchments, and it was said that he proposed to cross the Appomattox river and advance on Petersburg; but before his plans could be put into execution General Grant ordered the Eighteenth Army Corps and a portion of the Tenth Army Corps to reinforce the Army of the Potomac at Cold Harbor. This was a disappointing blow to Butler at this time, depriving him of the means of making any move whatever, "bottling him up,"[15] as he expressed it in a letter to General Grant. General Butler was an ambitious man as well as an able one, and he may have been a great military genius, but the result of the battle of May 16 did not prove it, and failed to satisfy General Grant.

The Regiment was permitted to remain quiet in camp, taking a rest that was so much needed, until the afternoon of the 20th, when they were ordered out for the purpose of cooperating with the balance of the Brigade in the recapture of a line of rifle-pits that the enemy had wrested from our troops a few hours previously. The preceding attack had been made during the night by the rebels and was chiefly directed against the line held by the Brigade under command of General Ames. For the space of half an hour the cannonading was terrific, and the volleys of musketry were incessant. Twice the enemy attempted to break through the lines and came forward with a rush—screaming and howling like a pack of hungry wolves, but each time they were hurled back with fearful slaughter and only succeeded in occupying the first line of rifle-pits, which our Brigade was ordered to recapture. The Brigade was under the temporary command of Colonel Joshua B. Howell, and we cannot do better than give Colonel Howell's report of this engagement that it fails to mention the fact that when the charge was made the Thirty-Ninth succeeded in occupying their part of the line, while the Sixty-Seventh Ohio, which charged with them, found their work too hot and fell back, which necessitated the falling back of the Thirty-Ninth.

Both regiments soon reformed and again advanced, carrying everything before them until the line of pits was occupied, the "rebs" slinking back to the cover of the woods, leaving their dead and wounded behind them.

---

[15]Beauregard's defenses across the neck of the Bermuda Hundred peninsula only prevented Butler from moving his forces west against the Richmond and Petersburg Railroad. He was however, capable of moving any other direction. The Eighteen Corps departure and Buter's raid on Petersburg disclosed that ability.

COLONEL HOWELL'S OFFICIAL REPORT

"Headquarters First Brigade,
First Division Tenth Army Corps.
May 21, 1864

Captain Adrian Terry, Asst. Adj't General

"Captain: I have the honor respectfully to report to you for the information of the Brigadier-General commanding the Division, the operations and result of the fight of yesterday by the troops under my command.

"At two p.m. yesterday, I received the order from Brigadier-General Terry, commanding the Division, to take with me the Thirty-Ninth Illinois and Sixty-Seventh Ohio Volunteers, two regiments of my Brigade—the Eighty-Fifth Pennsylvania Volunteers being already there at the front and under fire—and the Sixth Connecticut Volunteers, and proceed to the front, assume command of all the troops already there, and retake the ground and position which had been lost in the morning, and recapture the rifle-pits, and reestablish the line and hold it. It was suggested to me by General Terry, that I should go out in advance of my Brigade to the picket line and see the state of things existing, then the nature of the ground, etc. I went out at once, and the wisdom and propriety of the General's direction struck me as soon as I came on the ground. I found the Eighty-Fifth Pennsylvania Volunteers in very imminent peril of being overwhelmed by the superior force of the enemy. It was boldly sustaining itself. The Lieutenant-Colonel (Campbell) commanding that regiment has since told me that ten minutes later and my old Regiment would have been crushed.

"The Sixth Connecticut Volunteers had been ordered out before I left the entrenchments—I passed them on my way out. That regiment came promptly and boldly up under its brave and gallant leader, Major Kline. I formed it in line of battle, threw it rapidly forward. It was succeeded by the Sixty-Seventh Ohio Volunteers (noble and brave Regiment—officers and men); they came up on the double-quick. I threw that regiment forward, also the Thirty-Ninth Illinois Volunteers; they came up bravely on the double-quick and were formed in the general line of battle on the run. These three regiments went forward with cheers, directing their fire rapidly, steadily and with low aim. I never saw troops behave better; the fire of the enemy was very rapid and very heavy, but my brave boys dashed forward gallantly. We drove the enemy, and soon made a connected line of battle with the Eighty-Fifth Pennsylvania Volunteers, Lieutenant-Colonel Campbell, and with the 142nd New York Volunteers, Colonel Curtis commanding.

"I communicated the fact to General Terry by Captain Hooker, my acting Assistant-Adjutant-General, that my troops were all engaged. I received an order from General Terry directing me to swing my right towards the left and recapture the rifle-pits and hold them. That order was promptly obeyed and carried into successful execution. We drove the enemy like the wind, captured and re-occupied the rifle-pits and held them firmly. Directly after taking the rifle-pits, Brigadier-General Walker of the rebel force dashed out on the road in front of the rifle-pits and was wounded and immediately captured by Company C of the Sixty-Seventh Ohio Volunteers and sent in as a prisoner.

"It was a brave and gallant fight by all the brave and gallant officers and men who constituted my command, and engaged in it. I never saw officers and men behave better. Their promptness, zeal, dashing and daring courage was beautiful—their fire steady and deadly to the enemy.

"I beg leave respectfully to recapitulate the name of these regiments, for I love to repeat them and honor them. The Sixth Connecticut Volunteers, Major Kline commanding, temporarily assigned to me; the Eighty-Fifth Pennsylvania Volunteers, Lieutenant-Colonel Campbell commanding; Sixty-Seventh Ohio Volunteers, Colonel Voris commanding, Thirty-Ninth Illinois Volunteers, Lieutenant-Colonel Mann, commanding.

"I regret to have it to say that the brave and valuable officer, Lieutenant-Colonel Mann, was badly wounded in the leg in the action. It is an honorable mark of distinction, and was gallantly won by him. I am glad to say he is now doing very well. There were two brave officers of the Eighty-Fifth Pennsylvania wounded also.

"You can for an idea of the severity of the fire through which my command dashed and drove the enemy, when I say to you that in about thirty minutes I lost 149 men, killed and wounded. The casualties of the fight have already been reported to you. They amounted to some 300 killed and wounded; none missing. The enemy's loss we now know to be 800 in killed and wounded.

"I beg leave to speak in the highest terms of praise of the valuable services rendered me by the officers of my staff in that action—Captain Hooker, my acting Assistant-Adjutant-General, Captain Dawson, Brigade Inspector, and Lieutenant McGregor my Aide-de-camp. Their promptness, activity and efficiency are deserving of the highest praise.

"In this connection, Captain, I beg leave to refer to the valuable service of my Medical Director, Dr. Charles M. Clark, Surgeon of the Thirty-Ninth Illinois Volunteers. His zeal, energy, courage and skill are deserving of the highest praise. His thorough knowledge of his profession and his skill in the practice of it, secures to all the wounded the greatest care and attention and has saved many a limb from the amputating knife.

"I am grateful to know that my brave command and myself received the commendations of our gallant and distinguished leaders, Major-General Gillmore and Brigadier-General Terry.

"I have to honor to be, Captain, with great respect,

Your Obed't Servant,
Joshua B. Howell"

Lieutenant-Colonel Mann was wounded in the early part of the engagement by a musket ball in the lower third of the left leg. The ball passed completely through the large bone (tibia) of the leg, lodging beneath the skin; and the curious circumstance in the case was, that the bone was not fractured—merely a hole punched through it. After his wound was dressed, he was sheltered for the night in a corn-crib near by, and the next morning was sent on a stretcher with a detail of six men to the hospital boat at the landing, and taken to Chesapeake Hospital at Fort Monroe.

Private George Riddle, Company I related to Dr. Clark,

"There is one thing I do feel proud over, and always shall, and that was carrying Captain Sam Gilmore off the field at Drewry's Bluff on the 16th of May 1864, when he was wounded. When we started to leave the works, I was with him alone, but soon came across comrade Asa Wren. He helped me a short distance. We put the Captain astride of my gun, and then put the gun on our shoulders, the Captain holding around my neck. We carried him some distance in this way until Wren gave out. I then took the Captain on my shoulder, and had carried him a short distance when I saw the rebel cavalry gaining on me, and also saw a number of our cavalry about the same distance away from me that the rebels were. I told the Captain that I couldn't carry him any further. He said, 'Oh, God! George, don't leave me!' I told him that I would save him, and laid him down and started for out for our cavalry, and fortunately one of them saw me. I beckoned him to me, and placed the Captain behind me. By this time the rebels were within a short distance of us. The cavalryman asked me, 'What, in the name of God, are you going to do?' I told him to take care of the Captain and I would take care of myself, and when he started I grabbed hold of the stirrup of his saddle, and I tell you, I held on for dear life until we reached the railroad, where I saw an old log lying partly up off the ground. I was 'play'd out,' so I threw myself down under it, panting like a lizard. Lots of our wounded had been left there. The rebel cavalry had come up by this time. All at once I saw comrades John Berry and Jeff Everts pop out of the brush just as the 'Johnnies' came along, and the 'rebs' called upon Berry to surrender or they would fire upon him. Berry was an Englishman, and as brave as a brick! He looked up at the 'rebs' and told them to go to 'y-ell!' for he had been under a 'ot fire all day, 'eny 'ow; and he struck out for the brush with the rebels after him, while I crawled from behind the log and struck for the brush also. We all three came out all right, and the cavalryman brought in the Captain."

Riddle also commented that "I had some pretty close calls—was at 'Wagner,' had my gun smashed in my hand at Drewry's Bluff, a button shot off my coat at Hatcher's Run, and several other close calls too tedious to mention."

The loss sustained by the Regiment in this engagement amounted to seventy officers and men, killed and wounded; no missing; and the loss to the Brigade was 300.

The following is General (then Lieutenant-Colonel) Mann's account of this battle:

"After the repulse the Army of the James had met with on the 16th of May at Drewry's Bluff, there had been more or less severe fighting almost daily, and on the morning of the 20th, at Ware Bottom Church, the enemy seemed determined to crowd our forces as near to the James River as was possible. Soon after two p.m., a vigorous charge was made by a Confederate division, led by General Walker of South Carolina, on a Brigade of General Terry's Division, under command of Brigadier-General Ames. The enemy were driven back after a stubborn resistance and gained an eminence of advantage to them and soon began to throw up earthworks.

"An hour later General Terry rode to our camp, and calling together the Brigade and Regimental commanders, spread out a chart of the field to be retaken, and said he 'expected the First Brigade to do the work with neatness and dispatch.'

"The Brigade, under the command of the brave and venerable Colonel Howell, moved out with promptness to its bloody task. Less than two miles from camp they reached the contested ground and deployed into line to the left of the main road, cheered by the roar of artillery whose shot and shell soon began their deadly work, and the hiss of smaller missiles whose mission was equally fatal. The Thirty-Ninth was on the extreme right and like the other regiments, was soon almost lost to view in the dense undergrowth which all this time had veiled the enemy from us, although we were constantly receiving their metallic and murderous compliments. The Thirty-Ninth was making its way through the thick chaparral, firing, in the meantime, like the veterans they were, when an officer rode up to me and said:

"For God's sake, cease firing! You are killing the men of a New York Regiment in front of you. Cease! Cease!"

"Are you sure of that?" I inquired.

"Certainly I am; the rebels have fallen back sometime ago."

"I then gave the command to cease firing, ordered the acting adjutant to pass the word down the line, and requested my informant to order the New York regiment in our front to 'cease firing' also.

"A few moments later Lieutenant-Colonel Cumminger of the Sixty-Seventh Ohio Volunteers, appeared on the right, mounted on his old iron-gray horse, and said to me, 'Why are you not fighting?' The reason was given, when Lieutenant-Colonel Cumminger replied, 'Not so, at all!! Nothing but rebels in our front. I have just seen them there, and rode here to ascertain why you were not firing.'

"I was about to order the Regiment up and forward, when I thought I would mount an old pine stump of great size near by and see what I could for myself. The large stump proved a mere shell from decay, and I had scarce mounted when it collapsed and encase me in the ruins. The few of the Regiment who saw the ridiculous plight I was in, rushed to my assistance, thinking I had been wounded. I saw nothing, however, but some of the enemy's dead and wounded just in our advance, and was satisfied as to whom we were facing, and the boys were soon on their feet again and doing splendid execution, through fighting by faith rather than by sight.

"Well under way again, I found myself to the right and front of the Regiment, urging them forward and hurriedly sighing for the brave fellows who were falling in the ranks, when I received a bullet in my left leg below the knee joint which barred me from active field duty during the continuance of the war. We had been under fire for about twenty minutes and had crowded our way over a broad space of contested ground, but excepting the dead and wounded over whom we passed I did not see a Confederate soldier in that battle.

"Captain Baker of Company A now took command and most ably led the Regiment out of the entangling bushes into a small open space. In the woods, at the further border of this clearing, the 'Johnnies' were plainly visible, some throwing up earthworks and others hastening their retreat behind them. It was but the work of a few moments and the Brigade was charging on the double-quick over the open space upon the rebels, who, surprised at the audacity of the assault, fled in confusion to the dense woods beyond. Our orders were to capture and hold the line of works, hence there was a halt here. Orders were issued to 'change front to rear' on the works the rebels had commenced.

"At this time, and before skirmishers had been sent into the woods, there appeared a Confederate mounted officer issuing from a thick growth of young pines. He saw that he was covered by a regiment of Union guns, and he subsequently told me at Chesapeake Hospital, that his first impulse was to surrender, so complete was his surprise; then he thought that by means of a little strategy he might escape. He would impersonate a Union officer. So raising his hand, he shouts: 'Hold your position firmly, boys, I will ride back for reinforcements and we will drive these rebels to hell!'

"Here the fine charger he bestrode presented a broad side to a score of hungry muskets in the hands of men whose keen and experienced eyes had discerned the ruse, and the next moment the rider and horse lay bleeding at our feet. The horse was dead, the receptacle of ammunition to make a 'brevet' arsenal. The gallant rider was General [William S. 'Live Oaks'] Walker of South Carolina, whose division had been making the day lively from the time of their arrival from Charleston early that morning. Our prisoner was wounded in the arm, in the right side, and in the left leg so severely that amputation was necessary, which was performed that night at the headquarters of the Corps Commander, General Q. A. Gillmore, with whom our distinguished prisoner had been a classmate at West Point.

"It was on this occasion that the great kindness of heart and the matchless courtesy of Colonel Howell were very pleasingly illustrated. The moment General Walker fell, Colonel Howell bounded over the earthworks and approaching him asked, with a preliminary salute, if he could assist him in any way. "Certainly," said the prisoner. 'Take me into your lines as soon as possible; my entire division will be here in a few moments and I shall be under a crossfire if not removed."

"Thank you, Sir!" said Colonel Howell, this time lifting his hat—"thank you, Sir! order them on at once; I shall be very glad to meet your entire division." General Walker was taken to the rear, but his entire division failed to make their appearance."

It may be interesting to comrades to know what Thomas P. Kettell, a noted historian of some note if not of accuracy, says of this engagement in his history of the "Great Rebellion" published in 1865. He says:

"In an attempt to retake the rifle-pits, the Ninety-Seventh Pennsylvania Volunteers [it should be the Eighty-Fifth] and the Thirteenth Illinois [it should read the Thirty-Ninth] Regiment were ordered to move through the skirt of the woods to cooperate with a movement made by another portion of General Gillmore's forces. Misunderstanding the order, the troops were moved by the flank along the skirt of the woods. Marching steadily forward, they came unexpectedly upon a battery, which opened a murderous crossfire, literally mowing them down. It appeared to the looker-on as though the entire force melted away before this terrific rain of grapeshot and canister. The loss is estimated at 300. The rebel General Walker was dangerously wounded, and captured."

If this author had watched the course and conquests of these two regiments until they stood victors at Appomattox, he would have concluded that the "melting away" process had not been very effective. They fought in the same Brigade on the 20th of May 1864, and did not march under any crossfire of the enemy.

The Field Hospital.

Doctor Clark later related a ludicrous incident which occurred at the field hospital just after the fight at Ware Bottom Church.

"When night approached, Colonel Mann, who had passed through the ordeal of Surgeon Clark's anesthetics, scalpels, and prophylactics, was removed from the shade of a spreading oak and placed by the Doctor's order, in a large brick smoke house for the night, it being the best accommodation at hand. Near midnight, an officer displaying the rank of a Lieutenant of Cavalry stuck a light at the door and desired to know who was there. On being told, he demanded that the patient vacate the place at once, as it was to be searched for silver plate which one of his dusky attendants, now as soldier, assured him had been buried there by his former master.

"A little deliberation, and the patient told the officer that it would be necessary for the surgeon to direct his removal, and a guard stationed nearby was sent for Dr. Clark. The door was closed, and it was determined that the Doctor should send for assistance and a stretcher, and the prospectors were so advised.

"A moment later the Doctor returned, and with him a corporal and four armed soldiers. The Surgeon now placed the Lieutenant and his two soldiers in arrest. A parley followed, in which the Lieutenant insisted that the wounded officer was resting over much wealth, and that one-half of it was at the Doctor's disposal if he would let the search be made. The bribe was refused, and the intruders were marched beyond the hospital lines and ordered to 'git.'

"It is hardly necessary to say that early the next morning Dr. Clark and his patient both thought it admissible to have the premises searched, and a careful investigation was made, but without discovering any plate or treasure."

This reminded the writer of more remunerative "diggings" discovered by some of the Thirty-Ninth's boys and others, the following winter, near General Butler's famous "Dutch Gap" canal.[16]

Fatigue-parties prosecuted this work on this great scheme for getting nearer to Richmond, in reliefs, and those off duty frequently killed time by fishing in the James River. In searching for bait, a soldier lifted a board that rested beneath a large apple tree, and began digging for worms with his bayonet. A few inches deeper he came in contact with another board. This was found to cover a small iron kettle which contained about $3,500 in gold and silver coin. A great scramble followed, in which the Thirty-Ninth's chaps got away with about one-tenth part of the plunder.

This money had evidently been buried there in July of 1862, when the Army of the Potomac was approaching Harrison's Landing, nearby. The occupants of the place had fled, and the house had been burned, probably by shells from our gunboats in that region.

In connection with this engagement we relate a little anecdote in which the late Colonel Howell, who commanded the Brigade at this time, was the hero.

---

[16]This enormous effort allowed the troops to travel by barge cross-country. If they had to travel on the river, the journey would have been six miles further.

The Dutch Gap Canal

The day following the fight Colonel Howell, who was "officer of the day," made the "grand rounds," and at a particular point of our line our men were greatly annoyed by a sharpshooter, who would pick off, from his ambush, any man who dared to show his head. Various attempts had been made to finish the career of this rascal, who had succeeded in wounding several, and at last the gallant old Colonel came to the rescue, and hit upon the following expedient, which was ingenious though dangerous.

"Boys," said he, coolly, "you look out where the smoke comes from; for as soon as the traitor sees me he will let fly"; and getting deliberately up from the trenches where he had been watching operations, the Colonel walked a few paces and calmly seated himself on a stump. Scarcely had he done so, when bang! went a rifle, and a minie ball flew past in too close proximity to be agreeable; but ere the smoke had cleared away half a dozen bullets had sped on their way to the spot where the rebel lay, and in a few moments after, the body of a "Johnny," reeking with gore, was dragged from the spot with no less than three bullets through it.

"There!" said the Colonel, "did I not tell you that I could draw his fire?"

Colonel Howell was brave, even to desperation. He would on all occasions expose himself at the front, and seemingly courted death at the hands of the enemy. But he bore a charmed life, and bullets were not yet made to kill him. It was ordained that he should meet death in a sadder and less heroic form, the circumstances of which will be detailed further on, when in this history we reach the place, and the time.

The Regiment was now lying close to a large entrenchment under shelter tents, or as we termed them "button hole" tents, from the fact that four men each carried a piece that when brought together was pitched and buttoned together. It was scarcely large enough for four men, yet was made to answer the purpose.

The camp was situated on rolling ground, sparsely timbered, with good running water near by. The soil was a mixture of clay and sand, which, when sunbaked, was hard and unyielding, and the yellow glazed surface could be kept clean with a broom; but let rain come, and the hard flooring of camp was soon converted into the vilest of mud.

On the left, some 300 yards distant from the entrenchments, was a battery called No. Six, which was garrisoned by details from the different regiments, and the men there immured suffered great hardships, the least of which was the want of water. Diagonally at the right was another fort or battery, some six hundred yards distant, and armed "at all angles." Not a day passed without more or less skirmish firing, and we lost several men from the constant fusillade kept up from the enemy. The batteries would at times open up, and the dodging of shells was made a pastime both day and night.

May 23, Private Amos Reese, Company H, was wounded through the thigh by a stray ball from the enemy while asleep in his quarters at dead of night, and in the early morning of the 25th, Lieutenant James Burrill, while asleep was wounded by a stray bullet which passed through the neck. The same ball struck Private John Scanlan of Company A in the breast, but did not penetrate the skin by reason of its striking a button; the ball distinctly bearing the impress of the eagle, when picked up.

Jacob C. Franks, Private of Company B, was drowned on the 25th while swimming in the James River.

From May 20 to the June 2 there was comparatively quiet along our part of the line. We had been constantly annoyed by the desultory firing the "rebs" gave us both day and night, which had occasioned the loss of some five or six men from the Regiment. The enemy had put forth every conceivable effort to dislodge us, but had failed each and every time.

On June 2, at three o'clock in the morning, they made their last and grandest effort. Beauregard opened lively with his heavy artillery and pushed his troops forward to our lines. This action was undoubtedly precipitated by the knowledge of the departure of General Smith's Corps and two of General Gillmore's divisions, and the enemy naturally inferred that we had not troops sufficient to hold the fortifications in our front. But alas! for the "rebs;" they did not know that the First Division of the Tenth Corps, Brigadier-General Alfred H. Terry commanding, was holding the right of our lines, and that the center and left were equally well guarded, although not so easily assailable. With their accustomed insight they chose the most exposed and open part of our position as the point to be attacked. The time was also well selected—when night shrouded everything in impenetrable gloom.

After the heavy fire of the batteries, which was mainly directed on our center for the space of an hour and promptly replied to by our own, there was a cessation on both sides and quiet was restored almost as suddenly as it had been broken.

Soon we perceived the rush of a large body of rebels who had been massed and who came yelling like demons on our thin line of pickets. They took our line in reverse and broke it in two places, and forming in the rear took a large number of our men prisoners, chiefly belonging to the Third New Hampshire and Sixth Connecticut Regiments. The enemy was gallantly met by our boys, who after a protracted struggle sent them back with thinned ranks and a higher opinion of what the veterans from Morris Island could achieve.

During this engagement Second Lieutenant A. W. Fellows, Company I, was killed by a bullet passing through his brain. Lieutenant Al C. Sweetser of Company B was wounded through both legs. The wound of the left leg was not serious, the ball making merely a flesh wound. The right limb fared worse, the bullet passing through the knee joint and so disrupting the articulation that amputation at the lower third of the thigh became necessary.

We shall never forget the courage and fortitude of Lieutenant Sweetser while on the operating table, or while suffering for long months at Chesapeake Hospital by reason of hospital gangrene and the subsequent operations that became necessary from the necrosis of bone. He came back to the field hospital on a stretcher, calmly smoking a cigar, and after an examination, and when told that he must sacrifice a limb, he said, "Well, Doc, just go to work, and do the very best you can for me." Lieutenant Sweetser was a brave and gallant officer.

The other losses to the Regiment amounted to thirty-three enlisted men in killed, wounded and missing. The rebel loss was much heavier than our own, and must have been, when we consider with what desperation they faced our fire.

Colonel Dantzier of the Twenty-Second South Carolina Regiment, which attacked our left, was left wounded in our hands, and on June 2 he was taken within the rebel lines under a flag of truce. Our division captured some eighty prisoners.

General Terry, who commanded our Division of the Tenth Army Corps, was always spoken of as a cool and able soldier as well as a polished and courteous gentlemen, and he is to this day respected by each and every member of the Regiment as well as by the whole command which he so ably and surely conducted. He has won his present rank, Major-General U. S. A., by hard service in the field, and it is our wish that he may long live to wear the laurels that have been bestowed on so generous and brave a soldier by the grateful nation. His command was made up of veteran soldiers who had become hardened to the vicissitudes of camp and field, and presented the bronzed and "brawny" look of experienced men. They were as familiar with battlefields as with their muskets, and could always be relied upon in any emergency.

A Reminiscence from Captain Botsford, Company F

"In the early part of June 1864, when General Grant extended his lines on the north side of the James River, and order came to the headquarters of the Regiment for a detail of 150 men to report at the pontoon bridge at night.

"About dark, the acting Adjutant (Lieutenant Knapp) formed the command, and there was not a commissioned or non-commissioned officer to be found, when he turned it over to me. Of course there was no alternative, only to go as directed.

"In the meantime it had become rumored about the camp that we were to go back to our old quarters at Bermuda Hundred, and everybody volunteered to go. It was a queer command at best, only one officer.

"The bridge was not far away, and about ten p.m. a mounted officer rode up to me with orders to place my men in three pontoon boats and proceed to the creek called Deep Run, where I was to establish a post. In case of an attack, the gunboat *Hunchback*, anchored nearby in the James River, would support me, etc., etc. Some of the boys heard the order and didn't like the situation of affairs, and at once attempted to run the guards at the bridge, and a few succeeded in getting away.

"Having had some experience as a sailor when a boy, it served me to good purpose on this occasion, for we reached our destination safely. Climbing the steep bank of the creek, I divided my command into three reliefs and posted them as pickets. The line had scarcely been formed when rapid firing from a post in the advance indicated an attack by the enemy. Just then a private of Company F thought it about time to retreat, and made a break for the gunboat. In his haste and fright he stumbled and rolled down the steep and stony bank into the river and them swam to the gunboat; but the sentinels on board refused to assist or let him come on board, and he swam back to the shore again. The early morning revealed a wet, bruised and crestfallen soldier who never heard the last of his visit to the *Hunchback* to escape from the enemy. In a search made in the morning to ascertain the cause of the firing during the night, we found only a cavalryman's coat and belt, and nothing more, to account for it.

"We were relieved on the third day by the Twenty-Fourth Massachusetts Volunteers, having had rather a pleasant time. We were on the same ground where the disastrous charge was made on August 16 following, by our Brigade. I remember that on the morning of that day our Regiment could muster only 260 men for duty, and at the close of it only ninety-five men answered to the roll-call; and out of the eleven officers who went into that charge seven were either killed or wounded. I was the only lieutenant that was not wounded, and the first on the rebel works. It was myself who took the 150 prisoners and flag and turned them over in charge of a sergeant whom I did not know, but afterwards learned that it was a sergeant of Company G, Thirty-Ninth Illinois, who was afterwards commissioned by General Birney for the gallant act, a clear case of 'stolen thunder.' But, poor fellow, he was killed soon after, in front of Petersburg, Virginia. It was the excessive heat of that day, together with the extraordinary excitement and fatigue and the rain of the next night, that brought me down with typhoid fever, and which nearly terminated my life."

CHAPTER SIXTEEN

"Charge those works!"

There was comparatively little to do from this time until June 14, and the men were free to pursue their pleasures in camp with "turn about" for picket duty, and appearance at "dress parade" in the evening.

Occasionally there would be a man wounded from the almost continuous fire of sharp-shooters in our front. We remember that Captain George O. Snowden of Company D was wounded, June 3, through the right thigh, in this manner, and on June 12 there were other casualties. But there was, otherwise, little to do under the little huts of canvas that sheltered the men on the hard-baked yellow clay camp back of the entrenchments.

The thermometer ranged from 103° to 105° in the shade and evergreen boughs and brush were plentiful, brought into use in shielding the men from the glaring rays of a hot sun. Occasionally the General would come to inspect, or the Regimental Band would come out and enliven the scene with lively music; otherwise the men would seem to hibernate, except when running to the Sutlers sweetmeats, or a pack of cards for a little game of "poker," or "seven-up."

On June 16 the men were called on for a march of several miles out on the Richmond Pike, together with the balance of the Brigade and Division. The reason for this move was that we had found the enemy in our front evacuating their line, which as we moved forwards proved only too true. Our line of march was directly through their late position, and we followed on through the timber and clearings until we reached Ware Bottom Church, where we met the "rebs" in large force. In fact, the whole of Lee's army was in motion to oppose General Grant, who visited us on the 15th, whose army, after battling in the Wilderness for days, had crossed the James River and was advancing on Petersburg. The Eighteenth Corps and that portion which had gone to reinforce the Army of the Potomac had returned and was again behind the entrenchments in Butler's army. The principal force that the Thirty-Ninth met with on this day was Pickett's Division, and a lively time was had with them for some hours. It was said that Generals' Lee, Beauregard and Longstreet were present at the front, witnesses of the engagement. The Regiment was thrown out as skirmishers, and suffered considerably. Captain Oscar F. Rudd, Company G, was mortally wounded, and twenty enlisted men were killed or wounded. Captain Rudd was brought back to Dr. Clark who had followed his Regiment to the front that morning, shot through both shoulders, the ball, in its passage, injuring the spinal cord. He was given a hasty examination and dressing and sent to the rear, as the shells and bullets were flying around thickly. At nightfall, two successive assaults were made by the enemy and were handsomely repulsed each time with great loss on both sides.

The morning hours were very sultry and oppressive, and when the enemy was met the fighting was fierce and most bloody for several hours.

On the morning of the 17th the rebels again assaulted our picket line and were again repulsed and driven back, the Regiment taking twenty-six prisoners. The whole number of prisoners taken by the Thirty-Ninth during the two days' fight was ninety-six. At four p.m. the same day the enemy opened with a heavy artillery fire followed by another assault that resulted most disastrously to them, and where they lost many men taken prisoners. The Sixth Army Corps came to our relief at this juncture, and Terry's Division, thus strengthened, felt that it could withstand Lee, Beauregard, and the devil, if necessary.

General Gillmore at this time was relieved from the command of the Tenth Army Corps, and was succeeded by General Brooks. It was also rumored through camp that Grant had taken Petersburg, and that General Hunter had possession of Lynchburg, Virginia; but these rumors proved to be nothing more than that.

We returned to our old camp on June 18, and were glad to receive the order, for we had no food except what could be gathered from the surrounding country and that had been pretty thoroughly gleaned by the Confederates.

Letter from Sergeant E. J. Thayer to Captain George O. Snowden

Camp Thirty-Ninth Illinois, June 18, 1864.

"Dear Captain: Your letter of the 14th found me on the picket line yesterday. I was very glad to hear from you and that you were doing so well, and that the rest of the officers were doing finely. Remember me to the Major and tell him our boys are paying the 'rebs' for damage done, and we think have from the start. Day before yesterday the 'rebs' abandoned our front, so the picket reported at midnight; by eight o'clock they had advanced to the big forts in Howlett's Field and found all gone. Got thirty or forty prisoners, some muskets, etc. The troops were speedily put under arms and marched to the front. Our Regiment was deployed as skirmishers, and from the forts to the pike had the extreme front. Saw no 'reb,' however, save about 100 that give themselves up. As soon as we struck the pike the pioneers pitched into the telegraph wire and before we left had cut three miles, removing the wire and burying it. A couple of regiments also went to the railroad and tore up a mile or so of track, warping the rails with fire. As soon as we were on the pike we moved by the right flank about three-quarters of a mile to that house, we lay in line of battle across the road the evening of the 16th. On the other side of the field was plenty of 'rebs.' We held them as long as we could and then fell back slowly to the first line of rebel pits. The Third New Hampshire were on our right. Captain Rudd got an ugly wound in the rear of the picket line. From there we went back to camp and got supper, and then out on picket. After we left, the 'rebs' drove our forces from the fort and our advance was in that ditch we dug on the 20th. The 'rebs' had filled them up, but as soon as we were posted I took some men and went to camp, got a lot of shovels, and opened them again.

"All was quiet until three a.m., when the murmur of voices told us that 'Johnny Reb' was getting ready for a spree. As soon as it was light enough to see, the videttes reported two lines of 'rebs' in our front, covering a fatigue party building an abatis. We hauled in the videttes and opened out heavy on them about 300 yards distant. They gave us a volley or two and then broke for their pits. Then all day there was the devil to pay. If you didn't want to be shot at, keep out of sight. About two o'clock they made a break on the Seventh New Hampshire in about the place they came to us on the 2nd, and sent them back kiting. The 'rebs' opened the Eighty-Fifth Pennsylvania and they fell back and that left us open. A, B and part of K were on the reserve. Captain Williams was in command of the picket line and Baker of the whole. Williams was at the reserve when the fuss commenced, and John found himself the only officer in the three left companies. Not thinking it prudent to let them get too far to the left and rear of us, he ordered a retreat, and we fell back to what used to be the 'rebs' advance pits. Taking the shovel again, we soon reversed them, and with our reserves made a good line of battle. Company I and the Twenty-Fourth Massachusetts kept their position on the old line, and Companies F, G, and K were deployed as skirmishers to protect their flank.

"In this position we lay until night, when we again took our pits as far as where that road crosses the pits to the right of where we were on the 2nd, and Company B was put out on our flank as skirmishers and at right angles with our line. H did not come up, so D was the left of the line. We had not been there more than five minutes when they opened a fire from a line of battle on our flank and at the same time from the front. B left us in no time, and D, E, and I and F moved by the right flank until we found ourselves in line of battle; then I broke round about half of D for flankers. As I was going to the left of the line a shell passed and exploded right by my head, knocking me on my hands and knees. I thought I was hit, but not finding any blood I did not mind it until the fuss was over, when I found I was stunned and hurt a good deal. I was sick when I went into camp, and the hard work on the skirmish and digging puts, the excitement and shell, quite laid me up, so after all was quiet and no prospect of a relief I came to camp about midnight. The Company had not lost any at noon today, and about fifteen or twenty in the Regiment. Two or three killed; one in K, and Sergeant Harris of Company A.

"The Sixth, Second and Fifth Corps are here, and I expect that they will charge the 'rebs' tonight, or at least relieve our 'boys,' who have now been on picket forty-eight hours, and that after a big day's work in skirmishing through the most infernal hot hole on a hot day. General Terry, when we deployed, ordered us to fix our bayonets. Wan't that smart? Godfrey was on vidette on the pike, and seeing two 'Johnnies' advanced alone and ordered them to throw down their arms and surrender, which they did, but felt rather cheap when they saw only one little 'Yank' to yank them in. Our company took four.

"Rumor says that we have twenty-five pieces of cannon at headquarters captured at Petersburg yesterday and day before. They have been on a big fight there for two days now. I have commenced on our rolls.

"Hoping you may be soon with us, I am, with respect,

Yours truly, E. J. Thayer."

On June 22 President Lincoln, accompanied by General Butler and a brilliant staff, rode along our line of entrenchments and was greeted with hearty cheers.

Nothing of any particular interest took place after the fight of June 16 until August 13, there being a great lull in military operations along our line. Some of the Tenth Corps had been removed to join the army in front of Petersburg. On July 29 we heard of a great assault and the mine explosion at Fort Harrison in the front of Petersburg—another great blunder of the war, accompanied by a useless sacrifice of life. General Brooks, commanding our corps, was succeeded by Major General D. B. Birney on July 22.

During this period of inaction the writer had permission to go to Fortress Monroe to look after the wounded of the Regiment in that hospital. He found Colonels Osborn and Mann occupying a room together on the second floor of the hospital. They were both under the care of Assistant Surgeon David G. Rush, U.S.V, but were both still confined to bed and suffering with the pain of their wounds.

Dr. Rush was much respected by those who were so fortunate as to come under his care. The acquaintance there formed with the officers of the Thirty-Ninth who were under his special care doubtless had some influence in the Doctor's selection of Chicago as his future home, and the same may perhaps be said concerning Dr. Daniel R. Brower, whom we first met with at Norfolk, Virginia, but who was formerly on the medical staff of Chesapeake Hospital.

In this connection we may mention another medical gentleman, Dr. Daniel T. Nelson, now a prominent physician of Chicago, whom the writer first met in March 1864, when he was an acting Assistant Surgeon, and had been assigned to the flying hospital of the Twenty-Fourth Army Corps by Medical Director J. B. Morrison. The Doctor was with us some months, and was assigned to the duty of keeping the hospital records. We found him to be a very capable and pleasant addition to our staff.

Captain O. F. Rudd occupied a room in the near vicinity, and his wife was with him, but the Captain was fast failing and could not possible survive more than a day or two. Lieutenants Sweetser and Butterfield, and the other wounded officers of the Regiment were in the large ward on the first floor and were not doing as well as could be desired, especially Lieutenant Sweetser, who had been attacked with hospital gangrene and had undergone some painful operations; but he was still happy and hopeful, and said that he would see us later in the war, and he did, for when the writer took charge of the hospital at Ferry Point, Norfolk, Virginia, he came over and remained until he left for home.

The hospital was in a very bad condition, hospital gangrene being very prevalent, and it was a most unfit place for wounded men—especially the main hospital building. It was under the control of Assistant Surgeon McClellan, U. S. A.

The enlisted men of the Thirty-Ninth who where at this place were located in tents, and seemed to be well cared for, yet there were many complaints made relative to the manner of treatment and the quality of rations that were furnished; but this was to be expected in even the best regulated hospitals.

Great dissatisfaction was often expressed at the conduct of the chaplains, and with good reason, too, in many instances, for their ministrations often resulted in doing more harm than good, especially where they were so persistent and officious in looking after the spiritual interests of the men as to worry and irritate them. The chaplains, as a class, were noble and patriotic men, and were as zealous in caring for the physical wants of the wounded and dying as their spiritual, both on the field of battle, in hospital, and in camp. But then there was a large number of clerical parasites clinging to the hospital who were too timid to take the field or even accompany their regiments. They were Pharisees, who made it a business to pray aloud in public places that they might be seen and heard of men—they were rotten to the core, not caring half as much for their soul's welfare or "anybody else's" as for the dollars they received per month from "Uncle Sam."

One of our boys made a grievous complaint to me about the religious counselor that frequented his ward. He would come half a dozen times a day, scattering tracts; and sitting down on the cot would tell him that he was looking very poorly and must prepare to die; that if he did not repent of his sins he would surely go to hell.

"Now," said the boy, "I don't waste any such sycophant coming and preaching to me, disturbing the rest that I so much need—irritating me beyond all control by his canting about my sinfulness and telling me that I must die and go to perdition. He is doing me harm all the time! I feel that I shall get well if I have proper care; and if I don't, I am ready to go when the time comes. It was only the other day that one of the sick men here got so incensed at him that he threw a plate at him and told him to go to the devil, and whenever he comes palavering round me I feel like doing the same thing."

This forcing of religious counsel upon men at such times and under such circumstances was most unwise and reprehensible. No good came of it, but rather great injury sometimes.

The writer has stood beside hundreds of soldiers when dying from disease or wounds, and he has never yet seen one manifest the least fear in facing death. Often have they expressed themselves as willing and glad to go. One case is well remembered, that of a young drummer boy suffering with chronic diarrhea and under his care at the post hospital Norfolk, Virginia, in 1865. He knew that he could not get well—was wasted away to a mere shadow which was growing darker and darker for him each day. In visiting through his ward one morning he found him clothed and sitting up beside his bed. Says he: "Doctor, I want to ask you a question. You know that I cannot live, and I want to know how long it will be before I die."

"Why, Johnny, you seem pretty strong and cheerful this morning, and you must not go so gloomily."

"Yes, I know, Doctor, that I feel a little better, but it's all owing to the milk-punch and the stimulants. I want to know how long you think I can live. I am getting tired of living, for I feel myself a nuisance to everybody and I want to go. I have got a mother and sisters at home, and oh! I should be so glad to see them and have them here with me for a little time; but I shall never see them again in this world."

He was told that it was impossible to say how long he might live, but that he would soon be released from his troubles. It was promised to write to his friends. In making the evening round through the wards his bed was found vacant—he was in the dead-room.

While on the subject of army chaplains it may be proper to mention a little incident connected with our Chaplain, the Rev. C. S. McReading. While we were at Winchester, Virginia, in 1862, Chaplain Mac, as we termed him, was invited to pray in a Methodist church presided over by the Rev.

Dr. Brooke. It was seldom, during our stay near Winchester, that public service was held in the churches on Sabbath day, for the reason, as a soldier said, "the people were afraid to show themselves in their homemade clothes"; and it was a fact that even wealthy families were obliged to wear clothing of the coarsest description. The chaplain, who was invited to occupy the pulpit and assist in the services, was called upon to make the prayer, and he invoked the Deity most fervently for the "success of the Union armies"—"the speedy suppression of this wicked and causeless rebellion"—"for Abraham Lincoln, the President of the United States," and for "the Congress then in session at Washington"—a style of invocation that was new to the people of Winchester. He was never again invited into the pulpit at Winchester during our stay.

On August 13 the Regiment, then in command of Captain Leroy A. Baker, the senior officer present, was called upon to move out of camp to once more face the enemy. The movements of the Thirty-Ninth on this day, and the fierce and bloody battle that followed on the 16th of August, are graphically described by Homer A Plimpton, who took an active part in it, as follows:

An Account of the Battle of Deep Run, Virginia, August 16, 1864.

"When we broke up camp on the 13th of August, we concluded, from the nature of the orders, that we were to embark on transports and proceed to some point which, according to various surmises, was supposed to be somewhere between Washington and Mobile. When, however, we reached the river where we naturally expected to find the transports with steam up and everything in readiness for our reception, we beheld not the above, but a long line of pontoons stretched across the river. Over these we went 'marching on,' and did not stop until we found ourselves massed in a piece of woods near the enemy's line of advanced works not far from Deep Run. When morning dawned, skirmishing commenced, and it was not long before our brigade was in motion and in readiness for a charge. We charged the rebels and drove them from their first line to a second, more formidable.

"During the balance of the day we moved about from one place to another, and at night went on picket. At one o'clock, however, we were quietly withdrawn and moved back to the pontoon bridge, crossed over, and moved down the stream about half a mile recrossed on another pontoon, and found ourselves with the Second Corps, General Hancock commanding. Both corps commenced moving towards Richmond. We advanced to within about eight miles of the city, when we came in contact with the enemy entrenched. Our Regiment supported a battery all day and the next night. No general engagement took place that day.

"On the morning of the 16th, the day following, our Brigade received orders to move to the right of the rebel works in support of regiments thrown out as skirmishers. We were soon brought under fire, and were not long in ascertaining that the force before us was by no means small. We found that the enemy had been driven from their rifle-pits, and were now inside their main works. We soon moved forward over the line of skirmishers to within 200 yards of the rebel entrenchments, screened, however, from view by dense woods. We here received notice from our Division General A. H. Terry, that our Brigade had been selected to 'charge those works!' Between us and 'those works,' was a strip of slashing about 100 yards wide, and it was no easy matter to cross such obstacles under a galling fire. We formed just inside of the woods, out of sight, but near enough to the rebels for them to hear our commands:

Members of the Thirty-Ninth guarding a pontoon bridge over the James River

"The Brigade was formed in double column on the center at half distance by regiments, the Thirty-Ninth being on the extreme left. When all was ready, the command 'Forward!' was given, and we moved off on common time, with arms at a 'right shoulder shift,' but as soon as we reached the edge of the slashing we received a deadly volley from the enemy which brought the guns down to a 'trail,' and our colors to the ground. These were immediately picked up by an officer [Lieutenant Norman C. Warner, Company E], and away we went with a regular Western yell, on the full jump, over logs, tree-tops and stumps thrown about in inextricable confusion.

"The scene that now presented itself to my view I shall never forget—whole divisions of the advancing column swept down in the twinkling of an eye. On every hand could be seen the dead and dying men—our own comrades, who but a short time before were buoyant and hopeful, with no thought of death to make them sad.

"But notwithstanding this terrible slaughter, the old Western brigade did not stop, but made directly for the rebel breastworks bristling with bayonets and alive with men; nor did the enemy give way, but fought us hand-to-hand as we attempted to mount the works. Our colors were again shot down. Lieutenant Warner, who was carrying them, losing a leg. Another officer snatched them up and sprang upon the parapets, followed by scores of others, who leaped over right among the 'Johnnies,' and commenced using the bayonet and clubbed musket. Soon a break was made and then began the capturing of prisoners. After we got over the works, we immediately swung to the left and moved down the trenches, hauling out the 'graybacks,' who begged lustily for mercy. In a short time we had possession of the line and nearly 800 prisoners and five stands of colors.

"A brave young private, Henry M. Hardenburgh, of Company G, captured one of the latter after a hand-to-hand fight with the color-sergeant of the Tenth Alabama, whom he left dead on the field. General Birney, our Corps Commander, to whom he delivered the flag, complimented him very highly. Since coming here, while on duty in the trenches, he was mortally wounded by a piece of shell. A day or two after his death his appointment as First Lieutenant in the Thirty-Sixth United States Colored Troops was received at our headquarters from Major-General Butler, for gallantry on the field, but it came too late. He is silent in the grave, all unmindful of earthly rewards.

"After getting possession of the works spoken of before, the fighting by no means ceases. The enemy was constantly receiving reinforcements, and by some means or other succeeded in regaining possession of a portion of the line on our left, to which another brigade had been sent. Having gained this advantage, which uncovered our left flank, they soon rendered our position untenable, and we were, per consequence, compelled to give back, which we did under a raking fire.

"We remained on the north side of the James, skirmishing and fortifying, until the 20th, on the night of which we returned to our old camp. Our loss while on the north side was ninety-seven men and seven officers killed, wounded, and missing. Three of the seven officers are among the killed."

The morning report of the Regiment on August 16 showed only 228 men fit for duty, fifteen of whom were on detail, leaving only 213 with eleven officers to enter into this assault. The loss was ninety-seven men and seven commissioned officers, and when it retired and returned back to camp it did so with 116 men commanded by four officers, of whom Captain Plimpton, Company G, was the senior officer.

Scene of Assault, August 16, 1864.

Captain Leroy A. Baker, who commanded the Regiment, fell, struck by a bullet that so shattered his leg that amputation was found to be necessary.

Lieutenant Norman C. Warner, Company E, was struck down while gallantly bearing the colors of the Regiment, which he had torn from the bloody hands of Sergeant Henry M. Hardenburgh, Company G, and so tight was the grasp of Hardenburg upon the folds that the piece grasped by him remained within his hand when the banner was taken by Lieutenant Warner. Lieutenant Warner was also compelled to lose a leg, and as he was being borne back to the hospital his thoughts reverted to the mother at home, whom he was so anxious should be spared the intelligence of this calamity until able to communicate the matter in his own way, that he cautioned the boys, "Don't tell mother! Don't tell mother!" This seemed to occupy his mind more than the painfully shattered leg that was being borne back to the surgeon's knife.

Lieutenant Butterfield escaped with a severe flesh wound of the face and was soon able for duty. Lieutenant Horace Knapp, Company D, received a bad wound in the shoulder, the ball having to be cut out.

These officers together with our other wounded were placed on the hospital transport near by, after being attended to, and sent to general hospital.

The wounds received in this assault were more than usually severe in character, a great number requiring amputation, excision of bone and resection of joints. The number of wounded that our Division of the Flying Hospital disposed of in the ensuing forty-eight hours was 900, who were placed on board the *Hero of Jersey*, under the medical charge of Surgeon A. C. Barlow of the Sixty-Second Ohio Volunteers. The entire list of casualties on June 16 at Deep Bottom and Strawberry Plains amounted on the Federal side to 5,000, and it was impossible to say what had been accomplished, if anything, in our advance upon Richmond.

In closing this chapter the following lines from the pen of the Rev. William E. Miller, of Tompkins Cove, New York, seems to be appropriate.

"WOUNDED"

Let me lie down,
Just here in the shade of this cannon-torn tree;
Here, low in the trampled grass, where I may see
The surge of the combat; and where I may hear
The glad cry of victory; cheer upon cheer:
Let me lie down

Oh, it was grand!
Like the tempest we charged, the triumph to share;
The tempest! — its fury and thunder were there.
On! On! O'er entrenchments; O'er living and dead,
With the foe under foot and the flag overhead:
Oh, it was grand!

Weary and faint,
Prone on the soldier's couch, oh! How can I rest?
With this shot-shattered head and saber-pierced breast?
Comrades! At roll call, when I shall be sought,
Say I fought 'till I fell, and fell where I fought!
Wounded and faint.

Oh, that last charge!
Right through the dread host tore shrapnel and shell,
Through without faltering — clear through with a yell!
Right in their midst, in the turmoil and gloom,
Like heroes we dashed at the mandate of doom:

Oh, that last charge!

It was duty!
Some things are worthless, some others so good
That nations who buy them pay only in blood.
For freedom and Union, each man owes his part;
And here I pay my share, all warm from my heart:
It is duty.

Dying at last!
My mother, dear mother! With meek tearful eye,
Farewell! and God bless you and aye:
Oh, that I now lay on your pillowing breast,
To breathe my last sigh on the bosom first prest:
I am no saint!

But, boys, say a prayer; there's one that begins
"Our Father!" and then says, "forgive us our sins"
I'll try to repeat it, and you'll say Amen!
Oh, I'm no saint.

Hark! there's a shout!
Raise me up, comrades! We have conquered, I know!
Up, up, on my feet, with my face to the foe!
Oh! there flies the flag, with its star spangles bright,
The promise of glory, the symbol of right!
Well may they shout!

I'm mustered out!
Oh, God of our fathers! Our freedom prolong,
And tread down rebellion, oppression and wrong.
Oh, land of earth's hope! On they blood-reddened sod,
I die for the Nation, the Union, and God!
I'm mustered out.

CHAPTER SEVENTEEN

"Where are the rest?"

Those were very busy days in that hot August month. Fighting was almost constant at some point along our lines. General Ord had succeeded to the command of the Eighteenth Army Corps. General Butler had commenced operations of his "Dutch Gap" canal. On the 19th General Birney, commanding the Tenth Corps, issued the following congratulatory order to his troops:

> Headquarters Tenth Army Corps
> Fussel's Mills, Virginia, August 19, 1864.
>
> ### GENERAL ORDERS.
>
> "The Major-General commanding congratulates the Tenth Corps upon its success. It has on each occasion, when ordered, broken the enemy's strong lines. It has captured during this short campaign four siege guns protected by the most formidable works, six stands of colors, and many prisoners. Much fatigue, patience and heroism may yet be demanded of it; but the Major-General commanding is confident of the response.
>
> Major-General D. B. Birney
> Edward W. Smith, Lt-Col. and A. A. G."

The afternoon of August 21 the Regiment—if it could be so called, for there was but a mere fragment left of it—moved back to our old quarters, but had no sooner disposed of ourselves for a comfortable rest than orders were received to prepare for another move. We were like the men set out upon the chessboard—subject to the will of the players in this great game for National existence.

It was not, however, until August 24 that our Division filed out from behind the entrenchments at Bermuda Hundred and took up its march to the trenches in front of Petersburg. We reached the vicinity of the works on the evening of the same day and bivouacked for the night. The following day the Division took position near the huge works that rise some six or more feet above the level. Our Brigade (the First) spread their shelters in the open timber some yards back from the line of entrenchments, and protected their quarters by throwing up heavy embankments on the side fronting the enemy.

The Regimental camp was near Cemetery Hill, where General Burnside exploded the heavy mine on the evening of July 29 which was to have accomplished such wonders, and would, possibly, had the affair been properly managed; but it was successful only in a great and useless slaughter of human life. In the rear of our position, distant about one mile, and on higher ground, Surgeon Clark established the Brigade Hospital, marking its position with the hospital flag run to the top of a high pole; and during our stay in the front of Petersburg not a day passed without receiving wounded from some point along the line occupied by the Brigade.

August 25, Sergeant Henry Hardenburgh, Company G, was killed in camp by a fragment of shell which penetrated his left side. He lived but a short time after being brought to the hospital.

Near the hospital and to the right there had been placed in position a 15-inch mortar which was named the "Petersburg Express," and every half hour both day and night it sent a messenger, in shape of a 15-inch shell, over into the city of Petersburg. At night when the lit fuse of this monster shell could be seen, it was a sort of satisfaction to watch its progress through the air and to hear its explosion over that stronghold of treason.

About this time we heard that Colonel Osborn and Lieutenant Colonel Mann had so much improved in health that they had departed for home on "leave of absence."

Corporal Ely's Foraging Experience

"While on a foraging experience all alone by himself while the Regiment was in front of Petersburg, Ely discovered in his preliminary searches an old blind horse which he pressed into the service, and mounted, with a halter to guide him, and found him to be quite a help. He had secured several turkeys and had attached them to the saddle by strings, and was returning to camp, when he was surprised by a party of guerrillas who sprang out from their ambush in his front and opened fire on him. The rattle of the muskets and the sudden clamor frightened not only himself but the horse, which turned and went off on a jump through a 'stake and rider' fence, scattering the rails in all directions. The horse fell down in a pasture field, and Ely made a run for the woods near by, leaving turkeys and everything else, and succeeded in getting safe shelter and finally reached camp. The next morning as he passed the place with the Regiment he saw the horse lying dead where he fell, having been shot in several places."

September 3, news came that General Sherman had taken possession of Atlanta. It was received with general rejoicing.

The rebel fortifications in our front were most formidable, and some of the forts and redoubts on the left were very strong, especially Forts Sedgwick and Steadman. The length of the rebel line of fortification was some forty miles, extending from the left bank of the Appomattox River around to the western side of Petersburg and to the James River, and thence to the east of Richmond. The opposing line of Grant was equal in length but not so heavy and strong. General Grant's headquarters were at City Point, and there had been constructed a railroad from that place to the extreme end of the lines, and as trains passed to and fro they were made the target for numerous "Whitworth bolts" sent over with the design of disabling the locomotives; but as a rule they seldom did any damage. We often went out and picked them up as curiosities where they had fallen.

On September 3 the First Division of the Tenth Corps was called out to witness the execution of a young soldier belonging to a New York regiment who had been tried and convicted by court-martial, and he had been sentenced to be hung by the neck until dead. At two p.m. the division marched to the place of execution and was formed in hollow square, enclosing the gallows, which had been erected during the morning. The condemned man was escorted to the platform of the gallows by a file of soldiers. He mounted to the trap with apparent indifference, where the charge and sentence of the court-martial were read; after which he was asked if he wished to say anything; but he remained silent. A white cap was then drawn over his head and face, the chaplain made a short prayer, the signal was given, and in a moment the young "homicide" was dangling at the end of the rope, and soon he was pronounced dead. His soul had advanced to judgment.

Affairs remained comparatively quiet in our front, and there were no very exciting episodes connected with the daily routine of duty.

On the morning of September 13, we were painfully shocked to hear that Colonel Howell, then temporarily commanding the Third Division, had been seriously injured the previous evening by the falling of his horse. The orderly who brought the intelligence also conveyed a request from General Birney for Surgeon Clark to come and attend to the Colonel. The writer immediately proceeded to Corps Headquarters accompanied by an ambulance.

Colonel Howell was found in a small tent near General Birney's headquarters, alone and unconscious, no attention what ever having been paid to him. His clothing and even his sash and sword were still on him, and the front of his coat was encrusted with rejections from his stomach. Calling an orderly, and assisted by the driver of the ambulance, the Colonel was placed aboard and taken to the Brigade Hospital. No person about Birney's quarters seemed sufficiently interested to put in an appearance. The Colonel had been placed in that tent at the time of his injury and had remained there during the night without care of any attempt being made to ascertain the nature of his injuries. On reaching the hospital a thorough examination was made. No bones were found to be broken, but he was suffering from a severe concussion of the brain, and possible hemorrhage. It was evident, however, that he could not live. He remained unconscious up to a few moments before dissolution, when he opened his eyes and made an effort to speak, but was unintelligible. He died at sundown on the evening of the 24th.

Thus closed the life of as gallant and brave a man as ever entered the service. After death he was embalmed, and his brother, Dr. Howell, was informed by telegram of the sad event. As soon as his death was known, and which was wholly unexpected by his late comrades, large numbers of his friends came to do him honor. General Terry came, and sincerely mourned over the old comrade and officer whom he so lately seen in the full enjoyment of health, and so full of enthusiasm over the news of Sherman's victories on his "March to the Sea." All the members of his own regiment (the Eighty-Fifth Pennsylvania) came to look upon their dead commander as he lay under the shelter of the boughs, with the sharp cracking of musketry and the booming of rebel cannon for a requiem. The burial service for the dead was conducted by his brother officer of the Masonic fraternity, and the remains, in the care of his brother, were sent home.

September 18, the sharp and continuous crack of musketry still echoed and re-echoed along the whole picket line, accompanied now and then by the fierce screaming of shells and the loud detonation as they exploded overhead, carrying death and wounds in their course.

Preparations were making for the departure of the Eighteenth Army Corps and a portion of the Tenth, and our Division was in a constant state of expectancy, for orders might be received at any moment.

The troops in front of Petersburg at this time were disposed of in a semicircular line. Our left (the Army of the Potomac) extending across the Petersburg and Norfolk Railroad on the south, and the right resting on the Appomattox River at the Mills house, four miles north of the city. The Army of the James (Butler's) occupied a position on the right and front, to the north and westward, near the Petersburg and Richmond Railroad.

At about this time commissioners from the various States were coming into camp for the purpose of taking the vote of the soldiers for the coming election, and it was a busy and quarrelsome time. We had for a long time expected that we would be permitted to proceed home as a regiment for the purpose of voting, but it was not to be, for active preparations were being made for a movement against the enemy.

We had received the full details of the Chicago Convention, the platform adopted, and heard with dismay of the nomination of McClellan for the Presidency. But we were convinced that George B. McClellan, the hero who had won no battle and captured no city except Trenton, New Jersey, would appear "non est investus" when the result of the November election was known. Considerable excitement was rife, and we took some pains to ascertain the feeling of the soldiers in the matter and to probe the popular sentiment. In several of the brigades the election had already been held with the result of a seven-eighths vote for "Old Abe Lincoln"—the man whom the soldiers considered as best fitted to hold the helm of State until our cruise through the troubled waters of a treacherous rebellion was finished.

The commander of an Eastern regiment had told us that there were six officers and many men in his command who had openly declared their intention to support McClellan for the presidency, but who after reading his platform turned completely about and voted for Lincoln. "Little Mac" had but few friends in the army operating against Richmond.

We as a Regiment were loud in expressing our condemnation of the Illinois Copperhead Legislature in not permitting us to vote, and a meeting was held and resolutions passed to that effect.

On September 25 the First Division of the Tenth Army Corps had orders to move, and left camp in light marching order at eight p.m., and after marching until near midnight, turned into an open field and bivouacked, with a single blanket to each man for covering. Ah, me! What an uncomfortable night was passed, and how cold it turned before morning in the spacious and breezy dormitory of Nature's!

Light marching order in those days consisted in being equipped with gun and bayonet, cartridge-box filled with "sixty rounds," haversack containing five days' rations, overcoat and blanket, canteen of water and drinking cup. Quite enough to keep a man from flying. We remained in camp until the following evening, and then resumed the march.

On the 28th, we reached the James River and crossed it at Deep Bottom, on the pontoon bridge, after a most fatiguing march, and bivouacked. A portion of the Tenth Corps which had preceded us, together with the Eighteenth Corps, had advanced below Chaffin's Bluff, and on September 29 had taken a large portion of the enemy's fortified line, with fifteen guns and many prisoners. General Ord, commanding the Eighteenth Corps, was badly wounded, General Godfrey Weitzel succeeding to the command. General Birney had taken the enemy's fortified lines at New Market Heights, and had attempted the taking of Fort Gilmer at Laurel Hill, within six miles of Richmond, but the assault proved a failure. This was the same works that the First Brigade of the First Division, Tenth Corps, attempted later on at the battle known as "Darbytown Cross-Roads" on October 13, in which the Thirty-Ninth lost more than sixty men and the Brigade over 300.

September 30 the rebels made an effort to retake their line, but were repulsed; and another and more vigorous effort was made on the evening of October 6, when a terrible battle ensued, that resulted most disastrously to the Confederates. The Thirty-Ninth had taken no active part in these movements and assaults, but had moved to a position connecting with the Eighteenth Corps, the line of the First Division of the Tenth Corps extending from Chaffin's Bluff on the left to the New Market road on the right, and had been busy in throwing up entrenchments, with now and then a skirmish with the rebels.

On October 9 the enemy came in force to drive us from our position and turn our flank, but were repulsed with great slaughter and driven back some miles.

At three o'clock on the morning of the 13th we had orders to advance on a reconnaissance. We found the enemy strongly entrenched, and after some lively skirmishing the First Brigade was selected to make a charge.

The following from the diary of Lieutenant-Colonel Homer A. Plimpton describes the battle of Darbytown Cross-Road, October 13, 1864:

"On the 13th of October we advanced on to the Darbytown road about three and a half miles from Richmond, where we found the enemy strongly entrenched. We skirmished with the 'rebs' until about two p.m., when our Brigade was ordered to charge the works. The circumstances surrounding us at the time were very discouraging indeed. We were compelled to charge their works at a point where they had a heavy flank fire upon us, and through thick underbrush and small timber, and then over heavy slashing where their artillery could rake us. The men all knew before going in the difficulties ahead; all the officers of the Brigade were opposed to the charge, and reported so to the General commanding the Corps; but it made no difference. Charge we must, and charge we did, and Death reaped a rich harvest as the result.

"Nobly did our old Brigade stand up before that terrible storm of lead and iron, but human endurance could not withstand it, and it was hurled back with fearful loss. Our little

Regiment lost sixty brave men in less time than it takes to tell it. Our colors were completely riddled, and the color-guard all killed or wounded with the exception of three."[17]

THE ASSAULT.

Lieutenant-Colonel Plimpton continued:

"There was one sad incident connected with that color-guard that will never be forgotten by any who survived that desperate charge. Our Color-Sergeant, George W. Yates, of Company A, while deliberations were going on in relation to the expected charge upon 'those works,' took our all of his letters from his pocket, read them over, and then tore them to

---

[17] Among the Rebel units involved in the attack, perhaps the most famous was Lee's Texas Brigade. During the battle their commander, Brigadier-General John Gregg was killed along with about six hundred other Confederates casualties. Federal casualties totaled 458 killed, wounded or missing. This would be Lee's Army of Northern Virginia's last major offensive of the Civil War north of the James River.

pieces and scattered them to the winds. He then called his guard about him and told them that in all probability a charge would be made at the point and it would be a desperate affair; and 'Boys, I shall in all likelihood fall. When the order is given to charge, let not one of you desert those colors. Save them, whether I am lost or not.' When the order was given to charge, Sergeant Yates sprang forward with the colors like a deer, but no sooner did he come in sight of the rebel works than he became the target of a terrible volley from their guns and fell pierced with four balls. It was at this point that the Regiment was hurled back and the rebels sprang over their works in hot pursuit. Yates hung to the colors, and when one of their guard sprang to snatch them from him to save them from capture, he was compelled to tear them from the Sergeant's hands. And when the rebels took the bleeding and dying Sergeant, they found him clinging to a fragment of the old flag dripping in his own blood. He was paroled at once, and died at Annapolis, Maryland, October 26.

"It was a sad sight to look upon the colors after the fight, and when on our next inspection, the day after the charge, they were brought out, and only one line officer, and he a First Lieutenant, it made my heart grow sad. The question would arise, Where are the rest? Sleeping beneath the sod, or scattered in hospitals suffering from wounds? The Regiment is now commanded by a First Lieutenant. The only officers we have present for duty, aside from the one just referred to, are a Second Lieutenant (acting Adjutant), and myself. I am now the only officer belonging to Company G. My Captain, O. F. Rudd, died of wounds; the two Lieutenants are discharged, one by reason of expiration of term of service, the other on surgeon's certificate of disability. There are no other Illinois regiments in this Department; we are all alone and a long way from home; and although we are the sole representative of the Prairie State, we have ever endeavored to acquit ourselves like men and not bring dishonor upon her fair name."

* * * * * * * * * * * *

"January 28, 1865, everything in our front remains quiet at present, although on the 24th all was excitement and a desperate struggle was expected. Three rebel rams, the *Drury*, *Virginia*, and *Richmond*, came down the river with the intention of breaking our pontoons and destroying our stores at City Point. Having cut our communications, their army in our front was to come down upon us and capture us, i.e., if they could. This was the movement which General Lee had intimated, when made, would "startle the world." By the interference of Providence and our heavy Parrott guns their scheme was thwarted. The *Drury* was blown up by a shot from our land battery. The other two got aground and had to remain there under the fire of our batteries until high-tide, when they succeeded in getting of and putting back. The *Drury* went to the bottom. The failure of this part of the game, of course compelled the abandonment of the other.

"It has been reported that Semmes, of "piratical fame," had charge of the naval part of the program."

General David B. Birney, commanding the Tenth Corps, was sick at the date of this battle (the 13th), and the Corps was in command of Brigadier-General Alfred H. Terry, the First Division being temporarily in command of Brigadier-General Ames, and our Brigade was commanded by Colonel A. C. Voris of the Sixty-Seventh Ohio Volunteers.

At a Regimental reunion held at Marseilles, Illinois, February 4, 1885, Sergeant D. H. Slagle, Company K, made the following remarks in relation to this battle:

"At two p.m. we are in front of the enemy's works at Darbytown Cross-Roads. Our Regiment and Brigade are deployed in close column by division; the order comes down the line to charge! You all recall that terrific yell, as we made the assault through the brush, the air seeming filled with whizzing bullets, the scream of solid shot and shell; the rattle and sweep of grape and canister through our ranks. Comrades fell on our right and on our left; we find the 'Johnnies' too many. Their force behind protected works outnumbers ours two to one. The old Brigade find they cannot take the works this time, and are compelled to fall back and reform their line. That day myself and many others were wounded and made prisoners at the abatis of their fort. Our killed were quickly despoiled of their clothing by the enemy; the wounded are quickly hustled away by their ambulance corps at early moonlight, and that autumn evening finds us landed in Castle Thunder at Richmond."

Collecting the wounded

In 1887 Sergeant Slagle wrote to Dr. Clark that

"Your attention is called to my observation of the successful scheme of a Pennsylvania soldier who planned to get away from Castle Thunder—myself being wounded and captured at Darbytown Cross-Roads. A few hours after, we were landed in this notorious Bastille. It so happened at that time, the Confederates were massing a boatload of Union prisoners at this prison preparatory to sending them down the James River to near City Point, to meet Colonel Mulford's Exchange Boat, who would return a corresponding number of Confederates, the boats meeting under a flag of truce. This particular boatload of prisoners eligible to be included in this batch for exchange had to be badly wounded, or so reduced from sickness that they would hardly last till the exchange boats swapped prisoners or, to be more explicit, all the Union soldiers placed on this exchange roll had to be carried aboard on a stretcher, unless minus a limb, they could use crutches.

"We had been in this prison from the 13th till the 20th, when the rolls were complete for exchange. These 400 for exchange had occupied the four floors of the building. During this time, on the first floors of at least fifteen had died. On each floor the Confederates had a detail of four or five able-bodied Union soldiers to act as nurses for the sick and wounded. These nurses were not included on the roll for exchange. I must state these nurses were very kind and attentive, and did the best they could for our men, considering they had but very little to do with. One of these nurses dropped on a plan to get away in this manner:

"On the night of October 20 was to commence the transfer of the sick and wounded prisoners from Castle Thunder to the boat to go down the river. The rolls had been called two or three times during the afternoon. Just before night, on a cot near me was a Pennsylvania soldier (I cannot now recall the name) who was delirious, and about ready to answer the roll-call from on high. Presently he pulled his remnant of blanket over his head—and died. Those around him could not tell just the time, within an hour, when he passed away. Shortly after, one of the able-bodied nurses came around and raised the blanket and discovered the lifeless form. No one around recollected his name, although they had heard him, but a short time before, answer to it when the exchange-roll was called. The nurse then examined his memorandum-book and found his name; he then took possession of the contents of the deceased man's pockets, requesting those nearby to keep quiet. He then covered the man over with the blanket, and went away. Shortly, the hospital steward came around. This nurse returned, and, in an innocent way, discovered the dead man—the steward could not learn his name. The remains were, by steward's orders, removed to the dead-house and given a number as one of the 'unknown.'

"Just after dark this nurse came and laid down on the cot lately occupied by the dead man, and covered up his head. About midnight the transfer commenced. The officer would call a name; they would answer 'Here!' 'Are you able to walk?' 'No.' 'Send him a stretcher.' Then the nurses would place the soldier on the stretcher and carry him out to the ambulance. After awhile they reached the name of the dead soldier that occupied this cot. The name was called; the nurse made a faint reply, 'Here!' 'Are you able to walk?' 'No.' 'Send him a stretcher.'

"They lifted the form on the stretcher. He was 'not as light as the usual loads,' they remarked, as they lugged him away; 'this fellow has not fallen away much! Guess we had better leave him till he gets thinner!' But they did not happen to detect the game, and placed him in the ambulance. When I was taken on the boat I happened to be placed by the side of this nurse, and when they carried him off to the Union boat the same remarks were made about him being so heavy. Just as soon as the boats separated, the Union boat returning down the James, and the Confederate up towards Richmond with a load of able-bodied men in return for our lot of invalids, there was one of our number that very suddenly bounded on this feet and turned a hand-spring, to the delight of those interested in the successful scheme of escape.

"The nurse now declared that as soon as he could obtain a furlough, he would go to the family of the deceased prisoner and deliver to them the articles taken from the body, and also give them the number he was buried under. You may judge how happy this fellow was to get away from prison.

"Our reunions are to recall the unwritten incidents of our active service; to mention the valor of those that bravely fell on the field of battle, some of whom are sleeping in unmarked graves.

> "Far from their own proud land's heroic soil,
> which should be their fitter tomb!"

"Color-Sergeant George W. Yates, Company A, who sleeps in the cemetery near by, that day received his fatal wounds and was made prisoner. I was transferred in the same ambulance with him to Richmond, blood from his wounds trickling along the pike the entire distance from Darbytown battlefield to the city, he having received four severe wounds that proved fatal a few days after our parole and arrival at Annapolis, Maryland.

"You will recollect that just before the order came to make the assault our mail arrived and was distributed. Company A was on the skirmish line; their letters had been handed to Sergeant Yates, of the color-guard, who placed them in his left breast coat-pocket. In the assault he received a bullet which pierced those letters and also his watch, and penetrated his side, the letters turning the bullet from the heart. The next day I noticed those letters saturated with blood, and I have often wondered if they ever reached the parties to whom they were addressed, or whether the writers ever knew that their letters had helped to turn a rebel bullet from the heart and for a brief period spared the life of one of our brave men."

In that charge the Thirty-Ninth lost one-third of the number engaged. There Lieutenant Wilder, of Company H, fell; also Sergeant William E. Steele of Company E. The latter fell near me. A bullet struck him in the center of the forehead, and when he fell on their works he retained a firm grip of his musket at "charge bayonet," with his eyes firmly set on the enemy dying in the perfect attitude of a brave and fearless volunteer soldier yielding up his life in the defense of and for the perpetuation of the Union.

The writer's experiences at this battle were unusually disagreeable. On the 7th he had established a hospital at Temple Hall Church, about one mile in advance of the Tenth Corps field hospital, which was located at Chaffin's Farm, in charge of Surgeon S. W. Richardson, Seventh New Hampshire Volunteers. On the morning of the 13th, he with other surgeons of the First Division of the Tenth Corps was ordered by the Medical Director to take the field and follow the command, with strict orders to keep within 300 yards of the line of battle. When the First Brigade were preparing and forming to assault the rebel redoubt, he took the position behind a corn-crib in the yard of the Gerault house. As the Brigade advanced, there was a painful hush, like that of an audience awaiting some terrible denouement. Then came the roar and rattle of guns and a rain of shell and grapeshot in a most careless manner, shattering the old crib and scattering splinters and debris in all directions. One ambulance horse was killed and the driver wounded, and much other damage done. The wounded soon came back in numbers, and among them Captain George Heritage, Company B. Finding our position untenable, we felt justified in transgressing orders and removed to the left and rear inside an old earthwork, where at last we could give our undivided attention to our work without fear of being either killed or wounded. The wounded, as fast as they were temporarily dressed, were sent back to the corps hospital some three miles distant. At about four p.m. our troops fell back, and having sent all the wounded to the rear, the surgeons retired to the Corps Hospital. On the way back the writer met Lieutenant-Colonel Peter Pineo, Medical Inspector Army of the James, who said, "Doctor, you have anticipated my wishes, for I have already sent an order for you to report to the operating theater, where your services are much needed; and," he continued, "I shall make it my first duty to inquire if surgeons are to be compelled to stand as targets on the field of battle, or be placed in a position where they can do some good."

Captain Heritage had received two wounds, one a slight flesh wound of the side, the other more serious, the ball entering at the outer border of the left scapula, passing through to the left shoulder, where it lodged and was cut out. In its passage it had struck the spinal column slightly, and today Captain Heritage is much disabled from the results of that wound, suffering attacks of epilepsy.

Lieutenant Nathan E. Davis, Company E, had received a ball in the right shoulder joint, destroying the head of bone and a portion of its shaft, so that resection of the joint with removal of four inches of the humerus was necessary. He was sent to Chesapeake Hospital, where hospital gangrene attacked the wound, and by reason of having been in poor health at the time he was wounded, he soon died from blood-poisoning.

James G. Hamilton, Company G, was so badly wounded that amputation of the leg was required.

George Howell, Company E, and John Larking, Company C, each suffered the loss of an arm.

William H. Jenkins, Company C, received a wound of the thigh which two years later required amputation.

Lieutenant Charles J. Wilder, Company H, was killed.

The loss in this assault was fifteeen officers and men killed, and forty-seven officers and men wounded and taken prisoner. The losses to the Regiment on the 7th of October had been one man killed, fourteen wounded, and one taken prisoner. Among the wounded was E. J. Thayer, Company

D, who received severe wounds in both legs. The main strength of the Regiment present after this battle was less that 300 men, and there were but three officers left to command them—one Captain and two Lieutenants.

There is one incident connected with this battle that will bear relating. While the doctors were located back of the corn crib, near the house before mentioned, there was great consternation and excitement reigning therein. It was occupied by a German family, consisting of man, wife and child, named Gerault. We found them huddled together in a room that they had fortified by placing barrels and sacks of potatoes and furniture around the exposed sides. As the battle waxed warmer and the shells and bullets screamed and whistled loud and fast, the woman and child took refuge under a big feather bed. But alas! a shell exploded directly over the house and the fragments penetrated to the room, scattering feathers in all directions and severely wounding the woman in the leg so that amputation became necessary back at the hospital, which was performed by Surgeon M. S. Kittinger, 100th New York Volunteers, assisted by Miss Clara Barton. In conversation with Mrs. Gerault shortly afterwards, she seemed to deplore the loss of her feather bed more than the loss of her leg.

Miss Clara Barton was present at the Corps Hospital at this time and rendered most effective and grateful service in ministrations to the wounded both day and night. She was a "Florence Nightingale" in her devotion to the sick, wounded and dying that came and went from the hospital during the following winter. She was placed in charge of the "light diet department," and furnished with untiring zeal delicacies and appetizing dishes for the many sick. She only left us when we were again ordered to advance "On to Richmond." After these many years, her memory is still fresh and green with us; and we wish her Godspeed in her philanthropic mission as President of the "Red Cross" Association of America.

The last of our wounded was sent away on the afternoon of October 14, when the writer returned to his old quarters at Temple Hall Church.

On the morning of October 15 the surgeons and attendants at the church suffered a big scare—in fact, became somewhat demoralized for the time.

Several companies of Kaautz's cavalry who were on picket duty in our front, came flying back in the greatest excitement and disorder and cried out to us, "The rebels are coming!" and from appearances we thought it must be a fact, and at once prepared to vacate. Looking up the road toward the front could be seen a mass of disordered and tangled-up cavalry in a wild stampede; some horses were riderless, with saddles turned and the stirrups swinging and flapping about, which served to increase their speed. Troopers, hatless, with hair flying, rushed frantically by, whooping and cursing; scabbards and canteens swinging and clanging amid the clatter of hoofs, made up the scene of a most disgraceful rout. There seemingly was no one to command, and the horses were as frantic as the riders. Hospital Steward DeNormandie of the Thirty-Ninth, with his assistants, soon had our equipment aboard the wagon, and the six-mule team in place and speedily joined in the retreat, the surgeons bringing up the rear. We had not proceeded more than 100 yards, however, when an officer made his appearance and succeeded in checking the retreating cavalry.

It seems that the enemy in considerable force had made a sudden and unexpected attack on that portion of our line guarded by Kaautz's cavalry, and had routed them and created a panic. The First Division, Tenth Corps, were soon in line, however, and turned the rebels back with some considerable loss. On visiting the scene of the attack soon after we found a large number of dead rebels lying promiscuously around.

On the 18th we heard of the death of our Corps Commander, General David B. Birney, who was a brave and efficient officer, and his loss was deeply felt and was deemed irreparable. General Terry, who had previously commanded the Corps during the illness of Birney, now succeeded to the full command.

October 20, the writer was permanently detailed to the flying hospital of the Tenth Corps as Chief Operating Surgeon, and was succeeded by Surgeon Samuel Kurtz, Eighty-Fifth Pennsylvania, as Brigade surgeon. He therefore took up quarters at the Corps Hospital located at Chaffin's Farm. On the evening of this day, the Corps celebrated another victory of Sheridan's in the valley of Virginia, and salvo after salvo of artillery at our front proclaimed or emphasized the fact to the rebels opposite.

October 25, a grand review of the Tenth Corps took place on a broad "plateau" near the hospital. President Lincoln, Secretary Stanton, Secretary Fessenden, Surgeon-General Barnes and many other notables from Washington were present to witness the "fighting stock" of the Army of the James. The old Corps never appeared to greater advantage, and everything passed off creditably. Our Division had been almost decimated and did not present the same appearance as regards to numbers that it did when the President last reviewed us, some six months previous. The Thirty-Ninth at this time numbered only 225 men for duty and had but two commissioned officers with it, aside from medical staff.

October 26, orders were received to prepare for an advance which was to commence in the early morning, and there was every prospect for more bloody work. The following morning, the 27th, the Corps advanced to the front again, near the scene of the late engagement on October 13, where they met the enemy, and for two days more or less fighting was done. The Thirty-Ninth were not at this time compelled to take a very active part, and hence the losses during these days to the Regiment were small. The Corps suffered to the extent of some four hundred officers and men, 311 of whom were brought back to the hospital, and the number of severe and serious casualties was greater than in any other fight of this campaign. Out of this number it was necessary to perform ninety capital amputations and twenty-three excisions of bone, chiefly of the femur and humerus and the inferior maxillary.

After this battle a large number of deserved promotions were made for brave and gallant conduct on the field. Among these was our friend Colonel N. M. Curtis, of the 142nd New York Volunteers, who was in command of a brigade at the time. The Colonel took the field when he was scarcely able to stand from illness, and strange to say, was knocked down four different times on the 27th by spent balls. His escape from death was simply among the greatest of marvels.

At this time there seemed to be a general cessation of operations at our front, and the whole army prepared to go into winter quarters.

Winter Quarters at Chapin's Farm.

Pleasant camps were selected near our line of works, which were very heavy and complete, and the men, when off duty, went vigorously to work in building log houses. Timber was cut and hauled to the ground, and layer after layer of logs arose until the desired height was obtained and then covered with their shelter tents or boughs from the pines. The interstices between the logs were filled in with clay; the door hung with leather hinges, or, if possible, with stronger ones from the doors of the many vacant houses in the vicinity; and the same source supplied the necessary window-sash for the soldier's dwellings. The huts or cottages were arranged in conformity to army regulations and presented a very interesting appearance. The men built like structures for some of the officers, and the regimental medical officers were thus favored. Each little building was furnished with a fireplace or else a sheet-iron stove, and many of these buildings were very cozy and comfortable.

The headquarters of the Brigade and Division were under canvas shelters, but with good frames of timber to support them in lieu of poles, and besides had good flooring.

Officers' Quarters, Chapin's Farm.

The Thirty-Ninth's Band, which had a position at Brigade headquarters, were prolific in putting up shelters and digging wells, and theirs was among the best.

About this time, (October 31) General Butler left his command for a few days' recreation at Fort Monroe, leaving it in charge of General Terry.

Butler was quite popular with his command, winning our respect and confidence by unwearied attention to the details that make up the sum of a soldier's comfort. He was better at planning than executing, yet his record in this capacity will compare well with that of other Generals who were placed in the same position. He was no friend of those who did not perform their duty in all and every respect, as the following orders show, which we have copied for insertion in order to exhibit the character of the man:

"Headquarters
Department of Virginia and North Carolina,
Army of the James
In the Field, Virginia, October 29, 1864

ORDERS

I. It having been certified to me by Colonel Abbott, commanding Seventh New Hampshire Volunteers; Brigadier-General Hawley, commanding Brigade; Brigadier-General Ames, commanding Division; and Major-General Terry, commanding Tenth Army Corps, that Captain Joseph E. Clifford has tendered his resignation in the face of the enemy, and that he is guilty of "skulking" in the face of the enemy, and of absence without leave, he is hereby dishonorably dismissed the service of the United States, with forfeiture of all pay and allowances.

II. Citizen Joseph E. Clifford, having declared that he desired to get out of the service, and was bound to do so, either honorably or dishonorably, is hereby ordered to set at work under the charge of the superintendent of prison labor at Norfolk.

By command of Maj-Gen'l Butler.
Ed. W. Smith, A. A. Gen'l.

ORDERS

Special Orders, No. 372

III. David B. White, late Major of the Eighty-First New York Volunteers, who has left the service, cannot be elected as Sutler in this Department. Field officers leaving the service voluntarily cannot take the place of bootblacks here. If they have no more respect for the service which they have left, they will find that officers here have. David B. White will at once leave the Department.

By command of Maj-Gen'l Butler.
Ed. W. Smith, A. A. Gen'l

Other orders of a like nature could be given, but the foregoing will suffice.

Matters remained quiet at the front during the months of November and December, with the exception of some artillery practice occasionally, and now and then a little musket firing. Colonel Osborn returned to the front during the month of November, after a "leave of absence" home, and was soon placed in command of the First Brigade of the First Division.

CHAPTER EIGHTEEN

Reorganization

In December the work of reorganizing the Tenth and Eighteenth Corps was commenced, comfortable to the following order:

> War Department
> Adjutant-General's Office
> Washington, December 3, 1864

GENERAL ORDERS NO. 297.

By direction of the President of the United States, the following changes will be made in the organization of the "Army of the James."

I. The Tenth and Eighteenth Corps will be discontinued.

II. The white infantry troops of the Tenth and Eighteenth Army Corps, now with the Army of the James, will be consolidated under the direction of the Major-General commanding the Department of Virginia and North Carolina, and will constitute a new corps, to be called the Twenty-Fourth Corps.

III. The colored troops of the Department of Virginia and North Carolina will be organized into a new Corps, to be called the Twenty-Fifth Corps.

IV. The present corps staff and the artillery of the Eighteenth Corps will be transferred to the Twenty-Fourth, and the present corps staff and artillery of the Tenth to the Twenty-Fifth Corps.

V. Major-General E. O. C. Ord is assigned to the command of the Twenty-Fourth Corps, and General Godfrey Weitzel to the command of the Twenty-Fifth Corps.

> By order of the Secretary of War.
> E. D. Townsend, Asst. Adj't-General.

December 3, the Twenty-Fifth Corps was ordered away, and also a portion of the Twenty-Fourth Corps. The surmise was that they were going to aid Sherman, but their destination proved to be Fort Fisher; and on January 15, 1865, we had the pleasure of knowing that the expedition had been successful, the fort having yielded to our old commander, General Alfred H. Terry, and Admiral Porter, but not without severe loss, the casualties amounting to some 900. The loss in the land forces under Terry amounted to 691; the Navy losing a little more than 200 in killed and wounded.

Three of our best and most active surgeons lost their lives by disease contracted during the operations against Fort Fisher. They were Surgeon A. J. H. Buzzell of the Third New Hampshire, acting Chief Medical Officer of the Division; Surgeon Palmer of the Fourth New Hampshire; and Surgeon Washburne of the 112th New York Volunteers.

Our winter quarters were fully completed at this time and we commenced a life of partial hibernation. Even at the field hospital we had completed a system of permanent wards for the sick, constructed of pine posts set upright in the ground and covered with hospital tent-flies. Three wards, each 100' in length by 25' wide, were constructed on this plan, while hospital tents joined together and supported by inside frames made two other wards for surgical cases. The smallpox hospital consisted of a single hospital tent which was located 100 yards in the rear. Walks were laid, ever greens planted, and everything was done to embellish and add comfort. At the front we had erected a large flagstaff which flaunted the hospital flag and could be seen from all the camps.

A Medical Examining Board had been instituted, consisting of the Chief Medical Officers at the hospital, which met in session each week for the purpose of examining all applicants for furlough or discharge from service, as well as those presenting for the position of assistant surgeon.

Our work on the Board was decidedly heavy and lively, for a large number of both officers and men were making applications for either a "leave of absence" or a discharge from the service by reason of disability. We are sorry to say that many presented who had not the least claim to this indulgence, and they were sent back to camp, "disapproved."

A large number of men who had been drafted and forwarded to our Corps gave us more trouble and annoyance than all the old soldiers put together. Men were drafted in New York City who had but lately landed from emigrant-ships, and pushed forward to the front. They, on reaching the army, would malinger and feign all sorts of disorders.

We remember meeting with two persons of this class who were sent to the hospital for examination. They both claimed to suffer from acute rheumatism, and had suffered for years with the complaint until their limbs had been contracted. They were brought in an ambulance to the hospital and placed in bed. On examination day they were conveyed on stretchers to our room, and a thorough investigation was made. Both protested that they could not walk by reason of the contraction of tendons and muscles, and in fact our efforts to bring the limbs into normal position caused a great outcry. We placed them on a table and administered chloroform, when lo and behold! they each, during the exciting stage of the drug, moved their limbs as vigorously and with as much suppleness as we could wish to see. After they had regained consciousness their limbs relapsed back to the former condition with a power of will that was astonishing. We all agreed in pronouncing them a fraud, and so told them; but instead of confessing, they persistently clung to the falsehood they had agreed upon.

We had a summary way of punishing this class. They were told to get up and proceed to their regiment; and calling two men of the guard to take position behind them with fixed bayonets, with orders to march at a "charge bayonet," and if the villains faltered, to run them through, they were told to Forward, march! and they finally concluded to go nimbly to camp.

One other case of this character we will mention. A man from a New York regiment had been lying in hospital for some weeks with what he termed "hip-joint disease." During a meeting of the "Board" he was brought in for examination, and was accompanied by the assistant surgeon in charge of the ward, who stated that the man had been under treatment there for some weeks, and after doing all that he could for him, there was no improvement in his case. The assistant also stated that he had carefully watched the man and had noticed him at times walking naturally, when he thought himself unobserved. Each of the four surgeons constituting the examining board gave his opinion, after a full and free examination, and we all concurred in pronouncing the case one of fraud. Chloroform was administered, and the limb put through all its motions and examined thoroughly, and we were more fully convinced that he was malingering. We told him our conviction, but he stoutly maintained that he was an invalid.

The steward of the hospital was called and directed to place two irons or pokers in the fire, and we would soon cure the man. He watched the irons until they assumed a white heat, and was ordered to uncover his hip, which he did without any protest, and then, one after the other, the burning irons were applied over the hip-joint. He made no exclamation until the third application, when he confessed that he had been "playing off" on the doctors, and if we would let him go he would never do so again. We kept the man in hospital until he recovered from the cautery, and they sent him to his company, where he proved a good soldier afterwards.

December 24, the Band of the Thirty-Ninth came to the hospital in the evening chaperoned by the Hospital Steward Anthony DeNormandie. After some music in front of our headquarters, we showed them the way to the quarters of Miss Barton, where several pieces were played, and at last we were invited in to take a little milk-punch, provided for us, together with a "Christmas eve" collation. After doing the "nice thing" by the band we returned to the writer's quarters, where we found the band of the Eighth Connecticut, who had also come down for a little stimulation. In proceeding farther we met with General Osborn and his acting Assistant-Adjutant-General, Captain Nevins, and at once ordered in eggnog, for this was possible, as we had a large number of hens connected with the hospital and belonging to Surgeon Richardson. The affair was enjoyed amazingly, and the "wee sma' hours" approached before we were permitted to go to bed.

The Thirty-Ninth and Eighth Connecticut Bands took turns in giving us music, and when invited inside were as zealous in appropriating "something to wet their lips." The whiskey was brought from the division commissary, and how they ever got home was a "nine days' wonder" to us.

Before leaving, the bands got considerably mixed, and in playing their "finale" it was impossible to state whether it was "Schubert's Serenade," the "Mocking Bird," or the "Volunteer's Return." However, they did their best, and we have never yet seen members of a band who could not keep their legs, and the necessary "pucker" of lip.

During the winter, although a most ominous quiet had been observed at the front, the men were detailed to go out on picket duty at the front and at the rear near where a cut was being made which would save some six miles journey by river, and was known as the "Dutch Gap Canal" of General Butler. The men at work on this canal were continually harassed by the shot and shell of the enemy from the Howlett House battery, and they had the range so completely that it was dangerous to work at any time. The details that were sent there excavated pits in the embankment where they were comparatively safe during bombardment from the battery.

The canal was finally completed, with the loss of many a good man, and had, up to this time, been of no particular benefit, and we counted it as so much lost time.

January 24 we were awakened by the heavy booming of cannon, and at each discharge of the heavy guns our rooms fairly quivered and the window-sashes seemed to have the ague. On getting out of bed in the early morning the cannonading was still in progress and continued for perhaps an hour in great fury.

The occasion was the appearance of the enemy's gunboats. The result was, the destruction of one rebel ram, and two others ran aground in attempting to get down the river to "Dutch Gap Canal," and they, before getting off, were severely injured.

In the early part of February we received some visitors from the North. Among them was Joseph A. Cutler, our former quartermaster, and a Mr. Garrison from Chicago, who had come down on a semi-political mission pertaining to the promotion and commissioning of several officers.

February 11, Mr. Garrison took his departure for Washington via Norfolk to see Lieutenant-Colonel Mann, and was accompanied to the landing by several officers, including General Osborn, who was to accompany him to Norfolk on a few days "leave of absence." The Regimental Band had preceded the party and met them at the boat.

In this connection is mentioned a little incident that happened during the evening on board the gunboat *Hunchback*, were the band, Surgeon Clark and Dr. Woodward had been invited. The following version of the affair from the pen of Edward Conley, a former member of the band from Wilmington, Illinois, and who was the editor of the *Wilmington Advocate*, but not of the *Joliet Signal*, is inserted:

"On the evening of February 11 the Band proceeded on foot from the Brigade encampment on the New Market road, near the outer defenses of Richmond, to the 'landing' at Deep Bottom—about four miles distant, with a view of visiting the medical purveyor (Dr. Woodward, of the Thirty-Ninth), and his barges on the James River, and of seeing Colonel Osborn and his Chicago guest off to Norfolk on the steamer *Thomas Powell*. On arriving we gave some music, and as soon as the *Powell* departed we descended the hatches of the purveyor's barge, where a genial and hospitable circle, including Surgeon Clark, greeted us. The evening passed with vocal and instrumental music, pleasant repartee and general hilarity; all, however, within the bounds of decorum.

"At about eleven o'clock, a signal lantern appeared on the *Hunchback*, a 'double-ender' gunboat lying off a 500 yards distant, guarding the approaches to 'Four mile Run,' and forming the extreme right of the Union lines, at that time. To be brief, our Band and the officers were invited on board; and having accepted the courtesy, were conveyed to the vessel in a cutter and the captain's gig, the former for the Band and the latter for the 'shoulder straps.'

"The crew were in their hammocks and asleep, but not so the commander, Captain Fyfe, a splendid specimen of humanity, six feet in his stockings, if an inch, a handsome, swarthy, robust, daredevil sea-captain of the regular services.

"The officers of the vessel had now assembled in the cabin, and the immediate program may be easily guessed. Music, wine and song ruled the hour; there was indeed 'a sound of revelry by night'.

"Captain Fyfe felt 'mellow' and hurled his jokes at the volunteer service generally; as though volunteers on land or sea were a sort of nondescript when compared with 'regulars.'

"The Band, being his guests, threw aside rigid formality, and parried his thrusts freely; in fact, all in the cabin appeared to have ignored or forgotten the existence of such a thing as rank for the time.

"Suddenly a gong sounded, and all hands beat to quarters. The men sprang from their hammocks and rushed to their respective posts, armed for action, in a moment of time. We 'land-lubbers' thought that an attack had certainly been made on the line, not having noticed the Captain secretly and quietly giving the command to 'beat to quarters' a few minutes previously.

"We were assigned a place on the larboard bow; while a platoon of sailors with cutlasses line the starboard wheel house and gunwales, supported by a platoon of musketeers in the rear.

"Captain Fyfe, jolly enough, raised his trumpet to his lips and gave the command, 'Repel boarders!' which rang out on the frosty midnight air like a clarion; then in succession came the commands, 'Fire!' 'Board with cheers!!' At the second command a volley of musketry shook the vessel, and the report resounded for miles around, through Federal and rebel camps alike. The next command was heartily responded to by the jolly tars with echoing and re-echoing cheers. It was with difficulty that the Captain was restrained by Dr. Clark from firing his heavy broadside Dahlgen guns.

"The band looked on in amazement, just realizing the fact that all these noisy and alarming proceedings with an imaginary rebel craft were for our surprise and entertainment.

"Soon the ship was hailed from the shore and a cutter came alongside conveying an aid from General Weitzel, commanding all the forces in that vicinity. The officer stepped on deck and said: 'The Major-General commanding sends his compliments to Captain Fyfe, and desires to know the cause of this alarm and firing.'

"Captain Fyfe responded: 'Give General Weitzel my compliments; tell him I'm at the top of my profession, and have such a lot of damned green Ohio volunteer recruits on this vessel that I sometimes have to drill 'em all night; also say to your superior officer that I have instructions from the Navy Department to drill my men whenever I choose, and damn me if I don't do it! Good morning, Sir.'

"Our Band saw the 'situation' at once and took leave of Captain Fyfe for the shore, where we felt safer, and soon were toddling back to camp over four miles of corduroy road, and reached our bunks just before sunrise. The following day the New York papers reported 'heavy firing was heard last night near Deep Bottom. Troops were put in the trenches and awaited an attack until daylight.'

"The affair was signaled and telegraphed to General Grant's headquarters at City Point, and we afterwards learned that Captain Fyfe was arrested, tried by court-martial, and finally sent with the *Hunchback* out of the James to the coast of Hatteras, with loss of pay for six months.

"So much for the spree and Captain Fyfe's entertainment of the Thirty-Ninth Band."

February 19, we at the hospital, not having much to do except making "sectio cadaveris" of the dead who were brought to us with a new malady called "spotted fever," which takes men off suddenly, turned our attention to removing a bullet from the hip of Surgeon Richardson's horse where it had remained since May 16, 1864. The horse was cast and the bullet removed, and it is presumed that the poor brute felt grateful.

During the evening a large body of "rebels" came within our lines, consisting of two colonels, six captains, and 250 enlisted men. They all deserted in a body. They expressed themselves as having no confidence in the success of their arms; that the Confederacy was built upon sand, and the tidal-wave that Grant and Sherman were sending was fast crumbling the whole fabric of their superstructure.

February 21, official news came of the occupation by our forces of Branchville, Columbia and Charleston, South Carolina, and at noon 100 guns were fired along our line. The Richmond papers of that date acknowledged the fact of the surrender of these places, and they seemed to know that the "bogus Confederacy" was fast falling.

Day after day succeeded with unvarying uniformity—the same duties to be performed at the front, in camp, and elsewhere. In fact, life was monotonous, and we all wanted a change. To be sure there was novelty enough in the various circumstances that were daily occurring to keep us from brooding, but we were in haste for active service to commence that we might finish the work so near completion and return to our homes.

During the long winter in camp we had been comfortably housed and provided for. The daily routine of duty was made as pleasant as possible, and there was ample time and opportunity for amusements and social interchanges, and we made many valuable friendships with officers and enlisted men from all parts of the Union. The paymaster did not forget us, and came regularly through the winter bringing us the "promises to pay" of "Uncle Sam," and his arrival was always the anticipated event of all, the sutler especially. After pay day, old scores were settled, furloughs applied for and granted, and games of "draw poker," "seven-up," etc., indulged in by many without limit, and 'every thing was lovely' for a short time.

March 11, the Division was again called out to witness the execution of a soldier who had been guilty of deserting to the enemy. He had been tried, found guilty, and was sentenced to be shot to death with musketry. The day previous two others had been shot for a like offense, and others were yet to follow if they were not pardoned.

The Division was formed in hollow square, and in one corner a grave was dug and a coffin placed near it. After all was in readiness the man, who belonged to a New York regiment, a bounty-jumper and a most reckless piece of humanity, was brought forward and commanded to kneel on his coffin. After his arms had been secured and his eyes bandaged, a firing party consisting of twenty-four men in two platoons was marched up within six paces of the victim, and when the signal was given by the commanding General, the officer in command of the firing party gave the order, "First Platoon! make ready! aim! fire!!" and twelve muskets belched forth a volley that completely riddled the man. Dr. Barlow, Sixty-Second Ohio, and Dr. Clark stood within three paces of him, and when the orders were given we watched the man closely, but not the least tremor or motion could be detected except the nervous twitching of some of the facial muscles.

Immediately after the volley the surgeons went to the man, or rather to the corpse, to see if life were extinct. The firing party had done their work well. We found that nine bullets had penetrated the body—two through the heart; six within a circumference of four inches of it; and one through the brain. When the volley was fired the man jumped up and backwards at least four feet. If the volley that was fired had not done its work, the other platoon behind would have finished it, as was necessary on the day previous when the two that we have mentioned were executed. One of the men was killed, the other only wounded, and it was necessary to put him in position again.

We have often tried to conjecture what the feelings of that man was when he was made to kneel on that coffin that was to enclose him, and near the grave that was to contain him, and especially when he heard the snap and decisive commands that were so soon to send him on his last journey. They must have been terrible beyond expression.

CHAPTER NINETEEN

"There was some terrible hot work going on."

March 12, 1865, the First and Second Divisions of the Twenty-Fourth Army Corps, under the command of General John Gibbons, the only representatives of the Corps in the Army of the James, were reviewed by General Grant. Many ladies in carriages were present; also many notables from Washington.

General Grant had a numerous and brilliant staff with him; the day was fine and the troops were in excellent spirits and trim. Our Brigade, in command of Brevet Brigadier-General Osborn, elicited much admiration for their soldierly bearing and behavior, and was commented upon much to its advantage. The balance of the Division appeared fully as well and the occasion was one of satisfaction to all concerned.

March 17 General Grant and staff, on their way to the front, stopped at the hospital. The General dismounted and came forward unattended and was met by the writer. He said that he wished to write some dispatches and requested the favor of using the desk for the purpose. He remained for nearly half and hour, writing several orders, and after inquiring for the nearest telegraph station took his departure. While he was seated at the desk we had an excellent opportunity to observe the Commander-in-chief of the armies of the United States. He wore his uniform coat unbuttoned; a slouch hat encircled with a gilt cord; but had no sash or sword on his person. He was not arrogant, conceited or at all formal in speech or manner; and to one ignorant as to who he was and the position he occupied, and not bearing the insignia of his rank, he would have passed for some ordinary mortal connected perhaps with the commissary or quartermaster's department. His face wore a look of anxiety, but withal there was an expression of satisfaction noticeable, as if affairs were progressing in the right channel. We looked upon this man, who was burdened with so great a responsibility and on who the hopes of a great nation were centered, with feelings approaching to awe and wonder as well as admiration, and heartily wished him God-speed in his efforts to crush the great rebellion. Before the General took his leave he asked for a drink of water, which was given. After he was gone, an officer who had been present wished to know why he was not given something stronger, as he looked tired and dusty; but we felt somewhat diffident in the matter, although having seriously thought of doing so.

After dinner we rode to the front to witness another grand review of the "Army of the James" by General Grant, Secretary Stanton, Secretary Seward, Generals Ord and Gibbons, and there was also present a large number of ladies.

In the evening we received a visit from Generals R. S. Foster, commanding the First Division, Thomas O. Osborn commanding the First Brigade; and Colonel Dandy of the 100th New York Volunteers. They expressed themselves as well pleased with the review and the compliments that had been paid the troops under their command, and as Colonel Dandy expressed it, "were feeling like green bay trees!" but after being introduced to the several varieties of Surgeon Richardson's "milk punch" it was difficult to say how they felt; possibly they felt as if a cyclone had struck them, for they gathered themselves together and silently rode away.

March 21 orders came to prepare for a move, and we were directed to turn over tents and camp equipment. The sick and disabled were to be examined and sent away, and everything foretold of forced marches and lively times for the Army of the James. Over 400 sick and disabled were sent to hospital at Fort Monroe.

March 26 General Sheridan with his cavalry arrived and crossed the James River at Deep Bottom. President Lincoln also came and reviewed the First Division, Tenth Corps.

March 27 the order came to move, and the troops marched out of their winter quarters fresh and active at sundown. We were in motion all night and part of the succeeding day, making 40 miles, and reached the extreme left of the Army of the Potomac and expected to remain in the place of the Second Corps, but on the 29th were again ordered to move.

Here again is introduced the narrative of Captain Homer A. Plimpton, commanding the Regiment at this time, which fully describes the movements and operations of the Thirty-Ninth from March 27 to the surrender of Lee at Appomattox April 9, 1865. There is also presented the official report of Brevet Brigadier-General Osborn, who commanded the First Brigade, First Division, Twenty-Fourth Army Corps.

Extracts from a letter written near Richmond, Virginia
April 28, 1865.

"When we crossed the James, which was on the night of March 27, we marched to the defenses on Grant's left, which we occupied, while the Second and Fifth Corps, with Sheridan's cavalry, moved farther to the left to initiate the long talked of movement which was to wrench the strong holds of Petersburg and Richmond from the grasp of the enemy.

"The Sixth and Ninth Corps broke the enemy's line on the morning of the 2nd, when we were called upon to hasten to the assistance of the Sixth Corps, the principal part of which, after breaking through the works, had swung to the right towards Petersburg.

"Our Division, the First, commanded by General R. S. Foster, of Indiana, went through the line on the double quick, and passed the Sixth Corps, charged two of the enemy's redoubts, capturing them and turning the guns upon the flying foe. We advanced to within a short distance of a stronghold or work called Fort Gregg, where the enemy made a bold stand. This was a key to all the forts about Petersburg, and its capture necessitated the fall of the city, as well as Richmond.

"Fort Gregg commanded five other forts. It was built upon a high prominence, the country about it open, affording no covering. It was an enclosed fort; surrounding it was a ditch ten or twelve feet deep and same in width. It was garrisoned with nearly 500 picked men who swore to hold the fort against all odds or die in the attempt. General Lee visited the fort about two hours prior to our arrival and exhorted them to hold it at all hazards, for the salvation of Petersburg and the safety of Richmond depended upon the fate of that fort; and nobly did they endeavor to carry out his instructions, but it was all in vain. They were not counting on meeting with Western men in the coming conflict.

THE ASSAULT OF FORT GREGG, APRIL 2, 1865.

"Our Brigade, composed of the Thirty-Ninth Illinois, Sixty-Second and Sixty-Seventh Ohio and 199th Pennsylvania Volunteers, was soon in position in line of battle, ready to try its mettle. As soon as we started, the enemy arose from behind their parapets, where they had been compelled to keep down by our sharpshooters, and poured into our ranks a destructive fire of musketry and grape, which mowed down our men most unmercifully; but we faltered not. On we went; we reached the ditch, the Thirty-Ninth reaching it first, and was first in planting her colors upon the fort; and, by the way, our colors are to be sent to Washington to have an eagle, cast for the purpose, placed upon them, by our Corps Commander, General Gibbons, in honor of the event. Into the ditch we plunged; it was there we encountered a difficulty unforeseen when we started. The steepness and slippery nature of the sides of the fort for a time rendered futile all our efforts to scale them. The excitement that now prevailed beggars description. The men were nearly frantic in their attempts to gain the top of the works. The enemy continued to fire grape and minié balls at all who attempted to come to our assistance. It was only by digging footholds with bayonets and swords that we were enabled to work our way up inch-by-inch, fighting all the time. We finally gained the top of the parapets, and now the fighting was hand-to-hand, and continued for twenty-four minutes by the watch. It was the first time since entering the service that I ever thought it necessary to use my revolver in battle; this time I made good use of it, as I stood near our Colors and fought the enemy on the parapet. I was one of the first of the officers to enter the fort, and was not even touched by the missiles flying on all sides of me. When we rushed over the top the sight was truly terrific—dead men and the dying lay strewn all about, and it was with the greatest difficulty that we could prevent our infuriated soldiers from shooting down and braining all who survived of the stubborn foe. Not a rebel escaped; those not killed were captured.

"Immediately after the capture of Fort Gregg, two others nearby were evacuated. And during the night succeeding this, Petersburg was abandoned; and no sooner did we hear of that than the announcement ran along our line that Richmond, too, was ours, and Lee's army was on the retreat for Lynchburg.

"Our Brigade and Division gained quite a reputation in this brilliant affair at Fort Gregg. It was witnessed by thousands of spectators in both armies, who crowded by surrounding hills and housetops; and the Thirty-Ninth Illinois stands Number One in the Brigade.

"Out of 150 men, the number I took in of my Regiment, the balance being on picket duty at the time, sixteen were killed outright and forty-five wounded; six of whom, I understand, have since died. They lie buried where they fell.

"It has appeared good in the eyes of the commanding generals to reward your friend the writer for what they were pleased to denominate 'gallantry at the battle of Fort Gregg.' At least my Brigade Commander informed me, soon after the affair was over, that my name had been sent on to Washington to the War Department, with a recommendation for Brevet-Major, and also to the Governor of Illinois, for the regular commission as Major in my Regiment."

OFFICIAL REPORT OF COLONEL OSBORN

"Headquarters First Brigade,
First Division, Twenty-Fourth Army Corps,
Appomattox C. H., April 14, 1865

Major P. A. Davis, A.A.G.

"Major: —I have the honor to forward the following report of the operations of this Brigade since leaving the north bank of the James.

"The Brigade, preceded by a battalion of sharpshooters under command of Captain Curtis, moved from camp on the New Market road at 6:45 p.m. March 27, 1865, crossing the James river at Deep Bottom at eleven p.m. crossed the Appomattox at Broadway landing at daylight, halting about two hours, a mile beyond, for breakfast.

"Marched during the day toward Hatcher's Run on the left, bivouacking for the night near Humphrey's Station. At four a.m. March 29, 1865, moved forward and relieved General Miles (First) Division of the Second Army Corps, occupying his entire Division front at three p.m. on March 31, and Third and Fourth Brigades of this Division being engaged on our left; our pickets were strongly reinforced in accordance with orders of the Brigadier-General commanding, and a brisk skirmish was commenced with the enemy's pickets which continued about two hours, drawing heavy reinforcements to the line. But two of our men were wounded, one of the Thirty-Ninth Illinois Volunteers and one of the Sixty-Second Ohio Volunteers; both slight.

"Being relieved by a Brigade of colored troops April 1, 1865, at seven p.m., I moved my Brigade to the left in accordance with orders, reporting to the Brigadier-General commanding. Arriving on the ground designated, my command was placed in readiness to charge. In the meantime, by direction of General Foster, I sent six men forward to ascertain, if possible, the strength of the enemy, and the nature of the ground and obstructions intervening between our forces and the enemy's works; which was satisfactorily accomplished, the scouts giving full and reliable information.

"At five o'clock on the morning of April 2, I ordered forward one regiment of my command, the Thirty-Ninth Illinois Volunteers, by direction of the General commanding, to support the Third Brigade which was skirmishing with the enemy. At six a.m. I withdrew the Regiment, and in accordance with orders from the Brigadier-General commanding I moved left in front to the grounds of the Sixth Army Corps, some four or five miles to the right, nearing the front of the Sixth Corps; and word having been received that the enemy were re-occupying a portion of the line of works from which they had been driven early in the morning, the command 'double-quick' was given. Passing through the lines of the Sixth Corps, the Sixty-Second Ohio Volunteers being in advance, I threw them forward as skirmishers while the other regiments of the Brigade were in position 'in echelon' in the following order: the 199th Pennsylvania Volunteers on the right; their right resting on the line of the rebel works; the Sixty-Seventh Ohio Volunteers in the center, the Thirty-Ninth Illinois Volunteers being on the left. At once pressing rapidly forward we drove the enemy from their position, capturing some twenty-five prisoners, with two pieces of artillery; and turning these guns upon the enemy moved forward until we gained the hill, immediately in front of Fort Gregg and the chain of forts in the interior line of the defenses of Petersburg, which we wound to be strongly defended by artillery and infantry.

"At this point I halted my Brigade and prepared to charge the fort. The Third and Fourth Brigades moving up formed on my left at fifteen minutes past noon. At one p.m. orders were received to move forward and carry the enemy's works. I moved my command forward about half the distance in quick time at 'right-shoulder-shift arms,' and having passed a deep and difficult slough gave the command to 'charge' when the Brigade with cheers swept up the ascent at the double-quick under a terrible fire of grape, canister and minié balls tearing through the ranks. The Thirty-Ninth Illinois Volunteers moving straight forward struck the angle of the fort on the left and next the angle on the road; the Sixty-Second Ohio Volunteers and the 199th Pennsylvania Volunteers, striking this angle and the angle still further on the right, swept around to the rear, striving to gain an entrance, but it was found to be an enclosed fort admirably constructed for defense. The men rushed into the moat, and clambering up the exterior slope fought hand-to-hand across the parapet with the enemy, who stubbornly refused to surrender, although surrounded on all sides. The fighting lasted 24 minutes, when we forcibly burst over the parapets and the fort was ours. The redoubt on the right of the fort was also carried in the charge, by a portion of the skirmish line of the Sixty-Second Ohio Volunteers, assisted by two companies which had been detached from the 199th Pennsylvania Volunteers for this purpose, capturing a number of prisoners together with two cannon and five caissons.

"In this assault on Fort Gregg, Captain Patrick O. Murphy and First Lieutenant Robert McMillen, 199th Pennsylvania Volunteers, were killed; as also First Lieutenant William Lamb, Thirty-Ninth Illinois Volunteers; Captain O. M. Eddy and Captain Ansil, Sixty-Seventh Ohio Volunteers; Lieutenant Neil, Thirty-Ninth Illinois Volunteers, and Captain Gregory and Captain Beppus, Lieutenants Williams, Patton and Allison, 199th Pennsylvania Volunteers. Captain Hitchcock and Lieutenant Murry, Sixty-Second Ohio Volunteers, were wounded. The 199th Pennsylvania lost fourteen enlisted men killed and sixty wounded; the Sixty-Second Ohio Volunteers, three killed and twenty-five wounded; the Thirty-Ninth Illinois Volunteers, nineteen killed and forty-four wounded; and Sixty-Seventh Ohio Volunteers, seven killed and fifty-four wounded."

Narrative of William H. Howard, Company G, of the Thirty-Ninth Illinois stated:

"On the night of April 1, 1865, after our Regiment had reached the left of the line in front of Petersburg, I lay down for a little rest; but soon there came an order for me to report to General Terry, and he sent me out through our lines to locate the enemy's batteries and to ascertain the nature of the ground in our front. I was sent out without arms, and if possible

I was to get inside the rebel lines and find out what I could; and if captured, to play the part of a deserter. I started out, and had proceeded some distance when I was shot at while crossing a little stream on a log. I soon found out that I could not get through, and returned at three o'clock in the morning and reported to General Terry the position of the rebel batteries to our left and right, and what other facts I had gathered.

"We were in line at four o'clock for an assault, but at seven o'clock we were ordered to the right again, where we made preparations to assault Fort Gregg. While we were standing in line in the advance of the assaulting column I asked Captain Plimpton, commanding the Regiment, to let me advance as a sharpshooter. He at first declined, but finally said that I might go. I advanced about half way to the fort to a good sheltered position, and made several pretty fair shots at the rebel gunners. When the command to 'charge' was given, I started to the left oblique for a trench that ran out from the fort, but before I reached it there was some terrible hot work going on. I could see our 'boys' falling thick and fast. After reaching the trench I noticed a rebel officer with his hat in one hand and sword in the other, advancing from the rear to get into Fort Gregg. Two of Company D's boys who were with me fired at him, but missed. I then jumped out of the ditch near the stockade and took am at the officer's belt-plate, fired and the officer fell dead. As I rose up to get back to the ditch I was struck in the neck by a rifle-ball and knocked down, but it was a nearly-spent ball and did no great damage.

"After the fort had been taken, I went out where the dead officer lay and took his spurs and a pair of sleeve buttons, also some Confederate money. Some soldier from another regiment took his sword, which was a beauty. This officer, I have good reason to believe, was General A. P. Hill."

CHAPTER TWENTY

"End of this wicked rebellion"

In the previous chapter Captain Plimpton's letter of August 28, 1865 wrote of the attack on Fort Gregg, Virginia. His letter continues with the next phase in the final days of the war for the Thirty-Ninth Illinois.

"In our marches and fighting's from Petersburg to Appomattox Court-House where we compelled General Lee and his army to surrender on the 9th, it would run my letter out to too great length to give you a full account. Suffice it to say, our Corps, the Twenty-Fourth, followed the route along the Southside Railroad, marching day and night, skirmishing with the enemy wherever he would make a stand. It was by this rapid marching, some days without stopping for meals or sleep, that we succeeded in getting around in Lee's front and heading him off at Appomattox Court-House about twenty-two miles from Lynchburg.

"Our Division was in the lead of all the infantry when we arrived at that place, and our Brigade in the advance of the Division, and the Thirty-Ninth Illinois in the advance of the Brigade.

"We did not arrive upon the scene of the conflict five minutes too soon—Lee's advance was steadily pushing Sheridan's cavalry back, which he was determined to do before we could get up. General Sheridan sent work back to us for instant assistance. We arrived on the ground at the double-quick and immediately flew into line of battle, six companies of my Regiment being thrown out as skirmishers. A narrow strip of timber concealed us from the advancing rebels. As soon as we formed, we emerged from the woods with a regular Western yell, pouring a volley into the astonished rebels. At our first fire they halted and seemed to be dumbfounded, and as they saw the lone line of blue coats continuing to emerge from the woods they began to falter, and soon to break, and as we continued to advance, firing at every step, away they went in all directions, over the hills and down the gullies. I never, since entering the service, saw such a general "skedaddle." It was our sudden appearance directly across their only avenue of escape, and that right in their immediate front, that told them that their doom was sealed.

"We had not advanced over a quarter of a mile after the flying rabble ere the announcement ran along our line like wildfire, 'Lee had surrendered!' The white flag was sent out from his army in front of our Division."

"It was useless for me to attempt to give a description of the scene that followed the tidings. The tears rushed to my eyes—my heart was too full for utterance. There I stood at the head of my Regiment on the very ground where the Army of Northern Virginia, led by their pet General, Robert E. Lee, was compelled to surrender by our brave boys. It was to accomplish this very end that they had left home and friends, and periled their lives time and time again; and oh! how many of them are now sleeping the soldier's long, long sleep, unmindful of this great achievement! Here we recognized the end of this wicked rebellion, and you may be sure gratitude filled our hearts when we contemplated this grand result of all our tolls, our hard marches, hard fighting and exposures.

"I saw General Lee when he took his leave of General Grant after the papers were all signed, and I watched the countenance of our gallant chieftain as he came away, and I shall never forget it. It was beaming with a smile of satisfaction; and as he raised his hat when passing one of our sentinels who presented the proper salute, I knew that he did it as a mark of homage to the noble boys who had so gloriously accomplished this great work.

"We left Appomattox Court-House on the 16th and arrived at this place on the 25th. It was when were on the march back that we were shocked, yea horrified by the tidings of the death of our beloved President—killed by the cowardly hand of an assassin. Deep and revengeful was the indignation of the army when the truth was known. Emblems of mourning meet the eye on all sides. We never knew the depth of our love for that noble man until we heard of his cruel murder.

"This morning we heard of the death of the assassin. Vengeance is mine, and I will repay, saith the Lord. Amen, So let it be."

Colonel Osborn's Offical Report

"At eight a.m. on the morning of April 3 the Brigade moved at the head of the Division, the right in front, and marched toward Lynchburg, bivouacking for the night about eighteen miles distant from Petersburg. On the 4th reached Wilson's Station, halting at Ford's Station for dinner. On the 5th, after a long and tedious march of twenty-five miles, by was of Nottoway Court-House, we arrived at Burke's Station at eleven p.m. At one o'clock on the 6th of April we marched, in accordance with orders, towards Rice's Station. Arriving there were found the enemy in heavy forces throwing up entrenchments at the station to oppose us. In accordance with orders from the General commanding, throwing forward skirmishers, I formed line of battle and moved forward the Sixty-Second Ohio Volunteers and the 199th Pennsylvania Volunteers to the left and in advance of the Thirty-Ninth Illinois Volunteers, which was held in reserve, its right resting upon the railroad; the Sixty-Seventh Ohio Volunteers upon the right of the Thirty-Ninth Illinois Volunteers, the railroad intervening, and connecting with the Fourth Brigade on our right. I advanced my line as far at the Phillips House, nearly one mile southeast of the station, under a severe shell and musketry fire, driving back the enemy. Halting at this point, we remained during the night sleeping upon our arms.

"In this engagement Lieutenant-Colonel West of the Sixty-Second Ohio Volunteers and Captain Oliver C. Gregory of the 199th Pennsylvania Volunteers were wounded. The 199th Pennsylvania lost also in wounded, three enlisted men; the Sixty-Second Ohio Volunteers, thirteen enlisted men; the Sixty-Seventh Ohio Volunteers, seven enlisted men.

"At six a.m. April 7, my Brigade, advancing upon the enemy's works and finding them abandoned, moved out, taking the advance, following closely after the enemy; our skirmishers under command of Lieutenant-Colonel R. P. Hughes of the 199th Pennsylvania constantly engaging their rear, taking several prisoners. Crossing Sandy river, where General Crook's cavalry division came up on our right, we moved forward to Bush river, where we found the enemy inclined to dispute the passage. By direction of the General commanding, I formed line of battle, the 199th Pennsylvania on the right, its right resting upon the left of the road; the Sixty-Second Ohio in the center; the Sixty-Seventh Ohio on the left; the Thirty-Ninth Illinois supporting—and moved forward to the bank of the river, which was impassable except at the bridge. The 199th Pennsylvania, being on the right, was immediately thrown across the river, moved to the top of the hill, the enemy falling back before them. Moving across with the remainder of the Brigade we arrived at Farmville at five p.m., and encamped for the night on the west side of town.

"At six a.m. April 8 the march was resumed, bivouacking at midnight, having marched a distance of thirty-seven miles. Moving forward again at half-past three a.m. on the 9th inst., we halted at six a.m. for breakfast. At seven o'clock, heavy skirmishing being heard in advance in the vicinity of Appomattox Court-House, my Brigade moved rapidly forward to the scene of the action, arriving on the ground at the 'double-quick,' the cavalry falling back in confusion; and having thrown out a portion of the Thirty-Ninth Illinois as skirmishers, and throwing my Brigade forward into the line, the Thirty-Ninth Illinois on the right, the 199th Pennsylvania in the center, the Sixty-Second Ohio on the left, the Sixty-Seventh Ohio in reserve, I charged with a yell upon the enemy, giving them notice that the old Twenty-Fourth Army Corps was again in their front. Moving forward at 'doublequick,' I soon gained the edge of the woods, where I halted until the Third Brigade coming up extricated my left, which had become enveloped; when I again advanced, driving the enemy from the field, capturing one heavy piece of artillery.

"Changing direction by the left flank, in accordance with orders, I was passing the enemy's right when I was ordered to halt, word having been received that the Army of Northern Virginia had surrendered to the Army of the United States.

"In this engagement the 199th Pennsylvania Volunteers lost five enlisted men killed and twenty wounded; the Thirty-Ninth Illinois Volunteers, one commissioned officer and six enlisted men wounded; the Sixty-Seventh Ohio Volunteers lost one enlisted man killed and six wounded; the Sixty-Second Ohio Volunteers, eighteen enlisted men wounded. Two commissioned officers and thirty-eight enlisted men captured.

"Of the endurance and patience of the officers and men of this command during the tedious marches, and of their heroism and gallantry upon every battlefield I cannot speak too highly. I cannot close this report without speaking in high terms of the officers of my staff, Captain Childs, Captain Denny, Lieutenant Doud, and Lieutenant Ripple, for their heroic conduct. "I have to honor to be, Major,

Very respectfully, Your ob'd't serv't,
T. O. Osborn, Colonel Thirty-Ninth Ill. Vols, Com'd'g Brigade."

The letter of Major Plimpton and the official report of General Osborn have given a full and detailed account of the operations of the Thirty-Ninth from March 27 to the April 9, 1865. The writer now goes back a little and takes up the thread of his narrative. It will be remembered, however, that he was with the flying hospital of the Twenty-Fourth Corps, and what is said cannot very well be dissociated from the operations of that branch of his service. In fact, it has been the intention of the writer to give some prominence to the medical service of the army, which has never received the recognition that was its due except in the *Medical and Surgical History of the War* of *the Rebellion*. It was the general impression that the medical staff of the army—the "doctors!" as they were called, were exempt from the dangers and chances of war; but the following figures from the Surgeon-General's Report show to the contrary: thirty-two surgeons were killed in battle; nine by accidents; eighty-three were wounded in action, of whom ten died; four died in rebel prisons; seven of yellow fever; three of cholera; and 271 of other diseases incidental to camp-life and exposures. The medical staff as a body were efficient and faithful in the performance of duty; and were actuated by the highest motives of National and professional pride. They not only underwent the fatigues and exposures of the march and the chance on the field of battle, but many of them were also exposed to the contagion of disease.

Some idea of the labor performed by the medical department of the armies may be had when it is stated that 5,825,480 cases of wounds and diseases occurred among the white troops, and 629,354 among the colored soldiers.

The work devolving upon the flying hospital during this short but decisive campaign was enormous. The troops had been engaged with the enemy almost every day since March 27. We had stopped at eight different points along the line of advance since leaving Petersburg and put up our tents, tables and cots, and had cared for 1,200 wounded men, and 400 out of this number required operations. At the time the Army of Northern Virginia was paroled we received 200 of the enemy's wounded into our care, and after giving them all the attention they required sent them back where they could reach their homes as soon as able. We had been a flying hospital in so far as clarity could make it. We sooner was one lot of wounded disposed of, that we started onward again, keeping pace with the army.

We reached the scene of the assault on Fort Gregg in time to witness the return of our victorious troops, and in ample time to received the wounded of the First Brigade. After they had been cared for, which consumed the most part of the night, the writer rode into the city of Petersburg to gratify a curiosity to see the stronghold that our troops had been pounding at for so long a time and at so fearful a cost. On reaching the city the first party to encounter was made up of President Lincoln, Secretary Stanton and Generals Grant, Meade and Sheridan. Little did he think at that time that it would be his last look at the noble Lincoln, our beloved President. After riding through the district that had suffered so severely from the Federal shot and shell while on the other side of the river, and witnessing the great destruction to property, he rode back to quarters through the almost deserted streets of the fallen city. The only persons met with were groups of joyous Negroes who seemingly could not repress their enthusiasm, and they all wanted to see their great emancipator "Massa Linkum."

On getting back, the Twenty-Fourth Corps was in motion, advancing in the pursuit of Lee's army. Cannon were already booming at the front; aids-de-camp were hurrying to and fro, delivering orders; batteries of artillery were swiftly wheeling to the front, and the various regiments of infantry were deploying into marching order. The scene was grand and inspiring. The men looked weary and worn, but their spirits were jubilant and flowing over at the prospects before them of soon ending the rebellion.

At about noon of April 3 we came across the remains of the brave Assistant-Adjutant-General Theodore Reed, of General Ord's staff, who had been killed the day previous, and who had been buried in a very rude way by the rebels; his feet protruding out of the ground. In a short time we had his body exhumed and sent back, much to the satisfaction of his many friends.

Thus we followed on. Occasionally there was a lively brush with the rear-guard of Lee's army, and some quite severe battles until Appomattox Court-House was reached on April 9, where we set up our tables for the last time on the field of battle, and dressed the last man wounded in the finishing campaign of the war, belonging to the Twenty-Fourth Army Corps.

We started out on the preceding morning, April 8, and six a.m. and continued to press forward, with an occasional halt for rest and to await the movements of the advance guard, until midnight, when we turned into a field for bivouac. It was a brief one, however, for at three a.m. the call to "fall-in" sounded, and we were soon in motion, encouraged and stimulated by the reports that reached us, to the effect that Sheridan's cavalry was in the front and flank of the enemy, and fighting desperately to arrest the progress of Lee's army, and the orders were to "hurry up." The boys were very weary and foot-sore,-but courageously pressed onward, feeling—yes, knowing that the Confederates would be forced to surrender.

At six a.m. a halt was ordered for breakfast, but before the coffee was ready orders came to move forward on the "double-quick." Sharp firing was in progress at the front, and under this incitement the old Brigade started out at a swinging gait and soon covered the mile of distance that separated them from the advance of Lee's army. They were immediately formed in line of battle as they ran, with the Thirty-Ninth in the advance as skirmishers.

The rebels were totally unaware of the presence of infantry, the timber which we were hiding them from view, but they were soon apprised of the fact by hearing the unmistakable crack of the Springfield rifle, which was easily distinguished from the cavalry carbine. The surprise was as complete as unexpected, and we had not pressed forward on a forced march of forty-five miles in the past twenty-four hours for nothing. The enemy stood their ground faithfully, and even desperately, until either shot down or taken prisoner. "At one time," said Charles C. Hudson, Company E, "we thought the rebels had gained an advantage and got in our rear, as we heard lively volleys of musketry in the direction, but it proved to be a volley fired by a Negro regiment to celebrate the news of the surrender of the 'Army of Northern Virginia,' which fact had not yet reached us; but soon the welcome order 'Cease firing!' came to us, with the glad tidings that Lee was capitulating."

Appomattox Court-House was a town of about 200 buildings. It lay in a valley which divided the two armies. On hearing that Lee surrendered it was almost too good news to be believed all at once, but later, on riding out of the timber, we saw the wagons of the enemy perched on the slope beyond the town, and little white flags all along their line. Negotiations were then pending between Grant and Lee at McLean's house down in the town. We finally fully comprehended what this scene meant, all this quiet. It meant that the war was practically to an end; it meant that millions at our homes away in the northland were filled with joy and thanksgiving. There was as yet no cheering or manifestations of feelings, as the terms of the surrender were still being considered. It was about four p.m. when the capitulation was announced. Even then there was no outbreak among the victorious soldiers, flushed as they were with the greatest triumph of the war. Soldier grasped the hand of soldier in honest pride, and to his honor be it said, he was not wanting in a God-like charity and sympathy for the remnant of that misguided, fallen and half-starved army over there on the slope beyond.

McLean's House—Place of Lee's Surrender.

The writer rode over into Lee's camp, and mingled somewhat with the poorly-clad and emaciated rebels who had proved on many occasions foemen worthy of our steel. We outnumbered Lee's army three to one, and such sorrowful-looking men and beasts we had seldom seen. Many of the officers wished to sell their horses, or any other valuables they possessed, in order to get the means to return home. One officer came riding up to the writer, mounted on a splendid thoroughbred horse, who sent him to General Osborn, who had no horse, "Old Mack" having been killed while bearing the General gallantry forward to intercept Lee. "Old Mack" was so well thought of, having been with us throughout the war, that almost martial funeral ceremonies were paid him. The General purchased him, horse of the rebel staff officer, and brought it home with him. On our return to our own camp, there was noticed a large crowd of officers and soldiers surrounding a small apple tree near the borders of a small stream, and they were all busy in securing trophies, for they stated that the tree marked the spot where the terms of surrender had been decided upon by General Grant and Lee; and the hundreds securing pieces of the bark and limbs believed it too, and before night-fall that tree was gone—a victim to the relic-hunters. That Sunday Eve, April 9 at Appomattox Court-House, at the vesper hour, the Federals, in the true spirit of charity, divided their "hardtack" bread with their late bitter, uncompromising and deadly foes.

General Lee and many of his officers departed for their homes that evening, and the following is the General's last order to his Army of Northern Virginia.

GENERAL LEE'S LAST ORDER.

"Headquarters Army Northern Virginia.
10th April, 1865.

General Order No. 9

"After four years of arduous service marked by unsurpassed courage and fortitude, the Army of Northern Virginia had been compelled to yield to overwhelming numbers and resources. I need not tell the brave survivors of so many hard-fought battles who have remained steadfast to the last, that I have consented to the result from no distrust of them.

"But feeling that valor and devotion could accomplish nothing that would compensate for the loss that must have attended the continuance of the contest, I determined to avoid the useless sacrifices of those whose past services have endeared them to their countrymen.

"By the terms of the agreement officers and men can return to their homes and remain until exchanged. You will take with you the satisfaction that proceeds from the consciousness of duty faithfully performed, and I earnestly pray that a merciful God will extend to you His blessing and protection.

"With an unceasing admiration of your constancy and devotion to your country and a grateful remembrance of your kind and general consideration of myself, I bid you an affectionate farewell.

(Signed)   R. E. Lee, General.

After the surrender the First Division of the Twenty-Fourth Corps was ordered to guard, collect, and send back the war material that had been surrendered by the enemy. This duty occupied the attention of officers and men until April 17.

CHAPTER TWENTY ONE

"On to Richmond"

At five o'clock, April 17, we commenced the march to Richmond. Before leaving, however, the news came of the President's assassination. We could not at first credit the report; but the telegraph soon confirmed it, and when we reached Burkeville we received news of his death. It would be impossible to give expression to or present a word-picture of the feelings each and all shared alike. A great sorrow possessed our minds as we thought of Lincoln dead! He whom we had so lately seen in health, and so apparently satisfied that his armies had at least reached the "beginning of the end." And to think that the hand of an assassin should strike him down just as the great "sunburst" of victory was dispelling the gloom that had hung like a pall over the Nation for nearly four years! All of our gladness was gone. Tears and mutterings of Revenge were seen and heard on all sides. It seemed that all hope had departed. A few days ago were the happiest of our lives, but now the most sorrowful; each felt as though the loss was a personal one. The gaily swinging "route step" of our march on to the late rebel capital changed to the mournful cadence of a funeral pace. The men of the First Division were burdened with woe. The President's death called to mind some stanzas of his favorite poem.

"Oh! Why should the spirit of mortal be proud?
Like a swift fleeting meteor, a fast flying cloud,
A flash of the lighting, a break of the wave,
He passes from life to his rest in the grave.

"The hand of the king that the scepter hath borne,
The brow of the priest that the miter hath worn,
The eye of the sage, and the heart of the brave,
Are hidden and lost in the depths of the grave.

"'Tis the wink of an eye, 'Tis the draught of a breath,
From the blossom of health to the pallor of death;
From the gilded saloon to the bier and the shroud;
Oh! Why should the spirit of mortal be proud?
THAT
"Heroic soul, in homely garb half hid,
Sincere, sagacious, melancholy, quaint,

> What he endured, no less that what he did,
> Has reared his monument and crowned him saint."

We reached Farmville April 19, where the Division went into camp for a few days. The surgeons took possession of a large building where there were some 140 sick and wounded of the late Confederate army, as well as some of our own.

April 20, late in the afternoon, some twenty-two young ladies, escorted by Confederate officers, who were on their way to Richmond, came to us, seeking accommodations for the night, having been sent by General Meade. They were provided for and entertained as well as possible under the circumstances, and on taking their departure the following morning confessed to having a pretty fair opinion of the "Yankees." The string band of the Engineer Corps came over and gave them a serenade in the evening.

April 22, at four a.m. orders came to move forward to Richmond, which at last was to be our destination. The after noon of April 24 we reached Manchester, opposite Richmond, and went into camp, and where preparations were made for our triumphal entry into the capital of the exploded Confederacy. At nine a.m. the following morning we crossed the James River on the pontoon bridge and were received by the Third Division of our Corps, which had been the first of our troops to enter the city with General Weitzel. It was a grand and imposing sight to see the old war-worn veterans of the First and Second Divisions of the Twenty-Fourth Army Corps moving up Main Street with tattered banners flying, bayonets gleaming in the warm sunlight, and the troops marching and displaying as became them when entering the capital of the conquered, and especially after we had been so long a time in getting there.

The uniforms of officers and men were weather and travel stained, but this made little difference at such a time; all was happy within, and, to the music of the Union, the "boys" marched proudly and firmly over the pavements of the long-sought for, long-fought-for, and at last won! — the late throne of "Rebeldom," Richmond.

We passed through the city, between two lines of the Third Division, who "presented arms" and lustily cheered the heroes who had followed the army of Lee to the extremity of surrender.

The great victory that had been achieved was mainly due to the Twenty-Fourth Army Corps [of the Army of the James], and the First Brigade of the First Division of that Corps was entitled to the credit of being the first infantry to intercept the army of Lee which was pushing on toward Lynchburg as fast as possible. There were no war correspondents for the press with our Division at the time, which accounts, probably, for the little notice we received. From the tenor of the dispatches to the New York papers at that date it would appear that the Fifth, Sixth and Ninth Corps of the Army of the Potomac had done all the fighting and deserving of all the honors.

Since leaving our encampment at Chaffin's Farm on March 27, the Thirty-Ninth had marched over 250 miles; had fought or participated in eight engagements with Lee's army, one of which (the assault on Fort Gregg) had carried the key-point of the defense of Richmond, and which rendered both Petersburg and Richmond untenable; and besides, it had outflanked the advanced portion of the rebel army, compelled its surrender, and afterwards assisted in the disposal of the captured property.

The Regiment went into camp about two miles from the city, together with the balance of the Division, where a pleasant encampment was made.

General Osborn received his commission as Brigadier-General here, and planted a "star" on his shoulder. Captain Plimpton also secured his commission as Major, and was in command of the Regiment.

After we were established in quarters we rode to the city to look over the burnt district. It was sad to behold such a wanton destruction of property in the business district, and to know that it had been caused by rabid and lawless ruffians who, in the absence of the military and under no restraint, had fired the city for the purpose of plunder. There must have been a fearful state of affairs in the city of Richmond in the interval between the departure of Jeff Davis and his minions and the arrival of the Federal force under General Weitzel.

The city of Richmond, like ancient Rome, sat upon seven hills; and (to carry the parallel a little further) like Rome, it has fallen. "Pompey" Davis, after having exhausted all his resources and means for defense, had been overcome by the rapidly moving columns of "Caesar" Grant, who had passed the "Rubicon" (James) and created such alarm that the Senate and "Pompey" Davis party abandoned the city, leaving all the treasure (that he could not carry away) behind. The great King of the South was politically dead and buried, and we had assisted at the funeral with as joyous feelings as would well comport with such a disaster.

The people of the city seemed disposed to accept the situation as graciously as possible, and extended to us, in many ways, a cordial greeting. How honest it was at that time was not questioned.

May 5, the Army of the Potomac passed through the city on its way to Washington for the Grand Review, and to be mustered out of the United States service. The Twenty-Fourth Corps did the honors of receiving them. On May 10 General Sherman and his army of veterans reached Richmond and passed through on the way to Washington, and were also heartily received by the Twenty-Fourth Corps. All the inhabitants of the city had turned out to see them, and were amazed at their strength and equipment, and the fine soldierly appearance of officers and men. They often remarked that "they did not see how their army had held out so long as it did," having to antagonize such well-equipped, well-fed and disciplined soldiers as they had seen pass through Richmond. Some hours were occupied in their passage through the city. It was a grand and imposing spectacle to witness these bronzed and hardy veterans, some 60,000 strong, fresh from the "March to the Sea," passing on homewards for "muster out."

Our old commander, now Brevet Major-General Alfred H. Terry, the "Hero of Fort Fisher," was in command of the Department of Virginia and North Carolina with headquarters at Richmond, and Brigadier-General Joseph R. Hawley was his chief-of-staff. General Terry had been with us since July 1863, with the exception of the interval when he took command of the land forces in the expedition against Fort Fisher and the subsequent reinforcing of General Sherman at Raleigh, North Carolina. Our "boys" had confidence in Terry, and he was entitled to it; and besides, he had won their respect by his uniform kindness and courtesy of manner. He was a firm disciplinarian but never exacted anything from his command that he was not willing to share in. He was the friend of orderly and willing soldiers but despised shabbiness in either dress or action. His figure was commanding, tall, and straight as an arrow; manner dignified, but nothing approaching austerity; and one could seek his presence without the fear of being incontinently snubbed in so doing.

Major-General John Gibbons commanded the Twenty-Fourth Army Corps and Brigadier-General Robert S. Foster the First Division, while Brigadier-General Thomas O. Osborn was in command of our Brigade.

Soon after reaching Richmond a grand review of the Corps was held, and was made the occasion for the presentation of a new flag to the Thirty-Ninth by General Gibbons. On the standard was perched a magnificent bronze eagle which had been especially ordered by him and suitably engraved, to commemorate the gallant conduct of the Thirty-Ninth at the assault on Fort Gregg, Virginia, April 2, 1865.

One of the Ohio regiments of the brigade was likewise honored in the same manner.

This was the last general review before the disbanding of the old Corps, and it passed off in the most satisfactory manner to all concerned, and especially so to the officers and men of the Thirty-Ninth, who were proud as well as grateful to be honored in such a complimentary way and in so public a manner.

The duties of the men at Richmond were not excessive or burdensome, only such as the exigencies of the situation required. It was principally camp and provost-guard duty in and around the city.

The Corps Hospital was located at Camp Lee, formerly a camp of conscription and instruction for the Confederate army. The buildings upon the ground had been built before the war by the State Agricultural Society and were well adapted for hospital purposes. Soon after getting established, Miss Dix, Chief of the Nurse Department of the Army, made us a visit of inspection, and expressed herself as well pleased with our surrounding and accommodations for sick and wounded.

Surgeon Simonds, U. S. A., was our Medical Director, and is gratefully remembered for the interest he manifested in the welfare of our sick and disabled men.

In the early part of June the following General Order was promulgated, which was congratulatory and promissory, and we looked forward to a speedy muster out of service; but we were destined to remain yet longer in Virginia before that much-desired event.

"War Department,
Adjutant General's Office,
Washington, D.C., June 2, 1865.

GENERAL ORDER NO. 108

"Soldiers of the Armies of the United States: By your patriotic devotion to your country in the hour of danger and alarm—your magnificent fighting, bravery, and endurance—you have maintained the supremacy of the Union and the Constitution, overthrown all armed opposition to the enforcement of the laws, and of the Proclamation forever abolishing SLAVERY—the cause and pretext of the Rebellion—and opened the way to the rightful authorities to restore order and inaugurate peace on a permanent and enduring basis on every foot of American soil.

"Your marches, sieges, and battles, in distance, duration, resolution and brilliancy of result, dim the luster of the world's past military achievements, and will be the Patriot's precedent, in defense of Liberty and Right, in all time to come.

"In obedience to your country's call, you left your homes and families and volunteered in its defense. Victory has crowned your valor and secured the purpose of your patriot hearts; and with the gratitude of your countrymen, and the highest honors a great and free nation can accord, you will soon be permitted to return to your homes and families, conscious of having discharged the highest duty of American citizens.

"To achieve these glorious triumphs, and secure to yourselves, your fellow-countrymen, and posterity the blessings of free institutions, tens of thousands of your gallant comrades have fallen, and sealed the priceless legacy with their lives. The graves of these a grateful nation bedews with tears, honors their memories, and will ever cherish and support their stricken families.

U. S. Grant, Lieutenant-General."

War correspondents for the New York and other papers were still numerous around headquarters, and for the most part were jovial and interesting associates. We still bear in memory William H. Merriam, reporter for the *New York Herald*, a genial old soul done up in a wrapper of adiposity, and who was as broad as tall, and rolled and trundled about in a sea of humor. We had first met him in May 1864, at General Butler's headquarters, when he had a great appetite for news items of all kinds. He was full of "wise saws and modern instances," and when he would relax from his sphinx-like dignity of manner and expression, would entertain his friends with his store of anecdote and adventure, containing so much dry humor that it was necessary to wash them down with a bottle of his imported (?) champagne that he kept for these special occasions. He had his quarters in the State House, and seemed to be the custodian of the Confederate archives, or what was left of them, and was constantly circulating "Senate Journal Documents" among his friends.

The Richmond ladies, in course of time, having doubtless become convinced that the "Yankees" did not "wear horns," only drank them, began to show themselves more freely; and here it may be of interest to mention that Sam Greenbaum, of the band, was fortunate enough to secure a wife, who he says has been a blessing to him ever since. Sam was always on the lookout for chances.

Some of the Thirty-Ninth will remember Dr. Mayo and his brother, the mayor of Richmond, the former of whom gave the writer a lock of hair from the head of "Stonewall" Jackson, who died at Dr. Mayo's house. And some will recall with pleasant memories Governor Pierpont and the members of his staff; also Drs. Cabell, Hancock, and others who paid us friendly attention.

Some of you will remember old George Fitzhugh, a most bitter and uncompromising rebel, who had written several books in defense of Southern institutions—"Sociology for the South," "Cannibals All," and others of like stamp, but who now accepted the situation and the favors of the "boys in blue." You will recall pleasant memories of the Richmond Theater and its manager, R. D'Orsay Ogden, and Staples, his executive, and the actors—Frank Drew, Brink, William. H. Leake; and the

Misses Annie Waite, Revell and Tillinghast; and there will be some remembrance of the banquet that DeNormandie spread for them one night at Camp Lee when Generals Foster and Osborn and Colonel Dandy honored the occasion with their presence. And then there was the grand "blowout" at Division headquarters, given by Surgeon A. C. Barlow of the Sixty-Second Ohio, acting Division Surgeon, to the medical profession of Richmond as a return for like civilities, and where the extra, double B commissary whiskey so astonished the nerves of the invited guests that they were soon paralyzed and laid out—another "victory!" establishing the superiority of Yankee whiskey over that of the F. F. V.'s.

On or about the July 10 the Thirty-Ninth were ordered to City Point, Virginia, where they remained for a period of three weeks guard duty. While there they were called upon to suppress a riot between some cavalry soldiers and the Negroes, but happily they were not forced to use their guns. From City Point they proceeded to Norfolk, Virginia, and reported to Brevet Brigadier-General O. L. Mann, who was in command of the South eastern District of Virginia. General Mann, after recovering from the wound received at Ware Bottom Church, had been assigned to duty as provost-marshal at Norfolk and afterwards succeeded to the command of the district.

August 1 the Twenty-Fourth Army Corps ceased to be an organization, but a sufficient number of troops were retained at Richmond to maintain order and await the time when control of the State could be turned over to the civil authorities, the election for State officers having taken place on July 25, which passed off very quietly. The Corps hospital, also was soon closed out, and after the settlement of its affairs the writer reported to the Medical Director for orders, and was soon sent with orders to report to Surgeon J. J. Craven at Fort Monroe, who assigned him to duty at Norfolk, as Chief Medical Officer of the District and to take charge of the post hospital, reaching Norfolk with hospital steward DeNormandie about September 6, where he was once again among the members of his old regiment. Affairs at Norfolk were in the control of the Thirty-Ninth. The Regiment was pleasantly encamped in the open square of the city, fronting on Church Street.

The district was now under the command of Brevet Major General A.T.A. Torbert, who had succeeded General Mann, September 4. Captain Myers, Company K, had command of the hard-labor prison; Captain Samuel Gilmore was acting as provost-marshal, and afterwards was appointed on the staff of General Torbert, as Assistant General Inspector; and Lieutenant Leroy Doud was acting Assistant Adjutant-General on Torbert's staff.

The post hospital, called DeLamater Hospital, was under charge of acting Assistant Surgeon W. F. Litch, and was located in the court-house; and when the writer took possession was in bad shape and overcrowded. On representing the matter to General Torbert, the hospital was transferred to the old Marine Hospital situated on Ferry Point, midway between Portsmouth and Norfolk, after the premises had been inspected by Generals Torbert and Mann. It was then in possession of the Freedmen's Bureau, and was occupied as a school; but it was soon scrubbed out and whitewashed, and made most admirable quarters for the sick of the Thirty-Ninth and the Ninth Vermont Infantry, stationed at Portsmouth. Many of the Thirty-Ninth remember the hospital and the cry of "Ferry Point in a minit!" of the Negroes who conducted the little ferryboat that ran hourly between the hospital and Norfolk.

The duties at Norfolk were rather pleasant then otherwise, but we were not contented or satisfied. The war was finished and we wanted to go home, having filled our contract with the Government to the very utmost, and we were in daily expectancy of being "mustered out."

General Mann we remember as being very pleasantly and comfortably situated in fine quarters on one of the desirable residence streets near the bay, and had his wife with him. General Pennypacker, who had been seriously wounded at Fort Fisher, was still an invalid, and was located nearby, and under the care of Surgeon D. R. Brower. The writer remembers both gentlemen with much satisfaction. Dr. Brower, prior to our leaving Norfolk, went to Richmond and accepted some position under the new State Government.

The District of Southeastern Virginia embraced the counties of Princess Anne, Norfolk, Nansemond, Southampton and Isle of Wight, and there was a large Negro element to be cared for and kept at work. The Negroes had become possessed of the idea in some manner that on Christmas Day they were each to receive from the United States Government large quantities of land, and in consequence of this impression many of them refused to make any contracts to labor after Christmas. In order to correct this impression General Terry issued an order for the detail of proper officers to be sent into every county, and as far as possible in to each neighborhood, to explain that the Government had no intention, even if it had the power, to do anything of the kind. This entailed a great deal of labor, but ultimately saved a great deal of trouble.

CHAPTER TWENTY TWO

"School is out!"

On December 1, orders were received for the "muster out" of the Ninth Vermont Volunteers. Prior to their departure the officers of that regiment gave a grand military ball, and cordial invitations were extended to the Thirty-Ninth, who gladly responded. The affair passed off with much satisfaction and enjoyment.

On December 3, 1865, orders came for the Thirty-Ninth to prepare for "muster out." It is quite unnecessary to add that the tidings were received with great rejoicing. This formality took place on the afternoon of December 6, and at nightfall we were safely on board a steamer for Springfield, Illinois, via Baltimore and Chicago.

On the boat, and well assured that we were on the way home to stay, everybody was jolly and happy, and the jollity was long-drawn-out, lasting until we reached Baltimore early the next morning. After breakfasting, the Regiment took its place on the train awaiting it on the Pennsylvania Central Railroad and was soon speeding to Chicago. The journey was safe, comfortable and afforded enjoyment to all. We felt that at last "school is out!"

At Chicago a bountiful repast was spread at Bryan Hall by the noble-hearted ladies of the "Soldiers Aid Commission." The ensuing morning, after breakfast at the same place, we took the cars for Springfield. Our march to the cars was accompanied by cheers and shouts, the waving of hats and handkerchiefs by the loyal people of Chicago.

We reached Springfield the morning of December 9 without the occurrence of anything worthy of mention, and proceeded to Camp Butler, where we encamped. Here the time was fully occupied in turning over all government property in our possession and in making out the final discharge papers and payroll of men and officers, and on December 16 receiving the pay due from "Uncle Sam" and assembling once more together as an organization before Adjutant-General Haynie to surrender our war-worn, battle-torn and well-loved flags that the Regiment had carried through four years and two months of active service.

We met together for the last time, soon to be separate in widely diverging paths. The following exercises took place in the chapel.

The Regiment, under command of Brevet Brigadier-General O. L. Mann, was massed in the chapel of the camp, where the ceremony of surrendering the flags of the Regiment to the State authorities transpired. The flags were three in number, and were severally presented. Number One was a "prize flag," awarded by the State Agricultural Society, as a premium for superior drill and discipline, and was called "The Agricultural Flag." The brazen eagle, ball and socket, attaching to this flag, were presented by Major-General John Gibbons, commanding the Twenty-Fourth Corps, for gallant conduct in the assault on Fort Gregg, Petersburg, Virginia, April 2, 1865. Number Two had been presented by Governor Yates, and contained a life-size picture of His Excellency. This flag,

General Mann said, had been consigned to the care of a Sergeant of the same name, who had been shot down in one of the engagements, while unfurling it to the breeze, and when his lifeless body was about to be removed for burial, it was discovered that his right hand still grasped a shred of the flag, and that its folds were saturated with his life blood. The name of Sergeant Yates should therefore be associated with that old flag, and his memory should be dear and sacred to every patriotic heart in the State. Number Three, in its tattered, riddled and ragged condition, bore unmistakable traces of original beauty, and was the give of a young lady named Miss Arion, and had been tenderly and sacredly regarded for her sake. The flags were all literally in ribbons, and bore incontrovertible evidence of the fiery ordeal through which they had passed. General Mann observed that these old flags were very dear in the sight of the men of the Thirty-Ninth Regiment, and he hoped that if the State possessed no secure and proper receptacle for them and others of like history, that she would lose no time in providing one.

General Haynie, in taking charge of the precious relics, observed that he had no language in which to express the emotions of his soul on that occasion. He regretted that the State possessed no fireproof building in which to deposit them, and keep them secure against casualties, and earnestly hoped that the matter would engage the early attention of our Legislature. He said that these old, tattered and riddled banners constituted the jewels of the State, and, if lost or destroyed, could never be replaced. Diamonds or precious metals, if lost, could be made good again, but these were priceless and invaluable, and no pains on his part would be spared to protect them against any possible contingency. They were made sacred by the blood, which, they had been told, was shed upon them.

Turning from the flags to the men, on behalf of the State and its Executive, Governor Oglesby, who was absent therefrom, General Haynie bid them a most hearty welcome back to its generous soil, and gratefully thanked them for the noble and heroic services they had rendered to the Nation. In conclusion, he hoped that on their return home to the quiet pursuits of civil life, they would not abandon the principles they had fought for in the field; that they would be true to their own record, and true to the Union and its friends. There were, unfortunately, still rebels at home, who had kept up a fire in the rear while they were in the field, and there was no reason why they should change front at home and vote in favor of the party and principles against which they had fought and bled in the field. This part of the General's speech was received with rounds of applause, amid which he retired from the platform, the band striking up a stirring air.

At the conclusion of General Haynie's speech, General Mann again ascended the platform, and for the last time demanded the "attention" of his command, on this occasion to deliver to them his last "order" and take his final leave as their commander.

"Soldiers: The period toward which your attention has been directed for a long time is at hand. Having served your country faithfully for nearly five years, you are today honorably discharged from the army of the United States. You will soon leave off your veteran garb of valiant blue, and, putting on another suit, become honorable citizens of an honorable State—a State that has sent over 260,000 troops to the field, and given to the country a President who has fallen a martyr to that cause which, like the voice of God, called you from your homes to engage in the stern realities of fierce and bloody warfare. In parting with you, it is not necessary for me to remind you of the different departments in which you have served with distinction. The graves of your fallen but gallant comrades, in Missouri, in Maryland, in the Carolinas and in the Virginias, will keep them fresh in your memories. Nor need your commanding officer enumerate the many stormy moonless nights you have passed on picket, guarding your sleeping comrades from the midnight assaults of those who sought alike your lives and the life of your country—these will never be forgotten. The sanguinary fields which you have gallantly fought, and the frowning, formidable forts you have heroically stormed, you will always remember. Some of you will remember them by the wounds which are still fresh in your bodies, and by the limbs you have left to bleach on Southern soil, while on all your memories they are as deeply engraved as they are on your victorious old battle-flags, which you today turned over to the authorities of your State, unsullied by even an imaginary shade of dishonor.

"The fortunes of war have been such as to prevent your commander from participating with you in the final campaign that crowned our common country with Victory and Peace. Yet from his post of duty elsewhere he watched your interests with a jealous eye, and heard of your deeds of valor with feelings of pride and regret. To your gallantry and efficiency in the field is he largely indebted for his present rank and position, and he therefore most cheerfully embraces this last opportunity to thank you, one and all, for your soldierly bearing towards him, and for the promptness with which you have observed and executed his orders. He will ever regard it his sacred duty to contribute in any way to your individual prosperity, wherever he can, and bespeak for you that recognition of the glorious services you have rendered your country, and so nobly and dearly earned. Go to your homes, Veteran Soldiers, and strive to perpetuate that peace, whose purchase was effected at so vast a price, which has made your once long lives short, and your full ranks thin. But should the emergency again arise, when either National honor must be compromised, or personal life laid on the alter of your country, let no member of the Yates Phalanx be slow in rushing to the conflict as a representative of the honored old Thirty-Ninth.

"Urging upon you, possibly for the last time, the vital importance of maintaining characters of honesty, integrity, industry and stability, and hoping that again in the peaceful circles of home and friends you will leave far behind any habits contracted in the army that may tend to retard you in a manly career in the great campaign of life, your commander bid you, officers and men, one and all, an affectionate Farewell!"

For some moments after the General ceased speaking, a deep silence prevailed, which was then relieved by a burst of loud and prolonged cheering. The old colors were again, and for the last time, saluted, when the men passed out of the chapel to join the Paymaster, who had established a "headquarters" at another point, and was ready to distribute a large quantity of promissory notes, issued on the credit of Uncle Sam.

The men who participated in the final "muster out" have sought homes in almost every State and Territory of the Union, and have proved good citizens and worthy members of society. The number is growing less and less as each year makes its changes. Soon "taps!" and "lights out!" will be sounded for the last one of our number by the grim camp-follower of us all—Death! only to awake at the "reveille" of Gabriel as he summons us for final account; and we earnestly hope and trust, in closing this faithful yet imperfect record of your history in the War of the Rebellion, that there may be a balance in our favor at the Judgment.

Comrades, the following letter will explain itself. It is introduced here thinking that it would prove eminently satisfactory to yourself and your posterity to know the opinion of Major-General Alfred H. Terry, concerning your conduct during the nearly three years you were in his command. He is seriously ill from Bright's disease of the kidneys with its many complications. His sufferings make writing a difficult task, and hence his letter is to be the more appreciated by us all.

"New Haven, Conn. May 14, 1889.

My dear Doctor:

"You ask me to express my opinion about the 'Old Thirty-Ninth Illinois.' What can I say about it—what can any one say about it except that it was one of the most gallant of Regiments and was as distinguished for its discipline and good order in camp and on the march as it was for its gallantry in action.

"Sum up all soldierly qualities and attribute them to the Regiment and you will do it no more than justice.

Sincerely yours,
Alfred H. Terry"

One last word before you close this poor recital of your heroic deeds on many fields and under varied circumstances.

Do you not, all of you, comrades, feel gratified and proud of the noble and active part the dear old Regiment took in the "War of the Rebellion?" In tracing out its movements the writer has lived over again the days when this history was made; forms and faces, together with events almost lost to memory, have appeared with a brightness that seemed impossible; and so, doubt less, have appeared to you.

This history of the Thirty-Ninth has been written, not alone for your satisfaction, but for the gratification of your children and your children's children, who will hand it down to still remoter generations with the pride and boast of an ancestry who fought and died and were crippled in order to sustain and perpetuate the Union of the States of North America.

The Wilmington Monument

The modest white shaft, but one foot square at its base and six feet in height, which marks the burial place of Adjutant Joseph D. Walker at Oakwood's Cemetery, Wilmington, Illinois, is also the cenotaph whereon is recorded the names of many comrades who fell in battle or died of wounds and disease from Companies A and E of the Thirty-Ninth Illinois Veteran Volunteer Infantry. It is located in a beautiful spot on the bluff of the east branch of the majestic Kankakee river, within 150' of the tranquil water, which is only disturbed by the occasional passing of a canal steamer, or ruffled by the storm-winds that whistle a requiem over the graves of fifty or more martyrs representing various commands in the great "War of the Rebellion." It is laden with flowers annually, often visited by the friends of those whose names are modestly chiseled in the snow-white marble.

On the front or east-side surface of the shaft are the names of —

Adjutant JOSEPH D. WALKER.
Lieutenant JOSEPH W. RICHARDSON, Company A.

On the south front is inscribed the names of —

Sergeant DAVID M. HANSON.
Sergeant GEORGE W. BURTON.
ALEXANDER GRAY.
ALMON MERRILL.
THOMAS STEWART.
WALTER VAN DEBOGART.
JAMES McMASTER.
All of Company E.

While on the north surface of the shaft appear the following names —

Sergeant GEORGE W. YATES.
WILLIAM BUTTERFIELD.
IRA NICHOLS.
ANDREW SEYBERT.
GEORGE LYONS.

HENRY STARKWEATHER.
JOSEPH CARTER.
HUGH ROURKE.
All of Company A.

And the name of Major S. W. Munn, who organized Company A, will be added before the regimental reunion of 1889.

Testimonial to Dr. Charles M. Clark

"Dear Sir and Comrade: You and the undersigned were selected to act as a committee to publish the History of the Thirty-Ninth Illinois Regiment, and upon you the committee placed the responsible duties as chief editor. We recognize, therefore, that it is a very delicate task for you to record the important part of history which you made, and the honorable relations which you sustained to the Regiment and to the medical department of the army.

"We therefore request and direct you to insert the following relating to your labors during the war, as prepared by one of your comrades, feeling assured that all the survivors of the Regiment will fully endorse what we have said, and heartily join in this testimonial to your efficiency and faithfulness while Surgeon of the Thirty-Ninth.

"There is no branch of military service on which the usefulness of an army depends more than on the medical department. In order that it may be thoroughly prepared for long marches and for desperate encounters with an enemy, the entire rank and file must be in the very best of physical vigor. It is one of the prime duties of the surgeon of a regiment to see that this desired condition is rigidly maintained. Is the location of the camp healthful? Is its sanitary conditions at as high a grade of excellence as is possible? Are rations properly prepared? Is the soldier too sick for duty, or shall he be returned to the ranks? Shall he be sent to a general hospital or discharged from the service? All these questions, and many more of kindred character, constantly confront the army surgeon, and to answer them for the best 'good of the service,' requires great skill and untiring devotion to public duty.

"Comrade Clark entered upon his duties as Surgeon of the Regiment well equipped to meet manfully all these stern requirements under very favorable circumstances. Though young, he had met with success in his practice and had attracted the notice of the medical fraternity. He had 'roughed it' in the gold fields of the Rockies, and hence took kindly to camp life. His post of duty was, from the first, with his regiment, and it never got so far to the front as to leave him in the rear. He was on detached service frequently, but seldom lost sight of his own command, for he invariably refused duty that would remove him from fields where wounds were found. He was a skillful surgeon, and many of his complicated field operations are of public record; and of the public records which surgeons were required to keep, those of Dr. Clark are said by competent authority at Washington to be among the very best returned, and they must be of great value to the Bureau of Pensions.

"When Dr. Clark reached Appomattox Court-House, he was the Chief Operating Surgeon of the Field Hospital of the Twenty-Fourth Army Corps, and yet he was in 'hailing distance' of the old Thirty-Ninth.

"Our medical comrade settled in Chicago at the close of the war, and is now there in the enjoyment of a remunerative practice.

Signed, Amos Savage, Al. C. Sweetser, O. L Mann."

APPENDIX I

Hugh R. Snee Letter To his Grandchildren

Private Hugh Rippy Snee was one of the men mustered out with the Regiment on December 6, 1865. His tale is one of great deprivation, pain and terrible suffering. Yet, filled too, with strength, determination and courage. On May 16, 1864 during the battle of Drewry's Bluff, Virginia, he suffered a head wound caused by a Confederate saber and was also wounded in the cheek by a musket ball. After the battle, he was considered "walking wounded" by the doctors and was assigned to duties of helping other injured comrades on the battlefield. During this assignment his position was overrun and he was forced to surrender. He was sent to Andersonville Military Prison.

During the next several months' Snee attempted escape by various means. The Rebels, trying to reduce the number of escape attempts from Andersonville, decided to move many prisoners, including Hugh Snee. As these Union soldiers were being transferred to another prisoner, the train derailed forcing the prisoners to be returned to the camp. Snee suffered dreadful injuries to his hands, feet and scalp, but since the Confederate doctors did not consider these wounds serious, they were left untreated. These were the cause of various health problems that would plague him all his life.

Snee remained a prisoner until late September 1864 when, by taking the name of a dead soldier, his final attempt at freedom was successful.

After his escape he wandered barefoot and alone until he reached the little station of Lovejoy on the railroad running from Atlanta east. Following the tracks, he entered the Union lines on approximately October 21, starving and suffering from scurvy, chronic diarrhea, and gangrene.

It was here he found a cousin who located his younger brother Nathan who was on detached service from the Seventy-Sixth Illinois. (In June 1863, Nathan had been injured during the battle of Vicksburg. He was in the skirmish line when the man next to him fired his musket so close to Nathan's head that a piece of the percussion cap flew into his ear, causing injury and perm anent deafness. The Army believed he was no longer capable of being an infantryman, however, he could fire a cannon. In January 1864, Nathan was transferred to the Fourth Ordnance Division, Seventeenth Artillery Corps near Big Shanty, Georgia.) Nathan and others cared for Hugh until he could be sent to a hospital. Snee was to spend the next several months in the Military Hospital in Cincinnati, Ohio and his home near Rockville, Illinois. There after, he returned to the Regiment at Norfolk in August 1865.

My Great-Great-Grandfather, Private Hugh Rippy Snee of Company E, wrote a letter to his father shortly after his escape from Andersonville that tells his tale far better than this writer. This missive became the basis for another letter he wrote to his grandchildren.

"My Dear Grandchildren—

At your earnest and often repeated request that I write an account of my capture, imprisonment and escape from the Confederate Military Prison at Andersonville, G.A. in 1864, I have concluded that with the help of a copy of the tale as written for my father soon after my escape from there to comply with your wishes.

"But I am aware that a gray head is very liable to contain a failing memory. I shall confine myself almost entirely to the letter as I wrote it when all the incidents were fresh in my memory.

"My Regiment, the Thirty-ninth Illinois Volunteers, at the time was a part of the Army of the James under General B. F. Butler pushing out from Bermuda Hundred to attack Petersburg from that side and we were attacked by Beauragarde at Dreuries Bluff, V.A. on May 16, 1864 and were driven back from the rear by a force which had broken through our lines to the right of us. But we cut our way through the attacking party and again on a hill not far to the rear of our former position where we supposed we would be safe, and from this new position, I with a few of my comrades were sent back to pick up some of the wounded of my Company whom we found and carried back to where a large number of wounded had been gathered to be placed on some flat cars standing on the track at that place. And while resting (after caring for the wounded) we were charged upon by the Rebel cavalry [Third North Carolina] from the timber on our right which at first took to be our own men for we were not aware that our own lines had fallen back while we were after the wounded. The Rebs cut us off and ran us up on the Railroad towards Petersburg at a double quick. At Petersburg we were confined in an old tobacco warehouse until we were started on our long railroad journey to Andersonville where we arrived about June 1, 1864 where we were assigned to the Forty-Second Detachment which was located in the new or East side of the Stockade. A detachment consisted of three messes of ninety men, each in charge of one man chosen by vote from their own ranks, and the head of each mess was chosen the same way. My Detachment was made up principally of Western men and stood the hardships of this terrible prison life much better than the Eastern men did. Consequently, the death rate was lower in my Detachment than in the Detachments on each side of us which were made up from a regiment of shoemakers from Lynn, Mass., and I got along very well under the circumstances. I made it a point to be busy at something as much of the time as possible, and to further this plan, I made long walks about the Prison and kept posted as to what was being done as far as I could.

"I checked two attacks of that deadly scourge, prison diarrhea, by as total abstinence from food and drink for three days and a careful diet as I resumed eating afterwards. I fear that very few could have lived through such a fast when half starved at best. Many tried it but very few succeeded. Most of them would have died, I think, ere there fast could have been prolonged enough to have done them any good.

"And now, all of you having read many better descriptions of this prison that it is possible for me to write, I will attempt nothing further. But taking my cue from the nature of the questions you have put to me, I infer that you are more interested in the manner of my escape from there than in a recounting of my sufferings while there.

"I made two unsuccessful attempts at escape, both on about the same general plan, and will describe the last one. And will say right here that there was not at any time the remotest chance of escape from that prison and every and all of such attempts were only a dangerous waste of energy and brought only punishment and despair.

"One morning myself and a comrade got detached to go outside under a guide to get wood for cooking purposes. We were placed under a boy of about 16 years of age, and on a pretense of searching for Herbs for medicinal purposes, we enticed the boy into the woods as far as possible where we attacked him from the rear, took his gun from him, covering his mouth with a part of his clothes, tied him to a tree, and started South in the direction of a River that we had been told entered into a larger one which went to the Sea. But we soon ran into the Cavalry Patrol which surrounded the Prison at no great distance from it. We told where the Boy was; We were taken back to the Prison gate where we expected to meet with severe punishment, but fortunately for us, there happened to be a good natured, kind hearted Lieutenant in charge of the gate that day. After giving us a good scare, finished up by saying —Yanks, I guess you will have to try some other trick if you get out of here— and chucked us back in the prison again.

"Sometime in September, Authorities made an attempt to move some of the Prisoners to some other Prison and to discourage any attempt to escape on our part, they gave it out that we were going to the front to be exchanged. The train that I was on ran off the track and was badly wrecked about three miles from the Prison and many were killed and wounded. I was badly bruised on both my feet and got a bad scalp wound, and a sliver from the wreck pushed into my shoulder and a finger on my left hand was broken. We were taken back to the Prison. My injuries were not considered serious enough to require treatment, and right there is where my sufferings began in earnest: The scurvy developed in my wounds and instead the flesh began to slough off, and I had witnessed some of the sufferings and death of others, that it was only a question of a very short time I would be passed out of the gate, feet foremost, to swell the number of that silent host on the hill who tell no tales of Andersonville.

"And from that time on I was ever on the lookout for something that might give me an opportunity to escape. I had become desperate and preferred to die in an attempt to escape rather than to rot to death in that loathsome Pen, and made two unsuccessful attempts at escape ere fortune threw a chance my way, which, in my desperation, I availed myself of.

"About that time General Sherman and Hood were fixing up an exchange of Prisoners. As the result of the surrender of Atlanta, Sherman was to have 2,000 of the fresh men that he could place in the field. And as I belonged to Grant's Army, and had been a long time in Prison, I was hopelessly shut out. But the weather being very hot at that time, all movements of Prisoners had to be made at night, which circumstances gave me hope and kept me on the alert. The names of the men in the list of exchange were sent in sometime before the cars could be obtained for their transportation to the front for exchange, and in the meantime, some of the men died and I learned of the death of a man in a mess that the Sargent of which was an acquaintance of mine, and I persuaded him (for a consideration to be paid when I got out) not to report his death as belonging to the Cartel and allow me to answer his name when called and pass out with the squad. But just before the Roll Call began, someone caught onto the trick and demanded of him that one of their own impersonate the dead man, or they would report him. So you see, my bubble was badly punctured. But as a result of this attempt to get out with this squad, I had familiarized myself with all the details of the exchange and was on hand and ready to avail myself of any chance that might turn up to my advantage. The Rebel Sargent who called the roll stood on a box and a man stood near him and held up a torch (as they had no other kind of light) as a light for him to read the list by, which only served to intensify the darkness and gloom just beyond the circle of light caused by the flaring torch. And right here I will suggest that I owe my escape to a strange peculiarity of some persons, which, I am sure any old soldier of long service will bear me out as to the truth and prevalence of; namely, that no matter what the occasion or how much there might be at stake, they were never quite ready but had something to do yet, or, at any rate, were out of hearing for some cause unknown to anyone but them selves. And as the roll call progressed, I noticed that now and then some man did not answer to his name, and was passed to be called later, and I had noticed that a man of the 17th Iowa had been called twice with no answer, and right there, I resolved that I would answer if the name was called again and take my chances of detection. For I felt sure that his immediate comrades had passed out and those remaining would not know that I was not the right man. And to favor my chances, another Sargent got upon the box to relieve the other, and he at once began to call the unchecked names and when he reached the Iowa man's name, I answered. And after a deal of profane discussion and advice on the duty of punctuality, I was passed out of the gate and joined the men to march over to the cars. But while we were still at the gate, the Iowa man came up, and after a long wrangle, part of which I could hear, was passed out. I stepped into the shadows of the gate to be out of sight in case they came out to verify the count of the car load. They passed him out and the car load started for the Depot where we were given a day's ration. But this time, the man was on hand and I got no ration, but I laid down until morning when I give it out that someone had stolen my ration and some of the boys divided with me and did very well. And when we got to Macon we changed cars, but I don't remember just how I managed to make the change without detection. But at Lovejoy Station the track was torn up from there to East Point where the exchange was to be made. At Sherman's Out Post and from there we were obliged to march about twelve miles. And here it was dark again, and again the Roll was called. As the Rebs had a suspicion that some Yanks had managed in some way to smuggling who did not belong to the exchange and for the purpose of detecting any smugglers, a row of pine knots were lighted and placed in a row across a small field, and as fast as a man's name was called, he was made to step across and form in line on the other side of the row of lights. I took in the situation and in the confusion of so long a roll call, quietly slipped into the brush which was very thick just to our left. I never knew if any others were there who did not belong in the exchange, but heard that there were. I laid down near by and waited until day light when I started along the torn up railroad track, but kept far enough from the track to be out of sight.

"I had a terrible march. I was very weak and bare footed with several running sores on my feet and limbs. My body was swollen almost to the bursting point and nothing to eat, and in rained most of the time. Some time in the afternoon, I laid down by a fallen tree and went to sleep. And on waking up, heard a murmur of voices but could not distinguish as to whether they were Union men, Rebels, or Negroes at work. But dare not show myself. And in an effort to learn who they were, I passed along the length of the log on all fours several times in an effort to catch sight of them without exposing myself, but could see nothing. But while I was asleep, the weather had cleared off and the sun shown out and there appeared to be great activity among those talking. And while continually peering over the log, I caught sight of a flag being raised up among the limbs of the trees and soon made it out to be the Stars and Stripes and knew I was saved.

"I had passed through the outpost while it was raining and almost ran into the reserve picket line. The 116th Illinois was on picket at that place, and with them I found a cousin, a fifer of the Regiment, who cared for me, sent word to my brother nearby on duty with the division quarter master, and by him was taken to his camp, placed in the care of a kind-hearted motherly old wench who was cooking for the mess to which he belonged where I improved rapidly until the Twenty-First Ohio Regiment (in which I had relatives and many old school mates) was mustered out of the service. When they started home they took charge of me and took me with them to Elmore, Ohio, where I was born and lived until 17 years of age. And from there, after a short visit among relatives and friends, I went home at Rockville, Illinois, where I got a furlough for sixty days, which was renewed from time to time until I was able for duty, [nearly 8 months later] when I joined my Regiment at Norfolk, Virginia."

Snee finished his account to his father by stating, "Here the old record ends." He resumes the account to his grandchildren:

"And I shall be obliged to depend upon memory entirely and I feel loath to add anything to it. But I am sure there are many interesting incidents that occurred to me as my memory reverts back to that six months of by life between the date of my capture and the day of my deliverance, many of which you have heard me relate and which I would take pleasure in recording were it not for the prominence of the pronoun I that must, of necessity, be unpleasantly noticeable in connection with what I am able to recall at this distant date, but will mention a few where I shall be obliged to recall an unpleasant failure and should not be open to the charge of vanity.

"Immediately after we were cut off from our troops at Duries Bluff and they were running us along the railroad towards Petersburg, I noticed that the brush and trees grew very thick on both sides of the track. And I resolved to make a break for liberty. I felt sure that if the first shot missed me, I would be out of sight and that they would have no time to follow me and that I would soon be inside of our own lines. And under pretense of being taken suddenly very sick, began to fall back. And a comrade slacked up with me and the Rebel Officer told a young soldier to slow down and guard us, and soon as I got a few rods behind the squad I reached down and grabbed a stone about the size of a goose egg, intending the knock the boy off his horse, and jump into the brush. But as I was raising up with the stone, my comrade knocked it from my hand with the remark— 'Do you want us both shot, you fool?'—which caused the boy to yell out to the Lieutenant, who rushed back in a great rage, swinging his saber about our heads, started us at a double-quick which we were forced to keep us until we caught up with the squad. I was holding fast to his saddle skirt just back of his seat and was clear of his sword arm, but my comrade was so close to me that he knocked the stone from my hand before I could throw it.

"Now the next incident that I recall happened after we arrived in Petersburg. As I have already stated, we were in a large building and were being used and fed as well as they were able to. Our cooking was done on the outside of the building by the prisoners in a yard surrounded by a heavy guard. And for the sake of fresh air and a chance to look around, I volunteered as one of the cooks. I knew that it was a hard and disagreeable task. I will mention right here so that you may better understand the situation, that the Rebel guard here was a company of North Carolina nine-month men, most of them were Union men at heart but were forced into the Rebel service. And I was not long in getting to that fact. And I soon made the acquaintance of a Sergeant who I concluded to trust. I had many long and pleasant talks with him.

"The Union lines at that time were only 9 miles from Petersburg and I had not yet abandoned all hopes of escape. The Drs. and Provost Marshal officers wee in the same room in the end of the building, and my duties as cook let me past the open door of this office many times in the course of the day. I had noticed that a few sheets of blank passes lay on the table or desk used in common by both of the officers. As the duties of the Provost kept him up in the City most of the time, where his main office was located, he was in the habit of signing some of these passes in blank to be filled out by the Dr. for the accommodation of persons who called for them in his absence. Now the Sergeant had told me that if I could get one of these passes for two, he would pass me out to the front. Now to get one of these sheets of signed blanks, I feigned sickness and went into the office at sick call for medicine, but before going in, placed some wax on the sole of my shoe, and while in, I managed to brush one of the sheets off the table. I placed my foot on it and backed out of the office, and after consulting with the Sargent, I filled out a pass for the front on outside guard. And we arranged to start Thursday night when we expected to take advantage of an appointment of a meeting by a Priest and a Sister of Charity to give us a religious talk, - When most of our guards would be admitted into the prison to hear the talk. Now I have no doubt you will think this a very foolish and dangerous undertaking and perhaps it was. The Sargent may have been drawing me on for purpose and had he done so, I would have been in a very unpleasant situation. But I had made up my mind to risk it. But in the afternoon of that Thursday, we got orders to march to the Depot to begin our long journey to Andersonville. So you see how my second grand scheme for liberty went glimmering. I do not propose to add anything to what has already been told by those far better qualified to do it justice that I could hope to, and will only say in conclusion that in all I have read and heard, I have never seen or heard the facts exaggerated in regard to what the men suffered there. I was summoned from home to testify at the trial of Wirz, the Superintendent of Andersonville and was in Washington all through his trial. But my evidence was of little importance and think amounted to very little in the verdict of guilty the commission found against him.

"Now like many others, you want to know about that wonderful providential Spring that so miraculously broke out somewhere in Andersonville prison. Now I will say that as to the Special providential theory concerning that flow of water, I have never heard of it until I had been out of the service many years and know nothing as to who the author or inventor of that pleasant fiction. It was nothing more or less than the successful fiction. It was nothing more or less than the successful effort of a dammed up stream of water to break through the obstruction and resume its old channel— with the aid of a hard and prolonged rain storm. In building the stockade, they had cut off just a few feet about its mouth on where it entered the brook that ran through the prison stockade, a small brook or branch that entered into the main brook. The work was done in a dry time and the logs of which the stockade was built were set into a ditch six feet deep and this wall being so near the mouth of the small brook, they thought it best to cut off and run it into the main channel on the outside of the stockade which worked very well until sometime in July when we were deluged by a terrible rain that lasted for several days which so thoroughly soaked the ground and brought such a pressure to bear from below that the brook broke through under the stockade and it being so close to where it formerly joined the other brook, it ran into the deadline on between the deadline and the stockade, consequently the Prisoners could not get to it only as they reached over the deadline. Now the water in this spring or brook was of, the same quality as that in the larger stream, but was protected from pollution by the deadline, and the men could only get water from it by attaching cans, pails, pots and any and all kinds of dippers obtainable to poles and sticks and ropes and reach across the deadline and fill them. And the only advantage this so-called spring possessed over the main brook was in the fact of its being impossible for the prisoners to pollute it. I am aware that this commonplace explanation of this mythical wonderful affair is not quite orthodox and will lay me open to the heinous crime of heresy. But I have lived through the facts, you are at liberty to credit the source to whoever you feel inclined. I have drawn a rude map or diagram of the outlines of the prison. Showing the deadline and stockade and the main and small stream and where the small stream broke out under the outside wall and ran down into the main stream between the wall and deadline."

So ends Hugh Snee's modest account of some "interesting incidents. . .that six months. . .between the date of my capture and the day of my deliverance. . ."

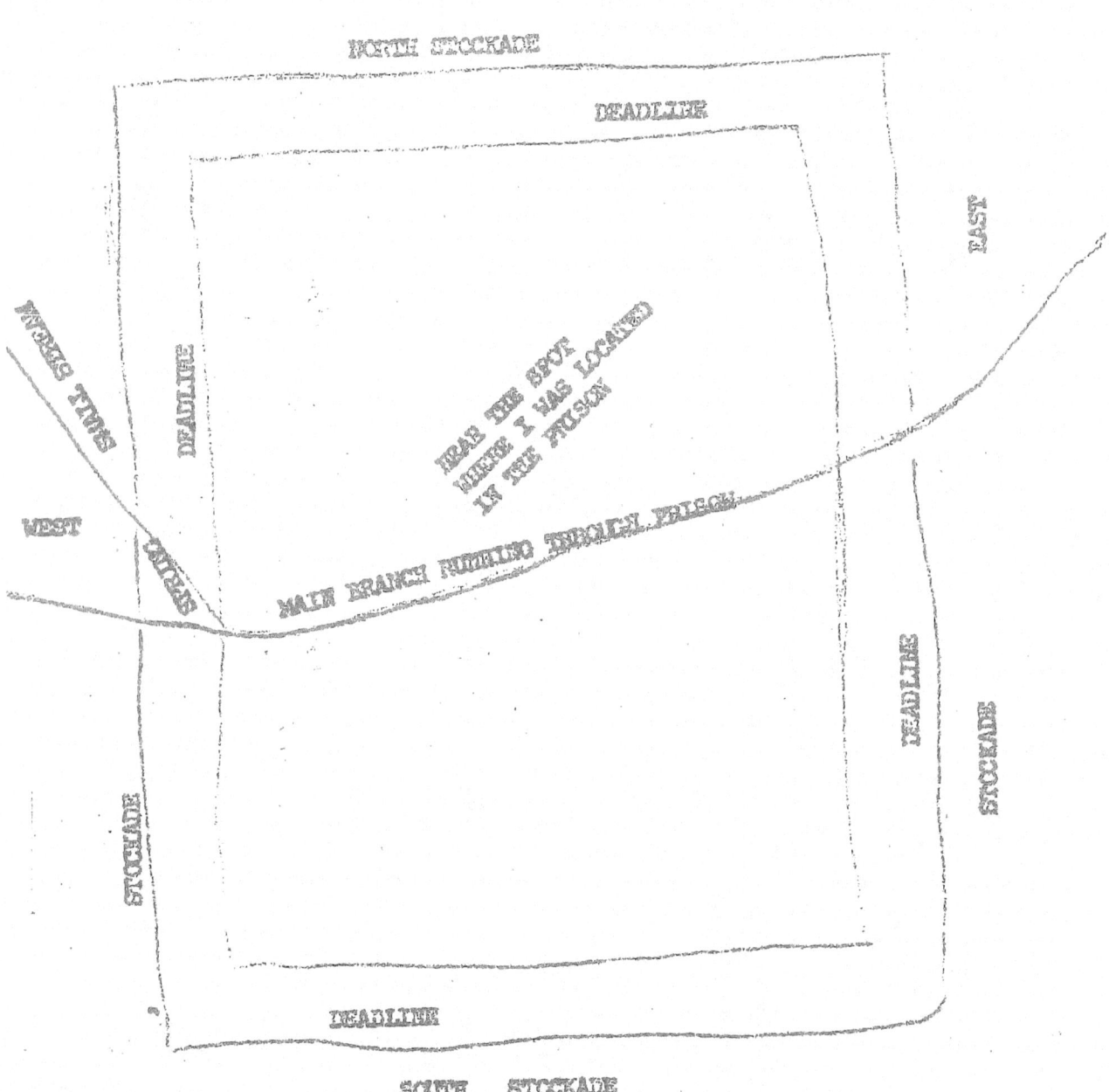

APPENDIX II

Trial Testimony of Hugh R. Snee

[Editors Note: In the summer of 1865, the Government began to collect it's testimony for the trial against Andersonville Commandant Henry Wirz. Thousands gave depositions, but only 148 were allowed to testify. My Great-Great-Grandfather Hugh Rippy Snee was one of the 148, and while he felt it did not amount to much, it was perhaps one more nail in the coffin of Captain Henry Wirz.]

The Trial of Henry Wirz
House Executive Document 23-23
Pages 352-354

"SEPTEMBER 20, 1865

Hugh R. Snee, for the prosecution:

'I was in the military service of the United States—in the Thirty-Ninth Illinois regiment. I was a prisoner at Andersonville about five months. I was captured May 16, 1864, and made my escape about the 9th of September following. I made my escape by smuggling myself out with a few prisoners who were to be exchanged on special exchange arranged between General Sherman and General Hood. When they called the roll of these men who were to be exchanged, it was after dark; that time being chosen on account of the heat, as men would faint during the day. When they called the roll they said they wanted none but able-bodied men—men who were able to go into the field; and as a test they have an order that any man who came out and was not able to walk eighteen miles would be shot. Of course every one was anxious to get out, and, among the rest, myself. I considered that I could walk eighteen miles, but I had no right to come out any more than my chances to get out. After I got out I fell into line. Others came out who could not walk. There were two men belonging to a western regiment—I think one belonging to an Iowa regiment; I am not certain as to that; they fainted before they got to the brook that ran, I think, between Captain Wirz's headquarters and the depot. They fell out of the ranks, and the guard shoved them to one side. A man ran back and wanted to know why they were out. They made a remark that they wished to get out of prison. The man said, 'I will help you out damned soon.' We were hurrying along at the double quick. I heard six discharges from a pistol; I supposed it to be a revolver, and I heard a cry, as if somebody was hurt. Presently a rebel officer, a lieutenant I think, came along, and he made the remark that it was a brutal act. Some one asked who did it, and he said the Captain. I have no means of knowing that they were killed, except that his lieutenant said that only one of them was killed. He said 'one of them is dead.' I have heard Captain Wirz's voice on several occasions. I cannot say positively if the voice I heard at that time had the accent of this voice. I thought at that time that it was his voice. We passed him soon afterward, perhaps not over fifteen minutes. He was sitting in his chair in front of his headquarters, and General Winder was sitting not a great distance from him. I supposed it was calculated that we were passing in review before them, and they were counting us. We were ordered to march in particular order so that we could be counted. That is all I know about that particular affair.

SHOOTING OF PRISONERS BY THE GUARDS.

'I saw three different men shot. One was either the sergeant-major or hospital steward of a New York regiment. He went outside the dead-line for the purpose of being shot. That was in August 1864. Some said that he was crazy; others said he was not. He was shot by the guard, and was killed instantly. The guards shot at him three times before they hit him. At the time the last shot was fired there was an officer in the sentry-box with the guard, but it was not Captain Wirz. It was a lieutenant of the guard. Another case was that of a man of the 21st Ohio. I cannot give his name. He was a German. He was living inside the dead-line asleep. Somebody raised a disturbance near the dead-line. A shot was fired which went through a man's shoulder and another man's foot. The man at whom they fired was missed. That was in July, I think. There was a crazy man—a German who was captured on the 16th of May. He seemed to be deranged from some cause. I think he was deranged when he was captured. He was shot; I think he staggered against the dead-line. I saw him when he was shot by the sentry. He was not trying to escape. The man was deranged; he did not know what he was doing. This happened near the north gate, close to the edge of the swamp. It occurred some time in July or August. I believe I don't know of any other occurrence of that character.

SHOOTING OF TWO PRISONERS BY WIRZ.

'Cross-examined by Counsel:

'I cannot tell the date precisely when I heard those six shots from a pistol or revolver. It was in September. It was at the time that exchange occurred.

Q. Was it the first part of the exchange or the latter part?

A. The last squad of prisoners that went away. Seven hundred were taken from the stockade, but I believe all of them were not exchanged. It was not as late as the 25th September. It was in the first part of September; it must have been, because I got within our lines on the 23rd of September. I was making my escape at that time. I followed the prisoners till I got to Lovejoy's station; there I broke away from them and got inside our lines at a little place called Eastport. I was only one day on my journey before I got away from the prisoners. I was four days with them before I got away from them. I think it was five days from the time I heard the pistol discharged till I got within our lines. It was about the 17th or 18th of September, as near as I can tell. I never say Captain Wirz shoot a man. I saw him shove a man; I did not se him strike a man with a pistol. I don't know that he bruised the man whom he shoved materially, but he was a sick man, and when Captain Wirz shoved him over, he got trampled on by the crowd. That is the only instance I ever saw.'"

APPENDIX III

Federal Forces - May 16, 1864

Army of the James

Major-General Benjamin F. Butler

Tenth Army Corps

Major-General Quincy A. Gillmore

First Division

Brigadier-General Alfred H. Terry

First Brigade - Colonel Joshua B. Howell, Commanding

Thirty-Ninth Illinois Infantry Regiment
Sixty-Second Ohio Infantry Regiment
Sixty-Seventh Ohio Infantry Regiment
Eighty-Fifth Pennsylvania Infantry Regiment

Second Brigade - Colonel Joseph R. Hawley, Commanding

Sixth Connecticut Infantry Regiment
Seventh Connecticut Infantry Regiment
Third New Hampshire Infantry Regiment
Seventh New Hampshire Infantry Regiment

Third Brigade - Colonel Harris M. Plaisted, Commanding

Tenth Connecticut Infantry Regiment
Eleventh Maine Infantry Regiment
Twenty-Fourth Massachusetts Infantry Regiment
100th New York Infantry Regiment

Division Artillery

Connecticut Light, First Battery
New Jersey Light, Fifth Battery
First United States, Battery M

Second Division

Brigadier-General John W. Turner

First Brigade - Colonel Samuel L. M. Alford, Commanding

Fortieth Massachusetts Infantry Regiment
Third New York Infantry Regiment
Eighty-Ninth New York Infantry Regiment
117th New York Infantry Regiment
142nd New York Infantry Regiment

Second Brigade - Colonel William B. Barton, Commanding

Forty-Seventh New York Infantry Regiment
Forty-Eighth New York Infantry Regiment
115th New York Infantry Regiment
Seventy-Sixth Pennsylvania Infantry Regiment

Division Artillery - Captain George T. Woodbury, Commanding

New Jersey Light, Fourth Battery
First United States, Battery B
First United States, Battery D

Third Division

Brigadier-General Adelbert Ames

First Brigade - Colonel Richard White, Commanding

Eighth Maine Infantry Regiment
Fourth New Hampshire Infantry Regiment
Fifty-Fifth Pennsylvania Infantry Regiment

Ninety-Seventh Pennsylvania Infantry Regiment

Second Brigade - Colonel Jeremiah C. Drake, Commanding

Thirteenth Indiana Infantry Regiment
Ninth Maine Infantry Regiment
112th New York Infantry Regiment
169th New York Infantry Regiment

Division Artillery - Captain Alger M. Wheeler, Commanding

New York Light, Thirty-Third Battery
Third Rhode Island Light, Battery C
Third United States, Battery E

Unattached Troops

First New York Engineers (eight companies)
Fourth Massachusetts Cavalry (First Battalion)

Eighteenth Army Corps

Major-General William F. Smith

First Division

Brigadier-General William T. H. Brooks

First Brigade - Brigadier-General Gilman Marston, Commanding

Eighty-First New York Infantry Regiment
Ninety-Sixth New York Infantry Regiment
Ninety-Eighth New York Infantry Regiment
139th New York Infantry Regiment

Second Brigade - Brigadier-General Hiram Burnham, Commanding

Eighth Connecticut Infantry Regiment
Tenth New Hampshire Infantry Regiment

Thirteenth New Hampshire Infantry Regiment
118th New York Infantry Regiment

Third Brigade - Colonel Horace T. Sanders, Commanding

Twenty-First Connecticut Infantry Regiment
Ninety-Second New York Infantry Regiment
Fifty-Eighth Pennsylvania Infantry Regiment
188th Pennsylvania Infantry Regiment
Nineteenth Wisconsin Infantry Regiment

Division Artillery - Major Theodore H. Schenck, Commanding

New York Light, Seventh Battery
Third New York Light, Battery E
First Rhode Island Light, Battery F
Fourth United States, Battery D

Second Division

Brigadier-General Godfrey Weitzel

First Brigade - Brigadier-General Charles A. Heckman, Commanding

Twenty-Third Massachusetts Infantry Regiment
Twenty-Fifth Massachusetts Infantry Regiment
Twenty-Seventh Massachusetts Infantry Regiment
Ninth New Jersey Infantry Regiment

Second Brigade - Colonel Griffin A. Stedman, Commanding

Eleventh Connecticut Infantry Regiment
Second New Hampshire Infantry Regiment
Twelfth New Hampshire Infantry Regiment
148th New York Infantry Regiment

Division Artillery - Captain Frederick M. Follett, Commanding

Seventh New York
Third New York, Battery E
First Rhode Island, Battery F

Fourth United States, Battery D

Third Division

Brigadier-General Edward W. Hinks

First Brigade - Brigadier-General Edward A. Wild, Commanding

First U. S. Colored Infantry Regiment
Tenth U. S. Colored Infantry Regiment
Twenty-Second U. S. Colored Infantry Regiment
Thirty-Seventh U. S. Colored Infantry Regiment

Second Brigade - Colonel Samuel A. Duncan, Commanding

Fourth U. S. Colored Infantry Regiment
Fifth U. S. Colored Infantry Regiment
Sixth U. S. Colored Infantry Regiment

Division Artillery

Third New York Light, Battery K
Third New York Light, Battery M
Second U. S. Colored Light, Battery M

Cavalry Division

Brigadier-General August V. Kaautz

First Brigade - Colonel Simon H. Mix, Commanding

First District of Columbia Cavalry Regiment
Third New York Cavalry Regiment

Second Brigade - Colonel Samuel P. Spear, Commanding

Fifth Pennsylvania Cavalry Regiment
Eleventh Pennsylvania Cavalry Regiment

Division Artillery

New York Light, Eighth Battery (section)

Unattached Troops

First New York Mounted Rifles
First U. S. Colored Cavalry Regiment
Second U. S. Colored Cavalry Regiment
Thirteenth Company Massachusetts Heavy Artillery

APPENDIX IV

Confederate Forces May 16, 1864

Department of Southern Virginia and North Carolina

General P. G. T. Beauregard

Ransom's Division

Major-General Robert Ransom, Jr.

Gracie's Brigade - Brigadier-General Archibald Gracie, Jr.

Forty-First Alabama Infantry Regiment
Forty-Third Alabama Infantry Regiment
Fifty-Ninth Alabama Infantry Regiment
Sixtieth Alabama Infantry Regiment
Twenty-Third Alabama Battalion of Sharpshooters

Terry's Brigade - Colonel William R. Terry, Commanding

First Virginia Infantry Regiment
Seventh Virginia Infantry Regiment
Eleventh Virginia Infantry Regiment
Twenty-Fourth Virginia Infantry Regiment

Barton's Brigade - Colonel Brikett D. Fry, Commanding

Ninth Virginia Infantry Regiment
Fourteenth Virginia Infantry Regiment
Thirty-Eighth Virginia Infantry Regiment
Fifty-Third Virginia Infantry Regiment
Fifty-Seventh Virginia Infantry Regiment

Hoke's Brigade - Colonel William G. Lewis, Commanding

Sixth North Carolina Infantry Regiment
Twenty-First North Carolina Infantry Regiment
Forty-Third North Carolina Infantry Regiment
Fifty-Fourth North Carolina Infantry Regiment
Fifty-Seventh North Carolina Infantry Regiment
First North Carolina Infantry Regiment
Twenty-First Georgia Infantry Regiment

Artillery - Lieutenant-Colonel Charles E. Lightfoot, Commanding

Hankin's Battery (Virginia Light)
Rives's Battery (Virginia)
Thornton's Battery (Carolina) Virginia

Cavalry

Fifth South Carolina Cavalry Regiment

Hoke's Division

Major-General Robert F. Hoke

Corse's Brigade - Brigadier-General Montgomery Corse, Commanding

Fifteenth Virginia Infantry Regiment
Seventeenth Virginia Infantry Regiment
Eighteenth Virginia Infantry Regiment
Twenty-Ninth Virginia Infantry Regiment
Thirtieth Virginia Infantry Regiment

Clingman's Brigade - Brigadier-General Thomas Clingman, Commanding

Eighth North Carolina Infantry Regiment
Thirty-First North Carolina Infantry Regiment
Fifty-First North Carolina Infantry Regiment
Sixty-First North Carolina Infantry Regiment

Johnson's Brigade - Brigadier-General Bushrod R. Johnson, Commanding

Seventeenth/Twenty-Third Tennessee Infantry Regiment
Twenty-Fifth/Forty-Fourth Tennessee Infantry Regiment
Sixty-Third Tennessee Infantry Regiment

Hagood's Brigade - Brigadier-General Johnson Hagood, Commanding

Eleventh South Carolina Infantry Regiment
Twenty-First South Carolina Infantry Regiment
Twenty-Fifth South Carolina Infantry Regiment
Twenty-Seventh South Carolina Infantry Regiment
Seventh South Carolina Battalion of Sharpshooter's

Artillery

First Company, Washington Artillery
Second Company, Washington Artillery
Third Company, Washington Artillery
Fourth Company, Washington Artillery

Cavalry

Third North Carolina Cavalry Regiment

Colquitt's Division

Brigadier-General Alfred H. Colquitt

Colquitt's Brigade - Colonel John T. Lofton, Commanding

Sixth Georgia Infantry Regiment
Nineteenth Georgia Infantry Regiment
Twenty-Third Georgia Infantry Regiment

Twenty-Seventh Georgia Infantry Regiment
Twenty-Eighth Georgia Infantry Regiment

Ransom's Brigade - Colonel Leroy M. McAfee, Commanding

Twenty-Fourth North Carolina Infantry Regiment
Twenty-Fifth North Carolina Infantry Regiment
Thirty-Fifth North Carolina Infantry Regiment
Forty-Ninth North Carolina Infantry Regiment
Fifty-Sixth North Carolina Infantry Regiment

Artillery

Macon's Battery
Martin's Battery
Payne's Battery (improvised)

Cavalry

Seventh South Carolina Cavalry Regiment

Whiting's Division

Major-General William H. C. Whiting

Wise's Brigade - Brigadier-General Henry A. Wise, Commanding

Twenty-Sixth Virginia Infantry Regiment
Thirty-Fourth Virginia Infantry Regiment
Forty-Sixth Virginia Infantry Regiment
Fifty-Ninth Virginia Infantry Regiment

Martin's Brigade - Brigadier-General James G. Martin, Commanding

Seventeenth North Carolina Infantry Regiment
Forty-Second North Carolina Infantry Regiment
Sixty-Sixth North Carolina Infantry Regiment

Cavalry Brigade - Brigadier-General James Dearing, Commanding

Seventh Confederate Cavalry Regiment

Sixty-Second Georgia Cavalry Regiment
Fifty-Ninth North Carolina Cavalry Regiment
Sixty-Fifth North Carolina Cavalry Regiment
Barham's Virginia Cavalry Battalion

Artillery

Blount's Battery
Bradford's Battery
Caskie's Battery
Graham's Battery
Kelly's Battery
Marshall's Battery
Miller's Battery
Pegram's Battery
Slaten's Battery
Sturdivant's Battery - Albermarle (Virginia)
Wright's Battery - Halifax (Virginia)
Young's Battery

APPENDIX V

COMPANY HISTORIES

&

SUMMARY

OF

CASUALTIES

History of Company A

This company was enlisted in the early part of April 1861, during that exciting period following the firing upon Fort Sumter, and within three days many more men had been enrolled than could be taken in one company, so that selection was made in securing what was considered the best material for soldiers. The election for officers resulted in the choice of—

Sylvester W. Munn for Captain.
Joseph W. Richardson for First Lieutenant.
Leroy A. Baker for Second Lieutenant.

The full muster-roll of 103 men was immediately forwarded to Springfield, for registry by the Adjutant-General of the State, and it should, by reason of precedence, have been assigned to the Twentieth Illinois Volunteer Infantry, but through some favoritism a second company, raised at Joliet received the place. The majority of the men who had enlisted were anxious to enter into active service, and the company was practically disbanded, many enlisted in the Twentieth Illinois and other organizations that were preparing to take the field. A sufficient number, however, remained behind to form the nucleus for another company. The Thirty-Ninth Illinois Infantry were organizing in Chicago and this company was offered a place as soon as the War Department would accept the Regiment.

After the first battle of Bull Run notice was received that the Thirty-Ninth was to be accepted, and measures were at once taken to recruit; and on August 5, 1861, Captain Munn with about fifty men proceeded to Chicago, and upon presentation of the muster-roll to Captain Webb, U. S. A., they were mustered into the service of the United States and assigned as Company A, Thirty-Ninth Illinois.

The Company was made comfortable in quarters in the building known as the Republican Wigwam on Market Street, and remained there until about September 1, when the Regiment encampment was established on vacant grounds on Indiana Avenue, near 26th Street.

The men forming this company were principally from the vicinity of Wilmington, and mostly farmers, or farmers' sons. They made earnest and loyal soldiers, ever maintaining a good state of order and discipline, each man contributing his due share in making the record of the Thirty-Ninth Regiment the peer of any that the State sent forth.

The Company took part in every battle in which the Regiment was engaged, as well as having several independent skirmishes in which it won commendations not only from its immediate commanders but from general officers.

It re-enlisted as veterans in January 1864, at Hilton Head, South Carolina, for three years, or during the continuance of the war.

Summary of Casualties

Killed in battle 6
Died of wounds 10

Died in prison 2
Died of disease 14
Lost limbs 6
Wounded 36
Discharged for disability 30
Transferred 7
Deserted 11
Taken prisoner 12
Mustered out at expiration of service 21
Re-enlisted as veterans 97
Recruits 61
Returned at muster-out of Regiment 57

History of Company B

This company was organized at Bloomington, August 12, 1861. After the old Eighth Illinois Volunteer Infantry had served its three months on the banks of the "Big Muddy" and at Cairo, Illinois, those who did not wish to re-enlist for the three years' service returned to their homes with their honorable discharge in pocket, feeling in a measure unsettled as to what they would do. The news of the first battle at Bull Run spreading over the country as fast as electricity could carry it—a battle and a defeat—so excited and stirred up the feelings of the boys that it soon decided the old members of Company K of the Eighth Illinois who had seen service as above mentioned, to re-enlist, and thus they became the nucleus of Company B, Thirty-Ninth Illinois Volunteers. These men were George T. Heritage, Al. C. Sweetser, James Gibson, D. F. Sellards, L. D. Kidder, Harvey Bailey, James S. Haldeman, Stephan Johnson, and others whose names we cannot at present recall. After a few days active work in recruiting we had a sufficient number on the rolls to call a meeting, which was held at No. 214 North Front Street, for the purpose of electing officers and perfecting the organization. At this meeting, which was largely attended by those who had enlisted, the following officers were chosen:

> For Captain, Isaiah W. E. Wilmarch.
> First Lieutenant, David F. Sellards.
> Second Lieutenant, James S. Haldeman.

The company proceeded to Chicago, where it was assigned to the Thirty-Ninth Regiment Illinois Volunteers as Company B, having at that time 34 enlisted men. While at Chicago thirty-six more recruits joined it before muster into the United States service October 11, 1861.

Company B participated in all the movements and battles the Regiment was engaged in, and won for itself an enviable reputation for soldierly conduct. At the battle of Drewry's Bluff on May 16, 1864, when the troops on the right of the line had been driven back, and the men on the right of our own Regiment were giving way file by file, stubbornly contesting every inch of the ground, and as the men of Company B were dropping back until Alexander Paul was reached, Sergeant Joseph Hallett said to him, "Aleck, there is no orders to retreat; hold your ground!" and then drawing his revolver and covering the "color bearer" commanded him to return with the colors, and at the same time called upon the Regiment to rally—which it did in grand style; and while the right of the line was making rapid strides to the rear, the Thirty-Ninth alone was advancing on the enemy and keeping his left in a spirited engagement, so much so, that General Alfred H. Terry was heard to say, "In the name of God! what troops are engaged on our left?"

On May 20, at Ware Bottom Church, Virginia, it did noble service, losing several men in killed and wounded. At this battle Lieutenant Al. C. Sweetser acted as Adjutant to the Regiment. On June 2, 1864, while it was on duty at the front near Ware Bottom Church, Lieutenant Sweetser was wounded through both legs. It took an active part in the battle of Darbytown Cross-Roads, Virginia, losing heavily in killed and wounded. Captain Heritage was severely wounded in this action and to his credit be it said, he entered into the engagement after his term of service had expired, and his order for "muster out" was at brigade headquarters.

At the time the Regiment was preparing to assault the rebel works, Companies B and G formed the Fifth Division of the Regiment under command of Lieutenant Harrington of Company G. The Lieutenant's term of service had expired, and not feeling willing to undergo the risk of his life, he turned his command over to Sergeant Joseph Hallett of Company B, remarking, as he did so, "I am a citizen, and by God it is getting too close for me, and I shall go where there is more room!" He did not stand long on the order of his going either, but went at once. Some may think that Lieutenant Harrington showed the "white feather," but we that knew him could vouch to the contrary, and we felt that under the circumstances he was fully justified in thinking the course he did. The company followed the fortunes of the Regiment through to its final "muster out" at the close of the was, and ever maintained a high order of discipline, especially after Captain Heritage was called to the command. It was always ready and willing for duty, and in its performance evinced those sterling qualities that give it the name of the "Old Reliable."

Summary of Casualties

Killed in battle 6
Died of wounds 5
Died in prison 1
Died of disease 6
Lost limbs 3
Drowned 1
Wounded 34
Discharged for disability 33
Transferred 3
Deserted 10
Taken prisoner 13

Mustered out at expiration of service 34
Re-enlisted as veterans 28
Number originally enlisted 94
Recruits 56
Returned at muster-out of Regiment 45

History of Company C

This company was organized and principally enlisted at Pontiac, Livingston county, Illinois, in the month of July 1861, through the efforts of John Gray, Simon S. Brucker and others. It numbered sixty-four men when it was offered to the Thirty-Ninth Regiment, and was the second company to be quartered in the Wigwam after Company A, although there were a few men, the nucleus of Company D, being recruited by S. S. Linton there at the same time. At the date of its muster into the United States service it numbered ninety-four men, eighty-three of them from the vicinity of Pontiac, and eleven recruited in Chicago.

The company was made up of first-class material, having in its ranks several men who had seen service in the British army; but it had not been fortunate in the selection of its officers, and there was more or less disaffection, and at times even mutinous conduct among its members up to the time that Lieutenant James W. Wightman was promoted to the captaincy, May 26, 1862, when it became almost perfect in discipline, and proved itself one of the most efficient companies of the Regiment.

It was one of the companies stationed at Alpine Station, West Virginia in the early part of January 1862, where they met a portion of the Confederate force under Jackson and Loring, and where they met their first baptism of fire and water, being compelled to make a hasty retreat and struggle through the icy water of the Potomac river across to Hancock, Maryland, the other companies being A, B, and F.

On March 21, 1862, this company, under command of Captain Gray, was sent out with one company of the Thirteenth Indiana in command of Lieutenant Hurd, on picket duty about two miles from Winchester, Virginia, the line extending from the Strasburg to the Front Royal turnpike. They had been out nearly twenty-four hours when they became aware of the approach, in force, of the enemy, which proved to be General Jackson's army. Word was immediately sent to General Shields. After several hours' skirmishing with Ashby's cavalry, in which two men of the Company were taken prisoners, Corporal Albert Fellows and Private William Hadley, the Company fell back until it met the advance of Shield's Division, when it again advanced, driving the cavalry back to Kernstown, where they were held in check until the following morning, March 23, which ushered in the battle of Winchester.

The Company did excellent service wherever engaged, and participated in all the battles in which the Regiment took part.

Summary of Casualties

Killed in battle 7
Died of wounds 2
Died in prison 4
Died of disease 7
Lost limbs 4
Wounded 32
Discharged for disability 27
Transferred 2
Deserted 8
Taken prisoner 13
Mustered out at expiration of service 18
Re-enlisted as veterans 39
Number originally enlisted 89
Recruits 62

History of Company D

This company was organized at Rochelle, by Samuel S. Linton. The larger portion of it was recruited from Ogle county, and some were from Lee county. It was among the first to be assigned to the Thirty-Ninth Illinois, and was for some weeks quartered in the old Republican Wigwam, on Market street, Chicago. At the time of its muster into the United States service it numbered some 88 young, robust and enthusiastic men. They were mostly farmers' sons, used to hard labor, and in good circumstances. They enlisted believing that their country needed their services, not for the novelty of wearing a uniform and enjoying camp-life, and their conduct throughout the whole war evinced how earnest and sincere was their devotion to their imperiled country. It was the first company to meet the advancing force of the enemy under General Jackson near Bath, Virginia, January 3, 1862, holding them in check for some hours, and finally retreating in good order with the loss of a few men taken prisoners.

This company was without a peer in skirmish tactics, consequently was often sent forward upon that duty, and did noble service. Nearly three-fourths of the members re-enlisted at Hilton Head, South Carolina, January 1, 1864, as veterans, and during the continuance of the war it proved a most prominent factor in all the battles and assaults the Regiment was engaged in. It is impossible, in the brief space allotted, to give a detailed account of its movements during the four years and two months of continuous service at the front. Suffice it to say that it was never found wanting when called upon, and never failed to do its full duty; and now, after more than a score of years, the few survivors look with pride and satisfaction upon what they helped to bring about, namely, a united, happy, and prosperous Nation.

Summary of Casualties

Killed in battle 10
Died of wounds 6
Died in prison 2
Died of disease 10
Lost limbs 2
Wounded 42
Discharged for disability 31
Transferred 4
Deserted 13
Taken prisoner 15
Mustered out at expiration of service 12
Re-enlisted as veterans 43
Number originally enlisted 88
Recruits 60
Returned at muster-out of Regiment 67

History of Company E

Some time in May 1861, soon after Stephan A. Douglas had returned to Illinois and made his memorable speeches in support of the Union, a band of young men in Wesley township, Will country, united and formed at the Wesley school-house a company which was called the "Florence Rifles." They met each Saturday afternoon for drill in company evolutions, and were uniformed in blue blouses. This continued up to some time in August, when they began to look for a Regiment in which to enlist for the war.

A company that had been formed at Wilmington, some six miles distant, and which had joined the Thirty-Ninth, or "Yates Phalanx" (Company A), had some influence in determining their choice of a regiment, and on September 12, 1861, they proceeded to Chicago, and entered that regiment at Camp Mather, forming the nucleus of Company E. While at Camp Mather the Company received a number of recruits from different places in the State. October 11, 1861, the membership numbered forty-six men. While at St. Louis, Missouri, Lieutenant Warner was sent home to recruit for the Company, and succeeded in taking quite a number of men with him when he rejoined his regiment at Williamsport, Maryland, in November 1861. The Company, however, never received its full complement of men until the return of the regiment from South Carolina on its "veteran furlough."

James H. Hooker was one of the principal organizers at the first attempt at the formation of a company, and it was he who bestowed the name of the "Florence Rifles." He did but little active service in recruiting, but furnished considerable money for the purpose. Lewis T. Whipple, who had picked up some knowledge of the "Scott Tactics," was the principal drill master.

At the election for officers held at Camp Mather, Chicago, James H. Hooker was elected Captain; Lewis T. Whipple First Lieutenant; and Norman C. Warner Second Lieutenant.

Company E was noticeable from the fact that the majority of its members were below the average stature of men, and there were many mere boys in the ranks; but what was lacking in this respect was more than compensated for in their soldierly spirit and behavior.

At the time General Jackson made his raid on the Union troops stationed on the line of the Baltimore and Ohio Railroad at Alpine Station, and other points, Company E was stationed at Sir John's Run, some six miles distant from Alpine, and held that place for the period of six hours against a brigade of the enemy, thus preventing their entrance into Maryland at that point. It took a prominent part in all of the battles and skirmishes with the enemy that the Regiment participated in, and acquitted itself most gallantly and heroically, as the record shows.

Summary of Casualties

Killed in battle	11
Died of wounds	5
Died in prison	3
Died of disease	7
Lost limbs	7
Wounded	41
Discharged for disability	25
Transferred	3
Deserted	16
Taken prisoner	13
Mustered out at expiration of service	4
Re-enlisted as veterans	42
Number originally enlisted	58
Recruits	78
Returned at muster-out of Regiment	59

History of Company F

The manner of recruiting Company F was not unlike that by which the other companies were brought into the service. Orrin L. Mann has the credit of enlisting the first body of men who formed the nucleus of the company which afterwards took the letter F in the Regiment. He was very active in this direction until he aspired to the position of Major, when his recruits were turned over to Amasa Kennicott, who continued the recruiting and was elected Captain. The men forming the company were principally from Cook, Lake, and McLean counties, and mostly farmers. They were a fine body of men and did most excellent service during the war.

It first met the enemy at Alpine Station on January 4, 1862, being the most advanced company at that post on the road leading to Bath. On the approach of the rebel cavalry from Bath this company, which was stationed at the summit of the mountain road from Alpine, fell back until it joined Company A, where they most effectually routed a large squadron of Ashby's cavalry. Forty of the original members re-enlisted as veteran volunteers at Hilton Head in January 1864, and forty-five members of the company returned home at the muster-out of the Regiment.

Captain Amasa Kennicott became tired of the "pomp and circumstance of the war," resigning his position in August 1862. He was succeeded by John W. McIntosh, who was dismissed from the service early in 1863. Lieutenant A. B. Hoffman was then promoted to the vacancy, but left the service at the expiration of his three year's term. The company came home under the able leadership of Captain R. S. Botsford.

The company made a good record, and the surviving may well feel a just pride in its military history.

Summary of Casualties

Killed in battle	10
Died of wounds	9
Died in prison	4
Died of disease	7
Lost limbs	2
Wounded	42
Discharged for disability	29
Transferred	7
Deserted	10
Taken prisoner	12
Mustered out at expiration of service	8
Re-enlisted as veterans	40
Number originally enlisted	75
Recruits	69
Returned at muster-out of Regiment	45

History of Company G

This company was recruited at Chicago, commencing on or about August 6, 1861, having been organized by the Rev. W. B. Slaughter, of the Methodist Episcopal Church, and Oscar F. Rudd and Amos Savage, who were elected as its commanders. It did most excellent service in whatever position it was placed, which may or may not have been in part attributable to the fact of its having a Slaughter and a Savage as leaders, and as a consequence its list of casualties were numerous, it having lost seventy-four officers and men in killed, wounded and taken prisoners.

At the time of the Jackson and Loring raid, January 4, 1862, the company was stationed at Great Cacapon, Virginia, to guard the Baltimore and Ohio Railroad bridge, being subsequently re-enforced by part of Company E; and while there, repulsed a whole brigade of the enemy, holding it in check for some hours, and made good their retreat under cover of darkness, without serious loss. It did guard duty, with quarters on board a train of freight cars, along the Baltimore and Ohio Railroad, from New Creek to Cherry Run, Virginia, up to March 13, 1862, when it joined Shield's Division at Martinsburg, Virginia, and participated in the victory over Jackson's army at Winchester, March 23, 1862. After this it shared in the campaign through the Shenandoah Valley, marching to Fredericksburg and back, then embarking at Alexandria, Virginia to join McClellan's army, and taking part in the last of the seven days' battle at Malvern Hill, Virginia. It took part in July 1862, in the grand retreat to Yorktown, and after a few days rest proceeded to Suffolk, Virginia, where winter quarters were established and where it participated in three different engagements on the Blackwater river, and in a reconnaissance to the Dismal Swamp.

In the early part of January 1863, it left Suffolk for New Bern, North Carolina, to take part in the Foster expedition for the reduction of Charleston, South Carolina, arriving and disembarking on Folly Island, April 4, 1863, after having spent some little time for drill and discipline on St. Helena Island. From July until October, 1863, it was actively engaged in the operations to effect the reduction of the batteries and fortifications in and around Charleston Harbor, being almost constantly exposed to the fire of the enemy and the no less active and merciless assaults of sand-flies, mosquitoes and fleas; but the loss from all causes was surprisingly small, being only two seriously wounded.

January 1, 1864, the company, while at Hilton Head, re-enlisted as veterans and received thirty days furlough home for recruiting. In February 1864, it was ordered to Washington, D.C.; remained for several weeks encamped at Arlington Heights, Virginia, then proceeded to Gloucester Point to join Butler's expedition up the James river, landing at Bermuda Hundred, and actively participating in the battle of Drewry's Bluff on May 15 and 16, in which the company lost four killed and thirteen wounded.

May 20, 1864, it was engaged in the battle of Ware Bottom Church, and then in the trenches at Bermuda Hundred; then followed the engagements of June 16, 17, and 18 at the same place, and where Captain O. F. Rudd was mortally wounded; then it crossed to the north side of the James river and took part in the charge upon the enemy's works at Deep Run, where Private Hardenburg captured the colors of the Eighth Alabama Regiment. August 8, 1864, it entered the trenches in front of Petersburg, where it remained constantly on duty and exposed to the fire of the enemy until September 28, when it again crossed to the north side of the James, and on October 8 assisted in repulsing an attack of the enemy on Chaffin's Farm, Virginia; and October 13 it was engaged in the charge on the rebel works at Darbytown Cross-Roads, where it was repulsed. Again, October 27, it had an engagement with the enemy at the same place. It went into winter quarters on the north side of the James, and during the winter received 13 recruits. March 27, 1865, it again crossed the river, moving to the extreme left of the army at Hatcher's Run, where, on April 2, it assisted in making a successful charge on Fort Gregg, near Petersburg, the key to the works around Richmond. It then engaged in the pursuit of General Lee's army to Appomattox Court House April 3 to 9, 1865. After remaining a few days to assist in guarding and collecting for transportation the captured property, it marched to Richmond where it remained until July 9, 1865. It was then ordered to City Point, Virginia, and from there to Norfolk, where, on December 6, 1865, it was honorably mustered out of the United States service and ordered to Springfield, for final payment and discharge, arriving there via Chicago, December 9, 1865.

Company G was called the "Preacher's Company," not alone from the fact of its having a clergyman for its commander, but because its rank and file had pretensions to more morality than the majority of their comrades; and, in fact, it well maintained its superiority in this respect for some considerable time after joining the Regiment. But, as is well known, evil communications and peculiar situations and surroundings are corrupting; so they soon lost prestige in this respect and became, in the esteem of their associates, "hail fellows, well met," at every turn, and could join in as noisy and abusive demonstrations as any when the commissary failed with rations or they were suspicious in quality; and in the long, discouraging marches, when foot sore, travel-stained and disheartened, they could generally find expression for a few modest "cuss" words to help maintain their courage. It possessed endurance, courage and eminent fighting qualities, as fully evinced on many occasions, and noticeably so at Great Cacapon, when they held a full brigade of the enemy, and at the last, when Lieutenant Rudd, in order to permit the larger part of his command to retire, placed himself at the head of twenty of his men and in a narrow pass successfully held the enemy at bay.

It can be fairly said of Company G that it did its full measure of duty, suffered its due share of hardships, and bore its proportion of loss. The reputations of the Regiment was never imperiled by its conduct in the camp, or on the march, or in battle; but on the contrary, the record of the "Yates Phalanx" has been made brighter by reason of its harmonious action in camp, its heroic and soldierly bearing in battle, and its prompt and intelligent response to every call to duty.

Summary of Casualties

Killed in battle 11
Died of wounds 6
Died in prison 2
Died of disease 19
Lost limbs 2
Wounded 50
Discharged for disability 34
Transferred 10
Deserted 10
Taken prisoner 6
Mustered out at expiration of service 25
Re-enlisted as veterans 41
Number originally enlisted 101
Recruits 68
Returned at muster-out of Regiment 52

History of Company H

Written by William H. Morley

"April 13, 1862, E. H. Wilson and myself went from Farmer City to LeRoy, Illinois, and were enlisted by Harvey Parks, who was there on recruiting service for Company I, Thirty-Ninth Illinois Volunteers. On the 15th, with one other recruit, we walked to Bloomington and there took the cars for Springfield, Illinois, and were assigned to the recruiting barracks at Camp Butler. April 17, Harvey Parks went back to the Regiment, and Charles J. Wilder took charge of the recruits. There were eight of us who were recruited for the Thirty-Ninth, being a larger number than for any other one regiment there present, and we organized a temporary company, calling it Company H, Thirty-Ninth Illinois Volunteers, selected C. J. Wilder as our Captain. Being a 'lost company,' we were kept at Camp Butler to guard the rebel prisoners, and there seemed to be no prospect of getting to our Regiment until about June 20, 1862, when Chauncey Williams of Company I came home on recruiting service and arrived at Camp Butler with a few men whom he had recruited at LeRoy. He was a favorite with the boys from the start, and he stated that if he was elected their Captain he would take us to our Regiment at once. During the time we had been at Camp Butler, all recruits who arrived in camp, and who had not been assigned to any particular regiment, and who had no choice as to where they went so long as they got to the front, were assigned to our barracks until we had a company numbering some seventy men from all parts of the State.

"On June 30, 1862, we held an election for officers which resulted in the choice of—

Chauncey Williams, Captain;
Charles J. Wilder, First Lieutenant;
George Searling, Second Lieutenant;

and we were mustered into the United States service as Company H, Thirty-Ninth Illinois Volunteers, dating July 11, 1862. July 16 we started to join the Regiment via Indianapolis and Washington, arriving at Harrison's Landing, Virginia, July 24, and were assigned our place in the Regiment. From that time to the close of the war our history is that in common with the Regiment, which we were never detached from, but were a part thereof at all times.

"This company participated in all the battles that the Regiment was engaged in excepting that at Drewry's Bluff, Virginia, May 16, 1864, when it was detailed as the guard to an ammunition train. It was proficient in drill, excellent in discipline, and did noble service during the continuance of the war, losing many officers and men killed in battle, wounded, and taken prisoners.

Summary of Casualties

Killed in battle 5

Died of wounds 5
Died in prison 1
Died of disease 5
Lost limbs 3
Drowned 1
Wounded 29
Discharged for disability 11
Transferred 7
Deserted 13
Taken prisoner 8
Mustered out at expiration of service 32
Re-enlisted as veterans 13
Number originally enlisted 77
Recruits 55
Returned at muster-out of Regiment 51

History of Company I

This company was principally recruited at LeRoy, by Hiram M. Phillips, who had seen some service in the Mexican War as a soldier, and found but little difficulty in gathering men to his standard for the "three years' service." It was organized on September 6, and mustered into the service October 11, 1861, at Camp Mather, Chicago.

Company I took part in the skirmish with Jackson's forces at Bath, some of the time being on the skirmish line or outpost duty; but the chief duty given to it on January 4 was supporting Lieutenant Muhlenberg's Artillery in its position on Warm Spring Ridge. It was a magnificent body of men—the majority of them were large in form, robust in muscle, young and spirited, and at the time of muster into the United States service was nearly full to the maximum limit. It took part in all the battles, skirmishes and movements of the Regiment, doing its full duty in the most acceptable manner. The First and Second Lieutenants were both killed in action, one (Lemon) on August 16, 1864 at Deep Run, Virginia, and the other (Fellows) on September 6 in a skirmish with the enemy near Ware Bottom Church.

Forty-one of the original members accepted veteran honors in January, 1864, determined to see the finish of the war or perish in the attempt. The roster will show how many of these were permitted to return home at the muster out of the Regiment. It is perhaps unnecessary to say that it always maintained a high order of discipline under the old veteran, Captain Phillips, who was wounded and taken to Libby Prison on May 16, 1864.

Summary of Casualties

Killed in battle 9

Died of wounds	7
Died in prison	3
Died of disease	5
Lost limbs	3
Drowned	2
Wounded	48
Discharged for disability	44
Transferred	7
Deserted	3
Taken prisoner	16
Mustered out at expiration of service	23
Re-enlisted as veterans	41
Number originally enlisted	85
Recruits	54
Returned at muster-out of Regiment	41

History of Company K

Prepared by Sergeant David H. Slagle

"In July 1861, Frank B. Marshall, a recruiting officer for the 'Yates Phalanx' (Thirty-Ninth Illinois), went to Marseilles, La Salle county, Illinois, where, he had been informed, a company was organizing for the three years' service. He had a conference with Joseph Woodruff, Andrew W. Wheeler and others, and suggested to them that if they could raise a company of men for the Thirty-Ninth in Marseilles and vicinity they could elect their own officers. Active recruiting was at once begun under very promising circumstances. On August 6 the first squad of recruits was forwarded to Chicago and quartered in the Old Republican Wigwam. Others were continually added, and when the Regiment went into Camp Mather the minimum number for a company organization was present for an election of officers, and the following were elected:

        Joseph Woodruff, Captain.
        Frank B. Marshall, First Lieutenant.
        Donald A. Nicholson, Second Lieutenant.

"Cyrus F. Knapp made some efforts for a commission, preferring the Captaincy, but could not control a sufficient number of recruits, and failed; but subsequently identified himself with Company D. Marshall was soon appointed Regimental Adjutant, leaving the place of First Lieutenant vacant. Oscar S. Belcher, then a Sergeant in Company B, claiming that he could procure the number of men yet wanted to complete the Company, was then elected to fill the vacancy; but his recruits did not materialize. He kept the position, however. Soon after this the Company received nineteen men that had enlisted in (the original) Company H, which had been organized at Bloomington by Captain C. S. Dirckes, who for some reason became dissatisfied and so neglected his Company that Colonel Light dissolved it and gave the members of it their choice between Companies F and K. Nineteen men came to Company K. These men had been enlisted by E. C. Myers, and he should have been elected First Lieutenant instead of Belcher. Myers and Terrell had been elected Lieutenants in Company H, but had not been commissioned; they had, however, gone to the expense of getting their uniforms, but like good patriots and soldiers they gracefully accepted the situation. Myers being appointed Second Sergeant and Terrell First Corporal. It was apparent, however, that Terrell was never fully reconciled; he lost his interest, became soured, and after being promoted to Sergeant was reduced to the ranks. For some time there was a little division in the company, the Bloomington men were clannish; but soon the line of formality was broken and the company became a unit, and a strong one. When Company K re-enlisted at Hilton Head, South Carolina in 1864, several of the members who on first enlistment were credited to La Salle county, on second enlistment were credited to Cook county, and received the $100 bounty offered by the county for men who re-enlisted in the field, while those who remained faithful to La Salle county received nothing—which was a source of much dissatisfaction.

"Captain Woodruff was the leading spirit in recruiting this company of men, from the very start, and was always the choice for leader. He proved worthy of the confidence reposed in him up to the date of his death, and his loss was deeply felt and sincerely mourned.

"The Company was made up of good material, and distinguished itself on many occasions, contributing thereby to the good name the Regiment had won in all the military departments in which it was called upon to serve."

Summary of Casualties

Killed in battle 7
Died of wounds 6
Died in prison 2
Died of disease 10
Lost limbs 2
Wounded 54
Discharged for disability 29
Transferred 2
Deserted 3
Taken prisoner 10
Mustered out at expiration of service 14
Re-enlisted as veterans 37
Number originally enlisted 80

Recruits 56
Returned at muster-out of Regiment 63

TOTAL
THIRTY-NINTH ILLINOIS VETERAN VOLUNTEER INFANTRY

Killed in battle 83
Died of wounds 61
Died in prison 25
Died of disease 90
Lost limbs 34
Drowned 4
Wounded 411
Discharged for disability 293
Transferred 52
Deserted 97
Taken prisoner 118
Mustered out at expiration of service 191
Re-enlisted as veterans 350
Number originally enlisted 844
Recruits 608
Returned at muster-out of Regiment 525
Enlisted men promoted to commissions 34
Medals of Honor awarded 2
Promoted to General Officer 2

APPENDIX VI

THE REGIMENTAL BAND

From its inception as a Regiment, the Thirty-Ninth Illinois had a band to perform during their various functions. The Regiment's original band was formed prior to leaving Chicago for the Camp of Instruction at St. Louis, Missouri. The Thirty-Ninth Illinois was to have plenty of music to relieve the monotony of camp life. The band also helped to relieve the tedium of the march. Moreover, during a battle it was the duty of the members to act as stretcher-bearers, and carry the wounded soldiers from the field.

By order of the War Department, the musicians of this original band were mustered out of service on June 4, 1862. This order dispensed with all regimental bands that had been enlisted.

A second band was organized by Philip M. Lace who re-enlisted and was placed on the non-commissioned staff as the Band Leader and Principal Musician. He was to be paid the same amount as a Second Lieutenant. However, this difference in pay was made up by tax on the Sutler. The members of the new band were enlisted soldiers detailed from the various companies.

This band returned with the Regiment to the front after veteran furlough in March 1864. Their instruments were bought with $600 subscribed by the officers of the Regiment while at Arlington Heights, Virginia, April 1864. The band, under the drill and teaching of Lace, was considered the best in the Twenty-Fourth Corps, and had the reputation of being the best band in the Army of the James.

For details of each musician of the new band, refer to the Roster, Appendix VII.

Original Band of the Thirty-Ninth Illinois Volunteers

Leader of Band

Lace, Philip M. - Enlisted September 22, 1861; discharged by order of the War Department June 4, 1862.

First Class Musicians

Bowman, N. B. - Enlisted October 2, 1861; discharged by order of the War Department June 4, 1862.

Hull, B. B. - Enlisted September 20, 1861; discharged by order of the War Department June 4, 1862.

Harrah, William C. - Enlisted September 20, 1861; discharged by order of the War Department June 4, 1862.

Hanning, William - Enlisted September 20, 1861; discharged by order of the War Department June 4, 1862.

Summers, Frank R. - Enlisted September 20, 1861; discharged by order of the War Department June 4, 1862.

Williams, Henry F. - Enlisted September 20, 1861; discharged by order of the War Department June 4, 1862.

Williams, Samuel R. - Enlisted September 20, 1861; discharged by order of the War Department June 4, 1862.

Second Class Musicians

Hannah, Calvin - Enlisted September 20, 1861; taken prisoner at Strasburg, Virginia, May, 1862. Was paroled, and discharged by order of the War Department June 4, 1862.

Lane, Edwin H. - Enlisted October 2, 1861; taken prisoner at Strasburg, Virginia, May, 1862. Was paroled, and discharged by order of the War Department June 4, 1862.

Pitcher, T. W. - Enlisted September 20, 1861; discharged by order of the War Department June 4, 1862.

Thaer, Andrew - Enlisted September 20, 1861; discharged by order of the War Department June 4, 1862.

Mears, D. C. - Enlisted October 8, 1861; discharged by order of the War Department June 4, 1862.

Towns, J. C. - Enlisted September 20, 1861; discharged by order of the War Department June 4, 1862.

Third Class Musicians

Johnson, James M. - Enlisted September 20, 1862; discharged by order of the War Department June 4, 1862.

Ladd, A. A. - Enlisted September 20, 1861; discharged by order of the War Department June 4, 1861.

Fisher, B. W. - Enlisted October 8, 1861; discharged by order of the War Department June 4, 1862.

Schermerhorn, Alford - Enlisted August 17, 1861; discharged by order of the War Department June 4, 1862.

Smith, C. E. - Enlisted October 5, 1861; discharged by order of the War Department June 4, 1862.

THE BAND OF 1864 AND 1865

Phillip M. Lace, Leader[18]	Eb Cornet, 1st.
Enoch C. Hedge	Eb Cornet, 2nd.
James A. Wilson	Bb Cornet, 1st.
Edward D. Conley	Bb Cornet, 2nd.
Henry T. Jones	Eb Alto, Solo 1st.
Charles A. McGregor	Eb Alto 2nd.
Edward A. Sackett	Eb Alto 3rd.
Samuel F. Hull	Bb Baritone Solo.
Samuel Greenbaum	Bb Tenor, 1st.
Frank L. Butterfield	Bb Tenor, 2nd.
William H. Brown	Bb Tenor, 3rd.
William C. Lace	Eb Tuba, 1st.
Theo W. Pitcher[1]	Eb Tuba, 2nd.
John Lewis	Cymbals.
James M. Johnson[1]	Cymbals.
Timothy Cannon	Small Drum.
William Hughes	Bass Drum.
M. H. Fuller	Bass Drum.

---

[18]Member of the Original Band

APPENDIX VII

ROSTER

OF

OFFICERS AND MEN

OF THE

THIRTY-NINTH ILLINOIS

VETERAN VOLUNTEERS

INFANTRY

1861 - 1865

[Spelling per Adjutant General's Report]

— A —

Abbott, William J. - Sergeant - Company F - Enlisted from Sandoval, Illinois, August 12, 1861. Discharged for disability, August 27, 1861.

Abrams, Frank - Private - Company A - Enlisted January 4, 1864. Captured May 20, 1864 at Ware Bottom Church, Virginia. Paroled and exchanged (date unknown). Mustered out with the regiment, December 6, 1865.

Adams, John Q. - Private - Company B - Enlisted March 1, 1865. Deserted September 2, 1865.

Adams, Samuel - Private - Company A - Enlisted August 5, 1861. Discharged for disability on June 1, 1862. (cause unknown) In 1889 he was living in Minooka, Illinois.

Adams, Thomas J. - Private - Company K - Enlisted from Marengo, McHenry County, Illinois, August 27, 1861. Promoted Corporal December 1, 1863. Discharged September 19, 1864 upon completion of military service. Native of Maine. In 1889 he was living at Ocala, Florida.

Agney, Washington - Private - Company G - Enlisted from Freeport, Illinois, February 29, 1864. Killed October 13, 1864 at Darbytown Cross-Roads, Virginia.

Ahishlager, Carl G. - Private - Company G - Enlisted from New Lenox, Illinois, September 7, 1861. Mustered out September 10, 1864 upon completion of military service.

Ahrens, Claus - Private - Company A - Enlisted August 5, 1861. Veteran. Wounded during the battle of Ware Bottom Church, Virginia, May 20, 1864. Mustered out with the regiment, December 6, 1865.

Aikins, Albert - Private - Company K - Enlisted April 11, 1865. Was a substitute. Mustered out with the regiment, December 6, 1865.

Akehurst, Henry C. - Private - Company C - Enlisted from Pontiac, Illinois, August 12, 1861. Discharged October 11, 1863 for disability. (cause unknown)

Akehurst, James S. - Private - Company C - Enlisted from Pontiac, Illinois, August 12, 1861. Wounded May 20, 1864 near Ware Bottom Church, Virginia. Arm amputated. Died in the hospital May 28, 1864.

Aldridge, Lawson - Private - Company H - Enlisted February 22, 1865. Mustered out with the regiment, December 6, 1865.

Allaban, Wilson S. - See Allahan, William S.

Allahan, William S. - Private - Company H - Enlisted from Palos, Illinois, February 1, 1862. Discharged March 3, 1863 for disability. [Allaban, Wilson S.]

Allen, Abner P.- Private - Company K - Enlisted from Bloomington, Illinois, September 2, 1861. Veteran. Promoted Corporal December 1, 1863. Member of the color-guard and carried the State flag at the surrender ceremony of General Lee, April 9, 1865. Allen accompanied General John Gibbon to Washington, DC with seventy-six stands of Rebel colors, and was presented with a **Medal of Honor** by Secretary of War Stanton for meritorious conduct in front of Petersburg. Mustered out with the regiment, December 6, 1865.

Allen, Andrew C. - Private - Company C - Enlisted from Esmond, Illinois, August 12, 1861. Taken prisoner May 16, 1864 at Drewry's Bluff, Virginia. Sent to prison in Florence, South Carolina where he died September 25, 1864.

Allen, James - Private - Company H - Enlisted April 11, 1865. Mustered out with the regiment, December 6, 1865.

Allen, James K. - Private - Company K - Enlisted from Bloomington, Illinois, September 2, 1861. Veteran. Promoted Corporal December 1, 1864; Sergeant January 1, 1865. Mustered out with the regiment, December 6, 1865.

Allen, John W. - Private - Company H - Enlisted from Chicago, Illinois, April 10, 1862. Deserted October 30, 1862.

Alles, Frank - Private - Company D - Enlisted from Winnetka, Illinois, February 20, 1864. Mustered out with the regiment, December 6, 1865.

Allison, John H. - Private - Company G - Enlisted from New Genesee, Illinois, August 28, 1861. Killed by a falling tree while cutting timber at Suffolk, Virginia, September 28, 1862.

Alsup, James M. - Sergeant - Company B - Enlisted August 12, 1861. Taken prisoner at Blackwater, Virginia, October 24, 1862; paroled and exchanged. Deserted in January 1863.

Alsup, John F. - Sergeant - Company B - Enlisted from LeRoy, Illinois, August 12, 1861. Promoted Sergeant May 26, 1862. To First Sergeant January 1, 1863. Wounded May 22, 1864 in a skirmish near Ware Bottom Church, Virginia. Wounded August 16, 1864 at battle of Deep Run, Virginia. Promoted Captain April 11, 1865, but could not muster. Discharged September 23, 1865 for disability from wounds.

Alsup, Robert D. - Private - Company B - Enlisted from LeRoy, Illinois, February 26, 1864. Mustered out with the regiment, December 6, 1865.

Ames, Jacob - Private - Unassigned Draftee - Drafted from Calhoun County, Illinois, April 8, 1865. Mustered out May 25, 1865.

Anderson, Alexander - Private - Company E - Enlisted February 23, 1865. Killed April 2, 1865 at Fort Gregg, Virginia.

Anderson, F. M. - Private - Company C - Enlisted from Indian Grove, Illinois, August 12, 1861. Discharged for disability in June, 1862.

Anderson, Henry - Corporal - Company B - Enlisted at Bloomington, Illinois, August 12, 1861. Mustered out September 10, 1864 upon completion of military service. In 1889 he was living in Xenia, Ohio.

Anderson, James L. - Private - Company B - Enlisted March 1, 1865. Discharged May 25, 1865 for disability. (cause unknown)

Anderson, James S. - Private - Company B - Enlisted December 15, 1864. Deserted August 2, 1865.

Anderson, John L. - Private - Unassigned Substitute - Enlisted October 20, 1864. Nothing further is known.

Anderson, K. - Private - Company C - Enlisted August 7, 1864. Died September 27, 1865. Cause unknown.

Andreas, William - Private - Company E - Enlisted from Wesley, Illinois, September 1, 1861. Wounded October 3, 1863 at Fort Wagner, South Carolina. Discharged May 16, 1864 for disability from wounds.

Andrews, Isaac B. - Private - Company G - Enlisted from Hartford, Michigan, September 10, 1861. Killed May 16, 1864 at battle of Drewry's Bluff, Virginia.

Angelen, Hicks - Private - Company H - Enlisted April 7, 1865. Mustered out with the regiment, December 6, 1865.

Angle, William - Private - Company G - Enlisted from Homer, Illinois, August 19, 1861. Veteran. Mustered out with the regiment, December 6, 1865.

Anthony, Herbert - Private - Company G - Enlisted from Bedford, Michigan, August 23, 1861. Veteran. Killed May 16, 1864 during the battle of Drewry's Bluff, Virginia.

Argubright, Caleb A. - Private - Company C - Enlisted from Livingston County, Illinois, February 10, 1864. Promoted Corporal July 1, 1865. Mustered out with the regiment, December 6, 1865. In 1889 he was living at Streator, Illinois.

Arlt, Otto - Private - Company F - Enlisted from Chicago, Illinois, August 6, 1861. Mustered out September 10, 1864 upon completion of military service.

Armstrong, Edward - Private - Company G - Enlisted from Chicago, Illinois, February 16, 1864. Wounded in the arm March 31, 1864. Mustered out with the regiment, December 6, 1865.

Armstrong, James - Corporal - Company H - Enlisted July 14, 1862. Reduced to the ranks May 19, 1863. Wounded in the foot, August 15, 1863 at Fort Wagner, South Carolina. Suffered amputation of part of foot. Discharged November 3, 1864 for disability from wounds.

Armstrong, Patrick C. - Private - Company A - Enlisted November 1, 1861. Taken prisoner in 1862. Mustered out August 6, 1863 for disability.

Armstrong, Thomas L. - Private - Company D - Enlisted from Willow Creek, Illinois, September 8, 1861. Discharged June 18, 1862 for disability.

Armstrong, William - Private - Company C - Enlisted from Chicago, Illinois, February 26, 1864. Mustered out with the regiment, December 6, 1865.

Aston, Daniel - Private - Company A - Enlisted August 5, 1861. Veteran. Captured at battle of Drewry's Bluff, Virginia, May 16, 1864. Mustered out under Order of the War Department, August 16, 1865 as a prisoner of war.

Atkins, Warran C. - Private - Company A - Enlisted August 15, 1861. Discharged for disability July 21, 1862.

Atkinson, Edward - Private - Company D - Enlisted from Willow Creek, Illinois, September 9, 1861. Discharged in June 1862 for disability.

Atwater, H. J. - Private - Company C - Enlisted from Esmond, Illinois, September 5, 1861. Wounded August 20, 1863 near Fort Wagner, South Carolina. Mustered out September 16, 1864 upon completion of military service.

Atwood, Joseph S. - Private - Company D - Enlisted from Paine's Point, Illinois, August 12, 1861. Veteran. Wounded in both thighs May 20, 1864 during the battle of Ware Bottom Church, Virginia. Was the Company barber. Mustered out with the regiment, December 6, 1865. Born in Canada, June 27, 1841, and remained there until his twelfth year, when his parents moved to Ogle County, Illinois. After the war he settled in Chicago and engaged in the salt fish business on Michigan Avenue.

Aurand, Robert D. - Private - Company G - Enlisted from Berryman, Illinois, March 15, 1865. Mustered out with the regiment, December 6, 1865.

Austin, Charles - Private - Company K - Enlisted from Chicago, Illinois, September 16, 1861. Discharged in 1862 for disability.

Axtell, Theodore F. - Private - Company E - Enlisted from Wesley, Illinois, February 27, 1864. Wounded August 16, 1864 in the battle of Deep Run, Virginia. Wounded again October 13, 1864 at Darbytown Cross-Roads, Virginia. Promoted Corporal April 1, 1865. Mustered out with the regiment, December 6, 1865.

— B —

Babbit, George M. - Private - Company F - Enlisted from Centralia, Illinois, August 13, 1861. Discharged September 10, 1864 upon completion of military service. [Bobbitt, George M.]

Babbit, Joseph - Private - Company F - Enlisted from Chicago, Illinois, September 4, 1861. Veteran. Mustered out with the regiment, December 6, 1865. [Bobbitt, Joseph]

Babcock, Ralph - Private - Company E - Enlisted from Chicago, Illinois, March 8, 1864. Wounded October 7, 1864 near Chaffin's Farm, Virginia. Killed April 2, 1865 during the assault on Fort Gregg, Virginia.

Baddow, Frederick - Private - Company H - Enlisted April 12, 1866. Mustered out with the regiment, December 6, 1865. [Baddoux, Frederick]

Baddoux, Frederick - See Baddow, Frederick

Baer, Joseph - Private - Company C - Enlisted from Rook's Creek, Illinois, August 12, 1861. Veteran. Wounded April 2, 1865 during the assault on Fort Gregg, Virginia. Promoted Corporal May 1, 1865. Mustered out with the regiment, December 6, 1865.

Bailey, David - Private - Company I - Enlisted from LeRoy, Illinois, September 4, 1861. Veteran. Killed April 2, 1865 during the assault on Fort Gregg, Virginia.

Bailey, Harvey - See Balley, Harvey

Bailey, James B. - Private - Company H - Enlisted from Springfield, Illinois, July 2, 1862. Deserted July 16, 1862.

Bailey, John - Enlisted from Chicago, Illinois, February 19, 1864. No further details known.

Bailey, Orin L. - Private - Unassigned Recruit - Enlisted from Chicago, Illinois, September 29, 1864. Rejected by Medical Board.

Bailey, Patrick - Private - Company A - Enlisted October 14, 1861. Transferred to regular army November 27, 1862.

Bailey, Perry - Private - Company I - Enlisted from LeRoy, Illinois, September 4, 1861. Discharged July 4, 1863 for disability.

Bailey, Robert - Private - Company B - Enlisted from Bloomington, Illinois, October 15, 1861. Deserted February 28, 1864.

Bailey, Robert - Private - Company F - Enlisted from Chicago, Illinois, August 22, 1861. Veteran. Mustered out with the regiment, December 6, 1865.

Baker, Israel S. - Private - Company I - Enlisted from LeRoy, Illinois, September 18, 1861. Drowned May 30, 1863 at Folly Island, South Carolina.

Baker, James W. - Private - Company I - Enlisted from LeRoy, Illinois, February 28, 1864. Wounded in the neck May 16, 1864 during the battle of Drewry's Bluff, Virginia. Mustered out with the regiment, December 6, 1865.

Baker, Lawrence - Private - Company E - Enlisted September 18, 1861. Veteran. Wounded May 16, 1864 during the battle of Drewry's Bluff, Virginia. Taken prisoner, and died as a result of his wounds, June 9, 1864 in Libby Prison, Richmond, Virginia.

Baker, Leroy A. - Captain - Company A - Commissioned Second Lieutenant August 5, 1861. Contracted typhoid fever at Williamsport, Maryland. Promoted Captain December 1, 1861. Rejoined Company in January 1862. At the battle of Drewry's Bluff, May 16, 1864, after Major S. S. Linton had been wounded, and Captain Hiram Phillips, of Company I, had been captured, Baker assumed command of the Regiment and retained it until relieved late that day by Lieutenant-Colonel Mann. When Mann was wounded, Baker again assumed command retaining it until August 16, 1864, when during the battle of Deep Run, Virginia, he received a wound to the right leg which so shattered the bones that amputation was necessary. Discharged from service for disability from that wound. Born

May 10, 1835 in Cortland County, New York. He moved to Will County, Illinois in 1855. After his return to civil life, he secured the position of postmaster at Wilmington, Illinois.

Baker, Levi - Private - Company E - Enlisted April 13, 1865. Mustered out with the regiment, December 6, 1865.

Baker, Thornton - Private - Company C - Enlisted from Sandwich, Illinois, February 2, 1864. Discharged March 28, 1865 for disability.

Baldwin, Charles - Private - Company E - Enlisted from Chicago, Illinois, September 28, 1861 under the name of Charles Creamer to elude his guardian and get into the service. Discharged September 18, 1862 for disability. [Creamer, Charles]

Ball, John T. - Private - Company B - Enlisted from Bloomington, Illinois, August 15, 1861. Discharged October 26, 1863 for disability.

Ballard, John P. - Sergeant - Company F - Enlisted from Bloomington, Illinois, August 12, 1861. Reduced to the ranks April 1, 1864. Veteran. Mustered out with the regiment, December 6, 1865.

Balley, Harvey - Corporal - Company B - Enlisted at Bloomington, Illinois, August 12, 1861. Wounded in the leg May 20, 1864 at Ware Bottom Church, Virginia. Died June 10, 1864 in the hospital from wounds. [Bailey, Harvey]

Barber, Alden - Private - Company K - Enlisted from Marseilles, Illinois, February 6, 1864. Wounded and taken prisoner May 16, 1864 at the battle of Drewry's Bluff, Virginia. Died of disease in Libby Prison, Richmond, Virginia in June 1864.

Barber, Cicero - Private - Company K - Enlisted from Marseilles, Illinois, August 16, 1861. Killed May 20, 1864 at battle of Ware Bottom Church, Virginia. Born in Saratoga County, New York on August 26, 1843. He had two brothers who enlisted in the service. John L. enlisted in Company A, Fifteenth Cavalry. Alden in Company K, Thirty-Ninth Illinois.

Barran, Dalace - See Barron, Dallas

Barrockman, B. C. - Private - Company A - Enlisted from Wilmington, Illinois, August 12, 1861. Deserted September 20, 1861.

Barron, Dallas - Private - Company F - Enlisted from Chicago, Illinois, December 19, 1863. Mustered out with the regiment, December 6, 1865. [Barran, Dalace]

Barron, William - Private - Company G - Enlisted from Orland, Illinois, February 1, 1865. Mustered out with the regiment, December 6, 1865.

Barry, Charles - Corporal - Company H - Enlisted from Kingston Mines, Illinois, February 1, 1862. Veteran. Wounded in the thigh May 20, 1864 at the battle of Ware Bottom Church, Virginia. Died June 17, 1864 from his wounds.

Bartlett, Asher - Private - Company H - Enlisted March 3, 1865. Mustered out with the regiment, December 6, 1865.

Barton, Samuel A. - Private - Company E - Enlisted from Bloomington, Illinois, December 16, 1862. Discharged July 4, 1863 for disability.

Barton, William H. - Private - Company B - Enlisted from Bloomington, Illinois, August 12, 1861. Discharged December 12, 1863 for disability.

Batchelder, Samuel C. - Private - Company E - Enlisted from Wilmington, Illinois, December 21, 1863. Discharged June 3, 1865 under order from the War Department.

Baur, Henry - Private - Company F - Enlisted from Elgin, Illinois, September 4, 1861. Discharged January, 1862. [Bour, Henry]

Baxter, William - Private - Company A - Enlisted August 5, 1861. Veteran. Wounded in the shoulder May 16, 1864 during the battle of Drewry's Bluff. Mustered out with the regiment, December 6, 1865. In 1889 he was living at Wilmington, Illinios.

Baxter, William - First Lieutenant - Company E - Enlisted from Wilmington, Illinois, September 20, 1861. Wounded through both thighs on May 16, 1864 during the battle of Drewry's Bluff, Virginia. Taken prisoner. He was a patient in the Pemberton Hospital in Richmond until exchanged on August 13, 1864. Promoted Sergeant November 1, 1864; to First Sergeant January 1, 1865; to First Lieutenant June 6, 1865. Mustered out with the regiment, December 6, 1865.

Beach, William H. - Corporal - Company D - Enlisted from Oregon, Illinois, September 5, 1861. Discharged May 30, 1864 for disability.

Beachy, Josiah F. - Private - Company H - Enlisted from Kingston Mines, Illinois, February 1, 1862. Wounded in the arm, June 2, 1864 in battle near Ware Bottom Church, Virginia. Arm amputated. Discharged March 3, 1865 upon completion of military service.

Beadles, Richard - Private - Company C - Enlisted April 6, 1865. Mustered out with the regiment, December 6, 1865.

Beam, Charles W. - Private - Company E - Enlisted from Gaines, Illinois, April 13, 1865 at the age of 15 years. Assigned guard duty at Richmond and City Point, Virginia. Was detailed as messenger for the telegraph service at Norfolk. Mustered out with the regiment, December 6, 1865.

Beamish, Thomas - Private - Company K - Enlisted from Elwood, Will County, Illinois, September 10, 1861. Veteran. Mustered out with the regiment, December 6, 1865.

Bean, B. L. - Private - Company I - Enlisted from LeRoy, Illinois, September 4, 1861. Discharged November 1, 1862 for disability.

Bean, John A. - Corporal - Company I - Enlisted from Santa Anna, Illinois, September 4, 1861. Reduced to the ranks, March 6, 1862. Killed October 27, 1864 in a skirmish near the Darbytown Cross-Roads, Virginia.

Beanblossom, Ira - Private - Company I - Enlisted April 11, 1865. Was a substitute. Mustered out with the regiment, December 6, 1865.

Beard, John P. S. - Private - Company I - Enlisted from LeRoy, Illinois, February 13, 1864. Wounded in the leg, June 2, 1864. Died of disease in Springfield, Illinois, February 1, 1865.

Beckwith, Lester S. - Private - Company B - Enlisted from Bloomington, Illinois, February 22, 1864. Wounded May 16, 1864 at the battle of Drewry's Bluff, Virginia. Again wounded May 20 at Ware Bottom Church. Was on furlough at muster-out of the regiment.

Beckwith, Walter J. - Private - Company B - Enlisted from Bloomington, Illinois, August 12, 1861. Promoted to Corporal October 31, 1863. Veteran. Reduced to the ranks May 1, 1865. Mustered out with the regiment, December 6, 1865.

Bedell, Ransom - Private - Company G - Enlisted from Cook County, Illinois, August 15, 1861. Veteran. Killed October 12, 1864 in a skirmish near Chaffin's Farm, Virginia.

Bedford, Peter Parley - Private - Company K - Enlisted from Marseilles, Illinois, February 24, 1864. Died of disease April 9, 1864.

Bedford, Wallace - Private - Company K - Enlisted from Marseilles, Illinois, August 14, 1861. Known as "Gunboat." Veteran. Wounded August 26, 1863 at Morris Island, South Carolina. Wounded October 13, 1864 at Darbytown Cross-Roads, Virginia. Mustered out with the regiment, December 6, 1865.

Beeler, Leonard - Private - Company G - Enlisted from Wood's Grove, Illinois, February 22, 1865. Mustered out with the regiment, December 6, 1865.

Begnall, O. B. - Corporal - Company K - Enlisted from Marseilles, Illinois, September 3, 1861. Discharged August 11, 1862 for disability. Was 57 years of age when he died April 1, 1866.

Belcher, Oscar S. - First Lieutenant - Company K - Enlisted in Company B in August 1861. Commissioned in Company K, September 20, 1861. Resigned May 11, 1862. In May 1863 enlisted as a private in Company M, Sixteenth Illinois Cavalry; was promoted to Sergeant; taken prisoner and sent to Andersonville Prison. Mustered out of the service, August 19, 1864.

Bell, John - Private - Company C - Enlisted August 29, 1864. Mustered out with the regiment, December 6, 1865.

Bender, Charles - Private - Company B - Enlisted at Bloomington, Illinois, August 30, 1861. Discharged June 16, 1862 for disability. Died in 1888.

Bender, Samuel H. - Private - Unassigned Recruit - Enlisted from Lexington, Illinois, February 26, 1864. No further details known.

Benson, Alexander - Private - Unassigned Recruit - Enlisted from Griggsville, Illinois, February 26, 1864. No further details known.

Benson, John H. - Private - Unassigned Recruit - Enlisted from Sandoval, Illinois, February 16, 1864. No further details known.

Benton, Silas - Private - Company E - Enlisted from Wilmington, Illinois, August 12, 1861. Veteran. Killed May 14, 1864 at Drewry's Bluff, Virginia.

Berget, Lancet - See Burget, Lawrence

Barns, James D. - See Burns, James D.

Berry, John - Private - Company I - Enlisted from Santa Anna, Illinois, September 4, 1861. Wounded May 16, 1864 at Drewry's Bluff, Virginia. Mustered out October 18, 1864 upon completion of military service.

Berry, Joseph - Private - Company B - Enlisted at Bloomington, Illinois, August 12, 1861. Wounded August 16, 1864 during the battle of Deep Run, Virginia. Leg amputated. Died September 4, 1864 in the hospital of those wounds.

Best, James F. - Private - Company K - Enlisted February 14, 1865. Died in the hospital at Norfolk, Virginia September 18, 1865.

Bias, John A. - Private - Company F - Enlisted from Centralia, Illinois, August 13, 1861. Promoted Corporal February 16, 1862. Veteran. Wounded May 20, 1864 and again August 16, 1864. Mustered out with the regiment, December 6, 1865. [Bras, John A.]

Bien, Frederick - Private - Company G - Enlisted from Milwaukee, Wisconsin, August 13, 1861. Deserted August 25, 1861.

Barber, Jonathan - Private - Company B - Enlisted from Bloomington, Illinois, February 6, 1864. Mustered out with the regiment, December 6, 1865.

Bierbower, Jonathan - Private - Company B - Enlisted from Bloomington, Illinois, February 6, 1864. Mustered out with the regiment, December 6, 1865. In 1889 he was living in Arrowsmith, Illinois.

Birch, William - Private - Company H - Enlisted from Ashore, Illinois, February 2, 1862. Wounded June 2, 1862; also April 2, 1865 at the assault on Fort Gregg, Virginia. Mustered out June 2, 1865 upon completion of military service.

Birge, Andreas - Private - Company K - Enlisted from Bloomington, Illinois, August 18, 1861. Veteran. Mustered out with the regiment, December 6, 1865.

Birkenbuel, Henry - See Burkenbuel, Henry

Bishop, Reese - Regimental Sergeant-Major - Enlisted in Company I from LeRoy, Illinois, October 18, 1861. Promoted Sergeant Major and transferred to non-commissioned staff July 15, 1862. Captured at Drewry's Bluff, Virginia, May 16, 1864. Died of disease in Andersonville Prison, Georgia on November 7, 1864.

Blake, Robert W. - Private - Company G - Enlisted from Chicago, Illinois, September 9, 1861. Wounded in the thigh June 17, 1864, and in the face on August 16, 1864. Discharged September 16, 1864 upon completion of military service.

Blake, Samuel C. - Regimental Surgeon - Commissioned August 5, 1861. Was responsible for General Bank's army general hospital in the Shenandoah Valley at Mount Jackson, Virginia. Organized three large hospitals near Strasburg, Virginia, and a field hospital in which he was responsible for 1,000 sick and wounded soldiers of both North and South. Resigned June 3, 1862 due to chronic hepatitis and diarrhea. Born in the city of Bath, Maine, July 25, 1826. The Doctor came from Revolutionary stock, his grandfather, John Blake, served at the age of eighteen years in the Continental Army as a member of his cousin's company, Captain Dearborn, afterwards Major-General Dearborn, for whom Fort Dearborn, Chicago, was named. On the maternal side, Dr. Blake is connected with John Hancock, the first signer of the Declaration of Independence. His father Rev.

S. P. Blake was a member of the Maine Annual Conference of the Methodist Episcopal Church for fifty years. Dr. Blake graduated in medicine at the medical department of Harvard University, July 20, 1853. He served as house physician in the Massachusetts General Hospital for one year. After practicing medicine in Boston for three years he went to Chicago in 1856. He leased the old City Hospital building and organized the second hospital in Chicago. In 1861 Dr. Blake was commissioned Surgeon of the Nineteenth Illinois Volunteers, and accompanied the regiment to Missouri. He organized the General Hospital at Quincy, Illinois. After the Thirty-Ninth was accepted, he transferred to it as the surgeon.

Blakesley, Samuel C. - Private - Company E - Enlisted from Durham, Illinois, September 18, 1861. Deserted, date unknown.

Blanchard, John - Private - Company B - Enlisted at Bloomington, Illinois, August 27, 1861. Discharged September 10, 1864 upon completion of military service.

Blanden, John K. - See Blandin, John K.

Blandin, John K. - Private - Company I - Enlisted from Santa Anna, Illinois, February 16, 1864. Wounded in the hip April 2, 1865 during the assault on Fort Gregg, Virginia. Discharged May 31, 1865 for disability from wounds. [Blanden, John K.]

Blevens, Sanford H. - See Blevins, Sanford H.

Blevins, Sanford H. - Private - Company B - Enlisted from Bloomington, Illinois, August 25, 1861. Discharged September 25, 1862 for disability. [Blevens, Sanford H.] He died shortly after the war. In 1889 his widow lived in Sebree, Kentucky.

Bobbitt, George M. - See Babbit, George M.

Bobbitt, Joseph - See Babbit, Joseph

Bogard, Levi W. - Private - Company D - Enlisted April 6, 1865. Mustered out with the regiment, December 6, 1865.

Bogart, Walter - Private - Company E - Enlisted from Wilmington, Illinois, September 17, 1861. Killed October 12, 1863 at Battery Gregg, South Carolina.

Bohmler, William - Private - Company E - Enlisted from Chicago, Illinois, September 26, 1864. Discharged June 20, 1865.

Bond, James - Private - Unassigned Recruit - Enlisted from Joliet, Illinois, September 20, 1862. No further details known.

Boone, William W. - Private - Company D - Enlisted from Chicago, Illinois, March 7, 1864. Mustered out with the regiment, December 6, 1865. In 1889 he was living Chicago engaged in the livery business.

Borchers, Hermanus - Private - Company G - Enlisted from Peoria, Illinois, August 30, 1861. Died of disease, February 13, 1862 in Cumberland, Maryland.

Bosworth, Isaac D. - Private - Company G - Enlisted from Mantenoo, Illinois, August 30, 1861. Discharged September 10, 1864 upon completion of military service.

Botsford, Reuben S. - Captain - Company F - Commissioned Second Lieutenant February 1, 1864. Wounded in the leg by a shell fragment, June 20, 1864 at the battle of Ware Bottom Church, Virginia. Promoted First Lieutenant August 13, 1864. Contracted typhoid fever after the battle of Deep Run, Virginia and sent to hospital. Promoted Captain, March 31, 1865. Mustered out with the regiment, December 6, 1865. Born in Albany, New York, July 1833, and came west to Waukegan, Illinois in 1854. After the war he moved to Huron, Dakota Territory and became an agent for American Express.

Boughton, Jehial - Corporal - Company G - Enlisted from Palos, Illinois, August 9, 1861. Veteran. Died from disease April 12, 1864 in Washington, D.C.

Bour, Henry - See Baur, Henry

Bowden, Ferdinand R. - Private - Company D - Enlisted from Oregon, Illinois, August 21, 1861. Veteran. Wounded September 25, 1863 at Fort Gregg, South Carolina., and again April 2, 1865 at the assault on Fort Gregg, Virginia. Mustered out with the regiment, December 6, 1865.

Bowen, Henry H. - Private - Company A - Enlisted from Florence, Illinois, December 26, 1863. Wounded and taken prisoner during the battle of Drewry's Bluff, Virginia, May 16, 1864. Nothing further is known.

Bowen, James R. - Private - Company I - Enlisted from Champaign, Illinois, October 3, 1861. Taken prisoner May 20, 1864 at Ware Bottom Church, Virginia. Discharged for disability, date unknown.

Bowen, Marion D. - Private - Company B - Enlisted from Chicago, Illinois, October 21, 1864. Wounded April 2, 1865 during the assault on Fort Gregg, Virginia. Died April 2, 1865 from his wounds.

Bowers, John - Private - Company B - Enlisted at Bloomington, Illinois, August 7, 1861. Taken prisoner May 1, 1862 at Strasburg, Virginia; paroled and exchanged. Wounded August 16, 1864 at the battle of Deep Run, Virginia. Discharged October 13, 1864 upon completion of military service.

Bowman, N. B. - Musician, First Class - Enlisted September 20, 1861. Discharged June 4, 1862 by order of the War Department.

Boyce, Hiram - Private - Company D - Enlisted from Odgon, Illinois, August 21, 1861. Veteran. Promoted Corporal August 4, 1865. Mustered out with the regiment, December 6, 1865. In 1889 he was living in Oregon, Illinois.

Boyd, Hiram C. - Private - Company H - Enlisted from Old Town, Illinois, February 12, 1862. Promoted Corporal March 20, 1863. Wounded in the thigh June 2, 1864. Discharged March 3, 1865 upon completion of military service.

Bradfield, Simon H. - Private - Unassigned Substitute - Enlisted April 5, 1865. Nothing further is known.

Brandon, Calvin K. - Private - Unassigned Substitute - Enlisted September 26, 1864. Nothing further is known.

Brannackman, B. C. - Private - Company A - Enlisted August 5, 1861. Dropped before muster.

Brasch, Frederick - Private - Company G - Enlisted from Palos, Illinois, February 15, 1864. Discharged for disability November 18, 1865.

Bras, John A. - See Bias, John A.

Brauer, August - See Brower, August

Breckenberg, Charles - Private - Company H - Enlisted March 2, 1865. Mustered out with the regiment, December 6, 1865. [Brickenberg, Charles]

Breninger, Benjamin - Private - Company G - Enlisted from Wood's Grove, Illinois, February 27, 1865. Mustered out with the regiment, December 6, 1865. [Brininger, Benjamin]

Breninger, David - Private - Company G - Enlisted from Hopkins, Illinois, March 29, 1865. Mustered out with the regiment, December 6, 1865. [Brininger, David]

Breninger, John - Private - Company G - Enlisted from Freeport, Illinois, February 27, 1864. Wounded in the head October 7, 1864 in a skirmish near Chaffin's Farm, Virginia. Mustered out with the regiment, December 6, 1865. [Brininger, John]

Brennan, John - Private - Company I - Enlisted from Santa Anna, Illinois, September 4, 1861. Veteran. Promoted Corporal September 1, 1864; Sergeant April 2, 1865. Mustered out with the regiment, December 6, 1865.

Brennan, Thomas S. - Private - Company H - Enlisted from Chicago, Illinois, March 29, 1864. Wounded in the thigh May 20, 1864. Died in the hospital July 22, 1864 from wounds.

Brickenberg, Charles - See Breckenberg, Charles

Brightman, William - Private - Company H - Enlisted March 1, 1862. Died of disease in the hospital at St. Augustine, Florida.

Brininger, Benjamin - See Breninger, Benjamin

Brininger, David - See Breninger, David

Brininger, John - See Breninger, John

Brink, Albert - Private - Company G - Enlisted from Sterling, Illinois, February 28, 1864. Mustered out with the regiment, December 6, 1865.

Brink, Samuel H. - Sergeant - Company G - Enlisted from Sterling, Illinois, August 15, 1861. Veteran. Promoted to First Sergeant January 1, 1864. Died of typhoid fever September 22, 1864.

Brogan, Daniel - Private - Company F - Enlisted from Benton, Missouri, October 15, 1861. Discharged December 18, 1861 for disability.

Brooks, James - Private - Unassigned Substitute - Enlisted April 12, 1865. Nothing further is known.

Brooks, Lysander R. - Private - Company A - Enlisted August 5, 1861. Veteran. Served 2 years as Brigade Postmaster. Mustered out with the regiment, December 6, 1865.

Broucket, Florence - See Brucket, Florence

Broughton, Charles - Private - Company K - Enlisted from Morris, Illinois, August 14, 1861. Discharged for disability in 1862.

Brower, August - Private - Company K - Enlisted from Bloomington, Illinois, September 5, 1861. Discharged June 18, 1862 for disability. [Brauer, August]

Brown, Ebenezer - Private - Company H - Enlisted from Downs, Illinois, March 1, 1862. Veteran. Injured while unloading a ship at Folly Island, South Carolina. Promoted Corporal April 16, 1865; Sergeant June 20, 1865. Mustered out with the regiment, December 6, 1865.

Brown, George - Private - Company F - Enlisted from Sandoval, Illinois, August 15, 1861. Deserted April 18, 1862.

Brown, George P. - Private - Company K - Enlisted from Bloomington, Illinois, October 17, 1861. Veteran. Wounded in the knee October 13, 1864 at Darbytown Cross-Roads, Virginia. Was absent (sick and wounded) at the time the regiment was mustered out.

Brown, George W. L. - Private - Company G - Enlisted from Orland, Illinois, February 29, 1864. Wounded in the thigh April 2, 1865 at the assault on Fort Gregg, Virginia. Discharged July 19, 1865 for disability from wounds.

Brown, Henry - Private - Company A - Enlisted December 26, 1863. Wounded May 16, 1864 at Drewry's Bluff, Virginia. Mustered out with the regiment, December 6, 1865.

Brown, John F. - Private - Company I - Enlisted from McLean County, Illinois, September 4, 1861. Wounded June 16, 1864. Discharged September 10, 1864 upon completion of military service.

Brown, John J. - Private - Company H - Enlisted from Downs, Illinois, March 1, 1862. Veteran. Promoted Corporal May 16, 1865; Sergeant June 20, 1865. Mustered out with the regiment, December 6, 1865.

Brown, Kental - Private - Company A - Enlisted April 5, 1865. Mustered out with the regiment, December 6, 1865.

Brown, Lewis - Private - Company B - Enlisted February 25, 1865. Mustered out with the regiment, December 6, 1865.

Brown, O. P. - Private - Company C - Enlisted from Esmond, Illinois, August 25, 1861. Discharged October 28, 1861 for disability.

Brown, Simon - Private - Unassigned Draftee - Drafted from LaSalle, Illinois, April 4, 1865. Mustered out July 8, 1865.

Brown, William - Corporal - Company E - Enlisted from Chicago, Illinois, September 27, 1861. Veteran. Detailed to the Regimental Band. Musician in Band of 1864 & 1865. Mustered out with the regiment, December 6, 1865.

Brown, William A. - Private - Company E - Enlisted April 11, 1865. Was a substitute. Mustered out with the regiment, December 6, 1865.

Brown, William H. R. - Private - Company A - Enlisted August 21, 1861. Wounded in the hand and finger at Ware Bottom Church, June 2, 1864. Finger amputated. Discharged upon completion of military service, August 1864. In 1889 he was living in Salida, Colorado.

Brucker, Simon S. - First Lieutenant - Company C - Commissioned Second Lieutenant August 12, 1861. Promoted First Lieutenant March 31, 1865. Resigned July 12, 1865. Born at Alzey, Germany in 1838. In May 1852 he emigrated to the United States locating in New Jersey. After a few months relocated to Pontiac, Illinois. In 1889 he was living at 259 Hermitage Avenue, Chicago.

Brucket, Florence - Private - Company A - Enlisted February 19, 1864. Taken prisoner May 16, 1864 at the battle of Drewry's Bluff, Virginia, and sent to Andersonville Prison. Muster out information unknown.

Brusch, Frederick - Private - Company G - Enlisted from Palos, Illinois, February 15, 1864. Wounded in the foot April 2, 1865 at the assault on Fort Gregg, Virginia. Discharged November 18, 1865 for disability from wounds.

Buchanan, John S. - Private - Company D - Enlisted from Clay County, Illinois, April 11, 1865. Discharged May 20, 1865 for disability.

Bullen, David - Private - Company G - Enlisted from Farmington, Illinois, September 9, 1861. Discharged June 2, 1862 for disability.

Bullis, Newman P. - Private - Company D - Enlisted from Lane, Illinois, August 12, 1861. Discharged September 10, 1864 upon completion of military service.

Bulter, Harrison - Private - Company B - Enlisted from Bloomington, Illinois, August 30, 1861. Severely wounded June 16, 1864 in a skirmish near Chester Station, Virginia. Left on the field and supposed to have been taken prisoner. Veteran. Nothing further is known. [Butler, Harrison]

Bunker, Nathaniel - Private - Company D - Enlisted November 4, 1862. Taken prisoner August 18, 1864. Died of disease in prison (probably in Florence, South Carolina), January 16, 1865.

Bunt, Francis P. - Private - Unassigned Substitute - Enlisted April 8, 1865. Nothing further is known.

Burden, John - Private - Company A - Enlisted August 17, 1861. Veteran. Killed during the battle of Deep Run, Virginia August 16, 1864.

Burdick, Charles L. - Private - Company F - Enlisted from Antioch, Illinois, February 13, 1864. Promoted Corporal August 1, 1865. Mustered out with the regiment, December 6, 1865.

Burdick, John H. - Private - Company F - Enlisted from Antioch, Illinois, February 13, 1864. Mustered out with the regiment, December 6, 1865.

Burget, Lawrence - Private - Company K - Enlisted from Marseilles, Illinois, August 27, 1861. Discharged August 17, 1863 for disability. [Berget, Lancet]

Burke, George - Private - Company B - Enlisted from Bloomington, Illinois, August 12, 1861. Killed September 11, 1863 at Fort Gregg, South Carolina.

Burke, Gerhard - Private - Company B - Enlisted from Bloomington, Illinois, August 12, 1861. Discharged September 12, 1864 upon completion of military service.

Burkenbuel, Henry - Private - Company D - Enlisted from Peru, Illinois, November 1, 1861. Wounded May 20, 1864. Promoted Corporal December 5, 1864. Discharged November 1, 1864 upon completion of military service. [Birkenbual, Henry]

Burnham, Freeman - Private - Company C - Enlisted from Pontiac, Illinois, August 12, 1865. Discharged June 26, 1865 for disability.

Burns, Charles - Private - Unassigned Recruit - Enlisted from Elk Grove, Illinois, January 6, 1865. No further details known.

Burns, Daniel - Private - Company B - Enlisted February 25, 1865. Mustered out with the regiment, December 6, 1865.

Burns, James D. - Private - Company K - Enlisted at Marseilles, Illinois, August 14, 1861. Promoted Corporal December 1, 1863. Mustered out with the regiment, December 6, 1865. [Berns, James D.]

Burrill, James - Second Lieutenant - Company A - Enlisted August 5, 1861. Promoted December 1, 1861. Wounded in the neck at Bermuda Hundred, Virginia, May 25, 1864. Discharged upon completion of military service. In 1889 he was living in Braidwood, Illinois.

Burt, John - Private - Unassigned Substitute - Enlisted February 24, 1865. Nothing further is known.

Burton, George W. - Corporal - Company E - Enlisted from Wilmington, Illinois, September 12, 1861. Veteran. Wounded in both thighs, August 16, 1864 at Deep Run, Virginia. Promoted Sergeant November 1, 1864. Killed April 2, 1865 at the assault on Fort Gregg, Virginia.

Burton, Lemuel J. - Private - Company H - Enlisted April 7, 1865. Mustered out with the regiment, December 6, 1865.

Bushnell, Albert - Private - Company G - Enlisted from Palos, Illinois, February 27, 1864. Mustered out with the regiment, December 6, 1865.

Butler, Harrison - See Bulter, Harrison

Butterfield, Augustus - Private - Company K - Enlisted from Marseilles, Illinois, December 16, 1863. Taken prisoner May 16, 1864 at Drewry's Bluff, Virginia. Sent to Andersonville Prison. Mustered out with the regiment, December 6, 1865.

Butterfield, Francis L. - Private - Company K - Enlisted from Marseilles, Illinois, February 4, 1864. Entered for service in the regimental band; was detailed as nurse to General Osborn, Colonel Munn and Major Linton when they were wounded in 1864. Musician in Band of 1864 & 1865. Discharged at Camp Lee Hospital, Richmond, Virginia, May 30, 1865.

Butterfield, Marion L. - First Lieutenant - Company K - Enlisted from Marseilles, Illinois, August 7, 1861 as a Sergeant. Promoted Second Lieutenant June 14, 1862; promoted First Lieutenant September 1, 1864. Wounded in the arm August 16, 1864 at Deep Run, Virginia. Discharged for disability December 7, 1864. Born at Antwerp, Jefferson County, New York on August 15, 1831. In 1855 he was married to Eliza Ferris of Owego, New York. In 1889 he was living at Marseilles, Illinois.

Butterfield, William - Private - Company A - Enlisted August 12, 1861. Veteran. Promoted Corporal August 22, 1863. Killed August 16, 1864 at Deep Run, Virginia, while member of the color-guard.

Button, Lorenz - Private - Company E - Enlisted from Wilmington, Illinois, October 2, 1861. Discharged for disability in 1862.

— C —

Caddigan, John - Private - Company K - Enlisted February 16, 1864. Wounded in the head May 20, 1864. Died from wounds, November 14, 1864. [Creddigan, John]

Cain, Christopher D. - Private - Company B - Enlisted from Bloomington, Illinois, February 24, 1864. Wounded August 16, 1864. Discharged March 23, 1865 upon completion of military service.

Cain, William B. - Corporal - Company G - Enlisted from Wilmington, Illinois, March 13, 1862. Reduced to the ranks, May 1, 1863. Discharged March 23, 1865 upon completion of military service.

Calbeck, William - Private - Company H - Enlisted February 28, 1865. Promoted Corporal May 10, 1865. Mustered out with the regiment, December 6, 1865.

Calhoun, William W. - Private - Company A - Enlisted August 15, 1861. Died in the regimental hospital, Patterson's Creek, Virginia, February 23, 1862. Cause unknown.

Call, Carlton - Private - Company B - Enlisted from Bloomington, Illinois, August 12, 1861. Discharged July 4, 1863 for disability.

Callahan, Calvin - Private - Company F - Enlisted August 10, 1861. Veteran. Wounded and taken prisoner May 16, 1864 at Drewry's Bluff, Virginia. Died of wounds in Andersonville Prison, August 21, 1864. Grave Number 6,356.

Callahan, Theodore - Private - Company G - Enlisted from Philadelphia, Pennsylvania, August 29, 1861. Discharged September 10, 1864 upon completion of military service.

Cambellick, William - Private - Company A - Enlisted October 8, 1864. Wounded April 2, 1865 at Fort Gregg, Virginia. Absent, wounded, at muster out of regiment. [Combelick, William] Last known to be living in Gettysburg, Dakota Territory.

Camp, Charles H. - Private - Unassigned Recruit - Enlisted from Chicago, Illinois, December 23, 1863. Nothing further is known.

Campbell, Alexander - Private - Company H - Enlisted March 3, 1865. Promoted Corporal May 14, 1865. Mustered out with the regiment, December 6, 1865.

Campbell, Merlin - Private - Company G - Enlisted from Newport, Michigan, August 29, 1861. Was Wagon-master. Discharged September 10, 1864 upon completion of military service.

Campbell, Samuel - Private - Company F - Enlisted January 14, 1864. Wounded June 18, 1864. Mustered out with the regiment, December 6, 1865.

Campbell, William - Private - Company G - Enlisted February 4, 1865. Was a substitute. Deserted May 12, 1865.

Campbell, William E. - Private - Company B - Enlisted from Bloomington, Illinois, February 22, 1864. Mustered out with the regiment, December 6, 1865.

Canaday, Calvin - Private - Company I - Enlisted from LeRoy, Illinois, February 26, 1864. Mustered out with the regiment, December 6, 1865.

Canaday, George W. - Private - Company I - Enlisted from LeRoy, Illinois, February 26, 1864. Mustered out with the regiment, December 6, 1865.

Cannon, John - Private - Company E - Enlisted from Wilmington, Illinois, October 21, 1861. Veteran. Discharged November 20, 1865 for disability.

Cannon, Patrick - Private - Company D - Enlisted from Oregon, Illinois, February 25, 1864. Wounded May 16, 1864 at the battle of Drewry's Bluff, Virginia, and also October 13, 1864. Died of wounds, October 22, 1864.

Cannon, Timothy - Musician - Company K - Enlisted from Troy, Wisconsin, September 27, 1861. Veteran. Regimental drummer in Band of 1864 & 1865. Mustered out with the regiment, December 6, 1865.

Carl, John - Private - Company G - Enlisted from Homer, Illinois, August 16, 1861. Discharged September 10, 1864 upon completion of military service.

Carl, Oliver C. - Private - Company B - Enlisted August 12, 1861. Deserted January 26, 1862.

Carman, Archibald L. - Corporal - Company B - Enlisted from Bloomington, Illinois, August 12, 1861. Promoted Sergeant May 26, 1862. Discharged September 10, 1864 upon completion of military service. [Corman, Archibald L.]

Carpenter, Adelbert F. - Private - Company A - Enlisted August 5, 1861. Promoted Corporal July 1, 1865. Mustered out with the regiment, December 6, 1865. In 1889 he was living at Wilmington, Illinois.

Carpenter, Charles - Private - Company F - Enlisted September 17, 1861. Veteran. Wounded June 18, 1864 in the arm, and suffered removal of about six inches of bone. Discharged December 8, 1864 for disability from wounds.

Carpenter, Joseph M. - Private - Company A - Enlisted August 5, 1861. Discharged February 16, 1862 for disability.

Carr, Henry - Private - Company H - Enlisted from LeRoy, Illinois, February 13, 1862. Transferred to Company I, August 1, 1862. Mustered out with the regiment, December 6, 1865.

Carr, James - Private - Company I - Enlisted from LeRoy, Illinois, September 4, 1861. Veteran. Promoted Corporal September 24, 1864. Mustered out with the regiment, December 6, 1865.

Carrigan, Hugh - See Corrigan, Hugh

Carroll, Harrison - Private - Company C - Enlisted from Chicago, Illinois, February 22, 1864. Mustered out with the regiment, December 6, 1865.

Carter, Joseph - Private - Company A - Enlisted August 5, 1861. Died of wounds received at Fort Wagner, South Carolina August 26, 1863.

Carter, William C. - Private - Company A - Enlisted August 5, 1861. Discharged November 15, 1862 for disability.

Case, Henry N. - Private - Company G - Enlisted from Thornton, Illinois, February 28, 1864. Died of disease, February 13, 1865, while home on furlough.

Casey, Edward - Private - Company H - Enlisted from Chicago, Illinois, February 28, 1862. Veteran. Taken prisoner October 13, 1864; was paroled and exchanged. Mustered out with the regiment, December 6, 1865.

Casey, James - Private - Company F - Enlisted September 20, 1861. Discharged October 22, 1862 for disability.

Casey, John - Private - Company E - Enlisted March 11, 1864. Joined the regiment at Camp Grant, Arlington Heights, Virginia. Was promoted Corporal. Mustered out with the regiment, December 6, 1865.

Cassady, James - Private - Unassigned Substitute - Enlisted April 8, 1865. Nothing further is known.

Cavanaugh, Michael - Private - Company H - Enlisted from Chicago, Illinois, October 9, 1861. Deserted March 17, 1862.

Cavett, John A. - Private - Company B - Enlisted from Bloomington, Illinois, August 6, 1864. Discharged July 6, 1865 under order of the War Department.

Chapin, Caleb F. - Private - Company G - Enlisted from Atlanta, Illinois, October 28, 1861. Veteran. Wounded June 2, 1864 at Hatcher's Run, Virginia and died of wounds the same day.

Chapman, Edward O. - Corporal - Company C - Enlisted from Cayuga, Illinois, August 12, 1861. Promoted Sergeant February 10, 1863. Discharged September 10, 1864 upon completion of military service. One of a party of eight soldiers that captured a blockade-runner in Broad River, near Bull's Island, South Carolina, in 1863. These men took the boat to Hilton Head and delivered it to General Gillmore for which they received special mention in Orders. He was wounded at Kingsland Creek, Virginia; also at Ware Bottom Church and again at Deep Bottom, Virginia. After the war he moved to Cayuga, Illinois where he became the Station Agent for the Chicago and Alton Railroad.

Charleston, Richard C. - Private - Company I - Enlisted from LeRoy, Illinois, October 13, 1861. Veteran. Taken prisoner May 26, 1862 at Strasburg, Virginia; was paroled and exchanged. Promoted Corporal October 9, 1865. Mustered out with the regiment, December 6, 1865.

Chasm, Thomas - Private - Company D - Enlisted from Oregon, Illinois, August 21, 1861. Died August 14, 1862 at David's Island.

Chatfield, Jesse - Private - Company G - Enlisted from Palos, Illinois, September 8, 1861. Promoted Corporal September 24, 1862. Wounded in the hand June 17, 1864 in a skirmish with the enemy. Discharged September 10, 1864 upon completion of military service.

Chatterton, Enoch - Private - Company K - Enlisted from Morris, Illinois, July 23, 1862. Discharged July 24, 1863.

Cheeseman, Charles W. - Private - Company B - Enlisted April 7, 1865. Mustered out with the regiment, December 6, 1865.

Cherry, Luke - Private - Company H - Enlisted from Chicago, Illinois, February 1, 1862. Veteran. Wounded in the arm and shoulder and taken prisoner August 16, 1864 at the battle of Deep Run, Virginia. Wounded, absent at muster out of the regiment. Died at Chicago, Illinois, October 7, 1887.

Chichester, Sanford H. - Private - Company D - Enlisted from Hennepin, Illinois, August 23, 1861. Discharged March 31, 1862 for disability.

Christian, Ackley - Private - Company C - Enlisted March 31, 1865. Mustered out with the regiment, December 6, 1865.

Churchill, John - Private - Company K - Enlisted from Marseilles, Illinois, September 16, 1861. Veteran. Promoted Corporal May 2, 1865. Reduced to the ranks, September 27, 1865. Mustered out with the regiment, December 6, 1865.

Claire, Hippolyte - Private - Company F - Enlisted February 29, 1864. Wounded in the leg August 16, 1864 at Deep Run, Virginia. Mustered out with the regiment, December 6, 1865.

Clapp, Frederick G. - Quartermaster-Sergeant - Enlisted August 5, 1861, from Chicago, reduced to private and assigned to Company A, September 30, 1861. Discharged September 9, 1864 upon completion of military service. Moved to Buffalo, New York after the war.

Clark, Charles - Private - Company G - Enlisted from Fremont, Illinois, February 12, 1864. Died of disease, April 8, 1864 in Chicago, Illinois.

Clark, Charles M. - Regimental Surgeon - Promoted June 3, 1862. Original member of Yates Phalanx formed in Thomas O. Osborn's office in April 1861. In April, 1863 was made Post-Surgeon and in charge of the hospital at Folly Island, South Carolina. On April 30, 1864, promoted to Chief Medical Officer of the First Division, Tenth Corps. On January 8, 1865 appointed Chief Operating Surgeon of Twenty-Fourth Corps. On June 18, 1865 appointed Surgeon-in-charge of the Twenty-Fourth Corps Hospital in Richmond. Mustered out with the regiment, December 6, 1865. Born October 8, 1834 at Manlius Square, Onondaga County, New York. He was married on February 22, 1866. After the death of his wife in 1872, he accepted an appointment in the Regular Army, and served at Fort Larned, Kansas, and then Fort Riley, from there to Fort Union, New Mexico and then to Santa Fe. He was then ordered back to Fort Union, where he acted as Post Surgeon until he left the service. He returned to Chicago where he again set up his medical practice and remained there until his death in 1904.

Clark, George A. - Second Lieutenant - Company E - Enlisted from Sheldon, Illinois, September 28, 1861. Veteran. Promoted to Corporal February 25, 1863; to Sergeant January 1, 1865, to Second Lieutenant October 6, 1865. Mustered out with the regiment, December 6, 1865.

Clark, Henry - Private - Company B - Enlisted from Bloomington, Illinois, August 27, 1861. Veteran. Taken prisoner May 1, 1862 at Strasburg, Virginia. Was paroled and exchanged September 14, 1862. Mustered out with the regiment, December 6, 1865.

Clark, James H. - Private - Company E - Enlisted from Channahon, Illinois, February 22, 1863. Killed August 16, 1864 at the battle of Deep Run, Virginia.

Clark, John W. A. - Private - Company B - Enlisted from Bloomington, Illinois, August 12, 1861. Discharged July 25, 1862 for disability. In 1889 he was living in Bloomington, Illinois.

Clark, Lake - Private - Company I - Enlisted from Santa Anna, Illinois, September 14, 1861. Discharged June 28, 1862 for disability.

Clark, Marion - Private - Company I - Enlisted from Champaign, Illinois, October 16, 1861. Discharged May 31, 1862 for disability.

Clayton, Francis M. - Private - Company H - Enlisted March 3, 1865. Mustered out with the regiment, December 6, 1865.

Clear, Peter - Private - Company K - Enlisted from Bloomington, Illinois, September 3, 1861. Died of disease July 11, 1862.

Clearwater, C. W. - Corporal - Company I - Enlisted from Santa Anna, Illinois, September 4, 1861. Discharged for disability November 20, 1863.

Clement, Frank - Private - Company K - Enlisted October 10, 1861. Discharged October 10, 1864 upon completion of military service.

Clifford, George A. - Private - Company H - Enlisted from Chicago, Illinois, February 4, 1864. Discharged by order of War Department July 7, 1864.

Clifford, James - Private - Company G - Enlisted October 15, 1864. Was a substitute. Discharged November 25, 1865.

Coate, A. D. - See Coats, A. D.

Coats, A. D. - Private - Company I - Enlisted from Franklin County, Illinois, April 11, 1865. Discharged August 18, 1865 by order of the War Department. [Coate, A. D.]

Cochlin, Davis - Private - Company H - Enlisted from Fairbury, Illinois, February 18, 1862. Wounded in the thigh August 16, 1864. Died of wounds in the hospital, August 20, 1864.

Cochran, David M. - Private - Company A - Enlisted August 8, 1861. Veteran. Promoted Corporal May 15, 1865. Mustered out with the regiment, December 6, 1865.

Colbert, William J. - Private - Company G - Enlisted from Chicago, Illinois, February 27, 1864. Promoted Corporal October 10, 1864. Died of disease at New Genesee, Illinois, April 15, 1865, while on furlough.

Cole, James - Private - Company K - Enlisted from Belleville, Illinois, October 11, 1862. Veteran. Died in Norfolk, Virginia, November 24, 1865, cause unknown.

Cole, Preston - Private - Company F - Enlisted August 15, 1861. Died of disease January 4, 1862.

Cole, William - Private - Company B - Enlisted March 1, 1865. Mustered out with the regiment, December 6, 1865. [Cowl, William]

Coleman, James - Private - Company K - Enlisted February 13, 1865. Mustered out with the regiment, December 6, 1865.

Collinge, Alexander J. - Private - Company A - Enlisted September 12, 1861. Veteran. Promoted Sergeant March 1, 1862. Injured in rail accident while on furlough. Transferred to Ambulance Corps. In 1889 he was living at Manchester, Iowa.

Collins, David - Private - Company D - Enlisted from Paine's Point, Illinois, August 29, 1861. Promoted Corporal December 7, 1861, to Sergeant July 1, 1862. Discharged September 10, 1864 upon completion of military service.

Collins, George - Private - Company K - Enlisted from Marseilles, Illinois, August 19, 1861. Died in the hospital at Hancock, Maryland, July 14, 1862. Cause unknown.

Collins, James - Private - Company I - Enlisted from New York City, New York, August 28, 1861. Mustered out with the regiment, December 6, 1865.

Collins, Lawrence - Private - Unassigned Substitute - Enlisted April 7, 1865. Nothing further is known.

Combelick, William - See Cambellick, William

Conklin, Lafayette - Private - Company B - Enlisted February 6, 1864. Died August 9, 1865 in City Point, Virginia, cause unknown.

Conley, Edward D. - Private - Company A - Enlisted January 5, 1864 from Wesley, Illinois. Brother to John Conley. Detailed to the regimental band. Musician in Band of 1864 & 1865. Mustered out with the regiment, December 6, 1865. In 1889 he was living in Wesley, Illinois.

Conley, James - Private - Company E - Enlisted October 18, 1861. Deserted May 1, 1862.

Conley, John - Second Lieutenant - Company E - Enlisted from Wilmington, Illinois, September 24, 1861 as First Sergeant. Promoted Second Lieutenant January 23, 1862. Resigned August 8, 1862 and died of disease shortly thereafter. Born in London, England March 19, 1838. His parents crossed the Atlantic in 1842 and settled for a time in Toronto, Canada, then moved to Buffalo, New York. In 1849, they moved to Wilmington, Illinois. Died of tuberculosis August 19, 1867 at the age of twenty-nine years and seven months. He is buried at Wilmington, Illinois, near the regimental monument in Oakwood Cemetery.

Conlin, Owen - Private - Company H - Enlisted from Chicago, Illinois, March 24, 1864. Mustered out with the regiment, December 6, 1865.

Connell, Charles C. - Private - Company A - Enlisted February 28, 1862. Discharged June 21, 1862 for disability.

Conner, Charles - Private - Company F - Enlisted August 3, 1861. Veteran. Wounded in the leg August 5, 1864. Taken prisoner August 16, 1864 at Deep Run, Virginia. Died at Camp Parole, Annapolis, Maryland in February 1865.

Connery, James - Private - Unassigned Recruit - Enlisted from Bremen, Illinois, December 28, 1864. Deserted January 8, 1865.

Conrad, Arthur - Private - Company C - Enlisted March 22, 1865. Mustered out with the regiment, December 6, 1865. [Coonrod, Arthur]

Conroy, Francis - Private - Company A - Enlisted October 1, 1861. Discharged May 25, 1862 for disability.

Converse, Charles - Private - Company C - Enlisted from Ocoya, Illinois, August 21, 1861. Wounded May 16, 1864 at the battle of Drewry's Bluff, Virginia. Discharged September 10, 1864 upon completion of military service.

Converse, Melvin - Private - Company C - Enlisted from Ocoya, Illinois, September 6, 1861. Discharged December 27, 1864 upon completion of military service.

Conway, Peter - Private - Unassigned Recruit - Enlisted from Chicago, Illinois, May 25, 1864. Discharged July 2, 1864.

Cook, Ezra A. - Private - Company G - Enlisted from Wheaton, Illinois, September 2, 1861. Wounded in the hand, May 16, 1864 at the battle of Drewry's Bluff, Virginia. Discharged September 10, 1864 upon completion of military service. Born in Windsor, Connecticut, November 5, 1841.

Cook, Levi - Private - Company B - Enlisted from Jacksonville, Illinois, August 28, 1861. Taken prisoner May 1, 1862 at Strasburg, Virginia. Paroled June 24, 1862. Died in Washington, D.C. October 17, 1862.

Cook, Methuselah - Private - Company B - Enlisted from Chicago, Illinois, October 19, 1861. Discharged December 20, 1862 for disability.

Coonrod, Arthur - See Conrad, Arthur

Coons, Montreville - Private - Company A - Enlisted February 20, 1864. Wounded and taken prisoner May 16, 1864 at the battle of Drewry's Bluff, Virginia. Paroled and mustered out July 12, 1864.

Cooper, William S. - Private - Company C - Enlisted from Fairbury, Illinois, August 28, 1861. Taken prisoner May 26, 1862 at Strasburg, Virginia; was paroled and discharged December 12, 1863. In 1889 he was living in Colorado.

Corbett, Frank M. - Private - Company E - Enlisted February 24, 1864. Wounded May 20, 1864 at Ware Bottom Church, Virginia. Mustered out with the regiment, December 6, 1865.

Corcoran, George - Private - Unassigned Recruit - Enlisted from Chicago, Illinois, March 9, 1864. Nothing further is known.

Cordell, Alex C. - Private - Company K - Enlisted from Bloomington, Illinois, October 10, 1861. Veteran. Promoted Corporal August 1, 1863. Wounded August 26, 1863 on Morris Island, South Carolina. Mustered out with the regiment, December 6, 1865.

Core, Robert - Private - Company D - Enlisted February 22, 1865. Wounded April 2, 1865 at Fort Gregg, Virginia. Mustered out with the regiment, December 6, 1865.

Corman, Archibald L. - See Carman, Archibald L.

Corrigan, Hugh - Private - Company A - Enlisted December 30, 1863. Wounded May 15, 1864 at Drewry's Bluff, Virginia. Died of wounds June 3, 1864. [Carrigan, Hugh]

Corrigan, William - Private - Company H - Enlisted from Mount Pleasant, Illinois, June 21, 1862. Deserted August 3, 1865 in Norfolk, Virginia.

Corsant, Henry - Private - Company D - Enlisted from Oregon, Illinois, September 5, 1861. Taken prisoner May 26, 1862 at Strasburg, Virginia. Discharged October 16, 1862 for disability.

Corwin, Horace T. - Sergeant - Company G - Enlisted from Homer, Illinois, August 16, 1861. Wounded in the leg May 20, 1864 at Ware Bottom Church, Virginia. Discharged September 20, 1864 upon completion of military service.

Coss, Alexander - Private - Company I - Enlisted from LeRoy, Illinois, September 23, 1861. Promoted Corporal May 1, 1864. Wounded in the leg May 16, 1864 at the battle of Drewry's Bluff, Virginia. Discharged August 5, 1865 for disability from wounds.

Cottle, Frederick - Private - Company E - Enlisted from Chicago, Illinois, April 16, 1865. Mustered out with the regiment, December 6, 1865.

Courson, Christopher E. - Regimental Quartermaster-Sergeant - Enlisted from Sandoval, Illinois, August 16, 1861, in Company F. Promoted Sergeant August 30, 1862 and to Quartermaster August 5, 1865 and transferred to non-commissioned staff. Mustered out with the regiment, December 6, 1865. Born September 4, 1837 in Tioga County, New York. He was brought up on his father's farm until the age of twenty-one when he moved to Illinois where he worked as a farm hand. In 1867 he married and settled on a small farm in Pennsylvania. In 1878 he moved to a homestead in Kansas. He was the Post master at Courson's Grove.

Covey, Albert - Private - Unassigned Recruit - Enlisted from Bloomington, Illinois, December 30, 1862. Nothing further is known.

Covey, Edmund - Private - Company B - Enlisted from LeRoy, Illinois, August 12, 1861. Veteran. Wounded in the arm June 16, 1864 at Chester Station, Virginia also October 13, 1864 at Darbytown Cross-Roads, Virginia. Mustered out with the regiment, December 6, 1865. In 1889 he was living in Welch, Missouri.

Covey, James R. - Sergeant - Company B - Enlisted from LeRoy, Illinois, September 19, 1861. Veteran. Promoted Corporal October 31, 1863. Wounded at Fort Wagner, South Carolina on September 14, 1863. Promoted to Sergeant August 27, 1864. Mustered out with the regiment, December 6, 1865. In 1889 he was living in LeRoy, Illinois.

Cowl, William - See Cole, William

Cox, Cornelius - Sergeant - Company G - Enlisted from Blue Island, Illinois, August 13, 1861. Promoted Corporal April 13, 1864; Sergeant July 5, 1864. Wounded in the arm October 27, 1864 in a skirmish near Darbytown Cross-Roads, Virginia. Suffered excision of some six inches of bone from the arm. Discharged June 8, 1865 due to disability from wounds.

Crabtree, George W. - Private - Company F - Enlisted April 4, 1865. Was a substitute. Died May 3, 1865 in Corps Hospital in Richmond, Virginia. Cause unknown.

Crabtree, John W. - Private - Company F - Enlisted April 4, 1864. Deserted August 2, 1865 at Norfolk, Virginia.

Craig, Henry - Private - Company K - Enlisted from Bloomington, Illinois, September 5, 1861. Veteran. Mustered out with the regiment, December 6, 1865 as a musician.

Craig, John - Private - Company I - Enlisted from LeRoy, Illinois, October 18, 1861. Died of disease on Folly Island, South Carolina, November 22, 1864.

Craig, L. E. W. - Private - Company I - Enlisted September 4, 1861. Taken prisoner May 20, 1862 at Strasburg, Virginia. Discharged for disability June 28, 1862.

Craig, William - Private - Company K - Enlisted from Bloomington, Illinois, August 14, 1861. Veteran. Promoted Corporal September 6, 1862. Discharged December 4, 1863 for disability.

Crandall, Christopher C. - Private - Company G - Enlisted from Joliet, Illinois, October 14, 1862. Wounded in the side, May 20, 1864 at Ware Bottom Church, Virginia, and in the head October 7, 1864. Discharged October 13, 1865 upon completion of military service.

Crandall, David G. - Private - Company F - Enlisted August 24, 1861. Veteran. Promoted Corporal November 1, 1862. Wounded May 16 and again August 16, 1864. Died of wounds August 16, 1864.

Crandall, James - Private - Company B - Enlisted from Bloomington, Illinois, November 20, 1862. Discharged November 20, 1865 upon completion of military service.

Cranston, Joseph H. - Private - Company B - Enlisted from Chicago, Illinois, October 19, 1861. Discharged December 30, 1862 for disability. In 1889 he was living at the National Soldiers' Home, Dayton, Ohio.

Crawford, John - Corporal - Company G - Enlisted from LaSalle, Illinois, August 14, 1861. Discharged September 23, 1862 for disability.

Creagar, James B. - Private - Company I - Enlisted from LeRoy, Illinois, October 6, 1861. Veteran. Promoted Sergeant June 27, 1862. Wounded in the chest October 13, 1864 at Darbytown Cross-Roads, Virginia. Discharged July 8, 1865 due to disability from wounds.

Creddigan, John - See Caddigan, John

Creswell, Samuel - Private - Company H - Enlisted April 8, 1865. Discharged August 18, 1865 for disability.

Crews, Harrison H. - Private - Company G - Enlisted from Joliet, Illinois, August 9, 1861. Discharged February 19, 1864 due to promotion to the Sixty-Fourth Illinois Volunteers.

Croop, George W. - Private - Company A - Enlisted September 16, 1861. Discharged July 21, 1862 for disability.

Croop, Jonas F. - Private - Company A - Enlisted August 5, 1861. Veteran. Wounded August 16, 1864. Discharged August 1, 1865 upon completion of military service.

Crossley, John - Private - Company B - Enlisted from Bloomington, Illinois, August 12, 1861. Discharged October 26, 1863 for disability.

Crotts, Silas - Private - Company B - Enlisted February 13, 1862. Killed September 23, 1863 at Fort Gregg, South Carolina.

Crozier, James - Regimental First Assistant Surgeon - Commissioned August 5, 1862. Mustered out with the regiment, December 6, 1865. Born in Davis, Edgar County, Illinois, April 8, 1834. His father was a soldier in the Indian war of 1832 and built the first house and the first mill in Davis Illinois. He attended Rush Medical College in 1858-1859. He was married in 1860. After the war he went to Clinton, Indiana, where he practiced medicine until 1883, when he went to Washington, DC, to serve in the office of the Medical Pension Examining Board.

Crum, Gabriel - Private - Company D - Enlisted from Oregon, Illinois, September 5, 1861. Discharged June 27, 1863 for disability.

Crum, William W. - Private - Company D - Enlisted from Oregon, Illinois, September 5, 1861. Taken prisoner January 3, 1862 at Bath, West Virginia. Discharged June 6, 1862 for disability.

Crummer, John - Private - Unassigned Substitute - Enlisted February 20, 1865. Nothing further is known.

Cubberly, Mills - Private - Company A - Enlisted April 6, 1865. Mustered out with the regiment, December 6, 1865.

Cubberly, William C. - Private - Company E - Enlisted April 4, 1865. Mustered out May 27, 1865.

Cullar, Benjamin - Private - Company B - Enlisted from Bloomington, Illinois, August 12, 1861. Taken prisoner May 1, 1862 at Strasburg, Virginia; paroled and exchanged. Discharged June 17, 1862.

Cummings, Timothy J. - Private - Unassigned Recruit - Enlisted from Chicago, Illinois, January 5, 1864. Deserted, date unknown.

Cummings, Williams S. - Private - Company D - Enlisted from Chicago, Illinois, September 4, 1861. Discharged June 1862 for disability.

Curry, James - Private - Company F - Enlisted from Bloomington, Illinois, October 9, 1861. Discharged for disability, date unknown.

Curtis, Cyrus - Private - Company A - Enlisted September 12, 1861. Veteran. Discharged September 2, 1865 under orders of the War Department. In 1889 he was living at Chanahon, Illinois.

Cutler, George O. - Private - Company D - Enlisted from Dwight, Illinois, August 28, 1861. Transferred to and discharged from the original band in 1862. Re-enlisted. Promoted Corporal December 15, 1862. Wounded in the head at Fort Wagner, South Carolina. Died September 11, 1863 from disease.

Cutler, Joseph A. - Regimental Quartermaster - Commissioned July 22, 1861. Discharged July 15, 1862.

— D—

Dabner, Leonard - Private - Company F - Enlisted January 28, 1864. Taken prisoner May 16, 1864 at Drewry's Bluff. Paroled, and died of disease December 12, 1864. [Dobner, Leonard]

Dagan, Patrick - Private - Company E - Enlisted from Wilmington, Illinois, September 25, 1861. Veteran. Wounded and presumed killed October 13, 1864 at the battle of Darbytown Cross-Roads, Virginia. Listed as missing on Company Rolls.

Dagnan, John - Private - Company D - Enlisted from Schaumbert, Illinois, September 26, 1864. Discharged June 10, 1865 for disability.

Dailey, Daniel - Private - Company A - Enlisted December 28, 1863. Wounded May 10, 1864 near Bermuda Hundred, Virginia. Died at New Bern, North Carolina, March 26, 1865 from wounds.

Dailey, John - Private - Company B - Enlisted from Bloomington, Illinois, August 23, 1861. Discharged December 1, 1862 for disability.

Dailey, John - Private - Company E - Enlisted October 2, 1861. Deserted October 1861.

Dake, John W. - Private - Company B - Enlisted from Bloomington, Illinois, August 12, 1861. Veteran. Killed August 16, 1864 during the battle of Deep Run, Virginia. [Doke, John W.]

Danely, Henry - Private - Company F - Enlisted February 23, 1864. Wounded October 13, 1864 at Darbytown Cross-Roads, Virginia. Discharged May 27, 1865 for disability from wounds. [Donnelly, Henry]

Dannable, William J. - Private - Company E - Enlisted from Wesley, Illinois, March 2, 1864. Wounded in the neck August 16, 1864 at Deep Run, Virginia. Discharged by order of the War Department for disability.

Darragh, George - Private - Unassigned Substitute - Enlisted February 1, 1865. Nothing further is known.

Davidson, James - Private - Company C - Enlisted from Chicago, Illinois, August 20, 1861. Discharged September 27, 1862 for disability.

Davis, Barnet H. - Private - Company B - Enlisted from LeRoy, Illinois, August 17, 1861. Taken prisoner May 1, 1862 at Strasburg, Virginia; was paroled and exchanged. Discharged April 11, 1863 for disability.

Davis, Charles O. - Private - Company F - Enlisted from Joliet, Illinois, December 17, 1863. Veteran recruit. Mustered out with the regiment, December 6, 1865.

Davis, Freeman - Private - Unassigned Substitute - Enlisted October 21, 1864. Nothing further is known.

Davis, George - Private - Unassigned Recruit - Enlisted from Wheeling, Illinois, January 6, 1865. Deserted January 15, 1865.

Davis, Isaac T. - Private - Company H - Enlisted from Monticello, Illinois, June 28, 1862. Deserted October 13, 1863.

Davis, James M. - Private - Company I - Enlisted from LeRoy, Illinois, February 22, 1864. Wounded in the head October 13, 1864. Promoted Corporal April 4, 1865. Mustered out with the regiment, December 6, 1865.

Davis, John - Private - Company K - Enlisted from Bloomington, Illinois, September 1, 1862. Discharged April 26, 1863.

Davis, John W. - Private - Company C - Enlisted April 7, 1865. Mustered out with the regiment, December 6, 1865.

Davis, Nathan E. - Second Lieutenant - Company F - Enlisted from Chicago, Illinois, August 22, 1861. Veteran. Promoted Sergeant November 1, 1862, promoted Second Lieutenant August 5, 1864. Wounded in the side and arm, October 13, 1864 at the battle of Darbytown Cross-Roads. Suffered removal of four inches of bone in arm. Died of his wounds November 16, 1864 in general hospital.

Day, Henry M. - Sergeant - Company A - Enlisted as Private August 5, 1861. Veteran. Promoted to Corporal March 1, 1862. Wounded April 2, 1865 during assault on Fort Gregg, Virginia. Promoted to Sergeant June 1, 1865. Awarded **Medal of Honor** for bravery at Fort Gregg, Virginia. Discharged for disability July 3, 1865.

Day, James O. - Private - Company D - Enlisted from Palatine, Illinois, December 28, 1864. Mustered out with the regiment, December 6, 1865.

Dean, Joseph - Private - Company C - Enlisted March 1, 1865. Discharged August 9, 1865 for disability.

Decker, Lester B. - Private - Company G - Enlisted from Orland, Illinois, February 23, 1864. Wounded in the thigh May 16, 1864 at battle of Drewry's Bluff, Virginia, and in the leg October 7, 1864. Mustered out with the regiment, December 6, 1865.

Decker, Lewis - Private - Company G - Enlisted August 9, 1861. Discharged August 30, 1861. Reason unknown.

Deeming, Thomas - Private - Company G - Enlisted from Homer, Illinois, August 15, 1861. Wounded in the head, March 23, 1862 at Winchester, Virginia. Veteran. Promoted Corporal November 1, 1864. Mustered out with the regiment, December 6, 1865. [Derming, Thomas]

DeLine, Thomas - Corporal - Company A - Enlisted August 5, 1861. Veteran. Taken prisoner near Drewry's Bluff, June 2, 1864. Mustered out under order of the War Department, August 16, 1864.

DeLong, Henry H. - First Lieutenant - Company C - Enlisted from Esmond, Illinois, August 28, 1861. Promoted Corporal May 29, 1863. Veteran. Wounded June 17, 1864 near Ware Bottom Church, Virginia. Promoted Sergeant October 1, 1864; promoted to First Sergeant March 31, 1865; promoted to First Lieutenant October, 1865. Mustered out with the regiment, December 6, 1865. In 1889 he was living at Canton, Dakota Territory.

Denline, John - Private - Company F - Enlisted February 28, 1864. Mustered out with the regiment, December 6, 1865.

Denline, John Jr. - Private - Company F - Enlisted February 12, 1864. Mustered out with the regiment, December 6, 1865.

DeNormandie, Anthony - Regimental Second Assistant Surgeon Enlisted August 5, 1861 from Gardner, Illinois in Company A and appointed Hospital Steward. Promoted Second Assistant Surgeon July 13, 1865. Mustered out with the regiment, December 6, 1865. After the war he moved to Braceville, Illinois.

DePuy, Hurlburt - Private - Company C - Enlisted from Chicago, Illinois, February 17, 1864. Mustered out with the regiment, December 6, 1865.

Derming, Thomas - See Deeming, Thomas

Derrick, Albert - Private - Company H - Enlisted from Padua, Illinois, February 12, 1864. Wounded in the leg October 13, 1864 at Darbytown Cross-Roads, Virginia. Mustered out July 25, 1865 for disability.

Deviney, Philip S. - Private - Company F - Enlisted October 28, 1861. Veteran. Killed April 2, 1865 at the assault on Fort Gregg, Virginia. [Devinney, Philip S.]

Devinney, Philip S. - See Deviney, Philip S.

Dewey, Thomas - Private - Company F - Enlisted from Northfield, Illinois, August 15, 1861. Veteran. Killed April 2, 1865 at the assault on Fort Gregg, Virginia.

Dickinson, James - Private - Company H - Enlisted from Pittsfield, Illinois, April 5, 1862. Discharged May 9, 1865 at completion of military service.

Dickinson, Joseph W. - Private - Company F - Enlisted from Chicago, Illinois, August 5, 1861. Veteran. Promoted Sergeant August 15, 1864. Discharged from regiment for commission as Captain in Twenty-First Regiment, U. S. Colored Troops on April 23, 1864.

Dickson, John - Private - Company H - Enlisted April 8, 1865. Mustered out with the regiment, December 6, 1865. [Dixon, John]

Dietz, Augustus - Private - Company D - Enlisted February 23, 1865. Mustered out with the regiment, December 6, 1865.

Dill, Willis A. - Private - Company I - Enlisted April 4, 1865. Mustered out with the regiment, December 6, 1865.

Dillon, Asbury P. - Private - Company B - Enlisted from Bloomington, Illinois, October 18, 1861. Veteran. Wounded May 20, 1864 at Ware Bottom Church, Virginia. Mustered out with the regiment, December 6, 1865.

Dillon, Orange W. - Private - Company B - Enlisted from Bloomington, Illinois, October 28, 1861. Discharged December 1, 1862 for disability.

Dilno, Aaron - Private - Company G - Enlisted from Bellevue, Michigan, September 5, 1861. Died of disease at Cumberland, Maryland, February 12, 1862.

Dilno, Henry - Private - Company G - Enlisted from Bellevue, Michigan, September 5, 1861. Discharged September 28, 1862 for disability.

Dircks, Casper S. F. - Captain - Company H - Enlisted August 5, 1861. Resigned, date unknown.

Dixon, John - See Dickson, John

Dobner, Henry - Private - Company F - Enlisted February 29, 1864. Mustered out June 16, 1865.

Dobner, Leonard - Private - Company F - Enlisted from Fremont, Illinois, January 28, 1864. Died December 12, 1864. Cause unknown.

Dobson, James - Private - Company A - Enlisted December 23, 1863. Wounded May 20, 1864, suffering the loss of an arm. Discharged November 3, 1865 for disability.

Dodge, James - Private - Unassigned Recruit - Enlisted from LeRoy, Illinois, January 5, 1864. Nothing further is known.

Doke, John W. - See Dake, John W.

Dolan, Timothy - Private - Company A - Enlisted December 26, 1863. Wounded May 16, 1864 at Drewry's Bluff. Transferred to Veteran Reserve Corps. Absent, due to wound, at muster out of regiment. In 1889 he was living in Joliet, Illinois.

Donahue, Patrick - Private - Company H - Enlisted April 8, 1864. Mustered out with the regiment, December 6, 1865.

Donald, George - Private - Company H - Enlisted February 24, 1865 under name of John O'Brien, in order to elude his guardians and get in the service. Mustered out with the regiment, December 6, 1865.

DonCarlos, Thomas - Private - Company I - Enlisted December 18, 1863. Discharged September 1, 1864 for disability. [Thomas, Don Carlos]

Donnelly, Henry - Private - Company F - Enlisted from Waukegan, Illinois, February 12, 1864. Discharged for disability June 22, 1865.

Doose, Casper - See Douse, Casper

Doran, James - Private - Company D - Enlisted from Pontiac, Illinois, November 22, 1863. Discharged June 23, 1865 for disability.

Dorr, Michael - Corporal - Company A - Enlisted August 5, 1861. Discharged September 10, 1864 upon completion of military service.

Dorsey, Peter - Private - Unassigned Recruit - Enlisted from Wheeling, Illinois, January 6, 1865. Nothing further is known.

Doud, Leroy - Regimental Adjutant - Enlisted from Bloomington, Illinois, September 12, 1861, as a private in Company B. Promoted to Sergeant, promoted First Lieutenant May 16, 1864 upon the death of Adjutant Walker. Veteran. Promoted Assistant-Adjutant-General of the First Brigade, First Division, Twenty-Fourth Corps. Mustered out January 1866.

Dougherty, William - Private - Unassigned Recruit - Enlisted from Cairo, Illinois, January 4, 1864. Veteran recruit. Nothing further is known.

Douglas, Aaron C. - Private - Company F - Enlisted February 23, 1864. Wounded September 16, 1864 in the chest and again wounded October 7 in the arm. Died May 11, 1865 from wounds.

Douglas, Edward - Private - Company C - Enlisted February 16, 1865. Mustered out with the regiment, December 6, 1865.

Douse, Casper - Private - Company A - Enlisted February 23, 1864. Mustered out May 22, 1865 under order of the War Department. [Doose, Casper]

Downey, John - Private - Company B - Enlisted from Bloomington, Illinois, August 12, 1861. Veteran. Mustered out with the regiment, December 6, 1865. In 1889 he was living in Lockport, Illinois.

Downs, William - Captain - Company H - Enlisted from Downs, Illinois, April 1, 1862 as Sergeant. Commissioned First Lieutenant October 13, 1864. Wounded in the side August 16, 1864 at the battle of Deep Run, Virginia. Commissioned Captain March 31, 1865. Mustered out with the regiment, December 6, 1865.

Doyle, John - Private - Company D - Enlisted from Chicago, Illinois, February 9, 1864. Wounded May 16, 1864 at Drewry's Bluff, Virginia and taken prisoner. Mustered out with the regiment, December 6, 1865.

Drake, George - Private - Company K - Enlisted from Marseilles, Illinois, August 11, 1861. Died at Cumberland, Maryland, from disease, July 20, 1862.

Drake, Jasper N. - Private - Company C - Enlisted from Fairbury, Illinois, August 20, 1861. Discharged June 18, 1862 for disability. In 1889 he was living at Wood River, Nebraska.

Drake, John C. - Private - Company F - Enlisted February 23, 1864. Promoted Corporal March 1, 1865. Mustered out with the regiment, December 6, 1865.

Draper, Abraham - Private - Company I - Enlisted from Mahomet, Illinois, September 14, 1861. Veteran. Wounded in arm and side October 13, 1864 at battle of Darbytown Cross-Roads, Virginia. Died in the hospital from wounds October 15, 1864.

Dresser, Lewis - Private - Company D - Enlisted from Lane, Illinois, August 29, 1861. Veteran. Killed October 16, 1864 at Darbytown Cross-Roads, Virginia.

Duff, Robert - Private - Company B - Enlisted March 2, 1864. Wounded June 16, 1864, and died of wounds shortly thereafter.

Dugan, Michael - Private - Company E - Enlisted from Wilmington, Illinois, October 2, 1861. Deserted October 1861. [Dagnan, Michael]

Dunham, Gideon - Private - Company E - Enlisted April 12, 1865. Mustered out with the regiment December 6, 1865. [Durham, Gideon]

Dunham, Hiram G. - Private - Company G - Enlisted from Hartford, Michigan, August 19, 1861. Died of typhoid fever at Cumberland, Maryland, February 23, 1865.

Dunlap, Lewis - Private - Company I - Enlisted from Cheny's Grove, Illinois, September 4, 1861. Veteran. Promoted Corporal October 27, 1865. Mustered out with the regiment December 6, 1865.

Dunn, Adam - Private - Company C - Enlisted February 1, 1865. Wounded in the leg April 2, 1865 at the assault on Fort Gregg, Virginia. Mustered out with the regiment, December 6, 1865.

Dunn, George H. - Private - Company E - Enlisted from Rockville, Illinois, October 6, 1861. Wounded May 20, 1864 at battle of Ware Bottom Church, Virginia. Reported missing. Supposed to have deserted. [Adjutant General's report shows him as mustered out June 3, 1865]

Durham, Gideon - See Dunham, Gideon

Dyer, Henry E. - Private - Company B - Enlisted March 1, 1865. Mustered out with the regiment, December 6, 1865.

— E —

Eastman, James P. - Private - Company H - Enlisted from Pecatonica, Illinois, May 1, 1862. Wounded in the foot June 7, 1864. Discharged May 9, 1865 upon completion of military service.

Easton, Lansom W. - Private - Company C - Enlisted from Long Point, Illinois, February 14, 1865. Mustered out with the regiment, December 6, 1865.

Edminston, Miles B. - Private - Company H - Enlisted February 13, 1862. Promoted Corporal and discharged October 9, 1862 for disability.

Edmonds, D. W. - Private - Company D - Enlisted from Lane, Illinois, August 18, 1861. Deserted August 20, 1861.

Eggenberger, Gallus - Private - Company C - Enlisted from Odell, Illinois, August 12, 1861. Transferred to Veteran Reserve Corps, September 20, 1863.

Egidy, Frederick - Private - Company B - Enlisted from Bloomington, Illinois, October 23, 1861. Discharged July 22, 1862 for disability.

Eigner, Louis - Private - Company F - Enlisted August 28, 1861. Discharged September 10, 1864 upon completion of military service.

Elick, Joseph - Private - Company E - Enlisted February 25, 1865. Mustered out with the regiment, December 6, 1865.

Ellinwood, Charles - Sergeant - Company C - Enlisted from Esmond, Illinois, August 12, 1861. Discharged July 4, 1863 for disability.

Elliott, John - Private - Company B - Enlisted March 1, 1865. Mustered out with the regiment, December 6, 1865.

Ellis, Dwight D. - Private - Company D - Enlisted from Dwight, Illinois, December 17, 1862. Killed August 16, 1864 at Deep Run, Virginia.

Ellis, William - Private - Company F - Enlisted September 10, 1861. Discharged September 10, 1864 upon completion of military service.

Ely, William W. - Private - Company F - Enlisted from Concord, Illinois, September 28, 1861. Originally enlisted in Tenth Indiana Volunteers for the three month's service; served in West Virginia, under McClellan and Rosecrans. Was wounded at the battle of Rich Mountain July 11, 1862. Was also wounded on Morris Island, South Carolina by a shell fragment while on duty with the Requa Battery. Re-enlisted as a veteran in Company E, and was again wounded at Bermuda Hundred, Virginia while helping to carry wounded men off the field. He served four years and seven months and was just 19 years of age at the muster out of the regiment, December 6, 1865.

Eteherson, William H. - Private - Company K - Enlisted April 12, 1865. Mustered out with the regiment, December 6, 1865.

Evans, Joseph S. - Private - Company E - Enlisted from Wesley, Illinois, December 21, 1863. Wounded in the neck August 16, 1864 at the battle of Deep Run, Virginia. Promoted to Corporal January 1, 1865, and to Sergeant May 31, 1865. Detailed as acting Commissary Sergeant; subsequently was detailed acting Sergeant-Major; was finally promoted to Commissary Sergeant. Mustered out with the regiment, December 6, 1865.

Everett, Eli J. - Private - Enlisted from LeRoy, Illinois, February 6, 1862. Transferred to Company I, August 1, 1862. Wounded in the shoulder at the battle of Drewry's Bluff, Virginia. Mustered out with the regiment, December 6, 1865.

Everett, Thomas J. - Private - Company I - Enlisted from LeRoy, Illinois, October 1, 1861. Discharged October 8, 1864 upon completion of military service.

— F —

Fagot, Jacob - Private - Company B - Enlisted from Peoria, Illinois, September 21, 1861. Transferred to the regular service November 28, 1862. Discharge information unknown.

Fagot, Matthias - Private - Company B - Enlisted from Peoria, Illinois, September 21, 1861. Taken prisoner May 1, 1862 at Strasburg, Virginia; paroled and exchanged. Discharged June 1862 for disability.

Fallon, Michael - Private - Company B - Enlisted from Chicago, Illinois, October 3, 1864. Mustered out October 9, 1865.

Farable, David E. - Private - Company A - Enlisted August 5, 1861. Died at New Bern, NC, April 22, 1862. [Farrabee, David E.]

Farbel, Joseph D. - Private - Company D - Enlisted from Oregon, Illinois, August 21, 1861. Was musician. Discharged August 18, 1862 for disability. [Frauble, Joseph D.]

Farley, Patrick - Private - Company D - Enlisted from Oregon, Illinois, August 12, 1861. Veteran. Wounded in the head May 16, 1864 at Drewry's Bluff, Virginia. Transferred to Veteran Reserve Corps May 15, 1865. In 1889 he was living at Oregon, Ogle County, Illinois.

Farrabee, David E. - See Farable, David E.

Farrance, Anthony - Private - Company K - Enlisted August 21, 1862. Wounded October 6, 1863 at Fort Wagner, South Carolina. Discharged June 20, 1863 upon completion of military service.

Fellows, Albert A. - Corporal - Company C - Enlisted from Pontiac, Illinois, August 1, 1861. Taken prisoner March 22, 1862 near Winchester, Virginia. Paroled February 1, 1863. Taken prisoner May 16, 1864 at Drewry's Bluff, Virginia. Discharged February 19, 1865 upon completion of military service.

Fellows, Albert W. - Second Lieutenant - Company I - Enlisted from Santa Anna, Illinois, September 6, 1861. Killed in battle near Ware Bottom Church, Virginia on June 2, 1864.

Fenlison, William H. - Private - Company C - Enlisted from St. Louis, Missouri September 19, 1861. Promoted to Corporal. Reduced to ranks June 7, 1863. Veteran. Wounded October 13, 1864. Mustered out with the regiment, December 6, 1865. [Fennelson, William M.]

Fennelson, William H. - See Fenlison, William H.

Ferrell, Jesse A. - Private - Company D - Enlisted from Oregon, Illinois, August 9, 1861. Veteran. Wounded and taken prisoner October 27, 1864. Died in prison at Florence, South Carolina, from wounds in November 1864.

Ferren, William H. - First Lieutenant - Company D - Enlisted from Paine's Point, Illinois, August 9, 1861. Promoted Sergeant March 1, 1863. Veteran. Promoted First Lieutenant March 31, 1865. Resigned August 16, 1865. [Ferrin, William H.]

Ferrin, William H. - Ferren, William H.

Fiddler, Henry - Private - Company F - Enlisted January 24, 1864. Killed August 16, 1864 at Deep Run, Virginia.

Finley, William J. - Private - Company E - Enlisted from Jefferson County, Illinois, April 4, 1865. Discharged May 27, 1865.

Finn, James B. - Private - Unassigned Recruit - Enlisted from Chicago, Illinois, December 28, 1863. Died at Camp Butler, Illinois, April 10, 1864. Cause unknown.

Fisch, James - Private - Company F - Enlisted February 27, 1864. Mustered out with the regiment, December 6, 1865.

Fisher, Burton W. - Musician, 3rd Class - Enlisted October 8, 1861. Discharged June 4, 1862 by order of the War Department.

Fisher, Lewis - Private - Company B - Enlisted from Enfield, Illinois, February 11, 1864. Wounded in the face August 16, 1864 at Deep Run, Virginia. Discharged February 28, 1865 for disability.

Fitts, William - Private - Company G - Enlisted February 29, 1864. Wounded in the hand June 2, 1864 in a skirmish near Ware Bottom Church, Virginia. Wounded again in the left arm, April 9, 1865 at Appomattox Court-House, Virginia. Mustered out with the regiment, December 6, 1865.

Fitzpatrick, Michael - Private - Company A - Enlisted August 14, 1861. Transferred to the regular army November 26, 1862. Discharge information unknown.

Flaherty, Michael - Private - Unassigned Substitute - Enlisted from Chicago, Illinois, August 17, 1864. Nothing further is known.

Flannigan, Rollin O. - Private - Company G - Enlisted from Thornton, Illinois, March 14, 1864. Discharged June 3, 1865 for disability.

Flickinger, Charles - Second Lieutenant - Company H - Enlisted August 3, 1861. Resigned March 11, 1862.

Flory, Thomas W. - Private - Company K - Enlisted from Bloomington, Illinois, September 19, 1861. Taken prisoner at Deep Run, August 16, 1864. Discharged June 2, 1865 upon completion of military service.

Flowers, Andrew J. - Private - Company E - Enlisted from Sheldon, Illinois, September 28, 1861. Deserted in October 1861.

Flowers, Lewis - Private - Company E - Enlisted October 17, 1864. Discharged October 18, 1865 for disability.

Flynn, William - Private - Company E - Enlisted from Chicago, Illinois, September 28, 1861. Died January 10, 1864 at Beaufort, South Carolina. Cause unknown.

Folsom, William F. - Private - Company D - Enlisted from Hennepinn, Illinois, August 21, 1861. Discharged May 31, 1862 for disability.

Foot, Jerome - Private - Company B - Enlisted from Concord, Illinois, February 24, 1864. Promoted Corporal September 14, 1865. Mustered out with the regiment, December 6, 1865.

Ford, Newton J. - Private - Company I - Enlisted from Santa Anna, Illinois, September 9, 1861. Wounded in the hand and neck May 16, 1864 at Drewry's Bluff, Virginia. Was taken prisoner and died of wounds in Andersonville Prison, October 15, 1864. Grave Number 10,881.

Fordyce, John K. - Private - Company B - Enlisted from Bloomington, Illinois, August 27, 1861. Wounded September 12, 1863 at Fort Wagner, South Carolina. Leg amputated. Discharged June 20, 1864 for disability from wounds.

Foster, Peter - Private - Company D - Enlisted from Chicago, Illinois, August 12, 1861. Deserted August 16, 1862.

Foster, Thomas - Private - Unassigned Substitute - Enlisted April 12, 1865. Nothing further is known.

Fowler, Jesse W. - Private - Company K - Enlisted from Bloomington, Illinois, October 10, 1861. Discharged in June 1862 for disability. Re-enlisted from Chicago March 29, 1864. Mustered out with the regiment, December 6, 1865.

Fowler, Josiah - Private - Company K - Enlisted from Bloomington, Illinois, October 10, 1861. Wounded in the head, June 11, 1863 at Folly Island, South Carolina by falling limb from a tree severed by rebel shell fired into camp. Discharged October 8, 1864 upon completion of military service.

Fowler, Lyford J. - Private - Company K - Enlisted April 11, 1865 as a substitute. Mustered out with the regiment, December 6, 1865.

Fox, Franklin L. - Chief Musician - Regimental Band - Enlisted from Chicago, Illinois, August 19, 1861 in Company G. Promoted Principal Musician July 11, 1865 and transferred to non-commissioned staff. Mustered out with the regiment, December 6, 1865. In 1889 he was living at 203 Thirty-Seventh Street, Chicago, Illinois.

Fox, Newton - Private - Unassigned Recruit - Enlisted from Chicago, Illinois, March 31, 1864. Deserted, date unknown.

Frane, John - Second Lieutenant - Company D - Enlisted as a sergeant from Paine's Point, Illinois, August 9, 1861. Promoted Second Lieutenant January 13, 1863. Killed in battle August 16, 1863 at Deep Run, Virginia.

Frank, Henry J. - Private - Company G - Enlisted from New Lenox, Illinois, September 22, 1861. Wounded in the side May 16, 1864 at the battle of Drewry's Bluff, Virginia. Discharged September 22, 1864 upon completion of military service.

Frankberger, Lee J. - Private - Company B - Enlisted from Bloomington, Illinois, February 20, 1864. Promoted Corporal. Mustered out with the regiment, December 6, 1865.

Franks, E. S. - Private - Company K - Enlisted from Seneca, Illinois, August 14, 1862. Discharged November 10, 1862 for disability.

Franks, Jacob C. - Private - Company B - Enlisted from Bloomington, Illinois, February 23, 1864. Drowned May 20, 1864 while swimming in the James River.

Frauble, Joseph D. - See Farbel, Joseph D.

Freeman, Edmund O. - Captain - Company H - Enlisted August 3, 1861. Resigned, date unknown.

Frink, Marcellus - Private - Company K - Enlisted from Marseilles, Illinois, August 19, 1861. Taken prisoner January 4, 1862 at Sir John's Run, Virginia. Paroled and discharged June 23, 1862. Returned to Marseilles, where he died before the end of the war.

Frisbie, Charles F. - Regimental Commissary Sergeant - Enlisted from Worth, Illinois, August 13, 1861. Veteran. Promoted Commissary-Sergeant and transferred to non-commissioned staff January 1, 1864. Mustered out with the regiment, December 6, 1865. In 1889 he was living in Chicago at 1335 West Fulton Street.

Frisbie, John - Private - Unassigned Recruit - Enlisted from Chicago, Illinois, January 18, 1864. Deserted, date unknown.

Fudor, Lewis - Private - Company G - Enlisted from Palos, Illinois, May 7, 1864. Mustered out with the regiment, December 6, 1865.

Fuller, George L. - Private - Company D - Enlisted from Oregon, Illinois, August 22, 1861. Promoted Corporal November 1, 1862. Reduced July 15, 1864. Discharged September 10, 1864 upon completion of military service. In 1889 he was living at Athens, Pennsylvania engaged in the confectionary business.

Fuller, Henry - Sergeant - Company K - Enlisted August 19, 1861. Taken prisoner at Bath, West Virginia. Paroled and discharged January 23, 1862. Re-enlisted in Company D, Eighty-Eighth Illinois Infantry, promoted to Sergeant and mustered out with that regiment June 9, 1865.

Fuller, Leander C. - Private - Company D - Enlisted from Oregon, Illinois, August 29, 1861. Discharged June 14, 1863 for disability. In 1889 he was living in Allerton, Iowa.

Fuller, Mahlon T. - Private - Company D - Enlisted August 21, 1861. Veteran. Wounded in the leg May 20, 1864. Promoted Corporal April 1, 1865. Mustered out with the regiment, December 6, 1865. In 1889 he was living at Lyons, Clinton County, Iowa.

Fuller, Myrex H. - Musician - Played in Band of 1864 & 1865. Mustered out with the regiment, December 6, 1865.

Fuller, Myron C. - Private - Company A - Enlisted June 5, 1864. Detailed to Regimental Band. Mustered out with the regiment, December 6, 1865. In 1889 he was living in Wilmington, Illinois.

Fuller, Thomas A. - Private - Company D - Enlisted from Rockvale, Illinois, March 1, 1865. Mustered out with the regiment, December 6, 1865. In 1889 he was living in Oregon, Illinois.

— G —

Gaddis, James I. - Private - Company K - Enlisted from White Oak, Illinois, February 22, 1864. Wounded in the arm August 16, 1864 at Deep Run, Virginia. Discharged August 7, 1865 for disability from wounds.

Gairon, Ulmer - Private - Company H - Enlisted from Kingston Miles, Illinois, February 27, 1862. Veteran. Promoted Corporal November 4, 1864; Sergeant April 2, 1865. Mustered out with the regiment, December 6, 1865. [Garren, Ulmer]

Galherer, John - Private - Company A - Enlisted December 28, 1863. Wounded in hand October 13, 1864. Discharged under orders of the War Department. [Gallaher, John]

Gallaher, John - See Galherer, John

Gallop, George - See Gallup, George

Gallup, George - Private - Company G - Enlisted from Worth, Illinois, February 23, 1864. Mustered out with the regiment, December 6, 1865. [Gallop, George]

Gambel, Harvey - Private - Company C - Enlisted from Rook's Creek, Illinois, August 12, 1861. Veteran. Mustered out with the regiment, December 6, 1865.

Gardner, Charles H. - Private - Company C - Enlisted from Thornton, Illinois, February 28, 1864. Mustered out with the regiment, December 6, 1865.

Gardner, John W. - Private - Company I - Enlisted from Delta, Illinois, September 17, 1861. Transferred to Company H, August 1, 1862. Discharged September 10, 1864 upon completion of military service.

Gardner, Mahlon - Private - Company I - Enlisted from LeRoy, Illinois, September 17, 1861. Veteran. Transferred to Company H, August 1, 1862. Promoted Corporal September 1, 1865. Mustered out with the regiment, December 6, 1865.

Gardner, Oscar - Private - Company C - Enlisted from Efford's Point, Illinois, October 24, 1861. Wounded in the arm May 20, 1864 at Ware Bottom Church, Virginia. Discharged October 14, 1864 upon completion of military service.

Garman, Lawrence - Private - Unassigned Substitute - Enlisted April 12, 1865. Nothing further is known.

Garren, Ulmer - See Gairon, Ulmer

Garrett, James - Private - Company D - Enlisted from Chicago, Illinois, October 9, 1861. Veteran. Wounded in right arm April 2, 1865 at the assault on Fort Gregg, Virginia. Deserted August 3, 1865. In 1889 he was living at Berlin, Wisconsin.

Garrett, Willis - Private - Company K - Enlisted December 23, 1862. Wounded in the thigh, August 16, 1864 at the battle of Deep Run, Virginia. Promoted Corporal in 1865. Mustered out with the regiment, December 6, 1865.

Garrison, John R. - Private - Company K - Enlisted from Manlius, Illinois, February 20, 1864. Discharged June 8, 1865 by order of the War Department.

Gaul, Cornelius D. - Corporal - Company D - Enlisted from Dwight, Illinois, September 21, 1861. Veteran. Received two accidental wounds, one in the thigh from a bayonet in July 1863, and one while cutting timber at Bermuda Hundred, Virginia in May 1864. Wounded in the head August 16,

1864 at Deep Run, Virginia. Promoted Sergeant on December 5, 1864. Mustered out with the regiment, December 6, 1865. In 1889 he was living near Cleveland, Ohio.

Gaurley, Alexander - Private - Company D - Enlisted from Dwight, Illinois, September 21, 1861, at the age of 67 years. Veteran. Detailed as company cook. Mustered out on May 6, 1865. In 1889 he was living at the Soldier's Home at Leavenworth, Kansas, and at the age of ninety-five years was the oldest living survivor of the Thirty-Ninth Illinois.

German, Allen - Private - Company D - Enlisted from Lane, Illinois, August 29, 1861. Deserted on December 18, 1861.

Gesford, William - Private - Company I - Enlisted from Santa Anna, Illinois, September 19, 1861. Discharged July 18, 1862 for disability.

Gibbs, Elias - Private - Company B - Enlisted from Bloomington, Illinois, August 12, 1861. Veteran. Promoted Corporal August 28, 1864. Wounded August 16, 1864 and October 7, 1864. Promoted Sergeant September 24, 1865. Mustered out with the regiment, December 6, 1865. In 1889 he was living in Climax, Missouri.

Gibbs, Jeremiah - Private - Company B - Enlisted from Bloomington, Illinois, August 12, 1861. Killed August 16, 1864 at the battle of Deep Run, Virginia.

Gibbs, Simeon - Private - Company I - Enlisted from LeRoy, Illinois, October 4, 1861. Discharged October 14, 1862 for disability.

Gibson, Hiram - Private - Company G - Enlisted from Bremen, Illinois, February 23, 1864. Wounded in the head October 13, 1864 at Darbytown Cross-Roads, Virginia and died of wounds October 27, 1864.

Gibson, James - Sergeant - Company B - Enlisted August 12, 1861. Promoted Second Lieutenant May 26, 1862. Resigned September 22, 1862. In 1889 he was living in Bloomington, Illinois.

Gillen, James R. - Private - Company B - Enlisted from Bloomington, Illinois, August 12, 1861. Promoted Corporal October 19, 1861. Dropped from the roll at expiration of service.

Gillett, Abner - Corporal - Company G - Enlisted from Homer, Illinois, August 29, 1861. Became ill in May 1864 and sent to general hospital at Fort Monroe, Virginia. Discharged for disability.

Gillett, Henry - Private - Company E - Enlisted from Wesley, Illinois, November 13, 1861. Died February 1862 in the hospital. Cause unknown.

Gillett, James - Private - Company E - Enlisted from Wesley, Illinois, November 13, 1861. Wounded May 16, 1864 at battle of Drewry's Bluff, Virginia. Died of wounds August 17, 1864.

Gillmore, Samuel - Captain - Company I - Enlisted October 16, 1861. Hospitalized at Bedloe's Island, New York with typhoid. Promoted Corporal, then Sergeant on June 27, 1862. Veteran. Promoted Second Lieutenant. Wounded through both hips by a musket ball during the battle of Drewry's Bluff, Virginia. Promoted First Lieutenant August 20, 1864. Promoted Captain September 5, 1864. First on the parapet at Fort Gregg, Virginia April 2, 1865. Commanded the first infantry troops that opened fire on the rebels between Appomattox Station and Appomattox Court-House on the morning of April 9, 1865. He was Provost Marshal at City Point, Virginia in July 1865 and later on the staff of Major-General A. T. A. Torbert at Norfolk, Virginia. Mustered out March 20, 1866. Born in Harrison County, Ohio, July 25, 1838. Moved to McLean County, Illinois in 1852. After the war he relocated to Chase, Kansas.

Girard, Hermann - Sergeant - Company C - Enlisted from Long Point, Illinois, August 28, 1861. Wounded October 9, 1863 at Fort Wagner, South Carolina. Veteran. Wounded May 16, 1864 at Drewry's Bluff, Virginia. Promoted Corporal November 1, 1864. Wounded April 2, 1865 during the assault on Fort Gregg, Virginia. Promoted Sergeant September 1, 1865. Mustered out with the regiment, December 6, 1865. In 1889 he was living at Long Point, Illinois.

Girardee, Hermann - See Girard, Hermann

Gitchell, John W. - Sergeant - Company D - Enlisted from Paine's Point, Illinois, August 9, 1861. Reduced to the ranks, May 10, 1862. Died from disease in Delhi, Iowa June 22, 1862.

Gladdis, John - Private - Company F - Enlisted April 14, 1865. Deserted August 2, 1865 at Norfolk, Virginia.

Glasson, Peter - Private - Company A - Enlisted April 11, 1865. Mustered out with the regiment, December 6, 1865.

Godfrey, Isaac W. - Private - Company D - Enlisted from Lane, Illinois, August 21, 1861. Veteran. Wounded in the leg August 16, 1864 at Deep Run, Virginia. Discharged July 20, 1865 for disability from wounds.

Goebel, John - Private - Company G - Enlisted from Chicago, Illinois, December 26, 1863. Wounded in the neck May 20, 1864 at Ware Bottom Church, Virginia and in the arm April 2, 1865 at the assault on Fort Gregg, Virginia. Mustered out with the regiment, December 6, 1865.

Goff, James O. - Private - Company H - Enlisted from Pecatonica, Illinois, March 17, 1862. Discharged March 25, 1865 upon completion of military service.

Goldsmith, Nicholas - Private - Company B - Enlisted from Bloomington, Illinois, February 29, 1864. Wounded in the face May 20, 1864 at Ware Bottom Church, Virginia. Discharged October 6, 1864 for disability.

Goltra, Joseph W. - Private - Company I - Enlisted from Lincoln, Illinois, October 19, 1861. Transferred to Veteran Reserve Corps November 15, 1863. No discharge information available.

Goodin, Hiram - Private - Company I - Enlisted from De Witt, Illinois, February 4, 1861. Wounded May 16, 1864 at battle of Drewry's Bluff, Virginia. Discharged July 22, 1864 upon completion of military service.

Goodman, Thomas - Private - Company G - Enlisted from Lockport, Illinois, December 29, 1863. Mustered out with the regiment, December 6, 1865.

Gopp, Seneca - Private - Company C - Enlisted August 12, 1861. Deserted December 6, 1861. [Yapp, Seneca]

Gorbett, George W. - Private - Company C - Enlisted from Rook's Creek, Illinois, August 12, 1861. Died April 17, 1864 in general hospital in Washington, D.C. Cause unknown.

Gorbett, Henry A. - Private - Company C - Enlisted from Rook's Creek, Illinois, August 12, 1861. Veteran. Mustered out with the regiment, December 6, 1865. In 1889 he was living at LaSalle, Illinois.

Gorbett, Quincy A. - Private - Company C - Enlisted from Rook's Creek, Illinois, August 12, 1861. Discharged August 6, 1862 for disability. Cause unknown.

Gordon, Henry - Private - Company B - Enlisted from Bloomington, Illinois, September 5, 1861. Discharged September 14, 1864 upon completion of military service.

Gorton, Silas - Private - Company C - Enlisted March 22, 1865. Mustered out with the regiment, December 6, 1865.

Gosan, Christopher - Private - Company F - Enlisted February 12, 1864. Discharged September 16, 1864 for disability.

Gosan, Jacob - Private - Company F - Enlisted February 12, 1864. Mustered out with the regiment, December 6, 1865.

Gosnell, Willis R. - Private - Company K - Enlisted from Howard, Illinois, December 23, 1863. Mustered out with the regiment, December 6, 1865.

Goss, Andrew - Private - Company A - Enlisted January 4, 1864. Died in Chicago, Illinois, August 11, 1864. Cause unknown.

Gott, Henry - Private - Company C - Enlisted from Rook's Creek, Illinois, August 28, 1861. Veteran. Taken prisoner June 2, 1864 at Hatcher's Run, Virginia. Died of disease June 15, 1865 in Andersonville Prison, Georgia. Grave Number 12,461.

Gough, William - Private - Company B - Enlisted from Bloomington, Illinois, August 12, 1861. Promoted Corporal January 1, 1863. Veteran. Wounded and taken prisoner May 16, 1864 at the battle of Drewry's Bluff, Virginia. Died in prison at Andersonville, Georgia, June 24, 1864 from wounds and disease.

Graham, John - Private - Unassigned Substitute - Enlisted from Joliet, Illinois, August 25, 1864. Nothing further is known.

Graham, Joseph - Private - Company I - Enlisted April 10, 1865. Was a substitute. Mustered out with the regiment, December 6, 1865.

Graham, William - Private - Company C - Enlisted February 15, 1865. Mustered out with the regiment, December 6, 1865.

Grant, James L. - Private - Company D - Enlisted from Paine's Point, Illinois, August 12, 1861. Taken prisoner January 3, 1862 at Bath, West Virginia. Discharged June 6, 1862 for disability.

Grant, James W. - Private - Unassigned Recruit - Enlisted from Chicago, Illinois, January 5, 1864. Deserted, date unknown.

Graves, James H. - Private - Company B - Enlisted from Bloomington, Illinois, August 12, 1861. Discharged December 20, 1862 for disability.

Gray, Alexander - Private - Company E - Enlisted from Wilmington, Illinois, October 6, 1861. Veteran. Wounded August 16, 1864 at the battle of Deep Run, Virginia. Mustered out with the regiment, December 6, 1865.

Gray, John - Captain - Company C - Commissioned August 12, 1861. Resigned May 26, 1862 by reason of failing health. Born in New York State. At the age of twenty, he moved to Michigan where he married. After resigning his Captaincy he returned to Michigan, and after a few years moved to Frazee City, Minnesota and started a stock farm. He was elected and served one term in the Minnesota Legislature.

Gray, Walter A. - Corporal - Company C - Enlisted from Rook's Creek, Illinois, August 28, 1861. Promoted Sergeant May 10, 1862. Deserted February 1, 1863.

Green, Henry - First Sergeant - Company G - Enlisted from Ottawa, Illinois, August 19, 1861. Veteran. Reduced to the ranks July 28, 1864. Wounded August 20, and again October 13, 1864. Promoted Corporal July 1, 1865. Mustered out with the regiment, December 6, 1865.

Green, Ira W. - Private - Company D - Enlisted from Marion, Illinois, February 27, 1864. Wounded in the arm May 16, 1864 at Drewry's Bluff, Virginia. Mustered out with the regiment, December 6, 1865.

Green, Martin - Private - Company B - Enlisted from Bloomington, Illinois, March 1, 1864. Deserted May 15, 1864.

Green, Martin R. - Private - Company I - Enlisted from LeRoy, Illinois, January 1, 1864. Deserted September 24, 1864.

Greenbaum, Samuel - Private - Company C - Enlisted from Chicago, Illinois, January 4, 1864 & detailed to regimental band. Played in Band of 1864 & 1865. Partially deafened due to being to near an exploding cannon. Mustered out with the regiment, December 6, 1865. After the war he married a lady he met in Richmond, Virginia. In 1889 he was living at Fairbury, Illinois.

Gregory, Orgro - Corporal - Company G - Enlisted from Bremen, Illinois, August 19, 1861. Reduced to the ranks January 1, 1862. Died in the hospital at Morris Island August 13, 1863. Cause unknown.

Gregory, Samuel - Private - Company D - Enlisted from Aurora, Illinois, August 16, 1861. Promoted Corporal September 11, 1863. Veteran. Promoted to Sergeant August 4, 1865. Mustered out with the regiment, December 6, 1865. In 1889 he was living at Lake Linden, Michigan.

Grice, Daniel S. - Private - Company E - Enlisted October 12, 1861. Discharged. Remainder of record unknown. [Grise, Daniel S.]

Griffith, Daniel - Private - Company I - Enlisted from Bloomington, Illinois, November 10, 1862. Wounded in the shoulder August 16, 1864. Discharged November 10, 1865 upon completion of military service.

Griffith, Edward - Musician - Company C - Enlisted from Chicago, Illinois, October 8, 1861. Discharged October 8, 1864 upon completion of military service.

Griffith, George - Private - Company D - Enlisted from Lane, Illinois, August 21, 1861. Wounded August 26, 1863 at Fort Wagner, South Carolina. Died August 31, 1863 from wounds.

Grimes, Thomas - Private - Company F - Enlisted February 8, 1864. Deserted February 8, 1864.

Grise, Daniel S. - See Grice, Daniel S.

Groesbeck, William D. - Private - Company G - Enlisted from Wood's Grove, Illinois, February 22, 1865. Mustered out with the regiment, December 6, 1865.

Gronigal, T. D. - Corporal - Company E - Enlisted from Wilmington, Illinois, September 12, 1861. Promoted Sergeant May 9, 1863. Veteran. Wounded and taken prisoner May 16, 1864 at the battle of Drewry's Bluff, Virginia. Died June 9, 1864 at Petersburg, Virginia from his wounds.

Grooms, John W. - Private - Company I - Enlisted from LeRoy, Illinois, September 4, 1861. Taken prisoner May 26, 1862 at Strasburg, Virginia; paroled and exchanged. Veteran. Mustered out with the regiment, December 6, 1865.

Grooms, Irwin M. - Private - Company I - Enlisted from LeRoy, Illinois, September 17, 1861. Veteran. Promoted Corporal October 24, 1865. Mustered out with the regiment, December 6, 1865.

Grooms, Martin V. - Private - Company I - Enlisted from LeRoy, Illinois, September 22, 1861. Taken prisoner May 26, 1862 at Strasburg, Virginia; paroled and exchanged. Discharged July 4, 1863 for disability.

Grose, John - Corporal - Company G - Enlisted from La Salle, Illinois, August 14, 1861. Discharged February 10, 1863 for disability.

Groves, Thomas - Private - Company B - Enlisted from Bloomington, Illinois, August 12, 1861. Veteran. Promoted Corporal October 30, 1865. Mustered out with the regiment, December 6, 1865.

Guernsey, Augustus C. - Corporal - Company C - Enlisted from Esmond, Illinois, August 12, 1861. Promoted Sergeant September 24, 1861. Discharged May 4, 1862 for disability.

Guisinger, Daniel - First Lieutenant - Company C - Enlisted from Rook's Creek, Illinois, August 12, 1861. Promoted Sergeant. Promoted First Lieutenant March 31, 1865. Resigned July 12, 1865.

Guntz, Emile - Second Lieutenant - Company K - Enlisted from Chicago, Illinois, August 6, 1861. Promoted Sergeant, August 1, 1863. Veteran. Wounded May 16, 1864 at Drewry's Bluff, Virginia. Taken prisoner and sent to Andersonville Prison. Paroled in November 1864 and returned to his company. Promoted First Sergeant October 1, 1865. Promoted Second Lieutenant October 4, 1865.

Mustered out with the regiment, December 6, 1865. Born in Alkirch, Alsace, Germany, March 27, 1844, and emigrated to this country in 1849 with his parents. Died in Chicago on May 7, 1889. Buried at Waldheim Cemetery, Chicago, Illinois.

Guntz, Francis P. - Private - Company K - Enlisted March 12, 1864. Wounded in the arm August 16, 1864 at Deep Run, Virginia. Mustered out with the regiment, December 6, 1865.

Gurrand, Francis L. - Private - Company G - Enlisted from Chicago, Illinois, December 21, 1863. Taken prisoner May 20, 1864. Mustered out with the regiment, December 6, 1865.

Guyott, Frank - Private - Company D - Enlisted from Willow Creek, Illinois, August 15, 1861. Veteran. Promoted Corporal November 22, 1862. Deserted March 9, 1864.

— H —

Hademan, Martin V. - Private - Company E - Enlisted from Wilmington, Illinois, November 13, 1861. Veteran. Wounded June 2, 1864 near Ware Bottom Church, Virginia and again April 9, 1865 at Appomattox Court-House, Virginia. Was one of the last men to be wounded at the close of the war. Mustered out with the regiment, December 6, 1865.

Hafer, John - Private - Company B - Enlisted from Bloomington, Illinois, August 27, 1861. Veteran. Promoted Corporal September 1, 1864. Killed October 13, 1864 at Darbytown Cross-Roads, Virginia.

Hagan, Henry - Private - Company K - Enlisted February 14, 1865. Mustered out with the regiment, December 6, 1865.

Hagen, Francis - Private - Company F - Enlisted from Waukegan, Illinois, February 12, 1864. Wounded May 20, 1864 at Ware Bottom Church, Virginia. Died of his wounds in general hospital. Date unknown.

Hager, James D. B. - Private - Company H - Enlisted March 16, 1862. Discharged March 23, 1865 upon completion of military service.

Hagins, Daniel - Private - Company H - Enlisted from Springfield, Illinois, April 14, 1862. Wounded in the arm May 20, 1864. Discharged June 20, 1865 upon completion of military service.

Hahn, Christian - Private - Company G - Enlisted from Homer, Illinois, August 13, 1861. Transferred to Veteran Reserve Corps April 10, 1864. Discharge information unknown.

Haines, Clayborn L. - Private - Company B - Enlisted from Bloomington, Illinois, August 27, 1862. Discharged June 28, 1865 upon completion of military service.

Haldeman, James S. - Second Lieutenant - Company B - Commissioned August 12, 1861. Resigned May 26, 1862. In 1889 he was living in Kansas City, Missouri.

Hall, Joseph - Private - Company F - Enlisted August 22, 1861. Discharged July 1862 for disability.

Hallett, Joseph - Sergeant - Company B - Enlisted for ninety days in Eighth Illinois. Enlisted in Thirty-Ninth from Bloomington, Illinois, August 12, 1861. Company bugler. Veteran. Wounded in the thigh May 16, 1864 at Drewry's Bluff, Virginia. Promoted Sergeant August 27, 1864. Mustered out with the regiment, December 6, 1865. Born in West Chennock, Somerset, England, May 9, 1843. Came to America in 1852 and located in Hamilton County, Ohio. Hallett remained there until 1857, when his family moved to Bloomington, Illinois. He was a marble cutter by trade. After the hostilities ended, he began the study of medicine and became a doctor. In 1889 he was living in Bloomington, Illinois.

Hallett, William D. - Private - Company B - Enlisted from Bloomington, Illinois, August 12, 1861. Wounded in the thigh May 20, 1864 at the battle of Ware Bottom Church, Virginia. Discharged October 13, 1864 upon completion of military service. In 1889 he was living in Bloomington, Illinois.

Halligan, Thomas - Private - Company K - Enlisted from Marseilles, Illinois, August 6, 1861. Veteran. Mustered out with the regiment, December 6, 1865.

Halloway, Phillip M. - Private - Company I - Enlisted from Santa Anna, Illinois, September 4, 1861. Discharged September 10, 1864 upon completion of military service.

Hallowell, John E. W. - Private - Company I - Enlisted from LeRoy, Illinois, September 18, 1861. Veteran. Taken prisoner May 16, 1864 at Drewry's Bluff, Virginia. Discharged June 29, 1865 for disability.

Hallowell, Robert C. - Private - Company I - Enlisted from LeRoy, Illinois, September 18, 1861. Promoted Principal Musician September 1, 1863. Veteran. Mustered out with the regiment, December 6, 1865.

Hamilton, Chester W. - Private - Company F - Enlisted from Goodale, Illinois, February 4, 1864. Wounded in the arm August 14, 1864 at Deep Bottom, Virginia. Mustered out with the regiment, December 6, 1865.

Hamilton, James G. - Private - Company G - Enlisted from Bremen, Illinois, February 26, 1864. Wounded in the leg October 13, 1864 at Darbytown Cross-Roads, Virginia. Leg amputated. Discharged June 3, 1865 for disability.

Hamilton, Lester - Private - Company C - Enlisted from Esmond, Illinois, October 28, 1861. Veteran. Killed May 20, 1864 at the battle of Ware Bottom Church, Virginia.

Hammock, Peter - Private - Company B - Enlisted from Bloomington, Illinois, February 13, 1864. Mustered out with the regiment, December 6, 1865.

Hammond, Morris - Private - Company B - Enlisted April 7, 1865. Absent, (ill) at muster-out of regiment.

Hammond, William - Private - Company G - Enlisted from Homer, Illinois, August 27, 1861. Veteran. Promoted Corporal November 1, 1864. Mustered out with the regiment, December 6, 1865.

Hancock, Erastus B. - Private - Company I - Enlisted from Randolph, Illinois, March 1, 1864. Wounded in the foot, April 2, 1865 at the assault on Fort Gregg, Virginia. Mustered out June 15, 1865 for disability from wound.

Hand, John M. - Private - Company I - Enlisted from Santa Anna, Illinois, September 20, 1861. Discharged September 20, 1864 upon completion of military service.

Handy, Austin A. - Private - Company G - Enlisted from Shabbona, Illinois, September 9, 1861. Discharged September 10, 1864 upon completion of military service.

Haney, James - Private - Company C - Enlisted from Nebraska, August 28, 1861. Veteran. Wounded October 13, 1864 at the battle of Darbytown Cross-Roads, Virginia. Mustered out with the regiment, December 6, 1865. In 1889 he was living at Keokuk, Iowa.

Haney, John - Private - Company C - Enlisted from Chicago, Illinois, March 4, 1864. Wounded May 20, 1864 at Ware Bottom Church, Virginia. Mustered out with the regiment, December 6, 1865.

Haney, Mathews - Private - Company C - Enlisted from Nebraska, August 12, 1861. Discharged August 21, 1862 for disability.

Hannah, Calvin - Musician, Second Class - Enlisted September 20, 1861. Taken prisoner at Strasburg, Virginia, May, 1862. Paroled and discharged June 4, 1862 by order of the War Department.

Hannum, James - Captain - Company C - Enlisted from Cayuga, Illinois, August 12, 1861. Promoted from First Lieutenant July 2, 1864. Mustered out with the regiment, December 6, 1865. In 1889 he was living at Garnett, Kansas engaged in farming.

Hanson, David M. - Sergeant - Company E - Enlisted from Wilmington, Illinois, September 12, 1861 as a Private. Promoted Sergeant January 16, 1862. Taken prisoner May 16, 1864 at the battle of Drewry's Bluff, Virginia. Died October 22, 1864 at Andersonville Prison, Georgia, of wounds received in a railway accident during transportation to another prison.

Hanson, Edward P. - Private - Company G - Enlisted from Orland, Illinois, August 29, 1861. Discharged September 3, 1862 for disability.

Hardenburgh, Henry M. - Private - Company G - Enlisted from Bremen, Illinois, August 15, 1861. Wounded in the shoulder August 16, 1864. Promoted to First Lieutenant in U. S. Colored troops for bravery on the field. Killed by a shell fragment in the trenches in front of Petersburg, Virginia August 28, 1864. His commission was posthumous.

Harding, Eugene H. - Private - Company D - Enlisted from Dement, Illinois, August 5, 1861. Veteran. Wounded in the arm August 16, 1864 at Deep Run, Virginia. Discharged June 13, 1865 for disability from wounds.

Hardman, John L. - Private - Unassigned Recruit - Enlisted from Lexington, Illinois, February 26, 1864. Nothing further is known.

Hare, John - Private - Company D - Enlisted from Lane, Illinois, August 9, 1861. Discharged March 5, 1862 for disability.

Harman, Thomas - Private - Company D - Enlisted September 10, 1864. Discharged January 10, 1865 by order of the War Department.

Harrah, William C. - Musician, First Class - Enlisted September 20, 1861. Discharged by order of the War Department, June 4, 1862.

Harrington, James M. - Second Lieutenant - Company G - Enlisted from Palos, Illinois, August 9, 1861. Promoted Second Lieutenant July 20, 1862. Discharged October 17, 1864 upon completion of military service. Born in the State of New York in 1831.

Harrington, Walter - First Sergeant - Company H - Enlisted from Pecatonica, Illinois, February 20, 1862. Veteran. Discharged for disability March 20, 1865.

Harris, William J. - Corporal - Company A - Enlisted September 19, 1861. Promoted Sergeant March 1, 1862. Killed June 17, 1864 in a skirmish near Chester Station, Virginia.

Harrison, John - Private - Company F - Enlisted from Sandoval, Illinois, September 6, 1861. Wounded May 16, 1864 at Drewry's Bluff, Virginia. Died July 1, 1864 from wounds.

Harrison, William - First Lieutenant - Company H - Enlisted from Kingston Mines, Illinois, August 16, 1864. Mustered out with the regiment, December 6, 1865.

Harsh, J. O. - Private - Company E - Enlisted from Rockville, Illinois, September 27, 1861. Discharged September 27, 1864 upon completion of military service.

Hartman, George - Private - Company E - Enlisted February 22, 1865. Discharged May 3, 1865.

Hartman, William H. - Private - Company A - Enlisted August 8, 1861. Died at Cumberland, Maryland, February 6, 1862. Cause unknown.

Hartry, Alfred - Private - Company B - Enlisted from Bloomington, Illinois, February 20, 1864. Taken prisoner May 16, 1864 at Drewry's Bluff, Virginia. Mustered out July 7, 1865 as a prisoner of war.

Hartry, Edmund - Private - Company B - Enlisted from Bloomington, Illinois, August 12, 1861. Promoted Corporal January 1, 1863. Veteran. Wounded and taken prisoner May 16, 1864 at Drewry's Bluff, Virginia. Died in prison at Andersonville, Georgia, June 24, 1864 of wounds. Grave Number 1,980.

Harty, James - Private - Company B - Enlisted from Bloomington, Illinois, August 27, 1861. Wounded August 16, 1864 at Deep Run, Virginia. Discharged October 19, 1864 upon completion of military service.

Harvey, Henry - Private - Company F - Enlisted from Avon, Illinois, February 29, 1864. Discharged July 17, 1865 for disability.

Harvey, Levi - Private - Company B - Enlisted from Pontiac, Illinois, August 12, 1861. Discharged September 10, 1864 upon completion of military service. In 1889 he was living in Bloomington, Illinois occupied as a railroad engineer.

Harvey, Louis - Private - Company F - Enlisted from Bloomington, Illinois, August 14, 1861. Veteran. Wounded August 16, 1864 in the arm. Arm amputated. Discharged for disability.

Hashman, Lewis - Private - Company I - Enlisted from Springfield, Illinois, December 30, 1862. Wounded in the neck May 20, 1864 in the battle of Ware Bottom Church, Virginia. Discharged June 15, 1865 for disability from wounds.

Haspel, Frederick - Private - Company B - Enlisted from Bloomington, Illinois, August 27, 1861. Discharged December 22, 1864 for disability.

Hauglebrock, William - Private - Company F - Enlisted September 2, 1864. Missing from the regiment since October 12, 1864. Supposed to have been captured. [Not listed in Adjutant General's Report.]

Hawath, John - Private - Company E - Enlisted from Chicago, Illinois, October 2, 1861. Deserted in February 1862.

Hawkins, Edwin - Private - Company G - Enlisted from Chicago, Illinois, September 4, 1861. Discharged June 2, 1862 for disability.

Hawkins, John J. - Corporal - Company G - Enlisted from Palos, Illinois, August 18, 1861. Discharged September 10, 1864 upon completion of military service.

Hawthorne, Ephraim W. - Regimental Sergeant-Major - Enlisted from Fremont, Illinois, February 9, 1864. Promoted Sergeant Major January 1, 1865. Transferred to U. S. Colored Troops for commission. No discharge information.

Hayes, James H. - Private - Company B - Enlisted from Bloomington, Illinois, August 27, 1861. Was injured in the back by falling timbers of a bomb-proof in front of Fort Wagner, South Carolina in 1863. Veteran. Mustered out with the regiment, December 6, 1865. In 1889 he was living in Saybrook, Illinois.

Hayes, John B. - Private - Company F - Enlisted from Chicago, Illinois, August 15, 1861. Veteran. Deserted, and died at his home March 16, 1864.

Hayes, Stephen - Private - Company F - Enlisted from Chicago, Illinois, August 5, 1861. Deserted in 1862.

Hayward, Stephen K. - Private - Company K - Enlisted from Bloomington, Illinois, August 14, 1861. Discharged March 13, 1864 upon completion of military service.

Hayworth, George - Private - Company E - Enlisted February 22, 1865. Taken prisoner April 9, 1865 at Appomattox Court-House, Virginia; paroled the same day. One of the last men to be captured by the Army of Northern Virginia. Mustered out with the regiment, December 6, 1865.

Hazzard, Monroe - Private - Company E - Enlisted from Chicago, Illinois, March 24, 1864. Was on detached service as orderly to General Osborn. Mustered out with the regiment, December 6, 1865.

Headley, William M. - Private - Company C - Enlisted from Chicago, Illinois, August 28, 1861. Taken prisoner March 23, 1862 at Winchester, Virginia. Discharged from the service on May 21, 1863.

Hedge, Enoch C. - Private - Company A - Enlisted August 15, 1861. Veteran. Played in the Band of 1864 & 1865. Took a rifle and entered the ranks at Drewry's Bluff and Strawberry Plains, Virginia. Mustered out with the regiment, December 6, 1865.

Heintz, P. H. - Private - Company G - Enlisted from Pekin, Illinois, August 30, 1861. Deserted September 12, 1861.

Heirsagle, Joseph - Private - Company F - Enlisted from Fremont, Illinois, January 28, 1864. Deserted July 17, 1864.

Helm, Willis N. - Private - Company G - Enlisted from Shabbona, Illinois, August 26, 1861. Died of typhoid fever April 10, 1862 at Cumberland, Maryland.

Hemmerling, Frederick M. - Private - Company D - Enlisted from Paine's Point, Illinois, September 6, 1861. Veteran. Promoted Corporal. Taken prisoner May 16, 1864 at Drewry's Bluff, Virginia. Promoted Sergeant 1, 1864. Mustered out with the regiment, December 6, 1865. In 1889 he was living at New Hartford, Iowa.

Henderson, James - Second Lieutenant - Company C - Enlisted from Rook's Creek, Illinois, August 12, 1861. Promoted to First Sergeant and commissioned May 26, 1862. Resigned June 28, 1863.

Hendrick, Henry - Private - Unassigned Recruit - Enlisted from Wheeling, Illinois, January 7, 1865. Rejected by Medical Board.

Hendricks, James S. - Private - Company K - Enlisted August 23, 1862. Discharged June 29, 1865 upon completion of military service.

Henner, John - Private - Company B - Enlisted from Bloomington, Illinois, August 12, 1861. Discharged August 2, 1863 for disability.

Hennings, John - Private - Company A - Enlisted February 28, 1864. Wounded in the head October 7, 1864 near Chaffin's Farm, Virginia. Taken prisoner and paroled April 9, 1865 at Appomattox

Court-House, Virginia. Mustered out with the regiment, December 6, 1865. In 1889 he was living in Wilmington, Illinois.

Henschod, Theodore - Private - Company B - Enlisted March 1, 1865. Discharged July 19, 1865 for disability.

Heritage, George T. - Captain - Company B - Enlisted at Bloomington, Illinois, August 12, 1861. Elected Orderly-Sergeant. Promoted to First Lieutenant May 26, 1862. Wounded in the shoulder and back October 13, 1864 at Darbytown Cross-Roads, Virginia. Discharged December 7, 1864 upon completion of military service. Captain Heritage was the only son of Thomas and Susan Heritage. He was born in Deddington, Oxfordshire, England on September 26, 1834. His mother died when he was very young, and his father emigrated to Canada and settled at New Hope. At the age of sixteen George went to Brantford, Ontario to learn the trade of carriage-making. In 1856 he went to Chicago, Illinois and then to Bloomington, Illinois. In 1859 he followed the gold trail to Pike's Peak. After limited success in finding gold, he returned to Illinois to join the Thirty-Ninth. In 1889 he was living in Bloomington, Illinois.

Herrick, M. B. - Private - Company F - Enlisted August 22, 1861. Discharged August 5, 1863 for disability.

Herrin, David O. - Corporal - Company A - Enlisted August 15, 1861. Reduced to the ranks January 1, 1862. Discharged July 20, 1862.

Herriott, John E. - First Lieutenant - Company A - Enlisted August 5, 1861. Promoted Sergeant March 1, 1862. Wounded in the face at Fort Gregg, South Carolina. Veteran. Promoted First Lieutenant March 31, 1865. Mustered out with the regiment, December 6, 1865. In 1889 he was living near Wilmington, Illinois.

Hertzog, Charles W. - Private - Company E - Enlisted from Rockville, Illinois, September 20, 1861. Transferred to Veteran Reserve Corps, November 16, 1864. Discharge unknown.

Hertzog, William F. - Private - Company E - Enlisted from Rockville, Illinois, September 20, 1861. Wounded in the thigh May 20, 1864. Killed June 18, 1864 near Ware Bottom Church, Virginia.

Herzog, Adam J. - Private - Company G - Enlisted from Lafayette, Indiana, August 15, 1861. Veteran. Wounded in the arm May 20, 1864 at the battle of Ware Bottom Church, Virginia. Promoted Corporal October 10, 1864; promoted Sergeant January 1, 1865. Mustered out with the regiment, December 6, 1865.

Hewill, Frank E. - Private - Company D - Enlisted from Lane, Illinois, August 6, 1861. Taken prisoner January 3, 1862 at Bath, West Virginia. Discharged January 9, 1863 for disability.

Hewitt, Charles - Private - Company F - Enlisted from Waukegan, Illinois, January 9, 1864. Mustered out with the regiment, December 6, 1865.

Hewitt, James W. - Private - Company K - Enlisted at St. Louis, Missouri, October 8, 1861. Promoted Sergeant April 15, 1862. Discharged July 22, 1862 for disability.

Hicks, Milton - Private - Company K - Enlisted from Chicago, Illinois, September 4, 1861. Veteran. Detailed as nurse and acting hospital steward of the regiment. Mustered out with the regiment, December 6, 1865.

Hicks, William - Private - Company A - Enlisted August 5, 1861. Died February 5, 1862 at Cumberland, Maryland, cause unknown.

Higgins, James T. - Private - Company A - Enlisted April 7, 1865. Mustered out with the regiment, December 6, 1865.

Hillsted, Errick - Private - Company C - Enlisted from Chicago, Illinois, September 24, 1864. Mustered out June 20, 1865 by order of the War Department.

Hilman, Henry B. - Private - Company B - Enlisted March 1, 1865. Mustered out with the regiment, December 6, 1865.

Hines, James H. - Private - Company A - Enlisted April 12, 1865. Mustered out June 3, 1865.

Hirst, James - Private - Company I - Enlisted from Champaign, Illinois, October 2, 1861. Discharged July 4, 1863 for disability that originated from a cold contracted in fording the Potomac River, January 4, 1862.

Hitcher, Chapman - Private - Unassigned Draftee - Drafted from Okaw, Illinois, April 12, 1865. Nothing further is known.

Hoffman, Stewart W. - Regimental Quartermaster - Promoted July 15, 1862. Mustered out with the regiment, December 6, 1865.

Hoisington, Henry - Private - Company B - Enlisted from Bloomington, Illinois, August 12, 1861. Died December 4, 1861 from disease.

Hollowell, Robert C. - Chief Musician - Regimental Band - Enlisted from LeRoy, Illinois, September 18, 1861. Discharged September 18, 1864 upon completion of military service. In 1889 he was living in LeRoy, Illlinois

Holt, Charles - Private - Unassigned Recruit - Enlisted at Chicago, Illinois, December 19, 1863. Deserted December 29, 1863.

Holter, John - Private - Company A - Enlisted August 17, 1861. Promoted Corporal March 1, 1862. Veteran. Wounded May 20, 1864. Promoted Sergeant April 1, 1865. Mustered out with the regiment, December 6, 1865.

Holz, Ernest - Private - Company A - Enlisted August 15, 1861. Veteran. Promoted Corporal January 1, 1864; promoted Sergeant July 3, 1865. Mustered out with the regiment, December 6, 1865.

Hontsinger, Benjamin F. - Private - Company K - Enlisted April 11, 1865. Was a substitute. Mustered out with the regiment, December 6, 1865.

Hooker, James H. - Captain - Company E - Commissioned August 12, 1861 from Wilmington, Illinois. Resigned May 26, 1862 due to ill health. Born at Rochester, New York, June 23, 1832. His father's name was Alexander A. Hooker and he had six sisters. His father served in the War of 1812 against the Indians, and in Canada, participating in the battles of Lundy's Lane and Queenstown Heights. His father died when James was only fourteen.

Hoover, Columbus - Private - Company I - Enlisted from Santa Anna, Illinois, September 21, 1861. Promoted Corporal May 11, 1862. Veteran. Promoted Sergeant October 10, 1865. Mustered out with the regiment, December 6, 1865.

Hoover, John - Private - Company I - Enlisted from Santa Anna, Illinois, September 4, 1861. Wounded in the thigh August 18, 1863 at Fort Wagner, South Carolina. Veteran. Taken prisoner May 16, 1864 at Drewry's Bluff, Virginia. [Adjutant General's Report shows him as missing since May 16, 1864.]

Hoover, Theodore - Private - Company I - Enlisted from Santa Anna, Illinois, February 18, 1864. Wounded in the arm May 16, 1864 at Drewry's Bluff, Virginia. Mustered out June 15, 1865.

Hopkins, Benjamin B. - Private - Company F - Enlisted from Chicago, Illinois, March 27, 1864. Killed in battle August 11, 1864 at Deep Run, Virginia.

Hopkins, Joseph - Private - Company A - Enlisted December 29, 1864. Mustered out with the regiment, December 6, 1865.

Hopkins, Thomas - Corporal - Company D - Enlisted from Hennepin, Illinois, August 22, 1861. Promoted Sergeant October 4, 1862. Veteran. Killed May 20, 1864 in battle at Ware Bottom Church, Virginia.

Horn, Gottlieb - Corporal - Company D - Enlisted from Lindenwood, Illinois, August 12, 1861. At his request was reduced to the ranks and made regimental bugler. Wounded in the leg, May 20, 1864 at Ware Bottom Church, Virginia. Discharge information unknown. In 1889 he was living in Holcomb, Illinois.

Hornberger, George - Private - Company H - Enlisted from Vermillion, Illinois, June 21, 1862. Wounded April 2, 1865 at the assault on Fort Gregg, Virginia. Discharged June 20, 1865 upon completion of military service.

Hotchkiss, Charles B. - Private - Company B - Enlisted from Bloomington, Illinois, August 26, 1861. Discharged September 10, 1864 upon completion of military service. In 1889 he was living at Covel, Illinois.

Houghton, Herrick - Private - Company A - Enlisted August 22, 1861. Veteran. Promoted Corporal April 1, 1865. Mustered out with the regiment, December 6, 1865. In 1889 he was living at Fairbury, Illinois.

Howard, Robert - Private - Company B - Enlisted from Bloomington, Illinois, August 12, 1861. Deserted October 28, 1861.

Howard, Stephen K. - Private - Company K - Enlisted from Bloomington, Illinois, August 14, 1861. Discharged for disability March 13, 1863.

Howard, William H. - Private - Company G - Enlisted from Lysander, NY, August 14, 1861. Veteran. Wounded in the neck April 2, 1865 at the assault on Fort Gregg, Virginia. Promoted Corporal April 3, 1865. Mustered out with the regiment, December 6, 1865.

Howden, Ephraim - Private - Company C - Enlisted from Rook's Creek, Illinois, September 6, 1861. Veteran. Wounded May 20, 1864 at Ware Bottom Church, Virginia. Promoted Corporal July 1, 1865. Mustered out with the regiment, December 6, 1865. In 1889 he was living at Pontiac, Illinois.

Howder, Martin - Corporal - Company C - Enlisted from Rook's Creek, Illinois, August 12, 1861. Promoted Sergeant May 12, 1862. Wounded and taken prisoner May 16, 1864 at Drewry's Bluff, Virginia. Died in prison at Florence, South Carolina, October 11, 1864.

Howe, Calvin H. - Private - Company E - Enlisted from St. Louis, Missouri, October 2, 1861. Deserted January 30, 1862.

Howe, Hermann H. - Private - Company E - Enlisted from St. Louis, Missouri, October 25, 1861. Deserted January 30, 1862.

Howell, Daniel - Private - Company E - Enlisted from Wilmington, Illinois, October 2, 1861. Discharged for disability (date unknown).

Howell, George - Private - Company A - Enlisted August 19, 1861. Discharged February 5, 1862 for disability.

Howell, George - Private - Company E - Enlisted from Wesley, Illinois, December 31, 1863. Wounded in the hand and side October 13, 1864. Hand amputated. Discharged March 30, 1865 for disability.

Howell, William - Private - Company H - Enlisted from Cerro Gordo, Illinois, June 28, 1862. Killed August 16, 1864 at the battle of Deep Run, Virginia.

Howland, Adelbert - Private - Company G - Enlisted from Genesee, Illinois, August 14, 1861. Killed August 16, 1864 at the battle of Deep Run, Virginia.

Hubbard, Albert - Private - Company K - Enlisted from Marseilles, Illinois, August 14, 1861. Discharged October 10, 1862 upon completion of military service.

Hudson, Arthur - Private - Company H - Enlisted from Pecatonica, Illinois, March 8, 1862. Discharged for disability, date unknown.

Hudson, Charles C. - Private - Company E - Enlisted from Wilmington, Illinois, September 17, 1861. Veteran. Promoted Corporal in 1864. Mustered out with the regiment, December 6, 1865.

Huff, Charles M. - Private - Company D - Enlisted from Oregon, Illinois, August 21, 1861. Deserted November 30, 1861.

Hughes, Edward - Private - Company C - Enlisted from Pontiac, Illinois, January 4, 1864, and discharged for disability.

Hughes, James H. - Private - Company K - Enlisted from Chicago, Illinois, January 4, 1864. Wounded, absent at muster out of regiment.

Hughes, R. E. - Private - Company C - Enlisted from Chicago, Illinois, August 21, 1861. Deserted August 21, 1861.

Hughes, William J. - Private - Company A - Enlisted February 24, 1864. Detailed to regimental band. Played in Band of 1864 & 1865. Mustered out with the regiment, December 6, 1865. Died in Chicago during 1886 of tuberculosis.

Hull, B. B. - Musician, First Class - Enlisted September 20, 1861. Discharged by order of the War Department, June 4, 1862.

Hull, Samuel F. - Private - Company E - Enlisted from Chicago, Illinois, February 27, 1864. Detailed to the regimental band. Mustered out with the regiment, December 6, 1865.

Hummell, Henry - Private - Company B - Enlisted from Bloomington, Illinois, August 12, 1861. Veteran. Wounded in the hand August 14, 1864 near Petersburg, Virginia. Promoted Corporal October 1, 1864. Reduced to the ranks April 30, 1865. Promoted Corporal September 24, 1865. Mustered out with the regiment, December 6, 1865.

Hummell, Lewis J. - Private - Company K - Enlisted from Chicago, Illinois, September 10, 1861. Discharged September 10, 1864 upon completion of military service.

Hummell, Robert N. - Private - Company D - Enlisted from Lane, Illinois, August 16, 1861. Veteran. Wounded in the head May 16, 1864 at Drewry's Bluff, Virginia. Killed April 2, 1865 during the assault on Fort Gregg, Virginia.

Humphrey, Thomas - Private - Company G - Enlisted from Orland, Illinois, August 29, 1861. Killed May 20, 1864 at the battle of Ware Bottom Church, Virginia.

Hunt, Loam J. - Private - Company D - Enlisted from Peru, Illinois, August 9, 1861. Wounded August 16, 1864 in the head. Promoted Corporal March 1, 1865. Wounded April 2, 1865 in the left cheek. Deserted August 3, 1865.

Hurlbut, Amasa - Private - Company A - Enlisted December 29, 1863. Discharged February 16, 1865.

Hurley, Lewis - Private - Company I - Enlisted from Santa Anna, Illinois, September 4, 1861. Veteran. Killed May 16, 1864 at the battle of Drewry's Bluff, Virginia.

Hurst, Edward - Private - Company I - Enlisted from Santa Anna, Illinois, September 9, 1861. Killed in battle August 16, 1864 at Deep Run, Virginia.

Hutchings, John A. - Private - Company F - Enlisted from Northfield, Illinois, August 21, 1861. Veteran. Promoted Corporal January 1, 1864. Severely wounded in the hand May 20, 1864 at Ware Bottom Church, Virginia. Reduced to the ranks at his own request. Sick and wounded, absent at muster out of the regiment.

Hutchinson, William - Private - Company B - Enlisted from Bloomington, Illinois, August 27, 1861. Veteran. Mustered out with the regiment, December 6, 1865.

— I —

Igsa, Henry - Private - Company I - Enlisted from LeRoy, Illinois, September 24, 1861. Veteran. Wounded in the head May 16, 1864 at the battle of Drewry's Bluff, Virginia. Severely wounded in the back, October 7, 1864. Mustered out with the regiment, December 6, 1865.

Inglehart, Charles - Private - Company G - Enlisted February 27, 1864. Wounded in the hand June 17, 1864 near Ware Bottom Church, Virginia, and in the leg April 2, 1865 at the assault on Fort Gregg, Virginia. Discharged October 30, 1865 for disability from wounds.

Ingleman, Augustus - Private - Company E - Enlisted from Cicero, Illinois, March 7, 1864. Mustered out with the regiment, December 6, 1865.

Irish, Franklin - Private - Company A - Enlisted February 19, 1864. Wounded October 7, 1864 near Chaffin's Farm. Mustered out with the regiment, December 6, 1865. In 1889 he was living at Wilmington, Illinois.

Isbester, John - Private - Company F - Enlisted from Waukegan, Illinois, January 25, 1864. Promoted Corporal August 1, 1865. Mustered out with the regiment, December 6, 1865.

— J —

Jackson, Charles A. - Private - Company E - Enlisted from Florence, Illinois, February 28, 1864. Wounded August 16, 1864 and arm amputated. Discharged November 7, 1864 for disability.

Jackson, James - Private - Company I - Enlisted from Bloomington, Illinois, February 12, 1864. Mustered out with the regiment, December 6, 1865.

Jacob, Bernard - Private - Company D - Enlisted February 21, 1865. Mustered out with the regiment, December 6, 1865.

James, Henry T. - Private - Company C - Enlisted from Chicago, Illinois, August 12, 1861. Discharged June 30, 1862 for disability. Re-enlisted February 29, 1864 and detailed to the regimental band. Mustered out with the regiment, December 6, 1865. In 1889 he was living at Atlantic City, Iowa.

Jared, Thomas - Private - Company H - Enlisted March 3, 1865. Promoted Corporal May 10, 1865; promoted Sergeant September 1, 1865. Mustered out with the regiment, December 6, 1865.

Jenkins, Isaac R. - Sergeant - Company C - Enlisted from Cayuga, Illinois, September 19, 1861. Veteran. Severely wounded in the chest May 20, 1864 at the battle of Ware Bottom Church,

Virginia. Promoted Corporal January 1, 1865; promoted Sergeant May 1, 1865. Mustered out with the regiment, December 6, 1865. In 1889 he was living in St. Paul, Minnesota engaged as a electrician for the city government.

Jenkins, Robert T. - Private - Company G - Enlisted from Coloma, Illinois, August 14, 1861. Discharged June 27, 1862 for disability.

Jenkins, Samuel N. - Private - Company G - Enlisted April 11, 1865. Mustered out with the regiment, December 6, 1865.

Jenkins, William H. - Private - Company C - Enlisted from Esmond, Illinois, December 30, 1863. Wounded in the neck and shoulder May 15, 1864 at Drewry's Bluff, Virginia. Wounded in the thigh October 13, 1864 at the battle of Darbytown Cross-Roads, Virginia. Suffered amputation of the leg. In the hospital at the time of the regimental muster-out. In 1889 he was living at Pontiac, Illinois.

Jenks, George W. - Private - Company C - Enlisted from Orland, Illinois, August 19, 1861. Discharged January 16, 1863 for disability.

Jewett, William O. L. - Private - Company E - Enlisted from Wesley, Illinois, September 12, 1861. One of the first to enlist in Company E. Sent home on recruiting service, became ill. In July, 1862 he was sent to the hospital in Washington, D.C. On recovery, he was sent to Rhode Island, where he remained until his discharge on June 6, 1863. Re-enlisted at Camp Butler, Illinois, and was sent to Memphis, Tennessee in command of 500 substitutes. After Memphis he was sent to Savannah with the First Illinois Artillery, to join Sherman's Army. He remained with Sherman's forces until the surrender, participating in the grand review in Washington, D.C., and returned home. Entered Michigan University at Ann Arbor, he graduated in 1866 and moved to Shelbina, Missouri to practice Law. In 1876 he was elected District Attorney. In 1886 he was elected to the Missouri Legislature.

Johnson, Abiram B. - Regimental Commissary-Sergeant - Enlisted from LeRoy, Illinois, September 12, 1861 in Company I. Promoted January 24, 1862 and transferred to non-commissioned staff. Discharged September 12, 1864 upon completion of military service. Born in Harrison County, Ohio, February 20, 1832. He was a carpenter. After the war he resided in LeRoy, Illinois.'

Johnson, Alfred - Private - Company B - Enlisted from Empire, Illinois, June 25, 1862. Mustered out with the regiment, December 6, 1865.

Johnson, Allen B. - First Lieutenant - Company A - Enlisted as First Sergeant July 1861; commissioned Second Lieutenant November 17, 1861; promoted First Lieutenant December 1, 1861. Died at New Bern, North Carolina, September 10, 1864 of yellow fever. Born in Pennsylvania.

Johnson, Ed. J. - Private - Company A - Enlisted August 5, 1861. Discharged March 19, 1863 for disability. In 1889 he was living at Kankakee, Illinois.

Johnson, Ezra E. - Corporal - Company D - Enlisted from Willow Creek, Illinois, September 4, 1861. Promoted Sergeant May 11, 1862. Discharged September 10, 1864 upon completion of military service.

Johnson, Franklin - Private - Company B - Enlisted from LeRoy, Illinois, June 5, 1864. Mustered out with the regiment, December 6, 1865.

Johnson, Frederick - Private - Company F - Enlisted from Waukegan, Illinois, February 4, 1864. Wounded August 16, 1864 at Deep Run, Virginia. Died August 24, 1864 from wounds.

Johnson, George - Private - Company F - Enlisted August 5, 1861. Discharged October 16, 1861 for disability.

Johnson, George W. B. - Private - Company I - Enlisted from Empire, Illinois, January 1, 1864. Wounded in the knee October 13, 1864 at the battle of Darbytown Cross-Roads, Virginia. Discharged May 2, 1865 under order of the War Department.

Johnson, Isaac R. - Private - Company B - Enlisted from Bloomington, Illinois, September 19, 1861. Discharged August 12, 1862 for disability. In 1889 he was living at Soldier City, Kansas.

Johnson, John H. - Private - Company I - Enlisted from Franklin County, Illinois, April 1, 1865. Mustered out August 18, 1865.

Johnson, James - Private - Company B - Enlisted from Bloomington, Illinois, August 27, 1863. Died October 26, 1864. Cause unknown.

Johnson, James M. - Private - Company B - Enlisted from Bloomington, Illinois, September 19, 1861. Veteran. Reported missing in action May 16, 1864 at Drewry's Bluff, Virginia was taken prisoner. Paroled and exchanged. Promoted Corporal May 1, 1865. Mustered out with the regiment, December 6, 1865. In 1889 he was living at LeRoy, Illinois.

Johnson, James M. - Private - Company E - Enlisted as Musician, 3rd Class on September 20, 1861. Discharged by order of the War Department, June 4, 1862. Re-enlisted from Chicago, Illinois, February 26, 1864. Played in Band of 1864 & 1865. Mustered out with the regiment, December 6, 1865.

Johnson, Joel B. - Private - Company I - Enlisted from Santa Anna, Illinois, March 10, 1864. Wounded March 16, 1864 at the battle of Drewry's Bluff, Virginia. Discharged June 2, 1864 for disability, at Point of Rocks Hospital, Virginia.

Johnson, John - Private - Company B - Enlisted from Bloomington, Illinois, August 22, 1861. Discharged June 28, 1864 for disability.

Johnson, John H. - Private - Company C - Enlisted August 12, 1861. Promoted Corporal. Wounded in the hip June 2, 1864. Promoted Sergeant July 2, 1864. Killed October 13, 1864 at the battle of Darbytown Cross-Roads, Virginia.

Johnson, John P. - Private - Company B - Enlisted April 8, 1865. Deserted June 4, 1865.

Johnson, John S. - Private - Company I - Enlisted from Santa Anna, Illinois, September 4, 1861. Discharged July 1, 1862 for disability.

Johnson, Joshua H. - Private - Company I - Enlisted from LeRoy, Illinois, September 4, 1861. Veteran. Wounded May 16, 1864 at Drewry's Bluff, Virginia. Promoted Corporal April 2, 1865. Mustered out with the regiment, December 6, 1865.

Johnson, Samuel B. - Private - Company C - Enlisted from Pontiac, Illinois, September 20, 1863. Died from disease at Hatcher's Run, Virginia, June 30, 1864.

Johnson, Stephan - Corporal - Company B - Enlisted from Bloomington, Illinois, August 12, 1861. Discharged July 22, 1862 for disability.

Johnson, Stephan - Corporal - Company C - Enlisted from Ocoya, Illinois, September 19, 1861. Promoted Corporal May 10, 1862. Killed in battle May 20, 1864 at Ware Bottom Church, Virginia.

Johnson, Thomas J. - Corporal - Company I - Enlisted from Santa Anna, Illinois, September 4, 1861. Veteran. Promoted Sergeant January 1, 1865. Mustered out with the regiment, December 6, 1865.

Johnson, William - Private - Company H - Enlisted from Hitesville, Illinois, June 16, 1862. Wounded August 16, 1864 at Deep Run, Virginia. Discharged June 20, 1865 upon completion of military service.

Johnson, William H. - Sergeant - Company A - Enlisted August 5, 1861. Reduced to the ranks March 1, 1862. Transferred to the regular army December 20, 1862. Discharge information unknown.

Johnson, William H. - Private - Company H - Enlisted April 7, 1865. Deserted October 27, 1865.

Johnston, Howard - Private - Company E - Enlisted from Channahon, Illinois, March 9, 1864. Wounded May 16, 1864 at the battle of Drewry's Bluff, Virginia, and suffered amputation of his arm. Discharged November 21, 1864 for disability.

Jones, Henry T. - Chief Musician - Regimental Band - Enlisted from Pontiac, Illinois, September 21, 1861. Discharged June 3, 1862 for disability. Re-enlisted in Band of 1864 & 1865. Mustered out with the regiment, December 6, 1865. In 1889 he was living in Atlantic City, Iowa.

Jones, Samuel - Private - Company I - Enlisted April 4, 1865. Mustered out with the regiment, December 6, 1865.

Jones, Thomas - Private - Company D - Enlisted from Taylorville, Illinois, April 14, 1865. Mustered out with the regiment, December 6, 1865.

Jones, William H. - Private - Company D - Enlisted from Lane, Illinois, September 3, 1861. Veteran. Wounded in the left thigh October 13, 1864 at Darbytown Cross-Roads, Virginia. Absent, sick and wounded at muster out of the regiment. After leaving the service, Jones attended Rush Medical College in Chicago and finally graduated from the College of Physicians and Surgeons, Keokuk, Iowa in 1874. He settled in Forest City, Iowa.

Jones, William R. - Corporal - Company A - Enlisted August 8, 1861. Transferred to regular army November 17, 1862.

Jones, William T. - Private - Company K - Enlisted from Bloomington, Illinois, October 19, 1861. Discharged October 26, 1864 upon completion of military service.

Joyce, Patrick F. - Private - Company F - Enlisted from Waukegan, Illinois, January 21, 1864. Promoted Corporal June 7, 1865. Mustered out with the regiment, December 6, 1865.

— K —

Kahler, Lloyd W. - Private - Company E - Enlisted February 24, 1864. Mustered out with the regiment, December 6, 1865.

Kalsthoff, Henry - Private - Company C - Enlisted from Chicago, Illinois, September 6, 1861. Taken prisoner May 23, 1862 near Warrenton Junction, Virginia,; was paroled and exchanged; recaptured May 30, 1862 near Front Royal, Virginia; was paroled and exchanged again. Veteran. Mustered out with the regiment, December 6, 1865.

Kame, Dennis - Private - Company F - Enlisted from Sandoval, Illinois, August 15, 1861. Died at Pittsburgh, Pennsylvania, November 1, 1861. Cause not recorded.

Kame, James M. - Private - Company F - Enlisted from Chicago, Illinois, August 22, 1861. Taken prisoner May 1, 1862 at Strasburg, Virginia. Died September 23, 1862 at Camp Parole, Annapolis, Maryland.

Katillinek, Albert - Private - Company G - Enlisted from Thornton, Illinois, August 15, 1861. Veteran. Promoted Corporal March 1, 1865; promoted Sergeant July 1, 1865. Mustered out with the regiment, December 6, 1865.

Kark, Frederick - Private - Company B - Enlisted from Bloomington, Illinois, August 5, 1861. Discharged March 3, 1863 for disability.

Karr, Elisha - Private - Company E - Enlisted from Iroquois County, Illinois, October 28, 1861. Killed May 14, 1864 at Drewry's Bluff, Virginia.

Kautz, George - Private - Company H - Enlisted March 31, 1865. Mustered out with the regiment, December 6, 1865.

Kearney, Michael - Private - Company C - Enlisted from Chicago, Illinois, February 24, 1864. Mustered out with the regiment, December 6, 1865.

Keepers, William A. - Corporal - Company A - Enlisted August 5, 1861. Veteran. Wounded at Fort Gregg, Virginia. Promoted to Sergeant April 2, 1865. Mustered out with the regiment, December 6, 1865.

Keith, E. H. - Corporal - Company I - Enlisted from LeRoy, Illinois, September 4, 1861. Transferred and promoted Hospital Steward, U. S. Army, September 2, 1862. Discharge information unknown.

Kelley, William T. - Private - Company E - Enlisted from Wesley, Illinois, November 13, 1861. Promoted Corporal May 1, 1863. Veteran. Promoted to Sergeant March 1, 1865. Mustered out with the regiment, December 6, 1865.

Kelly, John - Private - Company E - Enlisted from Orbisonia, Pennsylvania, February 12, 1862. Promoted Corporal January 1, 1864. Wounded June 17, 1864 in the shoulder. Wounded in the leg and side August 16, 1864. Died of wounds October 31, 1864, in the hospital.

Kelly, John - Private - Company F - Enlisted from Waukegan, Illinois, February 12, 1864. Wounded in the hand October 28, 1864 in battle near Darbytown Cross-Roads, Virginia. Mustered out July 15, 1865.

Kelly, John A. - Private - Company B - Enlisted from Chicago, Illinois, February 6, 1864. Transferred to Veteran Reserve Corps. Discharge information unknown.

Kelly, William - Private - Company E - Enlisted February 21, 1865. Mustered out with the regiment, December 6, 1865.

Kelsey, Albert - Private - Company E - Enlisted March 30, 1865. Mustered out with the regiment, December 6, 1865.

Kemp, Charles H. - Private - Company F - Enlisted September 21, 1864. Mustered out with the regiment, December 6, 1865.

Kemph, Fred - Private - Company F - Enlisted from Chicago, Illinois, September 28, 1861. Veteran. Wounded in the arm May 16, 1864 at the battle of Drewry's Bluff, Virginia. Mustered out with the regiment, December 6, 1865.

Kemph, William - Private - Company F - Enlisted from Lockport, Illinois, August 22, 1861. Veteran. Mustered out with the regiment, December 6, 1865.

Kendall, John - Private - Company C - Enlisted from Ocoya, Illinois, August 28, 1861. Promoted Corporal September 1, 1863. Discharged September 10, 1864 upon completion of military service.

Kendall, Neriah B. - Private - Company G - Enlisted from Joliet, Illinois, August 9, 1861. Promoted Corporal January 1, 1862. Veteran. Wounded in the head and taken prisoner May 16, 1864 at Drewry's Bluff, Virginia. Sent to Libby Prison for three months. Promoted Sergeant August 15, 1864, First Sergeant November 1, 1864, First Lieutenant April 29, 1865. Promoted Captain of the Company July 11, 1865. Mustered out with the regiment, December 6, 1865.

Kenhower, Thomas - Private - Company I - Enlisted April 12, 1865. Mustered out with the regiment, December 6, 1865.

Kennedy, Dennis - Private - Company B - Enlisted from Chicago, Illinois, October 25, 1861. Promoted Corporal January 1, 1863. Veteran. Killed August 14, 1864 in a skirmish at Deep Run, Virginia.

Kennedy, Thomas M. - Private - Company F - Enlisted from Antioch, Illinois, February 22, 1864. Wounded in the head August 16, 1864. Taken prisoner. Died in prison at Richmond, Virginia from wounds in September 1864.

Kennedy, Thomas W. - Private - Company F - Enlisted from Antioch, Illinois, February 22, 1864. Wounded August 16, 1864 at the battle of Deep Run, Virginia and left on the field. Reported as missing. [Adjutant General's Report lists him as "died in Virginia, August 16, 1864."]

Kennedy, William - Private - Company C - Enlisted from New Michigan, Illinois, August 12, 1861. Was discharged for disability.

Kennicott, Amasa - Captain - Company F - Commissioned August 27, 1861. Resigned August 27, 1862.

Keys, Daniel T. - Private - Company I - Enlisted April 5, 1865. Mustered out with the regiment, December 6, 1865.

Kidder, Lesmore D. - First Lieutenant - Company B - Enlisted at Bloomington, Illinois, August 12, 1861. Promoted to First Lieutenant December 24, 1862. Wounded May 16, 1864 at Drewry's Bluff, Virginia. In charge of ambulance train at the battle and was wounded in the leg. Was almost captured, but was able to escape despite badly fractured and shattered limb. Discharged February 9, 1865 upon completion of military service.

Killfoyl, James - Private - Company A - Enlisted September 10, 1861. Deserted March 17, 1864.

Kilmer, Egbert - Private - Company K - Enlisted from Marseilles, Illinois, August 14, 1861. Discharged October 26, 1864 upon completion of military service.

Kimbler, Benjamin E. - Private - Company I - Enlisted from LeRoy, Illinois, September 18, 1861. Discharged September 12, 1862 for disability.

Kimbler, Charles W. - Private - Company H - Enlisted from Downs, Illinois, May 28, 1862. Wounded and taken prisoner August 16, 1864 at Deep Run, Virginia. Discharged June 28, 1865 upon completion of military service.

Kimbler, Franklin - Corporal - Company I - Enlisted from LeRoy, Illinois, September 4, 1861. Reduced to the ranks March 6, 1862. Discharged September 11, 1864 upon completion of military service.

Kimbler, William - Private - Company I - Enlisted from LeRoy, Illinois, September 4, 1861. Discharged September 13, 1864 upon completion of military service.

King, George B. - Private - Company H - Enlisted from LeRoy, Illinois, March 4, 1862. Died of disease at Hilton Head, South Carolina, August 7, 1863.

Kingsbury, Elisha - Second Lieutenant - Company E - Enlisted from Wilmington, Illinois, September 12, 1861. Promoted Sergeant; promoted Second Lieutenant January 2, 1863. Wounded in the arm, May 16, 1864 at the battle of Drewry's Bluff, Virginia. Bone shattered so severely that amputation was necessary. Mustered out of service October 16, 1864 by reason of disability.

Kinnaw, Thomas - Private - Company D - Enlisted from Odgon, Illinois, September 21, 1861. Veteran. Wounded in the thigh August 16, 1864 at Darbytown Cross-Roads, Virginia. Absent, sick and wounded at muster out of regiment. In 1889 he was living at Kansas City, Missouri.

Kinney, Barney - Private - Company D - Enlisted February 22, 1865. Mustered out with the regiment, December 6, 1865.

Kinney, John - Private - Company D - Enlisted from Lane, Illinois, September 27, 1861. Veteran. Promoted Corporal April 1, 1865. Deserted June 25, 1865.

Kinney, Patrick - Private - Company D - Enlisted from Oregon, Illinois, September 22, 1861. Wounded January 3, 1862 at Bath, West Virginia. Discharged December 1, 1862 for disability. Re-enlisted February 25, 1864. Taken prisoner May 16, 1864 at Drewry's Bluff, Virginia; paroled and exchanged. Killed August 16, 1864 at Darbytown Cross-Roads, Virginia.

Kinney, Thomas - Private - Company E - Enlisted from Wilmington, Illinois, October 2, 1861. Wounded in the hand August 16, 1864 at of Deep Run, Virginia. Discharged June 20, 1865 for disability.

Kinsie, Franklin - Private - Company C - Enlisted August 20, 1861. Deserted December 3, 1864.

Kipp, John - Corporal - Company K - Enlisted from Marseilles, Illinois, August 14, 1861. Promoted Corporal August 1, 1863. Veteran. Wounded October 13, 1864 at the battle of Darbytown Cross-Roads, Virginia and died from his wounds November 5, 1864 in Chesapeake Hospital. Born at Chatham Four-Corners, Columbia County, New York in 1841. Buried in the U. S. National Cemetery at Hampton, Virginia, near Fort Monroe.

Kirby, John W. - Private - Company I - Enlisted from Santa Anna, Illinois, September 4, 1861. Wounded in the thigh May 20, 1864 at Ware Bottom Church, Virginia. Discharged April 13, 1865 for disability from wounds.

Kirschner, Thomas - Private - Company I - Enlisted from Okaw, Illinois, April 12, 1865. Mustered out November 23, 1865.

Kirkman, William G. - Private - Company K - Enlisted from Marengo, Illinois, August 19, 1861. Detailed as telegraph operator. Discharged August 19, 1864 upon completion of military service. Had two brothers, Albert, lost his life at Memphis, Tennessee, while on the way to rejoin his regiment. The other brother, M. M., was employed by the Chicago and Northwestern Railway as Comptroller.

Kitchens, Chapman - Private - Company E - Enlisted April 12, 1865. Mustered out with the regiment, December 6, 1865.

Klumpp, Jacob B. - Private - Company G - Enlisted from Peoria, Illinois, September 4, 1861. Veteran. Promoted Corporal October 12, 1864; promoted Sergeant May 1, 1865. While at Norfolk was detached as overseer of the Baxter Farm, worked by free Negroes. Mustered out with the regiment, December 6, 1865.

Klumpp, William - Private - Company G - Enlisted from Peoria, Illinois, August 30, 1861. Died at Morris Island, South Carolina, October 2, 1863. Cause not recorded.

Knapp, Cyrus F. - First Lieutenant - Company D - Enlisted as a Sergeant from Chicago, Illinois, August 12, 1861. Promoted Second Lieutenant September 4, 1862. Promoted First Lieutenant September 11, 1862. Wounded August 16, 1864 in the shoulder at the battle of Deep Run, Virginia. Mustered out December 17, 1864. It was reported that he moved to some place in Michigan, where it is reported, he died.

Knowles, Benjamin F. - Private - Company A - Enlisted August 22, 1861. Injured in the leg by a runaway wagon at Cumberland, Maryland. Discharged for disability July 22, 1862. In 1889 he was living in Chicago.

Knute, James - Private - Company C - Enlisted February 20, 1865. Was a substitute. Mustered out with the regiment, December 6, 1865.

Kockinkiniper, Francis - Private - Company K - Enlisted February 14, 1865. Was a substitute. Died at Richmond, Virginia, July 8, 1865. Cause not recorded.

Kohn, John - Private - Company H - Enlisted March 3, 1865. Mustered out with the regiment, December 6, 1865.

Kolldorf, Henry - Private - Company C - Enlisted from Lockport, Illinois, September 6, 1861. Veteran. Mustered out with the regiment, December 6, 1865.

Kramer, Jacob - Private - Company F - Enlisted from Bloomington, Illinois, September 8, 1861. Died June 14, 1864. Cause not recorded.

Krauskup, George - Sergeant - Company A - Enlisted August 5, 1861. Discharged February 5, 1862 for disability.

Kuyler, John W. - Private - Company D - Enlisted from Dwight, Illinois, September 5, 1861. Died October 24, 1861 at Dwight, Illinois. Cause not recorded.

Kyle, Joseph - Private - Company A - Enlisted October 8, 1864. Mustered out with the regiment, December 6, 1865.

— L —

Lace, Philip M. - Band Leader - Regimental Band - Enlisted September 22, 1861. Discharged by order of the War Department, June 4, 1862. Re-enlisted from Pontiac, Illinois, January 5, 1864. Played in Band of 1864 & 1865. Mustered out with the regiment, December 6, 1865. Died from tuberculosis in 1872 and is buried at Channahon, Illinois.

Lace, William C. - Musician - Played in Band of 1864 & 1865. Mustered out with the regiment, December 6, 1865.

Lacey, James L. - Private - Company D - Enlisted from Oregon, Illinois, September 21, 1861. Taken prisoner January 3, 1862 at Bath, West Virginia. Discharged June 6, 1862 for disability.

Lacey, Thomas - Private - Company C - Enlisted from Pontiac, Illinois, August 12, 1861. Transferred to Douglas Brigade.

Ladd, Atticus A. - Musician, 3rd Class - Enlisted in Company G from Chicago, Illinois, August 6, 1861. Transferred to regimental band October 5, 1861. Discharged June 4, 1862 by order of the War Department. Re-enlisted from Joliet, Illinois, October 27, 1862. Discharged October 27, 1865 upon completion of military service. In 1889 he was living in San Francisco, California.

Lafferty, William S. - Private - Company B - Enlisted from Bloomington, Illinois, February 24, 1864. On furlough at muster out of the regiment.

Lake, David - Private - Company F - Enlisted from Chicago, Illinois, September 28, 1861. Veteran. Promoted Corporal October 4, 1864. Wounded April 2, 1865 during the assault on Fort Gregg, Virginia. Discharged July 16, 1865 for disability.

Lakey, James A. - Private - Company H - Enlisted March 3, 1865. Promoted Corporal September 1, 1865. Mustered out with the regiment, December 6, 1865.

Lamb, M. W. - Private - Company I - Enlisted from LeRoy, Illinois, October 13, 1861. Veteran. Wounded in the head May 20, 1864. Died from wounds, October 29, 1864.

Lamb, William W. - First Lieutenant - Company F - Enlisted from Sandoval, Illinois, August 15, 1861. Corporal. Promoted Sergeant February 13, 1862. Veteran. Wounded in the foot August 16, 1864. Promoted First Lieutenant April 1, 1865. Killed at Fort Gregg, Virginia, April 2, 1865.

Lambert, William J. - Musician - Enlisted in Company G October 23, 1862. Transferred to regimental band. Discharged April 1864 by order of the War Department.

Lammy, Lewis H. - Private - Company K - Enlisted from Chicago, Illinois, August 6, 1861. Discharged October 5, 1863 for disability at Morris Island, South Carolina.

Lane, Edward H. - Musician, Second Class - Enlisted October 2, 1861. Taken prisoner at Strasburg, Virginia, May 1862. Paroled and discharged by order of the War Department, June 4, 1862.

Lane, William J. - Private - Company B - Enlisted from Bloomington, Illinois, August 27, 1861. Veteran. Promoted Corporal May 1, 1865. Mustered out with the regiment, December 6, 1865. In 1889 he was living in Hillsboro, Texas.

Langley, John - Private - Company D - Enlisted April 7, 1865. Mustered out with the regiment, December 6, 1865.

Lankenaw, Henry - Private - Company D - Enlisted from Lane, Illinois, August 21, 1861. Veteran. Killed during the battle of Deep Run, Virginia, August 16, 1864.

Lansing, John - Private - Company E - Enlisted February 26, 1865. Deserted August 5, 1865.

Larkins, John M. - Private - Company C - Enlisted from Esmond, Illinois, August 22, 1861. Veteran. Wounded October 13, 1864 at Darbytown Cross-Roads; arm amputated. Discharged June 19, 1865 for disability.

Larrett, Charles - Private - Company F - Enlisted from Chicago, Illinois, September 29, 1861. Veteran. Killed at Fort Gregg, Virginia, April 2, 1865.

Larsen, Thomas - Private - Company D - Enlisted from Lane, Illinois, September 19, 1861. Taken prisoner January 3, 1862 at Bath, West Virginia; paroled and exchanged. Veteran. Promoted Corporal September 2, 1865. Mustered out with the regiment, December 6, 1865. In 1889 he was living on Eighteenth Street, Chicago, Illinois.

Latimer, James A. - Private - Company K - Enlisted from Marseilles, Illinois, August 14, 1861. Promoted Corporal September 6, 1862. Veteran. Wounded in the neck May 20, 1864 at Ware Bottom Church, Virginia. Said to be the first man over rebel entrenchments during the assault at Deep Run, Virginia. Mustered out with the regiment, December 6, 1865.

Lattimer, Louis - Private - Company H - Enlisted February 15, 1865. Discharged May 27, 1865 for disability.

Laughlin, John - Private - Company E - Enlisted from Huntington, Pennsylvania, February 1, 1862. Died February 11, 1862 in the hospital of brain fever.

Lawler, Michael - Private - Company A - Enlisted September 16, 1861. Discharged July 1, 1862 for disability.

Lawrence, Daniel W. - Private - Company H - Enlisted March 1, 1865. Mustered out with the regiment, December 6, 1865.

Lee, Ditson - Private - Company E - Enlisted from Essex, Illinois, February 24, 1864. Taken prisoner May 16, 1864 at Drewry's Bluff, Virginia; paroled at Savannah, Georgia, November 19, 1864. Mustered out with the regiment, December 6, 1865.

Lee, Jefferson - Private - Company D - Enlisted September 30, 1861. Discharged September 30, 1864 upon completion of military service.

Lee, Orville - Private - Company K - Enlisted February 27, 1864. Wounded in the foot August 16, 1864. Mustered out with the regiment, December 6, 1865.

Leibo, Arthur B. - Private - Company B - Enlisted from Bloomington, Illinois, August 12, 1861. Veteran. Promoted Corporal January 1, 1864. Wounded in the foot May 20, 1864 at the battle of Ware Bottom Church, Virginia. Served in the Color-guard. Mustered out with the regiment, December 6, 1865.

Lemon, James D. - First Lieutenant - Company I - Enlisted from Santa Anna, Illinois, September 4, 1861. Promoted First Lieutenant May 14, 1862. Wounded in the chest August 16, 1864 at the battle of Deep Run, Virginia. Died in the hospital from his wounds, August 20, 1864.

Lemon, George W. - Private - Company B - Enlisted from Bloomington, Illinois, February 24, 1864. Wounded May 16, 1864 at the battle of Drewry's Bluff, Virginia. Mustered out with the regiment, December 6, 1865.

Lemon, Richard A. - Private - Company I - Enlisted from LeRoy, Illinois, February 26, 1864. Discharged June 1, 1864 by order of the War Department.

Levally, Charles T. - Private - Company E - Enlisted from Chicago, Illinois, March 14, 1864. Severely wounded in the right foot September 10, 1864 near Petersburg, Virginia. Transferred to Veteran Reserve Corps, November 3, 1865.

Lewis, Andrew J. - Private - Company G - Enlisted from Amboy, Illinois, August 9, 1861. Died of typhoid fever on Folly Island, South Carolina, July 4, 1863.

Lewis, Hermann F. - Private - Company B - Enlisted from Bloomington, Illinois, September 25, 1861. Discharged February 10, 1863 for disability.

Lewis, Jacob L. - Private - Company H - Enlisted from LeRoy, Illinois, March 10, 1862. Discharged March 23, 1865 upon completion of military service.

Lewis, John - Private - Company G - Enlisted from Amboy, Illinois, August 19, 1861. Discharged December 21, 1863 for disability.

Lewis, John - Musician - Played in Band of 1864 & 1865. Mustered out with the regiment, December 6, 1865.

Lewis, John - Private - Company K - Enlisted January 5, 1864. Taken prisoner May 16, 1864 at the battle of Drewry's Bluff, Virginia. Died in Andersonville Prison in June 1864 of disease.

Lewis, Lorenzo - Private - Company H - Enlisted from Clark, Illinois, June 26, 1862. Discharged June 20, 1865 upon completion of military service.

Light, Austin - Colonel - Received his commission July 22, 1861. Dismissed from the service of the United States, November 25, 1861. In 1889 he was living in Chicago, Illinois

Lilley, James - Private - Company C - Enlisted from Rook's Creek, Illinois, August 22, 1861. Wounded in the shoulder May 16, 1864 at Drewry's Bluff, Virginia. Discharged October 11, 1864 upon completion of military service.

Linton, George A. - Private - Company K - Enlisted from Bloomington, Illinois, September 21, 1861. Discharged September 21, 1864 upon completion of military service.

Linton, Jonathan F. - Regimental Quartermaster - Commissioned First Lieutenant of Company D, August 11, 1861. Promoted to Regimental Quartermaster June 12, 1862. Discharged July 15, 1862.

Linton, Samuel S. - Major - Regimental Staff - Commissioned Captain of Company D, August 9, 1861. Wounded through the side in April 1862 near Winchester, Virginia. Promoted Major January 13, 1863. Wounded through the lung, May 16, 1864 at Drewry's Bluff, Virginia. Mustered out November 10, 1864. Born in Miami County, Indiana, April 21, 1836, but was raised in Warren County, Ohio, about fifty miles from Cincinnati, near the village of Waynesville. After his muster out, he moved to Toledo, Ohio and engaged in the milling business. In 1876 he was elected sheriff of the County. He served for two years and moved to Missouri for a year and a half and then moved to Minneapolis, Minnesota where he established the grain commission, S. S. Linton & Co.

Littleton, Van Buren - Private - Company I - Enlisted from Bloomington, Illinois, September 24, 1864. Discharged June 21, 1865 by order of the War Department.

Littleton, William S. - Private - Company I - Enlisted from Mahomet, Illinois, September 4, 1861. Died from disease in the hospital at Cumberland, Maryland, February 25, 1862.

Litwiller, Charles - Private - Company F - Enlisted from Avon, Illinois, February 29, 1864. Wounded May 20, 1864. Mustered out with the regiment, December 6, 1865.

Livingstone, Lilsyth - Private - Company G - Enlisted from Chicago, Illinois, March 12, 1864. Deserted October 12, 1865.

Lonebarger, George - Private - Company I - Enlisted from LeRoy, Illinois, September 4, 1861. Veteran. Wounded May 16, 1864 at Drewry's Bluff, Virginia. Mustered out with the regiment, December 6, 1865.

Long, William P. - Private - Company C - Enlisted August 12, 1861. Promoted Corporal May 10, 1862. Discharged July 4, 1862 for disability.

Lookinbill, John H. - Private - Company C - Enlisted from Zion, Illinois, April 13, 1865. Mustered out with the regiment, December 6, 1865.

Lord, Wallace - First Lieutenant - Company C - Commissioned August 12, 1861. Resigned January 4, 1863 by reason of poor health. In 1889 he was living at Pontiac, Illinois engaged in contracting and building.

Lott, Theodore - Private - Company F - Enlisted from Washington, February 24, 1864. Died very suddenly of a heart attack June 5, 1864 while coming in from picket duty under fire.

Loughram, John - Private - Company F - Enlisted from Chicago, Illinois, September 6, 1861. Discharged May 8, 1863 for disability.

Loughram, Owen - Private - Company F - Enlisted from Sandoval, Illinois, August 15, 1861. Promoted Corporal December 7, 1861. Veteran. Promoted Sergeant February 1, 1864. Killed in battle October 13, 1864 at Darbytown Cross-Roads, Virginia.

Love, James - Private - Company G - Enlisted February 8, 1865. Mustered out with the regiment, December 6, 1865.

Low, Richard - Private - Company D - Enlisted February 23, 1865. Mustered out with the regiment, December 6, 1865.

Lucas, Henry - Private - Company H - Enlisted from Randolph, Illinois, March 31, 1862. Veteran. Wounded in the arm October 13, 1864. Promoted Corporal May 10, 1865. Discharged June 24, 1865 for disability.

Luce, Charles - Private - Company K - Enlisted from Marseilles, Illinois, December 16, 1863. Mustered out with the regiment, December 6, 1865.

Luce, William C. - Private - Company D - Enlisted from Chicago, Illinois, February 22, 1864. Mustered out with the regiment, December 6, 1865.

Lucen, Thomas - Private - Company D - Enlisted from Lane, Illinois, September 19, 1861. Veteran. Mustered out with the regiment, December 6, 1865.

Luscomb, Albert - Private - Company G - Enlisted from Bellevue, Michigan, August 15, 1861. Wounded and taken prisoner May 16, 1864 at the battle of Drewry's Bluff, Virginia. Died in prison at Petersburg, Virginia, from wounds June 26, 1864.

Lusk, Palmer - Private - Company F - Enlisted from Avon, Illinois, February 2, 1864. Wounded and taken prisoner May 16, 1864 at Drewry's Bluff, Virginia. Died in prisoner from his wounds June 5, 1864 at Andersonville, Georgia.

Lynch, John - Private - Company A - Enlisted October 31, 1861. Discharged upon completion of military service, October 30, 1864.

Lynch, John - Private - Company B - Enlisted March 2, 1865. Died March 30, 1865 at Point of Rocks Hospital, Virginia.

Lynn, George W. - Private - Company D - Enlisted from Lane, Virginia, September 21, 1861. Promoted Corporal November 1, 1862. Veteran. Wounded May 20, 1864 in the chest at Ware Bottom Church, Virginia. Wounded in the head on June 2, 1864. Promoted Sergeant September 1,

1864. Wounded in the thigh April 2, 1865 during the assault on Fort Gregg, Virginia. Mustered out with the regiment, December 6, 1865.

Lyon, Martin V. - Private - Company I - Enlisted from LeRoy, Illinois, September 4, 1861. Died from disease in the hospital at Hancock, Maryland, January 18, 1862.

Lyon, William W. - Corporal - Company I - Enlisted from LeRoy, Illinois, September 4, 1861. Discharged for disability July 7, 1862.

Lyons, George - Private - Company A - Enlisted August 5, 1861. Died February 23, 1863 on St. Helena Island, South Carolina. Cause not recorded.

Lyons, John - Private - Company D - Enlisted from Lane, Illinois, September 27, 1861. Veteran. Promoted Corporal April 1, 1865. Mustered out with the regiment, December 6, 1865.

Lyons, Sydney - Private - Company E - Enlisted from Florence, Illinois, September 12, 1861. Veteran. Wounded in the jaw October 13, 1864 at the battle of Darbytown Cross Roads, Virginia. Mustered out with the regiment, December 6, 1865.

Lysle, John - Private - Company I - Enlisted from LeRoy, Illinois, September 20, 1861. Transferred to Veteran Reserve Corps. Discharged September 20, 1864 upon completion of military service.

— M —

Magee, William T. - Private - Company G - Enlisted from Macomb, Illinois, September 5, 1861. Veteran. On detached service as hospital cook. Mustered out with the regiment, December 6, 1865.

Mahan, John - Private - Company E - Enlisted from Pittsburgh, Pennsylvania, February 24, 1861. Deserted April 20, 1862.

Maher, John - Private - Company A - Enlisted October 22, 1861. Discharged October 2, 1864 upon completion of military service.

Maher, John - Private - Company K - Enlisted February 6, 1864. Wounded in the hand May 20, 1864. Mustered out with the regiment, December 6, 1865.

Mahone, Michael - Private - Company A - Enlisted April 4, 1865. Mustered out with the regiment, December 6, 1865.

Mallett, Cyran - Private - Company E - Enlisted from Chicago, Illinois, March 24, 1864. Wounded October 13, 1864 at Darbytown Cross-Roads, Virginia. Deserted October 3, 1865.

Malone, Andrew J. - Private - Company C - Enlisted from Rook's Creek, Illinois, August 22, 1861. Veteran. Promoted Corporal September 4, 1864; promoted Sergeant May 1, 1865. Mustered out with the regiment, December 6, 1865.

Malone, William H. - Private - Company C - Enlisted from Rook's Creek, Illinois, August 22, 1861. Wounded in the face June 18, 1864 near Chester Station, Virginia. Discharged in September 1864 upon completion of military service.

Maloney, Richard - Private - Company H - Enlisted from Wilmington, Illinois, March 13, 1862. Discharged March 23, 1865 upon completion of military service.

Malony, James - Private - Company A - Enlisted December 4, 1863. Mustered out with the regiment, December 6, 1865.

Mann, Orrin L. - Colonel of Regiment - Commissioned Major July 22, 1861. Commissioned Lieutenant-Colonel December 1861. Seriously wounded in the left leg May 20, 1864 while leading a "charge" on the rebel works near Bermuda Hundred, Virginia. Promoted Colonel and Brigadier-General by "brevet" May 11, 1865. Mustered out with the regiment, December 6, 1865. Born in Geauga County, Ohio, November 25, 1833. His grandfathers on both the paternal and maternal side served in the Revolutionary War, and several of his uncles served in the War of 1812. General Mann's home was in Chicago. He was active in Republican politics and served in several elective offices.

Manzer, James - Private - Company F - Enlisted from Waukegan, Illinois, January 25, 1864. Wounded May 16, 1864 at Drewry's Bluff, Virginia. Discharged June 22, 1865 for disability from wounds.

Marcellious, Jacob S. - Private - Company I - Enlisted from Delta, Illinois, September 14, 1861. Veteran. Wounded in the leg October 13, 1864 at Darbytown Cross-Roads, Virginia. Promoted Corporal August 1, 1865. Mustered out with the regiment, December 6, 1865.

Marcellious, John J. - Private - Company I - Enlisted from Delta, Illinois, February 14, 1864. Discharged May 2, 1864 for disability.

Marrigold, Charles L. - Private - Company B - Enlisted from Chicago, Illinois, August 3, 1861. Promoted Corporal July 1, 1863. Veteran. Reduced to the ranks November 1865. Mustered out with the regiment, December 6, 1865.

Marsh, Lewis - Private - Company K - Enlisted from Marseilles, Illinois, August 6, 1861. Veteran. Wounded in the arm August 16, 1864 at Deep Run, Virginia. With his shattered arm, he assisted in carrying wounded men off the field. Arm amputated. Discharged November 19, 1864 for disability from wound.

Marshall, Frank B. - Adjutant - Commissioned August 5, 1861. Was on recruiting duty during most of his service. Resigned July 15, 1862.

Marshall, Peter - Private - Company F - Enlisted from Homer, Illinois, February 27, 1864. Wounded in the arm October 13, 1864 at the battle of Deep Run, Virginia. Mustered out with the regiment, December 6, 1865.

Martin, Albert - Private - Company D - Enlisted from Springfield, Illinois, December 17, 1862. Mustered out with the regiment, December 6, 1865.

Martin, Daniel J. J. - Private - Company H - Enlisted from Santa Anna, Illinois, June 13, 1862. Discharged June 20, 1865 upon completion of military service.

Martin, James - Private - Company A - Enlisted September 10, 1861. Mustered out with the regiment, December 6, 1865.

Martin, John - Private - Company D - Enlisted from Lane, Illinois, August 21, 1861. Taken prisoner January 3, 1862 at Bath, West Virginia. Discharged for disability on January 15, 1865.

Martin, John - Private - Company B - Enlisted from Bloomington, Illinois, August 15, 1861. Promoted Corporal June 1, 1863. Promoted to Sergeant September 1, 1863. Veteran. Killed August 16, 1864 at the battle of Deep Run, Virginia.

Martin, William - Private - Company E - Enlisted from Chicago, Illinois, March 8, 1864. Mustered out with the regiment, December 6, 1865.

Martuze, John - Private - Company D - Enlisted from Chicago, Illinois, September 13, 1861. Veteran. Wounded May 20, 1864 in the thigh at Ware Bottom Church, Virginia. Mustered out with the regiment, December 6, 1865 as a Corporal.

Marvin, Hannibal S. - Private - Company H - Enlisted from Chicago, Illinois, October 9, 1861. Deserted February 27, 1862.

Massey, Langdon S. - Private - Company K - Enlisted from Marseilles, Illinois, December 16, 1863. Mustered out with the regiment, December 6, 1865.

Matravious, John - Private - Company D - Enlisted from Lake, Illinois, January 6, 1865. Mustered out with the regiment, December 6, 1865.

Maxton, William - Private - Company K - Enlisted from Marseilles, Illinois, August 6, 1861. Veteran. Mustered out with the regiment, December 6, 1865.

May, William H. - Private - Company G - Enlisted from Genesee, Illinois, August 28, 1861. Killed May 16, 1864 at the battle of Drewry's Bluff, Virginia.

Mayer, Moses - Private - Company E - Enlisted from Florence, Illinois, September 21, 1861. Veteran. Wounded in both thighs at Ware Bottom Church, Virginia. Mustered out with the regiment, December 6, 1865.

McAree, Francis - Private - Company F - Enlisted January 28, 1864. Mustered out with the regiment, December 6, 1865.

McCann, James - Private - Company B - Enlisted April 10, 1865. Mustered out with the regiment, December 6, 1865.

McCarnley, F. S. - Private - Company D - Enlisted from Lane, Illinois, August 21, 1861. Taken prisoner January 3, 1862 at Bath, West Virginia. Veteran. Wounded October 13, 1864 in the leg at Darbytown Cross-Roads, Virginia. Mustered out with the regiment, December 6, 1865.

McCarthy, Michael - Private - Company F - Enlisted from Northfield, Illinois, February 19, 1864. Mustered out with the regiment, December 6, 1865.

McCarthy, Peter - Private - Company A - Enlisted August 12, 1861. Died June 12, 1862 in Alexandria, Virginia. Cause not recorded.

McClaime, William J. - Private - Company C - Enlisted February 28, 1865. Killed April 2, 1865 at the assault on Fort Gregg, Virginia.

McCoy, Orlando - Private - Company I - Enlisted from LeRoy, Illinois, February 23, 1864. Mustered out with the regiment, December 6, 1865.

McCracken, Solomon - Private - Company G - Enlisted from Thornton, Illinois, February 13, 1865. Mustered out with the regiment, December 6, 1865.

McCulloch, John - Private - Company A - Enlisted August 15, 1861. Discharged September 10, 1864 upon completion of military service.

McCullum, Alexander - Private - Company A - Enlisted from Gardner, Illinois, September 14, 1861. Veteran. Promoted to Corporal October 15, 1865. Was transferred from Company E November 16, 1861. Mustered out with the regiment, December 6, 1865.

McCurley, Michael - Private - Company F - Enlisted February 9, 1864. Mustered out with the regiment, December 6, 1865.

McDonald, James - Private - Company A - Enlisted September 10, 1861. Discharged September 10, 1864 upon completion of military service.

McDowell, George - Private - Company K - Enlisted March 3, 1865. Deserted May 23, 1865.

McDowell, Riley - Private - Company K - Enlisted February 13, 1865. Substitute. Mustered out with the regiment, December 6, 1865.

McElfreet, James - Private - Company C - Enlisted from Chicago, Illinois, February 16, 1864. Mustered out with the regiment, December 6, 1865.

McGinnis, Elijah - Private - Company F - Enlisted April 5, 1865. Died in the hospital September 30, 1865. Cause not recorded.

McGinnis, John B. - Private - Company F - Enlisted April 5, 1865. Mustered out with the regiment, December 6, 1865.

McGinnis, William - Private - Company F - Enlisted April 5, 1865. Discharged August 18, 1865 for disability.

McGinnis, William - Private - Company H - Enlisted from Kingston Mines, Illinois, February 1, 1862. Deserted July 4, 1862.

McGlasson, Leonard - Private - Company A - Enlisted April 1, 1865. Mustered out with the regiment, December 6, 1865.

McGrade, James - Private - Company I - Enlisted from McLean, Illinois, October 8, 1861. Discharged October 8, 1864 upon completion of military service.

McGraine, Constance - Private - Company A - Enlisted April 10, 1865. Mustered out with the regiment, December 6, 1865.

McGregor, Alonzo - Private - Company C - Enlisted from Pontiac, Illinois, August 22, 1861. Discharged September 10, 1864 upon completion of military service.

McGregor, Charles A. - Private - Company C - Enlisted from Chicago, Illinois, February 22, 1864 and detailed to the regimental band. Played in Band of 1864 & 1865. Mustered out with the regiment, December 6, 1865. After the war he entered into the pharmacy business and later had an Indian Agency out in Indian Terriroty. In 1889 he was living at Pontiac, Illinois.

McIntosh, James - Private - Company F - Enlisted from Bloomington, Illinois, October 5, 1861. Discharged June 1862 for disability.

McIntosh, James W. - Private - Company F - Enlisted from Bloomington, Illinois, August 27, 1861. Promoted Corporal November 1, 1862. Veteran: Mustered out with the regiment, December 6, 1865.

McIntosh, John W. - Captain - Company F - Commissioned August 7, 1861. Promoted Captain August 7, 1862. Dismissed from the service May 30, 1863.

McKee, Joseph - Private - Company G - Enlisted from Bremen, Illinois, August 13, 1862. Discharged November 25, 1862 for disability. Re-enlisted January 4, 1864. Wounded August 14, 1864 in a skirmish near Deep Bottom, Virginia. Promoted Corporal January 1, 1865. Again wounded April 1, 1865 at the assault on Fort Gregg, Virginia. Discharged July 22, 1865 for disability from wounds.

McKendrick, Michael - Private - Company A - Enlisted December 26, 1863. Wounded in skirmish near Chester Station, Virginia, and taken prisoner June 16, 1864. No other details known.

McKilley, Charles A. - Private - Company I - Enlisted from LeRoy, Illinois, October 13, 1861. Promoted Corporal January 1, 1863. Wounded in the side May 16, 1864 at Drewry's Bluff, Virginia. Wounded again, April 2, 1865 at the assault on Fort Gregg, Virginia. Promoted Sergeant August 1, 1865. Discharged October 1, 1865 by order of the War Department.

McLain, Marion - Private - Company D - Enlisted December 17, 1862. Died July 3, 1863 at Folly Island, South Carolina. Cause not recorded.

McLain, William - Private - Company C - Enlisted February 28, 1865. Was a substitute. Died at Petersburg, Virginia, September 27, 1865. Cause not recorded.

McLain, William - Private - Company D - Enlisted January 6, 1865. Mustered out with the regiment, December 6, 1865.

McLarkey, Hugh - Private - Company F - Enlisted from Chicago, Illinois, September 16, 1861. Discharged August 25, 1862 for disability.

McLaughlin, Dennis - Private - Company G - Enlisted from Chicago, Illinois, September 1, 1861. Transferred to Company F, October 1, 1861. Discharged January 1862 for disability.

McLaughlin, John - Private - Company D - Enlisted April 7, 1865. Mustered out with the regiment, December 6, 1865.

McLaughlin, Patrick - Private - Company G - Enlisted from Bremen, Illinois, September 1, 1861. Transferred to Company F, October 1, 1861. Deserted October 1, 1861.

McMaster, James - Private - Company E - Enlisted from Wilmington, Illinois, October 6, 1861. Died December 9, 1861 at Williamsport, Maryland. Cause unknown.

McMiller, James - Private - Company D - Enlisted February 22, 1865. Mustered out with the regiment, December 6, 1865.

McMurry, W. C. - Sergeant - Company I - Enlisted from Santa Anna, Illinois, September 4, 1861. Taken prisoner May 16, 1864 at Drewry's Bluff, Virginia. Discharged March 16, 1865 upon completion of military service.

McNally, John - Private - Company H - Enlisted from LeRoy, Illinois, December 6, 1861. Promoted Corporal July 24, 1862. Reduced to the ranks November 3, 1862. Transferred to the Fourth U. S. Artillery, December 5, 1862. Discharge information unknown.

McNally, Michael - Private - Company C - Enlisted from Pontiac, Illinois, August 29, 1861. Veteran. Wounded in the hand May 16, 1864 near Ware Bottom Church, Virginia. Discharged April 25, 1865 for disability.

McNight, William - Private - Company A - Enlisted from St. Louis, Missouri, October 22, 1861. Discharged October 21, 1864 upon completion of military service.

McQuillen, Patrick - Private - Company A - Enlisted from Guilford, Illinois, October 8, 1864. Mustered out October 11, 1864.

McReading, Charles S. - Regimental Chaplain - Commissioned October 9, 1861 from Channahon, Illinois. Resigned August 9, 1862 due to poor health.

McTravis, John - Private - Company D - Enlisted January 6, 1865. Mustered out with the regiment, December 6, 1865.

Mears, D. C. - Musician, Second Class - Enlisted October 8, 1861. Discharged by order of the War Department, June 4, 1861.

Melody, Patrick H. - Private - Company F - Enlisted from Waukegan, Illinois, January 21, 1864. Promoted Corporal March 15, 1865. Mustered out with the regiment, December 6, 1865.

Mendenhall, Absalom - Corporal - Company H - Enlisted from Wilmington, Illinois, March 15, 1862. Discharged March 23, 1865 upon completion of military service.

Merrill, Almon - Private - Company E - Enlisted from Florence, Illinois, September 12, 1861. Veteran. Promoted Corporal March 4, 1864. Wounded May 16, 1864 at the battle of Drewry's Bluff, Virginia. Died of wounds July 16, 1864.

Merrifield, Samuel - Private - Company B - Enlisted from Bloomfield, Illinois, August 12, 1861. Veteran. Mustered out with the regiment, December 6, 1865.

Meyers, Jacob - Private - Company D - Enlisted from Martinsburg, West Virginia, February 28, 1862. Died at Beaufort, South Carolina, December 15, 1863, cause unknown.

Meyers, John - Private - Company G - Enlisted from Thornton, Illinois, August 26, 1861. Veteran. Wounded in the face and neck June 2, 1864 near Ware Bottom Church, Virginia. Bullet cut out from right tonsil where it had lodged. Was again wounded April 2, 1865 in the shoulder at the assault on Fort Gregg, Virginia. Was 16 years of age when he enlisted. Mustered out with the regiment, December 6, 1865. Born January 3, 1845. Relocated after the war to La Delle, Spink County, Dakota Territory.

Meyher, Caleb - Private - Company E - Enlisted January 13, 1864. Wounded June 18, 1864 near Ware Bottom Church, Virginia. Mustered out with the regiment, December 6, 1865.

Mick, Parker - Private - Company K - Enlisted from Marseilles, Illinois, September 10, 1861. Died of chronic diarrhea, November 24, 1863 in St. Augustine, Florida.

Middleton, Daniel - Private - Company H - Enlisted April 4, 1862. Deserted August 3, 1865.

Miles, Charles - Corporal - Company D - Enlisted from Lindenwood, Illinois, August 12, 1861. Discharged for disability May 30, 1862. In 1889 he was living at Oregon, Illinois.

Milks, Hermann - Private - Company E - Enlisted from Gardner, Illinois, September 12, 1861. Veteran. Promoted Corporal March 1, 1865. Mustered out with the regiment, December 6, 1865.

Miller, Albert - Private - Company I - Enlisted February 16, 1864. Taken prisoner at the battle of Drewry's Bluff, Virginia, May 16, 1864. Mustered out with the regiment, December 6, 1865.

Miller, Anthony - Private - Company B - Enlisted from Bloomington, Illinois, September 18, 1861. Discharged October 18, 1864 upon completion of military service.

Miller, Eliott S. - Private - Company B - Enlisted from Chicago, Illinois, August 12, 1861. Veteran. Wounded in the arm May 30, 1864. Promoted Corporal September 15, 1864. Promoted Sergeant September 14, 1865. Mustered out with the regiment, December 6, 1865. After his service, Miller relocated to Jamestown, Dakota Territory. He became a contractor and builder.

Miller, G. D. - Private - Company C - Enlisted September 29, 1861. Deserted February 24, 1862.

Miller, Jacob - Private - Company K - Enlisted February 21, 1865. Substitute. Mustered out with the regiment, December 6, 1865.

Miller, Jacob S. - Private - Company A - Enlisted August 5, 1861. Deserted September 18, 1861.

Miller, John - Private - Company D - Enlisted from Lane, Illinois, August 28, 1861. Veteran. Wounded April 2, 1865 at the assault on Fort Gregg, Virginia. Discharged July 15, 1865 for disability from wounds.

Miller, John B. - Private - Company H - Enlisted April 8, 1865. Mustered out with the regiment, December 6, 1865.

Miller, Nichols - Private - Company F - Enlisted from Chicago, Illinois, September 16, 1861. Deserted in August 1862.

Miller, William - Private - Company E - Enlisted February 24, 1865. Mustered out with the regiment, December 6, 1865.

Milliman, Minor W. - Major, Regimental Staff - Enlisted from Wesley, Illinois, September 12, 1861 into Company E. Promoted Sergeant May 26, 1862; promoted First Sergeant January 1, 1863. Veteran. Promoted Captain of Company E December 6, 1864. Transferred to Regimental Staff. Had command of eight companies of the Thirty-Ninth on April 9, 1865. They were the first infantry that faced Lee at Appomattox Court-House, Virginia. Mustered out with the regiment, December 6, 1865. After the war he moved to Silver Creek, Merrick County, Nebraska.

Mills, Andrew P. - Private - Company E - Enlisted from Beaver Creek, Illinois, April 12, 1865. Mustered out with the regiment, December 6, 1865.

Miltmore, A. - Private - Company F - Enlisted from Avon, Illinois, February 29, 1864. Died March 23, 1864 of brain fever.

Milton, Sovereign - Musician - Company A - Enlisted from Chicago, Illinois, September 14, 1861. Mustered out September 10, 1864 upon completion of military service.

Miner, John - Private - Company C - Enlisted February 17, 1865. Deserted June 15, 1865.

Mitchell, W. R. - Private - Company K - Enlisted February 13, 1865. Substitute. Mustered out with the regiment, December 6, 1865.

Mitchell, William C. - Sergeant - Company H - Enlisted from Wilmington, Illinois, March 9, 1862. Mustered out March 9, 1864 upon completion of military service.

Mizell, John W. - Private - Company K - Enlisted April 11, 1865. Was a substitute. Mustered out with the regiment, December 6, 1865.

Monnier, Charles - Private - Company A - Enlisted from Guilford, Illinois, October 8, 1864. Mustered out October 11, 1865.

Monroe, James - Private - Company E - Enlisted from Florence, Illinois, September 17, 1861. Veteran. Wounded May 16, 1864 at Drewry's Bluff, Virginia. Mustered out with the regiment, December 6, 1865.

Monroe, John - Private - Company E - Enlisted from Florence, Illinois, February 22, 1864. Wounded May 20, 1864 at Ware Bottom Church, Virginia. Taken prisoner April 9, 1865; paroled the same day at Appomattox Court-House, Virginia. Discharged April 26, 1865.

Montgomery, George - Private - Company D - Enlisted March 29, 1865. Mustered out with the regiment, December 6, 1865.

Mooney, John - Private - Company F - Enlisted from Bloomington, Illinois, August 19, 1861. Veteran. Wounded in the leg August 16, 1864 at Deep Run, Virginia. Mustered out with the regiment, December 6, 1865.

Moore, Anderson L. - Private - Company C - Enlisted from Indian Grove, Illinois, August 28, 1861. Veteran. Promoted Corporal September 26, 1864. Killed April 2, 1865 at the assault on Fort Gregg, Virginia.

Moore, James - Private - Company K - Enlisted from Marseilles, Illinois, September 3, 1861. Veteran. Mustered out with the regiment, December 6, 1865.

Moore, Richard - Private - Company D - Enlisted January 5, 1865. Discharged June 23, 1865 for disability.

Moore, Thomas - Private - Company F - Enlisted from Chicago, Illinois, August 2, 1861. Promoted Corporal November 1, 1862. Veteran. Wounded August 16, 1864 at Deep Run, Virginia Promoted

Sergeant March 6, 1865; promoted to First Sergeant June 1, 1865, and commissioned Second Lieutenant October 10, 1865. Mustered out with the regiment, December 6, 1865.

Moore, William - Private - Company D - Enlisted from Lane, Illinois, August 26, 1861. Discharged September 10, 1864 upon completion of military service.

Moore, William T. - Sergeant - Company F - Enlisted from Chicago, Illinois, September 27, 1861. Promoted Corporal October 20, 1861. Veteran. Wounded in the shoulder June 5, 1864 near Petersburg, Virginia. Promoted Sergeant August 5, 1864. Promoted First Lieutenant May 9, 1865. Mustered out with the regiment, December 6, 1865. Born in England, January 20, 1826. Emigrated to the United States in 1848, going to Milwaukee, Wisconsin. After the war he moved to Rockton, Winnebago County, Illinois.

Moran, John - Private - Company G - Enlisted October 12, 1864. Deserted August 16, 1865 at Norfolk, Virginia.

Morey, Oscar R. - Private - Company E - Enlisted from Florence, Illinois, February 24, 1864. Promoted Corporal May 16, 1865. Mustered out with the regiment, December 6, 1865.

Morgan, Carlos - Private - Company K - Enlisted from Marseilles, Illinois, August 27, 1861. Discharged August 26, 1862 for disability. Later enlisted in a New York regiment, and died in North Carolina.

Morgan, E. A. - Private - Company H - Enlisted from Paris, Illinois, June 28, 1862. Died April 1, 1865. Cause unknown.

Morgan, George M. - Private - Company E - Enlisted from Sheldon, Illinois, September 25, 1861. Wounded and taken prisoner May 16, 1864 at Drewry's Bluff, Virginia; paroled and exchanged. Discharged February 2, 1865 upon completion of military service.

Morgan, Thomas J. - Private - Company D - Enlisted February 25, 1865. Mustered out with the regiment, December 6, 1865.

Morgan, William H. - Private - Company D - Enlisted from Chicago, Illinois, February 29, 1864. Wounded October 13, 1864 at Darbytown Cross-Roads, Virginia. Discharged September 1, 1865 for disability from wounds.

Morgan, William M. - Private - Company C - Enlisted from Chicago, Illinois, January 21, 1864. Killed in battle June 2, 1864 near Ware Bottom Church, Virginia.

Morley, William R. - Private - Company H - Enlisted from Santa Anna, Illinois, April 13, 1862. Discharged May 9, 1865 upon completion of military service.

Morris, James - Private - Company F - Enlisted from Bloomington, Illinois, August 10, 1861. Veteran. Wounded in the thigh May 20, 1864. Leg amputated. Died in Philadelphia July 9, 1864 from wounds.

Morris, John - Private - Company K - Enlisted from Chicago, Illinois, August 19, 1861. No further details known.

Morris, William M. - Private - Company H - Enlisted February 13, 1865. Mustered out with the regiment, December 6, 1865.

Morrison, William - Private - Company G - Enlisted January 23, 1865. Deserted April 2, 1865.

Morse, Ebenezer J. - Private - Company F - Enlisted from Centralia, Illinois, August 15, 1861. Veteran. Promoted Corporal August 16, 1864; promoted to Sergeant April 1, 1865. Mustered out with the regiment, December 6, 1865.

Morse, Jacob - Private - Company F - Enlisted from Chicago, Illinois, September 4, 1861. Deserted in 1862.

Morse, John - Private - Company K - Enlisted from Chicago, Illinois, August 19, 1861. While at Benton Barracks, St. Louis, Missouri he was, at his own request, transferred to the Seventh Wisconsin Volunteer Infantry in October 1861.

Mott, George - Private - Company A - Enlisted August 5, 1861. Died February 2, 1862 in Cumberland, Maryland. Cause unknown.

Mott, Leander M. - Chief Musician - Regimental Band - Enlisted from Chicago, Illinois, August 15, 1862 in Company D. Transferred to non-commissioned staff as principal musician. Discharged June 20, 1865 upon completion of military service. In 1889 he was living in Englewood, Illinois

Mott, William J. - Private - Company H - Enlisted from Chicago, Illinois, March 1, 1862. Transferred to U. S. Signal Corps April 23, 1864. Discharge information unknown.

Moulton, Belah - Private - Company G - Enlisted September 21, 1861. Discharged on Writ of Habeas Corpus.

Moxton, William - Corporal - Company K - Enlisted from Marseilles, Illinois, August 6, 1861. Veteran. Promoted Sergeant for meritorious conduct at the charge on the rebel fortifications at Deep

Run, Virginia, August 16, 1864. Detailed as Ordnance Sergeant. Mustered out with the regiment, December 6, 1865. Native of Pennsylvania.

Muller, John B. - Private - Company G - Enlisted from Pekin, Illinois, August 30, 1861. Discharged July 4, 1863 for disability.

Mulvaney, Barney - Sergeant - Company F - Enlisted from Sandoval, Illinois, August 13, 1861. Discharged July 27, 1862 for disability.

Munn, Sylvester W. - Major - Was first to report with full company and named Captain of Company A. Promoted Major January 1862. Resigned December 1862 because of disability. Born in 1824 in St. Lawrence County, New York. After the war served as State Attorney for the district of Will County, Illinois. Was a State Senator. Died in Joliet on September 11, 1888 at the age of sixty-four years.

Murphy, David - Private - Company C - Enlisted from Pontiac, Illinois, September 18, 1861. Discharged December 12, 1863 for disability.

Murphy, Orrin - Private - Company A - Enlisted September 10, 1861. Discharged September 4, 1863 for disability.

Murray, James - Private - Company A - Enlisted January 16, 1864. Wounded in the shoulder October 7, 1874, near Chaffin's Farm, Virginia. Mustered out with the regiment, December 6, 1865.

Murray, Levi - Private - Company G - Enlisted from Berryman, Illinois, March 15, 1865. Mustered out with the regiment, December 6, 1865.

Murray, Thomas - Private - Company B - Enlisted from Bloomington, Illinois, August 20, 1861. Deserted October 28, 1861.

Musselmen, Ephraim - Private - Company E - Enlisted from Pittsburgh, Pennsylvania, October 28, 1861. Died October 16, 1864 of typhoid fever.

Myers, Alden - Private - Company K - Enlisted from Bloomington, Illinois, September 3, 1861. Wounded in the arm August 16, 1864. Discharged September 3, 1864 upon completion of military service.

Myers, Ebanis C. - Captain - Company K - Enlisted from McLean County, Illinois, August 14, 1861. Appointed Second Sergeant. Promoted First Sergeant June 14, 1862. Promoted First Lieutenant October 24, 1864. Promoted Captain December 7, 1864. Mustered out with the regiment, December 6, 1865. Born in Licking County, Ohio, February 27, 1838. In 1889 he was living in Randolph, McLean County, Illinois.

Myers, Joseph - Private - Company D - Enlisted from Martinsburg, Illinois, February 20, 1861. Died September 15, 1864. Cause unknown.

Myers, Theodore - Private - Company C - Enlisted from Chicago, Illinois, August 6, 1861. Deserted February 4, 1862.

Myers, Thomas W. - Private - Company C - Enlisted March 22, 1865. Mustered out with the regiment, December 6, 1865.

— N —

Nash, L. N. - Private - Company C - Enlisted from Fairbury, Illinois, September 21, 1861. Discharged July 25, 1862 for disability.

Nason, Adam C. - Private - Company D - Enlisted from Rockford, Illinois, November 19, 1861. Taken prisoner March 28, 1862 at Winchester, West Virginia. Promoted Corporal September 1, 1864. Wounded in the thigh October 13, 1864 at Darbytown Cross-Roads, Virginia. Discharged June 16, 1865 and served until mustered out July 17, 1865.

Neal, Daniel - Private - Company K - Enlisted from Marseilles, Illinois, September 3, 1861. Injured by falling of a train en route from St. Louis to Williamsport, Maryland. Discharged for disability November 1, 1862. Re-enlisted in Company G, Eighth Illinois Cavalry, and was mustered out July 17, 1865. Neal committed suicide at Larned, Kansas, some time in February, 1889.

Neal, Henry T. - Private - Company I - Enlisted from LeRoy, Illinois, September 14, 1861. Discharged June 28, 1862 for disability.

Neal, John A. - Private - Company B - Enlisted from Bloomington, Illinois, September 12, 1861. Discharged June 11, 1863 upon completion of military service.

Neal, Joseph W. - First Lieutenant - Company I - Enlisted from Santa Anna, Illinois, September 4, 1861. Veteran. Wounded in the thigh June 16, 1864. Promoted First Sergeant September 5, 1864. Promoted First Lieutenant February 7, 1865. Wounded in the left arm, April 2, 1865; arm amputated. Mustered out with the regiment, December 6, 1865.

Neal, Silas - Private - Company I - Enlisted from LeRoy, Illinois, September 4, 1861. Veteran. Mustered out with the regiment, December 6, 1865.

Needham, Washington - Private - Company H - Enlisted March 31, 1865. Mustered out with the regiment, December 6, 1865.

Neff, Frederick - Private - Company G - Enlisted from Pekin, Illinois, August 30, 1861. Deserted September 12, 1861.

Nelson, James - Private - Company F - Enlisted from Sandoval, Illinois, August 15, 1861. Wounded in the head September 7, 1863 at Fort Wagner, South Carolina. Discharged September 10, 1864 upon completion of military service.

Nelson, James W. - Private - Company E - Enlisted from Wilmington, Illinois, September 12, 1861. Veteran. Promoted Corporal November 1, 1865. Mustered out with the regiment, December 6, 1865.

Nelson, O. P. - Sergeant - Company I - Enlisted from LeRoy, Illinois, September 14, 1861. Taken prisoner May 26, 1862; paroled and exchanged. Veteran. Taken prisoner again, May 16, 1864 at Drewry's Bluff, Virginia. Died in prison at Richmond, Virginia, from disease.

Nevil, Richard - Private - Company F - Enlisted from Bloomington, Illinois, August 20, 1861. Veteran. Mustered out with the regiment, December 6, 1865.

Newport, Henry - Private - Company H - Enlisted from Paris, Illinois, June 19, 1862. Wounded in the leg August 16, 1864. Discharged June 20, 1865 upon completion of military service.

Nichols, Benjamin - Private - Company A - Enlisted December 24, 1864. Promoted to Corporal September 28, 1865. Mustered out with the regiment, December 6, 1865. In 1889 he was living in Wilmington, Illinois.

Nichols, Ira - Private - Company A - Enlisted August 21, 1861. Veteran. Wounded and taken prisoner May 20, 1864; escaped, but was recaptured on June 16, 1864, and died of wounds in prison at Florence, South Carolina. Date unknown.

Nichols, Joseph T. - Private - Company K - Enlisted from Marseilles, Illinois, August 14, 1861. Veteran. Promoted August 16, 1864. Wounded in the leg, April 2, 1865 at the assault on Fort Gregg, Virginia. Died of wounds May 19, 1864 at Chesapeake Hospital, Fort Monroe, Virginia. Born at Austerlitz, Columbia County, New York, April 27, 1840. Buried at the U. S. National Cemetery at Hampton, Virginia.

Nicholson, Donald A. - First Lieutenant - Company K- Commissioned from Marseilles, Illinois, as a Second Lieutenant. Promoted First Lieutenant March 15, 1862. Contracted rheumatism and became disabled after being forced by the enemy to ford the Potomac River January 4, 1862. Resigned June 14, 1862. Born in Canada. In 1889 he was living in Marseilles, Illinois.

Niman, Henry - Private - Company A - Enlisted August 14, 1861. Deserted September 18, 1861.

Nobles, James R. - Private - Company E - Enlisted from Wilmington, Illinois, February 23, 1864. Mustered out with the regiment, December 6, 1865.

Norris, Henry D. - Private - Company G - Enlisted from Chicago, Illinois, August 6, 1861. Discharged June 1862 for disability.

Norton, Hiram - Private - Company A - Enlisted August 19, 1861. Deserted August 25, 1861.

Notmyer, Henry - Private - Company F - Enlisted February 8, 1864. Mustered out with the regiment, December 6, 1865.

Nutting, Harrison - Private - Company G - Enlisted from Champaign, Illinois, August 14, 1861. Wounded in the leg June 2, 1864 near Ware Bottom Church, Virginia. Died of wounds at Fort Monroe, Virginia, November 27, 1864.

Nye, Edward - Private - Company D - Enlisted from Lane, Illinois, September 3, 1861. Discharged October 12, 1864 upon completion of military service.

— O —

O'Brien, John - Private - Company H - Enlisted February 24, 1865. Mustered out with the regiment, December 6, 1865.

O'Brien, Patrick - Private - Company F - Enlisted from Bloomington, Illinois, August 20, 1861. Veteran. Wounded and taken prisoner August 16, 1864. Died at Camp Parole, Annapolis, Maryland, August 31, 1864, from wounds and exposure.

O'Connell, Charge - Private - Company A - Enlisted from Wilmington, Illinois, August 14, 1861. Deserted September 5, 1861. Re-enlisted February 28, 1862. Discharged for disability June 27, 1862.

O'Connell, John - Private - Company B - Enlisted from Bloomington, Illinois, September 27, 1861. Discharged March 15, 1862 for disability. In 1889 he was living in Bloomington, Illinois.

O'Conner, Patrick - Private - Company B - Enlisted from Bloomington, Illinois, September 12, 1861. Discharged July 11, 1862.

O'Harra, Henry - Private - Company E - Enlisted from Wesley, Illinois, March 1, 1864. Mustered out with the regiment, December 6, 1865.

O'Harra, James - Private - Company H - Enlisted from Springfield, Illinois, April 5, 1862. Discharged November 1, 1862 for disability.

Obenon, David - Corporal - Company A - Enlisted from Chicago, Illinois, August 15, 1861. Discharged for disability July 21, 1862.

Odell, John L. - Private - Company D - Enlisted from Oregon, Illinois, September 12, 1861. Veteran. Wounded June 2, 1864 near Ware Bottom Church, Virginia. Arm amputated at the shoulder. Died in the hospital June 29, 1864 from wounds.

Ogle, Daniel - Private - Company G - Enlisted from Sterling, Illinois, February 13, 1864. Mustered out with the regiment, December 6, 1865.

Ohlhues, Henry - Private - Company E - Enlisted from Florence, Illinois, February 23, 1864. Severely wounded in the chest May 20, 1864 at Ware Bottom Church, Virginia. Killed at Fort Gregg, Virginia, April 2, 1865.

Oleson, Jacob - Private - Company K - Enlisted from Marseilles, Illinois, September 25, 1861. Veteran. Wounded and taken prisoner May 16, 1864 at Drewry's Bluff, Virginia. Paroled in August 1864 and transferred to Company C, Veteran Reserve Corps. Discharged November 13, 1865.

Olmstead, Clinton - Private - Company K - Enlisted March 5, 1864. Discharged December 2, 1864 by order of the War Department.

Olmstead, Orlando - Private - Company K - Enlisted from Marseilles, Illinois, August 19, 1861. Wounded in the chest August 16, 1864. Promoted Corporal August 16, 1864. Court-martialed September 25, 1864 and reduced to the ranks. Mustered out with the regiment, December 6, 1865.

Onsoig, Frederick - Private - Company G - Enlisted from Chicago, Illinois, February 17, 1864. Mustered out with the regiment, December 6, 1865.

Osborn, Thomas O. - Colonel - Promoted after Austin Light was dismissed from the service. Wounded May 14, 1865 at Drewry's Bluff, Virginia, while leading the regiment to a position in support of a battery of artillery. After the engagement he was breveted Brigadier-General for brave and distinguished service. After his recovery he rejoined his regiment and assigned to command the First Brigade, First Division, Twenty-Fourth Army Corps. He led this brigade in the assault on Fort Gregg, Virginia, April 2, 1864; at Rice's Station on April 7, 1865 and at Appomattox April 9, 1865, where his horse was shot out from under him. Promoted to full Brigadier-General May 11, 1865 and received the brevet of Major-General of Volunteers. In 1868 he was elected County Treasurer of Cook County. He later received the appointment as one of the Board of Managers of the National Asylums for Disabled Union Soldiers. In 1873 he was appointed United States Minister to Argentina. In 1889 he was living in Buenos Aires, Argentina.

Osgood, Jerry - Private - Company A - Enlisted February 29, 1864. Mustered out with the regiment, December 6, 1865.

Osgood, Thomas - Private - Company A - Enlisted February 19, 1864. Wounded August 16, 1864. Died in the hospital September 28, 1864.

Ottenheimer, Solomon - Private - Company A - Enlisted October 1, 1864. Discharged June 21, 1865 by order of the War Department.

Owen, Leonard J. - Private - Company B - Enlisted from Bloomington, Illinois, September 12, 1861. Discharged July 11, 1862.

Owens, Thomas - Private - Company H - Enlisted April 7, 1865. Mustered out with the regiment, December 6, 1865.

— P —

Pacey, John - Private - Company G - Enlisted from Brimfield, Illinois, September 24, 1861. Wounded and taken prisoner May 16, 1864 at the battle of Drewry's Bluff, Virginia. Died of wounds while in prison at Richmond, Virginia, July 26, 1864.

Pacey, Richard - Private - Company G - Enlisted from Brimfield, Illinois, September 24, 1861. Transferred to the Veteran Reserve Corps. Discharge information unknown.

Page, Allen - Private - Company D - Enlisted March 23, 1865. Died at Point of Rocks Hospital May 12, 1865. Cause unknown.

Page, John G. - Private - Company I - Enlisted April 5, 1865. Mustered out with the regiment, December 6, 1865.

Palmer, Gersham - Private - Company C - Enlisted from Pontiac, Illinois, August 19, 1861. Died at New Bern, NC, February 21, 1863. Cause unknown.

Parker, Horace B. - Captain - Company A - Enlisted August 5, 1861. Promoted to First Lieutenant December 7, 1861. Veteran. Promoted to Captain March 31, 1865. Mustered out with the regiment, December 6, 1865. In 1889 he was living at Albaton, Iowa.

Parker, Nick - Private - Company K - Enlisted September 10, 1861. Died at St. Augustine, Florida on November 24, 1864. Cause unknown.

Parkhurst, Henry S. - Private - Company G - Enlisted from LeRoy, Illinois, August 20, 1861. Discharged June 29, 1863 for disability.

Parkinson, Isaac W. - Private - Company G - Enlisted from Wood's Grove, Illinois, February 22, 1865. Mustered out with the regiment, December 6, 1865.

Parks, Benjamin F. - Private - Company I - Enlisted from LeRoy, Illinois, September 4, 1861. Wounded in the hand August 16, 1864. Discharged October 8, 1864 upon completion of military service.

Parks, L. H. - First Sergeant - Company I - Enlisted from LeRoy, Illinois, September 4, 1861. Reduced to the ranks June 27, 1862. Discharged September 10, 1864 upon completion of military service.

Parrish, Harrison - Private - Company G - Enlisted from New Genesee, Illinois, August 14, 1861. Wounded June 2, 1864 in a skirmish near Ware Bottom Church, Virginia. Discharged September 10, 1864 upon completion of military service.

Parrish, Watson - Private - Company G - Enlisted from New Genesee, August 14, 1861. Wounded in the head May 16, 1864 at the battle of Drewry's Bluff, Virginia. Discharged September 10, 1864 upon completion of military service.

Parrish, William C. - Private - Company G - Enlisted from New Genesee, Illinois, August 14, 1861. Died of heart disease at Williamsport, Maryland, November 29, 1861.

Pate, Robert P. - Private - Company G - Enlisted August 6, 1861. Discharged September 30, 1861 for disability.

Patterson, John H. - Private - Company A - Enlisted August 5, 1861. Deserted August 20, 1861.

Patterson, William A. - Private - Company D - Enlisted from Oregon, Illinois, August 28, 1861. Wounded October 1, 1863 at Fort Gregg, South Carolina. Discharged September 10, 1864 upon completion of military service. Moved to Westminster, Los Angeles County and became a farmer.

Patton, Francis M. - Private - Company I - Enlisted February 10, 1864. Wounded in the right foot near Petersburg, Virginia, August 30, 1864. Mustered out with the regiment, December 6, 1865.

Paul, Alexander - Private - Company B - Enlisted from Bloomington, Illinois, September 26, 1861. Veteran. Wounded in the Knee May 20, 1864 at the battle of Ware Bottom Church, Virginia. Promoted Corporal August 27, 1864. Wounded in the foot October 13, 1864 at Darbytown Cross-Roads, Virginia. Mustered out with the regiment, December 6, 1865. Died at Allerton, Iowa in 1887.

Paul, Jacob - Private - Company G - Enlisted May 23, 1864. Mustered out with the regiment, December 6, 1865.

Peck, William - Private - Company F - Enlisted from Homer, Illinois, February 22, 1864. Wounded in battle near Ware Bottom Church, Virginia, June 18, 1864. Wounded in the head August 16, 1864 at the battle of Deep Run, Virginia. Discharge date unknown.

Pelton, Alsen D. - Private - Company A - Enlisted August 5, 1861. Taken prisoner at Strasburg, Virginia, May 1862. Discharged December 1, 1862.

Pemberton, Henry - Private - Company A - Enlisted January 1, 1862. Died June 18, 1864 in general hospital. Cause unknown.

Pembroke, Jerry - Private - Company C - Enlisted from Pontiac, Illinois, August 12, 1861. Discharged January 31, 1862 for disability. In 1889 he was living at Ottawa, Illinois.

Pennington, William H. - Private - Company E - Enlisted from Evanston, Illinois, March 15, 1864. Detailed as musician. Was Company bugler at Bermuda Hundred. Mustered out with the regiment, December 6, 1865.

Pernet, Joseph - Private - Company C - Enlisted from Odel, Illinois, September 9, 1861. Discharged September 10, 1864 upon completion of military service.

Perry, Arthur - Private - Company I - Enlisted from Waukegan, Illinois, February 10, 1864. Discharged August 20, 1864 for disability.

Perry, John J. - Private - Company E - Enlisted April 24, 1865. Mustered out with the regiment, December 6, 1865.

Perry, William H. - Private - Company C - Enlisted from Esmond, Illinois, August 12, 1861. Died at Cumberland, Maryland on February 25, 1862. Cause unknown.

Perkins, James - Private - Company A - Enlisted August 8, 1861. Died in Chicago, Illinois on September 7, 1861, cause unknown.

Peters, Benjamin - Private - Company K - Enlisted February 24, 1864. Died of disease April 9, 1864.

Peters, Martin Van Buren - Private - Company F - Enlisted from Elgin, Illinois, September 4, 1861. Veteran. Promoted Corporal February 1, 1864. Wounded in the hand June 18, 1864. Transferred to Veteran Reserve Corps March 17, 1865. Discharge information unknown.

Peterson, Ole C. - Private - Company D - Enlisted from Lake View, Illinois, September 22, 1864. Discharged June 10, 1865 under order of the War Department.

Pettijohn, James - Private - Company G - Enlisted from Orland, Illinois, February 23, 1864. Wounded in the hand May 14, 1864 in a skirmish near Drewry's Bluff, Virginia. Discharged May 23, 1865 for disability from wounds.

Phillips, Gideon - Private - Company H - Enlisted from Chicago, Illinois, February 12, 1864. Killed August 16, 1864 during the battle of Deep Run, Virginia.

Phillips, Hiram M. - Captain - Company I - Commissioned September 6, 1861. Wounded in the hand and taken prisoner May 16, 1864 at the battle of Drewry's Bluff, Virginia. Discharged December 5, 1864 upon completion of military service. Born in Piketon, Pike County, Ohio, February 1, 1822. At the age of seven he moved to Indiana. In 1846 he enlisted in Company G, First Regiment, Illinois Volunteers, and served in the Mexican War for one year. He participated in the Battle of Buena Vista. After his service in the Civil War was over, he moved to Bloomington, Illinois

Phillips, James - Private - Company D - Enlisted April 11, 1865. Mustered out with the regiment, December 6, 1865.

Phillips, James P. - Private - Company A - Enlisted August 13, 1861. Discharged June 8, 1863 for disability.

Phillips, John O. - Private - Company A - Enlisted September 20, 1864. Mustered out November 2, 1865.

Pickens, Samuel - Private - Company H - Enlisted from Paris, Illinois, June 17, 1862. Transferred to the Fourth U. S. Artillery November 4, 1862. Discharge information unknown.

Pike, A. H. - Private - Company F - Enlisted from Bloomington, Illinois, August 28, 1861. Veteran. Taken prisoner May 16, 1864 at Drewry's Bluff, Virginia. Sent to Andersonville, Georgia. Paroled, exchanged and discharged February 21, 1865.

Pitcher, Theo W. - Private - Company K - Enlisted from Marseilles, Illinois, August 17, 1861 as a Musician, Second Class in the regimental band. Discharged June 4, 1862 by order of War Department.

Pitzer, Henry - Private - Company G - Enlisted from Orland, Illinois, March 12, 1864. Wounded in the head October 13, 1864 at the battle of Darbytown Cross-Roads, Virginia. Mustered out with the regiment, December 6, 1865.

Platt, Charles D. - Private - Company B - Enlisted from Bloomington, Illinois, September 12, 1861. Veteran. Promoted Sergeant September 15, 1864. Wounded in the arm August 16, 1864 at the battle of Deep Run, Virginia. Promoted to First Lieutenant November 9, 1865. Mustered out with the regiment, December 6, 1865.

Plimpton, Homer A. - Lieutenant - Colonel of Regiment - Enlisted from Sterling, Illinois, August 14, 1861 as a private in Company G. Served one year in the ranks detailed to the regimental hospital department as a clerk, where he remained until January 1864. Veteran. After the battles of May 16 and May 20, 1864, he was made 5th Sergeant of his company to fill a vacancy and was detailed as Sergeant-Major. He was slightly wounded in the head by a shell fragment near Chaffin's Farm, Virginia, October 7, 1864. Soon after, he was commissioned First Lieutenant and on December 4, 1864 commissioned Captain of Company G. During the final campaign in Virginia, he was promoted Major of Volunteers by the War Department for gallant conduct in the assault on Fort Gregg, Virginia, April 2, 1865. On May 11, 1865 he received his commission to Lieutenant-Colonel. Mustered out with the regiment, December 6, 1865. Born on June 11, 1838 in Northeast Erie County, Pennsylvania. Moved to Illinois in 1840. Entered Northwestern University 1856-1860 and graduated with honors in June 1860. After the war, he filled the position of Assistant Assessor of the United States Internal Revenue Department. Later, he engaged in some mining operations in Colorado. At the time of the writing of the original book, he was occupied in stock-raising in New Mexico, while his family remained in Chicago.

Plimpton, Olin - Private - Company G - Enlisted from Sterling, Illinois, August 9, 1861. Discharged November 21, 1864.

Plowman, James - Private - Company F - Enlisted from Chicago, Illinois, September 15, 1861. Veteran. Wounded in the head June 2, 1864. Died November 14, 1864 from wounds.

Poff, Henry M. - Private - Company I - Enlisted from Santa Anna, Illinois, September 21, 1861. Discharged July 4, 1863 for disability.

Poffenberger, James - Private - Company D - Enlisted from Oregon, Illinois, August 28, 1861. Discharged December 15, 1862 for disability.

Pollock, George - Corporal - Company K - Enlisted from Marseilles, Illinois, September 3, 1861. Discharged July 18, 1863 for disability.

Pond, Henry D. - Private - Company G - Enlisted from New Genesee, Illinois, August 21, 1861. Discharged September 10, 1864 upon completion of military service.

Porter, A. C. - Private - Company E - Enlisted from Wilmington, Illinois, October 2, 1861. Veteran. Wounded May 20, 1864 near Ware Bottom Church, Virginia, and also wounded at Darbytown Cross-Roads October 13, 1864. Promoted Corporal August 16, 1864, and Sergeant June 1, 1865. Mustered out with the regiment, December 6, 1865.

Porter, James H. - Private - Company H - Enlisted March 16, 1862. Veteran. Wounded in the head November 1, 1863 on Morris Island, South Carolina. Deserted August 3, 1865.

Porter, John H. - Private - Company C - Enlisted from LeRoy, Illinois, March 21, 1862. Absent (ill) at muster out of the regiment.

Porter, John H. - Private - Company I - Enlisted from LeRoy, Illinois, September 4, 1861. Discharged October 12, 1864.

Porter, John S. - Private - Company H - Enlisted March 3, 1862. Transferred to Company C, April 1, 1863. Nothing further is known.

Porter, Joseph - Private - Company I - Enlisted September 22, 1861. Deserted October 30, 1861.

Postel, William S. - Private - Company D - Enlisted August 21, 1861. Transferred to Veteran Reserve Corps June 20, 1864. Discharge information unknown.

Potter, Isaac - Private - Company G - Enlisted from Johnson County, Kansas, August 19, 1861. Died of disease at Cumberland, Maryland, February 1, 1862.

Potter, William - Private - Company C - Enlisted from Rook's Creek, Illinois, August 28, 1861. Died February 20, 1863. Cause unknown.

Potts, Edward - Private - Company H - Enlisted from Randolph, Illinois, March 31, 1862. Discharged May 9, 1865 upon completion of military service. [Adjutant General's Report says he lost a leg.]

Potts, Frederick - Private - Company H - Enlisted from Randolph, Illinois, March 1, 1862. Veteran. Promoted Corporal January 13, 1865; promoted Sergeant March 20, 1865. Mustered out with the regiment, December 6, 1865.

Pratt, James - Private - Company G - Enlisted from Orland, Illinois, February 27, 1864. Died May 28, 1864 of scarlet fever.

Pratt, T. J. - Private - Company I - Enlisted February 23, 1864. Mustered out with the regiment, December 6, 1865.

Prebles, Edward - Private - Company K - Enlisted February 13, 1865. Wounded in the chest April 2, 1865 at the assault on Fort Gregg, Virginia. Mustered out with the regiment, December 6, 1865.

Prebles, Isaac D. - Private - Company K - Enlisted April 11, 1865. Was a substitute. No further details are known.

Preeler, J. Frank - Private - Company H - Enlisted from Chicago, Illinois, February 1, 1862. Veteran. Wounded October 13, 1864 at Darbytown Cross-Roads, Virginia; leg amputated. Taken prisoner; paroled and exchanged. Discharged October 17, 1865 for disability from wounds.

Preston, Dwight - Sergeant - Company F - Enlisted from Centralia, Illinois, August 15, 1861. Promoted Sergeant December 7, 1862. Veteran. Wounded in the arm May 20, 1864. Discharged June 1, 1865 for disability.

Preston, William - Private - Company A - Enlisted March 8, 1864. Discharged January 21, 1865 upon completion of military service.

Prey, Nelson - Private - Company I - Enlisted from LeRoy, Illinois, September 4, 1861. Discharged April 30, 1864 disability.

Price, Michael - Private - Company K - Enlisted at St. Louis, Missouri, August 21, 1861. Taken prisoner at Bath, West Virginia, January 4, 1862. Paroled. Wounded in the ankle April 2, 1865 at Fort Gregg, Virginia. Mustered out with the regiment, December 6, 1865.

Price, Robert - Private - Company H - Enlisted April 7, 1865. Mustered out with the regiment, December 6, 1865.

Price, William - Private - Company G - Enlisted May 23, 1864. Deserted August 14, 1865 at Norfolk, Virginia.

Prior, James - Corporal - Company G - Enlisted from Lockport, Illinois, August 13, 1861. Veteran. Wounded in both thighs June 2, 1864. Promoted Sergeant November 1, 1864. Transferred and promoted Second Lieutenant in the 122nd Regiment, U. S. Colored Troops. Discharge information unknown.

Proud, Samuel F. - Private - Company A - Enlisted August 8, 1861. Veteran. Wounded in the arm May 20, 1864. Killed at Fort Gregg, Virginia, April 2, 1865.

Purck, Henry - Private - Company D - Enlisted March 2, 1865. Wounded in the bowels April 2, 1865 at the assault on Fort Gregg, Virginia. Died April 4, 1865 in the hospital at Point of Rocks, Virginia.

Putham, John S. - Private - Company K - Enlisted from Bloomington, Illinois, October 3, 1861. Veteran. Wounded in the left arm June 2, 1864. Promoted Corporal May 1, 1865. Mustered out with the regiment, December 6, 1865.

— R —

Racker, Michael - Private - Company C - Enlisted March 7, 1864. Discharged July 5, 1865 under order of the War Department.

Raleigh, Thomas - Private - Company E - Enlisted March 7, 1864. Discharged July 5, 1865 under order of the War Department.

Randall, Frank R. - Private - Company A - Enlisted August 5, 1861. Discharged October 28, 1863 for disability.

Randolph, Valentine C. - Private - Company I - Enlisted from Lincoln, Illinois, September 16, 1861. Discharged September 17, 1864 upon completion of military service.

Raney, George S. - Private - Company I - Enlisted from Jefferson County, Illinois, April 5, 1865. Mustered out with the regiment, December 6, 1865.

Raney, Samuel - Private - Company C - Enlisted from Cayuga, Illinois, August 12, 1861. Veteran. Taken prisoner, June 2, 1864 near Ware Bottom Church, Virginia; paroled and exchanged. Discharged September 26, 1865 for disability.

Rapp, John W. - Private - Company I - Enlisted from LeRoy, Illinois, September 4, 1861. Veteran. Killed August 29, 1864, near Petersburg, Virginia.

Rarrick, Nathan - Private - Company F - Enlisted from Chicago, Illinois, August 22, 1861. Discharged for disability August 5, 1863.

Rawlins, Lemon P. - Private - Company A - Enlisted from Guilford, Illinois on October 7, 1864. Mustered out January 27, 1866.

Ray, Wilson - Private - Company C - Enlisted June 30, 1865. Contracted disease in October 1865 at Norfolk. Mustered out with the regiment, December 6, 1865 and died in 1870.

Rayner, Sylvester - Private - Company G - Enlisted from West Bend, Wisconsin, September 9, 1861. Discharged September 10, 1864 upon completion of military service.

Ream, Adam - Private - Company I - Enlisted from LeRoy, Illinois, September 25, 1861. Veteran. Injured on the ship coming from Hilton Head, South Carolina to New York on veteran furlough. Wounded June 18, 1864 near Ware Bottom Church, Virginia. Mustered out with the regiment, December 6, 1865.

Ream, Samuel - Private - Company I - Enlisted from LeRoy, Illinois, September 25, 1861. Veteran. Captured at the battle of Drewry's Bluff, Virginia, May 16, 1864. Paroled and exchanged. Mustered out with the regiment, December 6, 1865.

Redicks, Asa - Private - Company B - Enlisted from Zion, Illinois, April 12, 1865. Mustered out with the regiment, December 6, 1865.

Reed, Henry - Private - Company C - Enlisted August 25, 1861. Died at Hancock, Maryland on December 25, 1861. Cause unknown.

Reed, J. F. - Private - Company D - Enlisted April 11, 1865. Mustered out with the regiment, December 6, 1865.

Reed, John A. - Private - Company K - Enlisted from Marseilles, Illinois, August 19, 1861. Veteran. Detailed as a blacksmith. Mustered out with the regiment, December 6, 1865.

Reed, Stephan C. - Private - Company G - Enlisted from Palos, Illinois, December 31, 1863. Mustered out with the regiment, December 6, 1865.

Reed, William H. - Private - Company A - Enlisted August 15, 1861. Promoted Corporal March 1, 1863. Captured on June 2, 1864. Sent to Andersonville for 18 months. Mustered out August 15, 1865.

Reese, Amos B. - Private - Company H - Enlisted from LeRoy, Illinois, February 24, 1862. Wounded in the left thigh May 23, 1864 near Hatcher's Run, Virginia. Died in the hospital from wounds June 22, 1864.

Reese, John - Private - Company D - Enlisted from Lane, Illinois, August 9, 1861. Promoted Corporal September 1, 1863. Veteran. Promoted Sergeant April 1, 1865. Deserted August 5, 1865.

Reese, Isaac C. - Private - Company C - Enlisted from Joliet, Illinois, September 14, 1861. Discharged September 13, 1864 upon completion of military service. In 1889 he was living in Bloomington, Illinois.

Reeves, Joseph H. - Private - Company G - Enlisted from Palos, Illinois, February 29, 1864. Wounded in the thigh May 16, 1864; limb amputated. Discharged March 18, 1865 for disability from wounds.

Reigel, John - Private - Company G - Enlisted from Chicago, Illinois, December 29, 1863. Mustered out with the regiment, December 6, 1865.

Relae, George - Private - Company C - Enlisted September 4, 1861. Veteran. Wounded in the leg and taken prisoner May 16, 1864 at Drewry's Bluff, Virginia. Paroled and exchanged. Wounded in the right arm April 2, 1865 during the assault on Fort Gregg, Virginia. Arm amputated. Discharged June 17, 1865 for disability from wounds.

Riche, William - Private - Company G - Enlisted from Chicago, Illinois, December 31, 1863. Wounded October 13, 1864 at the battle of Darbytown Cross-Roads, Virginia. Mustered out with the regiment, December 6, 1865.

Richards, Dudley - Private - Company I - Enlisted from LeRoy, Illinois, October 6, 1861. Promoted Corporal March 1, 1863. Killed August 16, 1864 at the battle of Deep Run, Virginia.

Richardson, Jerry - Private - Company C - Enlisted from Sunbury, Illinois, August 21, 1861. Wounded and taken prisoner May 20, 1864 near Drewry's Bluff, Virginia,; paroled and exchanged. Discharged June 24, 1865 upon completion of military service.

Richardson, Joseph W. - First Lieutenant - Company A - Commissioned August 5, 1861. Died from typhoid fever at Williamsport, Maryland November 17, 1861. Born at Morriston, St. Lawrence County, New York, July 12, 1830. He took up the study of law at Ogdensburg, New York. After his admission to the bar he moved to Wilmington, Illinois where he became associated with S. W. Munn.

Riddle, George - Private - Company I - Enlisted from LeRoy, Illinois, September 17, 1861. Promoted Corporal June 27, 1862. Discharged September 17, 1864 upon completion of military service. Born in Warren County, New Jersey in 1840. In 1889 he was living in LeRoy, Illinois.

Riley, John - Private - Company G - Enlisted December 14, 1864. Mustered out with the regiment, December 6, 1865.

Riley, Newton - Private - Company E - Enlisted from Morris, Illinois, February 21, 1865. Mustered out with the regiment, December 6, 1865.

Riley, Thomas - Private - Company C - Enlisted from Rook's Creek, Illinois, August 12, 1861. Discharged May 9, 1863 for disability.

Ripple, John L. - Captain - Company E - Enlisted from Orbisonia, Pennsylvania, October 28, 1861. Promoted Sergeant January 16, 1862. Captured May 9, 1862 near Columbia Bridge, Virginia. Taken to Libby Prison, Richmond; finally to Belle Isle, Virginia. Paroled September 13, 1862. Taken prisoner again May 16, 1864 at Drewry's Bluff, Virginia, and sent to Andersonville Prison, Georgia. Paroled in Savannah November 19, 1864. Promoted First Lieutenant. Then Captain June 6, 1865. Mustered out with the regiment, December 6, 1865.

Ripple, William B. - Private - Company E - Enlisted from Orbisonia, Pennsylvania, February 1, 1861. Died at Alexandria, Virginia, on August 18, 1862 of brain fever. Buried in Monroe Cemetery at Huntington, Pennsylvania.

Roberts, Charles H. L. - Private - Company G - Enlisted from New Genesee, Illinois, August 28, 1861. Wounded in the knee September 1863 at Fort Wagner, South Carolina; wounded in the shoulder and face May 20, 1864 near Ware Bottom Church, Virginia. Discharged October 1864 upon completion of military service.

Roberts, Joseph - Musician - Company G - Enlisted from New Genesee, Illinois, October 5, 1861 as a drummer. Discharged November 12, 1861 for disability.

Roberts, W. H. - Private - Company K - Enlisted August 12, 1865. Mustered out with the regiment, December 6, 1865.

Robertson, George P. - Private - Company I - Enlisted from Santa Anna, Illinois, September 4, 1861. Discharged November 1861.

Robinson, George H. - Private - Company D - Enlisted from Hedgesville, Virginia, March 1, 1862. Wounded May 20, 1864 at Ware Bottom Church, Virginia. Leg amputated. Died May 25, 1864 in the hospital in Maryland from wounds.

Robinson, Hiram - Private - Company H - Enlisted from Fairbury, Illinois, March 29, 1862. Wounded in the side and hip September 7, 1864 near Petersburg, Virginia. Discharged May 9, 1865 upon completion of military service.

Robinson, Noah L. - Second Lieutenant - Company I - Enlisted from LeRoy, Illinois, September 4, 1861. Promoted First Sergeant February 7, 1865, and Second Lieutenant October 4, 1865. Mustered out with the regiment, December 6, 1865.

Robinson, William E. - Private - Company C - Enlisted from Rook's Creek, Illinois, August 22, 1861. Discharged March 8, 1863 for disability.

Robinson, William H. - Private - Company E - Enlisted from Wilmington, Illinois, October 6, 1861. Reported on Company rolls as a deserter.

Robinson, William H. - Private - Company F - Enlisted February 29, 1864. Promoted Corporal June 2, 1865 for meritorious service at the assault on Fort Gregg and at Appomattox, Virginia. Mustered out with the regiment, December 6, 1865.

Rodgers, Thomas - Private - Company A - Enlisted December 24, 1861. Discharged December 1, 1862 for disability.

Rogers, Alpheus W. - Private - Company E - Enlisted from Wesley, Illinois, December 31, 1863. Wounded in the hip and arm May 14, 1864 at Drewry's Bluff, Virginia; arm amputated. Discharged October 20, 1864 for disability.

Rooker, Vincent - Private - Company C - Enlisted from Amity, Illinois, March 7, 1864. Mustered out July 5, 1865.

Root, Charles - Private - Company D - Enlisted from Lane, Illinois, August 21, 1861. Killed September 9, 1864 in the trenches in front of Petersburg, Virginia.

Root, Luther J. - Private - Company D - Enlisted from Santa Anna, Illinois, April 10, 1864. Mustered out with the regiment, December 6, 1865.

Root, Pliny F. - Private - Company G - Enlisted from Greenwich, Mississippi, August 6, 1861. Died at Hilton Head, South Carolina of chronic diarrhea December 31, 1863.

Rose, Henry C. - Private - Company H - Enlisted from Pittsfield, Illinois, April 5, 1862. Reported as a deserter on January 5, 1863. Was taken prisoner January 5, 1863. Died of disease in Andersonville Prison, Georgia, September 27, 1864.

Ross, George - Private - Company G - Enlisted from Homer, Illinois, August 13, 1861. Discharged June 27, 1862 for disability.

Rost, Lewis J. - Private - Company D - Enlisted from Dwight, Illinois, September 21, 1861. Wounded August 16, 1864 in the arm and chest at Darbytown Cross-Roads, Virginia. Discharged September 21, 1864 upon completion of military service.

Rounds, John J. - Private - Company B - Enlisted from Bloomington, Illinois, September 12, 1861. Transferred to U. S. Army November 28, 1862.

Rourk, Hugh - Private - Company A - Enlisted August 20, 1861. Veteran. Killed April 2, 1865 at Fort Gregg, Virginia.

Rowley, Charles - Private - Company G - Enlisted from Homer, Illinois, September 10, 1861. Died at Cumberland, Maryland, of typhoid fever February 10, 1862.

Rowley, James - Private - Company I - Enlisted from LeRoy, Illinois, September 4, 1861. Died in the hospital at New Bern, North Carolina, October 11, 1864. Cause unknown.

Rudd, Oscar F. - Captain - Company G - Commissioned August 5, 1861. Promoted Captain July 20, 1862. Wounded June 16, 1864 in a skirmish near Chester Station, Virginia. Died in general hospital at Fort Monroe, Virginia, July 11, 1864.

Rue, John A. - Private - Company I - Enlisted from Mount Pleasant, Illinois, March 8, 1864. Wounded in the leg August 16, 1864 at the battle of Deep Run, Virginia. Died in the hospital from wounds on October 18, 1864.

Rumsey, Girard - Private - Company G - Enlisted from Manteno, Illinois, September 25, 1861. Veteran. Promoted Sergeant July 29, 1864. Discharged to accept promotion to First Lieutenant of Fifth U. S. Colored Troops.

Runyan, George W. - Private - Company I - Enlisted from LeRoy, Illinois, October 6, 1861. Discharged July 4, 1863 for disability.

Ruppenthal, Henry - Private - Company A - Enlisted January 1, 1862. Veteran. Wounded May 20, 1864. Arm so shattered that amputation was necessary. Died in general hospital June 18, 1864.

Rush, James - Private - Company H - Enlisted from Springfield, Illinois, April 5, 1862. Died from disease August 8, 1862.

Russel, S. S. - Private - Company C - Enlisted April 7, 1865. Mustered out with the regiment, December 6, 1865.

Russell, Edward - Private - Company H - Enlisted from Chicago, Illinois, April 5, 1862. Transferred to the U. S. Artillery.

Russell, John H. - Private - Company F - Enlisted from Northfield, Illinois, August 13, 1861. Promoted Corporal February 16, 1862. Veteran. Promoted Sergeant August 23, 1864. Discharged for promotion to commission in the Thirty-Sixth U. S. Colored Troops. Born at Northfield, Cook County, Illinois, July 16, 1843. In 1869 he married Cornelia E. Cadwell of Waukegan, Illinois and had two children—Jessie Eleanor and Gilbert Hamilton.

Russell, Lewis L. - Private - Company C - Enlisted from Alexander County, Illinois, April 7, 1865. Mustered out with the regiment, December 6, 1865.

Russell, William J. - Corporal - Company A - Enlisted August 15, 1861. Discharged for disability August 15, 1862.

Ryan, James - Private - Company C - Enlisted February 28, 1865. Was a substitute. Killed in battle April 2, 1865 at Fort Gregg, Virginia.

Ryan, Thomas - Private - Company A - Enlisted August 25, 1863. Acted as Orderly on General Osborn's staff during the spring campaign of 1865. Mustered out with the regiment, December 6, 1865.

— S —

Sackett, Edward A. - Private - Company E - Enlisted from Chicago, Illinois, October 10, 1861. Veteran. Detailed to the regimental band. Played in Band of 1864 & 1865. Mustered out with the regiment, December 6, 1865.

Sailor, Randolph - Private - Company E - Enlisted from Bear Creek, Illinois, April 13, 1865. Mustered out with the regiment, December 6, 1865.

Saint John, Seth - Private - Company C - Enlisted from Ocoya, Illinois, September 6, 1861. Promoted Corporal March 10, 1862. Veteran. Taken prisoner May 16, 1864 at the battle of Drewry's Bluff, Virginia. Sent to prison in Florence, South Carolina. Died in Florence Prison, January 23, 1865.

Sanborn, James - Corporal - Company K - Enlisted from Marseilles, Illinois, August 19, 1861. Promoted Sergeant September 1, 1862. Veteran. Killed during the assault at Deep Run, Virginia, August 16, 1864.

Sartell, Henry E. - Private - Company E - Enlisted from Wilmington, Illinois, October 27, 1861. Promoted Corporal May 1, 1863. Veteran. Wounded August 16, 1864 at Deep Run, Virginia. Discharged for disability March 30, 1865.

Sauers, Peter - Private - Company K - Enlisted from Bloomington, Illinois, August 14, 1861. Veteran. Killed during the assault on Fort Gregg, Virginia, April 2, 1865.

Savage, Amos - Captain - Company G - Commissioned Second Lieutenant August 5, 1861. Promoted First Lieutenant July 20, 1862. Commissioned Captain, but not mustered as Captain. Discharged October 28, 1864 for disability resulting from broken health and defective vision. Born June 18, 1836.

Savage, Patrick - Private - Company H - Enlisted March 12, 1862. Drowned in the Sangamon River, Illinois, June 1862.

Savitz, James - Private - Company G - Enlisted April 8, 1865. Mustered out with the regiment, December 6, 1865.

Sawin, Royal E. - Private - Company D - Enlisted from Lane, Illinois, August 12, 1861. Veteran. Promoted Sergeant May 20, 1864. Killed August 16, 1864 during the battle of Deep Run, Virginia.

Scanlin, John - Private - Company A - Enlisted August 5, 1861. Wounded at Bermuda Hundred, Virginia. Discharged November 20, 1864 upon completion of military services.

Schaefer, Frank - Private - Company H - Enlisted from Chicago, Illinois, March 31, 1864. Taken prisoner in Virginia, on October 2, 1864. No further information. Suspected to have died in prison.

Schafer, J. L. - Private - Company C - Enlisted from Cayuga, Illinois, August 12, 1861. Veteran. Wounded in the shoulder May 16, 1864 at Drewry's Bluff, Virginia. Promoted Corporal August 1, 1864; to Sergeant January 1, 1865. Mustered out with the regiment, December 6, 1865. In 1889 he was living at Tippecanoe City, Ohio.

Schermerhorn, Alford - Musician, 3rd Class - Enlisted August 17, 1861. Discharged by order of the War Department, June 4, 1862.

Schermerhorn, Almon L. - Private - Company G - Enlisted from Worth, Illinois, August 6, 1861. Veteran. Wounded in the neck May 16, 1864 at Drewry's Bluff, Virginia. Was Orderly for General Osborn at Richmond, Virginia, until the end of the war. Mustered out with the regiment, December 6, 1865.

Schlweis, Jacob - Private - Company C - Enlisted from Chicago, Illinois, January 25, 1864. Wounded April 2, 1865 during the assault on Fort Gregg, Virginia. Discharged July 20, 1865 for disability.

Schuman, Charles F. - Private - Company D - Enlisted from Lindenwood, Illinois, September 29, 1861. Discharged September 30, 1864 upon completion of military service.

Schwab, Jacob - Private - Company D - Enlisted from Willow Creek, Illinois, August 9, 1861. Veteran. Mustered out with the regiment, December 6, 1865.

Scott, John - Private - Company F - Enlisted April 6, 1865. Mustered out with the regiment, December 6, 1865.

Scott, Wesley - Private - Company C - Enlisted from Pontiac, Illinois, August 16, 1861. Wounded in the thigh May 20, 1864 at Ware Bottom Church, Virginia. Promoted Corporal September 4, 1864. Wounded and taken prisoner October 13, 1864. Paroled and died in Camp Parole at Annapolis, Maryland.

Scoville, John - Private - Company F - Enlisted from Chicago, Illinois, December 4, 1864. Transferred to Veteran Reserve Corps April 17, 1865.

Scoville, William - Private - Company F - Enlisted from Chicago, Illinois, February 4, 1864. Wounded in the leg May 20, 1864 at Ware Bottom Church, Virginia. Discharged for disability from wounds.

Scullion, William - Private - Company K - Enlisted from Marseilles, Illinois, August 14, 1861. Discharged July 10, 1863 for disability from disease.

Seaman, Allen M. - Private - Company K - Enlisted from Marseilles, Illinois, September 15, 1861. Died in June 1862 while home on medical furlough.

Searing, George - Second Lieutenant - Company H - Enlisted from Chicago, Illinois, July 11, 1862. Resigned September 6, 1864.

Seary, Patrick - First Lieutenant - Company F - Enlisted from Sandoval, Illinois, August 15, 1861. Commissioned Second Lieutenant August 15, 1861. Promoted First Lieutenant August 7, 1862. Resigned July 8, 1863.

Seavy, John - Private - Company F - Enlisted September 6, 1861. Deserted in 1861.

Sellards, David F. - Captain - Company B - Promoted Captain August 30, 1862. Resigned on account of ill health, August 31, 1862. After leaving the service, Captain Sellards moved to Iowa, locating near Mt. Ayr. He began the study of medicine and graduated as a physician in 1867. He died in 1877 from tuberculosis leaving a widow and a large family of children.

Selleck, Hiram - Private - Company K - Enlisted from Marseilles, Illinois, September 21, 1861. Discharged November 10, 1862 for disability from disease.

Sellman, John - Private - Company C - Enlisted from Rook's Creek, Illinois, August 18, 1861. Discharged September 10, 1864 upon completion of military service.

Sellman, M. B. - Private - Company C - Enlisted from Ocoya, Illinois, February 22, 1864. Promoted Corporal July 1, 1865. Mustered out with the regiment, December 6, 1865.

Sellman, S. H. M. - Private - Company B - Enlisted from Bloomington, Illinois, September 12, 1861. Discharged October 26, 1863 for disability. Relocated to Cecil, Kansas.

Seltzer, Peter - Private - Company F - Enlisted from Northfield, Illinois, August 5, 1861. Veteran. Mustered out with the regiment, December 6, 1865.

Seybert, Andrew - Private - Company A - Enlisted August 8, 1861. Veteran. Taken prisoner May 16, 1864 at Drewry's Bluff, Virginia. Died in Andersonville Prison August 11, 1864 from disease.

Grave Number 5,350.

Seymour, William H. - Private - Company H - Enlisted from Thornton, Illinois, March 12, 1862. Deserted May 12, 1863.

Shackley, Joseph - Private - Company H - Enlisted from LeRoy, Illinois, April 7, 1862. Discharged May 9, 1865 upon completion of military service.

Shade, Abraham - Private - Company E - Enlisted February 12, 1862. Deserted in September 1862.

Shafer, John L. - Second Lieutenant - Company C - Enlisted from Cayuga, Illinois, October 4, 1865. Mustered out with the regiment, December 6, 1865.

Shafer, John N. - Private - Company G - Enlisted from Scranton, Pennsylvania, September 19, 1861. Veteran. Promoted Corporal May 1, 1865. Mustered out with the regiment, December 6, 1865.

Shaw, James B. - Musician - Company K - Fifer - Enlisted at Marseilles, Illinois, August 14, 1861. Discharged June 1862 for disability.

Shea, James - Private - Company B - Enlisted from Bloomington, Illinois, September 20, 1861. Wounded August 16, 1864 at the battle of Deep Run, Virginia. Discharged October 10, 1864 upon completion of military service. Native of Scotland.

Sheets, Eli - Private - Company F - Enlisted September 27, 1861. Transferred July 1, 1863 to Veteran Reserve Corps. No further information known.

Sheffler, Moses F. - Private - Company E - Enlisted from Rockville, Illinois, September 27, 1861. Wounded in the head August 16, 1863 at Fort Wagner, South Carolina. Partially paralyzed. Discharged September 27, 1864 upon completion of military service. Died in 1867 after surgery required as a result of his wound.

Sherman, Martin - Private - Company A - Enlisted September 12, 1861. Veteran. Mustered out with the regiment, December 6, 1865.

Shero, Martin - Private - Company K - Enlisted from Chicago, Illinois, August 6, 1861. Veteran. Wounded October 13, 1864 at Darbytown Cross-Roads, Virginia. Mustered out with the regiment, December 6, 1865.

Sherwood, Daniel - Private - Company F - Enlisted from Waukegan, Illinois, January 25, 1864. Killed October 28, 1864 near Darbytown Cross-Roads, Virginia.

Sherwood, Frank - Private - Company G - Enlisted from Shabbona, Illinois, August 26, 1861. Promoted Corporal May 1, 1863. Discharged September 10, 1864 upon completion of military service.

Shields, Peter - Private - Company D - Enlisted February 20, 1865. Mustered out with the regiment, December 6, 1865.

Shinkle, Thomas W. - Private - Company I - Enlisted from LeRoy, Illinois, September 4, 1861. Veteran. Promoted Corporal June 1, 1864. Wounded in the side August 28, 1864. Killed at Fort Gregg, Virginia, April 2, 1865.

Shipley, Thomas - Private - Company G - Enlisted January 3, 1865. Discharged July 15, 1865 for disability.

Shoudorf, Ferdinand - Private - Company H - Enlisted February 27, 1865. Deserted June 22, 1865 at Richmond, Virginia.

Shultz, Valentine - Private - Company C - Enlisted from Nebraska, August 12, 1861. Wounded April 4, 1862 at Woodstock, Virginia. Discharged June 18, 1862 for disability.

Sifers, Theodore - Private - Company B - Enlisted from Jefferson County, Illinois, April 5, 1865. In prison by sentence of a general court-martial at muster out of the regiment. Discharged February 7, 1866.

Siggs, Francis - Private - Company F - Enlisted from Bloomington, Illinois, August 19, 1861. Veteran. Wounded in the head June 18, 1864. Died June 21, 1864 from wounds.

Silkwood, Brazil - Private - Company I - Enlisted from Franklin County, Illinois, April 11, 1865. Mustered out with the regiment, December 6, 1865.

Silkwood, Henry - Private - Company I - Enlisted from Franklin County, Illinois, April 11, 1865. Mustered out with the regiment, December 6, 1865.

Simpson, Charles - Private - Company K - Enlisted March 4, 1864. Mustered out with the regiment, December 6, 1865.

Slagle, David H. - Sergeant - Company K - Enlisted August 27, 1861. Wounded and taken prisoner October 13, 1864 at the battle of Darbytown Cross-Roads, Virginia. Discharged May 22, 1865 at Philadelphia, Pennsylvania because of disability from wounds.

Slagle, James - Private - Company K - Enlisted from Marseilles, Illinois, December 16, 1861. Wounded October 13, 1864 at Darbytown Cross-Roads, Virginia. Absent due to wounds at muster out of the regiment.

Slater, George - Private - Company K - Enlisted from Marseilles, Illinois, August 27, 1861. Discharged for disability September 1862. Enlisted January 20 in Eighth Illinois Cavalry. Discharged July 17, 1865.

Slater, William - Private - Company K - Enlisted from Marseilles, Illinois, September 10, 1861. Veteran. Mustered out with the regiment, December 6, 1865.

Slaughter, William B. - Captain - Company G - Commissioned August 5, 1861. Resigned July 20, 1862 at Harrison's Landing, Virginia.

Slayton, Reuben - Private - Company E - Enlisted from Chicago, Illinois, March 27, 1864. Wounded in the hand May 20, 1864. Absent from the Company since that date. [Adjutant General's Report lists Slayton as discharged July 16, 1865.]

Smith, Asahel - Private - Company F - Enlisted from Waukegan, Illinois, January 25, 1864. Discharged May 6, 1865 for disability.

Smith, C. E. - Musician, 3rd Class - Enlisted October 5, 1861. Discharged by order of the War Department, June 4, 1862.

Smith, Charles M. - Private - Company E - Enlisted from Wilmington, Illinois, September 20, 1861. Discharged February 14, 1863 for disability.

Smith, Charles W. - Private - Company A - Enlisted February 25, 1864. Deserted October 26, 1865.

Smith, Henry - Private - Company D - Enlisted April 5, 1865. Mustered out with the regiment, December 6, 1865.

Smith, Henry G. - Sergeant - Company A - Enlisted August 5, 1861. Wounded October 9, 1863 on Morris Island, South Carolina. Right leg amputated. Discharged for disability, date unknown. In 1889 he was living in Dawson, Sangamond County, Illinois.

Smith, Isaac - Private - Company H - Enlisted from Bloomington, Illinois, February 25, 1864. Wounded May 20, 1864 at Ware Bottom Church, Virginia. Wounded again August 16, 1864 at Deep Run, Virginia. Transferred to Veteran Reserve Corps April 17, 1865.

Smith, James J. - Sergeant - Company H - Enlisted from Pecatonica, Illinois, March 19, 1862. Discharged March 23, 1865 upon completion of military service.

Smith, John - Private - Company C - Enlisted March 14, 1864. Mustered out with the regiment, December 6, 1865.

Smith, John - Private - Company K - Enlisted from Chicago, Illinois, July 23, 1862. Discharged July 24, 1863.

Smith, Michael - Private - Company D - Enlisted from Lane, Illinois, August 21, 1861. Veteran. Mustered out with the regiment, December 6, 1865.

Smith, Nicholas - Private - Company A - Enlisted August 21, 1861. Wounded April 2, 1865 during the assault on Fort Gregg, Virginia. Died of wounds April 4, 1865.

Smith, Robert - Private - Company G - Enlisted from Sterling, Illinois, August 9, 1861. Discharged September 9, 1864 for disability.

Smith, Samuel - Private - Company E - Enlisted February 25, 1865. Mustered out with the regiment, December 6, 1865.

Smith, William - Private - Company H - Enlisted from Bloomington, Illinois, February 25, 1864. Died in the hospital of disease September 1864.

Smouse, Daniel - First Lieutenant - Company K - Enlisted from Bloomington, Illinois, August 19, 1861. Promoted Sergeant September 1, 1862. Promoted Second Lieutenant. Promoted First Lieutenant January 9, 1865. Mustered out with the regiment, December 6, 1865. In 1889 he was living in the Soldier's Home in Quincy, Illinois.

Snee, Hugh R. - Private - Company E - Enlisted from Rockville, Illinois, September 27, 1861. Veteran. Wounded in the cheek by a musket ball and suffered a saber cut in the head May 16, 1864 during the battle of Drewry's Bluff, Virginia; taken prisoner. Sent to Andersonville Prison. Escaped from Andersonville October 1, 1864. Mustered out with the regiment, December 6, 1865. After the war he married Moses Sheffler's sister, Sarah. They had two children, John and Nettie. They settled in Hayes Center, Nebraska where they maintained a farm and built and ran a hotel. Snee died in 1927.

Snowden, George O. - Captain - Company D - Enlisted September 12, 1861. Mustered into Company D as a private at Benton Barracks, Missouri. Promoted to First Sergeant. Commissioned First Lieutenant June 12, 1862 at Luray, Virginia. Wounded at Bermuda Hundred, Virginia, in the right thigh, June 3, 1864. Sent to Chesapeake Hospital, Fort Monroe, Virginia. Contracted hospital gangrene. Reported back to the regiment in October 1864. Unable to continue, he was mustered out November 10, 1864. Commanded the force in support of the "Swamp Angel" during the siege of Charleston, South Carolina. Born in Pittsburgh, Pennsylvania, December 31, 1835. In 1889 he was living in Waterloo, Iowa.

Snyder, Gottlieb - Private - Company F - Enlisted from Bloomington, Illinois, August 28, 1861. Discharged October 13, 1862 for disability.

Snyder, Nathaniel - Private - Company H - Enlisted from Kingston Mines, Illinois, February 1, 1862. Deserted February 28, 1862.

Sovereign, Milton - Private - Company A - Enlisted September 14, 1861 as a musician. Discharged September 10, 1864 upon completion of military service. In 1889 he was living at York, Nebraska and held the office of Clerk of the County Court.

Sparks, Ely - Private - Company K - Enlisted from Marseilles, Illinois, August 6, 1861. In May 1862, wandered outside of Union lines near Woodstock, Virginia, and was taken prisoner. Reported as a deserter. Paroled a few days later and mustered out of the service. Enlisted in another regiment and died of disease at Williamsport, Maryland.

Sparks, John B. - Private - Company K - Enlisted from Marseilles, Illinois, February 28, 1861. Discharged September 25, 1862 for disability.

Sparrow, Darwin M. - Corporal - Company B - Enlisted at Bloomington, Illinois, August 12, 1861. Reduced to the ranks on October 19, 1861. Discharged February 25, 1863 for disability.

Spencer, W. W. - Private - Company G - Enlisted from Bainbridge, Minnesota, August 15, 1861. Promoted Sergeant July 2, 1862. Wounded in the head June 1, 1864 at the entrenchments at Bermuda Hundred, Virginia. Died of wounds in Philadelphia, Pennsylvania July 5, 1864.

Spencer, William J. - Private - Company I - Enlisted from LeRoy, Illinois, September 22, 1861. Veteran. Wounded in the head June 17, 1864. Promoted Corporal September 10, 1864. Promoted Sergeant August 1, 1865. Mustered out with the regiment, December 6, 1865.

Spicer, Daniel W. - Private - Company G - Enlisted from Thornton, Illinois, February 29, 1864. Died of disease in Harword Hospital, Washington, D.C. April 14, 1864.

Spinnings, Clark - Private - Company D - Enlisted from Dwight, Illinois, September 3, 1861. Discharged June 22, 1863 for disability.

Spong, Augustus - Private - Company H - Enlisted from Kingston Mines, Illinois, February 27, 1862. Discharged February 27, 1863 for disability.

Spong, John - Private - Company H - Enlisted from Kingston Mines, Illinois, February 27, 1862. Discharged June 26, 1865 by order of the War Department.

Spratt, Thomas J. - Private - Company I - Enlisted from LeRoy, Illinois, February 22, 1864. Mustered out with the regiment, December 6, 1865.

Springer, R. - Private - Company C - Enlisted from Amity, Illinois, August 12, 1861. Discharged July 21, 1862 for disability.

Springer, Samuel A. - Private - Company F - Enlisted from Chicago, Illinois, August 24, 1861. Discharged September 11, 1862 for disability.

Sproul, William - Private - Company I - Enlisted from LeRoy, Illinois, September 4, 1861. Taken prisoner June 1862; paroled and exchanged. Veteran. Discharged March 22, 1865 for disability.

Staley, Abner - Private - Company D - Enlisted from Dwight, Illinois, December 17, 1862. Mustered out with the regiment, December 6, 1865.

Stanton, Albert - Private - Company F - Enlisted from Centralia, Illinois, August 13, 1861. Veteran. Mustered out with the regiment, December 6, 1865.

Stanton, William - Private - Company E - Enlisted from Rockville, Illinois, February 24, 1864. Detailed as Commissary of Subsistence. Mustered out with the regiment, December 6, 1865.

Starkey, Orlando - Private - Company C - Enlisted February 10, 1864. Wounded in the thigh August 16, 1864 at the battle of Deep Run, Virginia. Discharged July 20, 1865 for disability.

Starkweather, Henry - Private - Company A - Enlisted August 5, 1861. Died July 14, 1863 on Folly Island, South Carolina of unknown causes.

Starr, L. S. - Private - Company F - Enlisted from Newport, Illinois, February 13, 1864. Mustered out with the regiment, December 6, 1865.

Stebbins, Emory - Corporal - Company K - Enlisted from Marseilles, Illinois, August 19, 1861. Taken prisoner at Bath, West Virginia, January 4, 1862. Promoted Sergeant September 1, 1862. Discharged June 3, 1862 for disability.

Steele, William E. - Sergeant - Company E - Enlisted from Chicago, Illinois, October 2, 1861. Promoted January 16, 1862 from the ranks. Killed October 13, 1864 at the battle of Darbytown Cross-Roads, Virginia.

Steinkulan, Peter - Private - Company B - Enlisted March 11, 1865. Mustered out with the regiment, December 6, 1865.

Stephenson, Albert A. - Private - Company C - Enlisted from Nebraska August 27, 1861. Taken prisoner May 16, 1864 at Drewry's Bluff, Virginia. Died in prison at Florence, South Carolina October 11, 1864 from disease.

Stephenson, George W. - Corporal - Company B - Enlisted from Bloomington, Illinois, August 12, 1861. Promoted Sergeant January 1, 1862. Reduced to the ranks August 7, 1863. Discharged September 10, 1864 upon completion of military service.

Stephenson, John D. - Private - Company K - Enlisted from Marseilles, Illinois, September 3, 1861. Discharged for disability in 1862.

Stearns, F. L. - Private - Company E - Enlisted September 27, 1861. Taken prisoner May 26, 1861 at Strasburg, Virginia. Status unknown.

Stewart, James - Private - Company A - Enlisted August 5, 1861. Discharged August 4, 1862 for disability.

Stewart, John - Private - Company E - Enlisted from Wilmington, Illinois, September 20, 1861. Veteran. Wounded and taken prisoner October 13, 1864 at the battle of Darbytown Cross-Roads, Virginia. Paroled, and died on October 30, 1864 while in the hospital at Camp Parole, Annapolis, Maryland.

Stillhamer, William - Private - Company F - Enlisted from Bloomington, Illinois, March 9, 1864. Taken prisoner May 16, 1864 at Drewry's Bluff, Virginia. Paroled and exchanged. Killed April 2, 1865 during the assault on Fort Gregg, Virginia.

Stillyer, John - Private - Company D - Enlisted from Willow Creek, Illinois, August 9, 1861. Veteran. Mustered out with the regiment, December 6, 1865.

Stokes, Stephen N. - Private - Company K - Enlisted from Bloomington, Illinois. Taken prisoner May 17, 1862; paroled October 1862. Re-captured June 6, 1863. Veteran. Deserted August 25, 1864.

Stout, James - Private - Company F - Enlisted from Centralia, Illinois, August 14, 1861. Veteran. Wounded in the head and shoulder May 20, 1864. Discharged October 3, 1864 for disability from wounds.

Stout, John - Private - Company B - Enlisted from Bloomington, Illinois, September 12, 1861. Discharged March 23, 1863 for disability.

Stoval, Eden - Private - Company E - Enlisted February 25, 1865. Wounded April 9, 1865 at Appomattox Court-House, Virginia. Mustered out with the regiment, December 6, 1865.

Straub, Jacob - Private - Company H - Enlisted April 6, 1865. Deserted October 27, 1865 at Norfolk, Virginia.

Streeter, Charles - Corporal - Company C - Enlisted from Odell, Illinois, August 12, 1861. Discharged for disability June 5, 1862.

Stroban, George - Private - Company F - Enlisted from Waukegan, Illinois, February 26, 1864. Mustered out with the regiment, December 6, 1865.

Strong, Ambrose - Private - Company C - Enlisted February 17, 1865. Mustered out with the regiment, December 6, 1865.

Stumph, Michael - Private - Company A - Enlisted August 5, 1861. Discharged August 4, 1862 for disability.

Sullivan, George - Private - Company F - Enlisted from Libertyville, Illinois, February 26, 1864. Wounded in the knee May 16, 1864 at Drewry's Bluff, Virginia. Mustered out with the regiment, December 6, 1865.

Sullivan, Michael - Private - Company A - Enlisted August 22, 1861. Discharged May 19, 1862 for disability.

Sutter, John - Private - Company H - Enlisted April 12, 1865. Mustered out with the regiment, December 6, 1865.

Swab, Jacob - Private - Company D - Enlisted from Willow Creek, Illinois, August 9, 1861. Veteran. Mustered out with the regiment, December 6, 1865.

Swain, Royal E. - Private - Company D - Enlisted from Lane, Illinois, August 12, 1861. Veteran. Promoted Sergeant. Killed in battle at Deep Run, Virginia, on August 16, 1864.

Sweeny, Edward - Private - Company K - Enlisted February 15, 1865. Mustered out with the regiment, December 6, 1865.

Sweetser, Alphonse C. - Second Lieutenant - Company B - Enlisted August 12, 1861 as a Sergeant and promoted to Second Lieutenant October 11, 1861. Wounded through both legs June 2, 1864 near Ware Bottom Church, Virginia. Promoted to First Lieutenant December 6, 1865. Mustered out with the regiment, December 6, 1865. Born in Oxford County, Maine, February 23, 1839. While in his infancy, his parents moved to Mississippi, remaining there some years, then returned to Maine and located at Portland. After five years they moved to Columbia County, Wisconsin and made a trial at farming for four years. They then moved to Bloomington, Illinois. After his muster out and return to Bloomington he was elected to the office of city and town tax collector, and subsequently received the appointment of Deputy U. S. Collector of Internal Revenue, and held it until the administration of President Cleveland came in. In 1889 he was living in Bloomington, Illinois.

Sweiger, Jacob - Private - Company H - Enlisted February 25, 1865. Mustered out with the regiment, December 6, 1865.

— T —

Taggert, John - Private - Company D - Enlisted from Chicago, Illinois, December 29, 1864. Wounded in the arm at Ware Bottom Church, Virginia, May 20, 1864. Deserted on August 3, 1865.

Tanner, Andrew J. - Private - Company B - Enlisted from Bloomington, Illinois, August 12, 1861. Discharged September 10, 1864 upon completion of military service.

Tateburg, Ernest W. - Private - Company I - Enlisted from LeRoy, September 18, 1861. Veteran. Promoted Corporal May 16, 1865. Promoted Sergeant October 28, 1865. Mustered out with the regiment, December 6, 1865.

Taylor, Bufort - Private - Company A - Enlisted December 25, 1863. Died at Richmond, Virginia, May 14, 1865. Cause unknown.

Taylor, Galveston A. - Private - Company A - Enlisted August 5, 1861. Veteran. Promoted to Corporal September 10, 1864. Promoted Sergeant March 1, 1865. Promoted Second Lieutenant October 10, 1865. Mustered out with the regiment, December 6, 1865.

Taylor, John - Private - Company H - Enlisted from Springfield, Illinois, February 1, 1862. Promoted Corporal May 24, 1865. Reduced to the ranks June 10, 1865. Discharged June 20, 1865.

Taylor, Richard - Private - Company H - Enlisted March 12, 1862. Deserted May 25, 1862 at Springfield, IL.

Terrell, William - Corporal - Company K - Enlisted from McLean County, Illinois, August 18, 1861 in Company H. Transferred to Company K. Discharged for disability August 22, 1863.

Tewkey, Edward - Private - Company A - Enlisted August 14, 1861. Discharged September 10, 1864 upon completion of military service.

Thaer, Andrew - Musician, Second Class - Enlisted September 20, 1861. Discharged June 4, 1862 by order of the War Department.

Thayer, Edmond J. - First Lieutenant - Company D - Enlisted from Lindenwood, Illinois, August 21, 1861. Promoted Sergeant in 1863. Veteran. Wounded June 18, 1864. Wounded again, October 7, 1864, this time in both legs. Promoted First Lieutenant September 21, 1865. Mustered out with the regiment, December 6, 1865. Born August 22, 1840 at Chelsea, Vermont. Moved to Ogle County, Illinois in 1859. While home on veteran furlough in January 1874 he married Miss E. F. Benedict at Lindenwood, Ogle County, Illinois. After the war they went to Kansas, locating on a homestead near Fort Scott. He remained there until 1878 when he moved to Iola, Kansas. He had two sons and six daughters.

Thayer, George - Private - Company E - Enlisted from Wilmington, Illinois, September 17, 1861. Captured September 2, 1862 at Bull Run, Virginia. Veteran. Mustered out with the regiment, December 6, 1865.

Thewlis, William - Private - Company A - Enlisted February 19, 1864. Mustered out with the regiment, December 6, 1865.

Thomas, Francis Marion - Private - Company K - Enlisted from Bloomington, Illinois, August 14, 1861. Promoted Corporal October 1863. On June 17, 1864 at Hatcher's Run, Virginia, he was excused from duty due to injury to his neck. However, hearing the firing at the front, he rushed to rejoin his company. A few minutes later, he was killed.

Thomas, George N. - Private - Company K - Enlisted from Bloomington, Illinois, September 3, 1861. Veteran. Mustered out with the regiment, December 6, 1865.

Thomas, James M. - Private - Company I - Enlisted from Franklin County, Illinois, September 4, 1861. Discharged September 4, 1864 upon completion of military service.

Thompson, George - Private - Company F - Enlisted August 22, 1861. Discharged September 20, 1861 for disability.

Thompson, Henry V. - Private - Company K - Enlisted from Marseilles, Illinois, August 27, 1861. Discharged in 1862 for disability. September 1, 1863, Thompson re-enlisted in Henshaw's Battery, and on August 18, 1863 was again discharged for disability. He returned home and died soon after.

Thompson, James - Private - Company K - Enlisted from Chicago, Illinois, February 12, 1864. Wounded in the leg May 20, 1864 at the battle of Ware Bottom Church, Virginia. Discharged July 18, 1865 for disability and died shortly thereafter.

Thompson, Robert - Private - Company B - Enlisted April 5, 1865. Mustered out with the regiment, December 6, 1865.

Thornell, Jackson - Private - Company K - Enlisted from Marseilles, Illinois, October 4, 1861. Discharged March 7, 1863 for disability.

Timm, Christopher - Private - Company K - Enlisted from Marseilles, Illinois, December 16, 1863. Mustered out with the regiment, December 6, 1865.

Tindale, Daniel A. - Private - Company D - Enlisted from Chicago, Illinois, November 19, 1863. Wounded in the leg August 16, 1864 at Deep Run, Virginia. Deserted August 3, 1865.

Tobias, Nathaniel - Private - Company D - Enlisted from Lane, Illinois, August 29, 1861. Killed May 16, 1864 at the battle of Drewry's Bluff, Virginia.

Tomlinson, Andrew J. - Private - Company I - Enlisted from LeRoy, Illinois, September 4, 1861. Promoted Corporal March 1, 1863. Wounded in the leg August 16, 1864; leg amputated. Died in the hospital from wounds on September 14, 1864.

Tovera, Thomas J. - Private - Company H - Enlisted from Bloomington, Illinois, July 1, 1862. Discharged June 20, 1865 upon completion of military service.

Towner, Austin - Second Lieutenant - Company D - Commissioned August 9, 1861. Resigned September 4, 1862. In 1889 he was living at Quarry, Marshall County, Iowa.

Tower, Franklin H. - Private - Company A - Enlisted February 29, 1864. He was a company clerk; clerk in the Regimental Adjutant's office, the chief clerk of the First Brigade. Subsequently held the position of chief clerk in the office of the Assistant Inspector General of the Southeastern Department of Virginia, at Norfolk. Mustered out with the regiment, December 6, 1865. In 1889 he was living in Milwaukee, Wisconsin.

Towns, J. C. - Musician, Second Class - Enlisted September 20, 1861. Discharged by order of the War Department, June 4, 1862.

Tracy, Harvey - Private - Company A - Enlisted August 19, 1861. Taken prisoner May 16, 1864 at Drewry's Bluff, Virginia, and sent to Andersonville Prison. Exchanged and mustered out April 20, 1865.

Trapp, Augustus - Private - Company F - Enlisted from Northfield, Illinois, August 22, 1861. Discharged August 20, 1862 for disability.

Trumble, George W. - Private - Company H - Enlisted from LeRoy, Illinois, March 1, 1862. Wounded October 13, 1864 at Darbytown Cross-Roads, Virginia. Died in the hospital from wounds in November 13, 1864.

Turney, Daniel W. - Private - Company G - Enlisted from Orland, Illinois, March 7, 1864. Wounded in the face August 16, 1864 at the battle of Deep Run, Virginia. Was on detached service in Richmond and Portsmouth from April 20, 1865 until mustered out with the regiment, December 6, 1865.

Turill, John T. - Sergeant - Company B - Enlisted from Decatur, Illinois, August 12, 1861. Promoted Sergeant January 1, 1863. Died July 14, 1864 from disease.

Twigger, George - Private - Company H - Enlisted from Chicago, Illinois, March 25, 1862. Mustered out as a Corporal with the regiment, December 6, 1865.

Tyler, James - Private - Company G - Enlisted from Lockport, Illinois, August 13, 1861. Discharged June 2, 1862 for disability.

— U —

Underwood, George M. - Private - Company F - Enlisted September 4, 1861. Veteran. Promoted to Corporal January 1, 1865; promoted to Sergeant June 2, 1865. Mustered out with the regiment, December 6, 1865.

Unrine, Oscar - Private - Company C - Enlisted from Esmond, Illinois, August 28, 1861. Veteran. Promoted Corporal May 1, 1865. Mustered out with the regiment, December 6, 1865.

Urick, Samuel - Private - Company C - Enlisted December 22, 1864. Mustered out with the regiment, December 6, 1865.

— V —

Valentine, William - Private - Company H - Enlisted March 4, 1865. Promoted Corporal June 28, 1865. Mustered out with the regiment, December 6, 1865.

Van Buskirk, John - Private - Company F - Enlisted from Chicago, Illinois, September 1, 1861. Discharged July 1, 1863 for disability. [Vanbusker, John]

Van Court, Rufus - Private - Company F - Enlisted from Chicago, Illinois, September 12, 1861. Discharged May 9, 1863 for disability.

Van Doosa, Benjamin H. - Private - Company C - Enlisted March 27, 1862. Discharged April 12, 1863.

Van Dusen, John - Private - Company B - Enlisted from Chicago, Illinois, September 20, 1861. Died of disease October 4, 1862 at Suffolk, Virginia.

Van Patten, Adelbert - Private - Company F - Enlisted from Antioch, Illinois, January 18, 1864. Wounded and taken prisoner August 16, 1864 at Deep Run, Virginia. Paroled on August 16, 1864 and died of his wounds the same day.

Van Slet, Samuel - Private - Company K - Enlisted from Marseilles, Illinois, September 17, 1861. Discharged November 10, 1862 for disability.

Van Valkinberg, E. P. - Private - Company C - Enlisted from Odell, Illinois, August 30, 1861. Veteran. Wounded April 2, 1865 during the assault on Fort Gregg, Virginia. Discharged July 18, 1865 for disability.

Van Wermer, Chester - Private - Company K - Enlisted at St. Louis, Missouri, October 14, 1861. Was taken prisoner in the Shenandoah Valley, Virginia. Reported as a deserted on the company rolls. Mustered out May 21, 1862 as a prisoner of war. [Vanwormer, Chester]

Van Winkle, Willitt - Private - Company I - Enlisted from Enfield, Illinois, February 16, 1864. Wounded in the thigh October 13, 1864 at Darbytown Cross-Roads, Virginia. Discharged May 27, 1865.

Vanbusker, John - See Van Buskirk, John

Vandebogart, James - Private - Company E - Enlisted from Florence, Illinois, February 22, 1864. Promoted Corporal August 1, 1865. Mustered out with the regiment, December 6, 1865.

VanSchoick, John - Private - Company H - Enlisted from LeRoy, Illinois, April 8, 1862. Transferred to Company I September 1862. Taken prisoner May 15, 1864 near Drewry's Bluff, Virginia. Discharged May 7, 1865.

Vanschoyck, John - See VanSchoick, John

Vanwormer, Chester - See Van Wermer, Chester

Vaughn, William D. - Private - Company D - Enlisted February 23, 1865. Killed at Fort Gregg, Virginia, April 2, 1865.

Vermillion, Charles W. - Private - Company B - Enlisted from Bloomington, Illinois, August 12, 1861. Promoted Corporal August 7, 1863; promoted to Sergeant in 1863. Taken prisoner May 16, 1864 at Drewry's Bluff, Virginia. Mustered out July 15, 1864 as a prisoner of war.

Vetta, Osta - Private - Company I - Enlisted from Bloomington, Illinois, November 10, 1862. Sent from Folly Island to Beaufort, South Carolina and failed to report. Suspected to have drowned.

Vieux, Cassimire - Private - Company C - Enlisted from Fairbury, Illinois, August 16, 1861. Discharged December 16, 1862 for disability.

Vieux, John - Private - Company C - Enlisted from Odell, Illinois, September 10, 1861. Veteran. Taken prisoner May 16, 1864 at Drewry's Bluff, Virginia. Still reported as missing. [Adjutant General's Report lists him as killed May 16, 1864].

Vowalt, Charles - Private - Company A - Enlisted February 24, 1864. Mustered out with the regiment, December 6, 1865.

— W —

Wade, William - Private - Company D - Enlisted from Lane, Illinois, September 8, 1861. Nothing further is known.

Wadhams, Mortimer C. - Private - Company G - Enlisted from Joliet, Illinois, October 14, 1862. Died of small-pox at Bermuda Hundred, Virginia, on February 28, 1865.

Wagle, John J. - Private - Company C - Enlisted from Monroe, Illinois, February 28, 1865. Mustered out with the regiment, December 6, 1865.

Wagoner, William - Private - Company I - Enlisted from LeRoy, Illinois, January 1, 1864. Wounded in the head May 16, 1864 at Drewry's Bluff, Virginia. Taken prisoner. Discharged July 3, 1865 by order of the War Department.

Wagonrod, Henry - Private - Company G - Enlisted from Bremen, Illinois, September 12, 1861. Died on Folly Island, South Carolina, November 10, 1863. Cause unknown.

Waine, Thomas - Private - Company E - Enlisted from Chicago, Illinois, March 9, 1864. Mustered out with the regiment, December 6, 1865.

Waite, Malden C. - Private - Company D - Enlisted from Lane, Illinois, August 9, 1861. Taken prisoner January 3, 1862 at Bath, West Virginia. Discharged June 6, 1862 for disability.

Waite, Malden E. - Corporal - Company D - Enlisted from Oregon, Illinois, August 9, 1861. Reduced to the ranks December 7, 1861. Wounded in the arm June 16, 1864. Died July 2, 1864 in the hospital from wounds.

Walker, John W. - Private - Company G - Enlisted from Lockport, Illinois, December 29, 1863. Wounded in the hand October 7, 1864. Mustered out with the regiment, December 6, 1865.

Walker, Joseph D. - Regimental Adjutant - Enlisted September 19, 1861. Promoted Adjutant July 15, 1862. Shot through the bowels during the battle of Drewry's Bluff, Virginia, May 16, 1864 and died of wounds the same day.

Wallace, John - Private - Company I - Enlisted from McLean County, Illinois, October 22, 1861. Deserted November 26, 1861.

Waller, Emory L. - First Lieutenant - Company I - Enlisted from Santa Anna, Illinois, September 6, 1861. Resigned June 14, 1862.

Walls, Nelson - Private - Company D - Enlisted from Willow Creek, Illinois, August 20, 1861. Taken prisoner January 3, 1862 at Bath, West Virginia. Veteran. Listed as a deserter March 8, 1864. Known to have enlisted in the gunboat service on the Mississippi River, and served until the end of the war. No discharge information known.

Walrath, William - Private - Company E - Enlisted March 24, 1864. Mustered out with the regiment, December 6, 1865.

Walters, Barton S. - Private - Company A - Enlisted from Channahon, Illinois, August 17, 1861. Veteran. Died at Annapolis, Maryland April 1, 1865.

Walters, Charles - Private - Company A - Enlisted October 10, 1861. Taken prisoner May 16, 1864 at Drewry's Bluff, Virginia. Died at Camp Parole, Annapolis, Maryland March 26, 1865.

Ward, Lloyd S. - Private - Company D - Enlisted April 10, 1865. Deserted June 28, 1865.

Ward, Joseph R., Jr. - Private - Company G - Enlisted from Bremen, Illinois, August 29, 1861. Veteran. Promoted Corporal October 10, 1864; promoted Sergeant November 1, 1864; promoted Second Lieutenant October 16, 1865. Mustered out with the regiment, December 6, 1865.

Wardram, Charles A. - Private - Company H - Enlisted from Chicago, Illinois, March 4, 1862. Wounded in the arm August 16, 1864. Discharged March 23, 1865 upon completion of military service.

Wardram, R. S. C. - Private - Company H - Enlisted March 4, 1862. Discharged March 23, 1865 upon completion of military service.

Ware, Charles W. - Private - Company E - Enlisted September 14, 1861. Veteran. Promoted Corporal November 20, 1865. Mustered out with the regiment, December 6, 1865.

Warner, John - Private - Company K - Enlisted from Bloomington, Illinois, October 10, 1861. Veteran. Killed on May 16, 1864 at Drewry's Bluff, Virginia.

Warner, Norman C. - First Lieutenant - Company E - Promoted May 26, 1862. Commanded the Requa Battery on Morris Island, South Carolina. Breveted Major of Volunteers for meritorious conduct at the battle of Deep Run, Virginia, on August 16, 1864. Severely wounded in the leg the same day. Discharged for disability (loss of leg) December 15, 1864. Born in Lima, Livingston County, New York. Married to Edith Canmann in March 1879.

Warren, Richard - Private - Company G - Enlisted from Bremen, Illinois, September 5, 1861. Veteran. Taken prisoner June 2, 1864 near Ware Bottom Church, Virginia, and sent to Andersonville Prison. Paroled and exchanged. Promoted Corporal May 10, 1865. Mustered out with the regiment, December 6, 1865.

Warren, Stephen R. - Private - Company G - Enlisted from Bremen, Illinois, September 3, 1861. Deserted September 30, 1861.

Warren, William - Private - Company G - Enlisted from Lyons, Iowa, September 3, 1861. Wounded in the arm May 16, 1864 at the battle of Drewry's Bluff, Virginia. Discharged September 10, 1864 upon completion of military service.

Washburn, George W. - Private - Company F - Enlisted August 28, 1861. Promoted Corporal November 19, 1862. Discharged August 5, 1863 for disability.

Washburne, Charles - Private - Company K - Enlisted from Morris, Illinois, August 27, 1861. Discharged early in 1862 for disability. On December 6, 1862 he enlisted in Henshaw's Battery and mustered out with it July 18, 1865.

Watson, John - Private - Company C - Enlisted from New Michigan, Illinois, September 29, 1861. Discharged in May 1862 for disability. In 1889 he was living in Spencer, Iowa.

Watson, John M. - Private - Company A - Enlisted August 5, 1861. Discharged May 16, 1863 for disability.

Watts, Charles W. - Private - Company A - Enlisted August 15, 1861. Veteran. Deserted October 22, 1865.

Wayne, Thomas - Private - Company E - Enlisted from Chicago, Illinois, March 9, 1864. Mustered out with the regiment, December 6, 1865.

Wayne, Winters - Private - Company A - Enlisted March 11, 1865. Discharged by order of the War Department on July 21, 1865.

Webb, Daniel - Private - Company F - Enlisted from Antioch, Illinois, February 16, 1864. Mustered out with the regiment, December 6, 1865.

Webb, Wallace H. - Private - Company F - Enlisted from Antioch, Illinois, February 16, 1864. Wounded in the thigh June 18, 1864 in a skirmish near Ware Bottom Church, Virginia. Absent (ill) at the muster out with the regiment, December 6, 1865.

Webber, George A. - Private - Company E - Enlisted from Chicago, Illinois, March 8, 1864. Wounded in the hand October 7, 1864; finger amputated. Discharged August 21, 1865 by order of the War Department.

Webster, Levi - Private - Company K - Enlisted February 6, 1864. Promoted Corporal May 1, 1865. Mustered out with the regiment, December 6, 1865.

Weedman, Jacob F. - Private - Company I - Enlisted from Santa Anna, Illinois, February 11, 1864. Discharged June 2, 1865 by order of the War Department.

Weedman, John B. - Private - Company I - Enlisted from Santa Anna, Illinois, September 26, 1861. Discharged September 28, 1864 upon completion of military service.

Weedman, John W. - Private - Company I - Enlisted from Mount Pleasant, Illinois, September 4, 1861. Promoted Corporal June 27, 1862. Taken prisoner May 16, 1864 at Drewry's Bluff, Virginia. Died in Andersonville Prison, November 15, 1864 of disease.

Weedman, Norman A. - Private - Company I - Enlisted from Mount Pleasant, Illinois, February 17, 1864. Promoted Corporal. Mustered out with the regiment, December 6, 1865.

Weible, Nicholas - Private - Company F - Enlisted from Chicago, Illinois, October 4, 1861. Discharged October 4, 1864 upon completion of military service.

Weidman, W. M. - Private - Company C - Enlisted from Rook's Creek, Illinois, September 16, 1861. Veteran. Taken prisoner May 16, 1864 at Drewry's Bluff, Virginia. Paroled and exchanged. Died December 21, 1864 from disease.

Weiner, John - Private - Company E - Enlisted from Wilmington, Illinois, October 6, 1861. Veteran. Discharged November 20, 1865 for disability.

Weinholtz, John C. - Private - Company D - Enlisted from Chicago, Illinois, September 30, 1861. Deserted October 16, 1861.

Welch, William James - Private - Company A - Enlisted from St. Louis, Missouri, October 14, 1861. Transferred to Battery L, Fourth U. S. Artillery on December 29, 1862. No discharge information known.

Welcome, James - Private - Company K - Enlisted from Bloomington, Illinois, October 10, 1861. Promoted Corporal August 1, 1863. Killed at Fort Wagner, South Carolina, August 26, 1863.

Weldon, Jacob M. - Private - Company A - Enlisted August 8, 1861. Veteran. Mustered out with the regiment, December 6, 1865.

Wells, George W. - Private - Company D - Enlisted from Lane, Illinois, September 12, 1861. Veteran. Promoted Corporal September 5, 1864. Wounded in both knees October 13, 1864. Promoted Sergeant September 20, 1865. Mustered out with the regiment, December 6, 1865.

Wells, Mathew - Private - Company G - Enlisted from Orland, Illinois, March 9, 1864. Wounded in the arm May 16, 1864 at the battle of Drewry's Bluff, Virginia and taken prisoner. Discharged May 30, 1865 under order of the War Department.

Wells, Pomeroy - Private - Company A - Enlisted September 22, 1861. Discharged May 25, 1862 for disability.

Wemick, William - Private - Company C - Enlisted February 27, 1865. Deserted June 25, 1865.

Wengart, Henry - Private - Company G - Enlisted from Florence, Illinois, May 15, 1865. Mustered out with the regiment, December 6, 1865.

Wengler, Peter - Private - Company D - Enlisted February 22, 1865. Deserted September 1, 1865.

Werner, John - Private - Company K - Enlisted from Bloomington, Illinois, October 10, 1861. Veteran. Killed May 16, 1864 at the battle of Drewry's Bluff, Virginia.

West, George W. - Private - Company I - Enlisted from Hunter, Illinois, March 23, 1865. Discharged July 15, 1865 for disability.

West, James B. - Private - Company G - Enlisted from Homer, Illinois, August 1, 1861. Veteran. Promoted Sergeant September 10, 1864; promoted First Sergeant January 1, 1865; promoted First Lieutenant May 10, 1865. Mustered out with the regiment, December 6, 1865.

Westfall, Reuben - Private - Company I - Enlisted from LeRoy, Illinois, February 13, 1864. Wounded in the shoulder April 2, 1865 at Fort Gregg, Virginia. Discharged June 10, 1865 for disability due to wounds.

Weston, James D. - Private - Company H - Enlisted March 4, 1865. Mustered out with the regiment, December 6, 1865.

Weston, Perry E. - Private - Company G - Enlisted from Shabbona, Illinois, September 16, 1861. Discharged September 16, 1864 upon completion of military service.

Wetzell, Michael - Private - Company I - Enlisted from Santa Anna, Illinois, September 4, 1861. Promoted Corporal March 1, 1863. Veteran. Promoted Sergeant February 7, 1865. Wounded in the arm April 2, 1865; arm amputated. Discharged June 17, 1865 for disability due to wounds.

Wheeler, Andrew W. - Captain - Company K - Enlisted as First Sergeant August 14, 1861 from Marseilles, IL Promoted Second Lieutenant March 15, 1862. Promoted First Lieutenant June 14, 1862. Promoted Captain (date unknown). Wounded in the face October 13, 1864 at Darbytown Cross-Roads, Virginia. Discharged October 24, 1864 upon completion of military service. In February 1865, he again entered the service, as Captain of Company E, 153rd Illinois Volunteers, and served in several short campaigns in Tennessee and Alabama. On September 15, 1865 was commissioned a Major. He was mustered out with his regiment. Born September 6, 1830 in the State of New York. In 1889 he was living in Wadena, Wadena County, Minnesota.

Wheeler, John - Private - Company B - Enlisted February 28, 1865. Mustered out with the regiment, December 6, 1865.

Whipple, Lewis T. - Captain - Company E - Enlisted as private. Discharged October 26, 1864 upon completion of military service. Born in Miasisburgh, Ohio, on January 24, 1840, and died in Kankakee, Illinois on April 24, 1870. Parents (Ethan Allen Whipple and Martha, emigrated from Vermont and where pioneers in the settlement of the Miami Valley, Ohio. He married on December 18, 1867 in Kankakee to Miss Nellie Stiles. Died in April 1870 as a result of decreased brain function due to the effects of a terrific cannonading he was subjected to during the seven days' retreat with McClellan.

Whitaker, Alvin - Corporal - Company H - Enlisted from LeRoy, Illinois, February 13, 1862. Mustered out with the regiment, December 6, 1865.

White, G. G. - Private - Company E - Enlisted from Wilmington, Illinois, September 27, 1861. Discharged September 27, 1864 upon completion of military service.

White, James R. - Private - Company K - Enlisted September 19, 1861. Taken ill in May 1862 and sent to the hospital at Cedar Creek, Virginia. Discharged for disability at Williamsport, Maryland, June 19, 1862. Re-enlisted with the regiment March 4, 1864. Slightly wounded by a shell fragment May 30, 1864. Discharged December 16, 1865. Born in McLean County, Illinois September 26, 1844.

White, William D. - Private - Company I - Enlisted from Santa Anna, Illinois, September 4, 1861. Veteran. Wounded in the head May 16, 1864 at the battle of Drewry's Bluff, Virginia. Discharged June 16, 1865 for disability due to wounds.

Whiteman, John W. - Private - Company E - Enlisted from Concord, Illinois, September 28, 1861. Discharged September 27, 1864 for disability.

Whitney, Henry P. - Private - Company A - Enlisted August 5, 1861. Veteran. Wounded June 2, 1864 near Ware Bottom Church, Virginia, and suffered the amputation of his right arm. Discharged June 30, 1865 for disability due to his wounds. In 1889 he was living in Chicago.

Wightman, James W. - Captain - Company C - Enlisted from Odell, Illinois, August 12, 1861. Promoted Commissary-Sergeant November 28, 1861. Promoted from First Lieutenant May 26, 1862. Wounded in the head and lungs at Drewry's Bluff, Virginia, on May 16, 1864. Died in the field hospital May 17, 1864. Born in England.

Wilcos, James M. - Private - Company A - Enlisted August 19, 1861. Veteran. Wounded May 16, 1864 at Drewry's Bluff. Discharged June 30, 1865 due to wounds.

Wilcox, William - Private - Company A - Enlisted October 10, 1861. Veteran. Wounded May 16, 1864 at Drewry's Bluff, Virginia. Wounded, absent at muster out of regiment.

Wilder, Charles J. - First Lieutenant - Company H - Enlisted from Chicago, Illinois, March 24, 1862. Killed while leading a charge at the battle of Darbytown Cross-Roads on October 13, 1864. He was buried at the foot of a tree near where he fell. His comrades cut his name into the bark.

Wilhoite, Willis F. - Private - Company I - Enlisted from LeRoy, Illinois, October 2, 1861. Veteran. Wounded in the face May 16, 1864 at Drewry's Bluff, Virginia. Discharged May 4, 1865 for disability due to wounds.

Wilkins, Zephaniah - Corporal - Company H - Enlisted from LeRoy, Illinois, April 14, 1862. Mustered out May 9, 1865.

Willard, Cornelius S. - Private - Company A - Enlisted September 17, 1861. Wounded October 7, 1864 near Chaffin's Farm, Virginia. Wounded at Fort Gregg, Virginia, April 2, 1865. Discharged August 17, 1865 for disability.

Willard, William - Private - Company A - Enlisted December 26, 1863. Wounded May 16, 1864 at Drewry's Bluff, Virginia. Wounded October 13, 1864 at the battle of Darbytown Cross-Roads, Virginia. Mustered out August 11, 1865. In 1889 he was living in Channahon, Illinois.

Williams, Chauncy - Captain - Company H - Enlisted July 11, 1862. Killed in battle on August 16, 1864. His last words were "Boys, we will go into those pits, or die!" A rebel bullet pierced his brain, killing him at once.

Williams, Harry - Private - Company F - Enlisted February 25, 1864. Wounded in the foot October 13, 1864 at the battle of Deep Run, Virginia. No further details known.

Williams, Henry F. - Musician, First Class - Enlisted September 20, 1861. Discharged by order of the War Department, June 4, 1862.

Williams, Henry W. - Private - Company G - Enlisted from Neoga, Illinois, October 28, 1861. Discharged February 26, 1862 for disability.

Williams, John - Private - Company G - Enlisted as a substitute on February 7, 1865. Deserted August 14, 1865 at Norfolk, Virginia.

Williams, John W. - Private - Company B - Enlisted from Bloomington, Illinois, August 12, 1861. Wounded May 16, 1864 at the battle of Drewry's Bluff, Virginia. Discharged October 18, 1864 upon completion of military service. In 1889 he was living in Macon, Illinois.

Williams, Samuel R. - Musician, First Class - Enlisted September 20, 1861. Discharged by order of the War Department, June 4, 1862.

Williams, William - Private - Company H - Enlisted from Chicago, Illinois, February 11, 1862. Deserted June 22, 1862 in Springfield, Illinois.

Williams, William C. W. - Private - Company G - Enlisted from Palos, Illinois, February 29, 1864. Discharged May 19, 1865 for disability.

Williamson, James - Private - Company F - Enlisted April 7, 1865. Mustered out with the regiment, December 6, 1865.

Willis, Frederick - Private - Company D - Enlisted from Chicago, Illinois, February 29, 1864. Missing since August 19, 1864 at Deep Run, Virginia. [Adjutant General's Reports lists him as supposed killed August 19, 1864].

Wills, Elmore - Private - Company D - Enlisted March 23, 1865. Died June 16, 1865 at Richmond, Virginia, in the Twenty-Fourth Corps Hospital. Cause unknown.

Wilmarth, Isaiah W. - Captain - Company B - Commissioned August 12, 1861. Resigned May 26, 1862.

Wilson, Elias - Corporal - Company H - Enlisted from Santa Anna, Illinois, April 14, 1862. Mustered out May 9, 1865.

Wilson, James A. - Private - Company C - Enlisted March 14, 1864. Played in the Band of 1864 & 1865. Mustered out with the regiment, December 6, 1865.

Wilson, John S. - Private - Company H - Enlisted from Santa Anna, Illinois, August 20, 1861. Transferred from Company I September 1, 1862. Promoted Corporal May 1, 1863. Veteran. Discharged July 7, 1865 for disability.

Wilson, John T. - Private - Company E - Enlisted April 11, 1865. Mustered out with the regiment, December 6, 1865.

Wilson, William F. - Private - Company B - Enlisted from Bloomington, Illinois, September 30, 1861. Discharged February 5, 1863 for disability. In 1889 he was living in Bloomington, Illinois.

Wilson, William S. - Private - Company I - Enlisted September 4, 1861. Discharged September 12, 1864 for disability.

Winder, Joseph K. - Private - Company G - Enlisted from Lamoille, Illinois, August 29, 1861. Killed August 16, 1864 at the battle of Deep Run, Virginia.

Winder, Lorenzo D. - Private - Company G - Enlisted from Lamoille, Illinois, August 29, 1861. Discharged October 23, 1862 for disability.

Wingart, Henry - Private - Company G - Enlisted from Florence, Illinois, March 15, 1865. On special duty at the muster out of the regiment.

Winn, John - Private - Company E - Enlisted from Wilmington, Illinois, October 6, 1861. Discharged for disability November 20, 1861.

Winton, Wayne - Private - Company A - Enlisted from Luzerne County, Pennsylvania, March 11, 1865. Mustered out July 21, 1865.

Wirts, George - Private - Company A - Enlisted August 27, 1861. Discharged September 20, 1864 upon completion of military service.

Wise, Christian - Private - Company D - Enlisted from Lindenwood, Illinois, August 21, 1861. Wandered from camp near Edinburg, Virginia, in April 1862. Alleged to be insane. Listed as missing. Nothing further is known.

Wisner, Theodore S. - Private - Company A - Enlisted August 5, 1861. Wounded June 2, 1864. Discharged September 10, 1864 upon completion of military service.

Wogle, John J. - Private - Company C - Enlisted February 28, 1865. Mustered out with the regiment, December 6, 1865.

Wolcott, Edwin N. - Private - Company B - Enlisted February 28, 1865. Mustered out with the regiment, December 6, 1865. In 1889 he was living at Bloomington, Illinois.

Wolcott, William H. - Private - Company B - Enlisted from Bloomington, Illinois, September 5, 1861. Promoted Corporal January 1, 1863. Discharged September 10, 1864 upon completion of military service.

Wolfe, William - Private - Company G - Enlisted from Wood's Grove, Illinois, February 27, 1865. Mustered out with the regiment, December 6, 1865.

Wood, Andrew - Private - Company I - Enlisted from Okaw, Illinois, April 12, 1865. Mustered out with the regiment, December 6, 1865.

Wood, Samuel C. - Private - Company C - Enlisted January 11, 1865. Deserted August 12, 1865.

Woodard, Edward - Private - Company I - Enlisted from Santa Anna, Illinois, October 2, 1861. Veteran. Wounded in the side August 16, 1864 at Deep Run, Virginia. Promoted Corporal 1865. Mustered out with the regiment, December 6, 1865.

Wooden, Nathan J. - Company H - Enlisted from Chicago, Illinois, March 12, 1862. Discharged by Medical Department. Cause unknown.

Woodruff, Daniel - Private - Company A - Enlisted from Channahon, Illinois, October 13, 1862. Mustered out October 13, 1865 upon completion of military service.

Woodruff, Joseph - Captain - Company K - Commissioned August 24, 1861. Enlisted in 1846 at the age of 14 in a battalion of recruits to reinforce Illinois Volunteers during war with Mexico. In July 1861, he began recruiting for Company K; he was one of the first to enlist. Mortally wounded by a shell fragment near Fort Gregg, South Carolina, September 23, 1863. His body was returned home, and he is buried in Bluffside Cemetery in Marseilles. Born in Onondaga County, New York, September 7, 1829. In 1852 he became a resident of Marseilles, Illinois. He had three children, Nellie and Willie have died. The other name is Monroe. Before the war, Joseph was employed with his brother-in-law, James Fleming.

Wooding, Alfred - Private - Company B - Enlisted from Decatur, Illinois, August 12, 18161. Wounded and taken prisoner June 16, 1864 near Chester Station, Virginia. Mustered out July 6, 1865.

Woodward, William - Regimental Second Assistant Surgeon - Commissioned December 9, 1862 - In January 1865, he was appointed acting Medical Purveyor of the Twenty-Fourth Army Corps. April 11, 1865 he transferred to the Fifty-Eighth Illinois Volunteer Infantry; mustered out April 1, 1866. He died of tuberculosis in 1880.

Woodward, William B. - Private - Company I - Enlisted from Bloomington, Illinois, February 12, 1864. Wounded May 16, 1864 at the battle of Drewry's Bluff, Virginia. Also wounded October 13, 1864 at Darbytown Cross-Roads, Virginia. Mustered out with the regiment, December 6, 1865.

Woore, Henry - Private - Company F - Enlisted from Northfield, Illinois, August 5, 1861. Wounded by a shell fragment at Fort Wagner, South Carolina. Discharged September 10, 1864 upon completion of military service.

Worely, William F. - Private - Company B - Enlisted from Bloomington, Illinois, August 12, 1861. Deserted June 28, 1863.

Worth, William R. - Corporal - Company C - Enlisted from Esmond, Illinois, August 12, 1861. Veteran. Taken prisoner May 16, 1864 at Drewry's Bluff, Virginia, and taken to Libby Prison in Richmond and then to Andersonville Prison in Georgia. Paroled and discharged August 15, 1865. In 1889 he was living at Brookfield, Linn County, Missouri.

Worthy, Henry - Private - Company H - Enlisted April 7, 1865. Mustered out with the regiment, December 6, 1865.

Wren, Asa - Private - Company I - Enlisted from LeRoy, Illinois, February 13, 1864. Discharged July 20, 1865 by order of the War Department.

Wright, Richard - Private - Company K - Enlisted October 6, 1861. Discharged October 8, 1864 upon completion of military service.

Wurdenman, John H. - Private - Company D - Enlisted from Lindenwood, Illinois, August 28, 1861. Veteran. Promoted Corporal September 1, 1864. Wounded October 13, 1864 at Darbytown Cross-Roads, Virginia. Absent, sick and wounded at muster out of the regiment.

Wurts, George - Private - Company A - Enlisted from Wilmington, Illinois, August 27, 1861. Discharged September 10, 1864 upon completion of military service.

Wyatt, Edward - Private - Company H - Enlisted from Springfield, Illinois, April 8, 1862. Discharged July 13, 1865 upon completion of military service.

— Y —

Yapp, Seneca - See Gopp, Seneca

Yates, George - Private - Company A - Enlisted August 15, 1861. Promoted to Corporal August 1, 1862. Promoted to Sergeant August 8, 1864. Wounded at Darbytown Cross-Roads, Virginia, October 13, 1864. Yates was wounded by four bullets while carrying the Regimental Colors in the charge on the rebel works; he was captured and taken to Castle Thunder Prison, Virginia. He was paroled the same day and died from his wounds at Camp Parole on October 26, 1864. Shortly before his death, he was commissioned Captain in the United States Colored Troops.

Yoker, Jonathan - Private - Company A - Enlisted August 15, 1861. Deserted September 5, 1861.

York, John L. - Sergeant - Company D - Enlisted from Paine's Point, Illinois, August 9, 1861. Died at St. Louis, Missouri in October 1861. Cause unknown.

INDEX

100th New York Volunteer Infantry, 81, 85, 91-93, 129, 180, 194, 237
110th, New York Volunteer Infantry, 36, 37
112th New York Volunteer Infantry, 186, 239
199th Pennsylvania Volunteer Infantry, 196-198, 202, 203

Alexandria, Virginia, xiii, 64, 65, 120, 259
Alpine Station, ix, xii, 21, 23-26, 29, 32, 38, 40, 46, 48, 254, 257
Ames, Adelbert, 143, 147, 176, 183, 238
Andersonville Military Prison, v, xi, xvi, xviii, 142, 225-227, 231, 233
Annapolis, Maryland, 175, 178
Appomattox Court-House, 201, 202, 205, 207, 223
Appomattox River, 143, 170, 172
Arago, 79, 121
Arion, Miss Helen, xix, xxii, 3, 218
Arlington Heights, Virginia, 11, 119, 259, 267
Army of Northern Virginia, xvii, 201, 203, 204, 207
Army of the James, vii, xiv-xvii, 122, 136, 146, 172, 179, 181, 183, 185, 193, 194, 226, 237, 267
Army of the Potomac, 8, 65, 67, 122, 143, 150, 157, 172, 194, 210, 211
Ashby, Turner, 26, 34, 53
Atlanta, Georgia, 170, 225, 227
Augur General Hospital, 120

Baker, Leroy A., xxiii, 86, 120, 136, 148, 159, 162, 165, 251
Baltimore and Ohio railroad, xii, 16, 21, 24, 27, 37, 43, 44, 65, 257-259
Barton's Brigade, 180, 187, 238
Bath, West Virginia, 5, 21-27, 29, 31, 32, 35-38, 48, 52, 55, 76, 112, 255, 257, 262
Battery Gregg, 96, 107
Battery Wagner, 95, 96, 103, 105
Beacon House, ix, xiv, 93
Beaufort, North Carolina, 72, 80, 86
Beauregard, Pierre G. T., ix, xv, 106, 107, 122, 127, 131, 153, 157, 158, 243
Belcher, Oscar S., 23, 37, 263, 264
Benton Barracks, xii, 3, 5, 7
Berkeley Springs, (See Bath)
Bermuda Hundred, Virginia, ix, xiv-xvi, 122-124, 136, 138, 139, 141, 143, 154, 169, 226, 259
Big Cacapon, 31, 38, 39
Birney, David Bell, 155, 160, 164, 169, 171, 173, 176, 181
Blackwater River, xiii, 70, 259
Blake, Dr. Samuel C., 1, 18-20, 23, 24, 36, 43, 61, 65, 67
Bloomery Gap, 38, 47
Brucker, Simon S., 23, 50, 55, 70, 254
Bryan Hall, 115, 117, 217
Bull Run, Virginia, xii, 2, 58, 251, 252
Burnside, Ambrose E., 169
Burrill, James, 152
Butler, Benjamin F., ix, xv, xvi, 122-124, 127, 132, 135, 143, 160, 164, 169, 183, 184, 188, 217, 226, 237, 261

Camp Butler, 217, 261
Camp Distribution, 120
Camp Fry, 116, 117
Camp Lee, 212, 214

Camp Mather, 3, 256, 262, 263
Camp Seymour, 92
Camp Thirty-Ninth Illinois, 158
Cape Hatteras, 113
Castle Thunder, 176, 177
Cedar Creek, ix, 53, 58, 60
Charleston Harbor, xi, 1, 81, 92, 259
Cherry Run, 46, 49, 259
Chesapeake Bay, 70, 121
Chesapeake Hospital, 125, 146, 148, 153, 160, 179
Chester Heights, 122
Chester Station, 129
Chippewa, 96
Chowan River, 72, 73, 75
City of Bath, 76, 112
City Point, Virginia 121, 170, 175, 177, 190, 214, 259
Clark, Dr. Charles M., i, vii, xi, xiii, xxiv, xxv, 1, 3, 7, 24, 32, 44, 46, 48, 49, 55, 65, 67, 85, 91, 92, 113, 115, 118, 121, 124, 125, 135, 137, 141, 145, 146, 150, 157, 170, 171, 177, 188, 189, 191, 223
Cold Harbor, Virginia, xiv, 143
Columbia Bridge, Virginia, 61, 63
Company A, xii, xvii, 2, 13, 16, 19, 25, 114, 120, 136, 148, 152, 159, 174, 178, 221, 222, 251, 254, 256, 258
Company B, 16, 25, 51, 67, 114, 152, 153, 159, 179, 252, 253, 263
Company C, 2, 50, 55, 57, 67, 125, 135, 136, 145, 179, 254
Company D, 2, 22-24, 29, 37, 52, 60, 65, 84, 114, 135, 157, 165, 180, 254, 255, 263
Company E, iii, v, xi, xv, xvii, 21, 24, 31, 33, 38, 67, 100, 114, 120, 133, 140, 165, 178, 179, 205, 221, 226, 256-258
Company F, 25, 114, 141, 154, 257
Company G, v, 2, 16, 21, 24-26, 30, 31, 35, 67, 105, 124, 136, 138, 155, 157, 164, 165, 170, 175, 179, 198, 253, 258, 260
Company H, 3, 67, 77, 120, 152, 178, 179, 261, 264
Company I, v, 6, 22, 32, 50, 75, 114, 139, 146, 153, 159, 261, 262
Company K, xvii, 11, 22, 23, 37, 40, 67, 91, 100, 107, 108, 114, 115, 141, 176, 214, 252, 263, 264
Cook, Ezra, 33, 85, 119, 120, 138, 142, 230, 257, 264
Corse, Montgomery, xv
Cosmopolitan, 85, 94
Cossack, 86
court-martial, 47, 48
Cox, Corneluis, 105
Crozier, Dr. James, 70, 137
Cumberland, Maryland, vii, 9, 21, 29, 30, 33, 36-38, 43, 44, 46
Cumberland Valley Railroad, 9
Cummings Point, Virginia, 95, 96
Curtis, S. R., 3, 5, 7, 144, 181, 197
Cutler, Joseph A., 1, 65, 188

Dahlgren, John, 92, 95, 96, 99, 109
Dandy, G. B., 139, 194, 214
Darbytown Cross-Roads, vii, 75, 177
Davis, Jefferson, 45, 179, 197, 211
Deep Bottom, xiii, 166, 173, 190, 194, 197
Deep Run, vii, xvi, 154, 162, 259, 262
DeNormandie, 19, 44, 180, 187, 214
Department of Virginia and North Carolina, 183, 185, 211
Dircks, William, 1, 38
Dismal Swamp, xiii, 70, 259
District of Southeastern Virginia, 215
Dix, Miss Dorthea, 212
Douglas Brigade, 2
Drewry's Bluff, Virginia, xi, xiv, xvi, 75, 122, 126, 127, 135, 136, 141, 146, 225
DuPont, Samuel Francis, 81, 92
Dutcherage, William C., 30

Edinburg, Virginia, 58
Edisto Island, South Carolina, 81
Edisto River, South Carolina, 81
Eighth Connecticut, 187, 239
Eighty-Fifth Pennsylvania, 81, 84, 93, 95, 99, 121, 133, 144, 145, 159, 181, 237
Eighty-First New York, 183, 239
Eighty-Fourth Pennsylvania, 23, 25, 26, 29, 32, 33, 36, 42
Ellsworth Zouaves, 2
Ely, William W., 100, 103, 170
Eighteenth Army Corps, xv, 122, 133, 143, 169, 172, 185, 239
Eighteenth Virginia Infantry, xv
Farmville, Virginia, 203, 210
Fellows, Albert, 60, 87, 147, 153, 254, 260, 262
Ferry Point, 160, 214
Ferry, Orris Sanford, 23, 47, 67, 78, 81, 85, 114, 115
Fifth Corps, 159, 185, 186, 194
Fifteenth Virginia Infantry, xv
Fifty-Fourth Massachusetts, xiii, 96, 97
First Connecticut Heavy Artillery, 119
First Georgia, 35, 244
First Maryland Cavalry, 57, 86, 91
First Maryland Infantry, 17
First Michigan Cavalry, 53
First New Jersey Battery, 129
First U. S. Artillery, 93
First Vermont Cavalry, 61, 62
First Virginia Cavalry, 47
Folly Island, South Carolina, vii, xiii, xiv, 80-82, 84, 85, 87-89, 92-94, 103, 106, 111, 259
Folly River, 86, 88, 92
foraging, ix, 35, 48, 74, 75, 170
Forty-Eighth New York, 92, 98, 238
Fort Barnard, 119, 120
Fort Darling, xi, 68, 124
Fort Donelson, 45

Fort Fisher, 186, 211, 215
Fort Gilmer, 173
Fort Gregg, vii, x, xiii, xvi, xvii, xix, 103, 104, 108, 194, 196, 198, 199, 201, 204, 210, 212, 217, 259
Fort McAllister, 77
Fort Monroe, xvii, 70, 121, 124, 125, 138, 140, 146, 183, 194, 214
Fort Moultrie, 82, 103, 108
Fort Osborn, 22
Fort Sumter, ix, xi, 1, 83-85, 87, 91, 92, 96, 99, 108, 109, 251
Fort Wagner, vii, ix, xiii, xiv, 93-96, 98-100, 103-105
Foster, Robert S. "Sandy," 37-39, 73, 75-77, 120, 121, 194, 197, 212, 214, 259
Fourth U. S. Artillery, 22, 26
Fowler, Jesse W., 91
Franks, Jacob C., 152
Fredericksburg, Virginia, xiii, 64, 66, 87, 259
Fremont, Charles, 5, 8
Front Royal, 55, 56, 254

Gettysburg, xiv, 10
Gibbons, John, xix, 193, 196, 212, 217
Gillmore, Quincy, A., ix, xv, 91, 92, 95-97, 99, 103-107, 109, 112, 121, 124, 128, 129, 132, 145, 148, 158, 237
Gloucester Point, 120, 259
Grant, Ulysses S., 122, 143, 154, 157, 158, 170, 190, 193, 202, 204-206, 211, 213
Gray, John, xxvii, 57, 67, 147, 221, 226, 254
Great Cacapon, 21, 24-26, 29, 31, 38, 258, 260
Greek Fire, 107

Hagerstown, Maryland, xii, 8, 10, 16
Hamilton, Dr. Frank, 67, 179
Hancock, Maryland, xii, 21-27, 31, 33, 36-38, 42-44, 46, 61, 162, 213, 254
Hardenburgh, Henry, 164, 165, 170

Harrisburg, 9
Harrisonburg, 63
Harvey, Lee, 51, 252, 261
Haynie, Adjutant-General, xi, xii, 217, 218
Heritage, George, 179, 252, 253
Hero of Jersey, 166
Hilton Head, xiv, 76, 77, 79, 83, 86, 94, 98, 111, 112, 251, 255, 258, 259, 264
Hoisington, Henry, 16
Hooker, James E., 4, 26, 67, 144, 145, 256
Hopkins, Thomas, 52
Howard, William H., 86, 198
Howell, Joshua B., 84
Howlett House Battery, 124, 188
Hunchback, 154, 188, 190
Hunter, David, 77-79, 81, 84, 92, 158

Illinois Copperhead Legislature, 172
Imboden, Jno, 27
Indianapolis, 8, 9, 115, 261
Invalid Corps, 141

Jackson, Stonewall, xii, 24, 26, 27, 29, 31, 33, 34, 36, 37, 47, 57-59, 63, 65, 87, 93, 213, 254, 255, 257, 258
James Island, 92, 95, 104
James River, ix, xiii, xiv, 66, 68, 121, 123, 124, 138, 147, 150, 152, 154, 157, 163, 170, 173, 174, 177, 188, 194, 197, 210, 259
Jenkins, William H., 125, 179
Jersey City, 114
Jewell, William O. L., 33
Johnson, Bushrod, 63, 65, 82, 104, 245, 252, 268

Kaautz, August V., 241
Karr, Eilisa, 133
Kelly, General, 16, 24, 25, 29, 31, 32, 36, 37
Kendall, Neriah B., xxiii, 136
Keokuk, 83, 84

Kernstown, 57, 60, 254
Kettell, Thomas P., 148
Keyes, Erasum Darvin, vii, 67
Kimball, Nathanial, 57, 60
Kinney, Thomas, 100
Kipp, John, xvii, 107
Kittinger, Dr. M. S., 92, 93, 125, 180

Lace, Phillip M., 2, 8, 21, 50, 51, 137, 267, 269
Lamon, Ward H., 8, 36
Landers, Frederick, 24, 32, 34, 36, 44, 46, 47, 49, 80
Lankinaw, Henry, 24, 37, 84
Laurel Hill, 173
Lee, Robert E., xvii, 51, 122, 157, 158, 175, 194, 195, 201, 202, 205-207, 210, 212, 214, 255
Leonard, Colonel, 13, 16
Light House Inlet, 82, 88
Lincoln, Abraham, ix, xii, xvi, xix, 50, 58, 64, 65, 160, 162, 172, 181, 194, 204, 209
Linton, Samuel S., 22, 23, 25, 29, 37, 52, 65, 73, 88, 105, 125, 133, 135, 136, 254, 255
Longstreet, James, 60, 157
Long Hollow, 38
Luray, 61, 66
Lynchburg, 158, 196, 201, 202, 210
Lyons, Lord, 64, 221

Macon, 141, 228
Malvern Hill, xiii, 66, 259
Manassas, 55
Manchester, 210
Mann, Orrin L., xvii, xxiii, 1-3, 16, 20, 22, 23, 25, 26, 29, 34, 36-38, 42, 46-48, 50, 52, 70, 103-105, 111, 114, 115, 117, 123, 125, 133, 145, 150, 160, 170, 188, 214, 215, 217, 218, 223, 257

Martinsburg, 15, 18, 22, 23, 25, 29, 44, 46, 49, 51, 259
Mary Boardman, 112
Masonic, 13, 120, 171
Massanuton Mountain, 61
McClellan, 58, 69, 160, 172
McDowell, Irvin S., xiii, 64, 65
McReading, Rev. Charles S., 13, 23, 161
Meade, George, 204, 210
Mechanicsburg, 9
Middletown, 53
Miller, Rev. William E., 166
Mississippi, 5, 45
Missouri, xii, 1, 3, 11, 219, 256, 267
Mobile, 142, 162
Nahant, 83
Nantucket, 83
New Ironsides, 82
Montauk, 83, 96
Morehead City, 76
Morris Island, ix, xiii, xiv, 82, 83, 85, 86, 89, 92-95, 98, 106, 107, 109, 141, 153
Mount Alpine, 25
Mount Jackson, 59, 65
Muhlenburg, E. D., 22, 24, 26, 29, 33, 37, 43
Munn, Sylvester W., 2, 16, 18-20, 23, 32, 47, 48, 50, 52, 61, 65, 71-73, 222, 251
Myers, Ebanis C., 34, 40, 214, 264
Nahant, 83
Nansemond River, 70
Nantucket, 83, 87, 96
Neal, Daniel, 11
Nellie Baker, 86
New Ironsides, 82
New Creek, 36, 43, 44, 259
New Ironsides, 83, 87, 96
New Market, 61, 65, 173, 188, 197
New York and Erie railroad, 114
New York City, 114, 186
Ninth Corps, 194, 210

Ninth Maine, 92, 94, 100, 239
Ord, E. O. C., 169, 173, 185, 193
Orrick, Johnson, 21, 22, 35
Osborn, Thomas O., ix, xi, xii, xvii, 1, 3, 4, 7, 16, 17, 19, 21, 22, 24, 26, 32, 44, 46, 50, 73, 75, 99, 112, 115, 117-119, 124, 125, 133, 160, 170, 184, 187, 188, 193, 194, 197, 203, 204, 206, 211, 212, 214
Ottawa, 96, 108

Parrish, William, 16
Parris Island, 78
Parrott, 92, 175
Passaic, 83
Patapsco, 83, 96
Paul Jones, 96
Pawnee, 86
Paw-Paw, 46, 47
Peters, Martin Van Buren, 141
Petersburg and Norfolk railroad, 172
Petersburg, x, xiv-xvii, xix, 122-124, 129, 138, 140, 143, 155, 157-160, 169, 170, 172, 194-196, 198, 201, 202, 204, 210, 217, 226, 229, 230, 259
Phillips, Hiram, 22, 34, 50, 202, 262
Pineo, Peter, 179
Pittsburgh, ix, 8, 9, 11, 117
Pittsburgh and Fort Wayne Railroad, 117
Plimpton, Homer, xxiii, 129, 135, 162, 165, 173, 174, 194, 199, 204, 211
Pond, Colonel, 44, 46
Porte Crayon, 55
Port Republic, 66
Port Royal, 83, 85
Potomac River, xii-14, 21, 29, 33, 37, 254
Pulaski, 112
Putnam, Haldimand S., 97, 98

Reed, Theodore, 80, 205
Reese, Amos, 152
Regimental Band, viii, x, 2, 8, 24, 62, 157,

188, 267
Regimental Hospital, 13, 70, 111
Richmond, vii, x, xiii-xvii, 21, 51, 64, 66, 68, 84, 87, 122, 124, 129, 138, 143, 150, 157, 162, 166, 170, 172, 173, 175, 176, 178, 180, 188, 190, 194-196, 209-215, 259
Richmond and Petersburg Pike, 129
Riddle, George S., 6, 7, 32, 75, 146
Ripple, John L., xxiii
Romney, West Virginia, 16, 27, 29, 36, 44, 57

Sheridan, Phillip, 194, 201, 204
Sherman, William T., 142, 170, 186, 190, 211, 227, 233
Shields, James, 49-51, 53, 55, 57-59, 61, 65, 254
Sixth and Seventh Connecticut, 92, 98
Sixth Army Corps, 158, 197
Sixth Ohio, 85
Sixty-Seventh Ohio, 143
Sixty-Second Ohio, 44, 81, 85, 88, 166, 191, 197, 198, 202, 203, 214, 237
Sixty-Seventh Ohio, 44, 65, 81, 92, 93, 144, 145, 147, 176, 196, 198, 202, 203, 237
Slagle, David H., 114, 176, 177, 263
Slaughter, William B., 25, 29, 31, 38, 67, 143, 164, 169, 173, 258
Sleepy Creek, 25, 38
Smith, William 60, 124, 169, 183, 184, 239, 269
Smouse, Daniel, 100
Snee, Hugh Rippy, iii, v, viii, xi-xvi, xviii, 100, 103, 225, 226, 229, 233
Snowden, George O., 157, 158
Southside railroad, 201
Spencer, W. W., 139
spies, 14, 18
St. Augustine, 111
St. Louis, vii, xii, 3, 5, 8, 11, 256, 267

Stanton, Edwin M., xvii, 47, 64, 181, 193, 204
State Commissioners of Agriculture, 2
Steadman, Griffin A., 170
Secor, 86
Stono Inlet, 80, 81
Strasburg, 53, 55-61, 254, 268
Strawberry Plains, 166
Strobridge, Dr. J. H., 67, 70
Strong, George C., 1, 25, 29, 37, 38, 53, 61, 68, 92-94, 97-99, 104, 161, 169, 170, 194, 211, 264
Strother, David, 15, 23, 48, 55
Suffolk, xiii, 52, 70, 72, 259
Sullivan's Island, xiii
sutler, 6, 60, 86, 87, 91, 125, 183, 190, 267
Swamp Angel, ix, xiv, 107
Swan, 21, 22, 24, 35
Sweetser, Alphonse C., xxiii, 153, 160, 223, 252, 253
Temple Hall Church, 179, 180
Tenth Alabama, 164
Tenth Army Corps, xiv, xv, 120, 143, 144, 154, 158, 169, 172, 183, 237
Terre Haute, 8
Terry, Alfred H., 92, 98, 103, 104, 120, 144, 145, 147, 153, 154, 159, 162, 171, 176, 181, 183, 186, 198, 199, 211, 215, 220, 237, 243, 253
Third U. S.cavalry, 60
Third Arkansas, 30, 31
Third New Hampshire, 92, 98, 153, 158, 186, 237
Third North Carolina Cavalry, xv
Third Vermont, 100
Thirteenth Indiana, 25, 26, 33, 37, 39, 55, 56, 63, 65, 73, 75, 239, 254
Thirteenth Massachusetts, 13, 15-17, 19, 22, 51
Thirteeth Virginia Infantry, xv
Thirty-Seventh Virginia, 31

Thirty-Sixth United States Colored Troops, 164
Thomas Powell, 188
Trenton, 107, 172
tuberculosis, 16
Turner, John W., 34, 122, 238
Twenty-Fifth Corps, 185, 186
Twenty-Fourth Corps, 185, 186, 204, 205, 207, 211, 217, 267
Twenty-Fourth Massachusetts, 99, 103, 154, 159, 237
Twenty-Ninth Virginia Infantry, xv
Twenty-Second South Carolina, 153

Vogdes, Israel, 84, 85, 87, 89, 92
Voris, Alvin C., 44, 145, 176

Ware Bottom Church, xiii, xvi, 123, 146, 150, 157, 253, 259, 262
Warm Spring ridge, ix, xii, 22, 25, 29, 262
Warner, Norman C., 120, 164, 165, 256
Warrenton Junction, 65
Washington, DC, xiv, xvii, 46, 212, 259
Weehawken, 83, 96
Weitzel, Godfrey, 173, 185, 189, 210, 211, 240
West Virginia, xii, 15, 16, 18, 21, 29, 43, 46, 254
Whipple, Lewis T., 31, 33, 38, 39, 256
White House Bridge, 61-63
Williams, Chauncy, 34, 46, 61, 67, 120, 159, 198, 261, 268
Williamsport, xii, 8, 10, 11, 14, 15, 18, 19, 23, 36, 46, 256
Winchester, vii, xiii, 25, 35, 36, 44, 46, 47, 51, 52, 55-59, 161, 162, 254, 259
Wirz, Henry, 142, 231, 233-235
Wissahickon, 96
Woodruff, Joseph, 22, 37, 41, 59, 107, 108, 263, 264
Woodward, William, 70, 88, 89, 116, 188

Yates Phalanx, xi, 1, 219
Yorktown, xiii, 63, 68-70, 259
York River, 120, 121

ERRATUM

Wherever the name Sheffler appears, the correct spelling should be Shreffler.